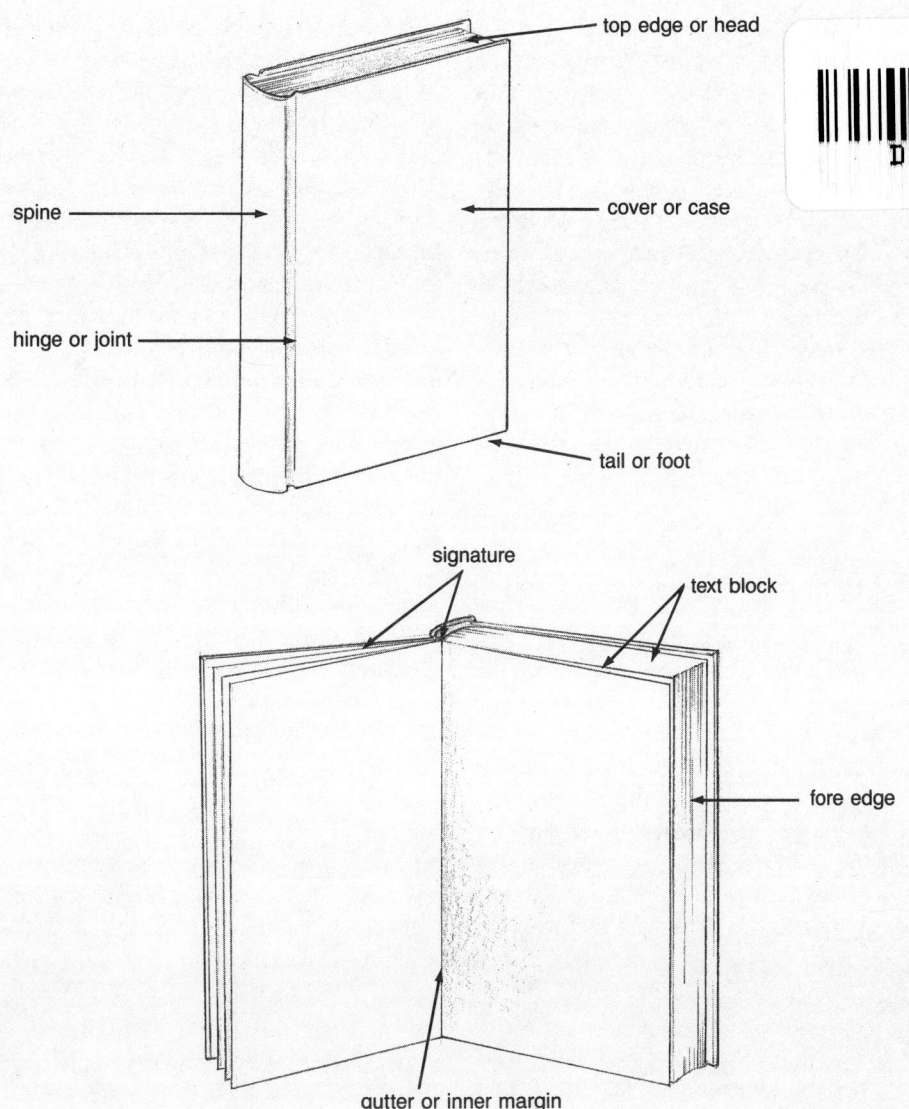

Figure 1. Parts of bound book

Review of Mission

In order to clearly establish the parameters of preservation activities in the small library, the mission of the library and the nature of the collection must be determined. Does the library serve the research needs of a small college community or the information and recreational needs of a small town? Clearly the preservation concerns of these two libraries differ. The small college library may have greater concern for extending the life of the majority of its collection because research requires historical as well as current materials. The small public library may be more concerned with maintaining current materials, which need to withstand high frequency of use for one or two years.

Within the individual library, specific formats and collections should be reviewed with the mission in mind. A paperback collection purchased to supplement the peak demand for best-seller hardbacks would not be targeted for long-term preservation. A paperback collection might be selected for preservation if it contained a certain literary genre or a particular author's works available only in paperback. Review should be made of the life expectancy goals and the kind and the frequency of use of formats and collections to establish limits and guidelines for preservation activities.

The reference and circulation staff and the staff or the volunteers who work with the physical preparation and mending of materials will be valuable resources from whom to obtain information about collection usage and typical repair problems. Keeping statistics on the classification of items that appear in the mending area and on the number of items that are shipped to the commercial bindery will provide information for planning a preservation materials budget and personnel needs. By focusing on the collection's goals and usage patterns, the coordinator should have a fairly well-defined picture of the short-range problems facing the library.

Physical Environment

A physical inspection of the library should also be part of the fact-finding stage. This is a very important component to document in the final written report, since the discovery of problems requiring repair or renovation may involve capital expenditures. On a smaller scale, such things as house cleaning may be conducted on a contractual basis and desired improvements in house-cleaning practices will be facilitated by written documentation.

While maintenance of the physical environment receives limited attention in many settings because it calls up the image of the librarian as "keeper of the books," it is one of the most important factors affecting the life of the collection.

It is important to remember that ordinary paper is an organic substance. The environment—temperature, humidity, and light—has a terrific impact on the life of paper. Fluctuations in the environment activate the destructive properties of the acid on the paper's fibers. It is a staggering but proven fact that every ten-degree shift in temperature in the library can either increase or decrease the life of the collection by a factor of two. At 80° F books will deteriorate twice as fast as those stored at 70°.

Cycling of heating and cooling systems creates stress on the paper, which is forced to respond to the upward and downward shift in temperature. The ideal temperature for paper is 60°, plus or minus 5°. If the ideal is not possible, the effects of temperature shifts can be minimized by less frequent, more gradual temperature changes that are less than 10°. Equipment, such as a hygrothermograph, is available to track the temperature and humidity over an extended period of time. Such equipment is relatively expensive. It probably will be necessary for the small library to use a thermometer to do in-house record keeping over a specified period of time, in both hot and cold months.

Humidity can also have an impact on the life of the library collection. If there is too much moisture in the air, the acidic reaction is speeded up. Mold and bacteria become problems. Too little moisture, however, may dry out the paper and cause it to become brittle. A relative humidity of 50 percent with a variance of plus or minus 3 percent is ideal.

Light presents another problem. Many new library buildings are designed with large expanses of glass. Fluorescent lighting is found in the stack areas as well as the reader and display areas. Visible light will yellow papers, a reaction seen often in newspapers. Invisible or ultraviolet light, found in sunlight and fluorescent light, will break down paper fibers over time, making the paper become brittle. Consequently, book stacks should not face out toward windows, and books should not be left open in display cases for long periods of time. If possible, inexpensive plastic sleeves should be placed on fluorescent tubes to help filter the ultraviolet rays. An alternative is the installation of low UV fluorescent lights. Windows should be tinted or shaded. The cost of these measures cannot compare to the expense of replacing the light-damaged materials.

Dust and dirt are also enemies of library materials. These particles of matter are abrasive to surfaces and actively contribute to the breakdown of paper fibers and the scratching of film surfaces. Dirt and dust also retain moisture and will increase the possibility of mold and fungi growth. Proper ventilation and air filters will help control dirt and dust and reduce the presence of other air pollutants. Simple housekeeping routines take on a new significance when their impact is understood.

The responsibility for monitoring these environmental factors belongs to the coordinator. The documentation of environmental problems should be conducted over an extended period of time. When a picture of the situation emerges, short-and long-range goals can be chosen. Solutions to problems may require the cooperation of those outside the library. If the library is housed within another structure, for example, a building also housing city offices, coordination will be required to regulate the environment within the library. Small college libraries may have their environment controlled by the physical plant personnel on the campus; their problems may have to be presented to the college administration.

Collection Maintenance and Circulation Practices

As previously discussed, proper housekeeping and environmental control prevent damage before it occurs. Collection maintenance activities are also integral to preventative care. Having reviewed the environment, the stacks and storage areas should be evaluated. Collection maintenance is generally the responsibility of the circulation librarian, who usually oversees the shelving staff. The coordinator should review with key staff the current practices for receipt, carting, and shelving of returned books, as well as short- and long-range planning for housing collection growth.

Are books returned in an outdoor book drop? Is there a book drop at the circulation desk? Book drops, as the words imply, do not safeguard the physical well-being of library materials. Cassettes, phonorecords, and videotapes should never be deposited in a book drop. Books also can be damaged in these mechanisms. Whether the drop is at an angle or completely vertical, the book will still suffer from the impact. Damage to the spine or pages may occur. This damage will be compounded as other books tumble on top. Consider as well how book drops are emptied or cleared. Are the contents dumped or tossed into bins? Book drops deserve careful review, and it is the considered opinion of most in the preservation field that they should be eliminated. If they are a necessity, they should empty into the interior of the building, since outdoor drops are subject to extreme fluctuations of temperature and humidity; the chute angle should minimize impact as much as possible; the book should land on a soft or spring-loaded surface; and the depository should be cleared frequently to reduce the pile-up of materials.

Books should be carted with care when reshelving. They should be placed upright on the book truck and should not protrude beyond its edges. Oversized books require flat-bed carts and should be laid flat on the cart's shelves. Never store an oversized book on its fore edge. The center of gravity on the loaded truck should be low to prevent tipping. Never overload a truck.

Shelving books is a very important activity, yet shelvers are usually the lowest paid staff in any library. In the small library, shelving may be assigned to volunteers. Libraries need to remember that a shelver is not the equivalent of a stock person in a grocery store. Getting the greatest quantity of "merchandise" out on the shelves with the greatest speed is not the goal of a library. Unlike canned goods, books cannot tolerate dropping or cramming.

Shelving deserves careful attention. The preservation coordinator should take a walk through the stacks with the circulation librarian and review the following questions: Are the shelf ranges stable and adequately spaced for book trucks and patron usage? Are books shelved within reach? Are step stools readily available where needed so that books will not be yanked from the shelves? Are all bottom shelves at least 4 inches off the floor to avoid dust and dirt from vacuuming and water from mopping?

Properly shelved books will not only add to the aesthetics of the library but also prolong the life of the collection. All books should be upright, resting on their base. Shelves should not be packed too tightly or too loosely. Book ends should support books on shelves that are not full.

Oversized books pose particular problems. The definition of oversized varies from library to library, but the term generally refers to a volume that exceeds the normal height and width of standard shelving. Ideally, oversized books should be housed in a separate location with appropriate shelving. Such a location can be provided in each classification area, or all oversized books can be removed to another location. Oversized books should be shelved flat with a maximum of four volumes in a stack. If flat shelving is not feasible, an oversized volume may be stored on its spine. Never shelve a large volume on its fore edge since its weight will pull the text block free from the spine.

Shelvers should be taught the proper way to remove and replace books on shelves. A book should be removed by moving adjacent books away from it, either by pushing them back to expose the spine of the desired volume or by gently pushing them away from the sides of the volume. Grasp the book by its sides in order to remove it. Do *not* hook a finger over the top of the spine and pull. Readjust the bookend to support the remaining books. (See figure 2 for instructions on removing books from the shelf.) Oversized books stored flat should be grasped with both hands after transferring upper volumes to an empty shelf or truck.

When replacing a volume, the bookend should be moved an adequate distance, and the books on either side of the needed space should be eased away. The book being replaced should not be used as a wedge to force a space between books on the shelf. Once the volume is in place, the adjacent books should be eased back into position and the bookend adjusted appropriately. Oversized volumes should be returned to their place on the shelf with the same care with which they were removed.

Excellent slide-tape presentations on proper handling and shelving practices are available on loan from the National Preservation Program Office of the Library of Congress as well as from other sources. Use of one of these in an in-house training program can convey important information to a large number of people.

The circulation staff can play a pivotal role in the success of a preventative maintenance program. Since they are in constant contact with the collection, they can spot areas requiring attention. Returned books should be inspected individually for damage or wear and tear. Problem items should be set aside. Shelvers should be trained to spot books in poor condition and instructed to pull these for treatment.

Crowded stacks noted by shelvers should be addressed by the circulation librarian and the preservation coordinator. The ability to house the collection adequately is critical to the collection's life. Overcrowding may indicate the need for withdrawal of outdated, worn, or unused materials or for shifting the collection to accommodate growth. Efforts to coordinate these activities can be integrated into the library's preservation activities.

Damaged Materials Treatment

Last, it is important to review existing practices for the treatment of damaged materials. Who oversees in-house repair and mending activities? Who determines what materials will be sent to a commercial binder? Who deals with the bindery representative? Are policies and procedures for these activities documented?

In the small library it is probable that the director determines the bindery budget and signs the contract. Someone in technical services may receive, with little question, whatever the circulation staff says needs to go to the bindery. The bindery representative probably has limited contact with the library staff and, once the contract is signed, may not reappear in the library. The books for the bindery may be picked up by a delivery person who does not discuss the shipment with a particular person but rather with any staff member who is available at the time. Finally, books that are to stay in-house for mending are likely to be handed over to a volunteer or a part-time staff person who determines the treatment and does what seems best to solve the problem.

The purpose of this hypothetical example is to demonstrate that in small libraries there often is little coordination of preservation activities. No one is focused on the total picture. A bindery budget should not be determined in a vacuum; a contract should not be signed without full understanding of the services offered and an assessment of past experience. The choice of appropriate treatment,

Push adjacent books back

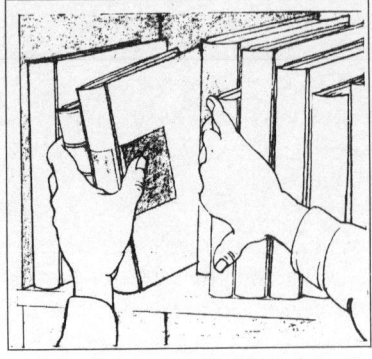
Grasp the exposed books with left hand

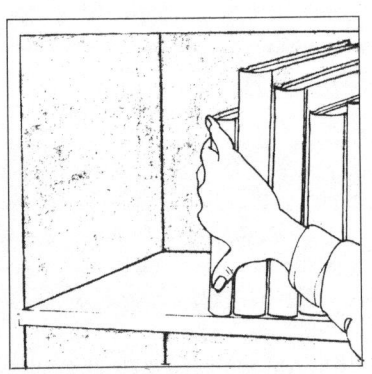
Support remaining books with right hand

Lay some books on their sides to act as support

Figure 2. Instructions for removing books from shelf

in-house or at a bindery, and the review of work quality should be the responsibility of one knowledgeable individual. Budget and contract terms for commercial binding should be suggested by this staff member. The in-house mending and repair processes should be carried out by volunteers or staff under his or her direction.

Assessments of environment, stacks maintenance, circulation practices, and damaged materials treatment, once documented, form the basis for the second component of the action plan, a realistic strategy. Considering the library's fiscal and personnel resources, where is attention most critically needed? What are the best means to address the need? What can be done immediately? What financial support should be requested for the future? The development of an action plan should provide overall direction as well as a benchmark from which to measure progress.

Preservation Options

All preservation programs ultimately deal with the day-to-day routine of treating the damaged item. Whether the library's staff is one or twenty, their knowledge and understanding of treatment options will ensure success.

Circulation staff and shelvers should be trained to spot the obviously damaged item and to understand the warning signs of a loose hinge or a loose page before further damage occurs. When books are sent to the designated mending area, the preservation coordinator should review them in a timely fashion and make one of the following decisions: replace, withdraw, repair in house, commercially bind, withdraw for limited circulation, or return to stacks. Each of these decisions should be based on criteria formalized in a procedures manual and on the mission and the resources of the particular library. There are some general guidelines for these decisions.

A decision might be made to withdraw and replace an item that circulates heavily yet is damaged beyond repair. Withdrawal without replacement might also be an option for an outdated book that is on its last legs. Since withdrawal is often an issue in preservation routines, it is very important to have a compatible weeding policy developed.

In-house repair is a decision that is contingent on staff skills, supplies, and budget. Generally an item is repaired in-house because of the simplicity of the problem, the economy of the process, and the expediency of getting the item back out for use.

Materials are sent to a commercial bindery if they require extensive repair and their value to the collection warrants the expense. As will be discussed later, the staff member should have a clear understanding of the processes available from the commercial bindery and be able to suggest to the binder the preferred option for treatment.

A decision to return a book to the stacks or restrict to limited in-house use may seem odd at first. A decision to do nothing to a damaged item is, however, a valid choice. Sometimes, for example, with a book containing brittle pages, there is simply no treatment available. The book may be out of print, but if it receives limited circulation it may survive some more use. Returning it to the stacks may also be the obvious decision when circulation staff misinterpret the warning signs of damage. Common sense and the library's collection goals will dictate the choice of this last treatment option. It is helpful, however, to note somewhere on the title page in light pencil the date when this option was chosen to avoid repetitive decision-making.

In-house Repair Options

In-house repair processes can range from the simple to the elaborate, depending on the library. The key point to remember is that very effective processes can be quite simple. The most common minor problems that occur in the library can be treated in-house with a minimum of staff, time and expense. Experience with mending minor repairs will increase dexterity and efficiency. This section will highlight five problem areas and briefly outline appropriate treatments. These are not sophisticated archival treatments designed for rare materials. They are the type of repair practices encountered daily in every small library—torn page repair, loose page hinging, repairing loose spine hinges, cleaning paper, and treating water-damaged or mildewed materials. The key point, however, is that unless the proper mending materials are used in these very basic repair processes, more harm than good will be done to the book. Only a select number of repair materials are recommended in this pamphlet; they have been reviewed by preservation specialists.

There are multiple sources for training and information, the key titles of which are cited in the bibliography. For a total expenditure of approximately $50, the library should purchase two outstanding books for learning "how-to": Carolyn Clark Morrow's *Conservation Treatment Procedures* and Heidi Kyle's *Library Materials Preservation Manual*. These sources are well illustrated with step-by-step instructions and will serve the staff for training and reference.

If the small library can manage it, a designated work area for in-house repair is helpful for several reasons. All materials and supplies can be readily accessible and no other process need be interrupted to conduct work. Not only will a clean, organized workspace increase efficiency but it will also encourage a professional attitude toward the project. The work table may be specially designed, but a large table will suffice. The top surface should be smooth, easily cleaned, and long and wide enough (approximately 6' x 2') to maneuver materials and books. It is desirable to have the table standing height, approximately 35". A drafting lamp provides very good lighting for repair work since it is adjustable for height and angle. Some procedures can be done sitting, so an adjustable stool is advisable. Peg board makes a good backboard for hanging needed tools by the work table within easy reach. Shelving is required to house paper and other supplies. The configuration of these elements should facilitate the work.

The initial cost of tools and materials may be kept to a minimum. A core of basic supplies is required to begin the operation. This area is not one in which to scrimp, since the quality of the repaired item is largely dependent on the quality of the material used. There are specialty suppliers for most conservation needs, but the local hardware or art supply store can also provide some of the products. A list of specialty suppliers is appended, and the supplier should be consulted for price lists of tools and materials.

There are two watchwords applied to conservation work—"non-damaging" and "reversible," meaning that the repair can be undone. Every repair process that is undertaken should aim at meeting these two criteria. Unfortunately, in many libraries the use of inappropriate repair materials results in more damage to the item. It is important to understand the chemical and textural properties of mending materials before use. Never mend with material that is heavier than the material being mended. Question the sales representative closely about the long-term effects of a product before buying; do not simply trust advertising. The term *archival* in the description of mending materials is used rather loosely by some suppliers.

Three mending materials to consider are paper, adhesive, and mending tape. All paper should be acid free, that is alkaline-buffered or pH neutral. Adhesives include pastes, glues, and synthetic adhesives (such as polyvinyl acetate or PVA). Ideally adhesives should be reversible (removable), flexible, and have an adequate shelflife.

Mending tapes include rubber-based tape and archival tape. Preservation professionals are united in their warnings not to use mending tapes in repairs. What are the reasons?

Common book tape is a rubber-based mending tape. Typically, a worn spine or a frayed book cover corner is mended with book tape. Use of this tape, however, is a classic example of creating more harm than good. The tape shrinks with age, oozes the gum base at the sides, and cannot be successfully removed from the book. The book must be removed from its covers and rebound at the bindery. Meanwhile, staff time and materials have been wasted.

Cellophane tape is another product. Cellophane tape has been used for everything from mending a torn page to reaffixing an entire text block to a cover. A fairly recent innovation is the use of wide cellophane tape to protect the spine of new paperbacks upon receipt. Once again, such measures are a waste of staff time and supply funds. This tape dries out, becomes brittle, and stains the surface to which it once adhered. The lack of flexibility of cellophane tape creates a stiff edge that may eventually cut the page or the paper cover that folds back against it. Inevitably the book will require more costly repair due to these incorrect mending materials.

Stitched binder tape also has a gummed back. Often this tape is used as a quick fix for reattaching a text block that has pulled free from the cover of the book. As with cellophane tape, the adhesive will dry and become brittle. Since the cloth binder tape is much heavier than the end paper, the paper will simply tear or be cut by the stiff edge of the tape.

Archival tape which is transparent, thin, acid-free, and removable is the only mending tape that preservation professionals will accept and they do so cautiously. As stated earlier, the word "archival" can be used loosely in supplier advertisements. One brand that is currently acceptable is Archival Aids.®

Torn Page Repair

One of the most common minor problems is the torn page. Batching books with torn pages or according to repair needs will increase efficiency. Three options for page mending include the use of heat set tissue, the use of archival tape or the use of mending tissue and adhesive. The choice depends on the type of item, the possibility of replacement, the time available for mending, and the cost involved.

Heat set tissue requires the use of a tacking iron, preferably one equipped with a teflon-coated bottom. The procedure is relatively simple and fast and is suited to slick or shiny paper, such as that found in art books. The transparent tissue is placed over the tear. The iron, set on medium temperature, releases the adhesive. The length of time and the pressure with which the iron is held on the tissue determine the adhesion.

Archival tape is very thin and pressure sensitive. The tape is simply placed over the tear and pressed smooth with a bone folder. (See figure 3 for repairing a leaf.) Both heat set tissue and archival tape can be removed; they will not become brittle and will not stain or leave residue as cellophane tape will. The trade-off for the speed and manageability of heat set tissue and archival tape is the higher cost involved.

The use of mending tissue and adhesive is the least expensive process. Heidi Kyle notes that this process costs as much as 20 percent less than the other two outlined. Although a certain degree of skill is required, the procedure is not difficult and can be learned easily. Materials needed include Japanese mending tissue—a long-fibered, thin paper particularly suited to mending because of its strength and non-acidity. Other supplies required are a small watercolor brush, bone folder, dissecting needle, metal ruler, scissors, wax paper, blotter paper, a piece of 100 percent polyester dress lining material (called terylene), two weights (a cloth-wrapped brick or a glass paper weight will do), and an adhesive mixture of polyvinyl acetate (PVA) and methyl cellulose (4:6 ratio). Preservation professionals are selective in their choice of PVAs available on the market. Among the best known are Elmer's and Sobo. These, however, become more brittle when dry than does product No. 834-403 (formerly Jade 403), which is available from Aabbitt Adhesives noted in the back of this pamphlet. The mixture of PVA and methyl cellulose is recommended because PVA alone cannot be removed in water. Remember that the ability to reverse a mending process is a critical requirement.

Select a tissue that is lighter in weight than the paper of the page being mended. A variety of weights is described in the suppliers' catalogs. Measure a piece of tissue slightly larger than the tear itself—about 1/2″ wider and 1/2″ longer. Score it by running a dissecting needle along the edge of the ruler, and tear it by pulling it apart along the score.

Prepare the book by opening it to the torn page and placing a weight on the opposite page to hold it open. Place a piece of wax paper under the torn page so that adhesive will not seep through.

Place the piece of tissue on a clean, smooth surface and paint one side with the adhesive mixture, thoroughly coating it. Lift one corner of the strip by sliding the dissecting needle under it, and carefully take the strip between the fingers. Place the tissue over the tear. The tissue should also extend about 1/4″ beyond the edge of the page. This will be trimmed when the repair is dry. Place a piece of terylene on top of the applied tissue and cover it with blotter paper. Rub down with a bone folder to set the tissue and to absorb as much excess moisture as possible. Place wax paper on top of the mended tear and a weight on top. Allow the mend to dry for an hour or two.

Page Hinging

Hinging is a repair procedure for reaffixing a loose page to the text block. Often loose pages are "tipped in," meaning that they are glued to an adjacent page along the inner margin. The two pages are stiff and not easily readable as a result. Hinging is preferable to tipping in since it allows

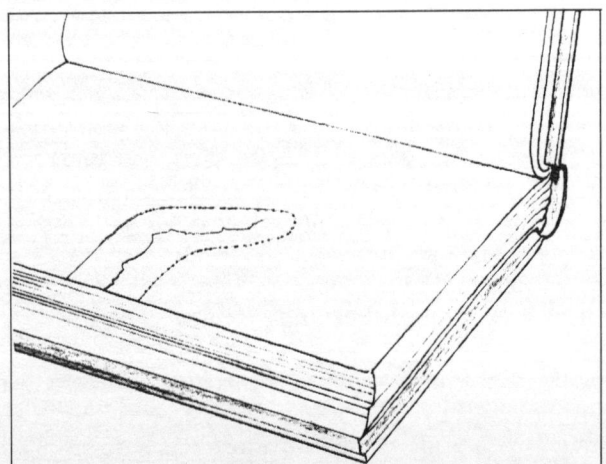

Figure 3. Repairing a leaf

the reaffixed page to swing freely on a hinge made of pliable Japanese tissue which is pasted to the adjacent page.

Materials needed for this process include Japanese mending tissue, a mixture of PVA and methyl cellulose, scissors, a medium-sized brush, a bone folder, two weights, a metal ruler, a dissecting needle, terylene, blotter paper, and wax paper.

Open the book to the place where the loose page will be reaffixed. Gently remove any ragged page edges remaining in the gutter of the book. (See figure 4A–D for description of page hinging.) Align the text block evenly and place a weight on top of the pages on the left. Place the loose page back into position on the right. Be certain to align the exterior edge of the loose page with the fore edge of the text block. Look at the loose page to determine if there is more existing margin on the left (interior margin) or the right (exterior margin). Trim approximately 1/4" from the larger of the two margins. This trimming is necessary because the new hinge will increase the width of the page. Be certain that the inner margin of the page is a clean straight edge. Replace the loose page in the book, aligning the exterior edge as before. (See figure 4B.) Place a weight on top of the page to hold it securely.

The Japanese tissue should be measured to extend approximately 1/4" beyond the text block on each end. It should be wide enough to overlap the interior margin of the loose page without covering the print and to extend fully into the gutter of the book.

With the grain of the Japanese tissue paper running parallel to that of the loose page, cut a strip to the specifications outlined above. Determine the grain by gently bowing the piece of paper between your hands. The paper will flex easily in the direction of its grain; resistance occurs when it is folded against its grain. Cut the paper by running the point of the dissecting needle along the edge of the metal ruler. Once scored, the paper should be gently pulled apart.

The simplest method to paste up the hinging strip is to spread the paste out evenly with the brush on a smooth, clean surface such as a piece of plexiglas. Place the hinging strip on this paste-painted surface. Place a piece of wax paper on top of the strip and rub the strip to coat it with the paste. Discard the wax paper and gently lift a corner of the pasted strip with the dissecting needle. Grasp this corner and remove the strip. Picking the strip up with both hands lay it, paste side down, on the loose page positioned in the book, placing it so that it overlaps the inner margin of the loose page and meets the gutter of the book. The space between the edge of the loose page and the gutter will allow the pasted hinge to affix to the page underneath. Place two strips of wax paper in the gutter between adjacent pages (see figure 4C) so that paste will not penetrate through and adhere them together.

Lay a piece of terylene on top of the hinge and top this with a piece of blotter paper. (See figure 4D.) Rub the hinge with a bone folder to absorb as much excess paste as possible. Placing a weight on the affixed page, allow the hinge to dry open for one to two hours. Complete the mending process by trimming the ends of the hinge the height of the text block and removing the two pieces of wax paper.

Tightening the Hinges of a Book

One of the most common problems found in a book is a text block that worked free from the spine of its cover. This often happens to large, heavy books such as those found in the library's reference collection. The repair process is simple and economical. A prompt five-minute repair may save the library an expensive commercial rebinding job later.

The procedure requires knitting needles (medium and long lengths), discarded card catalog drawer rods, a bone folder, an empty container approximately ten inches tall, a book press, wax paper, and PVA. Begin by placing the book on its tail, with the spine facing you. Open the covers. Press the text block forward away from the spine cover. Select a knitting needle slightly longer than the book is tall. Dip it in the container filled with PVA, diluted with water (7:3 ratio). When the needle is completely coated, insert it into the hinge area between the text block and the case. Roll the needle in this joint; then remove it. (See figure 5.) Repeat for the other joint.

Lay the book on its side and, using the bone folder, crease the exterior of the hinge to seal the pasted joint. Place wax paper between the case and the front and back end sheets. Place clean knitting needles or the rods from card catalog drawers on the top and bottom of the book, resting in the exterior hinge areas and put the book between the boards of a book press. Remove it from the press after fifteen minutes and leave it flat until completely dry.

Cleaning Paper

Most librarians have opened a returned book to discover that every other sentence has been underlined, editorial comments have been scribbled in the margins, or the book has become a baby's coloring pad. The best strategy for addressing this type of problem is an aggressive program of user education. Some damage to the paper's surface, wax crayon marks, for example, simply cannot be reversed. Ink presents special problems as well. Attempts to use diluted bleach to remove ink from paper will weaken the paper fibers. Dirt and pencil lead, however, can be cleaned from the paper, but this should be done with care.

To clean the pages of a book properly, the following supplies are needed: an Opaline pad, a Pink Pearl eraser, and a soft bristle brush. Begin by rotating and pressing the Opaline pad between the palms of the hands to release the pad's cleaning granules onto the paper. Gently rub the granules over the dirt or pencil lead with the fingertips. The granules will darken as they absorb the dirt. Brush them off the page with the soft brush. More difficult marks may be removed with a Pink Pearl eraser. Erase in small strokes with a light touch and always work from the interior of the page to the outer edge. Remember, overzealous erasing can cause more damage than did the original pencil mark.

Water, Mold, and Mildew

Whether the result of a leaky pipe or the negligence of a library user, water-soaked books present yet another problem for the librarian. A wet book should be treated immediately. Mold will begin to grow within forty-eight hours. If immediate treatment is a problem, freezing the book is the answer. Simply wrap the book in freezer paper and store it in the nearest freezer until treatment is possible.

Do not bake the book in the oven. Remember the detrimental effect of heat on glues and paper fibers.

Begin treatment for a wet book by standing it on its tail on a flat surface with its cover spread open. Place an electric fan about three feet from the fore edge of the book. If the book has been frozen, do not attempt to free any stiff pages. Let the fan do the initial work. If it is a cold day, set the book near an open window. Paper dries faster in cold air. Allow the fan, set on low speed, to dry the book, checking every so often to ensure that the pages are not bunched and are drying evenly. If the book is quite wet, insert paper towels every fifteen to twenty pages and change them every three hours. When the pages are dry to the touch, put the book in a book press for twenty-four hours to prevent the pages from buckling. Keep the dried book isolated for forty-eight hours to be certain that no mold will form.

Coated paper, such as that found in *National Geographic* or in fine art books, presents a particular problem when wet. Its clay-based coating will quickly seal pages together. Coated paper should never be frozen.

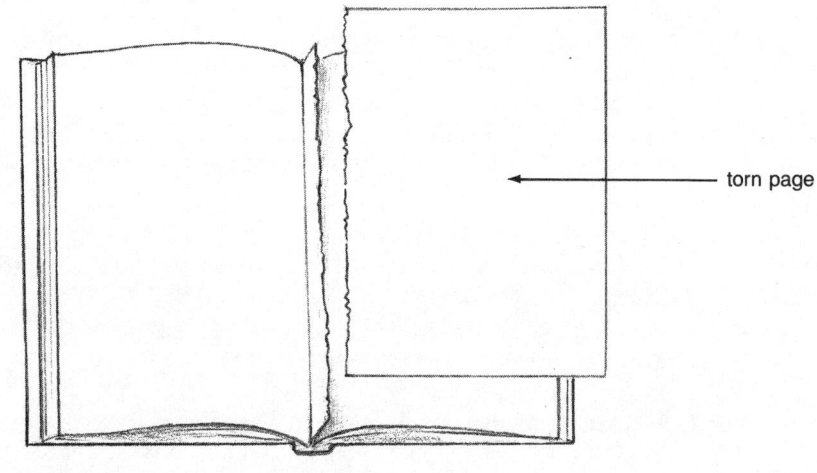

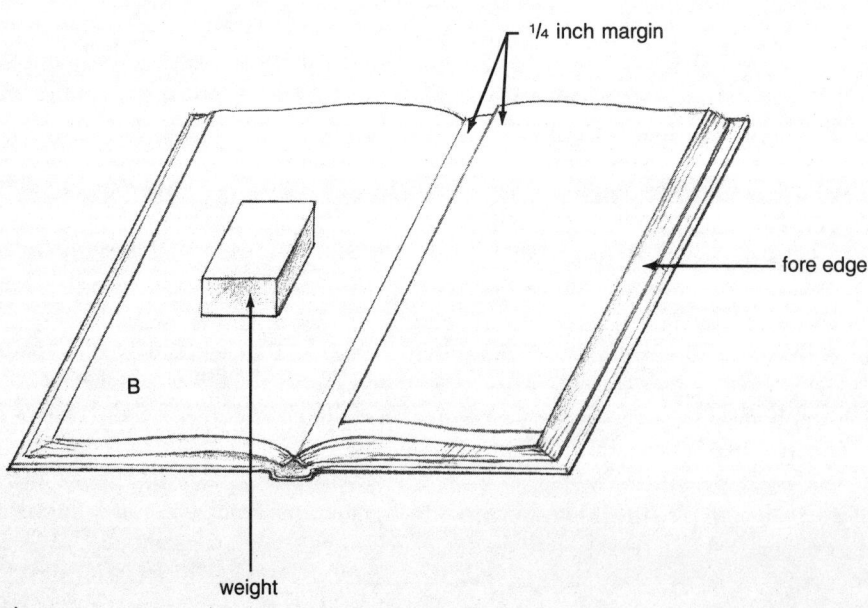

Figure 4. Steps in page hinging

Each page must be interleaved with tissue paper and then fan dried.

Should mold or mildew attack, the book must be decontaminated. Because mold and mildew spread, contaminated books should be isolated. Move such books to a well-ventilated dry area. With a soft brush remove all spores. If the mold is in a white powdery stage, standing the books fanned open for two to three days in a well-ventilated area may cure the problem. Standing the books in full sun for one hour can also kill the spores. More serious mold will require treatment with chemicals. The basic process is fairly simple, involving the use of a mixture of ethanol and a 10 percent solution of thymol. The infected pages can be sprayed with this solution to kill the active mold spores. However, any use of chemicals should not be undertaken by untrained staff. If professional help cannot be secured, seriously damaged items should simply be removed from the collection. Because mold and mildew do present such problems, book storage areas should be monitored frequently.

Commercial Book Binding

Most libraries, large and small, turn to a commercial library binder for the bulk of book repair. Too often, however, librarians relinquish all decision-making responsibility to the commercial binder. Although the binder has powerful tools and machinery at his disposal, the binder should not have all the authority to choose the appropriate binding method.

Preservation librarians and commercial binders have worked diligently over the past two decades to educate one

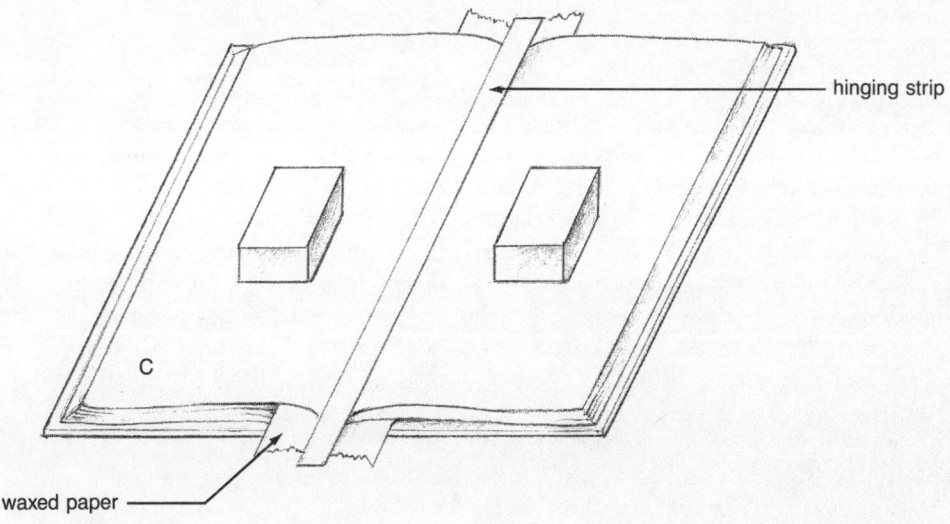

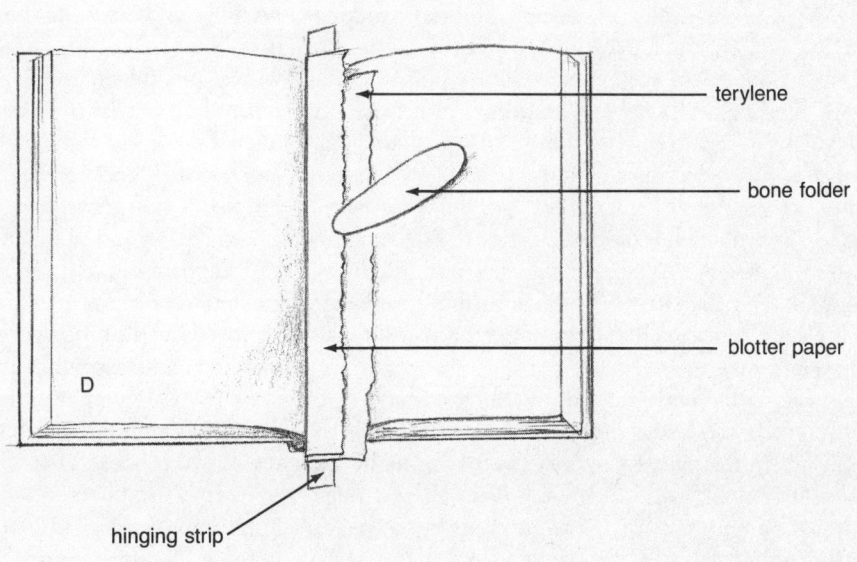

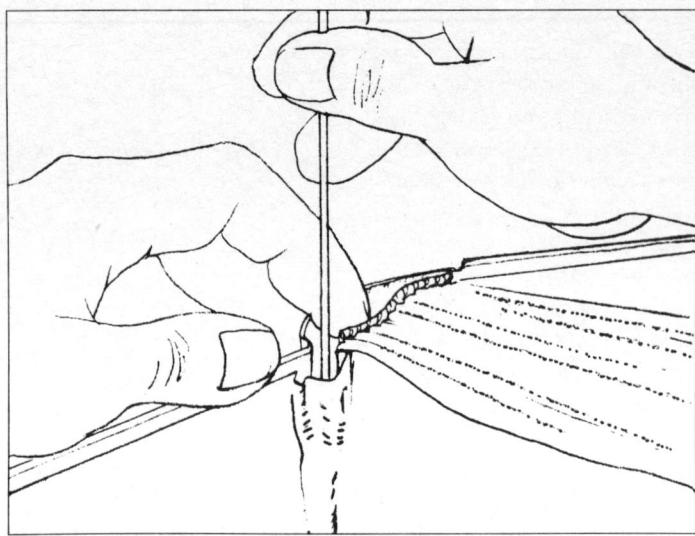

Figure 5. Applying adhesive into loose joint

another about their respective needs and to create an atmosphere of mutual trust and respect. Today it is the responsibility of the librarian to understand the construction of a book, to comprehend the variety of repair options offered by the commercial binder, and to request specific binding choices for each book. The binder, in turn, should offer a clearly stated contract with explicit pricing structure for each method and prompt, reliable, quality service.

The problem for small libraries is that they generally have a meager binding budget. This means two things. First, more costly quality options are sacrificed for economy. Second, a small budget may mean less clout with the bindery when poor quality is a problem since the loss of business will not be of great concern. There are no easy solutions to these inherent dilemmas. The issue of economy versus quality must be resolved, again, in terms of the library's mission statement. Are these sacrifices acceptable or should the library's budget be reviewed to allocate more to commercial binding? If quality is the issue, the unified action of several libraries working together in a geographic area may prove effective.

It is important to understand several key points about commercial binding. The library binding industry has traditionally considered strength of binding its primary goal. The industry requires that library binding be able to survive one hundred circulations. This sounds fine, but does every book need to survive one hundred circulations? Preservation librarians have stressed, instead, permanence and durability of binding and serviceability of the book as the criteria for adequate binding. A discussion of binding options will make these distinctions clearer.

The primary method utilized by library binders to achieve strength is a binding process called *oversewing* or *library binding*. In the oversewing process, the spine of the text block is trimmed, with the result that all the page signature folds are cut off. Holes are punched in the pages and a machine then stitches the pages together. The end result is a product that may be strong, but has drawbacks. An oversewn book will not open easily or lie flat when opened, tending, instead, to spring shut. The inner margin, or gutter, is greatly reduced because the spine has been trimmed. This means the text may be unreadable or the plates and illustrations may be partially concealed in the gutter. The book, because of tight sewing, is extremely difficult to photocopy and may be crushed under the cover of the copy machine. Should the book become damaged, rebinding is almost impossible. If the librarian does not indicate otherwise, this may be the method chosen by the binder to handle the library's book repairs.

Sometimes oversewing is an appropriate option. Children's books that receive extremely heavy use, are easily replaced, or intended for eventual discard are candidates for oversewing. If a book simply cannot be treated by any other binding process, oversewing becomes the necessary choice.

The most important point to remember in choosing a binding process is to have as little done to the book as possible. If the case is falling off but the text block is still whole and intact, there is no need to have the binder do more than *reaffix the case* or *case in* the book. The binder must be clearly instructed, otherwise the book may quite easily come back to the library with the spine trimmed, oversewn, and recased.

Why would the binder do more than is necessary? Commercial binding is an industry that operates on the principle of mass production. Thousands of books from hundreds of libraries come into the binding plant and are handled on an assembly line. If the librarian does not flag the book for particular attention, the book will undergo the basic process available. The bindery does not have the time to review each book. That is the business of the librarian.

It is important to note, however, that when the librarian asks for a binding process different from the mass-production approach, a higher cost is incurred. It is more expensive to recase a book than it is to oversew it because the book must be pulled off the assembly line and given special treatment. The librarian should make binding decisions based on intended use and desired life of the volume. Unlike research libraries, small libraries generally do not expect to retain everything that they acquire permanently. The librarian should, however, understand the binding processes available in order to make educated choices for the collection.

If the pages of the book are loose or falling out, determine if they are folded together in groups, or signatures. If folds are evident when looking at the head or tail of a book at the spine, then the inner margin or gutter in the center of each signature should reveal threads sewn to hold the text block together. These threads may become loose or break, and the loose pages must be reaffixed. The best method for treating this problem is to *sew through the fold*. The pages will be sewn back together as they were originally. Once again, this process will be more costly. Large art books printed on glossy paper with illustrations that spread across two pages are prime candidates for sewing through the fold. This type of binding will not trim off any of the fold or reduce the inner margin. Therefore, the illustrations will not be damaged, and the book can be opened easily.

If loose pages are a problem and there is no evidence of oversewing or sewing through the folds, chances are that the book was bound originally with adhesive. The process of *adhesive binding* began around 1900. In this method, the folds are cut so that the pages are in single sheets, and glue is applied to the spine of the text block. The process may also be called *budget binding* or *perfect binding*. If pages are loose, however, it is possible that poor glue was used in the process or that the spine of the text block was not properly prepared before gluing. Sadly, many new books arrive from publishers with such bindings. They are not as durable as those with sewn signatures.

Nevertheless, adhesive binding can be a very acceptable rebinding option. The method is a good choice if a book has been previously adhesive bound or oversewn, but it is important that the librarian request that a *double fan adhesive* binding process be used. In this procedure, the loose pages of the text are clamped together on the fore edge side while the spine edge is fanned in one direction and glued, then in the opposite direction and glued again. The glue thoroughly coats and penetrates between each sheet up to 1/16". Good quality glues must be used. This process gives a very strong bond and usually will be guaranteed by a binder for the life of the book. Books over two inches thick, however, generally cannot be bound by this method, nor can books with stiff or glossy paper because the glues do not penetrate or adhere well.

A review of the following columns should help in the decision-making process. The options are listed in priority order. Should the first option not be feasible with respect to the criteria, the next should be considered.

Binding option	*Criteria*
Recase	Although the case is loose or free, the text block is sewn and the original sewing thread is intact.
Sew through fold	The text block is composed of signatures; the folds of the signatures are intact, although they have become loose or free from the text block.
Double-fan adhesive binding	The text block is 2 inches thick or less, and the paper is not stiff or glossy.
Oversew	The text block has binding margins at least 5/8-inch wide, and the paper is sturdy.

The goals of rebinding are opening ease, permanence, and cost-effectiveness. Each volume returned from the bindery should be inspected carefully for quality workmanship. If binding instructions were disregarded, special note should be made to talk with the bindery. It is the bindery's responsibility to correct errors such as loose pages, pages out of order, etc. Records should be kept of problems. These can be consulted so that intelligent decisions can be made regarding contract renewal.

The commercial bindery and its representative are employed by the library. To ensure a good working relationship, the preservation coordinator should discuss the library's goals with the representative and establish a clear understanding of the library's and the company's responsibilities. A clearly stated contract is the first step in this direction. Binding specifications, pricing structure for various binding options, pickup and delivery dates, packing procedures, the contract period, and insurance requirements should be clearly covered. The bindery representative can be of great help to the librarian and can discuss the terms of the contract knowledgeably with the preservation coordinator. The contract should provide the basis for a sound business relationship between binder and library.

Preservation of Audiovisuals

The primary emphasis of this pamphlet is on book conservation since books make up the largest proportion of materials found in small libraries. However, because more and more small libraries house and circulate a variety of media, a few key points should be made regarding the care and handling of some of these formats.

Microforms

Microfilm and microfiche require much the same environmental controls as books. Fluctuations in temperature and humidity can encourage mold growth or cause film to buckle or become brittle. Dust and dirt can scratch the film surface. Microfilm and microfiche should be stored in appropriate acid-free boxes or envelopes. Metal paper clips, pressure sensitive tape, or rubber bands should be avoided since they will harm the film. Metal storage cabinets should be chosen so that there is no chance of film corrosion from the chemicals in wooden ones.

Film should be cleaned periodically with a soft lint-free cloth or brush to remove particles of dust and dirt. Equally important for the care of audiovisuals is proper maintenance of the machinery required for their use. Film and fiche readers should have their screens, lenses, and glass trays cleaned daily. Check to ensure that viewer bulbs are not left burning on film or a fiche that is no longer in use. Signs should encourage patrons to handle microforms with care and should provide instructions for proper use of the machinery.

Phonodiscs

Phonodiscs that are circulated to the public have a short life. Still, that life can be extended through proper library care and user education. Instructions for proper handling of phonodiscs can be affixed to the dust jacket. This will convey the message that the library cares about the treatment its materials receive as well as encourage concern from the user.

Upon receipt of phonodiscs in the library, the cellophane or plastic wrapping on the dust jacket should be removed since it will cause the record to warp. The dust jacket and inner liner will help extend the life of the recording. Shelved discs should be placed vertically at all times and never tightly packed. Slanted or horizontal shelving will also cause warping.

Temperature fluctuation in the library should be kept to a minimum, and patrons should be advised of the damage that heating and cooling will cause. It is important to handle discs as little as possible. Every attempt should be made to keep fingers off the playing surface. Oils in the skin help attract and hold dust particles in the grooves of the recording. Dust particles will cause a ticking noise when the stylus of a player hits the particle. Dust will also become impacted in the grooves, permanently damaging the recording. As with books, therefore, temperature and humidity control, cleanliness, and proper handling are important.

It is time-consuming but important to clean phonodiscs after use. A carbon fiber record brush is a helpful device that can penetrate the grooves of the disc and remove particles of dust safely. Patrons should be reminded that clean and properly operating equipment is also critical to the life of a recording.

Videotape

A relative newcomer to the library collection is the videocassette. While the book as we know it is over 1500 years old, videotape, as a medium for education and entertainment, is only a little over twenty-five years old. In most public libraries it is an extremely popular addition.

The care of videotape does not vary greatly from the precautions discussed for other audiovisual formats. Although figures are not exact, the average circulating life of a videotape is approximately two years or one hundred viewings. The primary cause of damage is from user negligence such as improper use of playback machinery or use of machinery that has not been cleaned. Once again, instructions affixed to the cassette's plastic case can educate users in proper care and handling.

If at all possible, tapes should be returned to the library before rewinding. During rewinding, the library staff can check for problems and damage. This practice will ensure that the tapes are rewound promptly and at a constant speed.

Videotapes should be shelved upright on grounded metal or wooden shelving to avoid any chance of demagnetizing the tape by exposure to an electromagnetic field. Control of heat, humidity, and dust are also important to the life of the medium.

In conclusion, collections of nonprint media have grown and will continue to grow in libraries of all sizes. The decision to acquire these formats should include consideration of their proper care and maintenance. The environmental requirements for their preservation do not vary greatly from those needed for books.

Special attention must be given to the handling, storage, and use of viewing or playback equipment, and the education of staff and patrons will be required. A chapter-by-chapter, in-depth discussion of these concerns for a great variety of nonprint materials can be found in *Conservation in the Library: A Handbook of Use and Care of Traditional and Nontraditional Materials,* edited by Susan Swartzburg. The book is recommended for small libraries that have extended their collections beyond the paper format.

Disaster Planning

The old adage states that an ounce of prevention is worth a pound of cure. Although everyone hopes that disasters such as fire or flood will never strike, the staff of the small library should consider these possibilities and be prepared to deal with them. A chain of command of library personnel with defined responsibilities at the time of crisis should be developed. A list of critical phone numbers of local services, such as the fire department, and of local businesses, such as plumbers and freezer warehouses should also be compiled. A list of collections to be salvaged, organized by priority, is advisable since clear thinking before the problem situation arises can determine the success or failure of rescue attempts.

The staff should become familiar with the fire protection and security systems in the library building. The fire marshal should be asked to review the building with the staff for potentially hazardous areas and to consult on a plan of action to be used in case of fire.

If water from a sprinkler system or fire hose is used to quench a fire, the library's collections will suffer additional physical damage. The National Fire Protection Association points out, however, that a sprinkler system does much less damage to library materials because of its design than do fire hoses.

Water damage from other sources should also be anticipated. Water pipes, sewer drains, roof-top air conditioning equipment, for example, should be inspected for safety and security. Books on top shelves are vulnerable to leaky pipes and roofs, books on bottom shelves may be subject to flood damage.

A good source for overall disaster planning is *The Library Disaster Preparedness Handbook*, published by the American Library Association. Some of its key points include the following: after a fire or flood, the building should be vented immediately to evacuate smoke and lower humidity; all floors that have been contaminated by smoke and water need to be scrubbed with a mold inhibitor; water logged books should be individually wrapped in freezer paper and frozen to -20° F or colder; slightly damp books should be air dried in a cool, dry place; books that are submerged in water should be left there until they can be packed off to a freezer facility such as a meat-packing house. This will reduce the chance of mildew developing.

The repair of library materials following extensive water or fire damage will require the assistance of professionals. According to the value and possibility of replacement of the materials, various options can be selected. The state library can be contacted for the names of facilities and professionals that can assist should disaster strike. The library's commercial binder may also have the capabilities to assist in repair. The advice of a professional conservator may be the library's best alternative, and the Restoration Office of the Library of Congress stands ready to serve as an information center. Nevertheless, replacement of items is nearly always less expensive than restoration. For the small library, this is an important point to bear in mind.

Preservation Networking

The physical well-being of library collections quite literally lies in the hands of concerned library staffs. Library literature in the 1970s alerted the profession to the critical nature of the problems facing book and audiovisual collections. Numerous workshops and seminars have been sponsored by the American Library Association and state and local library organizations during the 1980s in response to requests from those in the field for how-to and hands-on training and information.

Today, advice and assistance on preservation matters can be obtained through a phone call to the state library in almost every state or to the nearest regional network headquarters. The librarian in the small library can tap into a substantial body of literature and a large group of professionals with similar concerns. The small library in particular can benefit from the continued advances in preservation and conservation supported by the library profession.

The image of the librarian as keeper of the books need not be negative. In fact, it may become a rather unique one in the electronic world of the future. Intelligent and perceptive approaches to conservation and preservation are not small challenges. Extending the utility and life of a library's collection is an economically sound activity. Such pragmatic reasons argue for every library's involvement in educating staff and users in the proper care and handling of materials.

Bibliography

Books

Darling, Pamela. "A Local Preservation Program: Where to Start." *Library Journal* (15 November 1976): 2343-47.

DeCandido, Robert and Grace Anne Candido. "Micro-Preservation: Conserving the Small Library." *Library Resources and Technical Services* (April-June 1985): 151-60.

Horton, Carolyn. *Cleaning and Preserving Bindings and Related Materials*. 2d ed. rev. Chicago: American Library Association, 1969.

Hubbard, William. *Stack Management: A Practical Guide to Shelving and Maintaining Library Collections*. Chicago: American Library Association, 1981.

Kyle, Heidi. *Library Materials Preservation Manual: Practical Methods for Preserving Books, Pamphlets, and Other Printed Materials*. Bronxville, New York: Nicholas T. Smith, 1983.

Morris, John. *The Library Disaster Preparedness Handbook*. Chicago and London: American Library Association, 1986.

Morrow, Carolyn Clark and Carole Dyal. *Conservation Treatment Procedures: A Manual of Step-by-Step Procedures for the Maintenance and Repair of Library Materials*. 2d ed. Littleton, Colorado: Libraries Unlimited, Inc., 1986.

Swartzburg, Susan Garretson. *Conservation in the Library: A Handbook of Use and Care of Traditional and Non-Traditional Materials*. Westport, Connecticut: Greenwood Press, 1983.

Waters, Peter. *Procedures for Salvage of Water-Damaged Library Materials*. 2d ed. Washington: Library of Congress, 1979.

Winkle, Becky. "A Guide for Small Libraries: Preservation on a Shoestring, Low-and No-Budget Options to Get a Preservation Program Off the Ground." *American Libraries* (December 1985): 778-79.

Audiovisual Resources

Library of Congress. Preservation Office. *Handling Books in General Collections*. 35mm slide set and audiotape. Available on loan from the National Preservation Office, Library of Congress, Washington, DC 20540.

Simple Repairs for Library Materials. New Haven, Conn.: Yale University, 1981. 35mm slide set and audiotape. Available on loan from the National Preservation Office, Library of Congress, Washington, DC 20540.

Appendix

Suppliers

The following is a partial list of archival materials suppliers. Those listed should provide information on any of the equipment and supplies mentioned in this pamphlet. Contact each directly to request catalogs for pricing information. Visit booths at state library association conferences and the ARL conferences to obtain further information on suppliers.

Aabbitt Adhesives, 2403 N. Oakley Avenue, Chicago, IL 60647 (312-227-2700)

Aiko's Art Materials, 3347 N. Clark Street, Chicago, IL 60657 (312-404-5600)

Bookmakers, 2025 Eye Street NW, Room 502, Washington, DC 20006 (202-296-6613)

Brodart, 1609 Memorial Avenue, Williamsport, PA 17701 (1-800-233-8467)

Conservation Materials, 240 Freeport Boulevard, P.O. Box 2884, Sparks, NV 89431 (702-331-0582)

Light Impressions, 439 Monroe Avenue, P.O. Box 940, Rochester, NY 14603 (1-800-828-6216)

University Products, South Canal Street, P.O. Box 101, Holyoke, MA 01041 (1-800-628-1912)

Small Libraries Publications Series

The problems and challenges of operating small libraries are not a great deal different from those of large libraries. The administrator of the large library, though, normally has both more experience in various areas and more specialized help. The administrator of the small library, whether holding a library degree or not, is often thrown regularly and sometimes precipitately into "first-time" situations. This series is an attempt to provide some direction, reassurance, and practical help.

The series is directed primarily at librarians serving communities of 10,000 to 15,000 people, usually as administrators of independent libraries, although it is hoped that branch librarians and librarians serving larger communities may also find the pamphlets useful.

Copyright © 1989 by the American Library Association. All rights reserved except those which may be granted by Sections 107 and 108 of the Copyright Revision Act of 1976. Printed in the United States of America.

ISBN 0-8389-5718-8

Library of Congress Cataloging-in-Publication Data

Lowry, Marcia Duncan.
   Preservation and conservation in the small library / by Marcia Duncan Lowry.
   p. ; cm. — (LAMA small libraries publications series; no. 15)
   Bibliography: p.
   ISBN 0-8389-57188 (alk. paper)
   1. Library materials—Conservation and restoration. 2. Small libraries—Collection development. 3. Books—Conservation and restoration. I. Title. II. Series.
Z701.3.S53L69 1989
025.7—dc19
                                                             89-

Figures 2, 3, and 5 reprinted with permission from pages 6, 28, and of *Cleaning and Preserving Bindings and Related Materials*, 2nd ed. by Carolyn Horton, copyright © 1969 by ALA.

Library of
Davidson College

MARITIME STRATEGY AND THE BALANCE OF POWER

Admiral Jerauld Wright, Supreme Allied Commander Atlantic, and Vice-Admiral Sir John Eaton, RN, Deputy SACLANT, with President Dwight D. Eisenhower, SACLANT Headquarters, Norfolk, Virginia, 1957. *Reproduced with the permission of the Imperial War Museum, London.*

Maritime Strategy and the Balance of Power

Britain and America in the Twentieth Century

Edited by
John B. Hattendorf
Ernest J. King Professor of Maritime History
Naval War College, Newport, Rhode Island

and
Robert S. Jordan
Research Professor of International Institutions and
Professor of Political Science
University of New Orleans

Foreword by
Robert O'Neill
Chichele Professor of the History of War
and Fellow of All Souls College, Oxford

St. Martin's Press   New York

© John B. Hattendorf and Robert S. Jordan, 1989

All rights reserved. For information, write:
Scholarly and Reference Division,
St. Martin's Press, Inc., 175 Fifth Avenue, New York, N.Y. 10010

First published in the United States of America in 1989

Printed in Hong Kong

ISBN 0-312-03174-2

Library of Congress Cataloging-in-Publication Data
Maritime strategy and the balance of power: Britain and America in the twentieth century/edited by John B. Hattendorf and Robert S. Jordan; foreword by Robert O'Neill.
    p. cm.
Bibliography: p.
Includes index.
ISBN 0-312-03174-2
1. Naval strategy. 2. Sea-power—United States. 3. Sea-power—Great Britain. 4. United States—Military relations—Great Britain. 5. Great Britain—Military relations—United States. 6. Balance of power. I. Hattendorf, John B. II. Jordan, Robert S., 1929– .
V165.M37 1989
359.4′3—dc 19   89–5885
                                                                   CIP

This book is dedicated to our fathers:
Porter Maxwell Jarvis and Ralph Burdette Jordan

Contents

List of Plates	ix
Foreword by Robert O'Neill	xi
Acknowledgements	xv
Notes on the Contributors	xvi
Glossary of Abbreviations	xix

1 Introduction: The Balance of Power and the Anglo-American Maritime Relationship 1
   Robert S. Jordan

PART I THE BRITISH MODEL OF ORGANISING FOR TWENTIETH-CENTURY COALITION WARFARE

2 The Origins of Imperial Defence 23
   Norman H. Gibbs

3 The Chiefs of Staff and the Higher Organisation for Defence in Britain, 1904–84 37
   John Gooch

4 The Influence of the British Secretariat Tradition on Twentieth-Century International Peace-Keeping 56
   Robert S. Jordan

PART II ANGLO-AMERICAN MARITIME THEORY IN THE TWENTIETH CENTURY

5 Alfred Thayer Mahan and his Strategic Thought 83
   John B. Hattendorf

6 Mahan Revisited 95
   Donald M. Schurman

7 The Strategic Thought of Sir Julian S. Corbett 110
   Barry D. Hunt

8 Recent Thinking on the Theory of Naval Strategy 136
   John B. Hattendorf

PART III   ANGLO-AMERICAN RIVALRIES AND COALITIONS, 1898–1945

9   The Relevance of the Prewar British and American Maritime Strategies to the First World War and its Aftermath, 1898–1920   165
    Paul M. Kennedy

10 The Washington Conference and the Naval Balance of Power, 1921–22   189
    J. Kenneth McDonald

11 'Are We Ready?' The Development of American and British Naval Strategy, 1922–39   214
    Malcolm H. Murfett

12 Anglo-American Naval Co-operation in the Second World War, 1939–45   243
    Marc Milner

PART IV   PLANNING FOR A FUTURE WAR IN THE NUCLEAR AGE

13 Anglo-American Maritime Strategy in the Era of Massive Retaliation, 1945–60   271
    Eric Grove and Geoffrey Till

14 Anglo-American Maritime Strategy in the Era of Flexible Response, 1960–80   304
    Joel J. Sokolsky

15 Fleet Renewal and Maritime Strategy in the 1980s   330
    Robert S. Wood

16 Conclusions: Maritime Strategy and National Policy: Historical Accident or Purposeful Planning?   348
    John B. Hattendorf and Robert S. Jordan

Index   357

List of Plates

1. Captain A. T. Mahan
2. Sir Julian Corbett
3. HM the King's visit to the Grand Fleet, 21–24 July, 1918, HM the King receiving Admiral Rodman USN on board British battleship *Queen Elizabeth*
4. Admiral Sir David Beatty, Vice Admiral Sir John de Robeck and Rear Admiral Sir Hugh Evan-Thomas bidding farewell to Admiral William Benson USN after his visit to the Grand Fleet, 1918
5. Members of the Imperial War Cabinet, 10, Downing Street, London, 1918
6. Admiral Sir Bruce Fraser and US Admiral William 'Bull' Halsey discuss Occupation duties, Tokyo, 1945
7. Admiral H. Kent Hewitt USN presenting the US Legion of Merit to Admiral Sir Max Horton, RN, 4 June 1946
8. King George VI welcomed on board USS *Columbus* (CA-74) by Admiral Richard L. Conolly USN, 8 November 1949
9. Admiral Lynde D. McCormick, Commander-in-Chief Atlantic and Admiral Robert D. Carney, Commander-in-Chief, Allied Forces, Southern Europe, at Naples Airport, Italy, 6 October 1952
10. General Bernard Rogers, Supreme Allied Commander, Europe, Admiral Wesley MacDonald, Supreme Allied Commander Atlantic; Admiral Sir William Staveley, Commander-in-Chief Channel, 1987

Foreword

The nature of sea power has long been all too easily misunderstood. The very mention of the term conjures up visions of grey steel bows pitching as they slice through the turbulence of the slightly less grey North Sea in an urgent and vital quest for the enemy battle fleet. What seems much less interesting to call to mind is the picture of commerce sedately crossing the oceans in ordinary cargo vessels and huge tankers of ample beam. Yet it is that second picture which portrays the foundations of sea power more accurately than the first. Without a substantial merchant fleet nations have little foundation in terms of national wealth, tradition and seamanship on which to build sea power. It is easy to forget that the last great naval battles, those of the Pacific war from Midway to the Philippines Sea, are nearly two generations behind us and the types of ships that fought them were phased out or sunk long ago.

The drama of *Perestroika*, whatever its outcome, shows clearly that economic power rather than military might is now recognised by both East and West as the key element in determining the fortunes of nations. This same lesson is equally clear from the way in which Japan has returned to great-power status in the past twenty years. Whether or not there is ever another major naval battle, commerce will continue to flow in increasing quantities and the fortunes of nations will depend much more on trading profits than on numbers of capital ships in their navies.

Yet the world is a long way from being a sanctuary for maritime trade. The free use of the seas can always be challenged by any government or private agency which can threaten the security or liberty of an individual merchant ship. More severe threats still arise out of regional conflicts such as the Gulf War. The possibility of the outbreak of a world war continues to exist despite its generally perceived futility. The naval dimension of sea power may be subordinate to the economic but it continues to be important and will remain of great, although perhaps increasingly latent, significance until human society organises itself in some way to eliminate the use of force between its more significant sub-elements. The subject of this book will endure in importance, although perhaps in an increasingly speculative and theoretical way.

Because the seas are a medium inhospitable if not intrinsically fatal to man, naval strength is peculiarly sensitive to technological change. Defeated or dispersed armies can regroup and return to the attack. Defeated navies more frequently lie either at the bottom of the sea or in their enemies' harbours, their crews blown apart, drowned or imprisoned. Continuing increases in the accuracy and destructive power of weapons has for many years sharpened debate within all naval powers regarding the future development of warships and the ways in which they should best be used. Yet although the relative advantages of land-based strike forces and aircraft have increased *vis-à-vis* surface warships, they cannot exert the durability of presence in troubled regions nor the degree of physical control over maritime areas of which navies are capable. Technological change complicates life for the maritime strategist but it is a long way from making him redundant. Indeed, as we see in the cases of nuclear propulsion, electronic communications and defensive systems at sea, technology also continues to offer him new opportunities and scope for ingenuity. The ultimate threat to naval vessels, the nuclear warhead, has given navies the key role in maintaining the credibility of the second strike capabilities on which our system of stability through deterrence has rested for nearly thirty years.

Hence it is only prudent to re-examine our ideas on how naval force should be used and how the political problems of their command and control at both national and alliance levels might be handled. This book is both timely and appropriately broad in scope. It is also appropriate that the book gives detailed consideration to the ideas of the principal American and British naval theorists, Mahan and Corbett. Without disrespect to Mahan I believe that of all who have written on maritime strategy, nobody has given us a more cogent analysis of the topic than Corbett and it is pleasing that this book contributes further to his resuscitation from undeserved obscurity.

It has long been part of our thinking on war that there are two basic kinds of conflict: limited and unlimited. Corbett strove to differentiate clearly between them in a way which was both original and highly relevant to the analysis of conflicts and strategies today. In his examination of limited war, using the British conquest of Canada as his example, he emphasised the dual role of seapower, first to isolate the theatre of war from other external influences and second to secure the home base of the intervening power. The closest contemporary approximation to this case is that of operations in an island state or group, such as Grenada or the Falklands, where isolation was relatively easy to achieve and, after it had been obtained, victory was certain in the former case and highly probable in the latter. Without that isolation, as the Korean and Vietnam wars showed, prospects for conducting such a conflict successfully are highly problematical. Peninsulas are more suitable than states with long land borders for limited conflicts waged by naval powers because they offer more scope for attack from the sea and restrict the available areas of operations for enemy ground and air forces. However, as the Korean War showed, a determined enemy can still survive and sustain offensive action even when the connecting link between the front line and the support base is narrow. Obviously a naval power should not attempt to operate against an essentially land-locked state with several neighbours through which supplies can flow. Those charged with the conduct of a limited war could do worse than to study Corbett before evaluating their chances of success.

Foreword

Corbett's criticism of Mahan's more absolute doctrine of the command of the sea is even more relevant in the age of the Law of the Sea than when he first made it. More formidable obstacles now lie in the way of any state or alliance system which seeks to acquire command of the sea in the face of increasingly significant legal restraints and the growth in the numbers of sovereign states with maritime interests and capabilities. The seas can no longer be divided essentially between a handful of major maritime powers in peace or war. Their use must be concerted with substantial numbers of littoral powers who are likely to see their prime interests served by keeping trouble out of their region than by ready co-operation with one super-power or the other.

Increasingly the key element in the assertion of sea power has become recognised, as Corbett perceived, to be the security of communications routes. Commerce has to be able to move to keep major powers alive and forces have to be transported and maintained if they are to be of any use in the maritime environment. It is not essential to have full command of the sea to be able to secure communications and the burden on naval forces will obviously be the less if some reliance can be made on shore facilities for logistic and air support. The rising political unpopularity of foreign military bases in many of the states where they are situated suggests that such assistance will become increasingly difficult to obtain or to rely on once promised. These thoughts must already be troubling the minds of United States and possibly Soviet naval planners as they contemplate the future of their facilities at Subic Bay and Cam Ranh Bay. As developing states come increasingly to assert their independence and their rejection of involvement in the East–West rivalry, greater emphasis will have to be placed on more politically oriented strategies to build cooperation on a basis of sovereign equality rather than on the old one of dependence. The interesting question now is who is the better placed to gain from such a trend in international relations? If it is the West, then should not the West be doing more to encourage it by developing more positive relations with those who stand somewhat aloof, including the friends and allies of the Soviet Union?

This volume is, of course, concerned with a much wider topic than the theory of sea power. Essentially its scope is the period in which Britain passed the torch of leadership in sea power to the United States. Now it is the latter who is the troubled giant with never enough resources to cover all the tasks that are so readily delegated by those who rely substantially on America's protection of their interests. But British experience remains relevant to American policy-makers and their maritime advisers, particularly in the fields of planning, policy formulation and resource allocation. The lessons to be drawn are, for the most part, negative as study of the First World War and interwar periods readily attests. Despite the many differences between the positions of Britain in the world of the late nineteenth and early twentieth centuries and the United States in that of the late twentieth, some basic similarities stand out: responsibility for the management of a vast maritime network of bases; a need to control fleets spread over several oceans and seas; a position of leadership to maintain against a predominantly land-based rival; and a balance of power to preserve in the face of continuing change in the fortunes of nations. Both countries need the free use of the sea to sustain their trading economies and to meet their alliance commitments. Both remain keen practitioners of the art of maritime strategy. Both have flourishing communities of historians and contemporary policy analysts who can exchange ideas freely and with mutual benefit.

It is particularly fitting that the volume contains a chapter by Norman Gibbs because he did so much through his supervision and teaching of graduate students at Oxford between 1953 and 1977 to strengthen analytical capabilities on either side of the Atlantic. All of his students, of whom six are represented amongst the contributors to this volume, stand deeply in his debt for the care he took with their drafts, the encouragement and confidence he gave them when the going was difficult, and the wider view he offered of their own subjects from the perspective of his own experience and insights. The theme of the volume is closely related to his interests and indeed he laid its foundations not only in his supervision but also in his lectures on Corbett and his study of British and American systems of policy-making and operational command. Gibbs's students learned much from his gentle pragmatism in appraising their work and interpreting the wider world of scholarship to them. This book points to useful conclusions on maritime affairs that flow from British pragmatism in strategic policy formulation and alliance management before the torch was passed.

ROBERT O'NEILL

Acknowledgements

The idea for this book originated when we were colleagues in the Center for Naval Warfare Studies at the US Naval War College, in Newport, Rhode Island. We had both taken advanced degrees in military studies at Oxford University, under the guidance of Professor Norman Gibbs of All Souls College, and we had both been members of St Antony's College. It was, therefore, natural for us to think in an Anglo-American context about naval strategy, and the institutions of naval warfare.

We are grateful to many persons and institutions on both sides of the Atlantic for their support, including St Antony's College, Oxford; Dr Ian Bellany of the Centre for the Study of Arms Control and International Security, University of Lancaster; Dean Donald Hendricks of the Earl K. Long Library, University of New Orleans; and Dean Robert S. Wood of the Center for Naval Warfare Studies, Naval War College. Without the invaluable and dedicated assistance of Jane H. Jordan, who had to work with editors/authors located in different countries, along with Susan Parkinson of the Centre at the University of Lancaster, and Jim Collins of the Center at the Naval War College, this manuscript would not have been possible. Paul Sanchez-Navarro, a graduate assistant at both the University of New Orleans and the University of Lancaster, also deserves a word of appreciation, as does Robert H. Jordon.

Responsibility for the contents of these essays must rest with the contributors rather than with the institutions with which they are affiliated. It is our hope and purpose that this collective effort will find a useful place in the literature of Anglo-American maritime relations, and twentieth century international history.

JOHN B. HATTENDORF
ROBERT S. JORDAN

Notes on the Contributors

Norman H. Gibbs is Emeritus Fellow of All Souls College, Oxford. From 1954 to 1977, he was the Chichele Professor of the History of War in the University of Oxford. He is the author of *Rearmament Policy*, volume 1, in the *Grand Strategy* series of the official British History of the Second World War.

John Gooch is Professor of History at the University of Lancaster. In 1985–6, he was Secretary of the Navy Visiting Fellow at the US Naval War College, and in 1988 was Visiting Professor at Yale University. His most recent book is *The Prospect of War: Studies in British Defence Policy 1847–1942*.

Eric Grove now works as an independent defence consultant and Associate Director of the Foundation for International Security. A former Deputy Head of Strategic Studies at the Royal Naval College, Dartmouth, his most recent books are *From Vanguard to Trident: British Naval Policy Since World War II* and *The Future of Sea Power*.

John B. Hattendorf is the Ernest J. King Professor of Maritime History at the US Naval War College and director of the College's advanced research programme. In 1986, he was a senior associate member of St Antony's College, Oxford. His most recent book is *England in the War of the Spanish Succession: A Study in the English View and Conduct of Grand Strategy, 1702–1713*.

Barry D. Hunt is Professor and Chairman of the History Department at the Royal Military College of Canada. He is the author of *Sailor–Scholar: Admiral Sir Herbert Richmond*.

Robert S. Jordan is Research Professor of International Institutions and Professor of Political Science at the University of New Orleans. He was a member of St Antony's College in 1957–60 and was Distinguished Visiting Professor of Strategy at the US Naval War College in 1984–6. From January to August 1988, he was Fulbright Visiting Professor, Centre for the Study of Arms Control and International Security, University of Lancaster. His most recent book is *Generals in International Politics: NATO's Supreme Allied Commander, Europe*.

Paul M. Kennedy is the J. Richardson Dilworth Professor of History at Yale University. He was a member of St Antony's College in 1966–70, and is the author of *The Rise and Fall of British Naval Mastery* and, most recently, *The Rise and Fall of the Great Powers*.

J. Kenneth McDonald is Chief Historian of the Central Intelligence Agency. He was a commoner of St Antony's College, Oxford, 1958–61, and a Senior Associate Member 1967–69. At the US Naval War College he was Chester W. Nimitz Professor of National Security Affairs 1972–73, and Ernest J. King Professor of Maritime History 1973–74. His most recent publication is 'Thomas Hinman Moorer', in R. W. Love, Jr. (ed.), *The Chiefs of Naval Operations*.

Marc Milner is Associate Professor of History at the University of New Brunswick. He is the author of the prize-winning book, *North Atlantic Run: The Royal Canadian Navy and the Battle for the Convoys*.

Malcolm H. Murfett is Senior Lecturer in History at the National University of Singapore. In 1986–7, he was a senior associate member of St Antony's College, Oxford. He is the author of *Fool-Proof Relations: The Search for Anglo-American Naval Cooperation During the Chamberlain Years, 1937–40*.

Robert O'Neill is the Chichele Professor of the History of War and a Fellow of All Souls College, Oxford. He was the Head of the Australian National University's Strategic and Defence Studies Centre from 1971 to 1982, and Director of the International Institute of Strategic Studies from 1982 to 1987. He is the author of *The German Army and the Nazi Party* and *Australia in the Korean War* (2 vols).

Donald M. Schurman has recently retired as Professor and Chairman of the History Department at the Royal Military College of Canada. He is the author of *The Education of a Navy* and *Julian S. Corbett, 1854–1922: Historian of British Maritime Policy from Drake to Jellicoe*.

Joel J. Sokolsky is Associate Professor in the Department of Political and Economic Science at the Royal Military College of Canada. He is the co-author of *Canada and Collective Security: Odd Man Out* and *Canadian Defence: Decisions and Determinants*.

Geoffrey Till is Professor in the Department of History and International Affairs at the Royal Naval College, Greenwich, and lecturer in the Department of War Studies at King's College, London. He is the author of *Maritime Strategy in the Nuclear Age*; his most recent book is *Modern Seapower*.

Robert S. Wood is Dean of the Center for Naval Warfare Studies and Chester

W. Nimitz Professor of National Security Affairs at the US Naval War College. From 1980 to 1983, he was Chairman of the Strategy Department at the Naval War College. He is the author of *France in the World Community: Decolonization, Peacekeeping and the United Nations*.

Glossary of Abbreviations

AA/SSB	Anglo-American Allied Anti-submarine Board
A/C	Aircraft
A/S	anti-submarine
ACE	Allied Command Europe (NATO)
ASW	Anti-submarine warfare
AFAR	Azores Fixed Acoustic Range
AFCENT	Allied Forces Central Europe (NATO)
AFNORTH	Allied Forces Northern Europe (NATO)
AFSOUTH	Allied Forces Southern Europe (NATO)
BENELUX	Belgium-Netherlands-Luxemburg
BPF	British Pacific Fleet
CAS	Chief of Air Staff (UK)
CBO	Congressional Budget Office
CCS	Combined Chiefs of Staff
CDC	Colonial Defence Committee
CDS	Chief of the Defence Staff
CID	Committee of Imperial Defence
CIGS	Chief of the Imperial General Staff
C-in-C	Commander-in-Chief
CINCEASTLANT	Commander-in-Chief, Eastern Atlantic (NATO)
CINCHAN	Commander-in-Chief, Channel Command (NATO)
CINCNELM	Commander, Naval Forces Eastern Atlantic and Mediterranean
CINCSOUTH	Commander in Chief Allied Forces Southern Europe
CNO	Chief of Naval Operations (US)
CNS	Chief of Naval Staff (UK)
COMNAVSOUTH	Commander, Allied Naval Forces, Southern Europe
CONMAROPS	Concept of maritime operations
COS	Chief of Staff
CSG	Civilian Sealift Group (NATO)
CTF	Commander, Task Force
CVA	Attack aircraft carrier
CVBG	Carrier battle group
DNI	Director of Naval Intelligence
DOD	Department of Defense (USA)
DPC	Defence Planning Committee (NATO)
DRC	Defence Requirements Committee
FORACS	Fleet operational readiness accuracy check sites
G-I-N	Greenland–Iceland–Norway
G-I-UK	Greenland–Iceland–United Kingdom
GLCM	Ground launched ballistic missile
IBERLANT	Iberian-Atlantic Command (NATO)
JCS	Joint Chiefs of Staff (US)
LTDP	Long Term Defence Program
LRO	Long Range Objectives Group
MARAIRMED	Maritime Air Mediterrean (NATO)
MC	NATO Military Committee

Glossary of Abbreviations

MCF	Maritime Contingency Force
Mk	Mark
Mod	modification
MOD	Ministry of Defence (UK)
NAVOCFORMED	Naval On-call Force Mediterranean (NATO)
NCS	Naval Control of Shipping
NNAG	NATO Naval Armaments Group
NSC	National Security Council (US)
OKW	Oberkommando der Wehrmacht
PBOS	Planning Board for Ocean Shipping (NATO)
PHMO	Patrol Hydrofoil Missile Ship
PM	Prime Minister
RAF	Royal Air Force
RCN	Royal Canadian Navy
RMA	Royal Marine Artillery
RN	Royal Navy
SAC	Strategic Air Command
SACEUR	Supreme Allied Commander, Europe
SACLANT	Supreme Allied Commander, Atlantic
SIOP	Single Integrated Operation Plan
SPANS	Sealift Procurement and National Security
SLBM	Sea launched ballistic missile
SLOC	Sea lines (or lanes) of communication
SSBN	Nuclear powered, ballistic missile carrying submarine
SSN	Nuclear powered attack submarine
STANAVFORCHAN	Standing Naval Force, Channel (NATO)
STANAVFORLANT	Standing Naval Force, Atlantic (NATO)
TWOATAF	Second Allied Tactical Air Force (NATO)
UKAIR	United Kingdom Air Defence
USAAC	United States Army Air Corps (before 1942)
USAAF	United States Army Air Force (1942–7)
USAF	United States Air Force (after 1947)
USMC	United States Marine Corps
USN	United States Navy
VSTOL	Very short take off and landing
V/STOL	Vertical/short take off and landing
WESTLANT	Western Atlantic Area
WTO	Warsaw Treaty Organisation

1 Introduction: The Balance of Power and the Anglo-American Maritime Relationship

Robert S. Jordan

Great Powers employ a variety of maritime strategies, but these different national approaches have often been overlooked or inappropriately lumped together. Furthermore the concepts that were derived from these strategies can have effects that transcend the immediate historical circumstances that gave rise to them. Finally the methods of administration devised to implement governmental policy can either be viewed as a model for other rising Great Powers or can provide the means of making possible new institutions dealing with issues of concern to Great Powers. The purpose of this collection of essays is to examine the similarity in the Anglo-American perspective of Great Power maritime strategy and the role of navies in maintaining a balance of power. The institutions that emerged are very much a part of the life of all nations, great or small, and hence are worthy of careful examination.

CONCEPTS OF THE BALANCE OF POWER

Martin Wight, the historian, has observed that the balance of power appears to follow a cycle which he distinguishes as first forming a multiple balance (three or more), and then being transformed into a simple balance.[1] The multiple balance has been more characteristic of the modern state system but, when the Great Powers of the day find their interests conflicting directly, then the simple balance emerges. The simple balance is marked by heightened tension, arms races, and repeated crises which test the balance. As these crises persist, with the accompanying manoeuvrings for position and search for allies, they tend to spill over into open conflict. The run-up to the First and Second World Wars are usually cited as examples, with the post-1945 period seen as an exception, due primarily to the totality of the threat of nuclear weapons.

The decisive element as to whether war will in fact occur most probably falls to that state that 'holds the balance', which usually seems to be an insular or extra-continental Power. This role, deriving from maritime strength, was ascribed to Britain until well into the twentieth century. It had shifted to the United States by the period between the two World Wars.

Holding the 'balance' in this way is transitory because of the possibility that a condition of multiple balance may slip into a simple balance. This is evidenced in the immediate post-Second World War period by Britain's unsuccessful attempt to provide a 'bridge' or 'middle way' between the respective spheres of influence in Europe of the United States and the Soviet Union. It was not long before Britain came to rest in the American 'camp' as a simple balance, or bipolarity, emerged.[2]

A state that perceives of itself as a balancer usually also perceives of itself as holding some element of power that can be used to tip the scales, which gives this state freedom of action to influence events perhaps out of proportion to its total strength, as it threatens to combine with one or the other pre-determined coalition. This is more easily accomplished by an insular state, relying on a small army or on continental allies, thereby reserving to itself the preponderance of maritime power to throw in with one side or the other. For example, in the mid-1860s, the function of the British army was defined formally by Parliament to be 'the preservation of the balance of power in Europe'.[3] One of the early rationales for the British and French nuclear *forces de frappe* was precisely to hold in reserve a vital element of national power to be used in a manner that might tip the Cold War scales. Thus the inherent flexibility of maritime power can combine with the flexibility of being the balancer, to provide maximum freedom of national action. Unfortunately this condition has existed only relatively briefly in modern history, but the hope or search for such a role goes on in order to obtain the obvious advantages that it can afford to the state that achieves this level of influence.

Between the two concepts of a multiple balance and a simple balance, there can be interposed five other varieties:[4]

1 *The balance perceived as an even distribution of power*, in which no state is preponderant to the extent that it can successfully threaten the others. The nineteenth-century 'Congress system' was intended to do this, but first Britain and then Germany did not support it sufficiently to maintain an approximately even distribution of power. The condition of equilibrium implied under these circumstances was expected to operate more or less universally. But there was a mechanistic element in this approach, which aroused criticism in Britain:

> We fell into the habit of treating them [the Low Countries] as mere pawns in the game. . . . We were prepared to take part in handing them over to alien rulers . . . merely in accordance with the convenience of the general European situation. It was the bad side of the balance of power.[5]

2 *The balance perceived as power evenly distributed among otherwise unequal states.* The Security Council of the United Nations, with its right of veto for the five Permanent Members, illustrates this concept. Although the five might not in fact be equal in national power, they are considered by treaty as equals in protecting their respective interests. Apart from the legal aspect, states that possess approximately equal power are reluctant to leave matters as they are: they argue that there must be a margin of superiority precisely in order to preserve the even distribution by deterring the prospective enemy from overarming. Thus there is always the thrust to upset the balance in order to preserve it. The first decade and a half after the end of the Second World War can be characterised in this way, thus fuelling the arms race between the two superpowers, which in turn had brought about attempts from the 1960s onward to define the 'balance' between the two, known as 'arms control'. As one scholar put it:

> It is not the actual distribution of power which is vital: it is rather the way in which national leaders *think* that power is distributed. In contrast orthodox theory assumes that the power of nations can be measured with some objectivity... Indeed, it is the problem of accurately measuring the relative power of nations which goes far to explain why wars occur. War is a dispute about the measurement of power. War marks the choice of a new set of weights and measures.[6]

3 Thus *the search for a balance becomes an argument as to how the current distribution of power favours or injures one of the parties.* The *status quo* of the moment becomes the measure of the balance and by its very nature therefore becomes temporary. For example, the American notion of the balance – or distribution – of power during the immediate aftermath of the Second World War, when the United States was indisputably the greatest economic and military Power, was almost immediately challanged by the Soviet Union. When the United States attempted to preserve its advantage in atomic power through the so-called Baruch Plan, the attempt was doomed to fail precisely because the next greatest Power, the Soviet Union, would not accept permanent inferiority. There had to be a redistribution, or the establishment of a new *status quo*, which in turn, by 1957 and the advent of Sputnik, cast the United States into the role of attempting to restore its previously favourable balance – such are the ways of arms races.

4 *The special role of the balancer in maintaining an even distribution of power* provides another variation on the concept of balance. The dilemma in this instance is that, if the balancer state is weaker than the other Powers, then it will play the role of mediator, which is what Britain hoped to do after the Second World War. If the balancer state is stronger, then it will play the role of arbiter. Consequently the special advantage that the

balancer possesses can in time become an element of a reconstituted balance. Certainly Britain, for example, did not consider its influence outside Europe in the eighteenth and nineteenth centuries to be contained within a European-defined balance system of equilibrium, or rough equality, in the distribution of power. As far as the distribution in Europe was concerned Britain had reserved this balancer role to itself. Perceived another way, Britain, by maintaining supremacy through the Royal Navy outside Europe until the latter part of the nineteenth century (the arbiter), was able to contain the Powers of continental Europe within Europe through the balance of power concept that had Britain as the 'balancer' (the mediator). Thus two concepts of 'balance' coexisted in British policy during this period, both dependent on a strong and predominant navy.

5 *The balance of power seen as a self-regulatory mechanism*, in which, whenever a balance threatens to be disrupted, a countervailing power will emerge to deter it. Woodrow Wilson explained the American intervention in the First World War as being necessary to bring to bear 'the power of the New World in order to redress the balance of the Old'. (Not his phrase.) The balance is in this respect ever-changing, shifting and adjusting in order that no one state or group of states can gain permanent ascendency over the others. Thus war avoidance is linked to a dynamic concept of balance, with threat of the outbreak of war linked to a freezing of the balance that is then placed under constant disruptive pressure.[7] Superpower deterrence policy might fall into this category.

CONCEPT OF THE MARITIME BALANCE OF POWER

The political philosopher David Hume observed that the policy of the balance of power is founded 'on common sense and obvious reasoning'.[8] Unfortunately he might have been the only person to think so because, as discussed earlier, there have always been varieties of balance of power calculations. One, for example, is the argument between so-called navalists and continentalists, or the maritime and continental schools of strategy. To the continentalists, the ultimate determinant of war lies in conflict between armies in which maritime power becomes a supporting rather than a decisive ingredient. Landing troops ashore or protecting the sea lanes might be crucial for sustaining a conflict, but a further necessary ingredient has required the enlistment of continental allies to create a decisive countervailing military balance against a continental Power that threatened hegemony. Alternatively, if the First World War provides a lesson, it is that reverses for the British on land could be sustained, but, if Britain had suffered one decisive naval defeat, the war might well have been lost.

Fortunately, German prewar planning ignored the fact of the Allies' superior naval power or the offensive and defensive possibilities of their own navy.

For Britain, as Paul Kennedy has observed, 'this debate, about the balance that should be reached between land power and sea power, between Europe and the wider world, between the army and the navy, was always a contentious one ...'[9] The same can be said about the United States, especially in the twentieth century. As is discussed later, the key lies in the availability or utility of allies. Yet, perhaps even more important as far as the modern state system is concerned, the rise in the level of military power is directly attributable to the fact that for the past several hundred years there has been a steady increase in sea power as a component of power politics. Obviously the expansion of Europe into the non-European world, with all that this brought in wealth, power and glory, rested on the capacity to establish and maintain control over vital sea lanes on a global scale.

Yet, as Sir James Cable has commented, 'Power does not exist. Not in any absolute sense. It is the ability to apply appropriate force about a given point.'[10] Analytically, of course, this statement is a simplification of a more elaborate process of assessing the many ingredients of power – and especially of maritime power – that may or may not result in the direct application of force. What Cable was focussing on was the question: 'Power to do what?' The symbolism of 'showing the flag' is often used to justify a large fleet, even if the use of that fleet in the manner intended (or threatened) is problematical. President Theodore Roosevelt's sailing of the Great White Fleet around the world might fit this situation. But, whereas a fleet at sea was safe a century ago from everything but another fleet, with the advent of mines, torpedoes, aircraft, submarines and ballistic missiles, such is no longer the case.[11] Limited control of the sea for one's own particular and immediate purposes is all that we can hope for today, much in the way that Corbett modified Mahan's concept of 'command of the sea'.

Today there is talk of 'asymmetry' in weighing the balance of competing or comparable weapons, including maritime weapons platforms. Matching capability to missions has always been a risky business because it takes a long lead-time to create ingredients of maritime power, that is, ships, but missions can change almost overnight, as for example after an election or a coup. Calculations of the missions and forces of other states – friend and foe alike – go on continuously to sustain their own respective forces. For example, other advantages were gained from the world cruise of the US Atlantic fleet:

> The fleet left Hampton Roads in December 1907, an aggregation of tolerably efficient individual ships; it returned to the same anchorage late in February 1909, a veteran unit of power, a monument to the leadership of a President who had momentarily lifted the American people out of their traditional isolationism and, in the face of stubborn and growing

opposition, had led them with pomp and circumstance into the main stream of world politics.[12]

The Reagan administration's return of the battleship to active sea duty is another case in point. Can all that immense fire-power really deter or overwhelm a prospective enemy who, very probably, will be capable only of low-intensity maritime conflict? Or is the mere presence of this ship, with its escorting flotilla, a sufficient threat to deter hostile action or damage to American interests in some relatively remote corner of the world? In other words, in the absence of actual conflict, it is extremely difficult to weigh costs and benefits when it comes to assessing maritime power.

But one thing has been certain; if first the Royal Navy and later the United States Navy were ever incapable of keeping open the Atlantic sea lanes to enable the extra-continental Powers' resources to be brought to bear in a continental European war, then the navies' primary purposes would have been unfulfilled. Admiral Sherman, Chief of Naval Operations in 1951, in assessing the Cold War threat, foresaw two choices for the United States: 'to accept the necessity for deploying forces overseas ... troops, ships and aircraft – and to fight overseas if necessary', or 'to withdraw, abandon our allies, and later to fight alone'. He went on to conclude: 'I believe that the first course offers the greatest prospect of survival.'[13] For the threat in Europe currently posed by the Soviet Union, following threats in earlier times by France, then Russia, and finally by Germany, continues to be viewed essentially, although not exclusively, as a continental threat.

There has been a recent tendency towards fusion of sea power and land-based power, especially in regard to the maritime dimension of NATO *vis-à-vis* the Warsaw Pact. However, even though the smaller navies in NATO can act as advance land defences, can act to keep clear the avenues of re-supply and reinforcement to the continent, can provide air support for land operations, can facilitate sea-borne landings of ground forces, and can provide a degree of substitutability of land- and sea-based nuclear deterrents, the ultimate NATO maritime requirement continues to be to maintain the sea lines of communication from the United States to its allies in Western Europe (which would include the Scandinavian and Mediterranean flanks).[14] The way to do this has aroused much debate – should it be through a more aggressive 'forward strategy' which puts pressure early on in a crisis on the maritime flanks of the central front, thus serving, it is hoped, to deter an outbreak of hostilities (but also risking a premature engagement at sea that might lead to 'horizontal escalation'), or should the posture be one of 'wait-and-see', in which the NATO maritime forces stand astride the major international waterways and await the movement of hostile naval forces towards the Atlantic lifeline?

This basic strategic issue is discussed further later on, focussing in particular on the way in which Britain as an increasingly regional maritime

Power fits more into a Western European than into an Atlantic context (the Falklands War to the contrary notwithstanding). Before going any further, however, it is instructive to examine British conceptions of the balance of power.

BRITISH CONCEPTIONS OF THE BALANCE OF POWER

If a central theme of this book is that the United States, in its strategic thought and its capacity to act accordingly, was beholden to the prior British experience, it is equally the case that the larger conceptual framework within which American power was assembled and brought to bear in twentieth-century world politics derives from nineteenth-century British political conceptions of international order and the use of force. Put succinctly, American notions of the proper way to organise force in international society are outgrowths of British thought. This is an important point because, as the United States inherited the mantle of British Great Power leadership as the twentieth century unfolded, there was, inevitably, a lively domestic political debate as to the conceptual bases on which this leadership should rest.

One approach, articulated by Lord Castlereagh in defining his view of the Concert of Europe, linked the preservation of the territorial integrity – that is, boundaries – of the states of Europe as defined by the post-Napoleonic settlement, with the notion of a 'combination' of the Great Powers to make this possible. This was essentially a conservative idea of protecting the *status quo* as defined in 1815. As it was summarised:

> The three conceptions of the system of [19th century European] security related to situations of war, crisis and peace. They constituted a scale, ranging from temporary combination to permanent union, from physical intervention in the face of common danger to moral commitment on the basis of general agreement. Common to them all was that they presented the Concert of Europe as an instrument for maintaining the balance of power.[15]

Thus, through the Concert of Europe, the balance of power was used either to justify intervention or to preserve the territorial settlement of 1815. In this sense it was used as a conservative, *status quo*, instrument to justify British policy towards post-Napoleonic Europe. Another opinion evolved, however, which disapproved of the use of the balance of power to justify the 1815 settlement and the subsequent 'concert' of Great Powers. This other view was non-interventionist, with the balance itself being adapted to justify economic and social change and, in particular, 'progressive' change that might favour the weak as well as the strong. Specifically, Britain should remain out of European Great Power politics unless her vital interests were directly involved, precisely in order to conserve her power to perfect what then was viewed as a global system of trade and commerce not only led, but dominated, by Britain. 'Splendid isolation' was preferable to Great Power coalition politics, and all of this would be in the name of perfecting society within the context of spreading Christian principles. In other words, British nineteenth-century maritime strength could be viewed as useful in two ways: helping to preserve the European balance of power, and also helping to preserve a progressive notion of global trade, commerce and social development.

Both of these strands were reflected in parallel turn-of-the-century American concepts of the use of the balance of power to justify expansionism, viz Mahanian notions of command of the sea in the interests of trade, commerce and Christian principles. Also progressive social thought took up the strand of a 'concert' to employ the same principles that evolved through the 'Congress system' in the creation of the League of Nations; that is, the League being the organisation, in a 'higher' form, of the international community in the interests of minimising war among the Great Powers and, incidentally, preserving the territorial integrity of the smaller Powers. Along with this, the British method of organising its governmental machinery for planning and conducting war was transformed into the post-First World War League organisation created to bring about 'peaceful change'. As noted later, the influence of Britain not only in defining the type of international political system appropriate for a world Power, but also in creating the machinery to ensure the survival of this system, was a dominant one on American thinking. Wilsonianism is a direct descendant of British nineteenth-century social and political thought, as it either reflected accepted notions of the balance of power or rejected them, and the notion of an international secretariat derives directly from the British cabinet tradition.

CONCEPTS OF AN ANGLO-AMERICAN REGIONAL BALANCE OF POWER

The geographical separation of Britain, as the former colonial 'mother country' from the newly-formed United States afforded the evolution of a psychological buffer zone that gradually transformed intense antagonism into the shared conception described above of the two states' roles in world affairs.[16] The year 1898, according to one scholar:

> ... marked the close of the period associated with the Manchester school of economics, brought American influence to bear on English imperial policy ... [Chamberlain] had no doubt of the civilising role of Anglo-Saxons or the need of enlisting Americans in controlling the tropics; in

January 1899, he said, 'It will not be any longer the Imperial policy of England alone.'[17]

In truth, there never has been room enough in the world for coexisting British and American empires, a simple balance of power relationship and so, although logically there should have been intermittent warfare between the two English-speaking maritime Powers, no war has occurred since 1812. Why was this so? In the Western hemisphere, any attempt to allocate territories and islands to respective American and British spheres of influence ran up against the essentially monopolistic nature of maritime power, so that, as the Royal Navy drew back from overseas commitments as the nineteenth century gave way to the twentieth century, American maritime strength expanded concomitantly. This strength gradually brought about the primacy of America's interests over Britain's in this hemisphere.

Even though the balance of power concept, as articulated (not invented) by the British to justify containing the overseas maritime expansion of the Powers in Europe, could also have been applied against the United States, the sum total of Britain's capacity to do this was inadequate. With a navy second to Britain's, 'it was ... arguable that the United States had a vital interest in helping to maintain the European balance of power and, above all, the Anglo-German equipoise, which kept the two greatest European fleets, especially Germany's, confined to European waters'.[18] The United States Navy could keep either of the two hostile navies from destroying the other, which clearly gave the United States the 'balancer' maritime role.

For Britain it was easier, budgetarily, to relinquish primacy – but not hegemony – in the Americas to the United States in order to focus British maritime strength within a European power context. This was not because of any necessary affection for the United States on the part of British statesmen, but because of what was viewed as geopolitical necessity.

For example, Britain could have attempted to co-opt France in the mid-nineteenth century to block the American expansion in California which had opened up the United States to the Pacific, but did not. Nor did Britain enlist Germany in support of Chile to counter American expansion into all of Latin America.[19] But with whom, in fact, could Britain ally herself against the United States? Although Franco-British co-operation was instigated against the Russians in the Crimea in a containment coalition in regard to the Black Sea, could this co-operation be extended to contain the United States in the Caribbean? Would the United States, in turn, attempt to revive the Franco-American alliance that had proved successful once before against Britain? Concern over the British and American naval balance in the Caribbean and of commercial access to Latin America was perceived in London as being secondary to British concern over an industrialising expansionist Russia and an industrialised unified Germany. Ironically, although Britain sympathised with the Confederate South in the American Civil War, and doubtless would not have shed any tears over a Union dissolved into two hostile states, the subsequent threat from a unified Germany suggested that a strong America in its maritime rear could be a form of reassurance against a threatening Germany virtually in its front yard. By the turn of the century, as long as the two greatest navies confronted one another across the North Sea, there was little incentive for either to contemplate attacking the American navy which was, even prior to the First World War, a match for any navy except possibly the Royal Navy, and that navy had been 'frankly and openly excluded from the list of possible enemies'.[20]

Thus, although the expanding maritime power of the United States ought to have collided with the maritime–mercantile power of Britain, such did not occur.[21] Even though there were scares and, as revealed elsewhere in this book, planning and preparation for war between Britain and the United States well into the twentieth century, in actuality such a prospect was ruled out of the question.

Thus, prior to the First World War, even though the balance of power relationship between Britain and the United States was asymmetrical, this produced stalemate rather than conflict. Britain avoided conflict as the United States established its hegemony in the Western hemisphere and expanded into the rest of the world by surrendering effective balancing 'for the mirage of a concert and joint Anglo-American supremacy'. By not opposing growing American naval power, Britain hoped to replace the land–sea power asymmetry between them with a new solidarity, 'based on symmetry first in naval capabilities and eventually on that basis also in global concerns'.[22]

None the less each side during this period was willing to attempt subversion of the other. For example, the Americans were always willing to stir things up in Canada and, as mentioned, the British were not disinterested in the outcome of the American Civil War. Yet in spite of periodic bluffs and crises neither side attempted to apply effective force or counterforce against the other. As George Liska observed:

> Until the end of the nineteenth century, stalemate rested upon Britain's naval supremacy on the high seas, usable against the principal American coastal cities, and on America's ability to deploy against Canada a superior potential on land in prolonged hostilities and instant superiority on the Great Lakes.[23]

During this time the priorities were regional for the United States and global for Britain, in sharp contrast to the situation a century later. But the process of role reversal was shortly to begin as '... the United States evolved from being a devolutionary substitute for Britain regionally into a saviour and, finally, successor of Britain's empire globally'.[24]

One turning-point was the famous Naval Act of 1916, which provided an 'increase of appropriations over seven times more than the total increase by Great Britain in the ten years prior to the European war'.[25] Although the US naval budget was revised as the needs of naval warfare were redefined, from capital ship construction that would not come to fruition for several years, to a ship configuration more in keeping with convoying and anti-submarine warfare, naval policy and foreign policy were henceforth inextricably linked. The stage was set for the United States, after the Armistice in 1918, to challenge *both* British naval supremacy in the Atlantic and Japanese naval supremacy in the Western Pacific.

A further shift in the Anglo-American maritime balance of power revealed itself during the Second World War, most clearly over discussions in 1944 about the role of the Royal Navy in the Pacific. The American Chief of Naval Operations, Fleet Admiral Ernest J. King, was not enthusiastic about any British contribution to the war against Japan and, even when Churchill had obtained Roosevelt's endorsement, King commented that he did not think it wise if such participation were for political purposes. But the decision to tie the British fleet to the American in the central Pacific campaigns enabled the British to point out that the combined nature of their operations had been successful. As one commentator observed, 'It would be fatal for Anglo-American post-war relations if it could be said that America had made a great contribution to the defeat of Germany, whereas the British effort against Japan had been limited to the pursuit of her own selfish interests in Burma, Malaya and Hong Kong.'[26]

THE ANGLO-AMERICAN RELATIONSHIP IN THE EAST–WEST MARITIME BALANCE

Britain's share of the glory of the victory both in Europe and in the Pacific was considerable but, almost immediately, as evidenced by the crisis of the Greek civil war in 1946–7, actual British power went into rapid decline. Regionally the scenario was the defence of Western Europe. With great reluctance the Royal Navy had to give way in the Mediterranean to the United States' Sixth Fleet, and although within NATO a Commander-in-Chief Channel Command (CINCHAN) was created for Britain, this command was not equal to the other two NATO 'Supremos' – the Supreme Allied Commander, Europe (SACEUR) and the Supreme Allied Commander, Atlantic (SACLANT), both commanders being American.

Even though the Sixth Fleet was the predominant naval presence in the Mediterranean, the British felt strongly that one of their nationals should head a prospective NATO command through the traditional 'lifeline of the Empire' that would include the entire Middle – or Near – East, as a co-equal with the SACEUR and SACLANT, but this desire was not to be fulfilled.

The United States was not prepared to see the Sixth Fleet used for non-American 'out of area' purposes, and so a compromise was struck as reported by Lord Ismay, Secretary-General of NATO:

> At the end of 1952, it was decided that a further subordinate command should be set up under SACEUR with the title 'Allied Forces Mediterranean' and with headquarters at Malta. The first Commander-in-Chief was Admiral the Earl Mountbatten of Burma (UK), and his headquarters came into being in March 1953. Later that year the various national forces under his control were organised into six separate areas, each commanded by an admiral: one French, one Greek, one Turkish, one Italian, and two British. In time of war, Admiral Mountbatten would be responsible for the security of the line of communications through the Mediterranean.[27]

The compromise thus reached involved British acceptance of the necessity of making the new command subordinate to, not co-equal with, SACEUR, and American willingness to 'share' naval responsibilities in an area where existing naval power was overwhelmingly an American contribution, both by way of the Sixth Fleet and through naval vessels 'loaned' or given to France, Italy, Greece and Turkey.[28] The Sixth Fleet was redesignated for NATO purposes, as Naval Striking and Support Forces Southern Europe, and had elements of French and Italian naval strength attached to it for NATO training purposes.

The contingency plans put together during 1947–9, called *Half Moon*, *Fleetwood*, and *Trojan* foresaw a Soviet sweep to the Channel in 60 days or less, and within 200 days overrunning most of Turkey, Iraq and Iran. In the south-west, the Pyrenees would be the line.[29] All of these plans involved maintaining control of the Atlantic, which is why Admiral Richard Conolly did not agree with Admiral Arthur W. Radford, during the debate over carriers versus B-36s, that carriers were primarily justified as a strategic retaliatory weapons platform. Admiral Conolly had at that time the responsibility for protecting the Atlantic sea lanes, and to do so required both the maintenance of air superiority near land for the possible re-embarkation of an American army in retreat, and/or the use of naval air in anti-submarine warfare (ASW) to maintain re-supply and reinforcement.[30] None the less, by 1950–1 the Navy had succeeded in having its carrier task forces counted as part of the overall 'offensive striking power' under the doctrine of striking massively at the Soviet Union at the outset of hostilities.

By September 1952 the Atlantic Fleet (the Second Fleet) could rendezvous in British waters with almost 100 ships from the other NATO navies for Exercise *Mainbrace* in the Norwegian Sea. *Mainbrace*, the largest NATO naval exercise conducted up to then, with a total of almost 160 ships participating, was an exercise framed around the problem of the defence of Norway.[31] Britain's role was succinctly put: 'The direct defence of the United

Kingdom base is obviously vital as a forward base for operations in the Atlantic, a main base for operations in the Channel and North Sea and a rear base for operations on the continent.'[32]

However the progressive 'regionalisation' of British military power as the 1950s gave way to the 1960s, and the 'globalisation' of Soviet maritime power as the 1960s gave way to the 1970s, brought to light disparate tendencies between United States maritime perceptions and those of NATO. Whereas NATO, to which the bulk of British sea power is committed, remained more and more a regional maritime as well as army/air force alliance, the United States not only supports NATO's continental strategy, but also, through the 'forward' maritime strategy evolved by the Carter and Reagan administrations as the 1970s merged into the 1980s, supports a global strategy designed to counter a Soviet maritime war-fighting capacity that, for NATO purposes, is now concentrated in the Murmansk/Kola Peninsula area, as well as in the Black Sea/Eastern Mediterranean, but which is also global. The Royal Navy in early 1988 officially acknowledged that its primary role – other than its Polaris/Trident submarine strategic retaliatory force – was to support an American 'forward' strategy into the Norwegian Sea. In other words, the North Atlantic/Norwegian Sea and the Mediterranean Sea flanks of NATO are two of several flanks of the Soviet Union which the United States is prepared to attack. The reciprocal concepts of pincers, shared in regard to NATO/Warsaw Pact hostilities, have now become a global pincers operation of the United States *vis-à-vis* the Soviet Union, with the spearhead provided by maritime forces *in tandem* with amphibious forces.

CONTAINMENT AND THE SUPERPOWER NUCLEAR MARITIME BALANCE

From the end of the Second World War and the emergence of the Soviet Union as America's major threat, concern has been continuously expressed that the political–military goals of the United States were not in line with the means being provided to achieve them. This is, in a way, an echo of the debate carried on in Britain prior to the First World War. In part, this was a problem of reconciling a global policy of containment (read 'imperial' for Britain in an earlier age) with specific and shifting domestic and international political conditions. The dilemma has often been expressed as a 'mismatch', with the navalists calling loudly either for a scaling-down of the goals, or a beefing-up of the means, usually to no avail.

Stemming from the Truman Doctrine, containment has been vigorously debated both as a concept of American foreign policy *vis-à-vis* the Soviet (or at times, global communist) threat and as a justification for the defence budget. In a cogent statement of the most recent revival of this mismatch dilemma Roger Hansen put the issue thus:

> The Reagan Administration wagered that it could devise a military strategy whose goal (containment of the Soviet Union) would be matched by the resources made available by the American public through Congress ... Even if there had been no resource constraint, was the goal of global containment of Soviet power and influence plausible?[33]

He then went on to pose a more pertinent question:

> In short, we appear to have reached a point in postwar US foreign policy at which a heretical question is in order: is it possible that the American public is quite willing to distinguish – indeed may insist upon distinguishing – between vital national interests for which it will sacrifice, on the one hand, and morally sanctioned purposes such as a congenial world order and the spread of democracy for which it will not sacrifice, on the other?[34]

It is quite clear that the current warming of relations between the United States and the Soviet Union has resulted in increased tension among America's NATO allies, both with their patron superpower and among each other. In this sense, the political rule that the greater the East–West tension the lesser the inter-allied tension, and vice versa, is being borne out once again.[35] The current debate involves several interrelated aspects: (1) whether (as the West Germans prefer) further nuclear weapons cuts in Europe should involve the shortest-range nuclear weapons, that is, battlefield weapons – thus reducing the likelihood of the two Germanies becoming nuclear wastelands, or whether priority in further cuts should be given first to strategic weapons and then to reducing conventional forces and chemical weapons (as the British and French prefer); (2) whether rearranging the conventional inter-alliance weapons balance is politically possible, especially as either the deeper cuts would be required on the WTO side or, alternatively, NATO would need to build up its alleged weaker conventional forces to compensate for the, at least selective, de-nuclearisation of the European deterrent; and (3) what to do about nuclear forces at sea, which have not figured significantly so far in the current negotiations and only marginally in the attendant debate.[36]

Obviously the three aspects are interrelated although they have not heretofore been directly linked in the negotiations. In particular, the third aspect appears to have been set by the United States largely outside the context of the other two. In the first instance, as mentioned earlier, the grand strategy as to how NATO would fight its war at sea has rested almost entirely on how the United States viewed its maritime role.[37] Of course, until the rise of a 'blue-water' Soviet navy, the rationale for naval roles and missions, with accompanying ships and weapons, had as much to do with inter-Service rivalries for resources as with America's military activities outside Europe.[38] For the Navy, in the immediate postwar period of budgetary constraint, it was a race against the Air Force as to whether the Strategic Air Command (SAC) would monopolise the atomic capability to deal with the threat from the Soviet Union, or whether the Navy could carve out a role for itself that would further justify the new supercarriers that were becoming such a bitter bone of budgetary contention. Weapons systems – in this case delivery systems (SAC's B-36 or the Navy's supercarriers) – symbolised the struggle to justify a renewed naval role by attempting to share in co-opting the Bomb.[39] In this period a maritime balance of power concept still had an element of an Anglo-American balance because planning for possible war at sea in both Washington and London, at least theoretically, took account of a possible conflict of interest. To remain in the nuclear balance competition, Britain moved ahead to develop its own atomic and then nuclear capacity after the United States foreclosed further wartime sharing of information.[40] This was motivated in part by the notion that Britain would be able to continue to play an imperial role in postwar international politics as well as 'bridging' the East–West divide.[41] As Richard Rosecrance put it:

> Never suffering a cataclysmic reverse, Britain never was forced to rethink her patterns of foreign involvement. The imperial obligations of the nineteenth century could be seriously entertained in the twentieth. Fundamentally, Britain's reduced status was economic, not strategic; the need for a major national reorientation was not apparent.[42]

Since in the late 1940s neither the US Navy nor the Royal Navy had a major enemy to prepare itself to fight against, as discussed earlier, the only major rationale was to protect the Atlantic sea lanes and access to continental ports in the context of a strategy towards Europe that was designated as a replay of the Second World War, or to assist in restoring and/or relinquishing European control in the non-European world. In either respect 1949 was considered the critical year, not only because of Czechoslovakia and the Berlin blockade, but equally because the Soviet Union had by then demonstrated its capacity to acquire nuclear weapons. To quote Rosecrance again:

> Though the significance of the Soviet detonation was not fully appreciated at the time, its impact upon European strategy was fundamental ... 'Overlord' could not be successful against an air and ground atomic defense. If a ground strategy in the West were to be decisive, it had to stop the Russians at or near the onset of war ...[43]

Obviously, along with the growth of a Soviet blue-water maritime force, the development of various classes of nuclear and conventional attack and patrol submarines has played a large role in the transformation of the American maritime outlook and its relationship to NATO. An entirely new dimension of perceived missions and accompanying capabilities contains within it an almost instinctive tendency towards 'unilateralism' as regards the employment of American maritime forces that, unless carefully kept in check, could weaken NATO materially. The desire of the United States, within the context of its official maritime strategy, to prolong as long as possible an avoidance of using nuclear weapons (excluding the very short-range 'battlefield' variety which may be considered non-escalatory) is but one significant example of what some Europeans view as a weakening of American resolve to use nuclear weapons if deterrence were to fail. How is it therefore possible for the United States to contemplate fighting a global maritime war conventionally while at the same time NATO contemplates fighting a regional land war non-conventionally?

Paradoxically, if the American maritime strategy is intended to reinforce deterrence, it also has the potential implication of signalling to Britain and the other allies that perhaps another intention is to weaken the nuclear guarantee that, from the European viewpoint, lies at the heart of the Alliance. This raises the question as to how Britain and the other states of Western Europe can calculate accurately American intentions towards them. Such uncertainty has, of course, both a positive and a negative aspect. Positively, perhaps there may be more effort on the part of Britain to forge a stronger European conventional integrated force structure. Negatively, this could result in less of a political willingness on the part of the United States to maintain strong ground forces in Europe. In sum, a global American maritime strategy, linked but not restricted by or dependent exclusively on a regional NATO continental strategy, could diminish the importance of NATO in American eyes, and diminish the credibility of the American guarantee in European eyes.

SUMMARY AND CONCLUSIONS

As Richard Best concluded in his recent study of British influences on American security policy in the late 1940s, 'NATO arose out of the shared perceptions of British and American officials, representatives of "like-minded peoples", who had drawn similar conclusions about the nature of the Soviet challenge and the need for a consolidated Western response.'[44] This like-mindedness touches on the old debate between a blue-water strategy and a continental commitment. The experience of the twentieth century has given weight to Michael Howard's reappraisal of the history of the British way in warfare:

First, a commitment of support to a Continental ally in the nearest available theatre, on the largest scale that contemporary resources could afford, so far from being alien to traditional British strategy was absolutely central to it ... The flexibility provided by sea power made possible other activities ... but these were ancillary to the great decisions by land ... Secondly, when we did have recourse to a purely maritime strategy ... It was a strategy of necessity rather than of choice, of survival rather than of victory ... It gave us the breathing-space in which to try to attract other allies ... but it never enabled us to win.[45]

The importance of maritime strategy within European history lies in its relationship to land strategy and air strategy. These various military strategies working each within their own element, complementing diplomatic and economic affairs, form a nation's grand strategy, and thus a framework within which balance of power concerns are dealt with.

Part I of this volume of essays reveals one aspect of the extent of this dependence. In the light of the British model of organisation for coalition warfare, can, therefore, the creation of the League of Nations with its permanent secretariat, and the substitution of a new 'concert' under the guise of collective security, be seen as an Anglo-American turning-point? Or did this come earlier, with the shift in Anglo-American maritime responsibilities, especially in the Western hemisphere, and the justifications for the American imperial vision, based on maritime power? Parts II and III on theory and war-planning between 1898 and 1945 discuss the changing maritime relationships between the two Powers, suggesting, for example, that the Washington Conference made a notable shift in Anglo-American maritime power relationships. Then, of course, Lend-Lease, whereby American destroyers were turned over to Britain to reinforce the Atlantic lifeline, was also noteworthy. Clearly, however, the Anglo-American maritime balance had shifted irrevocably by the end of the Second World War. Therefore Part IV discusses how the advent of atomic and nuclear war-fighting maritime technologies including the famous Nassau agreement between President Kennedy and Prime Minister Macmillan – a possible turning-point – affected both Britain's search for continued Great Power influence, and the various strategic as well as tactical circumlocutions that were pursued in this search. These are the topics which are examined in detail in the essays which follow. They reveal what is not only a 'special' relationship, but also an 'enduring' relationship.

Notes

1. Martin Wight, *Power Politics*, Hedley Bull and Carsten Holbraad (eds), (New York, 1978) pp. 169–70. Carsten Holbraad, in his book, *Superpowers and International Conflict* (London, 1979), draws a distinction between a simple triangle and a complex triangle. In analysing the contemporary international system he does not rule out the eventual possibility of a pentagonal or hexagonal balance of power system.

2. A sophisticated attempt to analyse the impact of nuclear weapons on a systemic approach to bipolarity can be found in Arthur Lee Burns, 'From Balance to Deterrence: A Theoretical Analysis', *World Politics*, May, 1957, pp. 494–529.
3. Quoted in Wight, *Power Politics*, p. 172.
4. These points are discussed further, Ibid., pp. 173–9. See also Geoffrey Blainey, *The Cause of War* (New York, 1973), especially Chapter 8. Inis L. Claude, Jr, in his book, *Power and International Relations* (New York, 1962), classified balance of power in the following ways: (1) as a situation; (2) as a policy; (3) as a system (pp. 17–25).
5. As quoted in Claude, *Power and International Relations*, p. 87. See also Manus I. Midlarsky, 'Equilibria in the Nineteenth-Century Balance-of-Power System', *American Journal of Political Science*, vol. 25, no. 2, May 1981, pp. 270–96.
6. Blaney, *The Cause of War*, p. 114.
7. See Burns, 'From Balance to Deterrence'.
8. David Hume, 'Of the Balance of Power', in T. H. Green and T. H. Crose (eds), *Essays, Moral Political and Literary*, vol. 1 (London, 1982) p. 352 as quoted in Wight, *Power Politics*, pp. 168–9.
9. Paul M. Kennedy, *The Rise and Fall of British Naval Mastery* (New York, 1976) p. xvi.
10. Sir James Cable, *Diplomacy at Sea* (Annapolis, MD, 1985) p. 36.
11. Ibid., p. 37.
12. Harold and Margaret Sprout, *The Rise of American Naval Power, 1776–1918* (Princeton, 1967) p. 284. This event also, incidentally, 'revealed an unsuspected community of feeling among the English-speaking peoples'. (Ibid.)
13. Letter from Sherman to Bernard Baruch, 16 March 1950, as quoted in unpublished manuscript by Clark Reynolds, 'Forrest Sherman and the Development of Cold War Strategy. 1948–1951', pp. 32–3. As to the place of Europe in American overall maritime strategy, Sherman observed: 'I am inclined to believe that the significance of [the Russian naval buildup] may be as simple as a Soviet intention to create sea-borne trade with China and southeast Asia – undoubtedly paralleled by the development of naval forces in the same area. This leads me to wish that we might have a stronger Pacific Fleet. However, I still feel that Germany is the more critical spot, even though not so much a naval problem.' (Ibid., pp. 6–7).
14. Cable, *Diplomacy at Sea*, p. 88. See also William N. Still, Jr, *American Sea Power in the Old World: The United States Navy in European and Near Eastern Waters, 1865–1917* (Westport, Conn. and London, 1980).
15. Carsten Holbraad, *The Concert of Europe: A Study in German and British International Theory 1815–1914* (London, 1970) p. 152. As Lord Castlereagh put it, the combination was against any state 'whose perverted policy or criminal ambition shall first menace the repose in which all have a common interest'. (Quoted p. 137).
16. See, for example, Kenneth Bourne, *The Foreign Policy of Victorian England* (Oxford, 1970); *Britain and the Balance of Power in North America, 1815–1908* (Berkeley, 1967); and J. A. S. Grenville and G. B. Young, *Politics, Strategy and American Diplomacy: Studies in Foreign Policy, 1873–1917* (New Haven, 1966).
17. Richard Heathcote Heindel, *The American Impact on Great Britain, 1898–1914* (New York, 1968 and Philadelphia, 1940) p. 86.
18. Sprout, *The Rise of American Naval Power*, pp. 288–9.
19. For an expansion of these observations, see George Liska, *Quest for Equilibrium: America and the Balance of Power on Land and Sea* (Baltimore and London, 1977), especially Chapter V.

20. Sprout, *The Rise of American Naval Power*, footnote 8, p. 288.
21. As Liska observed: 'Reenacting the Rome–Carthage relationship between a land and a sea power, the collision would have occurred in Central America, the counterpart of the Sicilian land–sea area, and produced a matching amplification of American naval capability while Britain fell back on alliance with a continental European power just as Carthage had allied with Macedon in the earlier setting.' (*Quest for Equilibrium*, p. 84).
22. Ibid., p. 84.
23. Ibid., p. 86. Recognising this, President Theodore Roosevelt asserted that the navy's true function was not 'to defend harbors and sea-coast cities', but to attack and destroy the enemy's naval forces. In this way a battle fleet would contribute vitally, if indirectly, to coast defence. (Sprout, *The Rise of American Naval Power*, p. 283).
24. Ibid., p. 88. Put another way: 'The "American Peril" was more than an academic question for the United Kingdom. The potential strength of America, and the increasing manifestations of it from the nineties onward, made a deep impression upon the thought and activities of Great Britain.' (Heindel, *The American Impact*, p. 170).
25. Sprout, *The Rise of American Naval Power*, p. 344.
26. B. B. Schofield, *British Sea Power: Naval Policy in the Twentieth Century* (London, 1967) pp. 211–22. Schofield summarised: 'The Royal Navy reached its greatest strength at the end of the war in Europe with 1,065 warships in commission down to and including corvettes, to which must be added 2,907 minor war vessels and 5,477 landing ships and craft of various kinds. The personnel required to man this vast armada numbered 863,500.' (pp. 215–6).
27. Lord Ismay, *NATO: The First Five Years* (Paris, 1954) p. 73.
28. For a thorough examination of the British notion that the Mediterranean should have a 'Supremo' similar to SACEUR and SACLANT, and presumably be British, see letter from Admiral Robert Carney to General Eisenhower, FF5-3/A19, 8 March 1951, declassified (Eisenhower Papers, Eisenhower Library); see also Robert S. Jordan (ed.), *Generals in International Politics: NATO's Supreme Allied Commander, Europe* (Lexington, KY, 1987). Also see the unpublished doctoral dissertation by Philip A. Dur, 'The Sixth Fleet: A Case Study of Institutionalized Naval Presence, 1946–1968', Harvard University, December 1975.
29. See 'Cold War Navy', a history of the US navy prepared for the Chief of Information, Department of the Navy, submitted in March 1976 by Lulejian and Associates, Inc., unpub.; and Jordan, *Generals in International Politics*.
30. Admiral Conolly made the point that the entire Navy at this time would be getting less budgetarily than his command alone would need. Conolly was Commander Naval Forces, Eastern Atlantic and Mediterranean (CINCNELM). (See Admiral Richard L. Conolly, 'Reminiscences', (Oral History Research Office, Columbia University, 1960).)
31. As reported by *The New York Times*, 13 September 1952. See also Anthony Farrar-Hockley, 'The Alliance: Perceptions from the Northern Flank', *Defence Yearbook 1984* (London: Brassey's Defence Publishers, with The Royal United Services Institute for Defence Studies).
32. Cable, *Diplomacy at Sea*, p. 65. Central is the fact that military forces that Britain might need for operations 'out-of-area' from NATO would require the diversion of forces committed to NATO and trained and equipped for this purpose. For an expansion of these points, see Robert S. Jordan, 'The Maritime Strategy and the Atlantic Alliance', in *The Journal of the Royal United Services*

Institute for Defence Studies, September 1987. For a description of NATO's Standing Naval Force Atlantic, which shows the multilateral NATO flag in peace-time, see Admiral Richard G. Colbert, 'The Shifting Balance of Power at Sea', *The Atlantic Community Quarterly*, Winter 1972–3.

33. Roger D. Hansen, 'The Reagan Doctrine and Global Containment: Revival or Recessional', *SAIS Review*, Winter–Spring 1987, p. 41.
34. Ibid., p. 64. Clearly the Esher Committee report and the Fisher reforms in the light of the German naval challenge were based on the same awareness that the budget could not provide fully for both a British global imperial defence and a 'superpower' naval confrontation. For a brief historical summary of various British 'Grand Designs', see Peter Nailor, 'Britain and the Imperial Staff', in Robert L. Pfaltzgraff, Jr and Uri Ra'anan (eds), *National Security Policy: The Decision-Making Process* (Hamden, CT, 1984).
35. For a good review of the ebb and flow of inter-alliance/intra-alliance politics, see Richard Rosecrance, *Defense of the Realm: British Strategy in the Nuclear Epoch* (New York and London, 1968) especially pp. 93ff.
36. In regard to the third aspect, for a good overview, see Richard N. Fieldhouse, 'US Naval Strategy and Nuclear Weapons', in Carl C. Jacobsen (ed.), *The Uncertain Course: New Weapons, Strategies and Mind Sets* (London, 1987). For a brief overview of the INF Treaty, see Philip Windsor, 'The INF Treaty – Compensatory Adjustments', *Bulletin*, the Council for Arms Control, no. 30, February 1988; also Norman Polmar, 'The Missile Agreements', *US Naval Institute Proceedings*, February 1988.
37. See, for example, Jordan, 'The Maritime Strategy'; a revised version appears in Carol Edler Baumann (ed.), *Europe in NATO: Deterrence, Defence and Arms Control* (New York, 1987) pp. 145–61.
38. For the nuclear dimension, see William M. Arkin *et al.*, 'The Nuclearisation of the Oceans: Roles, Missions and Capabilities', in R. B. Byers (ed.), *The Denuclearisation of the Oceans* (New York, 1986). For the inter-Service rivalry dimension, see David A. Rosenberg, 'Origins of Overkill: Nuclear Strategy, 1945–1960', *International Security*, Spring 1983. See also Thomas H. Etzold, 'The End of the Beginning ... NATO's Adoption of Nuclear Strategy', in Olav Riste (ed.), *Western Security: The Formative Years: European and Atlantic Defence 1949–1953* (New York and London, 1985).
39. For a good discussion, see *Cold War Navy*.
40. See Rosecrance, *Defense of the Realm*.
41. See Elisabeth Barker, *The British Between the Superpowers, 1945–1950* (Toronto, 1983).
42. Rosecrance, *Defense of the Realm*, p. 4.
43. Ibid., p. 92.
44. Richard A. Best, Jr, *Co-operation with like-minded Peoples: British Influences on American Security Policy, 1945–1949* (Westport, CT, 1986) p. 194.
45. Michael Howard, *The British Way in Warfare: A Reappraisal*, The Neale Lecture in English History, 1974 (London, 1975), pp. 14–15; as reprinted in Michael Howard (ed.), *The Causes of War* (London, 1983).

Part I
The British Model of Organising for Twentieth-Century Coalition Warfare

'This long and curious history has left its trace on almost every part of our present political condition; its effects lie at the root of many of our most important controversies; and because these effects are not rightly perceived, many of these controversies are misconceived.'—Walter Bagehot

The machinery of government by which strategic decisions are made puts its own indelible stamp on the nature of the decisions which are reached through it. In this case, the British model of organising for twentieth-century coalition warfare has its roots in the British cabinet system of government, as developed through the experience of the Committee of Imperial Defence. This same approach was taken as the model for use in the major, international command and organisational structures developed in the twentieth century, including the League of Nations, the wartime Combined Chiefs of Staff, NATO and the US Joint Chiefs of Staff.

Part 1
The British Model of

2 The Origins of Imperial Defence*
Norman H. Gibbs

This chapter examines a comparatively unknown aspect of the foundation of the Committee of Imperial Defence (CID), the story as it refers to the Departments, to the actual machinery of government.

'Our policy', said Castlereagh, defending Britain's acquisitions by the Treaty of Vienna, 'has been to secure the Empire against future attacks. In order to do this we had acquired what in former days would have been thought romance – the keys of every great military position' in the world. Heligoland, Malta, the Cape, Mauritius, Ceylon, St Lucia, Trinidad, Tobago, Honduras, all bore witness to the truth of Castlereagh's claim. But the two generations after Waterloo, although they saw the acquisition, particularly as coaling stations, of further harbours and anchorages throughout the world, witnessed a decline, not an advance, in the conception of imperial defence. For this there were several reasons. In the first place, the grant of representative institutions to the now self-governing colonies was assumed to carry with it the obligation to protect themselves. 'Self-government begets self-defence.'

This phase reached its climax in the great Liberal administration of 1868–74 when separation from rather than preservation of the colonies was the imperial problem which chiefly exercised the Cabinet; and, as part of that problem, the last of that series of withdrawals of imperial troops from colonial garrisons which had gone on at intervals since at least 1830. For Richard Cobden – and there were many like him – colonies were economically useless in a period of increasing free trade. Indeed, they were worse than useless. They were a positive danger, for colonial rivalries might well involve Britain in otherwise avoidable war. In 1880, on becoming Prime Minister for the second time, Gladstone inherited from Disraeli a Royal Commission on the Defence of British Possessions and Commerce Abroad. When, much to John Bright's disgust, the Liberal Cabinet decided to allow the Commission to continue its unfinished inquiry, Bright's comment was typical of a great deal of Liberal thought. This was, he claimed, a 'fitting outcome to the folly or madness of our predecessors' who 'undertake to defend half the world'.

*This chapter is an edited version of Norman Gibbs's Inaugural Lecture as the Chichele Professor of the History of War, 8 June 1955, originally published by the Clarendon Press, Oxford, 1955, as a pamphlet. Reprinted here by permission of the author and Oxford University Press.

'We are not', he said, 'proposing to make war but to maintain peace. I suggest that the whole of this insane scheme be given up.' Gladstone's methods were more indirect but no more encouraging. 'Let it take its time', he wrote to the Commission, 'and perhaps make itself useless.'

To this particular attitude towards the colonies was added the more general mid-nineteenth-century attitude towards all expenses of government. At the root of the conception of 'Treasury control' lies the conviction that any man will privately spend his own money far better than any government will spend it for him. All government expenditures should therefore be reduced to a minimum. In no field did this belief work more strongly than in that of naval and military expenditures. Whatever the results of Cardwell's reforms at the War Office, their initial motive was economy. And it was the motive of economy which constantly reinforced the constitutional argument that colonies which governed themselves should pay for their own protection also. The estimates for Army colonial expenditure dropped by about 25 per cent in 1870 from the figures which had held good for the previous fifteen years, and dropped still farther subsequently. By the same year all imperial troops had left Australia and New Zealand, and those that remained in Canada and South Africa were there because of circumstances the Government would have avoided if it could.

To those who thought as did Cobden, Bright and Gladstone, any suggestion of organised defence planning, whether inside Departments or between them, was tantamount to a suggestion that Britain should plan aggressive war. Nor was this an idea that died with the elder generation of Liberal statesmen. One of the most important recommendations of the Hartington Commission on the Administration of the Naval and Military Departments in 1890 was that there should be, at the War Office, a Department of 'a Chief of the Staff who should be responsible for preparing plans of military operations and for collecting the intelligence on which those plans should be based'. Arguing against this suggestion in his Minority Report, Sir Henry Campbell-Bannerman claimed that in Britain, unlike the countries of Continental Europe, there was 'no room for "general military policy" in the larger and more ambitious sense of the phrase. We have no designs against our European neighbours'. Were such a Department of a Chief of the Staff set up 'there might indeed be a temptation to create such a field for itself; and I am thus afraid that while there would be no use for the proposed office, there might be some danger to our best interests'. 'Here,' writes Campbell-Bannerman's biographer, 'speaks the old Liberal with his rooted dislike of Continental ways and his suspicions of soldiers who "sit apart and cogitate".'

The work of the Prussian General Staff had naturally attracted attention in this period and much was being written, by Spenser Wilkinson among others, urging that the British Army should be provided with a similar 'thinking machine'. There were many who, like Campbell-Bannerman, feared that this would mean not merely planning for hypothetical wars but the precipitation of actual wars, a view which continued to find considerable support well into the twentieth century. Balfour's reasons for so long delaying his resignation as Prime Minister in 1905 were mixed. But among them was a genuine fear that the valuable work his government had accomplished in matters of national and imperial defence would – and that in the middle of a crisis – be discarded by his Liberal successors. In fact his fears were proved completely groundless.

Thus from Waterloo, at least until the long Conservative administration of 1874–80, imperial defence became simply a series of separate colonial problems, mostly distasteful, wherein strategy was rarely treated on its own merits and almost invariably ignored in favour of constitutional and financial arguments. In so far as there was any conception of the strategy of national and imperial defence in the mid-nineteenth century it served only to strengthen the effects of this purely political approach. British strategy in the wars of the eighteenth century was based upon a command of the sea which rendered the home islands safe from invasion and at the same time, by protecting trade routes and focal strategic bases, made the maintenance and increase of Empire possible. The sea was the common link which made of Britain and her colonies one continuous chain. The introduction of steam-driven ironclads in the mid-nineteenth century changed all this – at least, it changed men's views. And it coincided with Napoleon III's 'dangerous' period after the Crimean War. Steam, it was claimed, had 'bridged the Channel', and ironclads were becoming a match for shore-based guns. According to Palmerston, 30 000 Frenchmen could now be rushed across the Channel in the dark of a single night. According to Wellington, in one of those typical popular misrepresentations from which the Duke suffered more than most men, England would be open to invasion a week after war was declared. This violent and deep-rooted invasion scare of the early 1860s arose from a belief that the Navy was no longer sufficient to keep Britain safe against invasion, and that the only security lay in a well-garrisoned 'Fortress England' in which the bulk of the Army would be permanently stationed, and which would be protected by a combination of troops and heavily armed coastal forts. In this period, for example, were built those forts which still straddle the entrance to Portsmouth harbour and the enormous structures which still dominate the town from the chalk hills behind. The 'Fortress England' view was given official confirmation by the findings of a Royal Commission on the Defences of the United Kingdom set up in 1859. Further, it provided strategic justification for the withdrawal of colonial garrisons and their concentration at home, and entirely ignored the fact that Britain could be starved into submission, once command of the sea was lost, without the landing of a single invading soldier. And, by virtually ignoring the role of the Navy, it ignored the one factor which made a unified conception of national and imperial defence possible.

One certainly does not wish to suggest that these views about the defence of Britain and her Empire arose from the lack of any particular piece of governmental machinery. Obviously that lack was itself the product of far more general conditions. But there was, in fact, in the mid-nineteenth century an almost complete absence of departmental co-operation in matters of defence. Where such co-operation did exist, as sometimes between the War Office, the Colonial Office and the Treasury, it rarely reached the level of the Cabinet and was mostly concerned with economy and local reform. It needed a general change in political conditions, both domestic and foreign, accompanied by a radical alteration in opinion, both in Parliament and in civil and professional service circles, to make possible the administrative machinery at the highest level of policy making whereby the defence requirements of the British Empire could be dealt with according to a 'definite and harmonious plan'.

That change came about in the last twenty years of the nineteenth century. The growing rivalry of continental groups after the Franco-Prussian war led slowly in this country to a realisation of the need for increased naval and military strength even while 'splendid isolation' remained the political ideal. That realisation coincided with a period of increasing colonial rivalry, particularly in Africa and the Far East, which underlined the need for strength because of the danger that war against major European Powers might grow out of colonial quarrels. And, finally, the disasters of the first months of the Boer War, accompanied as they were by the evident hostility to Great Britain of nearly every major European Power, brought to a head agitation for careful and detailed planning in national and imperial defence which had been growing steadily for the previous twenty years. From that point of view, the Treasury Minute of 4 May 1904, finally constituting the Committee of Imperial Defence by making funds available for its permanent staff, is the end rather than the beginning of a story.

The story begins in the Departments rather than in the Cabinet. The war scare arising from the fear of hostilities between Britain and Russia which coincided with the later stages of the Russo-Turkish War of 1877–8 led to a revived interest in colonial defence. Isolated Russian naval units, it was feared, might break out of the Baltic and do damage as commerce raiders or attack naval bases at the Cape, Ceylon, Singapore, or Hong Kong. On 23 January 1878 the Cabinet in London ordered the Mediterranean Fleet to Constantinople. On 5 March a Colonial Defence Committee (CDC), appointed at the instance of the Secretary of State for the Colonies to inquire and report on the defences of the more important colonial ports, and specially directed to consider 'how to provide some early and temporary defence in case of any sudden outbreak of hostilities', was a small committee of three members, one senior service representative each from the War Office and the Admiralty and one representative of the Colonial Office. Its work does not seem to have reached Cabinet level and it died with the end of the crisis which gave it birth, having a life of little more than a year.

The value of the Committee's brief life lay in the evidence it provided of the difficulties of empire defence in such a sudden emergency, and of the need for much more careful investigation, particularly of problems which concerned more than one Department. Indeed, before the committee dissolved in April 1879, two of its members had formally submitted the suggestion that it, or at any rate its inquiries, should be extended beyond the scope of a sudden emergency arising from fear of war against one particular Power, and converted into a long-term inquiry designed to provide 'permanent defences for the more important Colonial ports, as also . . . the measures to be adopted for providing adequate garrisons and other accessories for them'. This suggestion was first received favourably by the Departments concerned. But in the end the inquiry was broadened, but also virtually postponed, by the appointment instead of a Royal Commission on the Defence of British Possessions and Commerce Abroad in 1879. This was the Commission much of whose work, as I have already pointed out, was negatived by the studied neglect of Gladstone's second administration.

In 1885, shortly before the fall of that administration, a new Colonial Defence Committee was, however, set up 'to consider representations as to their defence from Colonies which the Royal Commission on Colonial Defence made no provisions for'. The immediate problem which led to the setting up of this new Committee was the defence of Barbados and the problem was soon made more general and more urgent by a renewed fear of Anglo-Russian hostilities which arose from the Pendjeh incident and from the Bulgarian crisis in the autumn of the same year. The Colonial Office felt itself unable to act single-handed, and also considered that dealing with the problem by the ordinary methods of correspondence with the War Office and the Admiralty would be 'a long and unsatisfactory affair'. Therefore a small inter-departmental standing committee composed of representatives of the Colonial Office, War Office, and Admiralty was set up under the name of the Colonial Defence Committee and met for the first time on 22 April 1885.

The method of working was for the Colonial Defence Committee to consider a problem on receipt of dispatches from colonies requiring advice and help, and then to send their recommendations to 'those members of the Colonial Committee of the Cabinet departmentally concerned', and also to the Chancellor of the Exchequer if any question of the use of imperial funds arose. Thus it seems that there was also in existence a Colonial Committee of the Cabinet; but, so far, I have been unable to discover any useful information about its functions, its methods of procedure or its subsequent history. The absence of official records for a Cabinet committee at this date is not surprising. What is surprising and disappointing is that no serious mention of its work occurs in private records. Even Sir George Sydenham

Clarke (later Lord Sydenham of Combe) who was Secretary of the CDC for many years, and who was deeply interested in all problems of imperial defence, simply mentions the Cabinet committee in his autobiography, and then turns away from it in discreet silence.

The inter-departmental committee, the Colonial Defence Committee, had from now on a continuous existence; in 1902 it became a sub-committee of the Committee of Imperial Defence and in 1911 was renamed the Overseas Defence Committee. It is clear that the functions of the CDC, like those of its later parent the CID, were consultative and advisory only, and that there was no intention of conferring executive functions upon it. Indeed, when the Committee later trespassed in this respect it received a sharp rap over the knuckles. It was thought proper that its recommendations should go to the Department responsible for action on them, then to be sent out over the signature of a responsible officer of that Department.

The two committees, that of 1879 and that of 1885 and onwards, should really be seen as one. And they form a landmark. For the first time some degree of regularity and system was introduced into problems of imperial defence; information was carefully collected and became the common property of several interested and responsible Departments. The big difference between the two committees is that the later one extended its work beyond the demands of a single crisis and continued in its existence to ensure a permanent state of preparedness in the defence of the Colonies. Already, in August 1885, Sir George Sydenham Clarke wrote, 'The Secretary of State for the Colonies has expressed a wish that the Colonial Defence Committee should consider the practicability of compiling a record of all existing defences of British possessions abroad, to be afterwards corrected and supplemented as new works are completed and new guns mounted.' The new committee did in fact provide the elements of continuity which had been lacking in 1878–9. Otherwise the two bodies were essentially the creation of the Colonial Office and essentially designed for the same purpose.

That purpose was partly the product of existing influences which have already been described, and partly the product of a return to an older, wiser conception of imperial defence. In the first place, the motive of economy was still strong. The two committees were designed to advise the Colonies on how to provide for their own defence – both by fixed defences and by troops – for themselves. If London was to help, it was not by men and money. But behind that, and gaining ground all the time, was a move away from the strategic concept of 'Fortress England' and a return to the 'blue-water school', to the ideas which had governed the strategy of Chatham, St Vincent and Nelson. The Colonies persistently asked for local protection by units of the Fleet stationed locally. The Colonies were being urged and advised to develop their own local defence not merely because of the Treasury's unwillingness to bear the cost itself, but also because fixed colonial defences were regarded by the Admiralty as the complement of control of the High Seas by the Fleet. To this the Admiralty's answer was that the maintenance of maritime supremacy – the essential condition of Empire – depended upon the freedom of movement for the Fleet as a whole; that so long as freedom of movement was retained, no enemy could mount an invasion of the home islands or of the Colonies, on a scale sufficient for permanent occupation, without involving a major fleet action. Therefore what the Colonies needed was not dispersal of the Fleet, but only such local defences as would enable them to withstand the attacks of isolated raiders or small squadrons.

Writing in 1887 on the misunderstanding by the Australian colonies of this approach to the problems of imperial defence, Sir George Sydenham Clarke said:

> The whole standard of defence of the Australian Colonies is based on the fact that the enemy could send small squadrons only into their waters: that few, if any, ironclads would be able to reach Australian ports, and that considerable expeditions could not be undertaken. But these limitations to an enemy's action, which have been universally accepted, exist solely in consequence of the great ironclad fleet maintained by the Imperial Government in European waters, and based upon fortresses and coaling stations created and maintained without charge to Australian tax-payers.

This view, applied to the extreme case of the risk of the invasion of Great Britain herself, was confirmed by more than one official investigation in the early years of the twentieth century. By then the Fleet had recovered its position at the heart of the strategy of imperial defence.

The next stage began in 1886. In Lord Salisbury's second administration Lord Randolph Churchill, as Chancellor of the Exchequer, began the campaign for departmental economy which was the immediate cause of his resignation in December 1886. Lord Randolph Churchill focussed his attack on the Admiralty and War Office, and continued it as a private member after he had resigned. What had begun as agitation for economy continued as a demand for efficiency and, on the latter basis, enlisted the support of many who considered more and not less expenditure on defence necessary. In May 1887 a Parliamentary Committee on Army and Navy Estimates was set up. In June 1887 the Government went farther and appointed a Royal Commission under the chairmanship of Lord Hartington 'to inquire into the civil and professional administration of the Naval and Military Departments and the relation of those Departments to each other and to the Treasury; and to report what changes in their existing system would tend to the efficiency and economy of the Public Service'.

The main Report of the Hartington Commission concentrated on Army reform and is not of immediate interest here. An interim section of the Report, however, published in 1889, discussed a proposal from Lord Randolph Churchill to put professionals, an Admiral and a General, in charge of the two Service Departments, and to appoint virtually a Minister of Defence who, as a politician, would maintain a link between the two Services and between them and Parliament, 'so that one great object, viz. imperial defence, should be more completely attained'. The Commission rejected this proposal and, instead, recommended a naval and military council to 'be presided over by the Prime Minister and consist of the parliamentary heads of the two services and their principal professional advisers'. It was clear that co-ordination at the ministerial level, and the pooling of political and professional advice at that level were not seen to be necessary by the supporters of the Government as well as by its critics. But a committee was preferred to a Minister, and advice to control.

The Commission's suggestion, surely the germ which ripened later into the Committee of Imperial Defence, was not then accepted by the Government. Instead, another inter-departmental rather than a ministerial committee was soon afterwards set up. On 20 January 1891 the Secretary of State for War appointed, with the concurrence of the Admiralty, a Joint Naval and Military Committee on Defence; the President of the Committee was the Parliamentary Under-Secretary of State for War, there were three professional naval members, three military members, a Secretary, and an Assistant Secretary.

This Committee 'was a War Office Committee for the consideration of questions of coast defence in which the Admiralty and War Office' were jointly interested. In 1894 some slight reorganisation took place whereby the Committee became jointly responsible to the Admiralty as well as to the War Office, while the Directors of Naval and Military Intelligence were added to its members. In view of the Hartington Commission's work it is hardly surprising that the initiative came this time from the War Office. But the Joint Naval and Military Committee was basically concerned with much the same general problem – coast defence – as was the Colonial Defence Committee. In its terms of reference the Joint Committee was directed to consider questions of principle and policy, such as the proper types of armament for coast defence, and was empowered to refer the consideration of detail to the Colonial Defence Committee or any other suitable body. The new body seems to have been superior to the older one, and its agreement was necessary for sanctioning schemes of the Committee of 1885 'thought to involve a new departure in policy'. Further, the Joint Naval and Military Committee, when it did go into detail, was concerned with the defence of home ports and of those overseas bases required for the repair and refuelling of the Fleet; in other words, with bases which were an admitted charge upon imperial funds and resources. Thus the work of the two committees was complementary.

The functions of the new committee, like those of the existing one, were advisory only; executive action was left to the responsible officers of the Department concerned. The Joint Naval and Military Committee also continued in existence until absorbed by the Committee of Imperial Defence.

Whether or not its procedure was in the thoughts of those who later organised the CID it is difficult to say. But, in its two secretaries, one naval and one military, and with its general arrangements for the issue of papers, invitations to meetings, agenda and minutes, it calls strongly to mind that secretariat or Department which eventually came to be thought of as an essential feature of successful defence planning.

In 1895 yet a further step was taken, this time even more obviously in the direction of the Committee of Imperial Defence. At the beginning of his third administration Lord Salisbury appointed a Defence Committee of the Cabinet, under the chairmanship of the Duke of Devonshire, charged with the examination of defence problems in general. At last the top level of Government had been reached. And defence in general, rather than isolated bits of the problem such as coast defence, at any rate appeared to be the programme. The Defence Committee of 1895 lasted until 1902. Unfortunately, according to the existing Cabinet tradition, it kept, as a purely Cabinet Committee, no records; knowledge of its working comes to us primarily from criticisms made of it before the Royal Commission on the South Africa War, from a memorandum of 1902 containing suggestions for an improved committee, and from debates in Parliament when that new committee, the Committee of Imperial Defence, was eventually constituted.

Criticisms of the working of the Defence Committee of 1895 centred on two points. Firstly, it did not tackle the problem which – in the opinion of some – it had been originally designed to solve. That problem was how to settle the broad principles of national and imperial defence upon the basis of information from all the interested Departments, and then to lay down, again in principle, the size and composition of the military and naval forces necessary in peace to make such a defence policy possible. Instead, it was complained that the Committee had concentrated on inter-departmental disputes, especially of the financial sort. The incubus of the worst sort of Treasury control was a burden that left too little energy to spare for the construction of sound strategy; and the result was the usual departmental, piecemeal approach to the problem of defence.

Secondly, and this followed from the limitation of approach just mentioned, the Defence Committee of 1895 did not attempt to tap those sources of intelligence which alone could provide an adequate basis for high-level strategic plans. It was, of course, true, as the Hartington Commission, the South Africa War Commission, and the Esher Committee of 1904 pointed out, that War Office reform, particularly on its Intelligence side, was long overdue. The Esher Committee, especially, coupled War Office Reform and Defence Committee reform together as the essential ingredients of a sound defence policy. To some extent, therefore, the Defence Committee on its own was helpless, whatever its good intentions, since the vital Intelligence component of defence planning was lacking, at any rate so far as the War Office was concerned. No wonder that the Report of the Royal Commission on the South Africa War concluded: 'No plan of campaign ever existed for operations in South Africa.' The disasters of the early months of the war, culminating in the 'Black Week' of December 1899, were as much the result of ignorance as of defective leadership. And Lord Roberts, on his appointment as Commander-in-Chief, had to do for himself what an Intelligence department ought to have done for him.

Debates in the House of Commons in 1902 showed an acute awareness of the defects the Boer War had revealed. Then, in November 1902, the First Lord of the Admiralty and the Secretary of State for War placed before the new Prime Minister, Mr A. J. Balfour, a memorandum pointing out the limitations of the existing machinery for planning imperial defence. They stressed the fact that the Colonial Defence Committee dealt 'only with the organisation of the defence of each separate Colony', while the Joint Naval and Military Committee was concerned only 'with questions referred to it by the Admiralty or War Office, such as, for instance, the proper armament of the fortress of Gibraltar'. They pointed out that there was no machinery for dealing with the most difficult problems, 'those which are neither purely naval nor purely military, nor purely naval and military combined, but which may be described as naval, military, and political'. In other words, there was no person or group of persons explicitly entrusted with the task of providing for the defence of this country and her Empire as a whole. Where, as almost invariably happened, the task concerned several Departments of government, it was eminently possible for the views of one Department to prevail without any reference to genuine strategic considerations, or for another Department to avoid the unpleasant jobs because there was no one to fix responsibility.

In the face of this memorandum and of the criticisms of the Defence Committee made in Parliament and before the South Africa War Committee then sitting, the Prime Minister reconstituted the old Committee in December 1902. At its third meeting, on 18 February 1903, the new Defence Committee decided that its title should be the 'Committee of Imperial Defence'. From now onwards all the records of the new committee become part of a long and continuous series of records which – with a break during the First World War – end only in September 1939.

Early in March 1903 there was a debate in the House on the new Committee, and the Prime Minister gave a detailed account of its purpose, constitution and procedure. In the first place the new Defence Committee (that is, the CID) differed from the 1895 Committee, which it replaced, as regards the subjects with which it dealt. The general practice of the old Committee was to deal with points referred to it from time to time by the Cabinet. The Committee of Imperial Defence was much more ambitious in its scope. 'The idea the Government had in establishing it', the Prime Minister said, 'is not to take up from time to time questions referred to it by the Cabinet, but to make its duty to survey as a whole the strategical military needs of the Empire, to deal with the complicated questions which are still essential elements in the general problem, and to revise from time to time their own previous decisions, so that the Cabinet shall always be informed and always have at its disposal information upon these important points.'

In the second place, 'the old Defence Committee was, in the strictest and narrowest sense of the word, a Committee of the Cabinet', therefore keeping no records and admitting to its council no outsiders except as witnesses, not members. In both respects the new Committee was to be quite different. The conclusions of the Committee of Imperial Defence were to be embodied

> not merely in resolutions, but in reasoned documents in which the whole ground upon which those conclusions have been arrived at will be set out for the information, in the first place, of the Cabinet of the time; and in the second place of the same Administration at a later period, for revision if need be; and last, if not least, for the information of their successors in office.

The records of the Committee would thus provide a means of continuity in the military and naval policy of the Empire. Continuity, it was hoped, would also be ensured by providing the Committee of Imperial Defence with a fixed nucleus in its personnel, not large in number, but sufficient to avoid the complete recreation of the Committee for every topic that came before it or upon every change of government. The permanent nucleus provisionally decided upon consisted of the Prime Minister, the Lord President, the Secretary of State for War and the First Lord of the Admiralty as Cabinet members, and the First Sea Lord, the Commander-in-Chief, the Head of Naval Intelligence and the Head of Military Intelligence as non-Cabinet members. The Foreign Secretary, the Colonial Secretary and the Chancellor of the Exchequer would be very frequently consulted, and other members of the Cabinet would be asked to attend, according to the nature of the Committee's business, from time to time.

Thus the Committee of Imperial Defence differed from the old Defence Committee of the Cabinet in the scope of its investigations, in the possession of a nucleus of *ex officio* members, among them service experts who had previously been consulted only as witnesses, and in the keeping of detailed records. By treating the new Committee as a Prime Minister's committee, and not strictly as a committee of the Cabinet, it became possible to ignore the established conventions of Cabinet secrecy which, at their worst, made unbusinesslike methods inevitable. It met for the first time on 18 December 1902 and continued to hold regular meetings throughout 1903 and 1904, meeting on an average about once a fortnight. The Duke of Devonshire, the Chairman of the old Defence Committee, presided at first, but the Prime Minister attended regularly and, after the reconstruction of the Government in November 1903, himself regularly took the chair.

Thus the story of the Committee of Imperial Defence really begins not in 1904, the date usually given, but in December 1902. Already, by March 1903, its work was sufficiently recognised for the King to be provided with the conclusions reached at its meetings.

Although by now provided with a mixture of ministerial and professional members, and meeting regularly under the chairmanship of the Prime Minister himself, the Committee of 1902 still did not satisfy Balfour and his friends. In the first place, so large was the range and so varying the nature of the problems to be dealt with that only a committee of very elastic membership was thought to be adequate to the task. The constitution of 1902 prescribed a regular *ex officio* panel of members; many, and among them the Prime Minister himself, came to think this type of membership too rigid. At a meeting of the Committee held on 4 December 1903 Mr Balfour

> stated to the Committee, as he had previously done to the Cabinet, that, in his view, it would be best to consider the Committee of Defence as an advisory body with no *ex officio* members except the Prime Minister for the time being, who would summon to each meeting those persons whom he thought best qualified to advise upon the business to be dealt with at that meeting . . .

The advantage of this plan was the very great elasticity which would enable the committee to expand on occasion to include representatives of the great self-governing Colonies and of India. It would thus constitute a first attempt to form a constitutional machine dealing with imperial concerns in which representatives of the Empire beyond the seas might themselves take part. In fact, Sir Frederick Borden, Canadian Minister of Militia, attended the next meeting of the Committee of Imperial Defence.

In a Cabinet Memorandum of 1904 Mr Balfour repeated and expanded this point of view. After claiming that it would be easier to make the Committee of Imperial Defence a truly imperial body if it had no fixed constitution, he said that the suggested new arrangement would have the advantage that

> at each meeting all Members would be on an equality. Though in practice some of them would be summoned almost as of course, yet they would be there because they *were* summoned, and not as of right. There would, therefore, be no distinction of dignity between one Member and another; the Committee would be small enough to be effective; and its constitution would vary with the varying problems it was required to consider.

Here lay the essence of the argument which, when it was accepted and put into practice, enabled the Committee of Imperial Defence, particularly between the two World Wars, to include representatives of all interests and professions among the members of its sub-committees, and on occasion even leading members of the Opposition.

The second defect of the 1902 Committee lay in its lack of an adequate guarantee of continuity in membership. We have seen that the *ex officio* members were intended to provide a fixed and permanent nucleus as one means of ensuring continuity in the Committee's work. Yet clearly both Ministers and Service members must change. *Ex officio* membership could not in fact provide against changes of Government or the normal movements of Service personnel at the completion of a tour of duty. Again, the invariable inclusion of the Prime Minister could hardly solve this difficulty. As the Esher Committee pointed out, there had been 'in the past and there will be in the future, Prime Ministers to whom the great questions of Imperial Defence do not appeal'. What the Committee of Imperial Defence needed was a permanent staff to give it continuity or, as Lord Lansdowne expressed it, 'a continuous and corporate existence which did not belong to the old Defence Committee'. This was a matter of officials rather than members. Once more the Esher Report summed up the case in words worth quoting at length.

> A Committee which contains no permanent nucleus, and which is composed of political and professional members, each preoccupied with administrative duties widely differing, cannot, in our opinion, deal adequately with the complex questions of Imperial defence... The Committee is necessarily a changing body. It is not safe to trust matters affecting national security to the chance of a favourable combination of personal characteristics... For this reason we have suggested the creation of a 'Department', to use a well understood term for the Defence Committee, containing elements of a permanent character, following the well-tried and established precedents of British administration, located in close proximity to the residence of the Prime Minister, and under his exclusive control.

The Committee of Imperial Defence is usually assumed to begin with the acceptance of the recommendation of a permanent staff or Department embodied in Treasury Minutes of May and July 1904. The staff of one Secretary, two Assistant Secretaries, and half a dozen clerks so authorised is the seed from which has grown in fifty years the present Cabinet Office and Ministry of Defence.

In summary, three general observations can be made: one domestic, one imperial, and one foreign. In the first place, the Committee of Imperial Defence, developing into the War Cabinets of two World Wars and the present Ministry of Defence, provided a valuable object lesson in the methods of inter-departmental co-operation. On detailed investigation, that lesson will have, I think, two things to teach us about British administration.

One, that where detailed co-operation is necessary between Departments it is best achieved through advisory rather than through executive control. A genuine hierarchy of Departments has so far had no place in our system of government and even supervising Ministers have worked better when they have used the velvet glove of advice rather than the whip of orders. This is the essence of the Committee method. Two, the effective action is best achieved when those who plan and those who execute are the same individuals. If it is fair to complain of Ministers and Generals who are too busy to think, it is no remedy deliberately to separate planning and administration.

Secondly, it is too easy in the mid-twentieth century, when restricted resources force upon us new conceptions of national and imperial defence, to forget that it is barely a generation since defence was the one link which tended to bind the Empire closer together. The years I have described and the twenty years after them were a period when Britain could accept and fulfill the obligation to defend all her Dominions. Where attempts at closer economic and political integration failed, defence succeeded. The imperial meetings of 1907, 1909, and 1911 were devoted mainly to defence and the meetings of 1911 in fact took place as meetings of the Committee of Imperial Defence and are so recorded in its minutes. This was a phase that certainly remained true until the end of the First World War, reaching its peak in the meetings of the Imperial War Cabinet of 1917 and 1918.

Thirdly, although Britain was the last of the great nations to develop her own machinery for systematic defence planning, the popularity of the methods she adopted is now as great as that of the Prussian General Staff in earlier times. It was only to be expected that these methods would spread rapidly, as they certainly have done, to the great self-governing Dominions. But that is not all. The Committee of Imperial Defence, on its Chiefs of Staff Committee side – a committee originally set up in 1923 – has provided a model for the American Joint Chiefs of Staff and for the Allied Combined Chiefs of Staff of the Second World War. And today much of the experience of Britain, of the Dominions, and of the United States in these matters has been incorporated into the organisation of the North Atlantic Alliance. It is to be hoped that, in the process, we have taught only our friends and not our enemies the secret of losing all battles except the last one.

3 The Chiefs of Staff and the Higher Organisation for Defence in Britain, 1904–1984

John Gooch

The British chiefs of staff system first came into existence as part of a package of reforms designed to create a higher organisation for defence. Governments of the late nineteenth century increasingly felt the need to provide their service ministers with a spectrum of expert professional advice. As the Great Powers jockeyed with one another around the globe, they also grew aware of the need for specialised government machinery with which to consider defence policy. In Britain the customary solution to problems of coordination and of providing information across departmental boundaries was to create a committee of the Cabinet.[1] Thus, after some experimentation, the Committee of Imperial Defence (CID) was born in 1902: a cabinet committee presided over by the Prime Minister, with flexible membership, which could discuss pressing defence issues of the day.

In 1904, two years after its creation, the CID was provided with a permanent secretariat. The secretariat grew in power and influence by virtue of its position at the intersection between politicians and the military. Continuity allowed it to offer advice to premiers and ministers and, particularly under the hand of Sir Maurice Hankey, it became highly active in the higher organisation of defence, producing papers, offering opinions and formulating cabinet decisions as minutes.[2] The position of secretary of the CID was a powerful one and, when used with tact and diplomacy, it could exercise great influence; but when made the platform from which to make direct interventions in policy formulation it proved an insubstantial power base – as its first incumbent discovered.[3]

At the same time – though not as part of the same measure – a board system was introduced into the War Office. The Royal Navy had been run since the 1830s through a Board, which allowed specialisation and offered the First Lord collective advice. The Army, by contrast, was dominated by the single personage of the Commander-in-Chief, and attempts at the end of the nineteenth century to decentralise his responsibility had failed.[4] The deficiencies of this monolithic military structure were glaringly revealed during the

Boer War (1899–1902). Military efficiency demanded that traditional reservations be set aside and the British Army be provided with a brain in the form of a general staff; and political imperatives suggested that specialist advice also be available on other aspects of military organisation and structure. Accordingly, one member of the board was the newly-created Chief of the Imperial General Staff (CIGS).[5]

The mere existence of a CIGS did nothing to guarantee the development of comprehensive military plans. Much depended upon personality, and the founding head proved a poor choice: lazy but socially well-connected, Sir Neville Lyttelton's only real talent was his skill at lawn tennis. Of the first group of directors serving under him, most were no more distinguished; but within two years a cohort of highly able staff officers had entered the General Staff. War planning and military training improved markedly in quality in consequence. This was particularly obvious in the case of the mobilisation timetables drawn up after 1910 under the guidance of the Director of Military Operations, Sir Henry Wilson.

Although machinery now existed to co-ordinate government policy on defence, this did not of itself mean very much. How it functioned – and even whether it functioned at all – depended entirely on the Prime Minister of the day, for it was he who called the CID into session, determined its membership and set or agreed to the subjects for examination. Balfour, under whose premiership it came into being, used it with enthusiasm. His immediate successors were in varying degrees uninterested in it. No-one gave any thought to its role in war. More importantly, it was not used to integrate the two Services in joint planning. Admiral Fisher effectively withdrew the Navy from its deliberations in 1905 when it began to trespass into matters he regarded as his own preserve.[6] Left to itself, the Admiralty then set to work on plans for a series of amphibious operations which were distinguished by an 'excessive share' of fantasy.[7]

Demands from the CID for strategic advice exposed the Admiralty, for it had no specialised war planning staff through which to respond to them. Such war planning as there was came from the head of the First Sea Lord, who was also burdened with general responsibility for running the entire navy, unlike the Chief of the General Staff. If he felt the need for assistance, the First Sea Lord could call upon the Director of Naval Intelligence (DNI); however, the DNI's office was little more than an information-gathering organisation. In 1909, responding to the pressure from government and reacting to competition from the War Office (which was winning the arguments in the CID with discouraging frequency), the Admiralty established a Directorate of Naval Mobilisation and a Naval War Council. Within the new directorate the head of the War Division was given the task of war planning, but his powers were strictly circumscribed: his principal obligation was 'to edit the War Plan, and to make it workable by consulting the several authorities and ensuring that they were prepared to play the parts assigned to them'.[8] The Naval War Council met ten times between October 1901 and June 1910 and then went into a state of suspended animation for eighteen months, owing to lack of interest on the part of the new First Sea Lord, Admiral Sir Arthur Wilson.[9]

The two Services finally met on 23 August 1911 at a celebrated CID meeting held to consider naval and military planning for a war with Germany, at which the Admiralty unveiled a strategy of considerable ineptitude which was wholly at odds with accepted CID policy. As a result, Winston Churchill was imported into the Admiralty as First Lord to oversee the creation of a naval staff able to conduct proper planning. The new staff was viewed with considerable suspicion, and had barely taken root before war broke out in 1914.

In the first few months of war the extent to which planning had been limited, the problem of command in war unforeseen and co-ordination dependent upon political authority, was quickly revealed. The CID was closed down and Asquith tried to run the war through a series of large and unwieldy committees. By 1915 war by Cabinet government had completely collapsed.[10] In an ill-considered attempt to secure authoritative military advice, Asquith installed a soldier, Lord Kitchener, as Secretary of State for War in August 1914. Kitchener was totally unfitted for the post. Secretive, constitutionally unable to delegate authority and quite unfamiliar with the general staff idea, he confided in neither soldiers nor politicians. His experience and his talents lay in the field of administration, in which he continued to shine; but as a political head of the War Office he overbore his colleagues and ignored the planning machinery. This machinery was in any case in some disarray. The vast bulk of the General Staff left for the front in August 1914, and the 'dug-outs' who remained behind in their stead proved utterly incapable of standing up to Kitchener's forceful personality. They forebore to offer him any strategic advice, and he forebore to ask for it.

The Navy was afflicted by very similar problems. In October 1914, the 73-year-old Admiral 'Jackie' Fisher was recalled as First Sea Lord and brought back to Whitehall an obsession with amphibious landings on the Baltic coast which he refused to discuss either with his own staff or with Kitchener's. He also had to contend with Winston Churchill as First Lord of the Admiralty, a fact which meant (he remarked to Asquith) that 'he had to spend the whole of his time watching the First Lord instead of the Germans'.[11] His chief of staff, Admiral H. F. Oliver, was incapable of delegation and spent so much time allocating ships to different duties that he had little time left for strategy.[12]

Lack of determined leadership, Service compartmentalisation and an almost complete lack of forward planning created fertile soil for disaster. In an atmosphere of enthusiastic ignorance, and totally unencumbered by technical advice, amateur strategists with Churchill in the van devised the Dardanelles campaign in 1915.[13] Ill-conceived and spectacularly misconducted, the Dardanelles campaign did have one important long-term consequence: the report of the government enquiry into it, published in 1917, painted such a damning picture of the consequences of staff officers suppressing dissent that it acted as a spur to senior officers to speak their minds during the Second World War.[14]

Having at first paid too little attention to staff advice, the British now swung to the opposite extreme. In December 1916 Sir William Robertson took over as CIGS and Kitchener's powers were whittled down until he became little more than a cipher. Robertson demanded, and got, sole authority to sign orders on behalf of the Cabinet. Backed by Haig, who had taken over command of the British armies in France, he informed the government that Flanders was the decisive theatre of operations and that no more troops should be diverted to useless 'sideshows'. He then invited the government either to accept this policy or to formulate its own alternative. The government chose to accept professional advice, although Robertson was never able to close down peripheral operations and concentrate on the fighting in France and Flanders.

In June 1916 Kitchener drowned while on the way to Russia, and Lloyd George replaced him as Secretary of State for War for six months before taking over the premiership in December 1916. Lloyd George believed the strategy of attrition advocated by the General Staff to be wholly wrong. To redress a balance which had tilted to allow political authority to fall into military hands, he introduced a five-man War Cabinet under his own chairmanship to take executive charge of the war. However the Haig–Robertson axis prevented him from gaining full control of military affairs. He found it difficult directly to challenge the strategic arguments put up to justify concentration on the Western Front because of his amateur standing.[15] Rather than confront the soldiers directly he tried a number of political expedients: he attempted to encourage the Italians to launch an offensive in January 1917, which would justify switching troops and resources from France; then in April he subordinated Haig to the French general, Nivelle, in the hope that his plan to rupture the German lines would succeed. It did not. Haig's insistence on launching the Passchendaele offensive was impossible to overcome, not least because the First Sea Lord, Jellicoe, backed it in the hope that it would reach the Belgian coast and thereby end the submarine menace, about which he was extremely pessimistic.

Eventually, over the winter of 1917–18, Lloyd George broke the Robertson–Haig axis by skilful and contorted political manoeuvring, and was able to install a more pliant CIGS, Sir Henry Wilson, who was prepared to back peripheral operations. Prime Ministerial authority over the military was reasserted, although it proved impossible for Lloyd George to go one step further and take direct charge of the higher organisation for defence. However the lesson of the government's battles with its generals between 1914 and 1918 was not lost on Winston Churchill.

The Navy played a less direct part in the conduct of the war and occupied a less powerful political position, so that the government never lost control over it to the same degree. However its internal organisation and structure failed to meet the challenge of the war: staff work remained unco-ordinated and its administration grossly over-centralised. Fisher and Jackson, First Sea Lords during the first half of the war, continued to operate according to prewar notions of naval management and when Jellicoe succeeded Jackson, in December 1916, he made things worse by combining the posts of First Sea Lord and Chief of Staff. When the First Lord of the Admiralty, Sir Edward Carson, tried to lift some of the burden from his shoulders by establishing a planning section within the Directorate of Operations, Jellicoe refused point-blank to allow it to initiate plans, an action which he regarded as the prerogative of senior officers: 'Obviously our experience fits us better for this purpose than the experience of more junior officers; if that were not so, we should be unfit for our positions.'[16]

The Board organisation to which the Admiralty still clung was overwhelmed by the tasks imposed upon it by war. The revolution in communications which had occurred since the start of the century contributed very greatly to this. In the nineteenth century the Admiralty Board had been pre-eminently an administrative body, chiefly responsible for provision and maintenance. In the first decade of the twentieth century it had responded sluggishly to the demand for strategic plans. But from the outset of the war it found itself, as a consequence of the development of wireless telegraphy, the central controlling authority with direct responsibility for executive orders for the movement and operations of all ships. This direct command function was not shared by the War Office. The board structure was quite inappropriate for the complex obligations now resting on the shoulders of the Admiralty, and in the autumn of 1917 it was restructured into two separate committees, one for operations and the other for maintenance. At the same time the planning function was strengthened through the creation of a new post of Director of Plans.[17]

Released from the pressures of war in 1918, the higher organisation for defence slipped back into parochialism and inter-Service competition – the latter further intensified by the presence of a new arm, the Royal Air Force. During the 1920s successive Prime Ministers were largely uninterested in defence matters, and therefore the necessary political authority which alone could have compelled closer collaboration was missing. Nevertheless the need to make economies in government expenditure, together with the realisation that air power had thrown up new problems requiring resolution, led to official scrutiny of the system in 1922–3 with a view to deciding whether a co-ordinating authority was necessary.

Proponents of reform suggested a unified Ministry of Defence, reflecting the functional interrelationship of the three Services in war, or the creation of a single minister with a joint central staff, possibly working under the orders of a single chief. Sir Maurice Hankey, secretary to the Cabinet and formerly to the CID and a dedicated supporter of the bureaucratic system which he himself had done more than anyone else to create, marshalled the opposition and saw off this early attempt at unification by skilfully appealing to the self-interest of all parties. A defence minister, he suggested, would threaten the primacy and authority of the Prime Minister; an advisory central staff would replace the CID; a central staff with powers of control would interfere with departmental autonomy; and the Dominions would never accept it.[18]

One important development did, however, occur at this time. During the Chanak crisis of 1922, the three Chiefs of Staff began to meet informally in order to be prepared to take combined action if called upon to do so.[19] Sir Maurice Hankey suggested making this a permanent arrangement, and the Chiefs of Staff subcommittee met for the first time in formal session on 17 July 1923. The Prime Minister did not attend, and the chair was taken by the senior head of Service. The chairman had neither constitutional authority nor Prime Ministerial backing with which to impose unity on the new body.

The Chiefs of Staff liked to suggest that their new committee was a success: Admiral Beatty told the CID in 1926 that they 'were not three bodies working in opposite directions, but they were working in the same direction, each contributing towards the solution of the various problems of defence'. Even now, he remarked, their staffs were jointly considering war plans.[20] This was a gross exaggeration. The CIGS had torpedoed any strategic planning function two years earlier by stating that no plans of campaign were necessary except for the small wars incidental to Britain's imperial position: and it was not until 1933, when Lord Chatfield sought the Committee's approval for the decision that, in the event of war with Japan, the Royal Navy would hold Hong Kong, that the Chiefs of Staff gave any serious consideration to mutual strategy.

One reason for the failure of the Chiefs of Staff committee was the dispiriting economic climate of the 1920s. A second was that the Chiefs of Staff were given no guidance by the Foreign Office as to the political assumptions upon which war plans should be based, other than a generalised warning about the Russian threat to India. Left to their own devices the three Services usually differed. In 1924, for example, the Navy was alarmed at the situation in the Far East, the Army was worried about the Near East, and the Royal Air Force was deeply concerned at the menace of the French Air Force. When the Chiefs of Staff did invite the Foreign Office to react to strategic appreciations, their hopes were frequently dashed: in 1929 it responded to a string of annual estimates from the War Office chronicling rising German paramilitary strength by ridiculing them.[21] As late as 1937 the Chiefs of Staff were still complaining – with some justification – about the lack of clear political guidance by means of which to frame plans.

A major obstacle to co-operation between the Services lay in the issues raised by air power.[22] Its capacity to police the empire more cheaply than ground forces produced clashes between the Army and the RAF over which would have command in the event of operations in theatres where both Services would have to operate together, such as the Middle East. At another level the capabilities of the aircraft were unproved. The so-called 'bomber versus battleship' controversy, upon which hinged the decision as to which Service would have the lion's share in the defence of Singapore, rumbled on throughout the 1920s and into the 1930s. At a Chiefs of Staff meeting in January 1931 the new Chief of Naval Staff (CNS), Admiral Field, remarked despairingly that 'the air–gun controversy would never be satisfactorily settled until the respective merits of aircraft and guns were shown in the next war', to which Field Marshal Sir George Milne responded drily that by then it would be too late.[23] The dispute was resolved politically, and against the RAF, by Stanley Baldwin in 1932, but even then the question was regarded by the RAF as still an open one.[24]

Not only could the Chiefs of Staff not agree on how to use their own weapons, but they were also unable to agree on how other Powers would use theirs. Responding in 1934 to a questionnaire on the likely shape of a future war with Germany, the CNS replied that he expected a classic big fleet action from which a victor would emerge, the CIGS expected enemy air power to be used in support of the advancing German armies, and the Chief of Air Staff (CAS) thought that the Germans would go on the defensive against France and use air attack 'over these fortifications'.[25]

The failure of the Chiefs of Staff to reach agreement on such issues as the role of air power was partly due to the novelty and complexity of the problems they faced. But institutional factors were also at work to hinder co-operation at the highest levels. Writing in 1936, Admiral Lord Chatfield ascribed the 'difficulties of the past' to 'the personalities who composed the Chiefs of Staff subcommittee after the War, men who had risen chiefly by their forcefulness of character ... whose general line of argument was "what I say is right".'[26] Peace-time Chiefs of Staff frequently possessed similar characteristics. Among such men, disagreement was unavoidable; but without the firm hand of Prime Ministerial authority, it was also irresolvable.

With the ending of the Ten Year Rule in 1931 and the first steps towards rearmament two years later, the Chiefs of Staff were replaced by a system of direct Cabinet intervention in defence through ministerial subcommittees.[27] The first stage of Treasury control was now applied. In 1934 each Department submitted its estimates separately, assuming that taken collectively and developed over five years they would provide a reasonable level of rearmament. An unco-ordinated programme which overshot the financial target of £97,500,000 allowed the politicians to determine priorities according to non-strategic – or at best semi-strategic – grounds. Heavily influenced by Neville Chamberlain's economically based theory of parity deterrence, the government took the decision to put the bulk of the money into building a bomber force.[28]

The ineffectiveness of the Chiefs of Staff subcommittee was underlined in a different way by the Italo-Abyssinian crisis of 1935. Although confident that in the event of war Britain would win, the Chiefs could not agree on how to act and a bitter quarrel broke out in August 1935 over the correct tactical role of the RAF. The Air Staff wanted to use the bulk of its bombers in attacks on northern Italy, while the CNS and the CIGS demanded that priority be given to the protection of the fleet and the defence of Egypt.[29] The outbreak of war between Italy and Abyssinia on 3 October 1935 raised the even more fundamental question of whether the Chiefs of Staff had the authority to act executively as a battle headquarters. The then Prime Minister, Stanley Baldwin, said that he would be glad to consider this question and then, characteristically, did nothing about it. The Chiefs of Staff were never given Cabinet approval to exercise executive powers, and it was widely assumed that in war the government would establish a ministerial committee of control. The public disquiet aroused by the Abyssinian crisis did result in the creation in 1936 of a Minister for the Co-ordination of Defence, but the office lacked executive authority and its first incumbent, Sir Thomas Inskip, was not much respected within the Services.[30]

The onset of the German menace produced collective and individual acts of folly by the Chiefs of Staff. Collectively their hostile attitude towards the French and their absolute unwillingness to undertake staff talks at any meaningful level during 1938 irritated the Foreign Office beyond measure. Nor could they agree on what action to take when it became apparent after Munich that support of France would be necessary. In December 1938 the CNS favoured a limited land contribution to France, but the CAS absolutely opposed it. Then, in April 1939, when some form of combined contribution to France in the event of war seemed inescapable, the Air Staff declared that it regarded the Advanced Air Striking Force which would accompany the Expeditionary Force as primarily an integral part of Bomber Command which would participate in attacks on the Ruhr – not what the War Office was expecting or hoping for.[31] As war approached, this individualism increased rather than decreased, and Chamberlain took to making military decisions – such as the doubling of the Territorial Army in March 1939 – without consulting his professional advisers.

At the outbreak of the Second World War Chamberlain's lack of wartime experience – and Churchill's plethora of it – soon became apparent. A small War Cabinet was set up, including the Chiefs of Staff and all three Service ministers, but the military soon showed too much initiative for the newly-installed First Lord of the Admiralty. After a War Cabinet meeting on 21 September 1939, at which they resisted extending the war into the Balkans, Churchill suggested that politicians should be able to meet without servicemen present. Chamberlain responded by setting up the Military Co-ordination Committee, chaired by the Minister for the Co-ordination of Defence, Lord Chatfield, and comprising the three Service ministers and the Minister of Supply, assisted by the Chiefs of Staff, to scrutinise proposals for presentation to the War Cabinet.

The new body had a short and troubled life. Strategic differences were now debated three times instead of twice – in the Military Co-ordination Committee, the Chiefs of Staff committee and the War Cabinet – and unresolved disputes were simply passed up the line because Chatfield lacked the political authority to resolve them.[32] The machinery functioned fitfully and ineffectively for some six months, during which Churchill himself took the chair for a week, discovered how little could be done without Prime Ministerial authority and demanded to be appointed chairman of the Chiefs of Staff, before the German attack on France swept Chamberlain from office and Churchill succeeded him.[33]

Churchill moved swiftly and purposefully to reconstruct the higher organisation for defence. The War Cabinet was slimmed down by dismissing the Service ministers from it. The Prime Minister created and took for himself the new post of Minister of Defence; but instead of setting up a central staff to service him in his new role, he took over the Military Section of the War Cabinet secretariat under General Hastings Ismay, who became what he liked to call his 'handling machine'. The Military Co-ordination Committee disappeared into the limbo in which it belonged and was replaced by a Defence Committee with two panels, one for operations and one for supply. The operations panel varied in composition but always included the Prime Minister, the Deputy Prime Minister and the three Service ministers, with all three chiefs of staff in attendance. Recognising that the traditional attitude towards military planning, manifest in Jellicoe's attitude in 1917 and encapsulated six years later by Sir William Robertson in the formula, 'he who makes a plan ought to be responsible for its execution', represented an encumbrance to creative thinking, Churchill removed the Joint Planning Committee from the Cabinet Secretariat to work at his own orders, over the protest of the CIGS. Within a week he had invited its three senior members down to Chequers to discuss with him the campaign of 1941.[34]

Churchill's imaginative and far-sighted reconstruction of the defence machinery derived from a variety of sources. His participation in the higher direction of war between 1914 and 1918 gave him unparalleled experience, and his unique personal gifts both fostered the new system and empowered him to run it successfully. Additionally, as a result of his experiences since September 1939, he thought badly of the Chiefs of Staff organisation and of the individuals who ran it in the early stages of the Second World War: he called Sir John Dill, the CIGS until December 1941, 'the dead hand of inanition' to his face in the Cabinet.[35] Churchill had much to complain of, although some of the faults were to be found in the inadequacy of the system rather than of the men who ran it. He also regarded it as his duty as Prime Minister 'to use the power which Parliament and the nation have given him to drive others ... irrespective of anyone's feelings'.[36] Out of this crucible of experiences, beliefs and convictions, Churchill created a combined battle headquarters under the direct supervision of the head of government, through which he could exercise continuous direct and personal control over the formulation of military policy and the conduct of military operations. 'The practical effects', Lord Ismay later remarked, 'were revolutionary.'[37]

A system so highly centralised as the one Churchill had created could pose as great a danger as the one it replaced. Sir Alan Brooke, newly installed in the summer of 1940 in command of the defence of the United Kingdom, certainly thought so.

> It was a highly dangerous organization; had an invasion developed I fear that Churchill would have attempted as Defence Minister to coordinate the action of these various commands. This would have been wrong and highly dangerous; with his impulsive nature and tendency to arrive at decisions through a process of intuition, as opposed to 'logical approach', heaven knows where he might have led us![38]

No invasion ever came. But Churchill's system was tested in a different way in the early months of 1942 with the loss of Malaya and the fall of Singapore. Political pressure was exerted to change the Churchillian system and remodel it on the lines of the *Oberkommando der Wehrmacht* (OKW) (which contemporaries wholly misunderstood) as a 'system of unified military planning' which precluded the 'dangers of political misjudgement in military affairs'.[39] Churchill fought off this move in what was perhaps his most brilliant wartime speech. 'It is easy when the tide is adverse to contend that alterations in the structure of the war direction would have made or will make amends for the vast and gaping lack of men and resources or power of transportation,' he remarked. 'It is easy, but it may not be true.'[40]

The system worked because the Chiefs of Staff committee, under the chairmanship of Sir Alan Brooke from March 1942, provided the very necessary ballast which kept Churchill's fertile strategic imagination anchored to the shore of reality. General Sir Archibald Nye, Vice-Chief of the Imperial General Staff, succinctly summed up the priorities of the Committee:

> Our first commitment in this war is to impress the p.m. that his military strategy is incorrect and convince him of the unsoundness of his arguments; our second commitment is to put our views to the U.S. C.O.S. in such a way that they are not offended and agree to them; our third and last commitment is the war against Germany which is absolutely straightforward.[41]

Repeatedly the Chiefs of Staff had to stand their ground against Churchill in long, vigorous and exhausting debates before they could persuade him to abandon some cherished idea. Occasionally they simply withdrew support for a project before it had time to turn into a plan.[42] Sometimes – although rarely – Churchill overruled them on matters of policy.[43] Sometimes he ignored them.[44] Overall, however, the system produced good decisions. It did so because Brooke adopted three working principles and stuck to them. As Chairman of the Chiefs of Staff he believed they must always reach agreement; he did not believe in meddling with field commanders, and frequently stopped Churchill from doing so; and he always honestly spoke his mind, resisting Churchill's efforts to wear down his resistance to some pet idea with a battery of long dinners, late nights, brandy and cigars.

The appointment of two outstanding individuals ensured that the new integrated system worked to best effect. The first was Ismay. As head of the military secretariat, he, together with his deputies Hollis and Jacob, serviced the many formal and *ad hoc* committees and subcommittees spawned by the system; and as principal staff officer to the Minister of Defence, he attended all the meetings of the Chiefs of Staff committee. Ismay was thus in a position to act as a two-way communications channel, conveying information and impressions to and from the Prime Minister. The second was Brooke. Under his chairmanship the Chiefs of Staff committee became the very necessary ballast which weighed down the Churchillian imagination.

Although centralisation of the higher organisation of defence had worked well in wartime, when it had operated at theatre command level as well as in London, it had trampled on some of the most cherished Service principles. The war was scarcely over before an eagerness to re-establish patterns of prewar autonomy and independence re-surfaced. Nor did the immediate postwar experience of the Chiefs of Staff committee augur well for the future of inter-Service co-operation. Strong men were once again at the helm. As CIGS from 1945 to 1948, Montgomery displayed absolute contempt for his fellow chiefs, Tedder and Cunningham; according to a contemporary observer, all three men were caught 'in a sort of spell of hatred and spite which they could not break'.[45] Montgomery's subsequent chairmanship of the Western Union Commanders-in-Chief, marked as it was by a bruising feud with de Lattre de Tassigny, gave further ammunition to those who opposed efforts to impose centralisation in peace-time.

Between December 1945 and February 1946 a study group weighed the alternatives: absorption of the Service departments within a ministry of defence; a combined general staff on the lines of the OKW (which, since Germany had lost the war, was now regarded as a disaster); and a powerful independent chairman of the Chiefs of Staff reporting direct to the Minister of Defence. All these were rejected in favour of a Defence Committee of the Cabinet, including the three Service ministers and their Chiefs of Staff, and a Minister of Defence whose peace-time powers were drastically curtailed since the political heads of the three Services remained responsible to Parliament for expenditure.[46] Without Prime Ministerial authority the Minister of

Defence became, as Macmillan put it after a brief and unhappy sojourn in the job, 'a co-ordinator, not a master'.[47] To counteract any future moves towards undue centralisation, the 1946 Defence White Paper laid down as a cardinal principle of British organisation that 'it should be the men responsible in the Service Departments for carrying out the approved policy who are brought together in the central machine to formulate it'.[48]

The postwar system had to deal with familiar problems of demarcation, such as the struggle for control of Coastal Command, which went to the RAF. It also had to cope with the enormous problem of the development, production and control of nuclear weapons. The first effect of this was to set the Services against one another as they struggled for possession of a weapon which appeared to be appropriate to only one medium, and which would therefore enable one of them to claim the primary task in defence. In the pre-rocketry years it was the Royal Navy which felt most threatened: in a note to Lord Mountbatten urging him to take up the position of First Sea Lord, the Vice Chief of Naval Staff stressed the need to refute 'the "one big bang and it is all over" theory so cleverly sponsored by Jack Slessor and the U.S. Strategic Air Force'.[49] This problem was exacerbated when the RAF won control of ground-to-air missiles.

The second effect of the 'nuclear revolution' was to place the Chiefs of Staff in an environment in which the complexity of the new weapons and the pace of their development posed unforeseen problems of cost-control in a domestic environment in which economy was almost always the tune of the day. Research and development costs of the first generation of nuclear missiles were high, and budgeting was a total failure. This was largely the result of the absence of centralised control: until 1964 the Treasury negotiated with the separate Service departments once the broad totals had been settled between itself and the Ministry of Defence, dealing with the ministry only on service pay. Financial techniques were primitive: by 1957 cost projections only went forward three years. The 'scandalous inability to control weapons cost' was to be one of the most powerful factors in the move towards centralisation.[50]

Although Montgomery had been an ardent advocate of an independent chairman of the Chiefs of Staff committee since 1947, when he urged Mountbatten to use his influence with the Labour Prime Minister Clement Attlee to create such a post, there was little pressure from within the Services for further centralisation, since this inevitably meant the sacrifice of independence. Without Prime Ministerial interest and impetus, reform of the higher organisation for defence was impossible in other than trivial terms. In 1955, Anthony Eden took the first step down the path to full reorganisation: following the example of the United States, Canada and France, he created the position of Chairman of the Chiefs of Staff. The cause was the need to lighten the burdens imposed upon one man by the requirements of membership of NATO and the Western European Union. Almost immediately afterwards the new system was tested in the fire of the Suez crisis of 1956. It apparently had little influence on Eden's attitudes or behaviour.[51]

In 1957, Eden's successor, Harold Macmillan, appointed Duncan Sandys as Minister of Defence to 'work out a new defence policy in the light of present strategic needs which would secure a substantial reduction in expenditure and manpower'.[52] The result was Sandys' advocacy of an independent British nuclear deterrent. In devising policy Sandys worked largely through his own senior departmental staff and the chief scientist, prompting the Chiefs of Staff formally to protest in February 1958 that they were not being consulted over important decisions.

To some extent the Chiefs of Staff were themselves to blame for the position they now found themselves in. For one thing, as so often in the past, they were incapable of speaking with one voice on the desirability or otherwise of an independent British deterrent. In September 1958 the First Sea Lord and CIGS wrote a joint memorandum flatly opposing it, in direct contradiction to the view of the then current CAS. For another, in trying to block Sandys they worked independently of the new Chairman of the Chiefs of Staff, fearing that to do otherwise would be to contribute to a process of aggrandisement which would result in their losing control of their own affairs. The position of the first Chairman, Air Chief Marshal Sir William Dickson, grew so bad that in January 1958 he wrote to the minister complaining that the co-operation he was getting was 'reluctant almost to the point of nonexistence'.[53]

Macmillan reacted by strengthening the powers of the Minister of Defence, who now became responsible for 'the formulations and applications of a unified policy relating to the Armed Forces as a whole and their requirements' and by replacing the Chairman of the Chiefs of Staff with a Chief of the Defence Staff (CDS).[54] The CDS was given the responsibility of issuing operational orders; the Joint Planning Staff was put under his control; and he was also empowered to call on the staffs of the three Services for assistance. Macmillan's purpose in reconstructing the staff system was to produce an independent officer who could give the minister impartial advice. He was influenced in his actions by Montgomery, who had long proposed such a step.[55]

A year later, in July 1959, Lord Mountbatten was appointed CDS and began a personal crusade to centralise control of the armed forces. His experience in South East Asia Command during the Second World War had led him to favour unified control and he had many weapons at his disposal in trying to bring this about, not least some very good social connections. Centralisation was not a prospect the Services looked forward to with much relish: Marshal of the RAF Sir Dermot Boyle told Mountbatten to his face, 'I consider your appointment as Chief of the Defence Staff the greatest disaster that has befallen the British Defence Services within memory.'[56]

Mountbatten prepared the ground by setting up unified commands in the

Near East in 1960, in the Middle East in 1961, and in the Far East in 1962. Then, on 10 October 1962, he presented his proposals to the Minister of Defence, Peter Thorneycroft. They amounted to unification of the higher levels of the armed forces. A secretary of state for defence would be serviced by two functional ministers for personnel and research; a Defence Staff would be created to service the CDS, who would now only be 'advised' by the Chiefs of Staff; and the CDS would select and promote senior officers of one-star rank and higher from a single list. As a residual acknowledgement of their former independence, the three armed services were to have a junior minister each.[57]

All three Service chiefs were opposed in varying degrees to Mountbatten's proposals, a fact which Macmillan concealed from the Queen.[58] Their main grounds of concern were that those making plans and policy should not be divorced from those carrying them out (here the OKW was once again pressed into service as a good example of thoroughly bad practice); and that the new structure would prevent the Cabinet from having the opportunity to hear dissenting views.

Macmillan had shown by his previous actions that he was sympathetic to the policies which Mountbatten now suggested; and he had to hand a proposal which could be utilised to accommodate them. In September 1960 Montgomery had written to him urging that the Service empires be broken down and suggesting that the whole issue be examined by 'one, or at the most two, very high level persons – who would report to you'.[59]

Acting on this advice, Macmillan called Lord Ismay and General Sir Ian Jacob out of retirement to examine the proposals. They made one very significant change; contrary to Mountbatten's intentions, they recommended that the three Service Chiefs of Staff should continue to have access to the Prime Minister and that all alternative military policies originating in the Chiefs of Staff committee should always go up to the Defence Committee for decision.[60]

Accordingly, the 1963 White Paper set up a three-tier structure, at the top of which was the Defence and Overseas Policy Committee of the Cabinet, with the CDS and the Chiefs of Staff in attendance. Below this a Defence Council was established, to be chaired by the newly-titled Secretary of State for Defence. And the Chiefs of Staff committee remained untouched: chaired by the CDS, it was to be collectively responsible to the government for professional advice on strategy, military operations and the military implications of defence policy.

The position of the CDS was strengthened by the addition of a headquarters staff comprising a Defence Operations Executive, a Defence Signals Staff, a Defence Intelligence Staff, and a Defence Operations Requirements Staff.[61] These latter were small, and were intended to work alongside the existing Joint Planning Staff and Joint Warfare Staff. Constitutionally the

CDS was required to tender 'the agreed collective advice of the Chiefs of Staff Committee' or to report differing views and offer the Cabinet his own advice.[62] This formulation allowed for considerable individual latitude, and Mountbatten apparently took full advantage of it: on more than one occasion his fellow Chiefs of Staff caught him out misrepresenting the conclusions of the committee to the Minister of Defence.

The Labour government which came to power in 1964 considered the higher machinery for defence chiefly from the point of view of the degree to which it constituted an efficient and effective machine to control defence expenditure. Unacceptable cost acceleration and technological supercession – neither of which the military could do much about – had led to expensive cancellations of weapons systems.[63] The record, however, was undeniably poor: the RAF had spent £11,000 million between 1947 and 1965 and was left after the cancellation of TSR2 with an ageing fleet of 150 V-bombers and not very much more. The government intended to hold defence costs down to a fixed ceiling of £2000 millions, and to do this the new Secretary of State, Denis Healey, conducted a far-reaching Defence Review based on cost–benefit analysis. There was little input from the Services, and Healey apparently drew heavily on the expertise of his civil servants.

The government moved slowly forward towards Mountbatten's goal. In 1966 the Geraghty committee recommended a functional ministry, the elimination of the separate Service boards, a reduction in power for the Chiefs of Staff and a powerful new Defence Management Board. These reforms were not implemented; but two years later a single defence budget replaced the tri-Service budgets, and in 1972 managerial functionalisation on commercial lines reached new heights when a Minister of Defence Procurement was created to work under the Secretary of State. That same year the new post was dropped.[64]

The machine was struck by a second wave of managerial economies in 1974–5, when a Defence Review was again instituted with the aim of reducing expenditure from six per cent of GNP to four and a half per cent over ten years. Now, however, the machinery had learned better how to cope with the demands of politicians; and it had as its head a CDS who was willing to disregard official procedures in order to meet requirements. Care was taken to involve Treasury representatives in the review from the earliest stages in order to avoid producing a report which was financially unacceptable. The Assistant CDS on the review body worked to the brief of the CDS, who in turn brought round any recalcitrant Chief of Staff, either by individual meetings or through group discussion. And, thirdly, denied a satisfactory basis for setting strategic priorities, the CDS invented his own in which priority was given to NATO and within that to the Central Front and the Atlantic. In one respect the system hampered the CDS in his task: he was required by the rules to gain the agreement of his colleagues before taking the advice of either the Chiefs of Staff secretariat or his own Central Policy and initiating studies. This rule was overcome by the simple expedient of breaking it.[65]

The drawbacks to 'policy by council' were clearly revealed when the Defence Council was summoned to address the 1974 Defence Review. Under its terms of establishment the Council is not legally required to meet: whether it does so depends entirely on the wishes of the Secretary of State of the day, and its formal powers can be exercised by a quorum of two. In his early period of office Denis Healey apparently found it of value, since it met 26 times between 1964 and 1967. Thereafter it fell into complete disuse, being summoned once while Lord Carrington was Defence Secretary – to have its photograph taken.[66] When called together in 1974, it began to undermine the cohesive policy hammered together by the Chief of Defence Staff. Single-service junior ministers raised issues which had already been resolved in long and laborious discussion, threatening to erode an agreed Ministry of Defence position which had already been established in association with other departments, including the Treasury. Roy Mason quickly realised the dangers and reverted to the practice adopted by Lord Carrington of allowing the Chiefs of Staff Committee to function as the principal co-ordinating body within the Ministry of Defence.[67] His successor, Fred Mulley, felt differently, and the Defence Council was convened more than 30 times between 1976 and 1978.

The experience which followed the summoning of the Defence Council in 1974 illustrated the increasing difficulty in reaching agreement within the higher organisation for defence on the key question of resource allocation between the Services. In November 1981 the Chiefs of Staff used their collective weight to attempt to improve the defence budget, informing the government that unless more money was forthcoming they could not adequately fulfil defence commitments. The result was a Defence Programme Review which represented Defence Secretary John Nott's own view of the defence priorities, reached after consulting his advisers. The impotence felt by the CDS as a consequence of the manner in which this review was conducted led to an important revision of his terms of reference, announced on 11 November 1981. He was now given the task of tendering independent military advice to the Secretary of State for Defence.[68]

The centralisation of power and authority in the higher organisation for defence in Britain took a further step forward in 1984. Under proposals made by Defence Secretary Michael Heseltine the CDS continues to chair the Chiefs of Staff committee but tenders independent military advice on strategy, forward policy, resource allocation, commitments and operations; he will also plan, direct and conduct all military operations; and he will direct the work of the Central Defence Staff. In a major departure from all previous practice the appointment of a CDS will be at the discretion of the Prime Minister and the Secretary of State for Defence rather than being held on a 'turn and turn about' basis, and will be for an indeterminate period. Four Deputy Chiefs of the Defence Staff will be responsible for strategy and policy, for programmes and personnel, for systems, and for commitments.[69]

The process of squeezing the heads of the three armed services has been taken a step further, leaving them with responsibility for little more than morale, management, discipline and efficiency in their separate arms, although they retain the right of direct access to the Prime Minister. The proposals have drawn strong criticism from Admiral Lord Lewin and Field Marshal Lord Carver, both former Chiefs of Defence Staff, who argue that single-service Chiefs of Staff must be left with adequate staffs to enable them to fulfil their responsibilities as professional heads of Service and to contribute considered advice to the CDS on matters of strategy and policy, and that the single-service machinery is best qualified to determine the weapons system and organisation required.[70] However the evidence of the past twenty years suggests that, unless current trends are reversed, the power and authority of the CDS will continue to grow, at the expense of the individual Chiefs of Staff.

Notes

1. J. P. Mackintosh, *The British Cabinet* (London, 1962) p. 274.
2. S. W. Roskill, *Hankey: Man of Secrets*, 3 vols. (London, 1970–4), passim.
3. J. Gooch, *The Prospect of War: Studies in British Defence Policy 1847–1942* (London, 1981) pp. 73–9.
4. J. S. Omond, *Parliament and the Army 1642–1904* (Cambridge, 1933) p. 146; O. Wheeler, *The War Office Past and Present* (London, 1914) pp. 255–7.
5. N. H. Gibbs, *The Origins of Imperial Defence* (Oxford: Clarendon Press, 1955) pp. 2–9; J. Gooch, *The Plans of War: The General Staff and British Military Strategy c. 1900–1916* (London, 1974) pp. 32–59.
6. N. d'Ombrain, *War Machinery and High Policy: Defence administration in peacetime Britain, 1902–1914* (London, 1973) pp. 13, 99, 180, 211. See also Fisher to Tweedmouth, 9 July 1906, quoted in A. J. Marder (ed.), *Fear God and Dread Nought*, II (London, 1956) p. 83.
7. S. R. Williamson, *The Politics of Grand Strategy: Britain and France Prepare for War, 1904–1914* (Harvard, 1969) p. 50.
8. S. R. Freemantle, *My Naval Career, 1880–1928* (London, 1949) p. 151.
9. Public Record Office. Minutes of meetings of the Naval War Council, Adm. 116/3090. A. J. Marder, *From the Dreadnought to Scapa Flow*, I (Oxford, 1961) p. 248.
10. P. Guinn, *British Strategy and Politics 1914 to 1918* (Oxford, 1965) p. 115; John Ehrman, *Cabinet Government and War 1890–1940* (Cambridge, 1958) p. 61.
11. Crease to Jellicoe, 17 May 1915, quoted in A. Temple Patterson (ed.), *The Jellicoe Papers*, I, Navy Records Society 1966, p. 161.
12. A. J. Marder, *From the Dreadnought to Scapa Flow*, II (Oxford, 1965) pp. 89–90, 196.
13. Admirals Oliver and Jackson were subsequently very vague as to what they had actually counselled at the Dardanelles Committee; and the CIGS, Wolfe Murray, admitted that he left meetings of the War Council and the Dardanelles

Committee without having any idea that a decision had been reached at all: T. Higgins, *Winston Churchill and the Dardanelles* (London, 1963) p. 81; Gooch, *Plans of War*, pp. 303–4. See also Marder, *From the Dreadnought to Scapa Flow*, II, p. 218.
14. Personal information from Field Marshal Lord Harding of Petherton.
15. D. R. Woodward, *Lloyd George and the Generals* (London, 1983) p. 176.
16. Jellicoe, Remarks attached to Carson to Jellicoe, 7 June 1917, quoted in A Temple Patterson (ed.), *The Jellicoe Papers*, II, Navy Records Society 1968, p. 167.
17. Memorandum by Sir Eric Geddes, 10 September 1917. Ibid., pp. 211–17.
18. H. G. Welch, 'The Origins and Development of the Chiefs of Staff Subcommittee of the Committee of Imperial Defence: 1923–1939', unpublished PhD dissertation, University of London 1973, pp. 36–42.
19. Roskill, *Hankey*, II, p. 290.
20. Quoted in Welch, *Origins and Development*, p. 108.
21. Brian Bond, *British Military Policy between the Two World Wars* (Oxford, 1980) p. 93.
22. Roskill, *Hankey*, II, pp. 345–6.
23. Public Record Office. 97th meeting of Chiefs of Staff Committee, 26 January 1931. Cab. 53/3.
24. Gooch, *Prospect of War*, p. 22.
25. Welch, *Origins and Development*, pp. 163–4.
26. Public Record Office, Chatfield to Hankey, 17 February 1936, Cab. 21/424. Quoted in Welch, *Origins and Development*, p. 115.
27. The Ten Year Rule, instituted in 1919 and put on a rolling basis in 1928, guided British military planners by allowing them to assume that Great Britain would not be engaged in a major war for the next ten years.
28. M. S. Smith, 'Rearmament and Deterrence in Britain in the 1930s', *Journal of Strategic Studies*, vol. I, no. 3 (London) December 1978, pp. 313–37.
29. Welch, *Origins and Development*, p. 219.
30. Roskill, *Hankey*, III, pp. 52–3; Welch, *Origins and Development*, p. 250; M. S. Smith, 'The Development of British Strategic Air Power Doctrine and Policy in Period of Rearmament preceding the Second World War c. 1934–1939', unpublished PhD dissertation, University of Lancaster 1975, p. 107.
31. Welch, *Origins and Development*, p. 329.
32. Martin Gilbert, *Finest Hour: Winston S. Churchill 1939–1941* (London, 1983) pp. 38–40.
33. John Colville, *The Fringes of Power: Downing Street Diaries 1939–1955* (London, 1985) p. 108 (25 April 1940).
34. Gilbert, *Finest Hour*, pp. 753–4; Colville, *Fringes of Power*, p. 232. (30 August 1940). Robertson's observation, made in 1923, cited in Welch, p. 50.
35. Alex Danchev, ' "Dilly-Dally", or Having the Last Word: Field Marshal Sir John Dill and Prime Minister Winston Churchill', *Journal of Contemporary History*, vol. 22, no. 1, January 1987, pp. 21–44.
36. Charles Eade (ed.), *Secret Session Speeches by the Right Hon. Winston S. Churchill* (London, 1946) p. 35 (26 June 1941).
37. *The Memoirs of Lord Ismay* (London, 1960) p. 159.
38. David Fraser, *Alanbrooke*, London, p. 183.
39. Letter by Sir Edward Grigg, 2 May 1942, *The Times*, 5 May 1942.
40. Eade, *Secret Session Speeches*, p. 49 (13 April 1942).
41. Imperial War Museum, Earle Diary, 13 February 1944.
42. Joan Beaumont, *Comrades in Arms: British Aid to Russia 1941–1945* (London, 1980) p. 71.

43. Gooch, *Prospect of War*, pp. 25–6.
44. Roskill, *Hankey*, III, p. 506; D. Carlton, *Anthony Eden: A Biography* (London, 1981) pp. 168–9.
45. Quoted in Nigel Hamilton, *Monty: The Field Marshal 1944–1976* (London, 1986) p. 646.
46. Her Majesty's Stationery Office (hereafter, HMSO). Statement Relating to Defence, Cmd. 6743, 1946; Vice-Admiral J. Hughes-Hallett, 'The Central Organization for Defence', *Journal of the Royal United Services Institution*, CIII, 1958, p. 490.
47. Harold Macmillan, *Tides of Fortune* (London, 1969) p. 561.
48. HMSO Central Organisation for Defence, Cmd. 6923, 1946, p. 2.
49. Vice-Chief of Naval Staff to Lord Louis Mountbatten, 31 October 1954, quoted in Philip Ziegler, *Mountbatten: The Official Biography* (London, 1985).
50. F. A. Johnson, *Defence by Ministry: The British Ministry of Defence 1944–1974* (London, 1980) p. 42.
51. Ziegler, *Mountbatten*, p. 543.
52. Harold Macmillan, *Riding the Storm* (London, 1971) p. 244.
53. Dickson to Sandys, 2 January 1958. Quoted in Ziegler, *Mountbatten*, p. 562.
54. HMSO Central Organisation for Defence, Cmnd. 476, 1958, p. 1.
55. Harold Macmillan, *At the End of the Day* (London, 1973) p. 411.
56. Ziegler, *Mountbatten*, p. 582.
57. Johnson, *Defence by Ministry*, pp. 106–7; Ziegler, *Mountbatten*, pp. 610–11.
58. Compare Macmillan, *At the End of the Day*, p. 414, with Ziegler, *Mountbatten*, p. 613.
59. Montgomery to Macmillan, 2 September 1960, quoted in Hamilton, p. 922.
60. Johnson, *Defence by Ministry*, pp. 111–12.
61. HMSO Central Organisation for Defence, Cmd. 2097, 1963.
62. Lt. Gen. Sir Maurice Johnston, 'More Power to the Centre: MOD Reorganization', *Journal of the Royal United Services Institution*, vol. 128, no. 1, March 1983, p. 7.
63. Peter Nailor, 'Denis Healey and rational decision-making in defence', in I. F. W. Beckett and J. Gooch, *Politicians and Defence: Studies in the Formulation of British Defence Policy 1845–1970* (Manchester, 1981) p. 159.
64. HMSO Government Organisation for Defence Procurement and Civil Aerospace, Cmnd. 4641, 1971.
65. Personal information.
66. Brian Taylor, 'Coming of Age: A Study of the Evolution of the Ministry of Defence Headquarters', *Journal of the Royal United Services Institution*, vol. 128, no. 3, September 1983, p. 46.
67. Personal information.
68. Johnson, *Defence by Ministry*, p. 8.
69. HMSO Central Organisation for Defence, Cmnd. 9315, 1984.
70. *The Times*, 20 and 23 March 1984.

4 The Influence of the British Secretariat Tradition on Twentieth-Century International Peace-Keeping
Robert S. Jordan

INTRODUCTION

The evolution of one of the most effective means of achieving some measure of multinational co-ordination and possible amelioration of international political rivalries took place as a consequence of the great colonial – or imperial – expansion of Great Britain into the non-European world. One result of this expansion was the Boer War in South Africa. In the wake of the generally poor performance of Britain in this war, and because of the growing awareness in London that the Empire needed more systematic overseeing, a means of co-ordinating Britain's military affairs was introduced, called the secretariat method. In fact, stretching even from the Seven Years' War, as Peter Nailor points out, a new concept of imperial security was slowly evolving: 'The particular aspect of Imperial defense that pervades and illuminates the British experience is the cooperation (or lack of it) between the Imperial power and its self-governing possessions.'[1] More to the point of this chapter, Nailor observes:

> ... British Imperial defense is the story of a relationship that in some respects is more like that of an alliance than of central and dominant authority imposing and executing a series of objectives: a relationship in which persuasion and example – and indecision – have as much place as economic and political uncertainty or agreed strategic perspectives.[2]

As Britain's overseas involvements expanded, and the variety of conditions under which Britain could find herself embroiled militarily multiplied, innovative forms of administration to handle policy-making requirements took on more and more of an institutional character. What would begin as an improvisation, such as supplying a secretary or clerk to 'look after things' for an *ad hoc* committee or working group, gradually, over the years and especially by the first decade and a half of this century, evolved into a coherent concept of governmental procedure. This procedure was subsequently adapted to meet the needs of Allied war-making in the First World War. From that experience, the method served as the central concept of the formation of the international civil service of the League of Nations, and most of the other international organisations formed thereafter, including the United Nations and, more pertinent to this book, the North Atlantic Treaty Organisation (NATO).

THE COMMITTEE OF IMPERIAL DEFENCE

Initially the idea of a 'secretariat' grew out of the British notion that there should be a bureaucratic cadre of non-political officials who would serve whatever 'government of the day' the Sovereign had empowered to rule. Generally speaking, this cadre was not to be involved in policy-making – a political function – but rather in policy-implementing – an administrative function.

The immediate circumstances, however, which gave rise to the formation of a group of civil servants into a secretariat that would serve the needs of a government policy-making body, came from the external responsibilities of government, rather than from domestic sources. Just after the turn of the century, in 1902, the Prime Minister decided to set up a Committee of Imperial Defence (CID) as a subcommittee of the Cabinet, and in 1904 a small section of career civil servants and some military career officers was formed to co-ordinate its work. Franklyn Johnson has offered an explanation as to why this development had not taken place earlier within the full Cabinet itself to take care of overall policy-making needs:

> A weakness of cabinet government of the late nineteenth century was the lack of agenda or minutes. This was an especially serious failing because of the technicalities and delicate relationships among the strategic factors which accompany military activities, and their general lack of interest to politicians, who find it easy to overlook such problems in the absence of memoranda and records. Thus perhaps it was only natural that the need for an elaborate cabinet secretariat should first appear in the defence sphere, and then, under the pressure of a great military effort, the secretariat of the Committee of Imperial Defence should become a part of the cabinet machinery.[3]

Although it was not until 1916 that the secretariat system was introduced for the Cabinet generally, it had been long-established practice for the Prime Minister, the 'first among equals' in the Cabinet, to report its proceedings to the Sovereign. This was not, of course, in any way a substitute for the lack of a permanent record of the Cabinet's activities. None the less the CID carried on its work with the increasingly valuable – and valued – help of its small secretariat. The secretary to the CID, because of the nature of his work, possessed a significant potential for direct influence over much of the business of the Committee.

Under certain circumstances this influence could acquire political overtones if the secretary were to wander outside the nebulous boundary of his professional neutrality. This happened in 1907 when Sir George Clarke, the first secretary to the CID, was pressured to resign because he had openly advised the Prime Minister to oppose the construction of *Dreadnoughts*. Apart from the fact that the decision went against him, it was recognised that he had compromised his ability to deal effectively with many powerful naval leaders because this was an issue of great political and strategic significance. It was clear that a secretary who performed a co-ordinate role had always to maintain unobstructed channels to all the governmental bodies, groups and leading individuals in the policy-making process. While he might be asked his opinion on some issue – and he often was – he should not, according to the tradition which was being built up, have taken stands on issues in such a way as to interfere with his access to and credibility with those persons and organs that he was serving.

Rear Admiral Sir Charles Ottley succeeded Sir George Clarke (later Lord Sydenham) in 1907, and in 1908 Sir Maurice (later Lord) Hankey joined him as his assistant. Because both of these men were from the Navy (Hankey being a Marine), the lingering suspicion in naval quarters about the impartiality of the CID's Secretariat was dispelled. In 1912 Hankey succeeded to the secretaryship, holding this post – and after 1916 that of secretary to the Cabinet as well – until his retirement in 1938.[4]

It would be inaccurate to infer that the CID Secretariat had little power just because in policy-making it was to behave in a politically neutral manner. From its beginning, the Secretariat had the ability to initiate matters, and this can be a strong power indeed. The terms of reference, based on the *Esher Report*, provided that the Secretariat could 'consider all questions on the subject and anticipate'[5] the informational requirements of the Prime Minister. As Lord Hankey was to put it, retrospectively and quite candidly:

> The Government Departments looked at everything through departmental spectacles, and generally referred to us only questions in which their own business was crossed by or dependent on that of other departments. In these circumstances we secretaries soon discovered that we must find out ourselves what our work should be and then persuade either the Prime Minister himself or some department to refer it formally to us. In practice most of the initiative was taken by the staff of the Committee.[6]

Turning now to the Committee itself, we should note that its hallmark was flexibility of membership. The CID was a means by which the military leaders could communicate more or less systematically with the political leaders about security questions. As requirements dictated, the membership of the CID would change, but always under the chairmanship of the Prime Minister. He decided who should sit on the Committee. This was important, because the Committee was always advisory only: it, of itself, did not take the political decisions that lay at the heart of government. These were taken by the Cabinet under the leadership of the Prime Minister. But continuity and permanence of the CID Secretariat, in the face of the evanescent nature of the Committee membership, tended to give the secretary and his assistants an influence which otherwise would have been improbable. The Secretariat was 'the cornerstone of the whole edifice'.[7]

Initially the secretary to the CID was authorised several assistant secretaries, two junior officers each from the army, navy and Indian army, and from one or more colonies. India was viewed as the 'hub' of the Empire and '... the iron band that kept the wheel together was the Royal Navy ...'.[8] These persons succeeded William Tyrell, a Foreign Office official who had been asked to keep minutes of the CID. Tyrell was described by Lord Hankey as 'a part-timer who did not pretend to know the job'.[9]

From these beginnings, the place of the secretariat in the machinery of British government grew in importance to such an extent that the secretariat function, as mentioned earlier, was built into the work of the Cabinet itself during the First World War. It was no longer possible for the Cabinet, apart from the subcommittee which was the CID, to continue the informal and diffuse methods of the past. To meet the total needs of total war, authority and responsibility had to be defined by the primary policy-formulating bodies and the executive agencies of the government to a greater degree than ever before had been necessary. By the time of Hankey's retirement it was clear that his long tenure could be seen as a transition period between the days of informality and the 'gifted amateur' ruling Britain, and the coming into existence of the modern state requiring a large bureaucracy of professionals. It simply would be impossible today, even for a man as 'omnicompetent' as Hankey (as one observer described him) to hold all the main policy-making threads in his hands or in those of his secretariat. Lord Hankey, during his tenure of office, witnessed the development of Britain as a modern administrative state.

L. S. Amery, who had been a member of the CID Secretariat, put it thus: 'As for Hankey he had, in his quiet unobtrusive way, helped to prepare us for war, and had, in effect, both devised and continually oiled the machinery which won it.'[10] Even more complimentary – almost adulatory – was the comment in 1919 of Lord Riddell, a man who was not a leader but who was close to the leading figures of the time: 'The truth is that Hankey is one of the best-tempered, most agreeable, kindest men I have ever met – a real Christian in every sense of the word – as well as one of the most efficient.'[11]

In light of the fact that Hankey was able to maintain himself in the seat of power for so long, it must also be assumed that he had qualities of tough-mindedness and tenacity of purpose. He also, apparently, was a man who loved his work, as he freely admitted:

> ... the Committee was brought formally into existence by a Treasury Minute dated May 4, 1904. When I opened my newspaper at breakfast and read this item of news I remarked to my wife that the secretaryship of the new Committee was the post of all others to which I would aspire, adding that it was never likely to happen, and if it did, only late in life as the crown to my career. Little did I think that within less than eight years I was destined to realize my ambition, much less that I should hold the post for more than a quarter of a century, and that it would lead me into the vortex of national, Imperial, and international affairs during one of the most eventful periods in the Empire's history.[12]

THE WAR COUNCIL AND WAR CABINET

In November 1914, with the onset of the war, Prime Minister Asquith set up the War Council, which was composed of many of the same persons who sat on the CID. And, consistently, the Secretariat of the CID assumed the responsibility for the work of the War Council. There was a difference, however, between the functions of the CID and the War Council. The Council, which existed alongside the full Cabinet, was a more fluid body that proffered its advice only when asked to do so and then mostly on new departures of wartime strategy or about combined operations. In 1915 the War Council was replaced by the Dardanelles Committee, which soon in effect became the War Committee. The Secretariat of the War Committee, however, although deeply enmeshed in the problems of the British government as regards the waging of the war, was still serving an advisory and consultative body rather than a decision-making or executive body. This aspect was in the tradition of the CID. In contrast, when Prime Minister Lloyd George formed his War Cabinet in December 1916, the Secretariat's responsibilities changed by virtue of the altered role of the War Cabinet from that of the previous bodies. The War Cabinet was an executive body which was derived from the Cabinet itself. It was intimately involved in the prosecution of the war.

In the course of the war Britain had become increasingly engaged in working out collaborative relationships with its allies, especially with France, and later with the United States. As a consequence the Secretariat, once established, immediately began to take on not only an internal role but also a rapidly expanding international role as well. Furthermore, along with others,

Hankey was becoming more concerned about the kind of peace that should be obtained even while the war was yet to be resolved. Hankey's influence – apart from that of the Secretariat generally – on key decisions in the conduct of the war, is illustrated by an observation by Amery: '... Hankey, in close touch with junior officers in the Admiralty ... took it upon himself to state the case for convoys with overwhelming force in a memorandum early in February. Lloyd George caught fire at once, and never let the Admirals alone till they finally gave way in April, and very soon became whole-hearted converts to the new method.'[13] Amery also reveals how important the other secretaries could be in their work at this time:

> In January Hankey turned me on to act for him as secretary of the Inter-departmental Committee which had been set up by the late Government to study the question of the territorial changes outside Europe which we should aim at in the terms of peace, or might secure by exchanges with our own Allies. The secretary of such a committee, if he has any skill at drafting, and is supported by the chairman, can usually get what he wants, or most of it, for the simple reason that no one is prepared to take the trouble to recast the document from beginning to end. Consequently even the most drastic amendments usually end in a compromise that leaves the main argument substantially unaffected.[14]

Without a doubt, one of the major features of the secretariat system was the use of subcommittees. Lord Hankey thought that the parcelling-out of the work of the CID, and later the War Council and the various successor bodies, was one of his greatest contributions to good governmental management. Subcommittees, for example, could be useful to co-ordinate affairs among government departments or matters which might overlap departments. They could also help in dealing in greater detail with particular problems than the full Committee (or Cabinet) might have found would justify their collective attention.

Under the War Cabinet the system of delegation to committees and subcommittees was extended considerably. Even at that, from its formation in December 1916 to its dissolution in October 1919, the full Cabinet held more than 650 meetings, with over 500 persons who were not members of the War Cabinet and the Secretariat attending these meetings at different times.[15] The volume of business for the Secretariat must have been enormous.

It was at this time, after the evolution of the wartime planning function from the War Council, through the Dardanelles Committee and the War Committee to the War Cabinet, that the 'Cabinet Office' was created. Its duties, as written up by Hankey in a Rules of Procedure, were: (1) to record the proceedings of the War Cabinet; (2) to transmit relevant extracts from the minutes to departments concerned with implementing them or otherwise interested; (3) to prepare the agenda paper, and to arrange the attendance of ministers not in the War Cabinet and others required to be present for discussion of particular items on the agenda; (4) to receive papers from departments and circulate them to the War Cabinet and others as necessary; and (5) to attend to the correspondence and general secretarial work of the Office.[16]

Even though Hankey came to move among the highest-level wartime Allied decision-makers, there has been some disagreement as to whether the machinery which made this possible could be explained through institutional evolution, as had been suggested, or through the personal career of Lord Hankey, as has also been suggested. As John P. Mackintosh put it:

> The view that the Committee of Imperial Defence was the true ancestor of the War Council of 1914 and later of the War Cabinet comes largely from the writings of Lord Hankey ... this is largely a matter of pride of parentage, for there are evident connections – the main one being the Secretariat under Hankey – but for the purposes of the historian the important point is that before 1914 the Committee of Imperial Defence met occasionally and played a minor advisory role, while Lloyd George's War Cabinet was the executive body meeting every day and running the war. The latter took over the powers and outlook of the peacetime Cabinet and added some of the practices of the old Committee of Imperial Defence.[17]

Lord Hankey would put it somewhat differently: 'both before and during World War I we were always working, by trial and error, after nearly 100 years of freedom from major war, to build up a really reliable system. The big point was that at last we had in the C.I.D. the nucleus of a workable system'.[18]

THE IMPERIAL WAR CABINET AND IMPERIAL WAR CONFERENCE

As mentioned earlier, the dominion governments, reflecting Britain's world-wide commitments, had sometimes been consulted about questions of a political or strategic nature even before the outcome of the War. For example, representatives of the dominions had from time to time participated in meetings of the CID. This tradition of consultation was institutionalised by Prime Minister Lloyd George shortly after he came to office. He requested that the dominion governments should be involved in 'a series of special and continuous meetings of the War Cabinet in order to consider urgent questions affecting the prosecution of the war'.[19] The gathering together of this group, on a continuing consultative basis, came to be known as the Imperial War Cabinet. It was concerned with the planning of naval and military operations and of other broader issues affecting the Empire that the war had engendered.

In contrast, the Imperial War Conferences, under the chairmanship of the Secretary of State for the Colonies, was concerned with matters not directly connected with the war but which affected the Empire. The Conferences went on from 1917 to 1921. The Commonwealth Conferences held today can be seen as successors to these Imperial Conferences.

Noteworthy in the experience of the Imperial War Cabinet were the periodic meetings of dominion prime ministers with the British Prime Minister. Because the war came to a close fairly soon after this practice had developed, the procedures for its institutionalisation were not fully developed. However, the prime ministers did take up at their last session the question of the representation of the dominions at the Paris Peace Conference, which opened in January 1919. Canada, Australia, South Africa, New Zealand and India agreed that their own delegations at the Peace Conference should be included in the British Empire Delegation, which was seen as an extension of the Imperial War Cabinet. Significantly for our purposes, the War Cabinet Office provided most of the staff for the secretariat of the British Empire Delegation, with some of the staff coming from the dominions.

In summary, the records of the Imperial War Cabinet, the various meetings in London of dominion prime ministers, and the work of the British Empire Delegation were all served by the 'Cabinet Office' of the War Cabinet. In tribute to the work of Lord Hankey and his secretariat, the Machinery of Government Committee, which met in 1918 to consider postwar governmental organisation, made this recommendation:

> ... we think that there is one feature in the procedure of the War Cabinet which may well assume a permanent form, namely, the appointment of a Secretary to the Cabinet charged with the duty of collecting and putting into shape its agenda, of providing the information and material necessary for its deliberations, and of drawing up records of the results for communication to the Departments concerned.[20]

THE PARIS PEACE CONFERENCE

Regardless of the nature of the origins of the Cabinet Office – whether it was established owing to institutional evolution or personal leadership – the secretariat function had become central not only to Britain, but also, by 1919, to the conduct of Allied affairs and, especially as far as the future was concerned, to the making and keeping of peace. Because of the central position of Hankey in co-ordinating the British role in the wartime coalition, it was only natural that he and his secretariat would remain alongside the

Prime Minister as the process of peace-making began. In a sense, this aspect of proximity had evolved during the war. The emphasis had become *co-ordination* among the Allied states rather than joint execution of common projects. The secretariat style lent itself to this situation. It was good for planning and co-ordination, but not for execution. For example, a precedent for the League was described thus:

> [The Allied organisations'] powers were advisory, and they had no control over the resources of the different governments. The control was a national control ... The function of the Allied organisations was to make plans for the exercise of the national controls. It was their task to assemble the statistics and other data needed as a basis for correct decisions, to agree upon the accuracy of this information, to study it with the help of experts, and to recommend plans of action for the adoption of the several governments. Each government, however, was always free to reject any recommendation, if it was deemed contrary to the national interest. The Allied organisations, therefore, merely were machinery devised to secure effective co-operation among the nations fighting Germany for the purpose of utilising their full strength, with the least waste in carrying on the war.[21]

More and more, *ad hoc* groups composed of representatives of each Allied government were formed to deal with specific problems, and this practice brought with it an increasing requirement for secretariat support. The Wheat Executive, formed in 1917 in London by Britain, France and Italy, is an example. Its responsibility was to develop a comprehensive plan for the supply of wheat and to supervise the plan's execution. The Executive was composed of representatives of each participating country. Similar terms of reference were set for the Allied Maritime Transport Council. The Council's secretariat was non-national, charged to serve the organisation as a whole, but the Council was assisted by national staff members as well.

Because of the combination of the Prime Minister's decision-making habits and the growth of these Allied groups, the Cabinet Office Secretariat had become more involved in international affairs than perhaps otherwise would have been the case. The result was that within the British delegation to the Peace Conference there arose some disagreement about which part of the government – the Cabinet Office or the Foreign Office – should serve the policy-making needs of the delegation. Part of this disagreement stemmed from a general feeling of mistrust over the role which professional diplomats, employing 'traditional diplomacy', had played in the pre-1914 years, with what appeared to be disastrous consequences. This had led to a feeling of grievance on the part of the professional diplomats, as expressed, for example, by Sir Harold Nicolson: 'It is quite true that there was no time for much consultation: it is also true that there was little desire.'[22]

He went on to observe, 'haphazard methods [were] adopted for co-ordination between the Plenipotentiaries and the Delegation as a whole. We were seldom told what to do. We were never told what our rulers were doing'.[23] This was because the machinery of co-ordination had been set up by the Cabinet Offices under Hankey's direction. It operated very efficiently, but not in the service of the Foreign Office. Hankey served the Prime Minister's needs; furthermore, he was the only person to attend continuously the meetings of the Big Four (Lloyd George, Clémençeau, Orlando and Wilson). He had had experience in this situation, having headed the British Section of the Supreme War Council, which had been established near the end of the war. He thus had had an opportunity to meet his approximate counterparts in the French, Italian and American governments.

When the Peace Conference was held in Paris, it became inevitable that the French would be the hosts, and M. Clémençeau would be chairman, with the General Secretariat under French direction. This was generally considered to be unfortunate, for the French secretary was, in at least the British view, not as able as was Hankey and for a time this directly affected the ability of the Conference to proceed to its main task. As Nicolson put it:

> This defect in the Secretariat General was gradually remedied by the hearty British efficiency of Sir Maurice Hankey. Yet in the early stages it constituted a serious drawback. And for this reason. A really brilliant Secretary, a Gentz or a Massigli, might have remedied the omission of an agreed programme by the constant preparation of intelligent agenda papers. M. Dutasta was too flurried for any such acts of vision or responsibility. He took subjects in their order of temporal urgency, not in their order of actual importance. As a result, the first six weeks of the Conference were wasted in the discussion of *actualities* and were not devoted to the central purposes for which it had been convoked.[24]

The basic problem, of course, was that in distinction to the work of its predecessor, the Supreme War Council, the Conference could not take its agenda for events as they unfolded. Rather, the conferees needed the larger issues formulated for them. Only a strong secretariat, composed of persons with experience in working at the highest levels of governmental policy-making, could have overcome this deficiency.[25]

Another deficiency, as revealed above, was that the Secretariat, being composed of nationals from the participating states, had a tendency to suffer from a lack of strong centralised direction. This was a problem not only of language – each secretary having to have his work translated into the other official language – it was also a matter of national style. The success of the Peace Conference Secretariat, composed as it was of persons seconded from their governments, could not obviate the problem.

But, ironically, Hankey, who was able to work effectively under these circumstances, and who strongly recommended that the secretariat function in the League should be headed by a single person, did not support a strong centralised international secretariat for the League political organs. He favoured the retention of national secretaries, although working under a single Secretary-General. As he said: 'It is ... better to have a single secretary if one can be found who is acceptable to all. The authors of the Covenant did well to establish a single Secretary-General.'[26]

Sir Eric Drummond, the first League Secretary-General, summarised the different views:

> The first was that the Secretariat should be composed of national delegations of the various members of the League. Each delegation would be paid for by the Government of the country from which it comes and be responsible solely to that Government. The practice which had prevailed at international conferences previous to the foundation of the League of Nations would thus be continued, while the duties of the Secretary-General would be largely confined to the co-ordination on special occasions of the services of the national delegations on the Secretariat, and to the centralization of administrative functions.[27]

He went on to say:

> Those who advocated the second theory held that the Secretariat should form, as far as was practicable, an international Civil Service, in which men and women of various nationalities might unite in preparing and presenting to the members of the League an objective and common basis of discussion. They would also be entrusted, it was proposed, with the execution of any decisions ultimately taken by the Governments. Under this scheme the Secretary-General would not only be the co-ordinating centre of the activities of the Secretariat, but its members would be responsible to him alone, and not to the Governments of the countries of which they were nationals, and would be remunerated from the general funds of the League.[28]

Lord Hankey preferred that the League Council continue the role of the Supreme War Council into the postwar period. It would thus become a continuing international political conference of those states that felt they had a sufficiently strong and common basis of interests to co-operate continuously, or at least to consult together on a neutralised basis.

According to Lord Riddell, even though Hankey was sceptical about how the League might achieve this goal, he nevertheless had a strong opinion about the importance of creating machinery which could continue the collaboration of the victorious states:

[Hankey] told me that he himself had drawn up a scheme for a league of nations. His idea was that the Supreme Council should be maintained in a modified form. He was opposed to the formation of a body which would have no direct connection with actualities. For that reason he declined the Secretaryship of the League which was offered to him. He fears that the League in its present form is doomed to failure. He thinks that in some way the League should now be brought into direct touch with the Supreme Council, so that gradually the League may assume some of the Council's functions and ultimately replace it as peace-maker of the world.[29]

One of the reasons, possibly, why Hankey did not favour the introduction into the League of his demonstrably successful national administrative style was that the influence of national delegations might have been reduced. Since the services of the British delegation had proved effective in taking care of the work of the wartime Allied bodies and the Peace Conference, it would not be unlikely that Hankey foresaw with favour a continuation of Britain's influence if the national system were carried over into the League. Also it might be that the national predilection of Britain not to become too enmeshed in international organisations prevailed over the temptation to adopt the British model in the running of the various Allied councils and conferences.

Obviously opinion went against Hankey. The powers of the League Secretary-General and the Secretariat were formulated in three specific grants in the League Covenant. A general grant of power was contained in Article II, which stated that 'the action of the League under this covenant shall be effected through the instrumentality of an Assembly and of a Council, with a permanent Secretariat'. The Secretariat itself was defined in Article VI as comprising 'a Secretary-General and such secretaries and staff as may be required'. As to the specific role of the Secretary-General, Article VI provided that 'the Secretary-General shall act in that capacity at all meetings of the Assembly and of the Council'.

These provisions can be seen as a reaction against the failure of international diplomacy to prevent the war. The conferees in Paris perceived that it was vitally important, when international tensions arose in the future, that the protagonists should be able to continue to communicate with each other rather than to constrict or break off all forms of diplomatic intercourse. One way, it was thought, that this crucial international political communication could go on even as states were manoeuvring (or posturing) during a crisis, was to have in existence consultative machinery which could serve the needs of all parties, and thus provide a 'neutral' diplomatic arena.

Beyond these rather general observations and formal provisions, the statesmen at Paris left untended questions about the structure, form and nature of the new international Secretariat. They had had enough difficulty getting the Covenant negotiated without raising more and – politically speaking – relatively unimportant matters. As Leon Gordenker has observed: 'The idea and scope of the projected secretariat caused no real controversy at the peace conference, and as a result the delegates accepted a plan the implications of which had not been fully explored.'[30]

THE INTERNATIONAL SECRETARIAT OF THE LEAGUE OF NATIONS

An earlier expectation that the post of Secretary-General would initially be important politically proved short-lived. Originally it had been proposed during the Peace Conference that the office be given the title of 'Chancellor' and a distinguished international statesman was to have occupied the post. M. Venizelos of Greece, for whom the post was intended, turned it down, and so it was decided to give it to a civil servant. There was not complete agreement about this downgrading of the office, however. Lord Hankey, for example, has written:

> There was great and prolonged discussion on the term 'Chancellor'. I resisted on the ground that 'the tail must not appear to wag the dog', which would happen for certain by the adoption of so pompous a title as 'Chancellor' and eventually I got my way.[31]

Another observer at the time commented, in 1945:

> All things considered, it can be stated that it was a mistake on the part of the statesmen responsible for establishing the League to choose an administrator ... Experience proves that it is a statesman who must be chosen as head of a political agency. He must be an international leader. Unless he is that, no international agency can exhaust the possibilities inherent in its mission. The lesson of the League in this respect is as clear as possible, hardly open to contention, and absolutely convincing.[32]

With the change in the title also came a change in the authority of the office. For example, when M. Venizelos was in consideration as the possible head of the League Secretariat the officer was empowered to summon Council meetings on his own initiative. Afterwards, along with the change in name, Articles XI and XV were slightly altered to eliminate the Secretary-General's power of initiative. He became more akin to the model of the British Cabinet secretary, even though having in addition internal responsibilities as the chief administrative officer of the international organisation. The limitation placed on the Secretary-General's political power was that he could summon a meeting of the Council only if he had been notified by a government of the existence of a dispute, and thereafter if he and the president of the Council considered that the dispute warranted such action, or if he had been requested to do so by a member state. He was responsible for making 'all necessary arrangements for a full investigation and consideration thereof'.

In his position as administrative head of the League Secretariat, no limitation was placed upon the Secretary-General. Decisions as to the type of staff, its composition and functions, were left to him. He was subject only to the limits imposed by the nature of the work, the position itself and, of course, the budget. His authority for his actions was unquestioned.

With this constitutional framework, Sir Eric Drummond left his mark in two important respects: first, in the type of secretariat he established; and second, in his personal role both within the League and before the world. He justified the introduction of the British secretariat method into the workings of the League in an article published in 1924:

> International conferences in the past had often suffered from the lack of any organised international preparatory work, and we felt that it was exactly in this domain that a new system was required if the League were to fulfil the purposes for which it had been founded. It seemed to us that it would be of great value if an expert and impartial organisation existed which, before discussion by the national representatives took place, could draw up objective statements of the problems to be discussed, and indicate those points on which it seemed that the Governments were generally in accord. If this could be done, we held that discussion by the Government representatives would be automatically limited to matters where divergence of view really existed – and all who have had experience of international affairs know how much this increases the chances of reaching a definite and successful result. Further, we maintained that the execution of decisions should be entrusted to people who, being the servants of all the States Members of the League, could be relied upon to carry them out with complete freedom from national bias.[33]

Drummond's ideas were adopted, and he successfully created the first truly international civil service, based upon the principle of loyalty to the organisation rather than to the country of national origin.[34] As a former member of the League Secretariat observed, he 'ensured the Secretary-General of the League becoming a new and unprecedented institution in the history of the world'.[35] The testimony of the first Secretary-General of the United Nations also paid tribute to this innovation: 'His decision to create the first truly international secretariat was a decision of profound significance – surely one of the most important and promising political developments of the twentieth century. His place in history is secure.'[36]

As a public international figure, the Secretary-General's place in history is less secure. He did not enter the debates of the League organs unless it was absolutely necessary, and these occasions usually concerned personnel or budgetary matters. In the best secretariat tradition, he did not utilise his annual report either to dramatise his own role or to forward his own views. The annual reports, however, according to a Chatham House Study Group headed by Drummond 'provided the text of the chief debates in each body, and furnished delegates with all the material they required for the discussion of past and future policy'.[37]

At the national level, in 1921 the CID was reconstituted, with Lord Hankey as head of a secretariat serving both the CID and the Cabinet. He filled this dual role until his retirement in 1938 when Sir Edward (later Lord) Bridges became Secretary to the Cabinet and Colonel Hastings (later Lord) Ismay became Secretary to the CID.

Ismay came to this position with extensive experience. From 1926 to 1930 he had been an Assistant Secretary to the CID, and from 1936 to 1938 Deputy-Secretary.[38] When the Second World War began, the CID was once again integrated into the Cabinet, with Bridges as Secretary to the War Cabinet. Ismay became chief-of-staff to the Prime Minister, Winston Churchill, in Churchill's capacity as Minister of Defence, and his representative on the Chiefs-of-Staff committee. The CID–Cabinet structure was thus converted into an organisation called the 'Offices of the War Cabinet and of the Minister of Defence'.

The exact role of Lord Ismay during the war has been clearly explained. A White Paper of 1942 outlined Britain's war leadership structure:

> The ultimate responsibility for the conduct of the war rests with the War Cabinet, the Chiefs of Staff being their professional advisers. The Prime Minister and Minister of Defence [both Mr Churchill] superintends on behalf of the War Cabinet, the work of the Chiefs of Staff committee.[39]

Churchill himself said: '... the formulation of strategic plans and the day-to-day conduct of operations ... were settled by the Chiefs-of-Staff committee acting directly under the Minister of Defence'.[40] According to Churchill, Ismay fitted into the picture in this way:

> For the purpose of maintaining general supervision over the conduct of the War, which I do under the authority of the War Cabinet and the Defence Committee, I have at my disposal a small staff, headed by Major-General Ismay, which works under the long-established procedure and machinery of the pre-war Committee of Imperial Defence, and forms part of the War Cabinet secretariat.[41]

There is a significant difference between planning a war and fighting it.

Besides a qualitative difference in decision-making itself, the co-ordination necessary to conduct the war had to be both internal, that is, national, and external, that is, inter-Allied. Decisions made by the Chiefs-of-Staff committee might have been in agreement with, complementary to, or contradictory of decisions made in Washington, Moscow or elsewhere. There had to be some central agency or person in the British Government through whom the war-making threads would pass.

There was no doubt who this person was. Churchill has stated: '... as confidence grew the War Cabinet intervened less actively in operational matters, though they watched them with close attention and full knowledge. They took almost the whole weight of home and party affairs off my shoulders, thus setting me free to concentrate upon the main theme'.[42]

Since Churchill kept direct control over the functions of war planning and execution, the man who stood closest to him also stood closest to the major decisions taken in the British share of the war. Lord Ismay, because of his official standing and his personal influence, occupied this position. He was the pin-wheel in the British machinery for the conduct of the war. This is what he did:

> As Deputy Secretary (Military) of the War Cabinet, Ismay supervised the running of the military Committee and their relations with other interests; as a member of the Chiefs of Staff's Committee, he took his share of responsibility in its decisions, and geared the machine to its demands; as Chief of Staff to the Minister of Defence, he acted as the link between the machine, the Committee and the Minister, and as the link for the Committee with Washington and for the Prime Minister with allies and with commanders.[43]

In recognition of his service Ismay was awarded a barony in 1947. Under the postwar Labour Government he went to India as Chief-of-Staff to Lord Mountbatten, who as the last Viceroy had the difficult task of assisting at India's transition to independence. With the return of Churchill to power, Ismay became Secretary of State for Commonwealth Affairs, which post he reluctantly relinquished in 1952 to become Secretary-General of NATO.[44]

In sum, Lord Ismay was first a military staff officer, then a highest-level aide, co-ordinator, expediter, and diplomatist (he attended the Cairo, Malta, Teheran, Quebec, Moscow and Yalta Conferences) and then a Cabinet minister.[45] He had had dealings with the Russians, the French and the Americans on the highest plane, yet he was one of the second layer of public men by whom and through whom the top layer accomplished their affairs. He has been described as a 'tactful go-between, as "an interpreter, one among a thousand"; he explained, he soothed, he suggested, he harmonised ...'.[46]

THE FORMATION OF THE UNITED NATIONS

During the United Nations Charter-drafting days, when it was announced that the title 'Secretary-General' had been agreed upon, some of the people who had been intimately connected with the League protested that this title had been too restricting for the head of the League of Nations administration and would therefore be even more inappropriate for the head of the much larger administration of the United Nations. Even President Roosevelt found the title inadequate: he suggested the 'World's Moderator'.[47]

Trygve Lie, the first occupant of the office, also clearly did not subscribe to the limited concept of the office as it had existed under his League predecessors. He commented: 'In my view it was clearly not the intention of the Charter that the limited concept of the office of Secretary-General which Sir Eric evolved in the League should be perpetuated in the United Nations.'[48]

In fact the wording of the Charter's and the Covenant's provisions for their secretariats was similar. Article 97 of the Charter stated that 'the Secretariat shall comprise a Secretary-General and such staff as the Organisation shall require ... He shall be the chief administrative officer of the Organization'. Article VI of the Covenant said much the same. Article 97 of the Charter said that the Secretary-General 'shall be appointed by the General Assembly upon the recommendation of the Security Council'. The essential ingredient in both was the concurrence of the Great Powers.[49]

The chief difference between the two offices was that the Secretary-General of the United Nations could make recommendations directly to the organs of the United Nations on his own initiative. He could place items on the provisional agenda for meetings of the General Assembly and, more important, under Article 99 he could bring to the attention of the Security Council 'any matter which in his opinion may threaten the maintenance of international peace and security'. As the Preparatory Commission of the United Nations pointed out, Article 99 gave the Secretary-General 'a quite special right which goes beyond any power previously accorded to the head of an international organisation'.[50] Article 99 opened up possibilities for an active political role which under the Covenant had not been constitutionally open to Sir Eric Drummond (later Lord Perth). The Secretary-General of the United Nations had been clothed with powers of initiative until then reserved exclusively to member states in their sovereign entities. It is conceivable that the negative example of the League prompted the positive approach of the United Nations.

Mr Lie did not hesitate to adopt the 'expansive' approach to his office. In his submission of unsolicited memoranda to the United Nations organs and in his use of the annual report as a kind of 'State of the Union' message, he acted according to a broad conception of his office. He was also not as reluctant as Sir Eric Drummond to attribute world-wide significance to his public role. As he said:

> The Secretary-General might be the symbol of the Organisation as a whole – the symbol, in other words, of the international spirit. This, and his strategic situation at the very centre of international affairs as confidant of the world's statesmen and as spokesman to the world's peoples, attached significant influence to his position ... I was determined that the Secretary-General should be a force for peace.[51]

To be 'a force for peace' implied more than the role of a semi-anonymous 'civil-servant-type' official. To interpret the position as a symbol of the 'international spirit' gave an aura of ubiquity to it not claimed by Drummond. Even if the Secretary-General of the United Nations has perhaps not been able to operate in complete conformity with the assertions first of Trygve Lie and then of his successor Dag Hammarskjöld, the personalities of the two men and the interests they served gave the idea of their symbolic function a plausibility not possible for the League.[52]

The United Nations Charter in Article 98 granted that, in his secretariat role 'the Secretary-General shall act in that capacity in all meetings of the General Assembly, of the Security Council, of the Economic and Social Council, and of the Trusteeship Council ...'. The question again arises as to what was meant by the phrase 'in that capacity'. But by the time the Charter was drawn up the meaning had been affected not only by international and national traditions and by the legal provisions of the office itself, but also by the accrual of experience from the League.[53] From Britain, as discussed earlier, the process of governing by committees had thus been permanently transferred into international machinery for peace-keeping.

THE CABINET SECRETARIAT TRADITION AND THE FORMATION OF NATO

It is of special significance that Lord Ismay, in contrast to his predecessors in other international organisations, served in a dual capacity as head of the NATO International Staff/Secretariat and as Vice-Chairman (later Chairman) of the North Atlantic Council. The confluence of these two functions made the Secretary-General the point at which the purely political crossed with the administrative. Ismay was fully aware of this situation, and saw it as an opportunity for effective service.

Although no formal conditions were placed upon his acceptance of the post of Secretary-General, Ismay wanted it to be understood that he was to preside over the Council in the absence of the Chairman.[54] He also made it clear that he wanted freedom of action in his dealing with the Council, including the right to initiate business and to have direct access to member governments.[55]

As the *de facto* executive and presiding head of the Council, especially when it met at the Permanent Representatives' level, the Secretary-General could have used his position to propose his own programme or to adopt a critical (albeit constructive) attitude towards some of the workings of the Council. In view of the weaknesses displayed in the previous Deputies' structure and the increasing magnitude of the work to be performed (in 1952 it was full steam ahead for rearmament), an aggressive leader would have been strongly tempted to follow this course. Such a development would not have been entirely unexpected, for at the time the position was created the functions of the Secretary-General were characterised variously as those of a 'civil Eisenhower',[56] a 'super-expeditor',[57] and a director-general.[58] He was to possess 'drive, imagination and persuasiveness',[59] and should be a person 'of the highest caliber, a personage with an international reputation for efficiency and intellectual integrity, skilled in dealing with the kinds of problems certain to arise, within a group comprising the representatives of many nations'.[60]

The magnitude of the Secretary-General's task was measured in such statements as: 'The Secretary-General's chief function ... will be to speak directly to the member Governments with all the authority he can build up around his office as the voice of the NATO community as a whole';[61] 'this new permanent authority [the International Staff/Secretariat] would be placed under the chairmanship of a permanent secretary-general or chairman who would not be a member of any national delegation but would have an international status within NATO somewhat similar to that of Trygve Lie in the United Nations';[62] '[the] permanent chairman ... would thus clearly wield considerable authority and bear wide responsibilities'.[63]

From the American viewpoint these descriptions were apposite for, throughout the preliminary experience of NATO, the United States had advocated strong leadership for the Council and the civilian staff; most often it had been the British who had favoured more decentralised executive leadership. Ismay, as the first incumbent, could set the pattern for the Secretary-Generalship. As one observer put it: 'Working without direct precedents to guide him, the secretary-general has had to impose upon the new administrative machinery with which he was provided the cohesive stamp of an individual personality.'[64]

Ismay decided not to adopt an aggressive and independent role as Secretary-General. Though he had thought it necessary to claim unfettered authority at the time of his appointment, he did not assume the attitude of a full member of the Council, though in a sense he was one (especially after the Council Resolution of December 1956); he preferred to regard himself as 'an international servant of NATO', whose function was 'stewardship'.[65] Unlike his immediate successor, M. Paul-Henri Spaak, he considered it appropriate to wait for the Council to initiate or authorise a course of action before he promoted it publicly. He was also very careful not to appear to 'lecture' his Council colleagues. When Ismay began his term of office he was relatively unknown internationally although, as already pointed out, he was well-known in American and British military circles. He had been called to a position which, initially, had been the centre of lengthy discussions and speculation and, most important of all, he had to deal with fourteen (later sixteen) member states, each of which jealously guarded its own interests. For instance, in 1953 M. René Mayer, the French Prime Minister, complained that Lord Ismay was not being tough enough with member countries. Ismay replied: 'What would you expect? The first thing I would do would be to demand that France should increase its conscription term to twenty-four months. The next thing I would do would be to tell the British they must cut the expensive burden of their social services. Neither country would do this. I cannot get tough.'[66] The roles of arbiter, mediator, conciliator, and co-ordinator seemed to fit more appropriately his situation, his experience and his personality. The ultimate in tributes to his effectiveness in these roles was paid by William Batt, former chief of the United States Mutual Security Administration Mission and Chairman of NATO's Defence Production Board. He said, in a speech made at a banquet given by the English-Speaking Union:

> Looking back I am convinced that Lord Ismay was divinely chosen (although Sir Winston had something to do with it, too) for those difficult formative years of NATO. With no real constitutional authority, with little more than a hot office in the Palais de Chaillot, a limited budget and 14 prima donna nations, he produced all the harmony there was in the enterprise.[67]

Ismay had built a career in exercising his skills in the art of planning and then in executing those plans within the limits of feasibility. As discussed earlier, in the Second World War he had provided the 'lubrication' necessary to enable men of strong minds and enormous responsibilities to carry out their tasks successfully. NATO had men of equally strong minds, and certainly the magnitude of Lord Ismay's task was obvious to all. The traditions of the League Secretariat and the United Nations, and the British Cabinet system were valuable resources for the first Secretary-General of NATO to draw upon in accomplishing his task. The link – or common thread – from the CID to NATO is direct and can be traced without interruption through the organisation of the machinery of government to plan for and to carry forward the conduct of war when necessary, and to plan for and to carry forward common or collective efforts for peace.

Notes

1. Peter Nailor, 'Britain and the Imperial Staff', Robert L. Pfaltzgraff, Jr and Uri Ra'aman (eds), *National Security Policy: The Decision-Making Process* (Hamden, CT., 1984) pp. 3–4.
2. Ibid.
3. Franklyn A. Johnson, *Defence by Committee: The British Committee of Imperial Defence, 1885–1959* (London, 1960) p. 13. For Hankey's view of this book, see Stephen Roskill, *Hankey, Man of Secrets*, vol. I, 1877–1918 (London, 1970) pp. 138–42.
4. For a brief review of the evolution of the CID Secretariat, and the later career of one of Hankey's trusted lieutenants, Sir Hastings Ismay (later Lord Ismay), see Robert S. Jordan, *The NATO International Staff/Secretariat, 1952–1957: A Study in International Administration* (London, 1967) especially Part I. Sir Charles Ottley became unpopular because, rather than remain a passive secretary who synthesised other people's thinking, he preferred to advance his own ideas as well (interview of Robert Jordan with Lord Ismay, 28 May 1959).
5. Quoted in Johnson, *Defence by Committee*, p. 65. The *Esher Report's* full title was, *War Office (Reconstitution) Committee: Report of the War Office (Reconstitution Committee)*, Part I, dated 1904. Hankey retained his appointment as a Royal Marine through most of his career, even though his assignment was more that of a civil servant. However, his salary was not paid by the Navy.
6. Lord Hankey, *The Supreme Command 1914–1918*, vol. I (London, 1961) p. 52.
7. Quoted from the Esher Report, ibid., p. 46.
8. Nailor, 'Britain and the Imperial Staff', p. 5. Nailor went on to observe that: '... it was the contention of the "blue-water school" of naval thinkers (which for a long time dominated Imperial defense thinking in the high Victorian period) that it was command of the sea which provided both the basic security of the empire and the mobility which enabled local garrisons to be low and to be succored in time of need'. (Ibid.) See also John Gooch, 'The Army and Empire', in his *The Plans of War* (London, 1974) Ch. 2.
9. Quoted in Johnson, *Defence by Committee*, p. 56. Sir William Tyrell (later First Baron) had been senior clerk in the Foreign Office 1907–18, private secretary to Sir Edward Grey 1907–15, assistant under-secretary of state for foreign affairs 1918–25, permanent under-secretary at the Foreign Office 1925–8, and ambassador in Paris 1928–34. From his career it is evident that he was no 'minor clerk', as might be inferred from Hankey's comment.
10. The Rt. Hon. L. S. Amery, CH, *My Political Life, VII: War and Peace 1914–1929* (London, 1953) p. 172.
11. Lord Riddell, *Lord Riddell's Intimate Diary of the Peace Conference and After, 1918–1923* (New York, 1934) p. 69.
12. Hankey, *Supreme Command*, p. 46.
13. Amery, *My Political Life*, p. 120. Roskill's account of this episode, drawing on a wide range of sources, including Hankey's own papers, confirms the key role Hankey played in this crucial decision of wartime grand strategy (see Roskill, *Hankey*, pp. 256ff.).
14. Amery, *My Political Life*, p. 102. Insofar as this reflects sharp practices, this comment may suggest that Hankey might not have entirely trusted Amery.
15. Cab. 37/161/14, as given in *The Records of the Cabinet Office to 1922*, Public Record Office Handbook No. 11 (London, 1966) p. 3.
16. Ibid., p. 4. For a thorough and authorised history of Lord Hankey's career during this period, see Roskill, *Hankey*.

17. John P. Mackintosh, *The British Cabinet* (London, 1962) p. 272n.
18. Quoted by Johnson, *Defence by Committee*, p. 73.
19. *The Records*, p. 4 (quotation from CD. 9005).
20. Ministry of Reconstruction, *Report of the Machinery of Government Committee* (London, 1918) p. 6. The CID Secretariat was used by the Prime Minister, H. H. Asquith in his War Council, Dardanelles Committee, and War Committee, and then by Lloyd George in his War Cabinet and Imperial War Cabinet. Asquith said: 'We established the War Committee ... which took over to a large extent the functions of the Committee of Imperial Defence. Experts were present and we always had the leading representatives of the Army and Navy present, and a record was kept of their proceedings.' Lord Hankey, *Diplomacy by Conference: Studies in Public Affairs 1920–1946* (London, 1946) p. 72. Lord Hankey traced the development thus:

    As I always picture this story, it begins with Balfour's creation of the CID in 1904; the first phase of establishing principles for coordination of defence forces by Balfour; the successive stages of policy, plans and preparations by Asquith (the four Ps); and after the outbreak of war, the adaptation of the system by trial and error to the running of the war; that is to say first Asquith's War Council, then the first coalition's ... stupid Dardanelles Committee, followed by the War Committee; and finally, after Lloyd George became PM the War Cabinet. But under Lloyd George the system was extended to the coordination of the British Empire forces by the Imperial War Cabinet, and, after the Italian defeat at Caporetto the Supreme War Council of the Allies with a joint Secretariat, where the British section (a branch of my Cabinet office), took and held the lead. (Unpublished letter to Professor N. H. Gibbs, 31 August 1959.)

21. George Rublee, 'Inter-Allied Machinery in War-Time', *The League of Nations Starts: An Outline by Its Organizers* (London, 1920) pp. 30–1.
22. Harold Nicolson, *Peacemaking 1919* (New York, 1965) p. 110.
23. Ibid., p. 111.
24. Ibid., p. 120.
25. Sometimes this assistance might have been counter-productive, as Amery describes:

    Lloyd George, not having read the brief so carefully prepared for him, might start most eloquently arguing the very case we were concerned to oppose. Hankey would scribble a note in his large, legible hand which Lloyd George would glance at without interrupting the flow of his argument. Presently he would blandly explain that he thought he had done full justice to a view which, however, the British Government did not share, and would now expound our own real attitude. Meanwhile Hankey would draft a resolution which Lloyd George would then read out as representing the fully considered proposal which he had brought with him. (Amery, *My Political Life*, pp. 178–9)

26. Hankey, *Diplomacy*, p. 37.
27. Article in *The World Today*, March 1924, as quoted in C. Howard-Ellis, *The Origin, Structure and Working of the League of Nations* (London, 1928) p. 171.
28. Ibid., pp. 171–2.
29. Riddell, *Intimate Diary*, pp. 182–3. One of Hankey's protégés – Ismay – when he was setting up the International Staff/Secretariat of NATO, also conceived the proper function of an international secretariat in more narrow, or co-ordinative, terms. (See Jordan, *Study in International Administration*, Chapters 3 and 11.)

30. Leon Gordenker, *The UN Secretary-General and the Maintenance of Peace* (New York, 1967) p. 5. Gordenker traces this evolution thus:

> Official study groups produced textual suggestions for the League Covenant, mainly during the summer and autumn of 1918. Perhaps the earliest definite suggestion relating to a secretariat came from a French governmental commission, which showed more interest in a military staff than a civil service. The first official British draft of the Covenant, the product of the Phillimore Commission, did not even mention the subject of a secretariat. Nor did the first attempts by Colonel Edward H. House and President Woodrow Wilson. The most influential suggestion before the Versailles Conference came from General Jan Christiaan Smuts. In his seminal proposals for the League of Nations he projected a permanent secretariat, which was to keep alert to disturbances anywhere and to acquire first-hand information about them. A secretariat always appeared in subsequent drafts but not in well defined terms. (p. 5)

31. Private memorandum from Hankey to Robert Jordan, 31 August 1959.
32. Egon F. Ranshofen-Wertheimer, *The International Secretariat* (Washington, 1945) p. 49.
33. As quoted in Howard-Ellis, *League of Nations*.
34. The material contained in the following paragraphs is paraphrased from Jordan, *Study in International Administration*, pp. 6–9.
35. Howard-Ellis, *League of Nations*, p. 172. The International Institute of Agriculture, with headquarters in Rome, in theory had an international civil service prior to the League of Nations, but in practice the staff was entirely Italian because the salaries were too low to attract other nationalities.
36. Trygve Lie, *In the Cause of Peace* (New York, 1954) p. 41.
37. *The International Secretariat of the Future* (London, 1944) p. 8.
38. *Who's Who*, 1956, p. 1532. Hankey said of his thoughts concerning the recalling of Ismay to the CID in 1938:

> When I was nearing the age of retirement I brought Ismay back as head of the CID branch of the Cabinet Secretariat. My idea was that he should take over, on my retirement, two, and, if possible all three of the posts I then held, namely Secretary to the Cabinet, and to the CID (including Chiefs-of-Staffs Sub-Committee), and perhaps the Clerkship of the Privy Council. But Ismay would not take more than the CID; Bridges took the Cabinet; and Howarth (my Deputy for the Cabinet) took over the Privy Council. In retrospect I think that was right at the time with a war approaching – but, in the long run, after the war and after Ismay had left that office, the division went far towards spoiling the efficiency of the Cabinet organisation – but that is another story. (Private memorandum to Robert Jordan, 31 August 1959.)

39. Quoted in John Ehrman, *Grand Strategy* (London, 1956) VI, p. 322.
40. Winston Churchill, *The Second World War* (London, 1950) II, p. 16.
41. Winston S. Churchill, *The War Speeches of the Rt. Hon. Winston S. Churchill*, compiler Charles Eade (London, 1952) II, p. 217.
42. Winston Churchill, *The Second World War*, II, p. 18.
43. Ehrman, *Grand Strategy*, VI, p. 333.
44. *Who's Who*, 1956, p. 1532.
45. S. E. Morison, in *American Contributions to the Strategy of World War II* (London, 1958) did not mention Lord Ismay in his discussion of the British war planning system. This is unfortunate.
46. J. R. M. Butler, *Grand Strategy* (London, 1957) II, p. 250. General Eisenhower, in his memoirs, paid this tribute to Ismay:

Ismay's position ... was, from the American point of view, a critical one because it was through him that any subject could at any moment be brought to the attention of the Prime Minister and his principal assistants. It was fortunate, therefore, that ... his personality was such as to win the confidence and friendship of his American associates. He was one of those men whose great ability condemned him throughout the war to a staff position. Consequently his name may be forgotten; but the contributions he made to the winning of the war were equal to those of many whose names became household words. (*Crusade in Europe*, London, 1948, p. 487.)
Lord Ismay's chance to leap into the spotlight of history came in 1952.

47. Stephen S. Schwebel, *The Secretary-General of the United Nations* (Cambridge, 1952) p. 18.
48. Lie, *In the Cause of Peace*, pp. 41–2.
49. The variation in the method of renewal of Lie's appointment – the extension of his first term rather than a fresh appointment to a second five-year term – in the face of Soviet opposition to his taking a second term, did not mitigate the original intent of the Charter; in fact, if anything, it affirmed the necessity for the concurrence of permanent members of the Security Council if the Secretary-General were to provide effective leadership. In this sense the UN's experience was not very far removed from the workings of traditional coalition diplomacy.
50. Schwebel, *The Secretary-General of the United Nations*, p. 21.
51. Lie, *In the Cause of Peace*, p. 42.
52. See Robert S. Jordan (ed.), *Dag Hammarskjöld Revisited: The U.N. Secretary-General As A Force in World Politics* (Durham, NC, 1983).
53. The idea of an international secretariat performing secretarial duties for a governing council of member governments has been generally accepted; but the idea that an international staff should engage in activities of a technical or 'operational' nature, has not received universal acceptance.
54. Ismay's right to chair the meetings of the Permanent Representatives was never seriously questioned. However, the first time that the Chairman could not attend a meeting of the Council in Ministerial session, there was some talk of having another minister take the chair. Ismay objected to this, pointing out that the Council already had a qualified and logical chairman – meaning the Secretary-General – and should use him in this capacity. Thereafter the precedent was set for the Secretary-General to chair both Ministerial meetings and the Council of Permanent Representatives in the absence of, or at the request of, the chairman. In 1956 this procedure was officially confirmed when Ismay was made the Chairman of the Council and a Minister was elected on an annually rotating basis for the largely honorary and ceremonial post of President of the North Atlantic Council. (Interview with Ismay, 28 May 1959; *The North Atlantic Treaty Organization* (Paris, 1957) pp. 38–9.)
55. In retrospect, Ismay's insistence upon clarification of these matters may appear to have been unnecessary, but at the time of his appointment there was justification for it. When Sir Oliver Franks had declined the invitation to become Secretary-General, the Ministerial Council at Lisbon delegated to the Council Deputies the task of obtaining a Secretary-General and the Deputies had seriously considered narrowing the powers of the office if a person of sufficiently high rank could not be found to occupy it. Ismay felt that, if he did not have unfettered authority, he would be less of a figure than the Deputies' chairman had been, and consequently the aim of reorganising the civilian structure of NATO would be defeated in some measure from the outset. He was of course assured that he would have the powers he asked for.
56. *New York Times*, 27 February 1952.

57. *Daily Mail*, 22 February 1952.
58. According to some political scientists, this term implies stronger executive leadership than the term 'secretary-general', although perhaps more in the administrative than in the political sense.
59. *New York Times*, 27 February 1952.
60. *New York Herald-Tribune*, 28 February 1952.
61. *New York Times*, 13 February 1952.
62. Ibid., 18 February 1952.
63. *Manchester Guardian*, 27 February 1952.
64. *The Times*, 19 December 1953.
65. Speech delivered by Ismay, 12 March 1953 (NATO Speech Series No. 33). When Ismay talked of himself as the 'servant' of the Council he was thinking as much in terms of the military tradition as in the British civil servant tradition. He was fond of representing himself as an 'old soldier'. For instance, in a speech to the diplomatic correspondents in 1952, he said: 'It is an ordeal for a soldier – and a cavalry soldier at that – to address an audience who are not only masters in the realm of diplomacy, but who are also experts at giving expression to their views. My father would never let me forget the hackneyed story of the cavalry officer who was so stupid that his brother officers noticed it.' (NATO Press Release, 12 June 1952.) One observer saw him thus: 'Ismay, whose gentle, slightly protuberant blue eyes, turned-up nose and stubborn jaw have earned him the nickname of "Pug", likes to amuse strangers with a breezy impersonation of the simple old soldier. In fact, however, he has one of the sharpest minds in international public life.' (Edmund Taylor, *Washington Post*, 15 April 1956.)
66. As related by C. L. Sulzberger, *New York Times*, 22 May 1957.
67. *The Times*, 5 June 1957. The Hankey discussion in this chapter is based partly on my chapter in Robert S. Jordan (ed.), *International Administration: Its Evolution and Contemporary Applications* (London and New York, 1971).

Part II
Anglo-American Maritime Theory in the Twentieth Century

'Theory does not pretend to solve problems; it sheds light on problems and thus can provide guidance for those who have the responsibility for solving them.'—H. E. Eccles

Theory provides the intellectual framework from which practical activity can be planned and understood. This section traces the changing nature of naval theory in the twentieth century as theorists have attempted to respond to the changing strategic and technical nature of warfare. In the process, it identifies a tradition of thinking about the broad uses of naval power which is shared by Britain and the United States. While there have been policy differences between the two countries, their basic, theoretical understanding is similar. This tradition of naval thought is one which is different from that which other nations have developed. It has largely been formed by the similar circumstances which both Britain and the United States have shared in the way in which they have employed their navies as Great Powers.

5 Alfred Thayer Mahan and his Strategic Thought
John B. Hattendorf

Much was written by Mahan[1] and much has been written about him.[2] In the United States his name is known to every officer in the Navy and his authority is often evoked and applied to issues of naval strategy. By contrast, in Britain Mahan's works are now regarded as old and outdated. From either point of view, Mahan's contributions must be seen as part of the development of naval thought and, although he had precursors, Mahan is the proper starting-point in an outline of the progression and refinement of naval thinking in the English-speaking world during the twentieth century. Mahan found the literature of naval history largely a record of battles, and he was the first successfully to convert it to a subject which related activity at sea to foreign policy and the general activity of nation-states. In so doing he persuaded naval thinkers and writers to accept a new conceptual basis.

As with any writer or philosopher, the concepts he used were very much a part of his own culture and society. The purpose of this essay is to identify and to sketch those concepts as a means of providing a synthesis of Mahan's understanding of naval power and his view of the world in which it operated. His ideas were not static ones, but ones which evolved over the course of writing a body of works which included 20 books, 161 journal articles, 109 newspaper articles and a dozen pamphlets. Since he provided no summary of his own thought, one must examine his writings in the context of the events of the day. By understanding his thought in such terms one can begin to see more clearly his proper place in the development of naval theory and the process of refinement and change which has taken place since his time.

VIEW OF HISTORY AND INTERNATIONAL POLITICS

Mahan won his first public recognition with *The Influence of Sea Power Upon History 1660–1783*. It was an analysis of the relationship between war and national objectives in a period of European history marked by a series of wars which were fought for the limited purpose of adjusting or maintaining power relationships among European states, both in Europe and overseas. Moreover it was an era marked by the struggle for wealth and empire on the basis of a global economy. For Europe it was an age of spectacular enrichment and commercial expansion built, with strong national backing, on trans-oceanic trade. Mahan found, in that era of history, a broad and attractive similarity with the world about him in the period between 1885 and 1905. As one historian has written, these years at the transition point between the nineteenth and twentieth centuries were 'characterized by the continued economic growth of Europe, a process which absorbed much of the energy of her nations and acted as a safety valve; but this continued growth also had the effect of creating new or increasing old frictions among European powers, mainly out of their imperial expansion'.[3]

Mahan began his historical investigation for the US Naval War College in 1885 in order to lay the theoretical foundation for the study of navies.[4] 'The fundamental principles of warfare are the same on land and on sea,' Mahan wrote. 'Military war, commonly so-called, and naval war, are the two great principal subdivisions – specializations – of the military art. Each contains within itself certain minor specializations ...'.[5] In order to develop a specialised naval theory, Mahan began his work using an unusual methodology, then called the comparative method.[6] Mahan's mentor, Rear Admiral Stephen B. Luce, set the task by which Mahan proceeded to draw analogies from military operations and military history and to apply them to the data supplied from naval history. In this manner he could compare navies with armies as two specialised forms of activity and establish the basic characteristics of navies through contrast. To ease his task, both Luce and Mahan looked to the basic theoretical structure already established by Antoine-Henri Jomini. In this, all three men, Luce, Mahan and Jomini, shared a desire to identify fundamental principles of warfare.

The choice of Jomini was a natural one for a late nineteenth-century student of military affairs. He was indisputably the most prominent authority of the day, at a time when Clausewitz's work was little known. Moreover Mahan's father, Professor Dennis Hart Mahan of West Point, had been a pioneer among the interpreters of Jomini for the United States Army.[7] Today, when the name of Clausewitz has eclipsed Jomini's, we tend to think of Jomini only as a writer of aphorisms who built a conceptual framework around a complex pattern of strategic lines, strategic positions, points of manoeuvre, zones of operations and lines of communication. As Michael Howard has commented, Jomini's ideas 'fitted into a general synthesis in a manner calculated to baffle the simple and fascinate the worst sort of intellectual soldier'.[8] Despite those characteristics, one must recognise that Jomini's ideas remain a powerful force, often an unacknowledged and unrecognised one, even in military thinking in the late twentieth century.

For Mahan, Jomini's approach was the keystone for his own. As Mahan wrote to President Theodore Roosevelt in 1909, 'Jomini taught me from the first to scorn the sharp distinction so often asserted between diplomatic and military concerns.'[9] Uninterested in the philosophical nature of warfare,

Jomini looked to the more practical nature of strategy. In doing this he became in his own lifetime the great interpreter of Napoleon and he is often identified with ideas of Napoleonic warfare. A close examination of Jomini's writings shows that he did not stress the new elements which Napoleon brought to warfare, but showed instead the continuity which Napoleon shared with warfare in the eighteenth century. Although Jomini's name was so readily linked with Napoleon's, he admired Frederick the Great above all. Frederick had been the master of limited, national warfare.[10] Jomini thought that Napoleon 'fell from the topmost pinnacle of greatness through having forgotten that the mind and strength of man have their limits and that the more enormous the masses set in motion, the more the power of genius is subordinated to the unchangeable laws of nature and the less he can command events'.[11]

Mahan's world, both intellectually and contemporaneously, was a world of small and limited wars. When he generalised about the nature of naval warfare, even using examples from the Napoleonic wars, he tended to emphasise those elements which applied to his own times. Only in December 1912, as he observed the coming of the First World War, did Mahan hint that small wars could get out of hand. Writing in the preface to his last book on naval history, *The Major Operations of the Navies in the War of American Independence*, Mahan wrote: 'Wars, like conflagrations, tend to spread; more than ever perhaps in these days of close international entanglements and rapid communications.'[12] Not having dealt with this issue in his earlier writings, Mahan, in the bulk of his writing, expresses the view that war is justified by its results. The events which were performed on the world stage between 1890 and 1905 confirmed his belief that warfare would be beneficial in the present and foreseeable future. Writing on the moral aspect of warfare at the time of the First Hague Peace Conference, he wrote:

> Step by step in the past, man has ascended by means of the sword, and his more recent gains, as well as present conditions, show that the time has not yet come to kick down the ladder, which has so far served him.[13]

In writing this, Mahan had sincerely believed that war had always been fought and won by those with a moral purpose and for the good of all: the slaves had been freed by war in America; Prussia's wars had brought cultural and political unity accompanied by great economic and industrial progress. The call of humanity demanded a war to end Spanish rule in Cuba and in the Philippines, just as fair treatment, union and equality justified British action in the Boer War. Mahan concluded,

> What the sword and its supremacy, tempered only by the stern demands of justice and of conscience, and the loving voice of charity, has done for

India and for Egypt, is a tale at once too long and too well known for repetition here. Peace, indeed, is not adequate to all progress; there are resistances that can be overcome only by explosion.[14]

Such a view can only come from a man whose observations of war were conditioned by focussing on one type of warfare and were paralleled by continuing faith in imperial rule based on European and Christian values.[15] With these basic assumptions, Mahan described naval power as one of the positive forces which contributed to the rivalry of nations and which he believed represented 'the best hopes of the world'. The accentuation of differences and the conflict of imperial ambition preserved the martial spirit which Mahan thought was the only force capable of coping with the destructive elements that threatened the world's progress.[16]

THE RELEVANCE OF THE PAST

In his general understanding of war in the context of international politics, Mahan looked at naval history as a means to illustrate the general principles of maritime war which transcended scientific and technological advances. For Mahan, history was more than just a prologue to the present; it was the basis upon which to ground general principles which explained human actions. In his view,

> A precedent is different and less valuable than a principle. The former may be originally faulty, or may cease to apply through the change of circumstances; the latter has its root in the essential nature of things, and however various its application as conditions change, remains a standard to which action must conform to attain success.[17]

Mahan was keenly aware of the technological revolution which had swept navies within the time span of his own career. It had clearly raised in his mind the most important questions about the functions and purpose of navies. When Mahan described the events of the age of sail, he believed that he had focussed on and selected those aspects that were worthy of enduring consideration. In particular, as the new machines were coming into use during the wars at the end of the nineteenth century, Mahan believed that the old ideas of limited warfare were still valid. He made no suggestion that new technology brought with it weapons of uncontrollable force. Instead, he stressed the continuity between eighteenth century and contemporary practice, linking historical study as a guide to the present and future employment of naval forces:

> Steam has produced a relative certainty and precision into the movements

of fleets ... An art of naval war becomes possible; and it becomes imperative from the very fact that the rapid, many sided activity in the development of weapons produces a confusion in the mind which must by all means be ended.[18]

CONDITIONS ALLOWING THE GROWTH OF SEA POWER

In analysing his subject, Mahan came to the conclusion that the principal impetus behind the need for a navy was the need to protect merchant shipping. 'The first and most obvious light in which the sea presents itself from the political and social point of view is that of a great highway; or better perhaps of a wide common, over which men pass in all directions'.[19] Upon this fundamental basis a nation founded its relation to the sea and from it sprang the need, in wartime, to protect merchant shipping with armed naval vessels. It was commerce which was the driving force behind the need for secure and safe home ports, protection at sea, safe way stations and secure trading points abroad. Thus the principal geographical considerations for a sea power are, first, its geographical position, which induces it to seek trade across the sea. Secondly, its geographical conformation is a key consideration which allows port facilities to be built in accessible places and at key points in relation to its economic centres, while at the same time allowing its frontiers to be protected, and provides for a fertile soil for the production of merchantable products. Finally, the extent of a nation's territory can be either a weakness or a strength, depending on the character and strength of its people.

This observation led Mahan to consider three aspects of a nation's population: their number and availability, their character and aptitude for commercial pursuits at sea, and thirdly, the character of their government and national institutions which are able to promote and maintain activity at sea.

CONDUCT OF NAVAL STRATEGY

After considering the natural factors that promote or inhibit a nation's activity at sea, Mahan devoted the greatest bulk of his work to examining the exercise of naval strategy. After identifying sea power as the broad commercial interests of a nation in using the sea, Mahan went on to define his particular subject by saying that 'naval strategy has for its end to found, support, and increase, as well in peace as in war, the sea power of a country'.[20] Within this broad perspective, Mahan saw that much of the effect of sea power was indirect. For example, in considering the War of the Spanish Succession, he wrote of 'the noiseless, steady, exhausting pressure with which sea power acts, cutting off the resources of the enemy while maintaining its own supporting war in scenes where it does not appear itself, or appears only in the background, and striking open blows at rare intervals ...'.[21]

Turning to examine the conduct of naval strategy, Mahan used Jomini as his central guide, but he was selective in his approach, using only those aspects which he believed had validity at sea. In this regard, it is significant that Mahan never codified his principles. He focussed on a relatively small number of principles, but as he described them in his historical works he pointed out nuances of meaning. Reluctant to stress the principles alone, he returned again and again to lengthy narratives, and in doing so emphasised the importance of process and flexible application of strategy over a rigid, intellectualisation of it.

The 'use of naval power is naval strategy, whether applied in peace or war', Mahan wrote.[22] The first thing to consider is what position or chain of positions affect control of the sea. Applying Jomini, Mahan looked to (1) the principle of concentration of force; (2) the strategic value of central lines or central position; (3) the advantage of interior lines of movement; and (4) the bearing of logistics upon the tenure and success of combat operations.[23]

For Mahan, it was not position alone that mattered, but 'power plus position that constitutes an advantage over power without position'.[24] In naval terms, one needed to consider further that to control a commercial sea route, one needed:

(1) a mobile navy
(2) local ports near the route upon which the navy can base its operations.[25]

A naval base for such a purpose should be designed in relation to three factors: its situation, its military strength for offence and defence, and its resources.[26]

These bases represent strategic points which are not separate or disconnected, but are joined by strategic lines established by the shortest and most practicable sea route between them.[27] Since naval warfare connects strategic points not only within one theatre of war, but also to distant outlying and colonial possessions, the intermediate positions of strength are important. The most obviously important position, in this regard, is the fleet itself. The centre of an enemy's strength in the key intermediate areas is his organised force, that is to say his battle fleet. A crushing defeat of the enemy fleet, or its decisive inferiority, completely dislocates the enemy's lines of communication. The greater the distance involved, the greater the difficulty of defence or attack. Moreover, as the number of strategic bases increases, it becomes more difficult to defend them in proportion to their increased number, distance and relative dissemination.[28]

Colonies are open to attack, to harassment and even to invasion by another Power which seeks to obtain advantages of position for itself, or to obtain concessions of one type or another. The proper strategic response to this, Mahan believed, was to have an adequate, efficient and numerically superior fleet at sea. Having supremacy was, in fact, having tenure of the decisive position, in Mahan's view. The very existence of a numerically superior fleet tended to prevent the enemy from obtaining a concentration of force which could rival it.[29] At the same time, naval preponderance at sea means secure communications, the two ideas going hand in hand.

Going further, Mahan examined two related issues. One was the control of a distant maritime region. The other was the need to have a secure coastline and a navy adequate to dispute control of the sea with the enemy. With these additional factors in mind, a strategist can choose a base, an objective and a line of operations.

In the most important considerations, these factors coalesce around a position which is the strategic key to a maritime region. But to be useful, possession of that key point must be complemented by a naval superiority that is able to control the lines of communication. If a decisive naval superiority does not exist, one must fight a battle at sea, the outcome of which will determine control of the strategic position.[30]

When the strategic key to a maritime position has been won, the naval force which won that object passes from an offensive to a defensive role. In a joint operation, which is the characteristic type in overseas warfare, the navy is released to deal with communications, its true element, and the army assumes the defensive or continues prosecution of the campaign ashore. The navy can then move forward to maintain its lines of communication and to remove any further threat from an enemy fleet in the maritime area by destroying or blockading it. The aim of the weaker, opposing fleet is threefold: (1) to keep together, concentrating their force; (2) to endeavour not to be blockaded; and (3) to try not to be brought to action by the superior fleet.[31]

Throughout, the one great principle which governed Mahan's analysis was the need 'of being superior to the enemy at the decisive point, whatever the relative strength of the two parties on the whole'.[32] This, in a nutshell, is the scope of Mahan's theory of naval warfare. As he intended, it is a maritime counterpart of Jomini's work that is grounded on his principles and focussed on the idea that command of the sea required offensive and concentrated naval action. In Mahan's view the principles were simple, but their application was difficult. In the absence of a war, Mahan believed that the only way to learn about the subject was through the study of history, emphasising the process of strategy rather than the rules:

> The conduct of war is an art, having its spring in the mind of man, dealing with very various circumstances, admitting certain principles; but beyond

that manifold in its manifestations, according to the genius of the artist and the temper of the materials with which he is dealing. To such an effort dynamic prescription is unsuited.[33]

While the theorist understood that, Mahan was also the child of his own times. What he saw about him in his own era limited his vision. Like so many of his contemporaries, he was led astray from perceiving the nature of the war that would fall upon Europe in the summer of 1914, at the very time that Mahan himself lay on his deathbed.

In Mahan's day there were only two contemporary wars which involved large-scale naval operations: The Spanish–American War of 1898 and the Russo-Japanese War of 1904–5. Mahan stressed both as prime examples which illustrated his ideas and which conformed to his vision of future wars. To Mahan, the Spanish–American War served a valuable purpose for the United States in renewing and increasing its sense of national pride and its manifest destiny as a power in world affairs. In purely naval terms, Mahan believed that these wars confirmed the value of battleships and vindicated his concept of command of the sea, while also illustrating the limitations on navies caused by the need for fuel, service and repairs.[34]

Most importantly for Mahan, the Spanish–American War illustrated his view that decisive battle is necessary in obtaining command of the sea, and that battleships were the best weapons to employ for that purpose. 'If we lost ten thousand men, the country could replace them,' Mahan wrote;

> If we lost a battleship, it could not be replaced. The issue of war as a whole and in every locality to which it extended, depended upon naval force, and it was imperative to achieve, not success only, but success delayed no longer than necessary.[35]

In making this point, Mahan was arguing against those who stressed the 'fleet in being' principle, which was also illustrated by these wars. Mahan acknowledged that this idea was given concrete and convincing illustration by Admiral Cervera's squadron in the West Indies during the Spanish–American War, but, Mahan pointed out, it was not a decisive position; it was a game of evasion.

> A fleet in being is one the existence and maintenance of which, although inferior, on or near the scene of operations, is a perpetual menace to the various more or less exposed interests of the enemy, who can not tell when a blow may fall, and who is therefore compelled to restrict his operations, otherwise possible, until that fleet can be destroyed or neutralized.[36]

Cervera's fleet succeeded in doing this, but it created doubts and fears only until it could be destroyed. The Spanish admiral's action 'was opportunist, solely and simply', Mahan concluded. 'Such in general, and necessarily be that of any fleet in being, in the strict sense of the phrase, which involves inferiority of force; whereas the stronger force, if handled with sagacity and strength, constrains the weaker in its orbit as the earth governs the moon.'[37]

Mahan recognised the concept of the fleet in being as something distinctly British in origin and in statement.[38] In examining the other naval war of the period, the Russo-Japanese War, Mahan noted that the Russians employed a completely different conception which was distinctly Russian in character: the fortress fleet. Mahan saw them as opposites. The Russian idea stressed the fortress ashore and made the fleet so subsidiary that it had no reason for existence beyond helping the fortress. It was an idea which put the burden of national defence on coastal fortification. The British concept of the fleet in being discarded the fortress altogether, except as a momentary refuge, and relied upon the fleet alone for actual defence. Rather than to co-ordinate the two ideas, which Mahan believed to be the proper approach, the proponents of each idea tended to de-emphasise the other, to the point of exclusion.[39] After examining the misfortunes of Russia in the war, Mahan concluded that he needed to seek an adjustment of the two ideas, and to bring them into a composite theory which built on each of their desirable parts.[40]

The Russo-Japanese War was a case in which war existed between two enemies separated by the sea and in which one had taken the offensive and invaded overseas territory occupied by the other. In this situation, the Japanese Army invading Korea was the offensive force. The Navy made the invasion possible by preserving and assuring the communications of the invading army, but in this type of joint operation its function was defensive. In carrying out that defensive role, Mahan believed that a Navy's best course of action is to take offensive action as it pursued its defensive role. In other words, it should take the initiative in destroying the enemy's ships as the means to preserve its own army's line of communications.

Obviously the forces ashore which are attacked by an invading army take the defensive. However, Mahan argued, the obvious is only the apparent truth. The function of defensive works is to protect and to defend the offensive power under its walls. A coastal fortress defends a fleet 'by sheltering and sustaining that force which against an invader is the offensive arm'.[41] The advocates of the blue-water school based their arguments on the erroneous premise, Mahan believed, when they claimed that coast fortresses serve only for defence, that the navy defends better than a fortress, and therefore, money spent on fortresses is wasted and should be spent on fleets. 'Granting the premise, the conclusion follows', Mahan declared, 'but the premise is erroneous.'[42]

Mahan believed that the Russian admiral's failure to move his squadron out from its position as a supplementary defence to the fortress at Port Arthur was the central error of the war. The Russians should have used the fortress for preparation, then they should have moved out to strike offensively at the Japanese in a decisive battle, defeating the Japanese Navy and thereby cutting the lines of support to the invading Japanese Army. Mahan concluded, 'The Russian navy had the decisive part to play in the late war; and the war was unsuccessful, not because the Navy was not large enough, but because it was improperly handled.'[43]

Mahan used the Russo-Japanese War as a typical case of the type of naval warfare which he assumed would prevail in the future. This war between rival nations, both fighting for limited objectives outside their home territory, illustrated the validity of the capital ship theory, in which combat between battleships was the key to the war.[44] Mahan's criticism of the Russian Navy was meant to be a telling point that should have direct relevance for future naval preparations. Mahan criticised the Russian Navy for being on the defensive and trying to attempt to escape from Port Arthur to Vladivostok, instead of seeking out the Japanese Navy and destroying it. In Mahan's view, 'It was the cardinal, and, in view of the aggregate size of their navy, most discreditable feature of the campaign as a whole on their part, that no attempt was ever made to destroy the Japanese fleet by sheer hard fighting.'[45]

Moreover the war demonstrated another basic error that Mahan saw in Russian thinking: It was 'the position in which Japan caught Russia; with a navy in the aggregate superior, divided into two parts individually inferior to the Japanese navy'.[46] With that point in mind, Mahan warned, 'It is of vital consequence to the nation of the United States, that its people, contemplating the Russo-Japanese War, substitute therein, in their apprehension, Atlantic for Baltic and Pacific for Port Arthur, so they will comprehend as well as apprehend' the need to concentrate force in a single large fleet.[47]

Mahan's thought was thus composed of two strands. One was the application of Jomini's principles to maritime and naval problems. The other was his conscious attempt to link his ideas with the broad characteristics of the particular type of international situation which existed in the years between 1885 and 1905. His historical studies and the theoretical framework which he took from Jomini were all in harmony with the nature of his time, an era of distinctly limited warfare, national growth and imperial rivalry.

Notes

1. For published documents and bibliography, see Robert Seager II and Doris Maguire (eds), *The Letters and Papers of Alfred Thayer Mahan* (Annapolis, 1977) 3 volumes; John B. Hattendorf and Lynn C. Hattendorf, compilers, *A Bibliography of the Works of Alfred Thayer Mahan* (Newport, 1986). The main collection of Mahan manuscripts is in the Library of Congress, but for a guide to the complementary collection at the Naval War College, see John B. Hattendorf, compiler, *Register of the Alfred Thayer Mahan Papers* (Newport, 1987).
2. For the most recent works, see the notes to Chapter 6 by Donald M. Schurman.
3. René Albrecht-Carrie, *A Diplomatic History of Europe since the Congress of Vienna* (New York, 1973) p. 208.

4. John D. Hayes and John B. Hattendorf (eds), *The Writings of Stephen B. Luce* (Newport, 1975) p. 68.
5. Mahan, 'Sea Power in the Present European War', in *Letters and Papers*, iii, p. 706.
6. Ibid., pp. 54–7, 60, 65.
7. Russell Weigley, *The American Way of War* (Bloomington, 1973) pp. 81–9.
8. Michael Howard, 'Jomini and the Classical Tradition', in *The Theory and Practice of War* (Bloomington, 1967) p. 16.
9. Mahan to Roosevelt, 13 January 1909, *Letters and Papers*, iii, p. 276; also printed in Richard W. Turk, *The Ambiguous Relationship: Theodore Roosevelt and Alfred Thayer Mahan* (Westport, 1987) p. 154.
10. Crane Brinton, Gordon Craig and Felix Gilbert, 'Jomini', in Edwin M. Earle (ed.), *Makers of Modern Strategy* (Princeton, 1943) p. 90. See also John Shy, 'Jomini', in *Makers of Modern Strategy from Machiavelli to the Nuclear Age* (Princeton, 1986) pp. 143–85.
11. Jomini, *Traité des Grandes Opérations Militaires* (Paris, 1851, iii) pp. 57–8.
12. Mahan, *The Major Operations of the Navies in the War of American Independence* (Boston, 1913) p. 1.
13. Mahan, *Lessons of the War with Spain and other Articles* (Boston, 1899) p. 230.
14. Ibid., p. 231.
15. William E. Livezey, *Mahan on Sea Power* (Norman, 1981) p. 230. See also Mahan to Thursfield, 28 October 1899 in *Letters and Papers*, ii, p. 664.
16. Livezey, *Mahan on Sea Power*, p. 230.
17. Mahan, *The Influence of Sea Power Upon History 1660–1783* (Boston, 1890) p. 25.
18. Mahan, *Naval Strategy Compared and Contrasted with the Principles and Practice of Military Operations on Land* (Boston, 1918) p. 115.
19. Mahan, *Influence of Sea Power Upon History 1660–1783*, p. 25.
20. Ibid., p. 89.
21. Ibid., p. 209.
22. Mahan, *Naval Strategy*, p. 5.
23. Ibid., pp. 21, 25.
24. Ibid., p. 53.
25. Ibid., p. 68.
26. Ibid., pp. 93, 132.
27. Ibid., pp. 164–5.
28. Ibid., pp. 176–8.
29. Ibid., pp. 181–2.
30. Ibid., p. 204.
31. Ibid., p. 291.
32. Ibid., p. 297.
33. Ibid., p. 299.
34. Livezey, *Mahan On Sea Power*, p. 245.
35. Mahan, *Lessons of the War with Spain*, p. 186.
36. Ibid., p. 76.
37. Ibid., pp. 123–4.
38. Mahan no doubt had in mind the words of Torrington after the Battle of Beachy Head in 1690, '... I always said, that whilst we had a fleet in being, they would dare not make an attempt', as well as the writings of Vice Admiral P. H. Colomb. See in particular his *Naval Warfare*, annotated with an introduction by Barry M. Gough, Classics of Sea Power series (Annapolis, forthcoming).
39. Mahan, *Naval Strategy*, p. 385.

40. Ibid., p. 387.
41. Ibid., p. 435.
42. Ibid.
43. Ibid., p. 446.
44. Mahan, *Naval Administration and Warfare: Some General Principles* (Boston, 1908) p. 173.
45. Mahan, 'Reflections, Historic and Other, Suggested by the Battle of the Japan Sea', *Journal of the Royal United Services Institution*, vol. 50, part 2 (November 1906) p. 1330.
46. Mahan to Editor, *New York Sun*, 28 January 1907, in *Letters and Papers*, iii, p. 206.
47. Mahan, *Naval Administration*, p. 173.

6 Mahan Revisited*
Donald M. Schurman

Alfred Mahan was an outstandingly successful writer, both in terms of sales and in terms of influence, so far as one can measure influence. He was also a complex expositor, and it needs to be said at once that both the seeming contradictions in his work, and his sense of the need to qualify, make it necessary to clothe judgements on his work with seemly reserve. It is to be hoped that this article emulates the Master's caution without avoiding facts that need consideration seventy-five years after his death.

Mahan has been studied as a publicist of American sea power development; as a sort of naval Clausewitz, or universal thinker on war; as a standard thinker against whose views on strategy and tactics twentieth-century war actions and preparations may be judged. I have studied him as an historian (almost as a British historian) as opposed to a political analyst or naval prophet.[1] My own approach has been to measure Mahan, as an admitted non-technological person, against other historians who were his contemporaries. To me this latter approach revealed both strengths and weaknesses: strength in that his lack of technological preoccupation lifted his thought above the output of the bric-à-brac 'scientific' lore that passed for strategic thought in his time; weakness in that his need to be relevant always threatened to distort his real historical insights.

It is important to recognise that, in *Makers of Modern Strategy*, Margaret Tuttle Sprout took a semi-shelved Mahan and dusted him off in 1942 to suit wartime American naval instructional purposes. Her wartime scholarly achievement was great. From the point of view of maritime *Weltanschauung* her advancement of Mahan and sea power to centre stage was magisterial. Given her premises she constructed the masterly edifice from which Mahan is still viewed by most American navalists, propagandists of maritime determinants and naval historians. She described the effects of Mahan's words and tailored them for a second revival. This paper looks at what motivated Mahan to write what he did – in the 1880s, and to look at the constraints under which he wrote it.

This is not the first attempt to do this. Peter Karsten did it in *The Naval Aristocracy*,[2] which examined Mahan as a product of his time, service and social class. This book was the most innovative and courageous re-interpretive historian's attempt to deal honestly with the citadels of American

---

*A revised version of an article which originally appeared in *Militärhistorisk Tidskrift* (The Swedish Journal of Military History) 1982, pp. 29–43. Reprinted by permission.

naval complacency since Mahan fluttered the establishment himself. If the obsession behind this fine book seems excessive, continuous consultation of it improves the impression it creates. It was Karsten's view that Mahan was not so dominated by Jominian thought as he was by the mores of the naval service. Karsten could see that these were not the mores of Americans in general – and that even on the official level there was a wide divergence between naval purpose as apprehended from a naval – as opposed to a governmental – point of view. Paul Kennedy's discussion of Mahan vs. Sir Halford Mackinder in *The Rise and Fall of the British Naval Mastery*,[3] while interesting to the student of Anglo-German rivalry, builds on Margaret Sprout's article in *Makers*, and on its assumptions that most naval writers were blue-water determinists. He thus develops a case that historians like Julian Corbett conceded in the midst of the controversies he describes.[4] The new volume on *Makers of Modern Strategy*, edited by Peter Paret, has only one article on maritime strategy. It has been written by Philip Crowl, and is a careful work but traditional in interpretation. The same may be said of Robert Seager's biography.[5]

Perhaps the best judgement of Mahan was that he was a political scientist, who 'guessed right about the future'.[6] At the end of this essay the actual development of Mahan's ideas in the 1880s will be canvassed. Meanwhile it appears to be necessary to frame and discuss certain questions. First, what was Mahan's purpose? Second, how did Mahan view the British? Third, what were the British actually doing? Fourth, what agents – or forces – actually crafted British sea power? Fifth, how was naval power calculated by the British in the past – and in the 1880s? Finally, how did Mahan's purpose correspond to the realities of British maritime growth?

WHAT WAS MAHAN'S PURPOSE?

He aimed to show that warfare at sea could be conducted successfully by following proper scientific rules. He wrote at a time when deep uncertainty was present in the minds of planners who thought about what the next war would be like. This was so because of vast changes in the instruments of war (and this was especially true of sea power) that had not been tried out in any conclusive fashion, either in war or in peace. Mahan was asked to provide historical argument for a naval service requirement, viz a reassuring science of war. This was to be his task at the new Naval War College. He prepared his history lectures with this preoccupation dominant in his mind.

In order to do this in clear unmistakable fashion, Mahan turned for assistance to Jomini whose uncluttered mind had brushed aside the complications of international cause and effect in favour of a particularly military approach based on a theory of communications. Jomini was a sound thinker; the sort of theorist who is a great relief to the mind of any student fresh from a wrestle with Clausewitz. Mahan needed such a clear, uncomplicated method of exposition. Also it was natural for Jomini to be chosen since he had, for half a century, dominated the thought patterns of military instructors on the banks of the Hudson, at West Point. Chief among Jomini's admirers in America was Mahan's father, Dennis Hart Mahan, a professor at West Point.

HOW DID MAHAN VIEW THE BRITISH?

Good evidence that Mahan had fixed on both his purpose and his historical technique first, is provided by the fact that he chose British history between 1660 and 1815 as his model. For the command-of-the-sea theory did not fit classical and medieval models except in a random way. Certainly the Venetians, by all odds the greatest seamen between the Northmen and the Portuguese, did not exercise general maritime 'command' any more than did their great arch rival, the Byzantine state.[7]

Another example was Spain, where Fernand Braudel has shown how expensive and difficult it was for the Spanish to exert any consistent sea presence in the Mediterranean.[8] Overseas their problem was similar. The Spanish were successful in protecting trade from the 40 or so corsairs who preyed on their Caribbean shipping. They did not exercise command of the seas but rather command of the treasure fleets, and when sufficiently annoyed their instinct was to go for the English jugular,[9] without establishing sea command first. Similar comments might be made about the Dutch and later the French in response to English sea power.

The British suited Mahan's purpose because they continued to grow in a naval and maritime way until their general sea supremacy and wide range of action were everywhere acknowledged. It looked like a planned development carried out, from 1588 to 1815, by a people who had taken their instruction from Jomini. The history contained in the selected British time span exactly suited the Mahanite purpose of 'scientific' cause and effect.

WHAT WERE THE BRITISH ACTUALLY DOING?

Of course neither Drake nor Nelson ever read Jomini. No doubt they would have been surprised to find themselves acting on his principles. In fact, sea power in the age of fighting sail depended to a high degree upon geography. From at least 1565 on, it was discovered that a combination of wind and coast configuration produced advantages of military position and concentration that intelligent maritime men would use to good effect. The advantage related directly to the so-called ship-of-the-line and not to past galleys or to future steam vessels. Over and above ship safety problems, seamen could be ordered to take advantage of natural phenomena to achieve mercantile, indeed national, commercial advantages. The story of the harnessing of that mass fear, skill, prejudice, taciturnity and courage, that formed the British marine, to the counting-houses of the City of London, overseas roadsteads and increasingly perceived national purposes constitutes the real history of the Royal Navy.[10]

The application of these historical lessons, culled from experience, found their apogee in the age of Napoleon, where sea power exercised a powerful effect upon the history of Europe, as well as cementing colonial fragments into a great commercial Empire – an Empire of unparalleled range and scope.

Mahan's book showed British maritime growth in the period of Anglo-French rivalry, and it showed how maritime power appeared to be decisive. Later, when he turned to the war of 1812, it was to hammer home the message that single ship actions apart, a sea power was the one that could exercise overwhelming power in the line of battle numbers game. In 1813, when the British moved over to American big ships, grass grew in the streets of Boston.[11] Certainly the Royal Navy suited an approach whereby Jomini could be used to explain seemingly inevitable sea progress.

Both Margaret Sprout and lately Paul Kennedy have taken pains to show that land power and its theorists, such as Haushofer and Mackinder, posed special problems for naval mastery theorists. No one disputes (at least not the present author) that ships do not conquer land masses. What is more important is to note that Mahan consciously or unconsciously selected the illustrative material from a time when continentalist geographical theories of dominance seemed not to apply. *Some* blue-water theorists in England *circa* 1905 did eagerly accept the Mahan approach. In America many still do.

WHAT AGENTS OR FORCES ACTUALLY CRAFTED BRITISH SEA POWER?

So far the selection of Britain as a model has been described in almost Mahanian terms. However, if we wish to understand anything about the real nature of British sea power, it must be emphasised that in Britain monarchs after Henry VIII did not simply decree that state policy must conform to 'The Royal Will'. Rather, state policy was comprised of an increasingly complex number of factors, at home and abroad, that pressed for national policies to cover growing maritime commercial policies and activities. The commercial agenda for these developments at home in England were not simply port merchants but involved business men whose interests often reached through Parliament into the Royal decision-making processes. Socially all sorts of threads were woven together. As John Ehrman once put it, the Royal Navy was a slice not a layer of the national cake.[12] Agents of the government armed with wide regulatory powers lived at home and abroad, and their commercial brethren, who after all provided their salaries, lived cheek by jowl with them as formal control and support balanced and interwove with the logic of commercial profits. The precise tie between these various groups was financial and regulatory, and commercial agents operated not on the basis of any rigid principles or unlimited budgets, but by reference to that system of careful husbanding that one day would be known as Gladstonian finance.

All of these factors – the ship type, geographical position, carefully husbanded tradition based on a frank recognition of social possibilities – made for a British maritime and commercial greatness that found its ultimate expression in the word 'Empire'. The combinations of factors varied from time to time but it is true, allowing for short run setbacks, that progress in imperial maritime growth was constant over nearly three centuries. Perhaps the constant additive that made for success was, until 1807, the extra revenue generated commercially by the trade in negro slaves from Africa. Underneath the success of an Empire lay the seething moral sewer of trade in human flesh.

HOW WAS NAVAL POWER CALCULATED BY THE BRITISH IN THE PAST, AND IN THE 1880s?

After 1815 things changed for the British. They may not have been a satiated power, but they were an empire well spread out. From the end of the Napoleonic wars the very extent of the commerce and geographical growth dictated some priority system. Like Spain in the sixteenth century, Britain could not be strong everywhere and priorities were largely determined by periodic scares and, of course, by finance. When Robinson and Gallagher looked at the problem of the British African empire in the nineteenth century,[13] they concluded that in the final analysis it was not trade and money that generated funds for priority locations, but rather it was strategy. This view has been challenged by Marxists, non-Marxists and others – mainly those who write of unconscious or investment empire – as opposed to the economics of actual possessions. However, there is another way of looking at a place like, say, the Cape Colony with its naval base. One may concede at once that the Cape was of strategic importance (Suez notwithstanding) and the colonial policy towards, say, Rhodesia, might take its tone and strength from the relationship of the colony north of the Zambesi to the naval base at Simonstown. But what determined the *value* of the defences, floating and fixed, at the Cape? The answer is that the Carnavon Commission reporting in 1883, and its Colonial Defence Committee predecessor in 1878, both used the annual value of passing trade as a determinant.[14] The origin of this way of valuation was as old as the British Empire. For instance, Raffles had used it at Singapore in 1819. But in the 1880s, that the numbers of guns should be decided by relative value of commerce (for it was a comparative system *vis-à-vis* other strategic posts) was a crude correlation of the cash-box mentality with strategic general principles. These, incidentally, laid it down that Europe, where opposition to British trade success would probably be generated, was accorded the main strategic priority. For without the European heart being secure it was not considered by anyone that Imperial Britain would remain alive, let alone dominant. Even a Canadian nationalist could be expected to see that.

HOW DID MAHAN'S PURPOSE CORRESPOND TO THE REALITIES OF BRITISH MARITIME GROWTH?

In the 1880s, when Mahan was writing, these things were hidden from his eyes as he paraded his chosen aspects of social science and naval principles. The world was ready for crudities and it selected those aspects of Mahan which corresponded to their chosen dream. In England there was no General Staff. There was a Board of Admiralty where the nuances of government policy and commercial requirement were decided with a lordly disdain that had absolutely nothing to do with any kind of principle that a man like Mahan might deduce – or indeed any other principles that were not concerned with the hoar-frost of time. As the Board of Admiralty grappled with new ship types, new weapons and new problems, they had a kind of historical precedent to guide them.[15] This resembled nothing so much as the antithesis of, say, the Prussian General Staff. It was a modern farce played out against the background of outmoded, but firm, even confident tradition. It was not foolish; it was not magnificent: it was the Royal Navy painfully adapting to a less inviting age. All this was light-years away from the principles that Alfred Mahan expounded to senior officers at Newport in 1886 to 1893, and the real nature of the mainspring of the Royal Navy was not revealed to Mahan either through research or intuition. When he published, the British were grateful for his recognition of their genius but, as so often happens when they are written about by foreigners, they hardly recognised themselves.

MAHAN'S INTELLECTUAL ACTIVITY IN THE 1880s

Mahan's background and temperament were formed by his upbringing at West Point. He was a person of retiring habits and a reflective mind that neither cadet training at Annapolis nor service in the Union Navy during the War Between the States either disturbed or stimulated. In the sixties, he allowed himself to dwell on interpersonal relationships, both male and female, with the natural imaginative impetus of youth and the frustration that resulted from a strong, suffocating sense of duty, chivalry, honour and religious nature.

During the years 1867–9 this seething frame of emotional aspiration attached to an inquisitive mind was sent on sea duty, to the Far East. He served mostly in Japanese waters on board USS *Iroquois*, and he kept a diary[16] which mostly recorded the state of his bodily health, his Christian soul, and his fluctuating relationships with his brother officers. The introspective entries give off the oppressive steam of a hothouse environment. This serious young officer had not settled his matrimonial future and he was not the type to allow himself to be consoled by either geisha girls or wardroom companions, or even the comparative solace offered by food, drink, sailing, reading, prayer and sight-seeing. He also recorded the attempt to form a disciplined pattern out of this restricted choice of palliative opportunities. The fact is that, out of the sense of responsibility that he felt in the presence of his God, he elected to be a man of restraint. His responses to the irritations of daily life on board a relatively small ship matured him. It is to be noted, however, that he was not saved from the call of dissipation by intellectual activity. He tried. He wrote, after one bout with learning Greek, that he had 'constantly felt the perplexity between my active uncongenial professional duties and the desire for this religious or other study'.[17]

When he returned home, his marriage eliminated much of the ambivalent sexual uncertainty that had threatened to disrupt him. By 1875, Mahan was a disciplined personality pursuing a naval career that at no time called for joyous response from him, but one for whom purpose in life appeared to be nothing more than 'the gratifying feeling that his duty had been done'.[18] Although he had felt a 'capacity ... for more intellectual work', and that he had 'thrown himself away',[19] he had not proved capable of reorienting himself under his own steam.

Although he read widely, Mahan held the undisciplined opinions, prejudices and reflections of his naval contemporaries. He was sufficiently intelligent to be conscious of unfulfilled powers as he entered the 1880s at the age of 40. Mahan was turned towards his new calling of naval author and authority by the combined pressures of Admiral Stephen B. Luce and by the exigencies of Luce's new creation, the United States Naval War College at Newport, Rhode Island. These two forces shaped Mahan and gave his life singularity of purpose. Of course this has been commented upon before by other writers, but it needs emphasis if his historical responses are to be understood properly. Perhaps his new literary and pedagogical bent was shaped somewhat by his writing *The Gulf and the Inland Waters* in 1883. He did not, himself, think this was so in retrospect, but those who have written books will not dismiss this discipline of accomplishment so readily.[20] Nevertheless the decisive impetus was provided by Luce's call. Mahan wrote, 'at forty-five I was drifting on the lines of simple respectability as aimlessly as one very well could. My environment had been too much for one; my present call changed it'.[21]

Mahan was not Luce's first choice to give the historical evidence to support the latter's viewpoints at Newport. Mahan himself, somewhat unhappily stationed in the Pacific off the coast of western South America, saw the possibility of using this gambit to get home and he saw that, done properly, the work would turn out to be important. He returned to the historical narrative that would be used to illustrate cause and effect in naval war, 'thus enforcing certain general principles'.[22] This method might well serve for strategy: what it would do for tactics was more difficult to predict, and he knew it.

The problem fascinated Mahan and he worked away at it despite the fact that from November 1884 to September 1885 Luce left him to sweat it out with available books in the tropics.[23] It did not matter. By May 1885 Mahan had worked out a plan of attack that promised a general discussion of the elements of sea power – or affecting agents.[24] The list of geography, commerce and aptitude and so on reads remarkably like Mahan's arrangement in the beginning of his famous book – a logical arrangement of obvious 'elements' that most readers then and now skip to get at the subsequent history. He would then, he hoped, discourse on the effect of navies on great or small campaigns (for example, Hannibal). Next he would study great campaigns 'partly to clear up my mind on great questions of strategy' but also to enable him to deal with other matters such as the place of the ram and torpedo in modern war. This last is interesting, appearing as it does in direct response to a question from Luce, which indicated an intention to have him deal with the questions of which the *Jeune Ecole* in France were then the promoters. He concluded, strongly, 'of course I should introduce, what I have so far omitted, a study of great naval campaigns'.

These were his intentions, sent from exile. In November 1885 when he began work (under great pressure due to Luce's dilatory efforts at repatriation) he compared French and English sources as he studied campaigns,[25] and indicated his intention to use Jomini 'as a model possibly suggestive of manner of treatment'.[26] He stated that his chronological boundaries, 1660–1815, were largely set by the available material in French and English. For 'it is singular that the naval *history* of the world, for the most part, so far as records go, confined to the period between 1660–1815, the tactics and nautical conditions of those times are of the past – but the lessons and incitement of the part played by fleets remains and cannot I think but exact their progression in the eyes of officers'.[27]

By the middle of January 1886, he claimed to have understood the strategy (1660–1815). He discovered that it was not purely naval. To excerpt the general history of Europe for the period would be 'to capsize a proverb, Hamlet with all but the part of Hamlet left out'. Using this broad canvas had convinced him that the strategic effects of naval power on war situations or campaigns would always have pedagogic relevance. This is a partial answer to the question 'of what use is the knowledge of these bygone days'. The new technology makes the question more difficult to answer for tactics. Predictably he stated that efficiency, readiness and so on would always tell in ship-to-ship actions, but Jomini must help, for he would 'hope to detect analogies – and with an admirable system of one kind of war before one to contribute something to the development of a systematic study of war in another field'. These tactical remarks are not firm conclusions, but, in his own words, 'glimmers of light'.[28]

However, a month later, writing to his lifelong friend Ashe, he clearly revealed the priorities formed in his mind. He was assigned to teach 'the subject of Naval Strategy and Tactics' and this subject involved 'to a considerable extent Naval History as affording lessons'. That is to say, he went on, 'How to view the lessons of the past so as to mould them into lessons for the future, under such differing conditions, is the nut I have to crack'. He went on more startlingly: 'To excogitate a system of my own, on wholly *a prioric* grounds, would be comparatively simple and *I believe wholly useless*.' To show the connections between wooden walls and ironclads involved something more, and his effort, he hoped, would 'raise the profession in the eyes of its members by a clearer comprehension of the great part it has played in the world than I myself have hitherto had'. Finally, conscious of the importance and magnitude of the task he had set himself and, contemplating his progress, he wished he was 35 again and had 'two years for the work instead of one'.[29]

Mahan was not intellectually comfortable at the task of making tactics scientific. He knew that that was a part of Luce's purpose from the beginning but he shied at the gate. Would Jomini enable him to generalise the tactics of the olden days, let alone enable comparisons with the modern age to be made? The above letter to Ashe was written in February. In June he was writing confidently to Luce about how he was *now* writing on tactics for 'If I confine myself to history, the College would be blamed for not keeping me to things that were useful'. A revealing comment.[30] For by June 6 he was still prevaricating: 'I am anxious to get beyond *the mere historical part* if I can.'[31] And in a cry from the heart he admits that there is no clear detailed account of the Anglo-Dutch battle tactics, and 'I doubt if any has been preserved'.[32]

In the meantime he had received Luce's approval for what he had done so far. He acknowledged this with a recommendation to Luce that the *Revue Maritime* should be subscribed to 'when we have a library' for modern French tactical doctrine and because that periodical contained a good description of the Anglo-Dutch Four Days Battle of 1666.[33]

By August Mahan ceased to write to please Luce and wrote under the compulsion of making the College a success, for he had succeeded Luce as President of the new school at Newport. It will be remarked to this point that

Mahan had been selected to give lectures on naval strategy and tactics that Luce conceded would derive 'scientific' pedagogical substance from the use of history. Mahan in a remarkable eight-month blitz had mastered much of the secondary material for a study whose time-frame was set, in large measure, by the availability of secondary sources. It will also be obvious that although Mahan was reluctant to come to grips with modern tactical problems (perhaps because of temperament) he did see that history ought to provide a different perspective from which to view these problems, and hoped that Jomini might provide for the bridge between wooden walls and ironclads. Gradually his disinclination to grapple with tactical modernity forced him to deduce from history that French tactics *looked* better because they were theoretical propositions while English tactics *looked* worse because they tried them and sometimes failed. He was sailing comfortably towards a notion that allowed him to ignore small vessel or anti-commerce actions in that they were not ultimately *decisive*. This would, in time, lead him to expose the great French 'error' of *guerre de course* and to set up a concept of sea command that allowed him to ignore the commerce raiders of Louis Quinze and their subsequent modern version, the *Jeune Ecole*, at the same time. It is also clear, in retrospect, that he was writing lectures that were to cover the period between 1660 and 1815. Partly owing to time constraints he only got to 1778 by 1886 but saw that the work might be useful as a text and from the general tenor of the correspondence it is unlikely that he ever thought in terms of lectures divorced from publication. In other words he was writing a book from the beginning. The book, however, was shaped and would continue to be shaped by Luce and the general purposes and needs of the College, as well as by what Mahan read.

Thus it is clear then that Alfred Mahan's activity, from the time Luce appealed to him in 1884, was conditioned by certain factors. The first is that he was, like Stephen Luce, a creature of his times in that he accepted doctrines of progress, religion and social intercourse that were then current. Like Luce he appreciated the lack of sophisticated educational background, but unlike Luce he was unable to see naval problems whole. Luce quickly grasped the importance of Mahan's viewpoint. Genius is not too strong a word for Luce. Mahan was not a genius, but he had the instincts of a scholar, which Luce had not. Nevertheless Mahan was subject to the great overriding preoccupations of Luce's mind – which drove the latter to attempt to render all naval problems susceptible to 'scientific' solutions. Indeed the force of this viewpoint as set out by Luce penetrated to the fibre of Mahan's citadel. The idea that tactics, strategy, policy and 'principles' could be set up in a 'scientific' relationship to one another was not a concept outside the temper of the times; but the insistent strength of this synthesising thrust came from Mahan's mentor – the founder of the Naval War College – Stephen B. Luce.

Secondly, it is clear that if Mahan was aware that he was breaking new ground he was not doing it to placate any goddess of history. Mahan had a master, Luce, and a goddess – the United States Navy and its history – and they helped to make him a famous man. But history was a means to an end. Historical examples were mere pawns on the board of Mahan's game – the educational game of the Naval War College – where the total game plan was to convince naval officers that there was a scientific way to tackle problems of strategy and tactics.

As was fitting in a country where the army was the dominant service, Mahan had turned for his congealant force to the god of American army tactics, Jomini, that same Baron Henry de Jomini whose principles Mahan's father had persistently and for years incubated in the breasts of cadets at the US Military Academy, West Point. Jomini's view that there were immutable principles of war that held true for all historical periods of warfare struck Luce, not Mahan, as a worthy guide, for as Mahan worked on his lectures he constantly worried about whether these soldier rules could be applied to naval strategy and finally to naval tactics. Like Luce he held no brief for treating historical study in any cultivation of the mind context. Practicality was what the naval officers, and the watching authorities in Washington, would expect of him. He would be judged not on whether he fired the enthusiasm of his audiences for history, but rather to the extent that he could realistically show how the use of history would directly benefit the navy. The value of the history to the Naval War College would be in direct proportion to the simplification that the use of Jominian principles would bring to the study of history – in a specialised sense.

This viewpoint was rendered the more necessary by the fact that the only innovative naval thinking that was breaking in on what then passed for American naval thought was being done in France by Admiral Aube and the so-called *Jeune Ecole*. This policy of stealthy stalking, as opposed to committed mastery on the seas, did not commend itself to any American naval officers who, when they looked at foreign examples, saw the Royal Navy of Britain as top sea power, and the French naval thinkers as men who devised clever expedients for stealthily acquiring higher naval status. It was natural that American naval officers, who entertained dreams of one day surpassing the British, looked for a doctrine that venerated sure-fire principles that would permit them to do so. For the American Navy was no more interested in playing second fiddle to the Royal Navy than was the fledgling German Navy. The difference was that American political leaders were not as consistently amenable to the viewpoints of American navalism as the leaders in the Kaiser's Germany were to German navalism. Even Theodore Roosevelt, himself an expert on the naval aspects of the war of 1812, did not conceive of the Royal Navy as America's chief rival or enemy.

Thus it can be seen that Mahan approached the historical workbench in 1884–5 with purposes that were in no way divorced from the pressures induced by the naval aristocracy, the idea of the Naval War College and the personality of Stephen B. Luce. It also needs to be noticed that he worked in practical fashion and from hand to mouth. Without the careful and comprehensive training of the professional scholar, Mahan was faced with mastering modern political and naval history over two centuries, plus the strategic and tactical nature of line-of-battle warfare, in a little over a year. That he accomplished so much ought not to blind us to the fact that he owes his impact to the formula he devised both for mastering the material himself and for spoon-feeding his students at Newport. It is a military exercise that yielded some scholarly insights: not a scholarly search that yielded some military results.

The investigation led Mahan on to show that world power was oceanic power: that world dominance was founded upon the seas. After all, his models the British had proved it by inadvertently acting on Mahan's own principles. Paul Kennedy has paid Mahan the compliment of elevating his concepts to the position of challengers to Sir Halford Mackinder's later developed theories of heart land and land power. Certainly it was a theory of world dominance fit to stand beside Bismarck's wide-ranging European notions. The Kaiser recognised the naval power concepts in Mahan's works.

So Mahan, under great deadline pressure, goaded by his nemesis, and wrestling with history, used Jominian principles to put forward a theory of oceanic mastery and dominance. The flattered British, who always understood power, did him the honour to state that the Anglo-American navies, taken together, might rule the world. But Mahan's American audience was not interested in sharing naval power at the top with any nation – such obvious exceptions as Admiral Sims notwithstanding. At some time in 1943 the US Navy crossed the Rubicon by Mahanite standards. They were right to do so on their terms – for by those Mahan terms there can be only one naval power with command of the sea.

Looking back, the problem is that, while no one could accuse the English of being unconscious of Imperial Naval power, they had not arrived at it by Mahan's method or process. This may be hard to credit but Mahan's navalism does not, did not, and never has, represented a seaman's view of the universe. Furthermore the British Government – supporter of sea policies as it often was – did not have a Mahan outlook until it adopted him somewhat during the frenzy of that Imperial scramble that has since moved so easily into a sunset. And if in that sunset they twice mastered the Germans at sea they did not do it, some spokesmen apart, on the basis of Mahanite principles.[34]

The growth of English sea enterprise followed no Mahanite master-plan. It is necessary to understand that the first principle of a seaman's outlook is the safety of the ship. It was around this kernel of instinctive sailor reaction that the English, in the sixteenth and seventeenth centuries, sent out their commercial and military ships to achieve specific short-run purposes. Against the Spanish, the Dutch and the French the objects were not European dominance and obliteration but the protection of the growth of trade. This development led to the acquisition of bases and to the mastery of the consequent colonies that supported both the trade and the basis. Profits were guaranteed by the negro slave trade.

If ship owners and national policy once combined to carve a permissive area within the Spanish trading monopoly, so, in the same way, they came together in British–Dutch relationships after the Peace of Westphalia. The plain fact of the matter was, as the Duke of Albermarle stated in 1660, 'The Dutch have the trade and we want it.' Nevertheless, despite this blatant intention, some moderation ensued and London did not replace Amsterdam as the European money market until 1780. Similar comments could be made concerning competition with the French. Indeed it was the fact that the English appeared to be so commercially minded that dictated French sea policy from 1693 to 1815, towards *guerre de course* and not a war *à outrance* at sea.

Sea power was made up of practicalities at sea, and of government sea support. It also included home agents who provided capital and understood the logic of profits in sea policy, and who acted between the Government of which they were often members, and sea trading in which they were often investors. If there were times when national pride took these contributing factors to *national policy* and shook them into something resembling a *world policy*, these moments were fleeting and by no means the main ingredient in the formation of sea policy. This was so because the lowly Captain who only half-understood sea policy had to be forced to learn his true function by experience and the development of professional traditions.[35]

Eventually, ultimate policy was made by Parliament. That does not mean that it was based on some sort of top nation determination. A good example of the way sea power operated occurred after the Americans won independence. What should Parliament do about American vessels that had shot themselves into the West Indian Trade? There was no strong desire to smother the Americans as carriers. Adam Smith's arguments were well understood – and the general disposition was towards equality of treatment for American vessels. However the argument that loss in commercial trading volume meant fewer seamen to man the fleet in war prevailed, and British parliamentarians believed until very recently that control of trading privileges was the way to keep up a supply of mariners so that the navy could be manned – and the majority believed, rightly or wrongly, that Naval might was an essential guarantor of trading success.[36]

Notes

1. D. M. Schurman, *The Education of a Navy* (Chicago, 1965) pp. 62–3 and 81–2.
2. Peter Karsten, *The Naval Aristocracy* (New York, 1972) especially pp. 326–47.
3. New York, 1976.
4. Schurman, *The Education of a Navy*, pp. 170–1.

5. Philip Crowl, 'Alfred Thayer Mahan: The New Histories', in Peter Paret (ed.), *Makers of Modern Strategy* (Princeton University Press, 1986) pp. 444–77; Robert Seager II, *Alfred Thayer Mahan: The Man and His Letters* (Annapolis, 1977).
6. Albert Lepawsky, 'A Tribute to Mahan as a Social Scientist', USNI *Proceedings* (1940) p. 1625.
7. An awkward attempt was made by Frederic Lane to apply a Mahan yardstick to his otherwise learned discussion of Venetian seapower. See Frederic C. Lane, *Venice, A Maritime Republic* (Baltimore, 1973) pp. 67–8.
8. Fernand Braudet, *The Mediterranean and the Mediterranean World in the Age of Philip II*, 2 vols (London, 1973). See especially vol. II, pp. 836–91.
9. See Paul E. Hoffman, *The Spanish Crown and the Defense of the Caribbean, 1535–1585* (Louisiana, 1980). Aspects quoted in review by Julian De Zulueta in *The Mariner's Mirror* (vol. 61, no. 1) February 1981, p. 110.
10. Concisely expounded in Brian Tunstall, *The Realities of Naval History* (London, 1938).
11. A. T. Mahan, *Sea Power in its Relation to the War of 1812*, 2 vols (London, 1903). See vol. II, pp. 201–14.
12. John Ehrman, *The Navy in the War of William III, 1689–1697* (Cambridge, 1953) p. xxii.
13. R. Robinson and J. Gallagher with Alice Denny, *Africa and the Victorians* (London, 1961).
14. See D. M. Schurman, 'Imperial Defense, 1868–1887', unpublished PhD thesis, Cambridge University, 1955.
15. Indeed naval policy was what the Board of Admiralty actually sent as instructions to naval station commanders. See D. M. Schurman, 'An Historian and the Sublime Aspects of the Naval Profession', in A. M. J. Hyatt (ed.), *Dreadnought to Polaris* (Toronto, 1973) p. 2.
16. Robert Seager II and Doris Maguire (eds), *Letters and Papers of Alfred Thayer Mahan*, vol. 1, 1847–89 (Annapolis, 1975) pp. 145–332.
17. Ibid., p. 195.
18. W. S. Gilbert, 'The Gondoliers'.
19. *Letters and Papers*, vol. 1, p. 197.
20. Furthermore, the scope and numbers of books read by Mahan increased remarkably as he worked on *The Gulf*; see *Letters and Papers*, vol. 1, pp. 547ff. and especially p. 552.
21. A. T. Mahan, *From Sail to Steam* (New York, 1907) p. 290. For understanding Luce's almost dominating influence on Mahan I am much indebted to that carefully presented and annotated collection of Luce's work by John D. Hayes and John B. Hattendorf, *The Writings of Stephen B. Luce* (Newport, 1975). See especially pp. 45–68.
22. See Hayes and Hattendorf, ibid., pp. 69–97 for Luce's preoccupation with history and tactics.
23. Luce told him in June 1885 to let things take their course. *Letters and Papers*, vol. 1, p. 610.
24. Mahan to Luce, 16 v 85, ibid., pp. 606–7.
25. Mahan to Luce, 2 xi 85 and 4 xi 85, ibid., p. 617.
26. Mahan to Luce, 5 xi 85 ibid., p. 617.
27. Mahan to Luce, 14 xi 85 ibid., p. 618.
28. Mahan to Luce, 22 i 86 ibid., p. 223.
29. Mahan to Ashe, 2 ii 86 ibid., p. 625. All italics above are mine.
30. Mahan to Luce, 24 iv 86 ibid., p. 628.

31. Mahan to Luce, 6 v 86 ibid., p. 632.
32. Ibid.
33. Mahan to Luce, 31 v 86 ibid., p. 633.
34. These were, of course, alliance situations, and ones not easily reducible to Mahanite or any other kind of simplistic principles.
35. The best book in this genre of thinking was written by Gerald S. Graham and entitled *The Politics of Naval Supremacy* (Cambridge, 1965).
36. See Vincent Harlow, *The founding of the Second British Empire, 1763–1793*, vol. I (London, 1952) pp. 448–92. It should also be noted that Dr Kennedy has rightly spotted that the argument that trade and naval power are directly and clearly related is a difficult proposition to prove. See Paul M. Kennedy, *The Rise and Fall of British Naval Mastery* (London, 1976) pp. 42–43.

7 The Strategic Thought of Sir Julian S. Corbett
Barry D. Hunt

As the founding fathers of the 'historical school' of naval strategists, Sir Julian Stafford Corbett (1854–1923) and Captain Alfred Thayer Mahan (1840–1914) shared careers and convictions of sometimes remarkable similarities. Both turned to serious scholarship relatively late in their lives. Both thereafter committed themselves to bringing naval history into the mainstream of intellectual respectability. They were convinced of history's immense power as an educational tool and they looked to the past for insights that might guide their War College students and assist policy-makers in coming to grips with the changing technical and diplomatic circumstances of their own world.

In other respects, of course, their achievements should be carefully differentiated. Corbett was the superior historian and a more subtle and cautious strategic theorist. Since his first major book, *Drake and the Tudor Navy*[1] was published almost a decade after Mahan's first, he had the advantage of being able to extend the latter's first probes, as it were. But Corbett's refinements also entailed fundamental differences of approach and method as between Mahan's dependence on secondary materials and his own exploitation of primary sources. Indeed, in one of his rare public comments about his American colleague, Corbett wrote in 1916, 'the wonder is that Mahan could build as well as he did on a foundation so insecure'.[2] Yet, in terms of both immediate and longer-term impact, Mahan's books were far more successful and therefore influential. He is still the more familiar figure of the two. But for Professor Donald Schurman's research, Corbett's name and those of other important British writers of his generation would all but be forgotten, especially in North America.[3]

Timing had something to do with Mahan's greater popularity. So did his message. It almost perfectly complemented the aspirations of those Americans who recognised that greater international political and economic influence was directly linked to expanded naval strength. His ideas laid the foundation of 'blue-water' navalist thought to this day. Categorising Mahan's thinking has never been easy, however, for, gifted as he was as a narrative historian, he was more of a synthesiser than an analyst of ideas. Herbert Rosinski saw him as an 'epigrammatic' thinker:

Even his famous lectures at the Naval War College were nothing more than a series of case studies, strung together in a hardly perceptible general scheme; and when finally, towards the end of his life, he was induced to revise and publish them in 1911 under the title of *Naval Strategy*, that task was so uncongenial to him that the result proved, in his own words, 'the most perfunctory job I have ever done'.[4]

Corbett's *Some Principles of Maritime Strategy*, also published in 1911, was eminently more successful in this respect. It was more self-consciously systematic and analytical than anything else he wrote. It was also his last book before the First World War. Whether or not it was his best, it is the one for which he is most remembered and still consulted. Its claim on later generations stems from Corbett's role in the prewar reform of the Royal Navy associated with Admiral Sir John Fisher's name, and also from the fact that it was written as a deliberate counterpoint to Mahan and blue-water orthodoxy.

Between 1898, when his *Drake* book appeared, and the outbreak of war in 1914, Corbett wrote and edited more than a dozen major books, some multi-volumed, and numerous articles that are the real basis of his lasting significance in naval affairs. Their intrinsic scholarly importance derived from his combining of meticulous research with broad generalisations about national policy and grand strategy. Unlike Mahan, however, his goal was not a general or universalist theory of sea power. Rather he attempted to explain Britain's success as an imperial–maritime Power from the perspectives of the men who had actually developed and executed her policies. This was the basis of his most important contribution to maritime thought: the notion that Britain's 'success' as a first-rate Power had involved the combined interplay and exploitation of all her naval, military, economic and diplomatic resources in a comprehensive policy; that her established 'continental' and 'maritime' schools of strategy should be seen not as competing alternatives but as mutually reinforcing options. This 'British Way in Warfare' required that her statesmen, entrepreneurs and military leaders understood what it could and could not achieve; that therefore there was a good deal more to naval strategy than the seeking out and destruction of an enemy's fleet in a glorious culminating battle of decision on the Trafalgar model. In his view, the ultimate purpose of naval forces working in the service of the government's wider policy objectives was to pressure the enemy in various ways, to assist the army, the diplomats, the country's allies. Writing throughout the period when navalists questioned the value of any money spent on armies, and European general staffs were so preoccupied with their problems of mobilisation, train timetables and offensive short-war doctrines that they ignored the maritime dimensions of any future European conflict, Corbett stood virtually alone in his attempts to bridge that chasm.

His writing achievements were also bound up with his work with the Royal

Naval War College. His lectures there from shortly after the College opened in 1900 until the war in 1914 brought him contacts and even friendships with important Service and political figures, including Admiral Fisher. Corbett understood and, within limits, backed Fisher's controversial changes and he became an important publicist for them. The War Course itself, under its early Directors, Captains William J. May, and Edmond Slade, became with Corbett's help the only important centre of prewar naval strategic thought and, to a limited degree, war planning. As a lecturer, Corbett faced the problems of first winning his audience's interest and trust and then of offering history and strategy 'in a digestible form to the unused organs of Naval officers'.[5] That challenge conditioned his own research interests in the sense that the subjects he chose for his next books – *England in the Mediterranean, 1603–1713* (1904), *England and the Seven Years War* (1907), and *The Campaign of Trafalgar* (1910) – were expansions of his lecture series. Similarly, as will be seen, his *Some Principles*, and its earlier manifestation as the 1906 'Green Pamphlet', were tailored specifically to those classroom needs. He succeeded, though never completely. His impact therefore was limited because he could never entirely surmount his students' mistrust of civilian experts. The complexities of his subject and the fact that in certain key respects his ideas did run counter to Nelsonic lore antagonised more than a few of them.

So did his connections with 'Jackie' Fisher. Perhaps more than any other single factor, it was that association that was the actual focus of the resentment directed his way, before and during the war, by the so-called 'Syndicate of Discontent' led by Admirals Beresford, Custance and Noel and most of the Conservative press. In reality, by the time Corbett began to write *Some Principles*, the limits of his admiration for Fisher (who retired as First Sea Lord in 1910) had already been reached. Fisher's refusals to push seriously for inter-Service planning within the Committee of Imperial Defence or for the creation of a properly constituted naval war staff ultimately alienated Corbett and other backers like Admiral Slade and the young reformer Captain (later Admiral Sir) Herbert Richmond.[6] From then until the war, Corbett's influence on official naval affairs was confined to his continued friendship with Slade and Maurice Hankey, the CID secretary. He lectured at the War College until it was closed down for the duration of the war. The rest of his time was devoted to editing two volumes of *The Spencer Papers* for the Navy Records Society (1913 and 1914) and writing a two-volume confidential history of the Russo-Japanese War for the Admiralty.[7] These activities led to his selection to write *Naval Operations*, the official history of the war at sea, an appointment that kept him close to the centre of wartime developments. In this position he exerted more than an incidental influence, including the drafting of the general instructions to Admiral Jellicoe who as C-in-C Grand Fleet put into force the Distant Blockade and 'no risk' policy that characterised the handling of his critical command. But perhaps the true indicator of how far Corbett's thinking in strategic matters had permeated the Royal Navy's upper reaches only became obvious after the war, when Beatty's Admiralty issued its famous formal disclaimer to Corbett's third (Jutland) volume of *Naval Operations* on the grounds of his having played down the significance of decisive fleet action. Of course, the bitter and prolonged postwar Jutland 'controversy' cast a shadow dark and broad enough to obscure a string of careers, and also obscured issues that could have more profitably engaged naval professionals' minds.

SOME PRINCIPLES – SOME CONTEXT

Corbett's thinking had upset at least some naval experts for years of course. Indeed, when it had been first suggested in 1910 that he might write a book on 'The Principles' of naval strategy,[8] his publishers, Longmans, had just released his latest work, *The Campaign of Trafalgar*. It had already provoked controversy because of his apparent denigration of that great action's meaning and with it, presumably, Nelson's image. The book was conceived as a *strategic* analysis of the entire campaign at sea in 1805, and Corbett had quite consciously tried to place Nelson's contributions into a broader perspective by viewing developments through the eyes of the men in London: 'It is with them alone we may watch the inner springs at work, by which the fleets at sea were really controlled . . .'.[9]

The immediate occasion for the public agitation was his rendering of the actual battle off Cape Trafalgar. Its causes went much deeper. His critics, mainly retired Admiral Sir Cyprian Bridge and J. R. Thursfield, the *Times* naval correspondent (himself the author of a later book on Trafalgar), used the occasion to vent their doubts about Corbett's philosophy generally and more particularly his effect on the War Course where for five years he had included lectures on aspects of 'The Trafalgar Campaign'.[10] They succeeded in getting a special Admiralty committee of enquiry appointed whose purpose, Corbett worried, was to 'sit on my book', if not him.[11] In the end this highly unusual committee, composed of Admirals Sir Reginald Custance (Chairman) and Sir Cyprian Bridge, the historian Sir Charles Firth and, finally, as secretary, Mr W. G. Perrin the Admiralty Librarian, sensibly pronounced in Corbett's favour. It was a bizarre episode[12] by any standard and could have provoked some interesting legal arguments. How it affected Corbett's approach to his new book, that was to be a published version of the very ideas that had here drawn criticism, cannot be determined with any precision. The incident did demonstrate that he had not totally surmounted the basic prejudices of the naval officer corps. Corbett understood the problem and had consciously developed friendships with serving officers whose assistance he gratefully acknowledged; 'those of us who have dared walk upon the waters know well the need of their helping hands'.[13] Unfortunately his cultivation of those links may have only further alienated less progressive-minded officers.

Corbett had been brought in to lecture to the War Course by its founder and first Director, Captain W. J. May, because of his scholarly credentials, and because he would bring a civilian's perspective to bear. He therefore gave Corbett wide latitude, provided only that his lectures treated strategy in such a way 'that some lessons applicable to present-day warfare should be deductible from it'.[14] May's suggestion that his central theme might be 'The deflection of strategy by politics', reinforced by similar advice from Sir George Clarke (later Lord Sydenham), the first Secretary of the Committee of Imperial Defence, set the tone of his first lecture series and, as well, his 1903 Ford Lectures at Oxford, and his next book, *England in the Mediterranean: A Study of the Rise and Influence of British Power Within the Straits, 1603–1713*, published in 1904.

These early lectures ranged broadly from Roman examples through Napoleonic–Nelsonic themes to later nineteenth-century developments and, after 1906, the Russo-Japanese War. In 1905, his focus shifted quite dramatically when, following May's death, Captain Edmond Slade became Director of the College. By then Corbett, Slade and Captain Charles Ottley (Director of Naval Intelligence) were jointly pressing Fisher on a number of fronts, including the need for a proper naval staff and a general improvement in the Navy's strategic thinking and education. They succeeded only to the extent that Fisher was prepared to use the War Course as an *ad hoc* planning body.[15] Another result was Corbett's appointment for a new series of lectures 'with a view to a more thorough study of the laws of strategy on the part of naval officers'.[16]

This increased emphasis on theory corresponded to other general modifications to the Course in the autumn of 1905, when it was moved from Greenwich, first to Devonport and then, in early 1906, to Portsmouth where it remained until 1914. The student body was also enlarged from under twenty officers to thirty-six (four admirals, twelve captains, twelve commanders, four lieutenants and four Royal Marine or army officers).[17] The changed emphasis for Corbett also reflected his and Slade's sensing of what was needed to bring their students on side. In Professor Schurman's words:

> from the teaching point of view Corbett was faced with the almost insurmountable task of teaching strategy, and the history it was based on, at the same time. He had, as well, to entertain or be ignored.[18]

THE 'GREEN PAMPHLET' (1906)

Their joint response was a document, issued to the students early in 1906, entitled 'Strategical Terms and Definitions Used in Lectures on Naval

History' or, as it became more commonly known, the 'Green Pamphlet'.[19] It was re-issued in revised and stylistically improved form in 1909 as 'Notes on Strategy'.[20] Designed as a glossary of commonly used terms, it provided some common ground between teacher and students. In Slade's words, the intention was to 'fix the terminology, as the looseness with which men talked about strategy was one of the great hindrances to the proper appreciation of what it meant'.[21] They also saw it as a means of weaning their audiences from their instinctive adulation of Nelsonic ideals and folk-history approaches to strategy which Mahan's books tended to reinforce.

Rather than searching in conventional fashion for Jominian 'principles of war' or fundamental laws governing operational conduct, the 'Pamphlet' encouraged a Clausewitzian concern with first of all understanding the nature of war itself. From the outset, Corbett insisted that 'Naval strategy does not exist as a separate branch of knowledge. It is a section of a division of the art of war. The study for officers is the art of war ... The true method of procedure then is to get hold of a general theory of war and so ascertain the exact relations of Naval Strategy to the whole.'[22] Paraphrasing Clausewitz, he suggested that at the heart of this theory was the notion: 'War is a form of political intercourse, a continuation of foreign politics which begins when force is introduced to attain our ends.' Those ends or war aims, Corbett argued, would dictate or shape what he called 'Major' strategy. 'Minor' strategy, on the other hand, was concerned with the planning and execution of specific operations that gave substance to those higher ends. This important distinction underscored the point that the actions of fleets or armies were not ends in themselves but were rather instruments of those ends; 'Naval Strategy or Fleet Strategy is only a sub-division of strategy, and that, therefore, strategy cannot be studied from the point of view of naval operations only.'[23]

Careful definition of the nature of those political objectives would therefore determine the kind of strategy; whether 'offensive' (with a positive object) or 'defensive' (negative). The advantages and disadvantages of both were then compared. Initially he appears to endorse his contemporaries' faith in the offence's intrinsic superiority. 'The Offensive, being positive in its aims, is naturally the more effective form of war and, as a rule, should be adopted by the stronger power.'[24] Yet, in the next two sub-sections ('Functions and Characteristics of the Defensive', and 'Offensive Operations Used With A Defensive Intention') he went on to subtly make his case for the Defence's ultimate importance, especially for a sea Power.

> At sea we have had little occasion for the defensive as a general plan. But that is no reason for neglecting its study. In despising the defensive ourselves we have consistently ignored the strength it gives our enemies. The bulk of our naval history is the story of how we have been bluffed and thwarted by our enemies assuming the defensive at sea in support of their

offensive on land. We seldom succeeded in treating this attitude with success, and it is only by studying the defensive we can hope to do so.[25]

In highlighting these distinctions between offensive and defensive strategies defined by the nature of the ulterior object of the war, Corbett was following Clausewitz's lead. He also introduced here the further distinction between 'Limited' and 'Unlimited' wars based not simply on restrictions of weapons and means or of geographical extent but, more importantly, on political intentions. War with limited object was defined as 'where we merely seek to take from the enemy some particular part of his possessions or interests; e.g. Spanish–American War, where the object was the liberation of Cuba'. Unlimited war implied the complete overthrow of the enemy. Beyond these examples, however, Corbett went no further here in developing their implications. In *Some Principles* they became central to his whole argument.

The remainder of Part I of the 'Green Pamphlet' was devoted to some definitions of Plans of War, Objects and Objectives, Lines of Operation (Interior and Exterior), Lines of Communication, and Maritime Communications. In themselves they are straightforward and unremarkable definitions. How he used them was another matter:

> Maritime Strategy has never been regarded as hinging on communications, but (in fact) probably it does so even more than 'Land Strategy', as will appear from a consideration of maritime communications, and the extent to which they are the main preoccupation of naval operations ... all problems of Naval Strategy can be reduced to terms of 'passage and communications', and this is probably the best method of solving them.[26]

This theme provides the key to Corbett's whole theoretical structure and would dominate everything else he wrote.

In Part II of the 'Green Pamphlet', entitled 'Naval Strategy Considered as a Question of Passage and Communication', he turned to the troublesome concept of Command of the Sea:

> This means something quite different from the military idea of occupying territory, for the sea cannot be the subject of political dominion or ownership. We cannot subsist upon it (like an army on conquered territory), nor can we exclude neutrals from it. The value of the sea in the political system of the world is as a means of communication between States and parts of States. Therefore the 'command of the sea' means the control of communications in which the belligerents are adversely concerned. The command of the sea can never be, like the conquest of territory, the ulterior object of a war, unless it be a purely maritime war ...[27]

That control of communications, he suggested, could exist only in wartime. It could be General or Local, Permanent or Temporary in nature. The normal situation would be when Command had not been clearly decided and was in a state of Dispute, 'at least in the early stages of the war, and frequently all through it'. A 'preponderating' navy would usually want to end that state as quickly as possible by forcing a decision, usually through battle. The weaker navy conversely would avoid battle in order to prolong that state of dispute for as long as possible. Turning to 'Methods of Securing Command', he noted that 'Permanent general control' could only be won by a decisive fleet action, while 'Local and temporary control' could come from a partially successful action, by diverting forces to a concentration in another area, by masking enemy forces to deny their use in a particular theatre, and through blockade. This latter method, so frequently neglected or imperfectly understood, could be a Close Blockade designed to lock an enemy fleet in port, a Commercial Blockade that controlled both belligerent and neutral floating trade and, finally, an observational (or open) blockade which along with certain 'subsidiary operations' aimed at enticing enemy forces out to sea 'to bring him to decisive action'. These subsidiary operations would include diversionary attacks against the enemy's coast or important parts of his seaborne trade. Interestingly, in the light of later wartime developments, he sensed that both the Close naval and Commercial blockades would be more difficult to execute under modern conditions:

> owing to the existence of submarines and torpedo craft, the blockading ships have to remain further away from the port; there have to be inner lines of cruisers, scouts and destroyers; and quick concentration takes longer owing to the greater space covered by the blockading force, and more ships of all natures are required for the same reason.[28]

Concentration and readiness for immediate action remained, in his view, the 'guiding feature of modern preparation for war'. This did not imply, however, that old maxims such as 'keep your forces together' or 'never divide the fleet' required a single concentration of forces. Rather, the guiding principle should be '... to dispose the forces at sea so as to be able to concentrate them in time at the decisive point so soon as this point is determined, and also to conceal from the enemy what it is intended to make the decisive point'.[29] The right dispositions in this sense would simultaneously confer control over all lines of passage and the ability to meet any operation the enemy initiates.

On this note, the 'Pamphlet' concluded with a brief commentary entitled 'The Peculiarity of Maritime Communications'. The fact that at sea the communications of both sides were frequently identical or parallel, he observed, dominates and controls naval warfare. 'Nearly all our current maxims of Naval Strategy can be traced to the pressure it exerts on naval thought.' It was also 'at the root of the fundamental difference between Military and Naval Strategy, and affords the explanation of much strategical error and confusion which have arisen from applying the principles of land warfare to the sea without allowing for the antagonistic conditions of the communications and the operations against them in each case'.[30] The old aphorisms, such as 'the proper place for our fleet is off the enemy's coast', 'the enemy's coast is our true frontier', and 'the primary object of the fleet is to seek out the enemy's fleet and destroy it', retained their validity but should never be treated as immutable principles. 'Nine times out of ten', he noted, 'the maxim of seeking out the enemy's fleet, &c., is sound and applicable . . .' It should also be remembered, however, that 'nine times out of ten the most effective way of "seeking out the enemy's fleet" (i.e., of forcing an action upon him) is to seize a position which controls communications vital to his plan of campaign'. Perhaps the 'true maxim' would be: 'The primary object of the fleet is to secure communications, and if the enemy's fleet is in a position to render them unsafe it must be put out of action.' Two final caveats were inserted: '(1) That if you seek out the enemy fleet with a superior force you will probably find it in a place where you cannot destroy it except at heavy cost', and '(2) That seeing that the defensive is the stronger form of war than the offensive, it is *prima facie* better strategy to make the enemy come to you than to go to him and seek a decision on his own ground.'[31]

PITT'S 'SYSTEM'

This was the 'Green Pamphlet' – a bare-bones outline of Corbett's thinking at that point. The most fully fleshed-out version of the same ideas appeared in his next book, *England in the Seven Years War: A Study in Combined Operations*. Started at the same time as the 'Green Pamphlet' and finished in July 1907, this monumental two-volume study also grew directly out of his lectures and was in large measure another attempt to meet his students' needs for simultaneous instruction in difficult strategic concepts and the history from which they flowed. In Professor Schurman's words:

> *England in the Seven Years War* showed the exasperating complexity of the connection between military and political policy. Whether it demonstrated firmly the truth of all of the strategic philosophy it introduced is open to doubt. What is incontestable is that in this book for the first time theory of war and detailed naval history, on the grand strategy scale and taken from source materials, were made to illuminate one another . . .[32]

Corbett evidently settled on the theme of the Elder Pitt's 'system' of war-making on a global scale because it so aptly illustrated his lectures on limited war and combined operations.³³ Indeed it was *the* premier case study of the development and use of the kind of policies the need for which he had explored in his earlier studies of the Elizabethan and Stuart periods. 'Of all our wars', he noted in his opening chapter, 'there is none beside Pitt's war which is so radiant with the genius of a maritime state, and none which was so uniformly successful.'³⁴ And in Pitt's conduct of the war, as Peter Stanford has suggested,

> Corbett had found the ideal expression for the new idea of strategy he had been reaching for. It was as though, having followed the British maritime experience from its very source and spring in the Elizabethan age, Corbett's own ideas had been shaped as those of the great leaders whose naval and diplomatic policy he studied had been shaped, until at last he was able to state the meaning of the elder Pitt's consummate overall strategy in a theoretical framework large enough to accommodate its full meaning.³⁵

That framework also permitted him to extend his disagreement with naval conservatives regarding Command of the Sea and fleet actions. Although he was careful not to denigrate entirely the importance of seizing opportunities to secure command through such engagements, he again warned that such opportunities had been the exception in naval history. Moreover fixation on these 'rare moments' had the effect of obscuring their true significance and the circumstances that made them possible:

> The imagination comes naturally to concentrate itself upon such supreme catastrophes and to forget that war is not made up of them. Historians, greedy of dramatic effect, encourage such concentrations of attention, and the result is that the current conception of the functions of a fleet is dangerously narrowed, and our best minds cramp their strategical view by assuming unconsciously that the sole function of a fleet is to win battles at sea ... The great dramatic moments of naval strategy have to be worked for, and the first preoccupation of the fleet will almost always be to bring them about by interference with the enemy's military and diplomatic arrangements.³⁶

This suggested to him that modern planners and policy makers needed a much broader conception, a 'wider vision' of naval strategy:

> something that will keep before our eyes not merely the enemy's fleets or the great routes of commerce, or the command of the sea, but also the relations of naval policy and action to the whole area of diplomatic and military effort. Of late years the world has become so deeply impressed with the efficacy of sea power that we are inclined to forget how impotent

it is of itself to decide a war against great Continental states, how tedious is the pressure of naval action unless it be nicely coordinated with military and diplomatic pressure.

He called therefore for a rejection of easily remembered slogans and formulae in favour of reasoned historical argument as the basis of that broadening process.

> Instead of cramping our outlook by well-turned definitions, let us inquire of history what in past wars the functions of the fleet have been, what the actual objects for which it has been employed. For all that long series of wars which gave Great Britain first her position in Europe, and then in the world, the answer is simple and constant. The function of the fleet, the object for which it was always employed, has been threefold: firstly, to support or obstruct diplomatic effort; secondly, to protect or destroy commerce; and thirdly, to further or hinder military operations ashore.[37]

FISHER'S PEN

As he was completing *England in the Seven Years War*, Corbett's own efforts to apply some 'wider vision' to current questions took the form of writing several of his more important magazine articles,[38] his involvement in a secret Admiralty committee under Captain George Ballard to draw up war plans, and then helping to prepare the Admiralty's case before the CID Invasion Inquiry of 1907–8. In the latter case, the impressive analysis by Corbett and Slade (who by then was DNI) of the precedents for dealing with invasion threats, from the Spanish Armada to Napoleon, effectively silenced the 'bolt from the blue' alarms sounded by Lord Roberts and other army pro-conscriptionists, including the influential *Times* military correspondent Colonel à Court Repington.[39] That same research was developed into a new eight-lecture series on invasion plans and attempts which were delivered at Devonport in January 1907 and repeated over the next three months at Chatham and Portsmouth.

Corbett's contribution to the *ad hoc* Ballard war plans committee appointed by Fisher was much less positive in outcome and raises doubts about Corbett's actual influence on events by that time. Several authors have examined the committee's work and generally have concluded that this admittedly amateurish exercise in comprehensive planning – the only instance prior to 1914 – was devised by Fisher primarily to meet Admiral Beresford's charges that plans did not exist.[40] In Paul Haggie's judgement, the plans that were contrived demonstrated clearly

> the lack of an agreed basis for strategic planning within the navy, and how little notice had been taken of the revolutionary developments in sea

warfare [that is, mines and submarines in particular] that marked the latter half of the nineteenth century. Speed of execution may be to blame for some of the inconsistencies and omissions, but it cannot be held responsible for the fundamental confusion of thought revealed. Under pressure, Fisher's administration had produced war plans, and this in itself was undeniably an advance on the vague and woolly generalisations of the past; but the plans themselves serve only as proof of the distance the navy still had to go before it possessed a brain commensurate with the speed and sophistication of modern sea warfare.[41]

The main source of confusion was an obvious contradiction between Corbett's long introduction, which assumed that the foundation of any strategy would be an Open blockade, and the detailed Plans themselves, drafted by the other committee members, which in some instances presumed a Close blockade. This serious inconsistency arose from the fact that Corbett was called in only in March 1907 to assist the Committee. The other members, in addition to Ballard (Director of Naval Operations until July 1906), were Slade and Captain Maurice Hankey, RMA, who acted as secretary. They had been meeting secretly at the War College since the late summer of 1906. Corbett was never shown the latter sections of the Plans. His introductory section, entitled 'Some Principles of Naval Warfare', amounted to a précis of the 'Green Pamphlet's general principles to which he appended a compressed version of his more recent articles defending the *Dreadnought* battleship and battle-cruiser concepts and arguing the case for setting clear priorities in terms of cruiser needs between their work with the battle fleet and their commitment to protecting and controlling trade in war. Whatever Corbett had hoped ultimately to achieve here, it was not an attempt, as has been suggested, to apply Pitt's 'eighteenth-century recipes' to the solution of twentieth-century problems.[42] In any case, the plans failed to impress Beresford who derided them as 'the Pedagogue's Plan'. Fisher's successor as First Sea Lord, Admiral Sir Arthur Wilson, annotated his copy with the comment that Corbett's introduction 'does not require any remarks as it only deals with general principles'.[43] Fisher had pulled Corbett into this whole curious episode to add 'an epitome of the Art of Naval War' that was to be known as 'the Bible of the War Course'.[44] He never got it. Nor does it seem possible that he genuinely saw a highly secret war-planning exercise as the most propitious place or set of circumstances for it. In that respect, Admiral Wilson's remark was not misplaced. The attitude it reflected in a more general sense, however, was one that Corbett set out to confront when in 1911 he did produce his 'Bible'.

SOME PRINCIPLES OF MARITIME STRATEGY

The book is a much extended version of the 'Green Pamphlet', revised and tempered in its tone by his brushes with controversy. It is structured in three major segments: Part I, an overview of recent European writing on general war theory; Part II, an analysis of naval theory; and Part III, a discussion of naval operations. The introductory section on 'The Theoretical Study of War' obviously was written to head off the indifference and mistrust that Admiral Wilson's comments suggested many naval officers felt to any abstract approach to war.

He clarified his own expectations of theory's value: 'It does not pretend to give the power of conduct in the field; it claims no more than to increase the effective power of conduct.' Like Mahan, Corbett did believe in the existence of timeless features and concepts of strategy, but he never suggested that history's 'lessons' could produce prescriptions for the correct conduct of operations. For him study, discussion and reflection were essential parts of the processes of creating an educated mind, of nurturing intellectual reflexes that could distinguish from past patterns what had worked or had not. Using an analogy his students would appreciate, he explained theory's role this way:

> Navigation and the parts of seamanship that belong to it have to deal with phenomena as varied and unreliable as those of the conduct of war. Together they form an art which depends quite as much as generalship on the judgment of individuals. The law of storms and tides, of winds and currents, and the whole of meteorology are subject to infinite and incalculable deflections, and yet who will deny nowadays that by the theoretical study of such things the seaman's art has gained in coherence and strength? Such study will not by itself make a seaman or a navigator, but without it no seaman or navigator can nowadays pretend to the name. Because storms do not always behave in the same way, because currents are erratic, will the most practical seaman deny that the study of the normal conditions are useless to him in his practical decisions?[45]

Theory also provided a basis for 'mental solidarity' – between commanders and subordinates, and between commanders and their political masters. 'How often', he asked,

> have officers dumbly acquiesced in ill-advised operations simply for lack of the mental power and verbal apparatus to convince an impatient Minister where the errors of his plan lay? How often, moreover, have statesmen and officers, even in the most harmonious conference, been unable to decide on a coherent plan of war from inability to analyse scientifically the situation they had to face, and to recognise the general character of the struggle in which they were about to engage. That the true nature of a war should be realised by contemporaries as clearly as it comes to be seen afterwards in the fuller light of history is seldom to be expected.

At close range accidental factors will force themselves into undue prominence and tend to obscure the true horizon. Such error can scarcely ever be eliminated, but by theoretical study we can reduce it, nor by any other means can we hope to approach the clearness of vision with which posterity will read our mistakes. Theory is, in fact, a question of education and deliberation, and not of execution at all.[46]

For a maritime Power, an understanding of general warfare theory was especially important as the only means of grasping where naval and military strategy stand in relation to each other. 'It is the theory of war which brings out their intimate relation. It reveals that embracing them both is a larger strategy which regards the fleet and army as one weapon, which coordinates their action, and indicates the lines on which each must move to realise the full power of both.'[47]

Part I   Theory of War

At this point, Corbett very carefully spelled out his disagreement with the idea that there existed a distinct 'naval' school of strategy separate from the 'Continental' or 'German' school. Quite the contrary, his reading of history confirmed the existence of a specifically 'British' school or practice that defined maritime strategy as an extension of 'Continental' strategy, not a competing alternative. He saw Clausewitz (and to a lesser extent, Jomini) as the leading modern theorist whose unfinished work he wanted to push forward into its unexplored maritime dimension.

Standing at the final point which Clausewitz and Jomini reached we are indeed only on the threshold of the subject. We have to begin where they left off and inquire what their ideas have to tell for modern conditions of world-wide imperial states, where the sea becomes a direct and vital factor.[48]

His opening chapter was therefore an overview of contemporary European writing to show where Britain's case fitted into that continental mainstream. To a far greater extent than he had in the 'Green Pamphlet', Corbett acknowledged his debt to Jomini and Clausewitz. He also emphasised where he differed seriously with their military disciples in his own applications of their ideas. He had distanced himself from navalist extremists by insisting on a distinction between maritime and naval strategies. Here he also challenged what he called the 'cramping' effect of contemporary fascination with Napoleonic models that were assumed to have simply outdated all earlier experience and method.

Our teachers incline to insist that there is now only one way of making war, and that is Napoleon's way. Ignoring the fact that he failed in the end, they brand as heresy the bare suggestion that there may be other ways, and not content with assuming that his system will fit all land wars, however much their natures and objects may differ, they would force naval warfare into the same uniform under the impression apparently that they are making it presentable and giving it some new force.[49]

In resisting this forcing of all theory into Napoleonic garb, Corbett performed a service to subsequent strategic thought that would be hard to overrate. His reading of Clausewitz was unusual, especially for his generation. Most European soldiers had been profoundly affected by Clausewitz in some way. His impact on the German army probably resulted more from his associations with the earlier Prussian military reformers (Scharnhorst and Gneisenau) and the achievements of his later disciples (the elder von Moltke and von Schlieffen) than from any profound reading of his text or endorsement of his approach and methodology, which really were the basis of his most original achievement. Instead, they were drawn to the more practical and secondary aspects of his thought: the role of genius in war, of moral forces, offensive spirit, and the primacy of battle. In France, and to some extent Britain and the United States, Clausewitz assumed importance after 1870 as military fashion came to ape almost everything Prussian. With Ferdinand Foch and his more enthusiastic followers, Clausewitz's discussions of morale, the offensive, and decisive battle were given a uniquely French flavouring and formulated into a doctrine in which the problems of relating national war aims to practicable strategies were utterly lost to an exaggerated faith in the *offensive à outrance*. All the General Staffs ignored Clausewitz's insistence on the subordination of military means to political purpose, not because they considered the idea wrong so much as because, to them, it seemed anachronistic in a Europe of increasingly aggressive and mobilised nations. Wilfully or not, the General Staffs disregarded Clausewitz's more complex aspects. Corbett did not.

He grasped the significance of Clausewitz's distinctions between 'absolute' and 'real' war and, on an entirely different plane, 'total' and 'limited' war, that had led him to his well-known but elemental formulation 'that war is a mere continuation of policy by other means'.[50] That meant, Corbett sensed, that wars need not necessarily or automatically tend to become total or Napoleonic. This was not an argument for a return to an earlier golden age of limited wars. Quite the contrary; Corbett seems to have understood that Clausewitz was actually warning, not proposing, that wars shaped only by operational possibilities, free from overriding political reasoning, could and probably would of their own accord move towards the more absolute form. The 'primordial' strategic issue then, Corbett reasoned, was that of deciding upon the nature of the war to be fought. Only then could a suitable war plan or strategy be determined: 'To assume that one method of conducting war will suit all kinds of war is to fall victim to abstract theory, and not to be a prophet of reality, as the narrowest disciples of the Napoleonic school are inclined to see themselves.'[51] Implicitly, Corbett lumped Jomini (and therefore Mahan) within that group.

His discussion of Offensive and Defensive wars (Chapter II) and Limited and Unlimited wars (Chapter III) went beyond his 'Green Pamphlet' treatment of these definitions. Here it was the latter that he emphasised. The broad classifications of wars as 'offensive' or 'defensive', 'positive' or 'negative', were still useful, he suggested, though only insofar as they highlight the inherent advantages of each in specific situations. He still worried that military professionals instinctively regarded the offence as embodying the true 'military spirit' while the defence was 'always stupid or pusillanimous, leading always to defeat'.[52] Far more productive as a broad classification was that of 'limited' versus 'unlimited wars' which, as he explained, Clausewitz himself 'in the plenitude of his powers' had come to sense was 'the master key of the subject'. Corbett's description of the great Prussian thinker's late-life conversion on this question and his speculations on how it might have influenced the final form of his unfinished *Vom Krieg* manuscript was hardly remarkable, except that he was one of the very few in that pre-First World War generation to give it serious credence. When, however, Crobett determined to extend Clausewitz's unfinished speculations as a basis for demonstrating 'the radical and essential differences between the German or Continental School of Strategy and the British or Maritime School – that is, our own traditional School' and, further, to explore their application to contemporary British conceptions, he entered upon his own most important, and controversial, material.

In Chapter IV, 'Limited War and Maritime Empires', he showed that both Clausewitz and Jomini, naturally enough, had discussed limited wars from the perspective of land warfare usually between contiguous States. Depending on the geographical location of the disputed territory and also how far either belligerent was prepared to push events, it was not always possible to prevent a war of defined objectives from going total. Two conditions were therefore vital to the concept of a limited object:

> Firstly, it must not be limited merely in area, but of really limited political importance; and secondly, it must be so situated as to be strategically isolated or to be capable of being reduced to practical isolation by strategical operations.[53]

Citing examples of maritime or 'mixed' wars such as the Seven Years, the Crimea, the Spanish–American and Russo–Japanese, he argued that it was the peculiar ability of sea Powers to isolate their object and at the same time defend themselves against an unlimited counter-stroke that allowed them to meet these conditions. He concluded, therefore:

that limited war is only permanently possible to island Powers or between Powers which are separated by sea, and then only when the Power desiring limited war is able to command the sea to such a degree as to be able not only to isolate the distant object, but also to render impossible the invasion of his home territory.

In this proposition Corbett encapsulated his unmatched grasp of three centuries of naval history, his explanation of Britain's power world-wide and in Europe, and his conception of 'the true meaning and highest military value of what we call command of the sea'.[54]

In Chapter V, 'Wars of Intervention – Limited Interference in Unlimited War', he advanced what later critics considered his most questionable argument; namely, that Britain's sea-conferred imperviousness to invasion and control of inter-continental communications had allowed her to commit her limited military resources in support of her continental allies' larger operations without necessarily becoming entangled in their broader political objectives. Generally, these 'combined operations' as he called them were directed at overseas territorial goals or projections against the European coast in the form of raids, diversions or even invasions of more far-reaching effect. The classic expressions of this 'war with a disposal force' were Pitt's system of raids against France and operations against Canada, Wellington's actions in Portugal and Spain, and the Crimean War. The importance of these methods, that distinguished them from what Clausewitz labelled 'war by contingent' and gave British forces an operative impact far beyond their intrinsic military power, was determined by their 'touch with the sea'.

> It was not till the peninsular War developed that we found a theatre for war limited by contingent in which all the conditions that make for success were present ... The real secret of Wellington's success – apart from his own genius – was that in perfect conditions he was applying the limited form to an unlimited war. Our object was unlimited. It was nothing less than the overthrow of Napoleon. Complete success at sea had failed to do it, but that success had given us the power of applying the limited form, which was the most decisive form of offence within our means. Its substantial contribution to the final achievement of the object is now universally recognised.[55]

What perplexed later commentators was whether the ideal circumstances of the Spanish theatre could be duplicated, by design or by accident. And under modern conditions of vastly improved overland communications (rail and telegraph), could not such threats be neutralised or crushed, or even ignored?[56] Corbett himself raised the possibility that such conditions might not exist. In that case, British options would be reduced to directly reinforcing their ally's forces, or mounting coastal diversions whose effect he admitted might be marginal. 'The small positive results of our efforts to intervene in this way have indeed done more than anything to discredit this form of war, and to brand it as unworthy of a first-class Power.' Still, the strategic and psychological value of this form of war frequently outweighed its actual operational result.

> Its operative action was that it threatened positive results unless it were strongly met. Its effect, in short, was negative. Its value lay in its power of containing force greater than its own. That is all that can be claimed for it, but it may be all that is required.[57]

In Chapter VI, 'Conditions of Strength in Limited War', he followed this argument through to reinforce the point that although his limited war ideas were out of step with current European military fashion, they none the less reflected a 'sagacious instinct' for what best suited Britain's conditions and capacities. But, he also warned:

> The fact that the doctrine of limited war traverses the current belief that our primary object must always be the enemy's armed forces is liable to carry with it a false inference that it also rejects the corollary that war means the use of battles. Nothing is further from the conception. Whatever the form of war, there is no likelihood of our ever going back to the old fallacy of attempting to decide war by manoeuvres. All forms alike demand the use of battles. By our fundamental theory war is always a 'continuation of political intercourse, in which fighting is substituted for writing notes'. However great the controlling influence of the political object, it must never obscure the fact that it is by fighting we have to gain our end.[58]

Corbett's plea then was not for a return to eighteenth-century manoeuvre warfare when, supposedly, generalship was measured in terms of battles avoided: 'With such parading limited war has nothing to do.' What it did entail for navies was the subject of the next two sections.

Part II Theory of Naval War

Moving from the level of general theory to fleet or naval strategy, Corbett reiterated his thinking on Command of the Sea and the notion of common maritime communications that lay at its root. His arguments here (Chapter I, 'Theory of the Object–Command of the Sea', and Chapter III, 'Theory of the Method–Concentration and Dispersal of Force') regarding the place of battle and the various degrees of command are essentially those of the 'Green Pamphlet'. He added a section on blockade and the rights of belligerents to control neutral shipping in war. It incorporated the substance of his 1907 article, 'The Capture of Private Property at Sea'[59] that had been reprinted in Mahan's *Some Neglected Aspects of War* (1907). The significance of his defence of traditional British practice and claims would become evident during the War, and after as well, when Anglo-American differences on the question of belligerents' rights versus freedom of the seas brought relations between the two Powers almost to the breaking-point.[60] Here Corbett dispassionately marshalled the bases of Britain's long-standing opposition to any abolition or restrictions of those rights which would undermine the whole conception and utility of naval operations. 'Without it, indeed', he reasoned, 'naval warfare is almost inconceivable, and in any case no one has any experience of such a truncated method of war on which profitable study can be founded.'[61]

Chapter II of this section, 'The Constitution of Fleets', similarly reasserted the main burden of his arguments on ship design and functions, particularly those of cruisers, contained in his earlier articles, the 'Introduction' to the 1906 War Plans and his *Trafalgar* book. Once again he worried that current preoccupations with the role of cruisers for fleet protection and reconaissance functions could restrict their availability for blockade, control and convoy work. Invoking Nelson's wisdom, he pointed out that the 'Eyes of the Fleet' concept had never been seen as the cruisers' primary role. Their 'true function' was to exert the control won or sought by the battle fleets.

> Judged by his record, no man ever grasped more clearly than Nelson that the object of naval warfare was to control communications, and if he found that he had not a sufficient number of cruisers to exercise that control and to furnish eyes for his battle-fleet as well, it was the battle fleet that was made to suffer, and surely this is at least the logical view.[62]

Resolving what he called 'Nelson's dilemma' had never been easy, nor would it be in the future. The evidence suggested to him, however, that 'as a general principle cruisers should be regarded as primarily concerned with the active occupation of communications, and that withdrawals for fleet purposes should be reduced to the furthest margin of reasonable risk'.[63] This of course was one of the critical dilemmas of the First World War. Those, including Corbett, Richmond and his circle of reform-minded associates (most notably Commanders Reggie Henderson and Kenneth Dewar) and others who pushed for the introduction of convoys as an antidote to Germany's unrestricted U-boat offensive were able successfully to demonstrate that sufficient escorts were available provided destroyer resources so heavily assigned to the Grand Fleet could be diverted.[64]

Part III 'The Conduct of Naval War'

In the opening chapters ('Introductory' and 'Methods of Securing Command') of this final section of the book, Corbett retraced his earlier positions on battlefleet operations for winning command. His assessment here of blockade operations in their various naval and commercial forms and differing strategic purposes, reflected his feeling that modern conditions probably favoured the use of more distant or open forms. Still, by illustrating how in previous wars decisions between Close or Open blockades had never been based solely on naval needs, he reasoned that policy and grand strategy considerations would predominate in the future. He therefore reserved judgement, suggesting that:

> however high may be the purely naval and strategical reasons for adopting open blockade as the best means of securing a decision against the enemy's fleet, yet the inevitable intrusion of the ulterior object in the form of trade protection or the security of military expeditions will seldom leave us entirely free to use the open method.[65]

In the converse situation, 'Methods of Disputing Command' (Chapter III), he redeployed his discussion on 'Fleet in being' doctrine, tracing its development in French and British practice since the seventeenth century to show that defensive thinking was not heretical:

> with the voice of Torrington, Kempenfeldt, and Nelson in our ears, it would be folly to ignore [the defensive] for ourselves, and still more to ignore the exhausting strain its use by our enemy may impose upon us. It must be studied, if for no other reasons than to learn how to break it down. Nor will the study have danger, if only we keep well in view the spirit of restless and vigilant counter-attack which Kempenfeldt and Nelson regarded as its essence. True some of the conditions which in the days of sails made for opportunity have passed away, but many still remain.[66]

One such area he examined under the heading of 'Minor Counter-Attacks'. Although there were no historical instances of such attacks seriously threatening command, he wondered if torpedo attacks such as the Japanese had mounted against the Russian squadron in Port Arthur in 1905 represented a fundamentally new departure or merely a passing phase akin to the fireships of earlier days. The portents were anything but obvious. He worried, however, that 'The advent of the torpedo ... has given the idea [of minor counter-attacks] a new importance that cannot be overlooked.' Similarly, he withheld judgement on the potentials of submarines; their 'unproved value only deepens the mist which overhangs the next naval war'. Strategically, he concluded:

> we can say no more than that we have to count with a new factor, which gives a new possibility to minor counter-attack. It is a possibility which on

the whole tells in favour of naval defence, a new card which, skilfully played in combination with defensive fleet operations may lend fresh importance to the 'Fleet in Being'.[67]

Given the state of submarine technology to that point, it is perhaps not surprising that he considered submarines only in this limited role, and said nothing about their potential as strategic weapons in their own right. He was hardly unique in being unable to penetrate those overhanging mists; no one prior to the war foresaw German U-boats sheltering under the strategic umbrella of the High Seas Fleet in a complete reversal of their expected roles. More surprising, perhaps, was his failure even to mention the impact of aircraft.

Corbett's assumption that modern technological developments inherently favoured the naval defence raised some interesting points and contradictions in Sections I and III of his final chapter on 'Methods of Exercising Command'. In 'Defence against Invasion' he reinforced his CID Invasion Inquiry arguments, confident that success was assured in the future, providing the old policy of going first for the transports and not the escorting forces of the invaders was followed. Since the new weapons increased the flexibility and hitting power of the 'flotilla', that principle would not change, he felt. In the Second World War, Admiral Richmond would advance a similar argument when he suggested that the RAF's Fighter Command should be viewed as a 'highly formidable reinforcement' of the then overstretched anti-invasion flotilla of cruisers and destroyers.[68]

Much the same held true, Corbett suggested, with respect to British overseas combined operations. He manoeuvred around the apparent contradiction here about developments favouring the defence by arguing that, so long as general command existed, and naval units were deployed as independent or uncommitted covering forces to forestall enemy interference with the landing forces and their escorts, the defence would be overcome. These arguments, together with his plea for joint planning and the closest cooperation between the commanders, are reasoned and sensible, as might be expected in the light of Corbett's reputation as the leading exponent of conjunct strategies. This is not to suggest, however, that his estimation of the operational–tactical effects of mines, torpedoes and coastal artillery (and aircraft) and, at the strategic level, of railways, roads and telegraphic communications was not overly sanguine.

It was the penultimate section of this final chapter, on the 'Attack and Defence of Trade', that drew the most criticism for his underestimation of the importance of convoys in the coming war. The charge is justified, though of course it applied to virtually every writer at the time.[69] Indeed, as Professor Brian Ranft has shown, trade defence was perhaps the most neglected topic in the Victorian–Edwardian Navy.[70] Corbett, however, had not entirely ignored the subject. In company with Mahan, he was convinced that commerce attack had been and would continue to be an ineffective strategy against a major naval Power. Moreover, recent technical and other developments – the abolition of privateering (since 1856), steam technology and wireless telegraphy – as much as they assisted the potential attacker, also augmented Britain's ability to impose a crippling blockade. On balance, he remained convinced that the *guerre de course* threat to Britain was less than it had been. He was much less certain about the operational methods of trade defence, including convoy. As he admitted: 'Modern developments and changes in shipping and naval material have indeed so profoundly modified the whole conditions of commerce protection, that there is no part of strategy where historical deduction is more difficult or more liable to error.'[71] Perhaps it is worth noting that in early 1917, at the height of Germany's unrestricted U-boat offensive, many of the convoy's most ardent advocates looked upon it as useful only as an initial, even defensive, response. The ultimate solution, they expected, would come from an effective counter-offensive that stopped the submarines at their source. They were as surprised as anyone at the quick turnaround in the situation when in the late spring convoys were introduced.[72]

All this came later and serves mainly to make the point that the war held any number of surprises. When *Some Principles* was published, few of these deficiencies were detected. The reviews on both sides of the Atlantic were generally enthusiastic. The inevitable comparisons with Mahan were made, with Corbett in one instance referred to as a 'Super Mahan'.[73] Of course he was criticised, again mainly by those who had long resented his influence. The most vitriolic, perhaps, was a 'Captain R.N.' (presumably a former War Course member) who wrote that the book was the 'crowning mistake' of Corbett's career:

> For some years Mr. Corbett has, in the process of lecturing at the R.N. War College, permitted himself the indulgence of offering his audience his own views of the correctness or otherwise of the strategy adopted by naval officers in the past. His audience has usually treated his amateur excursions in to the subject good naturedly; nevertheless his presumption has been resented, and he has apparently been deaf to the polite hints thrown out to him that his opinion on strategy was of no concern to his listeners because as a civilian he was obviously incompetent to assess at their proper value the influences which purely naval considerations had on the problems which he was gratuitously attempting to solve.[74]

This must have stung Corbett. It could not have surprised him. His manner and his civilian status had always offended some officers, as his connections with Fisher had alienated others. The controversy surrounding his *Trafalgar* book the year before now resurfaced, this time led by Henry Spenser Wilkinson, a long-time Fisher critic and leading light in the 'Syndicate of

Discontent'. As military correspondent to the conservative *Morning Post*, Wilkinson had earlier attacked Fisher's use of the War Course as a *de facto* War Staff, and Corbett for teaching 'strategically false doctrine' there.[75] Now, in early 1912, he again warned that Corbett's book would have 'a disastrous effect upon the Navy, for it cannot but leave [naval officers'] minds in doubt upon every one of the principles which the strategists of the four great navies of the modern world are agreed as regarding as fundamental'. He warned against Corbett's de-emphasising of fleet actions, especially when it was so apparent that Germany's High Seas Fleet was designed to force a decision; 'it means to take the greatest risks for the greatest stakes'. He also challenged Corbett's views on limited war under modern conditions, recommending that his readers consult Mahan's 'admirable lectures' in preference to Corbett's 'confusing treatise'.[76]

How far Corbett's ideas, his lectures, his books or his connections actually did affect wartime events is treated elsewhere in this volume. Suffice it to note here that his prewar critics were the same individuals who, as the 'Victory School' during the war, publicly opposed the distant blockade and Jellicoe's refusals to risk unnecessarily the Grand Fleet as heresies perpetrated by Corbett.[77] In the light of the awful disappointment that Jutland was, it is not difficult to understand why such an inaccurate and unfair judgement could be made. Less easy to comprehend is the reality that another half-century would pass before a new generation of historians would finally sweep away the last of Jutland's dust and smoke that for too long obscured recognition of Corbett's gifts and legacies.

Notes

1. Julian S. Corbett, *Drake and the Tudor Navy* (London, 1898). That year he also edited for the Navy Records Society, *Papers Relating to the Navy during the Spanish War, 1585–1587* (London, 1898). His two earlier books for the 'English Men of Action Series' were *Monk* (London, 1898), and *Sir Francis Drake* (London, 1890).
2. 'The Revival of Naval History', *Contemporary Review* (Dec., 1916) pp. 734–5.
3. Donald M. Schurman, *The Education of a Navy: The Development of British Naval Thought, 1867–1914* (London, Chicago, Toronto, 1965; reprint Kreiger, 1984); and *Julian S. Corbett: Historian of British Maritime Policy from Drake to Jellicoe* (London, 1981).
4. 'Mahan and World War II: A Commentary from the United States', *Brassey's Naval Annual* (New York, 1941), reprinted in B. Mitchell Simpson III (ed.), *The Development of Naval Thought: Essays by Herbert Rosinski* (Newport, 1977) pp. 20–40.
5. National Maritime Museum, Greenwich, Corbett Papers, CP/B3, Corbett to Sir Henry Newbolt, 22 Oct 1905.
6. Schurman, *Education*, pp. 186–7; B. D. Hunt, *Sailor–Scholar: Admiral Sir Herbert Richmond, 1871–1946* (Waterloo, 1982) pp. 18–21.
7. J. S. Corbett, in consultation with Rear-Admiral Sir Edmond J. Slade, *Confiden-*

tial: *Maritime Operations in the Russo-Japanese War 1904–05*, 2 vols, issued under the direction of the Admiralty War Staff.
8. CP/B2, C. J. Longman to Corbett, 8 Aug 1910.
9. J. S. Corbett, *The Campaign of Trafalgar* (London, 1910) Preface, p. viii.
10. CP/'Deed Box', bound volume 'Lectures on Naval Strategy'.
11. CP/Diary, 2 April 1910.
12. See Schurman, *Corbett*, chapter VII, 'The Tactics of Trafalgar', pp. 113–30.
13. J. S. Corbett and H. J. Edwards (eds), *Cambridge Naval and Military Series*, University Press 1914–25, Volume I, *Naval and Military Essays*, 1914, 'Staff Histories', p. 31.
14. Schurman, *Corbett*, p. 33.
15. CP/B12, Fisher to Corbett, 22 & 24 May, 6 June 1905.
16. Richmond Papers (National Maritime Museum, Greenwich), RIC/9/1, Captain Charles Ottley to Corbett, 31 May 1905. Also, CP/'Deed Box', 'Lectures on Naval Strategy'.
17. 'Some Notes on the Early Days of the Royal Naval War College', *Naval Review*, vol. XIX, no. 2, (1931).
18. Schurman, *Corbett*, p. 44.
19. CP/B6, 'Strategical Terms and Definitions Used in Lectures on Naval History'. By Julian S. Corbett, Esq., LLM. (Proof corrected by Corbett with Slade listed as co-author).
20. RIC/2/2, Notes on Strategy. For the Information of Officers in H.M. Services Only. (RN War College, Portsmouth, No. 23, January 1909). No author is listed in this copy. It is the version currently issued to the Canadian Forces College, Toronto. Excerpts have also been published in G. E. Thibault (ed.), *The Art and Practice of Military Strategy* (Washington: National Defense University, 1984) Chapter IX. A full version is published as an appendix to the 1988 Naval Institute Press, Classics of Sea Power, edition of *Some Principles of Maritime Strategy*.
21. CP/B13, Slade to Corbett, 2 December 1906.
22. CP/B6, 'Strategical Terms', p. 2.
23. Ibid., p. 4.
24. RIC/2/2, Notes, p. 4.
25. Ibid., p. 6.
26. Ibid., p. 10.
27. Ibid.
28. Ibid.
29. Ibid., p. 18.
30. Ibid., p. 19.
31. Ibid., p. 12.
32. Schurman, *Education*, p. 169.
33. CP/'Deed Box', lecture notes.
34. J. S. Corbett, *England in the Seven Years War: A Study in Combined Strategy* (London, 1907, 2 vols), vol. I, p. 9.
35. P. M. Stanford, 'The Work of Sir Julian Corbett in the Dreadnought Era', *USNIP*, vol. 77, no. 1 (Jan 1951) p. 67.
36. Corbett, *Seven Years*, pp. 3–4.
37. Ibid., pp. 5–6.
38. 'Recent Attacks on the Admiralty', *Nineteenth Century* (Feb 1907); 'The Strategical Value of Speed in Battleships', *RUSI Journal* (July 1907); and 'The Capture of Private Property at Sea', *Nineteenth Century* (June 1907), reprinted in Mahan's *Some Neglected Aspects of War* (Boston, 1907).

39. Schurman, *Corbett*, chapter v, pp. 79–98. Copies of their submissions and supporting documents are contained in RIC/9/1, *Invasions and Raids* (Secret Admiralty Print). The full CID report is contained in PRO CAB 38/14, dated 22 Oct 1908.
40. See Schurman, *Corbett*, pp. 66–9; Paul Haggie, 'The Royal Navy and War Planning in the Fisher Era', in Paul Kennedy (ed.), *War Plans of the Great Powers, 1880–1914* (London, 1985) pp. 118–32; Lt-Cmdr P. K. Kemp (ed.), *The Papers of Admiral Sir John Fisher*, vol. II, Navy Records Society, 1964.
41. Haggie, 'The Royal Navy', pp. 124–5.
42. See Michael Howard, *The British Way in Warfare: A Reappraisal* (London, 1974) p. 12.
43. Schurman, *Corbett*, p. 69.
44. CP/B12, Fisher to Corbett, 17 March 1907.
45. J. S. Corbett, *Some Principles of Maritime Strategy* (London, 1911; New Impression, 1972) p. 2.
46. Ibid., p. 3.
47. Ibid., p. 8.
48. Ibid., p. 48.
49. Ibid., p. 14.
50. Ibid., p. 23.
51. Ibid., p. 25.
52. Ibid., p. 33.
53. Ibid., p. 52.
54. Ibid., pp. 54–5.
55. Ibid., pp. 61–2.
56. Howard, *The British Way*, pp. 12–13. See also Paul Kennedy, *The Rise and Fall of British Naval Mastery* (London, 1976) chapter VII, 'Mahan Versus Mackinder', pp. 177–204.
57. Corbett, *Some Principles*, p. 64.
58. Ibid., p. 82.
59. See note 38, above.
60. See Barry Hunt, 'British Policy on the Issue of Belligerent and Neutral Rights, 1919–1939', in Craig L. Symonds (ed.), *New Aspects of Naval History* (Annapolis, 1981) pp. 279–90.
61. *Some Principles*, p. 96.
62. Ibid., p. 112.
63. Ibid., p. 115.
64. See Hunt, *Sailor–Scholar*, pp. 56–81, *passim*.
65. *Some Principles*, p. 210.
66. Ibid., p. 228.
67. Ibid., pp. 233–4.
68. Hunt, *Sailor–Scholar*, pp. 226–7.
69. For example, Arnold White, 'The Chess Board at Sea', *Daily Chronicle* (13 Feb 1912). He wrote, 'we have probably seen the last of the convoy system'.
70. Brian Ranft (ed.), *Technical Change and British Naval Policy, 1860–1939* (London, 1977).
71. *Some Principles*, p. 269.
72. Hunt, *Sailor–Scholar*, pp. 74–5.
73. *The Standard*, 14 Dec 1911. Also, *The Times Literary Supplement*, 14 Dec 1911; *Pall Mall Gazette*, 14, 22 Dec 1911.
74. *Naval and Military Record, 1911*, p. 821. Viz., Fred T. Jane, 'Under the White Ensign', *Evening Standard*, 15 Jan 1912.

75. 'Strategy in the Navy', *Morning Post*, 13 Aug 1909.
76. *Morning Post*, 19 Feb, 24 April 1912.
77. A. J. Marder, *From the Dreadnought to Scapa Flow*, vol. IV, *1917: Year of Crisis* (Oxford, 1969) pp. 167–71.

8 Recent Thinking on the Theory of Naval Strategy
John B. Hattendorf

At the beginning of the Second World War, American naval strategists still based their fundamental concepts on the ideas that Alfred Thayer Mahan had expressed fifty years earlier. With Mahan, they shared the belief that the essential problem in naval warfare was to obtain 'command of the sea'. In other words, the way to protect oneself from the dangers which threaten across the vast, neutral expanse of the ocean is to deprive an opponent of his ability to move at sea. Mahan believed that there were two effective ways to do this. One could destroy an enemy fleet in a battle at sea, or one could blockade it in port in order to prevent its use. Fundamentally the Mahanian concept of sea power was based on the idea that the best defence is an offence. 'Command of the sea', which opens and assures the free use of the ocean to the victor, provides security by denying the use of the sea to the opponent.[1] The Navy that the United States built up so dramatically after 1940 was designed to perform this function.

NAVAL STRATEGY IN THE SECOND WORLD WAR

The experience of the Second World War tended to confirm for Americans the broad features of Mahan's thought, but the World War in two separate hemispheres brought home separate lessons.

The war in the Atlantic and in the Mediterranean was fought against naval Powers which did not share the concept of sea power held by the Anglo-American allies. The German and Italian navies persistently attempted to avoid the type of fleet battle sought by the Allies. Instead Germany and Italy concentrated on a single task: severing Allied lines of communication. The Axis Powers were initially in an advantageous position to undertake this. They had developed some very effective weapons, and German conquests on the continent placed Britain at a great disadvantage. Despite these initial strengths, the Allied defeat of this diametrically opposed system of strategy confirmed the basic correctness of Mahan's concept. Although naval battle seemed less important in the European theatre, the battle fleet had been essential in giving constant support and protection.[2] Analysts in America believed that the Allies had defeated the Axis navies by exercising command of the sea.

In the Pacific, Japan had gone to war with the notion that she could obtain victory, as she had in earlier wars, by maintaining a local 'command of the sea'. Japanese leaders failed to understand the full implications of what they had initiated, and they failed to prevent the transition from a 'limited war' to a 'total war'.[3] Surely this is what lay at the heart of Japan's defeat. Despite this, many Americans saw Mahan's ideas justified in the Pacific. They thought that the great battles of Midway and Leyte Gulf seemed conclusive proof that decisive victory in warfare was obtained through climactic battle between opposing fleets, and that these victories obtained command of the sea. This view tended to overlook the importance of amphibious operations, as well as the critical importance of American submarines and mines in destroying Japanese tankers and merchantmen, but Mahan had argued that this type of warfare was inconclusive.

MAHAN SINCE 1945

Mahan had been the first to explore rationally the fundamental problem of naval strategy. Despite some adverse criticism and developments which he could not foresee, many in America thought that his work had been vindicated by experience up to 1945.

Professional naval officers continued to employ his ideas and to structure the Navy's use and construction around them. At the Naval War College, for example, discussions and lectures on 'Mahan in the Nuclear Age' became commonplace. Many writers continued the effort to apply Mahan's ideas to the postwar world.[4] They were valiant attempts, but they raised some fundamental questions.

The questions came from a variety of sources. In the academic community, they came from both historians and political scientists. In the practical world of affairs, they came from those who were attempting to deal with the difficult problems of nuclear weapons and modern warfare, as well as from those who dealt in the day-to-day crises of cold war diplomacy.

Historians looked at the problem in two ways. One group looked at Mahan in relation to his own times, while another focussed on the same historical subject matter that he had studied. Historians have shown Mahan as a man within his own times, and a leader in the now unfashionable period of American imperialism. He was a 'navalist' who sought to enhance his own profession at the expense of others, and he was an advocate of the elitist, racist and social Darwinist ideas that were dominant in his day. As an individual, researchers found him to be the vaunted 'apostle of sea power', yet one whose personal characteristics were not those which the modern naval professional wanted to extol. To top it off, he was a naval officer who hated going to sea. None of these factors encouraged postwar students of naval strategy to regard Mahan as a prophet.[5]

Rejection of 'Scientific School' of History

Only a very few serious historians were working in the same field which Mahan had drawn upon for his ideas–naval history between 1660 and 1815. However historians in general had come to reject the so-called scientific school of history. Mahan had been a leader in the use of this nineteenth-century approach to historical study founded on the idea that basic principles of human action could be deduced from a study of history in the same way that scientists deduced laws from their observations of the physical world. By rejecting this approach, academic historians raised doubts about Mahan's conclusions and observations. The new schools of historians tended to study history with more attention to the factors that invited contrast rather than comparison to current situations. Students emphasised the past as a prologue rather than a pattern for the future. In general, when historical analogies were drawn, modern historians drew them with greater care and precision than Mahan had done.

Emphasis on Sea Battles Questioned

The few historians who were engaged in studying naval history of the seventeenth and eighteenth centuries began to re-examine the subject by comparing the results of their original research with Mahan's conclusions. Much of this work began to appear only in the 1970s,[6] but it showed that a careful examination of original source materials provided ground for a much different interpretation of the use of naval power. In particular, historians questioned Mahan's stress on battles at sea as the decisive factor in overall strategy. Readers of these new works were left with the general impression that naval power was important for the way in which the sea could be used to affect affairs on land, but in itself naval power was neither decisive nor a determining factor for national greatness.

Different Uses for Navies

Many historians continued to interpret history through Mahan's eyes, but some provided new insights in the process. One book, titled with Mahan's own phrase, *Command of the Sea,* made the original observation that different types of nations had different uses for navies.[7] Continental Powers, maritime–island nations, and small coastal states each valued and used navies in different functions, some playing a relatively more important role than others. Another student[8] developed these ideas further in terms of British maritime power, and explained naval dominance as a reflection of a unique system that was dependent on overseas trade in an era symbolised by 'guns, sails, and empires'.[9]

Mahan Evaluated

In post-Second World War America, Mahan's work came to be seen as the product of a particular person at a specific time in history, and as the application of Jomini's ideas to one peculiar set of historical circumstances. Yet Mahan's deeply detailed work was studded with flashes of great insight and originality as he suggested various shadings in the application of Jominian ideas in naval practice. In 1953, Rear Admiral John D. Hayes, USN, a prolific writer on strategy and naval history, acknowledged the problems with Mahan's thought, but concluded: 'Until there comes another like him to dissect, analyze, and codify the experience of our day, none of us can go wrong if we study Mahan's great historical works.'[10] This statement, more than any other, expresses the basic conflict in American thinking in this period. Admiral Hayes recognised the weakness of Mahan's ideas in the modern world, but saw the primary need to return to them until someone could provide a comprehensive statement that would supersede them.

CLAUSEWITZIAN THEORY IN US MARITIME STRATEGY

Some of the faults in Mahan's work led historians to the writings of Sir Julian Corbett who had used Mahan's ideas, but had presaged some of the criticisms. When first published in 1911, Corbett's *Some Principles of Maritime Strategy* had been largely ignored by American thinkers. In the 1950s and 1960s, however, it came to the attention of Americans,[11] and many of his works were reprinted.[12]

Political Policy and Diplomacy

One of the attractions of Corbett's work for American naval thinkers was his use of Clausewitzian theory. Many of Carl von Clausewitz's nineteenth-century German interpreters had emphasised only one aspect of his work, but Corbett had elaborated on the little-emphasised ideas of limited warfare and on the relationship of strategy to broad political policy. Political theorists in America had been developing concepts along these lines since the 1930s, but they had had very little impact in practical affairs until after the Second World War.

Americans continued, by and large, to see military and naval affairs as something quite distinct from political considerations and diplomacy. Academics imbued with Clausewitzian theory stressed the point that 'the political object – the original motive for the war – will thus determine both the aim of the military objective to be reached and the amount of effort it required,'[13] and that therefore 'war is not a mere act of policy, but a true political instrument, a continuation of political activity by other means'.[14] The shift in focus from the work of Mahan to that of Corbett reflected a fundamental change away from viewing naval strategy as one of autonomous concepts. The new focus was to see naval strategy as only an element within the broad spectrum of warfare and as one specialised instrument in the use of force for political purpose.

NAVIES IN LIMITED WARFARE

This line of thinking was developed further by many academics, and brought into practical use by a number of them who became advisers and officials in Washington. Among many others at various levels, Henry Kissinger was the most prominent.

Both Mahan and Corbett had been concerned entirely with the conduct of war at sea; however, the experience of the United States Navy after the Second World War emphasised the use of navies in limited warfare and in situations short of war. Both the Korean War and the Vietnam War had been limited wars, and there had been relatively little armed opposition to American naval operations. The focus on the Navy's work moved from events at sea to the effect which it had ashore. This was paralleled in other experiences. In 1946 the battleship *Missouri* had appeared in Turkish waters when the Soviet Union seemed to be making a threatening diplomatic move in that area. Friendly governments in the Far East were bolstered by the US Seventh Fleet after the collapse of Nationalist Chinese power in the Asian mainland. In other examples, American amphibious forces were landed in Lebanon in 1958 to support the government there. In 1983, amphibious forces landed on Grenada in the West Indies to prevent the further growth of Soviet and Cuban influence in that region. In April 1986, a joint US Navy–US Air Force strike against targets in Libya was designed to persuade the leaders of that country to stop their support for terrorist activities. Perhaps the supreme example is the Cuban Missile Crisis of 1962 in which the threat of US naval forces prevented the Soviet Union from following its own foreign policy objectives in the Caribbean.

These varied uses of navies in peace-time subtly brought with them a growing appreciation of the importance of geography and geographical position in relation to strategy. Rarely stated explicitly, it was nevertheless an increasingly clear part of the strategic statements that were made.[15]

EXPLOITATION OF POTENTIAL FORCE

The Clausewitzian emphasis on the relationship between military affairs and politics joined the practical naval experience to stimulate further thought in this area. Among notable works, civilian theorists such as Thomas C. Schelling began to apply the ideas of game theory to warfare.[16] In Schelling's view, the important focus was not the actual application of force, as it had been for Mahan, but the exploitation of potential force. In terms of naval power, however, no book of theoretical writing on this aspect of thinking appeared until the early 1970s. Since that time the subject has been explored by James Cable, Edward Luttwak, and Kenneth Booth.[17]

NEW ROLES FOR NAVIES

The work done by these men emphasised some additional functions of naval force. Kenneth Booth's work, *Navies and Foreign Policy,* was by far the most complete statement. He based his approach on a trinity of uses for the sea: (1) for the passage of goods and people; (2) for the passage of military force for diplomatic purposes or for use against targets on land and at sea; and (3) for the exploitation of resources in or under the sea. Navies, he argued, existed to further such ends, and it is appropriate that the military character of a navy forms the basis for two additional roles: a diplomatic and a policing role. In making this point, Booth emphasised that a navy's ability to threaten and to use force gives meaning to its other modes of action. In a policing role, a navy can extend sovereignty as well as defend offshore resources. In a diplomatic role, navies can provide the force which can change the political calculations of other nations as well as promote prestige.[18]

The use of naval force in these varied roles presented some new dimensions and emphasised some traditional usages. The problem which Americans first began to face seriously in the late 1960s was the rise of the Soviet Navy as a rival to the United States Navy. It is a rivalry very deeply enmeshed in the relationship between technology and strategy. When Mahan wrote his famous books, he had specifically argued that understanding of strategy transcended technological change. As he wrote, 'Conditions and weapons change; but to cope with the one or successfully wield the others, respect must be had to these constant teachings of history ... in those wider operations of war which are comprised under the name of strategy.'[19] Mahan's contention was first challenged by the naval employment of aviation and submarine, and it is challenged additionally by nuclear weapons and the guided missile.

In a book widely read in America during the late 1960s, L. W. Martin declared that the strategic world of Mahan and Corbett 'is no longer with us'

Similar battle fleets will no longer fight each other at sea; technological developments have altered the scene forever.

> Developments in naval propulsion, in aircraft, missiles, explosives and techniques of computation have overthrown completely the context in which fleet actions were the focus of strategy. Submarines, aircraft and missiles have become the most dangerous enemies of the larger surface ships, while those ships find their prime targets on shore. Bombardment of the land, once one of the most humble naval tasks, has become a dominant concern of the larger navies – strategically with missiles launched from submarines, tactically with aircraft based at sea.[20]

The Nuclear Age Navy

Nuclear weapons, of course, are supreme among new developments in technology. Since they were first employed in 1945, many observers declared that they had completely altered the nature of warfare. During the short period when the United States was the sole owner of atomic weapons, the government spent vast sums in developing military uses for them. Both strategists and budgets stressed the Air Force's ability to deliver nuclear weapons, while the other Services found waning support for their more traditional methods and roles. Many years later, observers have looked back on this period through the lens of Clausewitzian theory and have seen that the possession of this terrible weapon had only a very limited political effect on the outside world. Somewhat ironically, the possession of nuclear weapons has come to have a useful meaning only as a deterrent to the use of similar weapons by those who have now come to possess them.

Strategy of Deterrence

The complicated theories surrounding the use of nuclear weapons lie outside the scope of this book, but two dimensions apply directly to the Navy. First of all, there is the use of submarines to carry submarine-launched Polaris and Trident missiles. This is part of the strategy of deterrence, based on a weapon that could be kept safe from attack. Oskar Morgenstern described the idea as early as 1959:

> The principal aim of shifting the weapons carrier, of putting it one moment here, the other there, below the water and in the air, is of course to hide it ... This is achieved by combining the properties of speed and depth of water with erratic movements, with randomization. Instead of deploying forces to carefully selected places, of giving their placement of a pattern and formation such as fleets had to adopt by necessity even in the

last war, probability alone should determine the geographical spot where the weapon carrier (submarine, floating missile base, seaplane) is next to appear. This is what the combination of nuclear propulsion for missiles is making possible. Never before in warfare could a system be envisaged where mobile dispersal is combined with great power in each unit, the ability for all to act together from their dispersed points according to some previous plan, and be directed from a central point of command.[21]

The central purpose of all this is the ability to have a weapon which is still usable under attack. In view of the catastrophic implications of nuclear warfare, some observers doubted that such weapons could ever be used, and from this they argued that the deterrent effect of nuclear weapons was of no value:

> The trouble with this concept is faulty assumptions (for example, that civilian casualties and collateral damage can be kept to low levels); it ignores a basic lesson that the leaders of the U.S. Government in all crises have learned – that when faced with the decision to start a nuclear war, almost any other alternative looked better.[22]

Extrapolating from this, some American naval strategists in the late 1980s have argued that one can use conventional forces against nuclear armed forces, still keeping a war at the level of conventional weapons. Despite this, the submarine-launched Polaris missile remains a part of American strategy and performs a function while there is a reasonable suspicion that the United States might use nuclear weapons in retaliation against a nuclear attack.[23]

THE TACTICAL NUCLEAR WEAPON

In one respect, American military power was muscle-bound. In attempting to circumvent the problem of having too much power to be useful, some strategists hit upon the idea of the so-called tactical nuclear weapon. This is a small nuclear weapon used in conjunction with a gun or torpedo which would have an effect limited to the battle area. With this in mind, some naval strategists envisaged a nuclear war fought at sea between two opposing naval forces. The concept attracted those who wished to find a viable method to use nuclear weapons and still to confine warfare to struggle between military forces without damage to civilian populations. A knock-out blow could be delivered within the confines of a single battle area. It is an idealistic concept which suggests that naval forces could fight to the death in a duel which does little harm to anyone in a place which is of no great concern. The problem is that it reduces warfare to a boxing match and a sideshow while ignoring the military factor in the essential nature of international politics. The day is yet to come when weapons and force play no direct part in competing national interests and political goals.

At the same time, the increasing accuracy and explosive power of conventional naval weapons appeared to render unnecessary the potential use of 'tactical nuclear weapons'. A conventional weapon was soon able to deliver a knock-out blow without the danger of causing an all-out war that might follow the use of a nuclear weapon of any kind.

INTER-DEPARTMENTAL RELATIONS

While these ideas seem esoteric, they performed a very real and practical function in the matter of bureaucratic politics. In the late 1960s, academics began to explore the relationship of foreign and military policy with domestic affairs.[24] There are many aspects to this problem, but one very important side is the political relations of separate agencies and departments inside one governmental organisation. Each in its own way competes for a share of influence, position, or money. In the period following the Second World War, the Air Force had the primary position in defence because of its ability to deliver nuclear weapons. It became dominant in terms of money and its role in the defence establishment. The Navy's continual emphasis on its traditional roles, however correct, was not impressive when contrasted with the revolutionary innovations claimed for nuclear weapons. Submarines, amphibious forces, destroyers, cruisers, even aircraft carriers, seemed to be anachronisms. The ability of the Navy Department – either consciously or unconsciously – to connect the more traditional interests of naval power with nuclear warfare and nuclear deterrence played an important role in supporting the Navy's stake in national security affairs. There is no doubt that the Navy lost much, in terms of politics, finance and material, during the early period of development for nuclear weapons. However the Navy's successful effort to develop a credible maritime role for nuclear weapons served the political purpose of stemming the Navy's losses in Congress.

COPING WITH TECHNOLOGICAL CHANGE

Nuclear weapons are only part of a much broader issue. The essence of the matter lies in the very basic problem of man's ability to cope with technological changes which alter the very fabric of tradition, custom and society. For a century the Western world has largely agreed with Matthew Arnold that technology and machines appear to have very little to do with sweetness and light, the essential elements that create culture and the best that humans have thought and said.[25] Our experience in the technological world has caused us to be more aware of the various ways in which machines affect society. Their impact can no longer be ignored.

> Technology tends to create its own environment and set of conditions. Put even more simply, as the mechanism steadily increases in power and scale, the tendency is to fit men into machinery rather than to fit the machinery into the contours of a human situation.[26]

In 1948, the president of the US Naval War College observed this happening to naval strategy. 'So much of the old has broken down', he wrote, 'and so much of the new has been added that there no longer exists an accepted closely knit analysis of the whole of war and strategy. Instead, theories have tended to center around new technological developments which have given rise to more or less unconnected and very often contradictory doctrines, like sprawling limbs without backbone or head.'[27]

The means were stressed at the expense of the whole. Naval officers were becoming specialists in using a particular type of technology. They were aviators, surface ship officers, and submarine officers before they were specialists in the broader functions of armed force. Most naval officers saw the need for 'hard' technological training and expertise more readily than for the 'softer' understanding of political and military affairs. At the same time, naval men increasingly found that, in order to maintain a rational continuity, they resisted certain types of technological change, and moved to develop machines along already established lines: aircraft carriers, destroyers, ordnance, nuclear power. They avoided change that would sweep everything away, reacting in a way that was only gradually being understood about technological societies.[28] The daily life of the ordinary naval officer, in this period, became increasingly a problem in the care and feeding of machines rather than the examination of their utility.

The problem was the same that Mahan had encountered in the 1890s, but his answer was the opposite extreme. Mahan ignored technology and sought a higher understanding that was unaffected by change. The course of events between 1940 and 1970 demonstrated that technology and change could not be ignored. They have a deep and abiding effect on human behaviour, in both peace and war. They are necessary factors that must be considered in the rational use of armed force, yet American naval officers had not developed a balanced and systematic approach to strategic thinking that included these factors. They tended either to ignore the strategic implications of technological change or to be swept away in enthusiasm for their new machines.

ALTERNATIVES TO ARMED FORCES

The vast technological changes of these thirty years, particularly the development of nuclear weapons and the spectre of mass destruction which they carry, created another effect. Military force seemed less relevant and less useful to the modern world. All around the globe, people were increasingly aware of the cost of military functions at the expense of social services. As economic issues became more and more important and budgets became tighter, many nations found less to spend on armament. Many people believed that they saw a long-term but clear trend that showed the traditional reasons for conflict disappearing. The very standards of international conduct were slowly replacing the forceful assertion of national interests.

Yet there was a limit to change of this nature. The long-term trend had not reached its ultimate goal. Conflict and arms races continued. The nation still required protection, and potential enemies could still be deterred. The potential use of armed force still seemed to have persuasive value.

By 1970, American naval thinkers had not found a new conceptual basis upon which to formulate strategic ideas. The older ideas were still in use, but they had not been thoroughly reworked and adapted to new situations. New perceptions had been opened, and some of them suggested a viable way for the future.

As early as 1949, Rear Admiral C. R. Brown told the Naval War College that what was needed was not a new Mahan, but 'brilliant strategists, not of land power, not of sea power, and not of air power, but able, broad-gauged individuals who can view the whole picture of *military strategy*'.[29] It was this challenge that Rear Admiral J. C. Wylie took up in his successful book: *Military Strategy: A General Theory of Power Control*.[30]

STRATEGY AS 'COMPREHENSIVE DIRECTION OF POWER'

Another within the small group of individuals who responded to this challenge was Herbert Rosinski, a refugee from Nazi Germany and former lecturer at the German Naval Staff College. Rosinski's key contribution was his concept of strategy as comprehensive direction of power. Rosinski wrote:

> This definition required the recognition that there is much more to strategy than mere direction of action. It is a type of direction which takes into account the multitude of possible enemy counteractions, and thus it becomes a means of control. It is this element of control which is the essence of strategy ... It must be comprehensive in order to control every possible counteraction or factor.[31]

This concept was developed further by Rear Admiral Henry E. Eccles in the 1960s when he stressed the relationship between economic and industrial factors, policy, strategy, and tactics. 'Military strategy is subordinate to national strategy, so the selection of weapons to be used and the choice of tactics to be employed is subordinate to strategic objectives and factors', Eccles emphasised. 'Strategy must have at its disposal a variety of weapons and forces, so that the particular combination most suitable to a situation, as it actually arises, may be formed and swiftly and decisively employed in an appropriate manner.'[32]

Wylie, Rosinski and Eccles pointed the way out of the thicket in naval thinking. They provided the basic foundation stones for future development of a comprehensive theory of naval power, but it took a long period for them to begin to bear fruit. Until the 1980s, observers of naval thought in the English-speaking world since 1945 saw more disarray and confusion than cohesion and concise theoretical statements. By the mid-1980s, however, that picture had changed with the revival of some of the classical ideas about the use of naval power, and the modification of those ideas as they were adapted for use in the nuclear age, connecting them with both a broader conception of strategy which had emerged in the postwar years and new concepts for the peace-time use of naval force for political purposes. This change in understanding, made within the context of technological change, was largely due to the recognition that there was a role for conventional weapons, even within the nuclear context. The first and most obvious technological change was the introduction of nuclear weapons. When they first appeared they seemed to overwhelm the thinking of the day and to sweep away all that had gone before. At the same time, in a less obvious fashion, technology was changing the character of navies. Older ships gave way to the new, conventional weapons and sensors came to have longer ranges and greater power. Automation allowed men to use machines at sea with more precision, enhancing human control. More could be done with less. Men at sea came to have the power to have a direct influence on events ashore, when heretofore their influence had been distant and indirect.

The experience of the Vietnam War and the Soviet invasion of Afghanistan, among other events, helped to give credence to the growing perception that nuclear weapons had limited value. Together these two influences helped to bring wider support to the long-standing naval opinion that conventional weapons retained their utility. This change in opinion resulted in the reaffirmation of many ideas which were clearly resonant with the earlier thought of Mahan and Corbett. No recent writer has attempted to synthesise all the empirical evidence into a new and wider theory of naval strategy, but much of it has been tacitly applied in the US Navy's *Maritime Strategy*. First published in 1986, it had been under development since the 1970s. This essay is an attempt to piece together the various bits of theory that have been expressed in the postwar period and to try to outline a modern theory of naval strategy as it stands in the late 1980s, summarising the substantive contributions which have been made in thinking about the theory of naval strategy since 1945.

A TAXONOMY FOR A MODERN THEORY OF NAVAL STRATEGY

Strategy's aim is to establish control while it provides a common frame of reference for the specialised work of the soldier, sailor, airman, politician, diplomat, technologist and economist in their joint efforts to reach a mutual goal that reflects national policy and the basic interests of a nation. Strategy, as a concept, covers all kinds of conflict. It is not limited to wars or even to military application. The military or naval application of it is rarely inseparable from the broad social context within which and on behalf of which it functions as a part.[33]

Policy and strategy cannot easily be distinguished. They blend and overlap because both desire to achieve an effect related to or in support of an interest. However it can be said that policy provides the guidance under which officials work to attain a desired effect, while strategy is the plan for actions which brings fruition to the guidance, relating means to ends.

When applied to military and naval affairs, strategy can be understood only in relation to the other fundamental areas of the art of war: operations, tactics, logistics, intelligence and communications. Broadly defined, strategy is the comprehensive direction of power to control situations and areas to attain the broad objectives of policy. Strategy is carried out by operations which are a blend of logistics and tactical actions designed to achieve a hierarchy of primary and secondary, immediate and ultimate goals. This intermediate level is focussed on campaigns, in relation to which the term 'operational art' describes the skills required in the intermediate level between strategy and tactics, involving the broad use of force within a geographical context. A broad grand strategy on a national level involves the complementary use of various campaign strategies to achieve broad national policy objectives.

Each campaign is conducted within a maritime theatre, an area of potential wartime operations in which the lines of communication are primarily across water and in which key potential battlefields ashore are within reach of weapons launched from naval forces at sea. The conduct of operations within a maritime theatre require a close interdependence of land, air and naval forces with interlocking and complementary strategies for each type of force employed. In order to seize or to keep control of a maritime theatre, combat and support forces on land with ground-based air forces are essential elements of a campaign. These forces seize and protect territory, supply lines and bases, while others operate directly or indirectly with naval forces at the same time, amphibious naval forces serve to strengthen land and land-based air forces in combat ashore while also maintaining and protecting the sea lines of communication. Within the context of a geopolitical situation as well as in terms of the mutual supporting use of different types of force, the modern naval strategist defines the functions of a navy in both peace and war.

Strategy is the direction of power and involves consideration of

> What to control,
> For what purpose,
> To what degree,
> When to initiate control,
> How to control and
> How long to control.[34]

Every strategic plan or action should be additionally tested, not only for its logical relationship to policy goals, but also for its

> Suitablility: will its attainment accomplish the effect desired?
> Feasibility: can the action be accomplished by the means available?
> And acceptability: are the consequences of cost justified by the importance of the effect desired?[35]

Most importantly, these tests imply an examination of whether the end justifies the means in terms of the commonly accepted practice and ethics of a nation and the community of nations, including a careful assessment of the utility of force as well as an appreciation of everything which an enemy can do to influence materially one's own course of action.

All of the foregoing considerations are basic elements in the further examination of strategy in terms of three broad categories: the uses of nuclear weapons in the context of naval warfare, the uses of naval power in wartime, and the uses of navies in peace-time.

THE USES OF NAVIES IN PEACE-TIME

In peace-time, the navies of the major Powers and their allies operate within the context of nuclear deterrence. In a sense, nuclear deterrence is a negative aspect of strategy. It is founded on the concept that opposing Powers with the credible capability of using nuclear weapons against one another present to each other the probability of unlimited and unacceptable destruction through the potential use of these weapons. Because of this, they will not be used. This balance serves to prevent total wars which would seek to overthrow a nation which possesses credible nuclear defence or nuclear parity. At the same time, it leaves scope to use conventional weapons for limited political aims within the context of this overall balance of power.

The functions of navies may be conceived as a triangle around a basic understanding of the uses of the sea. The three functions are: military, policing and diplomatic roles. The policing and diplomatic roles are complementary to the military role and all are founded upon the navy's ability to be an effective fighting force in a future war. This gives the navy its power to succeed in war, and its latent power makes it an effective tool in peace. Nations without a navy or with a weak navy make themselves vulnerable to distant states which have a navy and would wish to pursue their own separate interests. From this military basis comes a police role by which a nation defends the sovereignty of a nation, ensures the enjoyment of offshore resources in contiguous areas and maintains good order. In addition, within this role comes the function of contributing to internal stability during times of turmoil and contributing to internal development, social cohesion and direct assistance in times of national or local emergencies.[36]

The third side of the triangle is a diplomatic role. The use of navies in peace-time is an expression of coercive diplomacy. As Sir James Cable defined it, this is 'a resort to specific threats or to injurious actions, otherwise than as an act of war, in order to secure advantage, or to avert loss, in the furtherance of an international dispute or else against foreign nationals within the territory or the jurisdiction of their own state'.[37] Coercive diplomacy may be attempted in any one of four main modes: (a) it may be *definitive* with the object of establishing a situation in which the victim can only acquiesce or else risk escalating the level of the conflict to a higher, and presumably unacceptable, level of destruction; (b) it can be *purposeful* with the object of threatening or inflicting so much damage that the victim will prefer to adopt an indicated course of action which would avoid further pain; (c) it can be *catalytic,* encouraging the victim to comply or to compromise in his aims, by creating a volatile general atmosphere in the absence of coercive measures directly related to the dispute; or (d), it may be *expressive,* emphasising more one's own attitude rather than directly influencing the conduct of an adversary.[38]

Peace-time Diplomatic Role

In peace-time, as in wartime, the use of armed force is never an isolated act. It involves both the employment of force by one participant, and a reaction to that use from others. In that light, the diplomatic uses of navies in peace-time may be subdivided by their main and subsidiary policy objectives. A nation may use its navy to *negotiate from a position of strength* by making a demonstration of naval force without actually violently destroying a target. Under this main category of diplomatic use, one may touch several countries within a short time to:

a   reassure and strengthen allies and associates;

b reassure and strengthen friendly governments threatened by serious internal challenge;
c reassure and strengthen friendly governments fearing external attack;
d change the behaviour of friendly governments when the latter are facing the threat of external attack;
e signal 'business as usual' during a crisis;
f support or threaten force from the sea to assist friendly governments contemplating acquisitive military action;
g improve bargaining position;
h threaten force from the sea to support policy;
i improve one's ability to affect the course of specific diplomatic negotiations.

One can use naval force for diplomatic *manipulation* by changing the political calculations of observers, and the perceptions of others to:

a manipulate bargaining positions within an alliance;
b demonstrate support for different countries;
c gain or increase access to new countries;
d build up foreign navies and create proxy threats;
e create a degree of naval dependency;
f provide standing demonstrations of naval power in distant waters to establish the right to be interested in the affairs of that area.

One can make a diplomatic use of naval force to promote the *prestige* of one's own country, to:

a provide psychological reassurances for the home country;
b project a favourable image of one's own country;
c project an image of impressive national power.[39]

Peace-time Military Role

The peace-time military roles of a navy may be categorised under several main functions: strategic deterrence, conventional deterrence, forward deterrence, and international order.

Navies can contribute to the broad area of nuclear deterrence by carrying nuclear weapons and providing a moveable location for them and thus attempting to hide them to make them usable even under attack. Under the general function of *strategic nuclear deterrence,* a navy can:

a deter attack on the homeland, and the homelands of the allies;
b provide a secure situation in which to promote foreign policy interests;

c   contribute to the nation's ability to negotiate from a position of recognised strength;
d   counter the deterrent forces of adversaries.

Through *conventional deterrence and defence,* a navy can be used in the waters contiguous to its own land area, by:

a   preparing for wartime tasks;
b   deterring hostile intrusion into maritime frontiers;
c   contributing to local maritime stability;
d   protecting national claims in contiguous seas;
e   extending national claims in contiguous seas.

Through deployment in distant seas, a nation may use its navy for *forward deterrence and defence.* Under this mission, it may function to:

a   protect its own national activities on the high seas;
b   protect the lives, interests and property of its nationals (and others) operating in distant waters;
c   protect the lives, interests and property of nationals (and others) threatened by local disturbance or natural disaster;
d   provide the local maritime defence of distant national territories, or serve to complement the forces of a distant state for the same purpose;
e   demonstrate commitment to allies;
f   develop operating techniques for essential wartime tasks in distant waters, thereby adding to the credibility of one's latent naval power;
g   build up an infrastructure (including bases and other shore facilities) for the performance of wartime missions, along the key routes to and in distant waters;
h   deter another nation from taking a forward position by sustained operations of one's own naval forces in waters adjacent to the nation.

The fourth category of military uses of naval power in peace-time is their relation to the structure of *international order.* Under this category, naval power may be used to:

a   maintain the *status quo;*
b   change the *status quo;*
c   establish an internationally recognised law of the sea;
d   challenge an internationally recognised law of the sea by promoting conflicting national claims.[40]

THE USES OF NAVAL POWER IN WARTIME

In the modern era, war and peace have lost their distinctive demarcation, and one sees only a spectrum of violence ranging in its intensity. One can see along it general war, conventional war, limited low-intensity wars, interventions and guerilla wars. The operational functions which a navy might perform within each type of warfare will vary enormously both in terms of scope and in the intensity of violence.[41] Whatever the nature of the war or its level of intensity, the basic objectives of naval force fall into three broad categories: (1) to secure the command of the sea, thereby obtaining control of maritime communications for oneself and denying it to the enemy; (2) to dispute command of the sea, thereby denying control of maritime communications to the enemy; and (3) to exercise one's own use of the sea whether or not one has command of maritime communications. The functions of naval power within these categories may be enumerated as follows:

Command of the sea may be secured by removing the possibility of a rival or potential rival naval forces from effectively using the common sea lanes to interfere with one's own use of the sea. This may be achieved by destroying the opposing forces in battle or by preventing them from using the sea lanes by isolating the enemy's naval forces from the use of the sea lanes, by forms of blockade such as offensive mining, or by forcing the enemy into a defensive position.

Command of the sea may be disputed by a Power too weak to obtain command of the sea for itself through offensive operations. This may be achieved by a nation which maintains an effective defence at sea against an opposing naval Power. This means maintaining an active fleet that uses the sea lanes, refuses to be placed in jeopardy by the opposing, offensive forces, and selects its own favourable time and place to make offensive strikes against the other Power. This allows the disputing nation to prevent another nation from having total control of the maritime communications which would be essential to its own offensive use of naval power. This may be complemented by counter-attacks against other targets, which serve further to challenge control and to dissipate naval assets.

The general theory of war establishes a great distinction between *offensive* and *defensive* strategy. In naval theory, however, the mobile nature of navies blurs this distinction, making the two forms of strategy complementary rather than mutually exclusive. Without entirely abdicating the use of the sea, a nation cannot secure a defensive position at sea until it first seizes command of the sea, either locally or generally, by offensive operations. Similarly, a naval power cannot dispute the command of the sea without offensive attacks from a position of defence. An offensive operation or the credible threat of an offensive operation is necessary to change a strategic situation that exists, for it is only by offence that action is taken. A strategic defence at sea is extremely strong when a naval Power restricts itself to its own waters close to base support, where it is usually extremely difficult for an enemy to attack with a decisive result. The weakness of this defensive strategy lies, first, in dissipating one's force in order to defend oneself against all possible attacks, thereby weakening one's force and making one vulnerable to attack by a more concentrated force. Secondly, a position of defence has historically led to a defensive mind-set which effectively has prevented the naval Power in question from making the necessary offensive counter-strikes required to dispute command of the sea. In such circumstances, a defensive strategy ceases to be a means of nurturing a weaker Power's assets so that they may be used in a timely manner for offensive strikes. A nation which adopts such a defensive strategy contributes to objectives by containing its own force. Conversely an offensive mind-set may lead a nation into failing to take advantage of a defensive position, plunging recklessly into attacks at inopportune times or places. In the most common situation, which is when the command of the sea is in dispute, a navy must use a combination of offensive and defensive operations, in the first place to attempt to secure control and, secondly, to dispute control, if it cannot be secured.[42] From this follows a further consideration that the exercise of the use of the sea requires a defence of oneself and one's vessels using the sea. This requires both the use of passive defensive measures which are alert to attack as well as offensive operations which can remove the potential threat.

Exercising the Use of the Sea in Wartime

Securing or disputing command are merely the means by which a nation obtains use of the sea. One exercises use of the sea in order to influence events ashore, and the process is a complex one, involving many functions. Under this topic, one must consider all forms of wartime naval activity which do not directly involve securing the command of the sea or preventing an enemy from securing the command of the sea. Although less attention is paid to it because it is less dramatic and exciting, exercising the use of the sea to achieve strategic objectives in wartime is the principal end of naval warfare. Naval warfare is not solely the destruction of the enemy's navy, but involves a myriad number of operations. Most importantly these[43] project a nation's power at a distant or increased range from what it might otherwise be, by:

a   interfering with the enemy's use of the sea;
b   moving troops strategically;
c   acquiring and establishing bases;
d   bombarding enemy territory or forces ashore;
e   landing troops on hostile shores;
f   protecting sea lanes of communications which support distant operations on land.

The last touches upon a whole category of operations which involve war, surrounding and centring upon communications. The *war of communications* may be divided into both offensive and defensive categories.[44] Under the heading of indirect defence, one may protect communications through distant operations that remove the threat or one may achieve this by both passive defence and active defensive operations in direct connection with the lines of communication. With an active defence one may attack both the logistical lines of communication as well as the lines of command and control used by the enemy. This may be extended to a general attack on the economic basis of a nation. At sea, this generally refers to an attack on commercial trade passing over the sea. Historical experience has suggested that the attack on trade cannot be of decisive military and political significance unless it is undertaken by strong states against other states which are, at the same time, weak, economically vulnerable and which cannot count on the support of powerful neighbours. In this situation, the determining factor is the vulnerability of the victim, not the strength of the attacker. Conversely, a weaker state may profitably attack a more powerful state's extensive sea trade with a relatively small scale offensive strategy which would lead to a disproportionate commitment of enemy resources. Although this kind of attack will not have a decisive effect, it will impede trade and strategic mobility, while forcing the enemy into diverting resources from offensive operations into defensive protection. Thus attack on trade can be a more effective strategy for the diversion of naval forces than for a decisive attack against a vital lifeline.[45]

In addition to the foregoing functions of a navy in wartime, one may also include the following:[46]

a   attack on ports, harbours and waterways;
b   protection of ports, harbours and waterways;
c   bombardment of fortified areas;
d   defending against enemy raiders;
e   gunfire support of troops ashore;
f   protection of coasts from attack;
g   support or seizure of isolated positions;
h   assistance in the tactical movement of troops and equipment;
i   surveillance and anti-surveillance operations;
j   tactical demonstrations of naval power;
k   strategic demonstrations of naval power;
l   evacuation of endangered troops;
m   attempt to deny enemy the use of his own or other ports;
n   rescue of friendly governments;
o   rescue of civilians;
p   showing the flag;
q   gaining local air and sea control;

r   port salvage and reopening;
s   supporting the establishment of peace-keeping operations.

Beyond these operations, one must also mention the role of *guerilla warfare* at sea, through the use of terrorist-like methods of random attack, the placement of obstacles and the use of weapons for harassment, sabotage and the creation of fear. Such methods are open to both major and minor naval Powers through the use of submarines, mines, land-based missiles and aircraft.

NUCLEAR WEAPONS IN THE CONTEXT OF NAVAL WARFARE

Navies are part of nuclear warfare in that they have become key parts of those weapons systems. Through nuclear weapons, navies have developed a means which makes a massive change in their strategic function, allowing them to strike effectively at the very heart of an enemy territory and to preserve a capability for a retaliatory second strike, if attacked. At the same time, such naval forces have become vulnerable to long-range attack through the use of space surveillance systems. Thus the advent of nuclear weapons along with other technologies places naval operations in a strategic context which changes their role. No longer limited as they were to the classical strategists, nuclear weapons at sea allow navies to play a direct role in the global balance of power affecting all nations. Because of the instantaneous and massive destruction which would presumably destroy all means of fighting or of obtaining any useful objective, full-scale nuclear war would make the use of navies nearly irrelevant. However, the more controlled the use of nuclear weapons and the more limited the destruction involved, the more exceptions one can make to that proposition. Thus there is a varying range of strategic uses for navies which have been, on the one hand, enhanced by the use of navies for nuclear deterrence, and which at the same time, are controlled and limited in their wartime use by the presence of the nuclear deterrent. These developments can be seen in the range of equipment which has come to support such concepts.

On the other hand, there is the nuclear-powered, ballistic missile-carrying submarine (SSBN) which represents a wholly new sea vehicle, not useful for anything but nuclear deterrence and absorbing vast amounts of money to build and to keep at sea. At the same time, it requires a special range of equipment to threaten and to counter it. At the other end of the spectrum, there is the development of nuclear weapons whose effects can be limited and directed: the tactical nuclear weapon. The presence of these weapons (and the potential for the development of conventional weapons of similar capacity) creates a great threat to large naval vessels that could previously survive a number of attacks. With these developments they become vulnerable to a single weapon. Across this spectrum, changing technology has allowed a greater interaction between forces based at sea and forces based on land. They can no longer be viewed in isolation as they once were, and thus conform more closely to the broader definition of strategy which encompasses all forms of national power. This is a key factor in the geopolitical context within which navies must operate. Within the context of nuclear strategy, navies are:

a   capable of fighting nuclear war, and
b   therefore they play a role in nuclear deterrence.

At the other end of the spectrum, navies are affected by deterrence in the following ways:

a   They are limited in their strategic objectives by the presence of a nuclear deterrent preventing nations from embarking on ventures which would cause another Power to use nuclear weapons in its defence.
b   For a nation which practises deterrence, there is a certain marginal freedom of action obtained in relation to secondary nations which do not possess nuclear weapons, to the extent that nuclear deterence guards against the main threat.
c   Third countries can profit from the limitations which deterrence imposed on the freedom of action of two nuclear weapons Powers opposed to one another, thereby allowing a third Power navy to operate where a major Power navy is restricted.
d   The presence of a nuclear deterrent may be used in the context of a conventional naval war between nuclear Powers to limit the extent of the war and even to assist in concluding such a war, thereby avoiding escalation in nuclear destruction.

These factors create a wide variety of situations in which naval confrontations can take place and in which the conventional range of naval functions can be used in varying degrees. Among these situations are:

a   Tension, where confrontation is a powerful hazard.
b   Continuing confrontation, represented at sea by a kind of preliminary naval warfare on a limited scale, without a nuclear threat, liable to last for years.
c   Serious crisis, represented at sea by highly developed naval warfare or skirmishing, although without actual bloodshed, under a nuclear threat, liable to last for several months and posing great maritime problems for merchant shipping as well as for naval forces.

d   A period of open conventional fighting, under a nuclear threat, for or against the freedom of action of naval vessels, liable to last for weeks or days.
e   A phase of amphibious landings with conventional opposition, under a nuclear threat.
f   A period of fighting between remnants, the survivors of a nuclear war, for control of the sea, which may or may not continue under a continuing nuclear threat.
g   A war whose purpose is to seize territory which is not truly vital between maritime nuclear Powers that do not want to escalate to the extremes.
h   A purely naval limited war, for or against commercial assets at sea, between nuclear Powers that do not want to escalate to the extremes.
i   A classical naval war between non-nuclear Powers or between a nuclear Power, behaving as if it were not a nuclear Power, and a non-nuclear Power.
j   A distant war between one maritime Power and a Power with a comparatively small navy capable of local maritime control or of substantially disputing control.[47]

Modern naval theory has thus expanded from major and clearly definable situations of warfare at sea between major naval combatants. It now includes the consideration of a much wider range of circumstances. Naval theorists no longer attempt to exalt naval power over other forms of armed force or claim for it an independent role. They see naval power as a specialised application of force and as a particular military instrument within the context of broader theories of power control. It is now firmly linked to the wide range of national power within the context of international politics. The additional aspect of thinking about the peace-time use of naval force and the new dimension of nuclear warfare has served to suggest that war is less useful in solving international issues, while there is at the same time a broadening range of naval functions in the prevention of war and in situations short of war. In modern theory the threat of force has a more useful and more common role to play in international affairs, while its use in major wars appears to have become remote. Paradoxically, the capability to fight successfully in wartime is the key to a navy's ability to play a role in peace-time. In modern theory, navies operate within the context of a far more complex *milieu* and function in relation to the entire spectrum of national power, both in peace and war, directly linked to the complementary use of ground and air forces for the achievement of national objectives.

Notes

Author's note: The limitations of this chapter are entirely my own, but I would like to express my appreciation to my colleagues who have given me useful, constructive criticism: Captain John Bonds, USN; Dr Donald Daniel; Mr John Hanley; Captain Kenneth McGruther, USN; Mr Frank Uhlig, Jr, at the Naval War College and at the Naval Postgraduate School, Captain Wayne Hughes, Jr, USN (Ret.). This is a rewritten and expanded version of my earlier essays, 'American Thinking on the Theory of Naval Strategy 1945–80', in G. Till (ed.), *Maritime Strategy and the Nuclear Age* (Macmillan, 1982) and 'Some Concepts in American Naval Strategic Thought, 1940–1970', in Joyce Bartell (ed.), *The Yankee Mariner & Sea Power: America's Challenge of Ocean Space* (Los Angeles, 1982).

1. B. Mitchell Simpson III (ed.), *The Development of Naval Thought: Essays by Herbert Rosinski* (Newport, RI, 1977) p. 24.
2. Ibid., pp. 34–5.
3. Ibid., pp. 102–20.
4. See, for example, Bernard Brodie, *Layman's Guide to Naval Strategy* (Princeton, NJ, 1942, and four other editions to 1965) and A. E. Sokol, *Sea Power in the Nuclear Age* (Washington, 1961).
5. The pre-eminent work in the iconoclastic school is Robert Seager II, *Alfred Thayer Mahan* (Annapolis, 1977).
6. See, for example, Geoffrey Symcox, *The Crisis of French Sea Power, 1688–1697: From guerre d'escadre to the guerre de course* (The Hague, 1974); J. F. Guilmartin, Jr, *Gunpowder and Galleys: Changing Technology and Mediterranean Warfare at Sea in the Sixteenth Century* (Cambridge, 1974); and J. B. Hattendorf, *England in the War of the Spanish Succession* (New York, 1987). See also, Michael Howard, *The British Way in Warfare: A Reappraisal*, Neale Lecture in English History, 1974 (London, 1975) which summarises the general trend of recent work.
7. Clark G. Reynolds, *Command of the Sea: The History and Strategy of Maritime Empires* (New York: William Morrow & Co., 1974), pp. 12–16. See especially, Rear Admiral J. R. Hill, *Maritime Strategy for Medium Powers* (Annapolis: Naval Institute Press, 1986) which develops the concept of a medium Power, that is to say those who have sufficient naval power to protect their own interests, but can not by themselves be a match for a superpower.
8. Paul M. Kennedy, *The Rise and Fall of British Naval Mastery* (London, 1976).
9. Carlo M. Cipolla, *Guns, Sails, and Empire: Technological Innovation and the Early Phase of European Expansion, 1400–1700* (New York, 1965).
10. John D. Hayes, 'Peripheral Strategy – Mahan's Doctrine Today,' US Naval Institute *Proceedings* (Nov. 1953), p. 1193.
11. Largely through the efforts of Donald M. Schurman, most notably in his book, *Education of a Navy: The Development of British Naval Strategic Thought, 1867–1914* (Chicago, 1965).
12. For example, *Some Principles of Maritime Strategy* (Annapolis, 1972) and *Campaign of Tralfalgar* (New York, 1976).
13. Carl von Clausewitz, *On War*, translated and edited by Michael Howard and Peter Paret (Princeton, 1976), p. 81.
14. Ibid., p. 87.
15. For geopolitics, see Hervé Coutau-Begarie, *La Puissance Maritime: Castex et la strategie navale* (Paris: Fayard, 1985); *Geostrategie de l'Atlantique sud* (Paris, 1985) and Colin S. Gray, *Maritime Strategy, Geopolitics, and the Defense of the West*, New York, 1986); *Geopolitics, Strategic Culture, and National Security*, forthcoming.

16. Thomas C. Schelling, *The Strategy of Conflict* (Cambridge, Mass., 1960): *Arms and Influence* (New Haven, 1966).
17. James C. Cable, *Gunboat Diplomacy: Political Applications of Limited Naval Force* (New York, 1971); Edward N. Luttwak, *The Political Uses of Sea Power* (Baltimore, 1974); Kenneth Booth, *Navies and Foreign Policy* (New York, 1977).
18. Booth, *Navies and Foreign Policy* pp. 15–25.
19. A. T. Mahan, *The Influence of Sea Power Upon History, 1660–1783* (London, 1965) p. 7.
20. L. W. Martin, *The Sea in Modern Strategy* (New York, 1967) pp. 9–10.
21. Oskar Morgenstern, *The Question of National Defense* (New York, 1959) p. 90.
22. A. C. Enthoven and K. W. Smith, 'What Forces for NATO? And from Whom?', in *Foreign Affairs* (October 1969) p. 82.
23. Linton Brooks, 'Tactical Nuclear Weapons: The Forgotten Facet of Naval Warfare', US Naval Institute *Proceedings*, January 1980; Donald C. F. Daniel, 'The Soviet Navy and the Tactical Nuclear War at Sea', *Survival*, vol. 29, no. 4, July/August 1987, pp. 318–35.
24. The most famous of these studies is Graham T. Allison, *Essence of Decision: Explaining the Cuban Missile Crisis* (Boston, 1971).
25. Matthew Arnold, 'Sweetness and Light' (1867), printed in E. K. Brown, *Four Essays on Life and Letters* (New York, 1947) pp. 44, 50, 52; and Elting Morison, *Men, Machines and Modern Times* (Cambridge, Mass, 1966) pp. 206–7.
26. Morison, *Men, Machines*, p. 211.
27. Naval War College Archives, RG8, Series II, XWAG: Enclosure B: 'Reassessment of the Fields and Value of Three Elements of Land, Sea and Air Power', in President, Naval War College, letter to Chairman, General Board, 30 April, 1948.
28. See Morison, *Men, Machines*, Ch. 2, and Stansfield Turner, 'Navies for Yesterday or Tomorrow?', a special university lecture in War Studies, King's College, London, 4 May, 1976.
29. C. R. Brown, 'The Role of the Navy in Future Warfare', *US Naval War College: Information Service for Officers (Naval War College Review)* (April 1949) p. 16.
30. New Brunswick, 1967.
31. Herbert Rosinski, 'New Thoughts on Strategy', in B. M. Simpson III (ed.), *War, Strategy and Maritime Power* (New Brunswick, NJ, 1977) p. 64. This was written in 1955.
32. H. E. Eccles, *Military Concepts and Philosophy* (New Brunswick, NJ, 1965) p. 262.
33. J. C. Wylie, *Military Strategy*, pp. 105, 108.
34. Henry E. Eccles, 'Strategy – The Theory and Application', *Naval War College Review* (May–June 1979) pp. 11–21.
35. *Sound Military Decision* (Newport, RI, 1942) p. 32, quoted in Eccles, 'Strategy', p. 15.
36. K. Booth, *Navies and Foreign Policy* (New York, 1977) pp. 15–17.
37. James Cable, 'Coercion, Compromise and Compliance', in *Diplomacy at Sea* (London, 1986) p. 18.
38. Ibid., p. 19.
39. Booth, *Navies and Foreign Policy*, pp. 18–20.
40. Ibid., p. 23.
41. Ibid.
42. Julian S. Corbett, *Some Principles of Maritime Strategy* (Classics of Sea Power edition. Eric J. Grove, editor. Annapolis, 1988) pp. 32–3, 34–40.
43. Frank Uhlig Jr, unpublished manuscript, 'Naval Warfare Since 1775'.

44. Hervé Coutau-Begarie, *La Puissance Maritime,* p. 199.
45. Nicholas Tracy, unpublished manuscript, 'Attack on Trade'.
46. Frank Uhlig, Naval Warfare since 1775'; Captain Wayne P. Hughes Jr, USN (Ret.), *Fleet Tactics: Theory and Practice* (Annapolis, 1986) pp. 227–32.
47. Hubert Moineville, *Naval Warfare Today and Tomorrow* (Oxford, 1983) pp. 26–7, 45–6.

Part III
Anglo-American Rivalries and Coalitions, 1898–1945

'The paramount concern ... of maritime strategy is to determine the mutual relations of your army and navy in a plan of war. When this is done, and not till then, naval strategy can begin to work out the manner in which the fleet can best discharge the function assigned to it.'—Sir Julian Corbett

At various times in the twentieth century, Britain and the United States have evolved maritime strategies that appeared to influence directly their roles as Great Powers. What has not been sufficiently appreciated, either by scholars or practitioners of politico-military affairs in either country, is the possibility that the strategies developed in peace-time might have been intellectual or analytical formulations rather than blueprints for national action. Another consideration is the fact that the merging of events and ideas, rather than being purposeful, may instead be so random that, in spite of the fact that a broad link might be found between strategy and policy, the conjunction may border on the purely fortuitous. In this section, one can see the continuing threads identified and one can note where cause and effect are linked or, alternatively, where cause led to irrelevance.

9 The Relevance of the Pre-war British and American Maritime Strategies to the First World War and its Aftermath, 1898–1920

Paul M. Kennedy

It may seem ironic, to some readers perhaps perverse, to begin an essay upon Anglo-American maritime strategies by reference to Lord Trenchard's doctrine of air power, since the Service of which he was head claimed to have made redundant every traditional strategy, whether land-based or sea-based. None the less the story of British air power in the decades after 1920 has a moral for any military organisation which asserts that it has a single strategic vision. In the Royal Air Force's case, there was an outspoken belief that 'the bomber will always get through'; more specifically, that its *own* bombers, provided they were produced in large enough numbers, would enable the nation to carry devastation to the enemy's heartland and, in a reasonably short time, induce it to surrender. If true, such a strategy made land-warfare appear irrelevant, and made naval warfare both indirect and marginal.[1]

Alas for this 'aerial strategy', the realities (or, in Clausewitz's term, the frictions) of actual warfare offered severe problems to the RAF's cozy assumptions. In the first place, an enemy air force – the *Luftwaffe* – turned out to be much more numerous and powerful by the mid-1930s, causing worried British politicians to seek to divert resources into aerial *defence*, not offence.[2] Secondly, while that defensive strategy clearly worked in the Battle of Britain, with German bombers suffering heavily at the hands of British fighters, it did not deflate the Air Staff's own firm belief in the efficacy of the strategic bombing campaign against Germany. Nor, indeed, did the increasing evidence that the RAF was ill-equipped for accurate bombing; that German radar and fighters and AA defences could match every new device which Bomber Command employed; and that, without the command of the air, which was finally secured by the American long-range Mustang fighter in daytime, the night-time offensive campaign orchestrated by 'bomber' Harris would have ground to a halt.[3]

Finally, *and perhaps the most important point of all*, British air power in the

Second World War was employed in a whole number of roles not envisaged in the Trenchardian doctrine of bombing the enemy's industrial heartland, viz, tactical operations in the North African and Normandy campaigns, aerial supply to Slim's armies in Burma, anti-submarine patrols in the Bay of Biscay, attacking German submarine pens at Brest and German warships in the Altenfjord, and carrying aid to European resistance movements, as well as the defence of the British homeland itself from all forms of air attack, from Dornier bombers to V-1 'doodlebugs'.

The relevance of this story of the dichotomy between the RAF's prewar aerial strategy and what actually happened when hostilities commenced may not be apparent to those who believe that 'the Great War at Sea 1914–1918 was an overwhelmingly successful demonstration of naval power along classical lines'.[4] To more thoughtful scholars, however, the point will be obvious. What one is dealing with here is the inexact and difficult relationship between a general theory of strategy and the unpredictable, complicated, random problems which are thrown up in wartime. To put it another way, there is a marked difference between what an armed service expects to be doing as a result of its prewar 'strategy', and what it actually turns out to be doing in consequence of the demands of war. As a minor consolation, the example of Trenchard and Harris provides the gloomy proof that strategic misjudgement is not confined to any one Service, or to any one period in history.

Apart from its utility as a cautionary tale, the above example suggests that any proper analysis of Anglo-American 'maritime strategies' in the first two decades of this century will need to incorporate the three separate stages which occur in the evolution of all strategic policies:

1 the doctrinal formulation of the strategy, that is, the cluster of ideas which, whatever the differentiation of emphasis within the Service, advocated a certain way of warfare;
2 the actual force-structure created during the years of peace by the Service, which will include overall size and organisation, weapons-systems, levels of technology and training, logistical support, location of major bases, and so on – and the degree to which all this conformed to the strategy envisaged in the doctrinal formulation itself;
3 the wartime experiences of the Service, and in particular the extent to which the prewar strategy proved itself relevant.

This implies an assessment not merely of whether the accepted strategy could in fact be successfully implemented, but also whether the real conditions of war compelled the Service to engage in roles which were downgraded or even totally ignored in the original peace-time conception of how victory was to be secured. It confronts, in other words, Lord Kitchener's rueful observation that 'Unfortunately we have to make war as we must and not as we should like to.'[5]

The first point to be ventured about Anglo-American maritime–strategical assumptions in this period is that they were much more *instinctive* than they were intellectual. That is to say, that few if any references to the 'classics' of naval thought can be detected in the policy documents of this time; and that successful naval officers made their reputations in gunnery practices and fleet manoeuvres, not in their knowledge of Thucydides, Clausewitz or other works of broad military history. There was, it is true, an immense public debate about 'sea power' in these years, carried on by the press and by the British and American navy leagues, but not much of that focussed upon a maritime strategy *per se*. In Britain, for example, far greater attention was given to the annual naval budget (especially when the Liberal government sought to limit the growth of defence spending), to the number of capital ships needed to maintain a lead over Germany, to the wisdom of newer types like the *Dreadnought* and *Invincible*, to Fisher's controversial 'scrapping' policies, and so on.[6] Journalists like Arnold White, Garvin, and Thursfield were deemed useful to Admiral Fisher when defending *his* policies in the press, but there is no sign that they influenced strategic thought in any way. Even within governmental circles, little effort was made by bodies such as the Committee of Imperial Defence to investigate the Navy's strategical assumptions; when Sir George Clarke tried to do so, he quickly earned Fisher's animosity and soon after moved to become Governor of Bombay.[7] Admiralty policy, it was clear, was the Admiralty's policy alone. It was *not* the result of a refined and open debate about strategical principles.

Part of the problem was institutional: there simply was no Royal Navy equivalent to a General Staff, trained to think through strategical issues. But that in turn was a reflection of Fisher's own lack of interest in strategy. In 1906, when under pressure from his many critics, he did create the small Ballard Committee (on which Julian Corbett was a member) to devise a set of 'War Plans'.[8] There is, however, very little sign that either Fisher or his successor Admiral Wilson paid attention to those plans – or that they were ever willing to set their own ideas on paper. When Wilson was forced to explain his own views, at the critical Committee of Imperial Defence meeting of 23 August 1911, his suggestions were (to use Asquith's later description of them) 'puerile'. But even the creation of an Admiralty War Staff by Churchill in 1912 did not solve the problem, because of its clumsy structure.[9] Institutionally, at least, the US Navy was in a better position to consider strategical issues, once the General Board had been set up in 1900.[10] As will be seen below, that did not necessarily mean that it possessed a maritime strategy which was intellectually well-grounded.

That said, it also has to be admitted that the maritime strategies of both the British and American navies did reflect the ideas of the one writer who had done so much to popularise the notion of 'sea power'. One cannot help being struck by how 'Mahanian' the British and American maritime strategies were, both before and even during the First World War. To begin, they presumed 'the influence of sea power upon history' without much or any appreciation of the fact that a struggle fought at appalling daily cost in such regions as Galicia, Flanders and the Isonzo might make a maritime strategy *less central* than had been the case in, say, the Anglo-Dutch wars. No doubt it is the habit of individual armed services everywhere to emphasise the strategical importance of their own campaigning: none the less, one cannot help being surprised by both admiralties' blithe disregard of the awkward fact that this particular war was one in which governmental and public concern was heavily focussed upon struggles on *land*. If nothing else, this prewar assumption about the superiority of sea power made the Navy intellectually ill-equipped to suggest campaigns in which it might work *in conjunction with* the Army: in other words, admirals who assumed that 'sea power' had 'influence' regardless of the actual circumstances were not likely to consider alternatives to their own maritime strategy.

More particularly, the official Anglo-American strategy followed Mahan in believing that sea power was manifested in the existence of a powerful battlefleet which would engage a similarly configured enemy force in a struggle for command of the oceans; the heavily-armed dreadnoughts of 1914, just like Nelson's line-of-battleships, thus represented 'that overbearing power on the sea which drives the enemy's flag from it ...'.[11] Every other weapons system was secondary for the impending Trafalgar in the North Sea, or west of Midway.

By extension, therefore, the Anglo-American maritime strategy was heavily *offensive* in its operational nature. This was perhaps most clearly spelled out by the British Admiralty's testimony to the 1902 Colonial Conference:

> the primary object of the British Navy is not to defend anything, but to attack the fleets of the enemy, and, by defeating them, to afford protection to British Dominions, supplies and commerce. This is the ultimate aim ... The traditional role of the Royal Navy is not to act on the defensive, but to prepare to attack the force which threatens – in other words, to assume the offensive.[12]

This was true of both schools in the acrimonious debate over 'speed versus armour' prior to 1914, for the point behind Fisher's increasingly unorthodox battlecruiser designs was to create a warship which could destroy the enemy battlefleet *before* ever coming under fire itself. And it remained true even when, in 1912, the Royal Navy reluctantly concluded that it would have to abandon its policy of close blockade, for it still planned to seek battle as soon as the enemy's fleet ventured into the open waters of the North Sea.[13] In the same way, although the US Navy envisioned its role as beating back either a German strike at the Caribbean or Japanese expansionism into the western Pacific (especially the Philippines), the actual naval campaign would involve seeking out the enemy's main fleet and destroying it.[14] Once that happy event had taken place, the war would essentially be over so far as the *battleships* were concerned, although of course smaller vessels (cruisers, destroyers) might be needed to maintain an economic blockade of the enemy's ports.

It was probably no coincidence, therefore, that the Anglo-American maritime strategy in this period contained many of the features of contemporary *military* thought, aptly described by Snyder under the term 'the ideology of the offensive'.[15] The impending war was bound to be swift: it would be decided by a few, early major battles; and everything depended upon getting one's larger forces into action as soon as possible.[16] A defensive posture spelt failure.

It is also proper to note that the period 1900–1920 also saw certain naval writers beginning to argue for a more subtle understanding of what 'command of the sea' meant – in particular, Corbett, in his *Some Principles of Maritime Strategy*. But the point about both Corbett and Richmond (who are discussed in Part II: see p. 81) is that their historical approach to naval strategy did not fit in well with services which had a distinctly *materialist* outlook.[17] After all, it could be argued, if one really needed to draw lessions from the past, were they not already at hand in the early chapters of Mahan's *The Influence of Sea Power upon History*? Why study it further, especially when the message was either wrapped up in Corbett's more abstract, Clauswitzian formulations (*Some Principles*), or buried within detailed multi-volume studies of the wars of 1739–48 (Richmond) and 1756–63 (Corbett)?

The prevailing suppositions of the maritime strategy structured the British and American navies in predictable ways. Although Fisher himself became mesmerised by the potentialities of an ultra-fast, lightly-armoured battle-cruiser type, the core of both fleets always remained the battleship itself, which since the 1905–6 'Dreadnought revolution' possessed uniform main guns of ever-larger calibre – 12-inch, then 13.5-inch, then 15-inch in the British case, 12-inch and 14-inch in the American – and an increasing displacement, from the *Dreadnought*'s 17,000 tons to the 29,000 tons of the *Queen Elizabeth* class and 32,000 tons of the *New Mexico* class.[18] Because this was 'The Battleship Era',[19] with more than a dozen navies acquiring these expensive weapons systems, the size of a country's battlefleet became the measure of its maritime power. The various naval 'races' of this period (Britain versus Germany, the United States versus Japan, Chile versus Argentina and so on) excited much public debate about the size of the respective battlefleets; Asquith's Liberal government, for example, was severely battered by the criticism made in 1908/9 that it was losing its numerical lead over Germany in this critical class of weapons.[20]

By comparison, therefore, all other types of warship were seen to possess only ancillary functions. The 'armoured' or heavy cruisers were to bustle between the battle-lines, if need be joining the line itself with their 9·2-inch guns. The light cruisers, just like Nelson's frigates, would act as 'scouts', bringing news to the battlefleet commander of the whereabouts of the enemy force – a task which was also given, in later years, to aircraft (launched from seaplane-carriers), Zeppelins and other airships, and even to submarines. Surrounding the battlefleet would be squadrons of fast destroyers, designed to deal with the threat posed to the large ships by torpedo-boats but also capable of launching their own torpedoes at enemy warships if that was required. All this meant that, because the force itself was so numerous (at Jutland, for example, the Grand Fleet consisted of 28 battleships, 9 battle-cruisers, and 113 smaller warships), plus the fact that a modern battlefleet could move three or four times *faster* than Nelson's line-of-battleships, the key problem for the Commanding Admiral was one of tactics: that is, of how to manoeuvre the massed columns of vessels so as to bring the greatest weight of shell upon the enemy's fleet.

In consequence prewar tactical training concentrated upon the three related aspects of gunnery, signals and formation exercises. Gunnery in particular was a Royal Navy obsession, and an officer's career could be greatly affected by his ship's performance during the Admiralty-designed firing competitions. The increased speed of warships, and the much longer ranges at which large-calibre guns could throw their shells, posed an enormous challenge to gunnery officers everywhere, and a vast amount of thought was given to developing new range-finders, spotting devices, calibration techniques and the like. In Fisher's view, this combination of faster warships, larger guns and better fire-control would enable an admiral to fight 'HOW you like, WHEN you like, and WHERE you like!'[21] But this also implied that a fleet commander knew the enemy's whereabouts and was able to place his own squadrons in the most advantageous position to fight: hence the importance given to the scouting cruisers, to visual signalling systems (wireless being too risky), and especially to the repeated tactical manoeuvre practices, such as changing the columns of warships into a line-ahead formation and back again.[22]

Such Anglo-American maritime strategies had obvious implications for their respective naval-base policies and their general operations plans. To a Royal Navy whose attention after 1905 was focussed almost exclusively upon the German challenge, it was the bases in the North Sea which mattered, not such historic ports as Plymouth, Gibraltar and Halifax. Sheltered in their various locations (Harwich, Rosyth and especially Scapa Flow), the British squadrons of the Grand Fleet would emerge to do battle once it became known that the enemy's forces were at sea. The US Navy's tasks were more complicated, simply because of geography. Apprehending a German challenge to the Monroe Doctrine and, more specifically, a German move into the Caribbean, American naval planners prepared to order their East Coast-based battlefleet down to Culebra, off Puerto Rico, to meet the oncoming enemy invasion force. In addition, however, the planners in Washington had to prepare against possible Japanese action in the Pacific – a contingency which could not be dealt with immediately, but only after sending large forces from the West Coast (or via the Panama Canal) to the critically important advanced fleet base of Pearl Harbor. Only when assembled in sufficient strength would the United States fleet steam westwards towards Midway, Guam, and the beleaguered Philippines.[23] Exactly like the British, however, the Americans looked forward to a decisive fleet battle to settle the issue of who had command of the sea, and to demonstrate once again the influence of maritime operations upon history.

Given this crudely[24] Mahanian vision of the workings of sea power, it was scarcely surprising that both navies ignored or at least heavily played down a number of alternative strategies and activities in the realm of naval warfare. Thus the heated public debate over maritime rights, especially at the time of the Declaration of London (1909) had certainly produced a number of Admiralty papers on the topic of economic warfare; nevertheless remarkably little concern was shown by either the British or the American naval authorities about the possibility of an enemy-conducted *guerre de course* against their own merchant shipping. Clearly geography played as great a role here as the predilection for battleship actions. With the British controlling the exits from the North Sea, and with the greater part of the German navy based in its home waters because of Tirpitz's opposition to an overseas commerce-raiding strategy,[25] the Admirality in London felt reasonably confident of being able to handle the few, scattered German squadrons in distant seas. (By comparison, it had worried a lot about the threat posed by French and Russian armoured cruisers in the 1890s to the British Empire's sea lines of communication, since that would have been much harder to contain.) In the same way, the geography of the Pacific basin meant that a Japanese threat to United States commerce was judged to be negligible; and even in the Atlantic theatre it was difficult for US naval planners to imagine German commerce-raiders dealing a heavy blow to trade (especially since so much of the USA's exports and imports were carried in British bottoms). Yet, however understandable this reasoning, it meant that, having discarded the *guerre de course* as a major danger to the Anglo-American command of the sea, the respective navies were not very well equipped, either intellectually or in any other respect, to grapple with the much larger threat which the fast-developing submarine would pose to the sea line of communications. Even the brilliantly insightful Fisher sometimes tended to think of what British submarines could do to enemy vessels and not (as Balfour reminded him on a number of occasions) of what French or German submarines could do to 'render *our* [Britain's] position untenable'.[26]

It was also not surprising, therefore, that the British and American navies paid little attention to a strategy of combined operations, particularly with respect to launching an amphibious force to affect the military campaigns on land. Theoretically this was an important part of the overall American strategy as outlined in War Plans Orange and Black, which could be viewed as an updated version of the 1898 expeditions to the Philippines and Cuba. In actual fact, the prevailing tendency within both the Army and the Navy was to see themselves as completely separate and independent bodies, with the consequence that the so-called Joint Board, in the view of one historian, 'lost rather than gained influence in these years'.[27] While the modest-sized US Army engaged in Mexican adventures in this prewar period, the Navy concentrated upon its beloved battleships. It was true that the Marine Corps was toying with the idea of an Advanced Base Force before the war, but there was opposition within its own ranks to that sort of activity, *and* a chronic lack of funds. Both of the major Services neglected the many logistical problems which would need to be solved before any fully successful execution of War Plan Orange:

> In 1914 the battleship fleet could hardly reach San Francisco, let alone make a voyage of 10 000 miles from their Atlantic base to the Philippines. Moreover, the construction of defences, docks, and the establishment of garrisons on United States Pacific islands had been neglected. The army in the Philippines could not hope to resist a Japanese assault for sixty days, while Guam, Midway and Hawaii were virtually defenceless and Pearl Harbor as yet could not even dock a battleship.[28]

In such circumstances it was inconceivable that the American plans for combined operations would be anything other than rudimentary.

The British neglect of this alternative strategy is also easily explained. Traditionally, combined operations – or at least 'descents' by British forces upon enemy coastlines – had formed a very familiar part of what was later to be termed 'the British way in warfare', although those operations had produced less operational success and much more tactical blundering than its chief protagonist, Liddell Hart, rosily suggested.[29] More to the point, Admiral Fisher was proposing a variety of combined operations against (say) Borkum or even the Pomeranian coast in these years, and the idea of amphibious operations was also attractive to such influential people as Esher and Hankey. In actual fact, however, the increasing interest shown by the Army after 1905 in developing a 'contintental commitment',[30] together with the growing awareness of the difficulties of landing an army on a hostile coast (as was revealed in the various prewar 'Invasion' enquiries), meant that Fisher's schemes were opposed by the Imperial General Staff, which simply required the Navy to safeguard the Expeditionary Force's transit to France.[31] With the two Services looking for a decisive battle in their own spheres of war, it was in vain that that thoughtful strategist, Julian Corbett, proposed 'conjunct' operations in keeping with Britain's geostrategical traditions.[32]

Finally there was the relative neglect of all of those ancillary activities required of a navy if it really intended to exercise full command of the sea. According to Professor Grenville, the 1914 War Plan Orange was undermined by the fact that, while 'Congress had approved appropriations for the construction of a battleship fleet superior to the Japanese, [it] had ignored the persistent requests of the General Board, passed on to them by the Secretary of the Navy, for adequate personnel to man the ships and for the necessary auxiliary ships, cruisers, destroyers, transports, ammunition ships and above all colliers on which the movement of the fleet depended.'[33] Colliers were obviously less impressive – and diverted less cash towards congressional districts – than battleship contracts. (The same was true, incidentally, of naval bases: because of pressures from Congressmen, the US Navy had an excessive number of *home* bases, but none adequately equipped overseas.) If the Royal Navy was in a better position with regard to smaller ships, that was simply because its global empire and trading and fishing activities had generated a large number of colliers, tramp-steamers, trawlers and other vessels which could be pressed into service. Nevertheless it still lacked a whole variety of the vessels which would be required for minelaying, minesweeping, escort duties and so on.

When it actually came, the 'Great War at Sea' did indeed turn out to be a much more variegated and complicated affair than that postulated in the prewar maritime strategies. There was, for example, *nothing* in the actual strategical circumstances of 1917–18 which conformed with the assumptions of the US Navy prior to 1914; and even in the case of the Royal Navy – which, because of its far more extensive wartime role, will be examined in proportionately larger detail below – the reality of naval warfare turned out to be significantly different from the earlier expectations.

The US Navy's dilemma is easily understood. Guided (if that is the right word) by prewar and wartime assumptions about likely enemies which often bordered on the absurd,[34] the Service found itself in April 1917 in a situation which seemed to render irrelevant a battleship-centred 'maritime strategy'. In the Pacific, Japan was already a member of the alliance against the Central Powers; and even if its expansion into the formerly German-controlled territories gave American planners cause for concern, and complicated War Plan Orange, there was certainly no case for instigating that plan.[35] In the Atlantic, battleships were close to being superfluous: the High Seas Fleet was bottled up by the Royal Navy and when the five American battleships under Rear-Admiral Rodman joined the Grand Fleet at Scapa Flow they reinforced a surface-vessel superiority that was already overwhelming. Needless to say, the prospect of the German navy penetrating the Caribbean – which was still the assumption of the 1915 war-game – was about as remote as a Martian invasion. All this, at first sight at least, makes the Naval Act of 1916, designed to give the Service 'a navy second to none' by the construction in short time of an additional ten battleships and six battlecruisers, appear to be the work of strategical dreamers.[36]

The experience of the British with their battlefleets in the First World War was, if anything, even more disappointing. There were, to be sure, individual surface-fleet victories – in particular, at the Battle of the Falklands, and another, if one discounts the many ominous signs of mistakes in tactics and communications,[37] at the Battle of the Dogger Bank. But that had to be set against the failure to catch the *Goeben* and *Breslau*, the disaster at Coronel, the inability to intercept the 1917–18 sorties of German warships into the North Sea; and, above all, Jutland. For however much that encounter confirmed the impossibility of the High Seas Fleet's overall strategical position, it also pointed to the weaknesses of the Royal Navy's prewar suppositions. The most immediate of these was the assumption that the British superiority in numbers of battleships and weight of shell would almost certainly translate into a smashing defeat of the German navy even in the unpredictable conditions of the North Sea and against a foe which, as it turned out, had better-compartmentalised vessels, better fire-control, and better tactical preparation for night-fighting.[38]

In addition, Jutland brought into the open the bitter disagreement between the *offensive* and *defensive* schools of thought in British naval circles. To Jellicoe, the inheritor of the many risky reforms of the 'Fisher era', the battle confirmed both his earlier worries about the capacity of British warships to withstand sustained enemy fire and his apprehensions, especially those of October 1914,[39] about the danger from torpedoes. It was therefore just a logical step for him – and also for his successor, Beatty – to firmly adopt a waiting policy, justifying it in terms which echoed Corbett's emphasis upon 'control of communications'. When Churchill, who at this time oscillated between a defensive and an offensive strategy, justified the former in September 1916 by publicly claiming that 'without a battle we have all the most victorious of battles could give us', he provoked the outrage of the so-called 'historical school', which claimed that the fighting traditions of Drake, Hawke and Nelson were now being abandoned.[40]

Acting offensively once a battle had commenced, by, for example, turning *towards* rather than away from enemy-launched torpedoes, was one thing; but critics of the Admiralty like Custance, Sydenham and Pollen could never satisfactorily explain exactly how the High Seas Fleet could be brought to battle in the first place, if the Germans declined to leave harbour. And behind the frustration of both schools there may have lurked the uncomfortable thought that even a result different from that which obtained at Jutland (that is, far fewer British and many more German warship losses) would not have had any real influence upon the epic, grinding struggle that was being fought across Europe.

At sea, it was true, the 1914–18 conflict produced its own epic, grinding struggle, the results of which determined the overall outcome of the war; but it was a campaign fought, not between battlefleets, but to defeat the threat posed by the U-boats to the Atlantic and Mediterranean lines of communication. By definition, the challenge to Allied merchantmen represented by German submarines was one that could *never* be settled by a single decisive encounter. It was, rather, a war of attrition in which the tonnage of merchant ships sunk each month had to be measured against those being launched. Even the number of U-boats destroyed by Allied counter-action was, in its way, a secondary (if useful) contribution; for the key problem was *to stop the submarines getting at the merchantmen*, and a policy of re-routing and evasion was as successful, strategically, as one of beating off the U-boats and deterring them from pressing home their attacks. As Winton remarks, 'the sinking of U-boats did not in the end matter very much. What counted was the safe and timely arrival of the merchant ships'.[41]

The consequences of all this for the prewar maritime strategy were serious and many. In the first place, it challenged the cozy assumption mentioned earlier that a *guerre de course* was irrelevant strategically. It was not the case, of course, that the defence of seaborne trade had been totally ignored by either the British or the American admiralties. In the British case especially, given its dependence upon foreign trade, commerce-protection had been a matter of constant concern during the late nineteenth and early twentieth centuries.[42] The replacement of France and Russia by Germany as the Power most likely to challenge Britain's command of the sea had eased that problem, although it was admitted that if the Germans deployed fast auxiliary cruisers in wartime they would cause trouble.[43] Nevertheless such interruptions to trade seemed small-scale to a service committed to retaining naval mastery by its own *offensive* maritime strategy, which would, in Churchill's view, dislocate the enemy's ability to do much damage to the sea lanes:

> A policy of vigorous offence against the enemy's warships whenever stationed, will give immediately far greater protection to British traders than large numbers of vessels scattered sparsely about in an attitude of weak and defensive expectancy. ... Enemy cruisers cannot live in the oceans for any length of time. They cannot coal at sea with any certainty. They cannot make many prizes without much steaming; and in these days of W/T their whereabouts will be constantly reported. If British cruisers of superior speed are hunting them, they cannot do much harm before they are brought to action.[44]

Behind this assumption, it is clear, there lay that Mahanian belief in the indecisiveness of the *guerre de course*, although few of the prewar planners seem to have considered whether lessons drawn from, say, the Napoleonic War might be fully appropriate for the changed economic and technological conditions of twentieth-century warfare. Linked with this assumption, however, was the Admiralty's worry that too great a concern about the protection of commerce would 'divert ships from the main theatre of war to the trade routes',[45] thus undermining their own offensive strategy. It was for this reason, for example, that British naval planners favoured war-risks insurance for shipping, to prevent a cessation of commerce and a public panic which might force a derangement of the intended British maritime strategy.

The second challenge posed by the U-boats was to the planned disposition of British warships and, in the longer term, to the *types* of vessel that proved most useful in maintaining command of the sea. Given the Admiralty's worry about a possible sortie by the High Seas Fleet, it was inconceivable for the Royal Navy to scrap or decommission, its own large fleet of battleships and to use their crews, and the smaller escorts, in other theatres of war. In just the same way, it was also held to be important to maintain the Harwich Force of scouting cruisers and destroyers. Nevertheless a larger and larger proportion of the Navy's warships and personnel shifted out of the North Sea as the war progressed. It was also natural that, as the U-boat war intensified, Admiralty planners looked longingly at the squadrons of destroyers residing at Rosyth and Scapa Flow. By early 1917, for example, 280 destroyers were available for anti-submarine warfare but there still remained about 100 with the Grand Fleet;[46] and Beatty found himself, like Jellicoe before him, fighting off Admiralty suggestions to reduce that total, that is, to quote again from the prewar memorandum, 'to divert ships from the main theatre of war to the trade routes'. For the same reason, British warship-building sharply changed its emphasis: in 1914 the Royal Navy had no less than 14 battleships and battlecruisers under construction, as compared with 20 destroyers; by 1918, only one battlecruiser was being completed, but so also were 108 destroyers.[47]

It was not only the destroyers which were drawn into the anti-submarine campaign. Winton notes that 'in one week of September 1916 three U-boats operated in the Channel between Beachy Head and the Eddystone Light, an area patrolled by forty-nine destroyers, forty-eight torpedo boats, seven Q-ships, and 468 armed auxiliaries – some *572* anti-submarine vessels in all, not counting aircraft'.[48] In the pre-convoy period, that was a quite disproportionate effort, akin to the proverbial hunt for the needle in the haystack. The U-boats on this occasion sank thirty ships and disrupted Channel traffic; they themselves were unscathed, despite the British patrols. When the British later turned to the scheme to block U-boats exiting into the Atlantic by the construction of an elaborate and expensive Channel Barrage, they still could not deal with the problem. This was also the case with the Allied efforts to prevent U-boats leaving or entering the Adriatic by constructing the Otranto Barrage (of nets and mines), with supporting warships. Winton's nicely-understated comments are worth reproducing *in extenso* here:

> The fixed barrage was supported by a mobile barrage force, of destroyers, flotillas of submarines, sloops flying kite balloons, American sub-chasers, torpedo boats, MLs and one yacht. The total number of warships was

some 300 and to provide them the convoys were stripped to their minimum escort, convoys of thirty ships often being escorted by one sloop and two trawlers. There were also lines of fixed hydrophones laid out under water, constant patrols along the length of the barrage, and air patrols (there were some seventy British aircraft, bombers, fighters and seaplanes, with Italian and French aircraft support, based at Taranto and Otranto).

There is no evidence that the U-boats were unduly bothered by the Barrage. They continued to make their passages more or less at will. The barrage forces sank two U-boats. The net itself claimed one. In the same period the much-depleted and often-disparaged convoy escorts sank eight out of the twelve U-boats sunk in the Mediterranean during 1917 and 1919.[49]

The last sentence brings us to the final impact of the emergence of this newer and deadlier form of *guerre de course*. It compelled a reluctant Admiralty not only to admit to the significance of commerce-protection – by 1917 both Jellicoe and Beatty were beginning to fear that they might lose the war at sea, and thus the *entire war*, regardless of the fire-power of the Grand Fleet – but also to acknowledge the critical importance of that long-disregarded method, the convoy. This is not the place to analyse all the arguments made for and against its introduction in 1917, or to speculate on the role of Lloyd George in imposing that system upon the Admiralty;[50] the point being made here is that this was yet another example of a prewar assumption which proved erroneous. Yet another offensive notion, that of going out to hunt for submarines (exactly in the same way that one 'hunted' for surface commerce-raiders) was made futile by the particular technological and geographical circumstances of the 1914–18 war at sea. By contrast, the *defensive* strategy of convoy protection was much more successful, since it forced the U-boats to expose themselves to counter-attack by the convoy's escorts whenever the submarines came close to the merchant ships. Ironically, just as in the great land battles along the Western Front (at least until 1918) the attacker was always tactically disadvantaged *vis-à-vis* the defender.[51]

Despite three years of observing the devastation which U-boats could inflict upon merchantmen, the US Navy was no better prepared to deal with *guerre de course*. Although the General Board in 1916 claimed that the navy was 'short' 125 cruisers, destroyers and other smaller warships, its own ambitions placed a heavy emphasis upon capital-ship building. Despite the urgings of Sims in London, and President Wilson's own feelings on the subject, the Navy Department was not enthusiastic about convoy, offering all the traditional arguments against that practice; if it had to be tried, it was argued, it should be in very small numbers, say four mechantmen escorted by two destroyers (a very uneconomic measure).[52] The Northern Barrage, laid with great expense at American insistence, showed Washington to be as naive about how to deal with the U-boat as Whitehall had been in the case of the Otranto Barrage.[53]

Furthermore, because of their battlefleet obsession, and continued fantasies about a German–Japanese combination against the USA, Benson and his colleagues resisted for months Sims' pleas to release more destroyers for escort in the eastern Atlantic. They also disliked the dispatch of a battle-squadron to Scapa Flow, partly out of the purportedly Mahanian objection that that would 'split' the main fleet, chiefly because they wanted to keep their force of battleships intact for future eventualities.[54] Finally the US Navy fought hard against the proposals that the critical nature of the U-boat campaign necessitated a halt to capital-ship construction, and the use of those resources for a crash programme of building destroyers and merchantmen. The Board's reluctance here was heavily influenced by their suspicions of the motives of the British (who had requested such a change in American shipbuilding policy), and their decision to suspend the capital-ship programme was reversed as the war came to its close. Throughout, the US Navy stayed wedded to the overriding importance of 'big ships'.[55]

Because the idea of combined operations had suffered from Army–Navy differences prior to 1914, and occupied no part in the Grand Fleet's maritime strategy, it was perhaps inevitable that wartime attempts to execute an amphibious landing proved so difficult. The Dardanelles campaign in particular showed weaknesses at all levels, operational, tactical and logistical. Theoretically it might have seemed that Britain and France were using their natural strengths (derived from the flexibility of sea power) to attack a weak member of the enemy coalition, to relieve Russia, and to influence the balance of power in the Balkans. But the problem with this essentially 'peripheral' and 'navalist' campaign was that it ignored the general technological trends (minefields, mobile shore-batteries, torpedoes) which rendered hazardous *close-in* operations by battlefleets in hostile waters; it ignored the specific assessments made prior to 1914 about the Royal Navy's chances of taking the Straits; and it ignored – or overrode – the doubts expressed by senior officers at the Admiralty in 1915 itself about the feasibility of such an action.

Equally damning was the fact that, for all the alleged preference by the British for 'conjunct operations' there simply were no supporting facilities for something like the Gallipoli landings. When General Hamilton was appointed to that command, there was no intelligence back-up at all, there were no maps of the area, and no awareness of the 1907 enquiry which pointed out how difficult such an assault from the sea might be. The Navy's minesweeping resources were inadequate, and the bombarding squadron lacked trained spotter–pilots and, indeed, aerial reconnaissance in general. Hamilton's troops were a veritable *mélange* of ill-prepared units. Artillery was well below standard issue, and ammunition stocks were far too small.

For the trench warfare which actually occurred, the landing force possessed neither mortars, nor grenades, nor periscopes. Water supplies and containers – absolutely vital in that heat – were dreadfully low; medical facilities were insufficient.[56]

Since the British had evolved no oerational/tactical organisations for amphibious landings, and since Gallipoli turned out to be such a disaster, there were no real developments in this field of warfare for the rest of the war. That more might have been done is suggested by the Zeebrugge Raid of April 1918. The force was trained for weeks beforehand in the Thames Estuary; special ships were requisitioned, or old ones reconstructed; special smoke-shells and other effects were produced; monitors with heavy guns were to give artillery support; and the landing-party consisted of 'picked companies of marines ... armed with the paraphernalia of trench warfare, howitzers, stokes-mortars, flame-throwers, and machine-guns'.[57] This was one of the very few (and very temporary) efforts made to create Special Forces, and was soon forgotten after 1919. No doubt much of this neglect was due to the very obvious fact that the Army disliked the idea of combined operations, and that there was no one in power (like Churchill between 1940 and 1945) to push its case. But it provides a reminder that 'alternative strategies' are not going to succeed unless considerable technical and tactical preparation is made for the operations which are being proposed. In an age when battlefleet actions dominated naval thought, such preparation was hardly likely.

Since the US Army, once it entered the war, found itself even more bound to a European 'continental commitment' than the British (who did at least carry out a number of mobile campaigns in Mesopotamia, East Africa and Palestine), the possibility of a special American contribution to amphibious warfare at this time was nil. Only in the 1920s, in fact, did some circles in the US Marines begin to develop ideas which would ensure that the 'maritime strategy' of the Allies in the Second World War was so much richer and more flexible than that of the First.[58]

Finally one is struck by the importance and ubiquity of *small* ships, the sheer variety of tasks they were required to carry out in the 'Great War at Sea', and the absence of any significant reference to them in the maritime strategy of both the British and American navies. The Mediterranean theatre between 1914 and 1918 provides an excellent example of this. In navalist–romantic histories, the war in those waters is usually depicted in terms of a few epic events or campaigns – the escape of the *Goeben* and *Breslau*, the fiasco of the Dardanelles, the sinking of the Turkish battleship *Messudieh* by the 'small, old and relatively primitive' British submarine B-11, and so on.[59] Professor Halpern's extraordinarily diligent and multi-archival reconstruction of the war in that theatre offers an important corrective. Of course battleships played a role; given the excessive Allied worries about a sortie by the Austro-Hungarian fleet or (near the end of the war) by a Turkish/German/(captured) Russian force from the Black Sea, it remained necessary to keep ready a considerable force of French, Italian and British dreadnoughts, since they still were 'the accepted standard of naval strength at the time'.[60] Nevertheless, whatever the assumptions of the various admiralties, the reality of the Mediterranean naval war was quite different. It was a campaign waged chiefly by smaller vessels: monitors bombarding the Albanian coast, supply-ships and hospital-ships attending to shoreline operations, minelayers and minesweepers and, above all, the submarine and its many enemies – destroyers, sloops, trawlers, sub-chasers, not to mention aircraft. Simply to patrol the coastal waters and to escort merchant shipping, there were over 850(!) armed Allied vessels in the Mediterranean in May 1917.[61]

All this helps to explain the curious fact that, although the overwhelming proportion of Britain's own battleships remained in the North Sea, the Royal Navy's 'influence' (to use Mahan's term) in the Mediterranean steadily increased. Halpern's comments upon this trend are particularly insightful:

> As the war progressed it turned out to be the light craft, the cruisers, submarines, destroyers, sloops and drifters which became all-important, while the powerful dreadnoughts played a subsidiary, though always potentially important, role as fleets-in-being. By the latter stages of the war there would be a correspondingly different definition of naval power – one based on these light craft. There is something essentially artificial in speaking of French predominance in the Mediterranean and treating Britain as a minor factor. ... The size of the British merchant marine and fishing fleet which was the source of the anti-submarine drifters and trawlers, and the capacity of British yards to turn out scores of escort craft as well as the ability of British industry to produce large quantities of anti-submarine nets and materials resulted in a steady increase in Britain's relative strength in the Mediterranean. The British would never have the strength in capital ships that the French had, but through the swarm of light craft they would gradually recover much of the influence they had been willing to relinquish in 1912.[62]

It was not surprising, therefore, that when the US Navy entered the war, its expensive new battleships were superfluous to the naval balance in the Mediterranean; what was needed instead was destroyers, gunships, sub-chasers and, perhaps above all, fast American supply-ships.[63] In the same way, when the Japanese government agreed to Allied requests to extend its assistance westwards, into the Mediterranean theatre, it was destroyers, *not* battleships, which were provided, proving especially valuable in escorting troopships.[64] It is true that neither the American nor the Japanese admiralty *wanted* to commit their heavy ships;[65] but even if some had been sent to the Mediterranean, it is hard to see what use they could have been.

Given the above-mentioned deficiencies in the Anglo-American maritime strategy before and during the First World War, it may strike the reader as odd that both admiralties, as well as their French, Italian and Japanese counterparts, approached the 1919 peace negotiations obsessed about battleship numbers and, in particular, about the disposition of the battle-fleets of the defeated Powers.[66] From the US Navy's viewpoint, Grenville has argued, the General Board had spent the period 1914–17 in 'preparing not for the First World War but for the war which would follow it'.[67] That is to say, Admiral Benson and his colleagues, admitting that the geostrategical conditions in the North Sea would not provide the fleet with a significant surface victory, chose instead to emphasise a future social–Darwinistic and mercantilist world order in which the US Navy would have to face the British and the Japanese fleets at the same time.[68] If the American admirals were the most fatuous of the end-of-war maritime planners, there was precious little enlightenment shown by the staffs of the other Allied powers. While the Sea Lords in London were doing detailed calculations of their battlefleets *vis-à-vis* the Americans and the Japanese, in the Mediterranean the French and the Italians were already squaring off against each other. This was why the disposal of the High Seas Fleet, and of the large warships of the Austro-Hungarian and Turkish navies, placed such a strain upon Allied loyalties in 1918–19.[69]

Why the British and American navies placed such emphasis upon the central importance of the battleship at the end of a war which had revealed the limitations of that particular weapons system had as much to do with politics as with strategy. To a considerable extent, it could be argued that it was necessary because all *other* major navies possessed battleships and that none of their admiralties was proposing (as Percy Scott did) that such warships were now redundant.[70] In addition, it could plausibly be maintained that, while conditions in the North Sea and Adriatic had restricted the employment of battlefleets in the 1914–18 conflict, those squadrons would again come into their own in, say, a future Japanese–American clash in the Pacific or in the British defence of their Eastern empire (now to be centred on the new *battleship* base at Singapore). There was also the technically correct argument that, since small vessels could be built so much faster than battleships, a shortage of, say, destroyers could more easily be made up in wartime (always provided one had not lost the naval war in the meantime!).

But quite apart from such diplomatic and strategical reasonings, there were also budgetary and psychological causes for the retention of the large battlefleet as the accepted standard of naval strength. A decision to order, say, another four battleships involved enormous sums of money, not just for the hulls, machinery and guns themselves but also for their large crews, and possibly for such ancillary items as dry-docks, new escort-vessels and the like: in other words, it involved a very *large* establishment, which was precisely why most admirals preferred a battleship-centred navy, and why they sought to fight off cost-conscious politicians and Treasury officials who were also aware of the consequential costs of building and maintaining such large ships. Finally, of course, there was the element of tradition. Virtually all of the Anglo-American admirals of 1919 had been brought up as 'battleship men', trained to extol the heavy gun and to be ready for the decisive fleet encounter. To admit that the battleship era might be drawing to a close would have been a dreadful psychological blow, equivalent to a cavalryman conceding that the horse was no longer of use on a modern battlefield. To think that way was virtual suicide for the service.

Nevertheless one detects an anxiety among British and American admirals as they turned from what had been a disappointing surface war to face the uncertainties of peace-time. This was admittedly less the case in the US Navy, since despite the limitations imposed by the Washington treaties it was able to consolidate much of its post-1916 expansion; and the 'threat' posed by aircraft to the traditional means of sea power could be incorporated into the fleet with the development of new carriers.[71] The erosion of funds for naval purposes by the late 1920s did depress morale, but the Service itself was still better treated than in most other countries and it could continue to feel that it had a distinct mission, to uphold the interests of an isolationist America and to prepare for a possible Pacific war. British admirals, one senses, were rather more desperate, not only because of the budgetary cuts demanded by Lloyd George and Geddes or even the cession of undisputed naval supremacy at the Washington Conference, but also because so many aspects of their own strategical thinking were coming under attack. The Service's strong rivalry with the newly-created Royal Air Force, which challenged the autonomy of sea power: the 1921 proposal at the Washington Conference to abolish all submarines – still regarded (to use Admiral Wilson's phrase) as 'underhand, unfair, and Damned unEnglish!' – precisely because it undermined the role of the battlefleets;[72] the Admiralty's disagreement with their own official historian, Sir Julian Corbett, for (in their words) minimizing 'the importance of seeking battle and of forcing it to a conclusion' in his account in *Naval Operations*,[73] not to mention their constant 're-fighting' of Jutland, whether at the Staff College throughout the inter-war years or in their memoirs and other acrimonious published accounts of the battle; their later reprimand of, and final break with, that other original naval thinker, Admiral Sir Herbert Richmond, because of his 1920s advocacy of 'mini'-battleships:[74] all suggests an organisation which was now repeatedly called upon to defend its 'maritime strategy' in a way that had rarely been necessary prior to 1914.[75]

What, if anything, could the above analysis contribute to the contemporary debate about the US Navy's proclaimed 'maritime strategy'?[76] In the first place, it suggests that those involved in thinking about future wars might occasionally profit from some knowledge of past conflicts. This is not a popular proposal among those who believe that advanced technology has so transformed the battlefield that it has made irrelevant the study of History. A similar view, it might be recalled, was held by Fisher:

> Whatever service the past may be to other professions, it can be categorically stated in regard to the Navy that history is a record of exploded ideas. Every condition of the past is altered....[77]

It is ironic to observe, however, that at least two of the members of what might be termed Fisher's 'brains trust' during his period as First Lord were none other than Corbett and Richmond; and that whenever their minds were able to turn from practical matters like naval education to the study and writing of History, they were drawn towards conclusions at variance with the prevailing 'maritime strategy': that is, they tended towards the view that the influence of sea power was not an absolute, but something determined by the historical and geographical circumstances of each particular conflict, that is, by time and space; that command of the sea need not always invoke a decisive naval battle, and that in some cases victory might be achieved without one's main fleet ever needing to be engaged; that trade protection and the *guerre de course* on the one hand, and combined operations on the other, might each be critical parts of a fuller and more successful 'maritime strategy', *always depending upon the nature of the war in question.*[78] But such voices offered little consolation to Beatty, who wanted to get his battlefleet into action on the open seas – and they were anathema to many other strategic commentators, who felt that the wartime Admiralty simply had not been aggressive enough. Ironically, while those critics were wrong about the 1914–18 war at sea, their constant emphasis upon *offensive* naval warfare probably had a useful influence upon naval conduct in the Second World War, when the changed geostrategical circumstances meant that the Allied fleets *had* to take the fight to their enemies, whether in the Mediterranean, off the North Cape, or across the Pacific.

The charge against the pre-1914 Anglo-American 'maritime strategy' is not that the construction and deployment of a fleet consisting mainly of large warships is always wrong, or that the search for offensive operations in enemy waters is always wrong; it is, rather, that those two strands of the strategy *might not always be the right ones for the war in question.* What is vital is context. The First World War, unlike either the Anglo-Dutch wars of the seventeenth century or the 1941–5 Japanese–American war in the Pacific, was chiefly a land conflict in which navies played an important but none the less indirect, supportive and essentially negative role. To put it crudely, if the German submarines had been able to interdict the Allied lines of communication in the Atlantic and Mediterranean, they would in all probability have won the land war as well; because they did not block those sea lanes, they lost the overall conflict.

In such circumstances, a 'maritime strategy' centred upon offensive battlefleet actions was simple-minded. The squadrons of British and American battleships at Scapa Flow *might* have had to go into action, but only if the numerically inferior High Seas Fleet had ventured forth to dispute command of the sea, which was always highly unlikely; a defensive, 'waiting' strategy therefore made sense for the Allies, as Corbett rightly argued. Conversely, the Anglo-American admiralties' fixation with the decisive battle not only distracted them from a more serious study of the alternative uses of sea power such as combined operations, but also left them badly equipped to handle the challenge thrown up by the U-boat menace. In terms of the ships and weapons systems required, in both the structure and deployment of their fleets and, perhaps most importantly of all, in their *mental* preparation of war, the two navies were not properly equipped for a conflict which turned out to be altogether more diffuse and variegated than that imagined in the prewar maritime strategy. Like the Generals on land, the Admirals made the mistake of assuming that they knew in advance exactly how the next war would be fought.

Notes

1. For Trenchard's views, see A. Boyle, *Trenchard* (London, 1962); and, with more nuance, M. Smith, *British Air Strategy between the Wars* (Oxford, 1984) chapter 2.
2. U. Bialar, *The Shadow of the Bomber: The Fear of an Air Attack and British Politics 1932–1939* (London, 1980); Smith, *British Air Strategy*, chapter 6.
3. The story is summarised in N. Frankland, *The Bombing Offensive against Germany* (London, 1965).
4. R. Hough, *The Great War at Sea 1914–1918* (Oxford, 1983) is a good example of this genre, but see also A. A. Hoehling, *The Great War at Sea: A History of Naval Action 1914–18* (London, 1965), and G. Bennett, *Naval Battles of the First World War* (London, 1968).
5. Quoted by P. Guinn, *British Strategy and Politics 1914 to 1918* (Oxford, 1965).
6. See A. J. Marder, *From the Dreadnought to Scapa Flow*, 5 vols (London, 1961–1970), i, chapters iv–viii; B. Semmel, *Liberalism and Naval Strategy* (London/Boston, 1986) chapter 8.
7. J. Gooch, 'Sir George Clarke's Career at the Committee of Imperial Defence, 1904–1907', *Historical Journal*, xviii, 3 (1975) pp. 67–8.
8. They are reproduced in *The Papers of Admiral Sir John Fisher* (ed.) P. K. Kemp (Navy Records Society, vol. CVI, London, 1974) Part 2; for a critique, see P. Haggie, 'The Royal Navy and War Planning in the Fisher Era', in P. M. Kennedy (ed.), *The War Plans of the Great Powers 1880–1914* (London/Boston, 1979) pp. 118–32.
9. *Fisher Papers*, Part 2; Marder, *From the Dreadnought to Scapa Flow*, i, pp. 265–7. For Asquith's quote, see S. R. Williamson, *The Politics of Grand Strategy: Britain and France Prepare for War, 1904–1914* (Cambridge, Mass., 1969) p. 193.
10. J. A. S. Grenville, 'Diplomacy and War Plans in the United States, 1890–1917', in Kennedy (ed.), *The War Plans of the Great Powers 1880–1914*, p. 28.
11. A. T. Mahan, *The Influence of Sea Power upon History 1660–1763* (London, 1965 edn) p. 138.

12. Quoted by W. C. B. Tunstall, 'Imperial Defence 1897–1914', in E. Benians *et al.* (eds), *The Cambridge History of the British Empire*, vol. iii (Cambridge, 1959) p. 571.
13. This is discussed in Marder, *From the Dreadnought to Scapa Flow*, i, pp. 367ff.; and it is further analysed in P. Kennedy, 'Strategic Aspects of the Anglo-German Naval Race', in *Strategy and Diplomacy 1870–1945* (London, 1983) pp. 147ff. For Fisher's battle-cruiser policy, see the brilliant article by J. T. Sumida, 'British Capital Ship Design and Fire Control in the *Dreadnought* Era', *The Journal of Modern History*, 51 (June, 1979) pp. 205–30, and his important forthcoming book.
14. American naval war planning in this period is best discussed in W. R. Braisted, *The United States Navy in the Pacific*, 2 vols. (Austin, Texas, 1958, 1971), but see again Grenville, 'Diplomacy and War Plans', *passim*.
15. J. Snyder, *The Ideology of the Offensive: Military Decision Making and the Disasters of 1914* (Ithaca, NY, 1984), *passim*.
16. See the discussion in the Introduction of Kennedy (ed.), *The War Plans of the Great Powers 1880–1914*, pp. 18–19.
17. Marder, *Dreadnought to Scapa Flow*, i, pp. 395–405.
18. For details, see A. Preston, *Battleships of World War I* (London, 1972).
19. To employ the title of P. Padfield's *The Battleship Era* (London, 1972).
20. Marder, *Dreadnought to Scapa Flow*, i, pp. 151ff.; P. Padfield, *The Great Naval Race* (London, 1974) chapter 9.
21. Quoted in Sumida, 'British Capital Ship Design and Fire Control', p. 221. See also P. Padfield, *Guns at Sea* (London, 1973) chapters 30 and 33.
22. Marder, *Dreadnought to Scapa Flow*, i, pp. 395ff.; iii, pp. 3ff.
23. Apart from Braisted's works (note 14 above), see once again Grenville, 'Diplomacy and War Plans in the United States, 1890–1917', and H. H. Herwig and D. F. Trask, 'Naval Operations Plans between Germany and the United States, 1898–1913', both in Kennedy (ed.), *The War Plans of the Great Powers*.
24. The adverbial qualifier is worth making: much of Mahan's writing is nuanced and subtle – see especially such later essays as 'Considerations Governing the Disposition of Navies' – but the overall message (especially as presented by his followers) usually comes over in the form of a few sweeping principles.
25. Kennedy, 'Strategic Aspects of the Anglo-German Naval Race', in *Strategy and Diplomacy*, p. 133.
26. Quoted from A. J. Marder (ed.), *Fear God and Dread Nought: The Correspondence of Admiral of the Fleet Lord Fisher of Kilverstone*, 3 vols. (London, 1952–6) ii, p. 485. See also R. F. Mackay, *Fisher of Kilverstone* (Oxford, 1973) pp. 303, 447.
27. R. D. Challener, *Admirals, Generals and American Foreign Policy 1898–1914* (Princeton, NJ, 1973) p. 401.
28. Grenville, 'Diplomacy and War Plans', p. 34.
29. B. H. Liddell Hart, *The British Way in Warfare* (London, 1942), especially chapter I; and compare with M. Howard, 'The British Way in Warfare: A Reappraisal' (London, 1975); and P. M. Kennedy, *The Rise and Fall of British Naval Mastery* (London, 1976).
30. M. Howard, *The Continental Commitment* (Harmondsworth, 1974), *passim*; and see the useful discussion in H. Strachan, 'The British Way in Warfare Revisited', *The Historical Journal*, 26, 2 (1983) pp. 447–61.
31. Apart from Howard, *The Continental Commitment*, chapter 2, see also Williamson, *The Politics of Grand Strategy*, chapters 4 and 7.
32. D. M. Schurman, 'Historians and Britain's Imperial Strategic Stance in 1914', in

J. E. Flint and G. Williams (eds), *Perspectives of Empire* (London, 1973) pp. 172–88, discusses why the proponents of 'conjunct' operations failed.
33. Grenville, 'Diplomacy and War Plans', p. 34.
34. Challener, *Admirals, Generals, and American Foreign Policy, passim*, and Braisted, *The United States Navy in the Pacific, 1909–1922*, have some remarkable examples.
35. Braisted, *The US Navy in the Pacific*, chapters 15 and 17.
36. Ibid., chapter 12; D. F. Trask, 'The American Navy in a World at War, 1914–1919', in K. J. Hagan (ed.), *In Peace and War: Interpretations of American Naval History, 1775–1978* (Westport, Ct, 1978) pp. 208ff.
37. For details, see J. Goldrick, *The King's Ships were at Sea* (Annapolis, 1984) pp. 247ff., which is full of telling details about the discrepancy between prewar expectations and the realities of the first year of naval combat in the North Sea.
38. Marder's analysis in *Dreadnought to Scapa Flow*, vol. iii (the revised second edition of 1978) is best here. But see also the comments in S. Roskill, *Admiral of the Fleet Earl Beatty* (London, 1980) chapters 8–9; and C. H. Fairbanks, Jr, 'Choosing Among Technologies in the Anglo-German Naval Arms Competition, 1898–1915', which will appear soon in K. Hagan and W. Cogar (eds), *New Aspects of Naval History* (Wilmington, Del., 1988?).
39. See especially Jellicoe's prescient memorandum, reproduced in Goldrick, *The King's Ships Were at Sea*, pp. 166–8.
40. The term 'historical school' needs to be used with caution here. Semmel, *Liberalism and Naval Strategy*, chapter 9, and A. Pollen, *The Great Gunnery Scandal: The Mystery of Jutland* (London, 1980) pp. 160ff., 226ff., employ it to describe those critics who pressed for 'Nelsonic' aggressiveness; and it is also true that Corbett and Richmond referred to the lessons of history to suggest a quite different interpretation: see D. M. Schurman, *Julian S. Corbett* (London, 1981) pp. 168–72. Marder prefers the more neutral terms of 'offensive' and 'defensive' schools, in *Dreadnought to Scapa Flow*, iii, pp. 314–20, and iv, pp. 167ff. (which nicely captures Churchill's contradictory moods).
41. J. Winton, *Convoy; The Defence of Sea Trade, 1890–1990* (London, 1983) p. 114.
42. For details, see Marder, *The Anatomy of British Sea Power: A History of British Naval Policy in the Pre-Dreadnought Era, 1880–1905* (Hamden, Ct, reprint, 1964); T. Ropp, *The Development of a Modern Navy: French Naval Policy 1871–1904* (Annapolis, Md, 1987) pp. 321–2; and especially B. Ranft's chapter on 'The protection of British seaborne trade', in B. Ranft (ed.), *Technical Change and British Naval Policy 1860–1939* (London, 1977).
43. Marder, *Dreadnought to Scapa Flow*, i, pp. 359–60.
44. Ibid., p. 365.
45. Ibid., p. 366.
46. Roskill, *Admiral of the Fleet Earl Beatty*, p. 218.
47. Compare *(Brassey's) Naval Annual, 1914* (London, 1914) pp. 81–2 and ibid., *1919* (London, 1919) p. 103.
48. Winton, *Convoy*, p. 40.
49. Ibid., p. 100.
50. Marder, *Dreadnought to Scapa Flow*, vol. iv, *1917: Year of Crisis*, and Winton, *Convoy*, chapters 5–7, are excellent here.
51. See, briefly, H. Strachan, *European Armies and the Conduct of War* (London/Boston, 1983) chapter 3.
52. Winton, *Convoy*, p. 67; but there is nothing of that in D. F. Trask's extremely thorough *Captains and Cabinets: Anglo-American Naval Relations, 1917–1918* (Columbia, 1972).

53. See Marder, *Dreadnought to Scapa Flow*, v, pp. 66–76, for a corrective of such older works as Josephus Daniels' *The Wilson Era: Years of War and After* (Chapel Hill, NC, 1946).
54. Braisted, *The United States Navy in the Pacific*, pp. 301ff.; and H. H. Herwig, *Politics of Frustration: The United States in German Naval Planning, 1889–1941* (Boston, 1976) p. 164.
55. Braisted, *The United States Navy in the Pacific*, pp. 307–9. See also the remarkable plans and conjectures outlined in Trask, *Captains and Cabinets*, pp. 285ff.
56. I have taken this summary from my own article on 'British Military Effectiveness in the First World War', in A. Millet and W. Murray (eds), *Military Effectiveness*, vol. i (forthcoming).
57. C. R. M. Cruttwell, *A History of the Great War 1914–1918* (London/New York, 1982 edn) pp. 537ff.
58. J. J. Reber, 'Pete Ellis: Amphibious Warfare Prophet', *United States Naval Institute Proceedings*, 103 (October, 1977) pp. 53–64; for a brief summary, see E. B. Potter, *Sea Power: A Naval History* (Annapolis, 1981) pp. 237–8.
59. Hough, *The Great War at Sea*, p. 182.
60. P. G. Halpern, *The Naval War in the Mediterranean 1914–1918* (London/Boston, 1987) p. 10.
61. Ibid., p. 348.
62. Ibid., p. 10.
63. Ibid., *passim*.
64. Ibid., pp. 332, 344, 388, 443–4.
65. Braisted, *The United States Navy in the Pacific 1909–1922*, p. 305.
66. Covered in Marder, *Dreadnought to Scapa Flow*, v, pp. 262ff.; and Trask, *Captains and Cabinets*, chapter 9.
67. Grenville, 'Diplomacy and War Plans', p. 38; and see again Braisted *The US Navy in the Pacific*, chapters 17, 23–33; Trask, *Captains and Cabinets*, *passim*; and Herwig, *Politics of Frustration*, p. 167.
68. Braisted, Grenville, and Trask all cover this (mis)perception.
69. Marder, *Dreadnought to Scapa Flow*, v, pp. 262ff.; Halpern *The Naval War in the Mediterranean*, *passim*; Trask, *Captains and Cabinets*, pp. 342–52; S. Roskill, *Naval Policy between the Wars*, vol. 1 (London, 1968) pp. 78ff.
70. Scott's proposal is covered briefly in Marder, *Dreadnought to Scapa Flow*, i, pp. 333–4. See also P. Padfield's biography of Scott, *Aim Straight* (London, 1966) pp. 223–6, 260, 270–9.
71. P. T. Rosen, 'The Treaty Navy 1919–1937', in Hagan (ed.), *In Peace and War*; A. Millett and P. Maslowski, *For the Common Defense* (New York, 1984) pp. 372–7, 386ff. Comparisons of the superior American use of carriers are made in Roskill, *Naval Policy between the Wars*, *passim*; G. Till, *Air Power and the Royal Navy 1914–1945* (London, 1979) *passim*; and T. C. Hone and M. D. Mondales, 'Interwar Innovation in Three Navies: U.S. Navy, Royal Navy, Imperial Japanese Navy', *Naval War College Review* (Spring, 1987) pp. 63–83.
72. Kennedy, *The Rise and Fall of Britain Naval Mastery*, p. 245; Roskill, *Naval Policy between the Wars*, i, pp. 326–8.
73. Schurman, *Corbett*, p. 193.
74. A. J. Marder, *Portrait of an Admiral: The Life and Papers of Sir Herbert Richmond* (Cambridge, Mass., 1952) pp. 28–31.
75. Beatty's own gloom about British naval policy after 1920 comes out clearly in Roskill, *Beatty*, pp. 297ff.
76. At least as outlined in 'The Maritime Strategy' articles of the supplement to the January 1986 issue of *The Proceedings of the U.S. Naval Institute*.

77. Quoted in Marder, *Dreadnought to Scapa Flow*, i, p. 402.
78. See, for example, not only Corbett's *Some Principles of Maritime Strategy*, but also his *England in the Seven Years War*, 2 vols (London, 1910), as well as Richmond's somewhat later *The Navy in the War of 1739–48*, 3 vols (Cambridge, 1923).

10 The Washington Conference and the Naval Balance of Power, 1921–2

J. Kenneth McDonald

Short of war, there is perhaps nothing like an imminent international disarmament conference to concentrate a government's mind on national strategy and policy. This essay therefore focusses on the second half of 1921 when Britain and the United States, having drifted into a post-war naval building race, revised their maritime strategies to make possible the naval settlement that resulted from the Washington Conference treaties.

From the Armistice in November 1918 to the call for the Washington Conference in July 1921, Britain and the United States had difficulty adjusting their naval policies to the shift in the world balance of power that resulted from the First World War. It is true, as Professor Kennedy's preceding essay explains, that the experience of the war did nothing to change either Power's Mahanian faith in the battlefleet as the ultimate weapon of naval warfare. Yet neither Britain nor America was prepared for the postwar world where the eclipse of Germany made their principal naval rivals now Japan – and each other.

In the years just before the First World War, British naval policy had been in principle a relatively simple matter. The Royal Navy's strategic thought, war plans, fleet distribution and construction policy had all focussed on the immediate threat of the Imperial German Navy. Accepting the sea power theories of the American strategist, Alfred Thayer Mahan, the British Admiralty expected a naval war with Germany to be decided by a great battlefleet action between the two navies. War plans to prepare for this ultimate test of naval power concentrated the British battlefleet in home waters, on the eastern coast of Scotland, across the North Sea from the German bases of the Kaiser's High Seas Fleet. This meant reducing to a minimum British naval commitments everywhere else in the world: a defensive alliance with Japan, secret naval staff talks with France, and naval negotiations with the dominions all supported this object. The navy and the empire accepted Admiral Mahan's 1911 dictum that 'so long as the British fleet can maintain and assert superiority in the North Sea and around the British Isles, the entire imperial system stands secure'. Finally, since ancient British practice as well as modern Mahanian theory agreed that capital ship battlefleet strength was the measure of naval power, Britain pursued a naval building race against Germany, to ensure that the Royal Navy never fell below a fixed standard of capital ship superiority over the German navy.[1]

Britain's prewar battlefleet strategy remained intact from the outbreak of war in 1914 to the armistice in 1918. It is true that the long-awaited decisive naval battle never came and the battlefleet proved helpless against the new German U-boat threat. Yet the ultimate Allied victory over Germany seemed to vindicate the British strategy of bottling up the Kaiser's High Seas Fleet by relentlessly maintaining battlefleet supremacy in home waters. Indeed, at the end of the First World War Great Britain had no idea of giving up the overwhelming naval pre-eminence that she had achieved by her victory over Germany. With the armistice and the internment of most of the German fleet, the Royal Navy was nearly equal, in tonnage and numbers of fighting ships, to all the remaining major fleets of the world combined. If world naval supremacy could be defined as simply having a bigger battlefleet than any other Power, or combination of Powers, then Britain clearly had this supremacy at the end of 1918. Moreover, whatever the faults of this Mahanian emphasis on capital ship strength, Britain's principal naval rivals fully shared her faith in the battlefleet as the measure of naval power.

Britain's battlefleet pre-eminence in 1918 made her government and navy slow to recognise how the elimination of Germany and other potential European naval enemies required her to reorient her naval strategy. Even in the Far East British naval policy had always been oriented towards European enemies, of whom Germany had been but the latest. When world politics were European politics, the Royal Navy's European supremacy gave Britain world supremacy. Yet by the beginning of the twentieth century Britain had also had to reckon with the growing naval strength of two non-European powers, Japan and the United States. This she had done by concluding and renewing an alliance with Japan, and by simply excluding the possibility of a conflict with the United States from her strategic planning. Well before 1914, as Britain concentrated on her naval race with Germany, Japan's navy had come to dominate her home waters, while the United States navy dominated the western hemisphere.

Although it is easy to see – and not only in restrospect – that the defeat of Germany would leave the United States and Japan as the only remaining major naval Powers apart from Britain, it was difficult for the British Cabinet or navy to foresee just what this would mean for Britain's postwar defence and foreign policy. The war's effects on the naval positions of Japan and the United States were dramatic enough, however, for them not to be entirely ignored even in the course of the war.

Both America and Japan prospered greatly during the war, both navies expanded steadily, and both profited from the elimination of German naval power that resulted from the terms of the armistice in 1918 and from the Versailles Treaty in 1919. Japan had achieved a great strategic advantage in

Far Eastern waters by seizing the northern German Pacific islands – the Marshall, Mariana, and Caroline groups – in the first months of the war. The new American naval position, on the other hand, was mainly the result of an enormous naval building programme first begun in 1916. Although the United States emerged from the war second only to Britain in naval power, President Woodrow Wilson had announced in 1916 that the United States was determined to become 'second to none'. This great American capital ship construction programme, authorised in 1916, delayed by the 1917 entry into the war, and begun again in 1918, would give the United States 16 new 'superdreadnought' battleships and battlecruisers by the mid-1920s. If Britain's faith in the dominance of the capital ship was undiminished by the experience of the First World War, the United States was no less a true believer.[2]

At the Paris Peace Conference in the spring of 1919, in what later became known as the 'Naval Battle of Paris', British Prime Minister David Lloyd George tried unsuccessfully to force the United States to give up its naval expansion policy. In the autumn of that year Lloyd George decided to try persuasion, and sent former Foreign Secretary Lord Grey of Fallodon, who opposed any form of Anglo-American rivalry, on a special mission to Washington to negotiate a naval agreement with President Wilson. Partly in support of Lord Grey's proposed mission, the Cabinet on 15 August 1919 adopted the famous 'Ten Year Rule', which in its original form instructed the Service departments to assume 'for framing revised Estimates, that the British Empire will not be engaged in any great war during the next ten years'.[3] When Grey's mission also failed, the British Government finally had to accept the idea of American naval equality with Britain. Almost two years before Anglo-American battlefleet parity was incorporated into the Washington naval treaty, the First Lord of the Admiralty, Walter Long, announced in the March 1920 navy estimates debate that the Government had adopted a 'One-Power Standard', the principle that the Royal Navy should not be inferior in strength to the navy of any other Power.[4]

Yet the Admiralty recognised that even parity with the United States Navy would be difficult to maintain. By around 1924 the completion of the American 1916 capital ship building programme would make the United States Navy both newer and stronger than the Royal Navy. In March of 1921 the British Government reluctantly accepted the American challenge by adopting a new capital ship construction programme, and Parliament voted £2.5 million to begin four 'Super-*Hoods*', giant battlecruisers of 48 000 tons.[5]

Anglo-American naval rivalry was primarily a matter of national prestige, since no responsible opinion in either country looked upon the other as a very probable potential enemy. While the British Naval Staff had undertaken new war plans by 1920, planning for a war against the United States was a largely theoretical exercise, which produced no proposals for bases in the Western Atlantic or Eastern Pacific. For a potential war against Japan, however, the Naval Staff in 1921 recommended building a new major Far Eastern base at Singapore. The United States similarly had no realistic plans for a war against the British Empire, although it continued to revise an implausible War Plan Red for this purpose right up to 1941. The British navy and government nevertheless believed that the traditional claim to naval supremacy would not allow Britain to drop below at least first-equal standing in naval strength. Meanwhile the United States government looked upon its navy's expanding power as necessary for America's increasing world importance, and for the protection of her Pacific possessions and interests against Japan. Thus, while the United States and Britain both worried about the threat of Japan, they set the naval standard for each other. Based on Mahan's battlefleet strategy, their naval rivalry was almost entirely expressed in the capital ship building competition. Having little to do with war plans or fleet distribution, it came to have a life of its own, as a classic case of something approximating to a 'pure' naval race.

The world's two leading naval Powers thus competed with each other almost entirely for prestige reasons. They were both uncertain, however, about the security of their Far Eastern interests and possessions in the face of the threat of the world's third great naval Power, Japan. The war and the peace settlement had made Japan the leading power in China, and her 'Eight-Eight' capital ship building programme, already begun during the war, ensured her continued battlefleet predominance in the western Pacific. Yet the potential threat of a powerful and aggressive Japan to their Far Eastern interests (many of which were mutual) did not bring the United States and Britain to a common policy towards Japan. Britain had been allied with Japan since 1902, while Japanese-American hostility had been mounting since the end of the Russo-Japanese War in 1905. In the 1919 peace settlement Japan got a League of Nations mandate to occupy and administer the German northern Pacific islands that she had captured in 1914. These islands straddled America's lines of communication to Guam and the Philippines, and made more vulnerable the already tenuous American strategic position in the western Pacific. Moreover President Wilson's unsuccessful support for China in her quarrel with Japan over Shantung at the Paris Peace Conference had renewed Japanese-American antagonism. Convinced of the threat of Japan, the United States Navy had strengthened the Pacific fleet, pressed for the completion of the mid-Pacific base at Pearl Harbor, and asked that Guam be prepared and fortified as a first-class base in the western Pacific. Belief in the Japanese threat gave impetus to the Navy's continued expansion, and aroused American opposition to the continuation of Japan's alliance with the world's largest naval power, Britain.

In turn, Japanese-American naval rivalry affected British policy. By the end of 1920, Britain desperately wanted to stabilise world naval strengths and to provide for an Anglo-American naval equality based upon the existing British battlefleet. Japanese-American competition both increased the size of the United States and Japanese navies and made the ageing British fleet obsolescent. Yet the British government could not expect the United States to ignore growing Japanese naval strength.

Indeed it was the British government's recognition of the potential Japanese threat to Britain's own position in the Far East that brought its decision in June 1921 to build a major naval base at Singapore. At the same time, Lloyd George's Government believed that the Anglo-Japanese Alliance (which came up for renewal in July 1921) helped to reduce Japan's threat to the British Empire. To renew this alliance, however, seemed increasingly likely to antagonise America and to accelerate the naval building race. The United States Government was convinced that the alliance strengthened Japan's position and encouraged her aggressive expansion, especially in China.

As the United States, Japan and Britain moved towards an all-out naval arms race in the first half of 1921, mitigating factors in all three countries converged. In Britain the severe economic recession that set in by the winter of 1920–1 made the Government anxious to stop this naval race, while the Japanese Government also recognised the strain which the building competition placed on Japan's limited resources. Furthermore, by the spring of 1921, many British supporters of the Anglo-Japanese Alliance – most notably the Prime Minister, David Lloyd George, and the Foreign Secretary, Lord Curzon – had begun to retreat from their previous proposals for outright renewal. In June 1921, when the six dominions' prime ministers met in London at the first postwar Imperial Conference, America's opposition to the alliance caused Canada to refuse to agree to its renewal. If some alternative acceptable to both America and Japan could not be found, the alliance would have to be dropped. In early July 1921 the British Government therefore approached the United States, Japan and China to arrange a conference on the problems of the Pacific and Far East.[6]

Although American opposition to the Anglo-Japanese Alliance was mounting in 1921, enthusiasm for large naval expenditures was waning. A popular American movement for naval disarmament had gathered enough momentum by July 1921 to force a drastic cut in the large naval appropriations proposed by the new Republican administration that had taken office in March. In response to this movement, President Warren G. Harding, on 10 July 1921, called for an international conference on the limitation of armaments to meet in Washington in the autumn. At the British government's request, he proposed that this conference also take up Pacific and Far Eastern questions.

In the summer of 1921, the prospect of a great disarmament conference in November meant that British and American governments and navies had to examine their naval policies carefully, both to decide upon their objectives and to determine what was negotiable and what was not. An account of

British and American planning for the Washington Conference reveals not only their general strategic assumptions, but also how they determined the specific levels of capital ship strength that they could accept for themselves and for others in a general agreement limiting all the major naval Powers. If both Powers had not shared the orthodox strategic view that naval power was measured almost entirely in capital ships – whose number was also assumed to determine the number of supporting ships needed – the work of naval limitation would have been vastly more difficult, and perhaps impossible. Moreover, since counting capital ships – the intercontinental strategic weapons of the time – was relatively easy, issues of inspection and verification did not bedevil planning or the conference itself. Since the British Government had a simpler task and the more orderly planning process, we shall first turn to its work and results.

As the United States was about to summon the Washington Conference in July 1921, the First Lord of the Admiralty, Lord Lee of Fareham, had convinced the Prime Minister that no scheme for naval disarmament could possibly affect the construction of the four new capital ships that parliament had authorised the previous March. Lee argued that of the three great naval Powers, only Britain had reduced her navy since the war, while Japan and America were both increasing theirs. No capital ships had been laid down in Britain since 1916. Indeed, since the launching of the light cruiser *Effingham* in June 1921, not a single ship was being built for the Royal Navy in the whole of the United Kingdom. The United States, on the other hand, was building 15 capital ships, while Japan had eight capital ships under construction. To reach equality 'in fighting force' with the United States Navy, the First Lord insisted that Britain had to lay down four capital ships in 1921, and four more the next year.[7]

In July 1921 this proposed second four-ship building programme was still secret, while no work had yet begun on the first four ships authorised in March. Certain that Japan and America would not stop their well-advanced programmes before the conference, Lee warned that if Britain alone stopped building, 'we shall enter the Conference stripped naked'.[8]

Convinced by these arguments, the Cabinet authorised the Admiralty to go ahead with the construction of the four capital ships in the new programme. Deciding that the British case for the conference should be prepared 'in a most serious and hopeful spirit', the Cabinet also asked the Committee of Imperial Defence for advice on the necessary preparations. Sir Maurice Hankey, the Royal Marine lieutenant-colonel who was Secretary of both the Cabinet and the Committee of Imperial Defence, took the initiative and asked the Admiralty, War Office, Air Ministry, and Foreign Office to prepare memoranda for the committee.[9]

Replying for the Foreign Office, the Permanent Under-Secretary, Sir Eyre Crowe, emphasised that the problems of disarmament and of the Pacific, although distinct in themselves, 'really hang together, and that one must to some extent at least turn upon the solution of the other'. Crowe nevertheless recommended that the Committee of Imperial Defence, in organising its ideas on disarmament, should assume that a solution to the Pacific question was attainable.[10]

The Foreign Office worked hard to prepare the British position on Far Eastern issues to be discussed at the conference, including the expected negotiations to find some replacement for the Anglo-Japanese Alliance.[11] The Admiralty followed Crowe's advice and prepared the British position for the arms limitation talks on the assumption – which proved sound – that a political settlement of the alliance and Pacific question could be reached.

In early October the Admiralty sent the Committee of Imperial Defence a secret memorandum on the issues that they thought most likely to be important at the Washington Conference.[12] In only six printed pages, the Naval Staff's paper presented a concise but thorough Admiralty position. The Plans Division under the direction of Rear-Admiral Sir Alfred E. M. Chatfield, Assistant Chief of Naval Staff, prepared the initial draft paper, which had then been extensively revised by Admiral of the Fleet, Earl Beatty, First Sea Lord and Chief of Naval Staff. It was this revised paper that Lord Lee of Fareham, First Lord of the Admiralty, submitted to the Committee of Imperial Defence.

The Naval Staff generally succeeded both in predicting the principal issues and in producing shrewd advice for the prospective negotiations. The Admiralty memorandum became the basis for the naval recommendations in the report of the Committee of Imperial Defence, which the Cabinet approved for the general guidance of the British delegation. This Admiralty paper reveals not only Britain's strategic policy on the eve of the conference, but also why she found so little difficulty in reaching a naval agreement with the United States and Japan at Washington.

Satisfied that no disarmament agreement could be achieved until the larger problems of the Pacific had been dealt with, the Admiralty offered several comments on the political issues in the Far East. To insure that Japan could not threaten Hong Kong by developing a naval base south of Formosa, the Admiralty recommended two steps: first, a reaffirmation of Japan's commitment not to build naval bases on her League of Nations mandated ex-German Pacific islands; and secondly, a new international guarantee of the territorial *status quo* in the Pacific. If Japan herself made it a condition for the reduction of naval armaments that no naval base should be developed in the western Pacific, Britain could agree, so long as it did not interfere with the development of Singapore as her main Far Eastern naval base.[13]

Before discussing various possible naval disarmament schemes the Admiralty recommended that

> no concrete proposals should, in the first place, emanate from our Delegates, but that they should restrict themselves to the consideration of

schemes brought forward by the United States or other foreign Delegates.[14]

Since the American Secretary of State, Charles Evans Hughes, immediately proposed a full-blown disarmament scheme on the opening day of the Washington Conference, the British delegation had no difficulty in following this Admiralty advice.

The rest of the Admiralty paper dealt entirely with the question of naval strength, and how to measure it to determine fleet limitations. It explained the objections to each of a wide variety of undesirable naval arms limitation schemes (such as limitation by size of naval expenditures, or by number of naval personnel) which might be proposed at Washington. It dismissed any proposal for a naval building holiday – 'freeze' we would say today – as entirely unacceptable. Britain had already indulged in a five-year holiday that had allowed the Royal Navy to fall below the Government's one-Power standard in capital ships. To agree to any further building holiday, the Admiralty contended, 'would place us in a position of permanent inferiority'. At the Washington Conference that autumn Britain found it hard to accept the American proposal for a ten-year freeze in capital ship building, and in the conference negotiations managed to provide for the completion of two of her four projected 'super-*Hoods*'.

The Admiralty paper also rejected the limitation of capital ships by total tonnage – the scheme America actually proposed – and opted for a limit on the total number of capital ships. Since the United States' plan allotted Britain both the most tonnage and the largest number of capital ships at the outset, the difference in concept proved no insurmountable barrier to agreement.[15]

To calculate the lowest number of capital ships that the British Empire could safely accept, the Naval Staff examined the British naval strength necessary in European waters, in the Pacific and in the Atlantic. Europe, where only France and Italy had to be taken into account, caused no concern; the peace settlement had disarmed Germany and dismembered Austria, while Russia was prostrate from revolution, defeat and civil war. For the Pacific, however, Britain needed a total strength equal to Japan,

> *plus* the percentage necessary to give reasonable certainty of success in battle, *plus* the percentage necessary to compensate us for the disadvantage of operating at a great distance from our main bases with the inadequate docking and repair facilities in the Far East, *plus* the percentage necessary to enable us to retain in Home Waters a force capable of dealing with any European Powers which might be drawn into the conflict, or to deter them from being so drawn.[16]

Although he recognised the significance of time and distance factors, by focussing on relative ship strength, Beatty implied that sheer numbers of ships could make up for a lack of adequate bases and enormously extended lines of communication.

Admiral Chatfield's initial draft memorandum had proposed a 100 per cent Royal Navy superiority – a battlefleet twice the size of Japan's – to meet these requirements. Admiral Beatty reduced the figure to 50 per cent superiority – a ratio of three British capital ships to two Japanese.

Beatty's calculation allowed Japan two-thirds (66 per cent) of the number of capital ships in the British battlefleet. This acceptable Japanese proportion was higher than the 60 per cent of the American or British capital ship tonnage that the United States actually proposed for Japan at the Conference.[17] In the negotiations at Washington, Britain supported the United States in rejecting the Japanese demand for an allowance of 70 per cent of the tonnage allowed the British and American battlefleets.

Turning from the Pacific to the Atlantic, the Admiralty noted that the Government was already committed to naval equality with the United States. At this stage in planning, however, the question was whether the United States would accept a 50 per cent margin of superiority over Japan as the basis for equality with the Royal Navy. The Naval Staff recognised that apprehension over the Anglo-Japanese Alliance might cause the United States to demand a greater superiority over Japan. 'This is a powerful argument', the Admiralty paper declared, 'in favour of an attempt to substitute a Tripartite Agreement for the present Anglo-Japanese Alliance'. Even though the measure of inferiority that the Japanese would accept was unknown, it was in Britain's interest 'that they should be inferior'. Britain should explain to Japan, the paper continued, 'that the U.S.A. has two oceans to think of whilst Japanese interests are confined to one'. The paper did not suggest what potential enemy the United States should arm against in the Atlantic.[18]

As usual in schemes that naval staffs work out to limit naval armaments, the Admiralty's proposal could actually have justified an enormous new British capital ship building programme. The limitation scheme was to apply only to capital ships of post-Jutland design, of which Britain had but one, HMS *Hood*. The paper argued that the lessons of the great 1916 battle at Jutland formed 'an epoch in naval design', so that 'post-Jutland ships automatically sound the death knell of their earlier sisters'. In the Committee of Imperial Defence it was pointed out that Britain would have to build 16 new capital ships to reach the ratio of three post-Jutland ships to two similar Japanese ships. Since the existing state of British finances made this impossible, the Admiralty representatives (Lord Lee and Admirals Beatty and Chatfield all attended) took the position that, once the conference had set an outside limit on armaments, the naval Powers should be at liberty to build up to their agreed allowances of post-Jutland ships as fast, or as slowly, as they liked. Within the allowances capital ships could be replaced when they were 20 years old. At Washington the scheme eventually adopted was not restricted to post-Jutland capital ships, but these ships' superior value was taken into account in the figures proposed for total tonnage allowances, and in the hard bargaining when Japan insisted on retaining her newest battleship, *Mutsu*.[19]

The Committee of Imperial Defence meeting of 14 October 1921 considered a whole range of conference preparations, including the Admiralty's exhaustive and highly secret memorandum. The committee's report, which the Cabinet approved 1 November, began with the assumption that

> the aim of the British Empire Delegation at the Washington Conference is to achieve the largest possible reduction in expenditure on armaments.[20]

This assumption was subject to two special considerations: first, that the vital interests of the British Empire were safeguarded; and second, that the conference settlement was not liable to be repudiated later by the American Senate – the Versailles Treaty's fate was still a lively memory. The committee endorsed the Admiralty's views on a Pacific *status quo* agreement, and agreed that to limit the total numbers of capital ships was the only scheme simple enough to be practicable. The committee also supported Winston Churchill's suggestion that the British Delegation be authorised to put forward – for bargaining purposes – a 'paper programme' of capital ship construction that the British Government was likely to undertake if the other Powers persisted in their own programmes. This device had worked well with the Germans before the war, Churchill observed, and he thought it might work again at Washington.[21]

The Cabinet gave the principal British delegate full discretion to use Churchill's paper programme stratagem. Without further comment on the naval issues, the Government on 1 November 1921 approved the report of the Committee of Imperial Defence as the British Empire Delegation's general guide for the naval disarmament negotiations at the Washington Conference.[22]

A few days earlier the Government had announced that its delegation to Washington would be headed by the former Prime Minister, Arthur James Balfour, supported by Lord Lee of Fareham, First Lord of the Admiralty, and by HM Ambassador in Washington, Sir Auckland Geddes. Admiral of the Fleet Lord Beatty and Rear-Admiral Sir Alfred Chatfield were to accompany the delegation as naval advisors. All of these British delegates and advisors – except for Sir Auckland Geddes – had played important roles, at more than one stage, in forming British naval policy and strategy for the conference.[23] Yet this well-prepared delegation was as surprised as the rest of the world by the American Government's initiative at the conference's opening session on 12 November 1921. It is now time to look at how the United States arrived at its 'stop now' naval disarmament plan.

In deciding to call the Washington Conference, President Harding had consulted neither his Secretary of Navy, Edwin Denby, nor anyone else in the Navy Department. The initiative came almost entirely from Harding's formidable Secretary of State, Charles Evans Hughes. The President's 10 July announcement of the conference found the US Navy preparing its recommended building programme for the 1923 fiscal year, which Secretary Denby had asked the Navy's General Board to submit by 16 July.[24]

The General Board was an advisory panel of eleven officers, which had been formed after the Spanish-American War 'to insure efficient preparation of the fleet in case of war'. Since its establishment, the General Board had been responsible for formulating American construction programmes. It was an efficient body with impresive expertise, whose recommendations for fiscal year 1923 were on Secretary Denby's desk by 15 July. Although the naval disarmament conference had only been announced on 10 July, the General Board's report took account of this new development. While the United States looked only to international law, and not to pacts or agreements, for her rights, the report explained, she needed not only justice and law on her side, 'but also force to sustain the right'. This required a navy 'second to none', a navy the United States would not have until the massive 1916 building programme of 16 superdreadnought battleships and battlecruisers was completed in 1924. The General Board therefore insisted that this 1916 programme should not be slowed down or suspended. 'We cannot afford to enter a disarmament conference', the board warned, 'with our position as a world power already compromised'. As had the British Naval Staff, the General Board approached naval disarmament by first insisting that its existing capital ship building programme must be completed.[25]

Assuming that a naval strength second to none would be achieved by 1924, the board explained that the Navy would then need a replacement programme, even if armaments were limited. Recommending that Congress appropriate money for one 'replacement' capital ship in each of the fiscal years from 1923 to 1925, the General Board assumed that the *status quo* – meaning ships built, building or projected – would be the basis for negotiations at the forthcoming conference. It therefore warned that to postpone this recommended replacement building programme could relegate the United States to a position of permanent naval inferiority.[26]

The General Board found it almost inconceivable that the 1916 construction programme – already delayed by the war – should not be completed. As it turned out, however, Secretary of State Hughes refused to propose a 'limitation' plan that would permit a large capital ship building programme to continue.

After recommending the new replacement building programme, the

General Board turned its attention to the projected disarmament conference. As the advisory body responsible for planning the Navy's shipbuilding programmes, it seemed the logical organisation to plan the international limitation of these programmes. On 27 July 1921 the board got formal terms of reference from the acting Secretary of the Navy, Theodore Roosevelt, Jr. Roosevelt, the 33-year-old son of the late president, was Assistant Secretary of the Navy, the job that his father had held from 1897 to 1898, and that his distant cousin, Franklin Roosevelt, had held from 1913 to 1920 in the preceding Wilson Administration. Young Roosevelt instructed the General Board to begin an immediate preliminary investigation of armament limitation by international agreement, and to report to the Secretary of the Navy by 20 September 1921.[27]

The specific instructions asked for the board's opinion on the 'equitable relativity' in the naval strength of the five Powers – America, Britain, Japan, France and Italy – taking part in the disarmament conference. It was to define a 'naval unit' – the measure of comparison for navies – and then use this unit to determine the strength ratios of the five Powers' existing navies, and of their future navies when their current building programmes were completed.

In determining this 'equitable relativity' of the American navy's size compared with the others, the General Board's instructions noted that the United States would not consent to limiting its sovereign powers, nor to any naval limitations that might imperil its territory or population. The United States must always have sufficient force to maintain the Monroe Doctrine, and to protect American commerce, policies and rights anywhere in the world. These were some of the least necessary caveats ever directed to the General Board, which was perhaps the last body in the world that would be tempted to limit American sovereignty, subvert the Monroe Doctrine, or jeopardise the rights of American citizens or commerce abroad.[28]

Assistant Secretary Roosevelt drafted these 27 July instructions (which the General Board referred to as its 'precept') without reference to the State Department or anywhere else outside the Navy. In late August, however, Secretary of State Hughes wrote to Secretary of the Navy Denby, asking for information about the Great Powers' existing naval armaments, and the economic and political policies that had determined their development. In his final paragraph, Secretary Hughes noted his difficulty in determining 'what I can perhaps best describe as a "yardstick"', which could be used as a standard of measure not only for existing armaments, but also in any general plan for reduction. What Roosevelt had called a naval unit, Hughes called a yardstick, and this was perhaps the easiest request for the General Board to meet. In assessing the relative strengths of navies, the General Board reported, it had always based its estimates on displacement tonnage of capital ships.[29]

From 12 September to 8 October 1921 the General Board submitted the first three parts of its report to Secretary of the Navy Denby, who then forwarded copies to the President, Secretary of State and members of the American Delegation.[30] Part I of the report discussed the national policies of the world's principal Powers, and their bearing on naval strategy and policy. Part II answered specific questions posed in the 27 July precept, while Part III presented the board's basic naval limitation plan.[31]

The first part of the General Board's report examined those points where American policies might clash with other nation's policies. 'The General Board heartily approves of the limitation of armaments', the paper began, and then described the dangerous world that America lived in. America's principal foreign policies were listed as 'No Entangling Alliances', the Monroe Doctrine, the Open Door in China, and Asiatic Exclusion. Its survey of American and other national policies identified Britain and Japan as the greatest threats to American interests and security.

According to the General Board, Britain demanded naval supremacy to dominate world markets, to defend its colonial empire, and to prevent any Power from achieving the hegemony of Europe. Although recognising Britain's need for a large and secure world commerce, the board railed against her efforts to stifle foreign competition and her defensive alliance with Japan. Yet the problems with Britain, the board observed, were problems with a state whose people, aims, ideals, standard of living and government were similar to America's. Britain could adjust and update her world commercial methods to prevent unfair trade competition and unlimited arms competition between the English-speaking peoples. In any event, since naval policy could not solve most Anglo-American problems, the General Board accepted that the United States needed only equality in naval power with Britain.[32]

The board pointed out, however, that the problems with Japan were problems with a state of dissimilar race, government, ideals and traditions. Japan had few friends in the US Navy, and the board's discussion of her policies reflected the Navy's hostile attitude. Japan, the report declared, sought territorial expansion (by conquest if necessary), eventual commercial and political control of the Far East, naval control of the western and southern Pacific, and overseas colonies, both for trade expansion and strategic advantage. Japan's feudal and militarist governing classes aspired to national greatness by building a great army and navy. Since Japan was poor, and had no threat from other nations, the board assumed that this expansion of her military and naval forces had aggressive purposes. Moreover the board feared that Japan might ally herself with a revived Russia or Germany – or both. This assessment of Japan's policies led the board to contend that the continuation of the Anglo-Japanese Alliance was a potential danger to American interests, and a threat to 'the solidarity of the Anglo-Saxon peoples'. Without the Anglo-Japanese Alliance, the report concluded, the United States would need a navy only twice as big as Japan's. If the

Alliance continued, however, the United States would need a navy at least as strong as the combined navies of Japan and Britain – a two-Power standard, giving the United States the greatest navy in the world. 'Today no power in the Atlantic save our own balances British sea power', the board declared. 'No power in the Pacific save our own checks Japanese sea power.' The board had little doubt that Japan would join in any war that Britain might undertake against the United States.[33]

The report's second part defined the 'equitable relativity' of naval strength among the major naval Powers. Assuming the early demise of the Anglo-Japanese Alliance, the board called for an American navy equal to Britain's and double the strength of Japan's. France and Italy were each to have a navy equal to Japan's, so that the General Board's 'fair, just and unbiased ratio' for America, Britain, Japan, France and Italy was to be 10:10:5:5:5.[34]

In preparing a specific plan for arms limitation, the General Board sought a scheme that would give the US Navy its desired 10:10:5 ratio with Britain and Japan, and also ensure the completion of the 15 remaining capital ships of the 1916 programme. Having decided to use total capital ship tonnage as the yardstick, the board still had to determine whether to compare strengths by counting only ships already built, or also those then building, or perhaps also those authorised but not yet laid down. In existing ships, the board discovered that Britain exceeded the American battlefleet by almost 40 per cent, while Japan in the autumn of 1921 had 68 per cent of the American strength – making her already markedly stronger than the 50 per cent ratio that the board felt was the maximum Japan could be permitted. A comparison of American, British and Japanese building programmes in 1928, when all the ships already authorised would be completed, was even more alarming. While the United States would catch up to Britain, and the two would have roughly equal battlefleet tonnage, Japan's capital ship strength would rise to about 85 per cent of America's. Not surprisingly the board discarded both of these approaches, having already decided that 'equitable relativity must mean such naval power as compared with Japan as to enable the United States to contemplate a war with her with confidence'.

To reduce Japan to this standard, the board landed on a 'keels laid' scheme, which purportedly would permit only ships already laid down to be completed. Actually, the board proposed to apply its keels laid principle only to the United States, to ensure the completion of the 1916 programme capital ships, all 16 of which had been laid down, and one already completed. Britain was to be allowed to build her four projected battlecruisers, which had not yet been designed, much less laid down, while Japan would be allowed to complete only seven of the 15 capital ships that the Japanese Government and Diet had already authorised. Although France and Italy had no capital ships then building or authorised, they were each to be allowed to lay down a new battlefleet up to equality with Japan's tonnage.[35]

The upshot of the board's plan was that by 1928 the United States and Britain would still be roughly equal, each with about a million tons of capital ships, while Japan would then have only about 56 per cent of the United States' battlefleet strength. This was rounded up to a ratio of 10:10:6:6:6 for the five naval Powers coming to the Washington Conference. The board called this a 'Naval Holiday' plan, to limit new construction. Actually it was a plan for continued naval expansion, which would eventually stabilise capital ship strength at a million tons each for the United States and Britain, and 600 000 tons each for Japan, France and Italy.[36]

The General Board's plan also provided that capital ships could be replaced, ton by ton, by new capital ship construction 20 years from the date of their original completion. Thus the completion of the existing programmes would be followed by regular replacement building. There was also a size limit: no ship laid down during the term of the agreement could exceed the tonnage displacement of the largest ship authorised by the plan. It was unofficially reported that the four projected British 'super-*Hood*' battle-cruisers would be 48,000 tons each – almost 5000 tons larger than the biggest American or Japanese ships then building. Thus 48,000 tons would probably have been the size limit for capital ships in the board's scheme. Qualitatively the United States would have a great capital ship superiority over both Japan and Britain. In 1928 the United States would have 18 'superdreadnoughts' of post-Jutland design, while England would have but five and Japan seven. This was why the General Board plan permitted Japan a 10:6 ratio, rather than the 10:5 that it had earlier pronounced the maximum safe ratio.[37]

Constantly returning to the problems of Japan, the Anglo-Japanese Alliance and the Pacific, the General Board's report insisted that it could offer only preliminary limitation proposals, which it would have to review after the conference had arrived at its decisions on political questions. In forwarding each of the first three parts of the board's report, however, Assistant Secretary Roosevelt told Secretary of State Hughes that they did not necessarily represent Secretary Denby's or his own views. All of these General Board reports, Denby wrote Hughes on 10 October, were simply memoranda containing information primarily for the Navy Department's use, although also available for the American delegation's study. If Hughes wished, Denby added with some diffidence, the Navy Department would give him 'in due course a suggested proposal of the American Government'.[38]

On 12 October 1921 Secretary Hughes, as Chairman of the American delegation, first met the other three delegates: Senator Henry Cabot Lodge (Republican, Massachusetts), Chairman of the Foreign Relations Committee; Senator Oscar Underwood (Democrat, Alabama), Senate Minority Leader; and the elder statesman, Elihu Root. Having distributed and discussed the General Board's report at this meeting, Hughes told Denby the next day that the delegates were now particularly anxious to have the views of the Navy Department, 'as such'. Hughes also impressed upon Denby that he wanted a radical cut in the board's plan.[39]

On instructions from Secretary Denby the General Board therefore submitted a 'Modified Plan' on 14 October 1921, which reduced the eventual capital ship allowance for Britain and the United States from a million tons to 820,000 tons each, and the allowance for Japan, France and Italy to 410,000 tons each. In slightly reducing British and American total tonnage, the board also returned to its earlier demand for a 50 per cent ratio for the three lesser naval Powers. An accompanying paper vigorously, if not very effectively, defended the original basic plan as safe, simple, sound and likely to be acceptable to all the Powers involved. The United States needed this large, million-ton capital ship fleet because 'Its interests and world policies are based on equity and altruism, and are in opposition to the selfish aims of other great powers.'[40]

Aware that the General Board's reduction would not satisfy Hughes, Secretary Denby informally appointed a special naval advisory committee to prepare the Navy Department's official proposal. The committee's three members were Assistant Secretary Theodore Roosevelt, Jr, chairman; the Chief of Naval Operations, Admiral Robert E. Coontz; and Captain William V. Pratt from the General Board. Roosevelt's diary gives a good account of how this committee collaborated with Secretary Hughes and the American delegation in preparing the American naval proposal, in the last three weeks before the Conference opened on 12 November 1921. Roosevelt was the key figure in the Navy Department's work, once the General Board had refused to endorse any plan that would not permit the completion of the 15 capital ships building in the American 1916 programme. Roosevelt had the confidence of both Secretary of the Navy Denby and Secretary of State Hughes, as well as an excellent working relationship with his two naval colleagues, Admiral Coontz and Captain Pratt. Moreover, as the energetic, intelligent and personable son of a recent president, he had an easy entrée almost everywhere in Washington, not least at the White House, where he played bridge and rode with President Harding.[41]

Roosevelt, Coontz and Pratt quickly set to work on three new plans to reduce capital ship strengths below the levels proposed by the General Board. These three plans, all incorporating the General Board's original 10:10:6:6:6 ratio, proposed that construction be stopped on either four, six or eight of the 15 remaining American capital ships. This would produce total capital ship allowances for America of either 809,600 tons, 731,250 tons, or 722,300 tons.[42]

In the meantime, on 21 October, the American delegates agreed that, since naval reduction should be the first emphasis of the conference, the United States should present a clear-cut and formal proposal. Secretary Hughes insisted, however, that they could not discuss the Navy programme or the

1. Captain A. T. Mahan. *Elliot and Fry*.

2. Sir Julian Corbett.

3. HM the King's visit to the Grand Fleet, 21–24 July 1918. HM the King receiving Admiral Rodman USN on board British battleship *Queen Elizabeth*. On the left with HM the King and Admiral Rodman are Admiral Sir David Beatty, Vice-Admiral Sir Charles Madden and Vice-Admiral Sir John de Robeck. Towards the right is Rear-Admiral Strauss USN. Others in the photograph are: Rear-Admiral Goodenough, Rear-Admiral Phillimore, Rear-Admiral Oliver, Rear-Admiral Clinton Baker, Rear-Admiral Fergusson (who was invested by HM the King with the CB Military), and Rear-Admiral Alexander-Sinclair. HM also invested Rear-Admiral Rodman USN with the KCB and Rear-Admiral Strauss USN with the KCMG. *The Imperial War Museum.*

4. Admiral Sir David Beatty, Vice-Admiral Sir John de Robeck and Rear-Admiral Sir Hugh Evan-Thomas, bidding farewell to Admiral William Benson USN after his visit to the Grand Fleet, 1918. *The Imperial War Museum.*

5. Members of the Imperial War Cabinet, 10 Downing Street, London, 1918.
Top, left to right: Sir W. Wier, Gen. Sykes, Col. G. Lambert, Col. Amery, Lt-Col. Sir Maurice Hankey, The Hon. A. Meighen, Sir S. P. Sinha, Col. Storr.
Middle Row, left to right: Sir Rosslyn Wemyss, Sir Joseph Ward, The Hon. N. W. Rowell, Mr Walter Long, Mr G. N. Barnes, Lord Curzon, Gen. Smuts, Mr Austin Chamberlain, The Hon. J. A. Calder, The Hon. M. Burton, Mr E. B. Montagu, Sir Joseph Maclay, Gen. Sir G. N. Mondonah.
Front Row, left to right: Mr W. F. Massey, The Maharajah of Patiala, Dr Bonar Law, Sir Robert Borden, Mr Lloyd George, Mr W. M. Hughes, Mr Balfour, Mr Joseph Cook, The Hon. W. P. Lloyd. *The Imperial War Museum.*

6. Admiral Sir Bruce Fraser and US Admiral William 'Bull' Halsey discuss Occupation duties, Tokyo, 1945. *The Imperial War Museum*.

7. Admiral H. Kent Hewitt USN presenting the US Legion of Merit to Admiral Sir Max Horton RN, 4 June 1946.

8. King George VI welcomed on board USS *Columbus* (CA–74) by Admiral Richard L. Conolly USN, 8 November 1949.

9. Admiral Lynde D. McCormick, Commander-in-Chief Atlantic (*right*) and Admiral Robert D. Carney, Commander-in-Chief Allied Forces Southern Europe, at Naples Airport, Italy, 6 October 1952. *National Archives, Washington.*

10. General Bernard Rogers, Supreme Allied Commander Europe; Admiral Wesley MacDonald, Supreme Allied Commander Atlantic; Admiral Sir William Staveley, Commander-in-Chief Channel, 1987.

General Board's report until he had an official programme prepared by the Secretary of the Navy.[43]

In fact, on the day before, Thursday, 20 October, Secretary Denby had met Hughes and President Harding in a long conference at the White House. Denby's report of this meeting convinced Theodore Roosevelt, Jr, that the United States Government had to propose a naval disarmament plan concrete and drastic enough 'to prove the honesty of our intentions to the country'. If one of the other naval Powers then balked at the American plan, Roosevelt observed, the Harding Administration, having proved its good faith, could hope to get public and congressional support for 'a proper defense'. Uncertain that a conference impasse would rally support for more building, Roosevelt in fact hoped that the conference would succeed. If it did not, he feared that Congress would reflect American public opinion and insist on reducing the navy 'willy-nilly'.[44]

Of the three new plans that Roosevelt's committee formulated, Secretary Denby submitted the most drastic reduction to the American delegation. Although this plan cut eight of the 15 remaining capital ships in the 1916 programme, it was not enough for Secretary Hughes. On 24 October when the American delegates next met Denby and his advisory committee, Hughes proposed what came to be called the 'stop now' plan. This would halt construction of all 15 American ships then building, with proportionate reductions in the other navies. Assuming that the United States brought its own building to a dead stop, Hughes asked the Navy what reduction in capital ship tonnage it would be fair to ask for Japan and Britain in return. As Roosevelt had expected, Hughes argued that only this kind of drastic American initiative would convince the country of the sincerity of the Administration's intentions.[45]

Hughes's request for the 'commensurate sacrifice' to ask of Britain and Japan was referred to both the General Board and the advisory committee. Both bodies responded by 26 October. For the advisory committee, Roosevelt and Coontz worked out a 'stop now' plan that they believed would leave the United States safe and give Japan no grounds for complaint, although it might arouse British objections. The United States was to stop construction on all 15 ships of the 1916 programme and scrap another 15 older battleships, to leave the United States with 18 battleships, totalling 500,650 tons. Britain was to halt the four projected 'super-*Hoods*' and scrap 12 older battleships, to leave her with 22 capital ships totalling 604,450 tons. Japan was to cancel her eight capital ships authorised but not laid down, stop construction on the seven capital ships already begun, and scrap 10 older ships. This would leave the Japanese with ten capital ships, totalling 299,700 tons. France and Italy were simply not to exceed the capital ship tonnage established for Japan. Twenty years after completion, capital ships could be replaced, ton for ton, by new capital ships up to a total of 550,000 tons for America and Britain, and 330,000 tons for Japan, France and Italy. This, of course, represented a 10:10:6:6:6 ratio. Slightly revised to provide for replacement allowances of 500,000 tons for America and Britain, and 300,000 tons for Japan (with France and Italy left for later determination), this plan was the basis for the 5:5:3 capital ships ratio that Secretary Hughes proposed at the opening session of the Washington Conference.[46]

The General Board's 'stop now' plan left the United States with the same 18 capital ships that Roosevelt's committee proposed. It allocated only 17 ships of roughly equal strength to Britain, however, and allowed Japan only eight capital ships, representing about half of the American strength. This was a 10:10:5 ratio. Having thus responded to the Secretary of State's request for a 'stop now' plan, the General Board then explained why such a proposal was entirely unacceptable and 'fraught with probable dangerous results'. Their report concluded:

> The proposition would probably be acceptable to Japan, as it reduces our Navy to a point where she would feel that the United States would be impotent to restrain her aggressive plans in the Far East. These fifteen capital ships brought Japan to the conference. Scrap them and she will return home free to pursue untrammeled her aggressive program.
> The General Board believes that the peace of the Far East and the safety of China is [sic] absolutely dependent upon the ability of America to place a force of unquestioned preponderance in the Western Pacific. If these fifteen ships be stricken from the Navy list, our task may not be hopeless; but the temptation to Japan to take a chance becomes very great.[47]

Negotiations at the Washington Conference demonstrated that the General Board was badly mistaken in believing that Japan would accept 50 per cent of the American or British capital ship tonnage. In the event, when offered a 60 per cent ratio by the American proposal, Japan demanded 70 per cent. After hard bargaining she only reluctantly accepted 60 per cent in return for two important concessions: first, a freeze on further naval fortifications in a specified area of the Western Pacific; and secondly, the retention of her newest super-dreadnought, *Mutsu*, which Hughes' plan had scheduled for scrapping.

Two days later the President of the General Board, Rear Admiral William L. Rodgers, who had recently commanded the US Asiatic Fleet, sent the Chief of Naval Operations, Admiral Coontz, the General Board's long statement of reasons why the US Navy should have double the strength of the Japanese navy. The General Board's efforts were unavailing, and Roosevelt's *ad hoc* advisory committee pressed on with its 'stop now' plan.[48]

Both Coontz and Pratt worked loyally with Assistant Secretary Roosevelt in formulating the final American plan. When they next met Hughes and his three colleagues on Monday, 31 October, the American delegation decided that the United States would definitely propose a 'stop now' plan along the lines of the advisory committee's 26 October draft. Meeting the advisory committee again two days later, the delegates came to a final agreement on the naval plan, which would apply only to Britain, the United States and Japan in the initial statement, leaving the French and Italian ratios and tonnages for consideration as the conference proceeded. Roosevelt noted that, while the aged Elihu Root was grasping the general situation well, Hughes was the only delegate who had any accurate knowledge of the Navy's plan.[49]

At the same meeting, the delegation insisted that the Navy must understand that

> the proposal in regard to the building program was not connected with the fortification of Guam or with the separate question of the fortification of the Mandated [Japanese Pacific] islands; nor, further, with the current construction of fortifications or bases in Hawaii.[50]

Although Secretary Hughes was determined not to link the Pacific bases and fortifications question with the capital ship limitation, this proved impossible to avoid at the conference. As we have noted, in return for accepting a capital ship tonnage of only 60 per cent of the American or British allowance Japan got the other four major naval Powers to agree to 'freeze' the development of certain western Pacific bases.

On Friday, 4 November 1921 – less than two weeks since Hughes had first broached his 'stop now' suggestion, and only a week before the conference convened – Assistant Secretary Roosevelt delivered the Navy Department's plan to the Secretary of State. Hughes carefully locked it in his own safe, and told Roosevelt that he would show it to no one. And indeed, Hughes did not even show it to Messrs Lodge, Root and Underwood, the other three American delegates. Roosevelt noted that Hughes planned 'to spring everything, including our definite naval program, on the opening day'. On 10 November Roosevelt and Pratt finished the final version of the plan, which also limited replacement ships to 35,000 tons, after a ten-year capital shipbuilding holiday. Pratt – who had just assumed the rank of Rear Admiral – personally mimeographed the copies that Roosevelt took to the State Department and left in Secretary Hughes's charge. 'Now', Roosevelt wrote, 'all that remains is twenty-four hours and then there will be no more reason for the intense secrecy that has had to be preserved'.[51]

Sir Maurice Hankey, who went to Washington as Secretary of the British Empire Delegation, wrote a private letter to the Prime Minister in London just after the conference convened. Noting the 'extraordinarily dramatic effect' of Hughes's opening speech, and how completely the Americans had kept their secret, Hankey told Lloyd George that he had heard that the proposals originally put up by the American naval experts were far from sufficient and that there was a battle royal before their assent was secured to the drastic policy of scrapping the old and new vessels. . . .[52]

As we have seen, Hankey's information was not entirely accurate. While the Administration had not accepted the General Board's proposals, there had been no 'battle royal'. There had been no need for one, since the General Board's assent to the final plan was neither sought nor received. Indeed the General Board never saw the new plan before Hughes announced it on the first day of the conference. Although highly respected, the General Board was only an advisory body, which could not speak for the Navy Department; civilian control was firmly in place. In September and October of 1921, when the Secretary and Assistant Secretary of the Navy saw the massive scale of the General Board's 'limitation' proposals, they could – and did – simply disavow the reports as they forwarded them to the State Department. In late October, when Secretary of State Hughes demanded an alternative to the General Board's plan, Secretary of the Navy Denby could co-opt the Chief of Naval Operations, Admiral Coontz, and the ablest officer of the General Board, Captain Pratt, to do the job with Assistant Secretary Roosevelt. This *ad hoc* naval advisory committee drafted the plan that the American Secretary of State announced to a startled world on 12 November 1921.

Colonel Hankey perhaps assumed that American naval staff work followed the same sort of orderly progression that had developed in the Admiralty since 1911. There, the British naval recommendations had proceeded from the Plans Division and Assistant Chief of Naval Staff to Admiral Lord Beatty, Chief of Naval Staff. Beatty then revised them for approval of the First Lord, who submitted a single document to the interdepartmental Committee of Imperial Defence as the Navy's agreed position.

Of course, the Naval Staff made its job easier by recommending that Britain should not first offer its own limitation scheme, but rather respond to the proposals of other nations. This, and the rest of the Admiralty's recommendations, were quickly accepted, first by the Committee of Imperial Defence, and then by the Cabinet.

There were other respects in which the General Board's task was more difficult than that of the British Naval Staff. The General Board's conception of America's maritime strategy made it unable to accept any actual reduction in naval armaments. The General Board's rationale for its proposals had three main points: first, that the United States must have a navy 'second to none'; second, that Japan was a serious threat to American Far Eastern interests; and third, that the United States must in any case complete its 1916 capital ship-building programme. Accepting the first two assumptions, the President and Secretary of State firmly rejected the third.

Public reaction, when Charles Evans Hughes announced the American naval proposals in his opening day speech, was overwhelmingly favourable, both in the United States and abroad. The American plan, which had been hammered out in great secrecy over the preceding three weeks, provided the basis for the eventual Five Power Naval Treaty signed on 6 February 1922. Hughes's initial proposal was not complete, of course, and capital ship allowances for France and Italy, a Pacific '*status quo*' agreement on fortifications, limitations on aircraft-carriers, and provision for some capital ship construction during the ten-year holiday were four major elements added to the treaty in the course of the negotiations. On the other hand, the original American proposal to extend the capital ship limitation ratios to all auxiliary – that is, non-capital – ships was not incorporated in the treaty. With these revisions and compromises, the four other major naval Powers were able to accept the American plan for naval limitation.[53]

The credit – or blame – for this acceptance must go mainly to Secretary of State Hughes. Once Hughes, with President Harding's approval, decided that the United States should present a dramatic disarmament initiative, he needed naval experts to organise a workable plan. Accepting the General Board's recommendation to use capital ship tonnage as the yardstick for naval limitation, he rejected any suggestion that battle fleet tonnage or ratios had to be calculated according to 'national needs'. Since no two nations could be expected to assess their own and others' naval requirements in the same way, Hughes decided to ignore the question of needs, and to base his plan on the maintenance of existing relative strengths. International stability, especially in the Pacific and Far East, and an end to naval building competition were Hughes's policy objectives, and he never let the naval experts divert him from these goals.

Hughes never doubted that the ten-year freeze in naval strengths was the key to his proposal's success. At the outset of the conference, when Theodore Roosevelt, Jr, reported to Hughes and the American delegates that Japan had demanded a ratio of 10:7 rather than the offered 10:6, the delegates unanimously insisted

> that the question of ratio had nothing whatever to do with the American proposal which was to stop at existing strength. The Secretary of State went so far as to say that if that proposal proved to result in establishing a ratio of even 10 to 8, he would still accept it in order to preserve the basic principle.

In Hughes's view, this basic principle eliminated both naval competition and the maintaining of any specific ratio 'based on alleged national requirements'.[54]

In fact, the 'stop now' plan that Hughes presented did not preserve existing relative strengths. His 'basic principle' was a myth, and Hughes's plan was actually based on ratios almost as arbitrary as those the General Board had proposed. In dreadnought capital ship tonnage, Britain's existing strength in late 1921 was over twice America's tonnage, while Japan's dreadnought tonnage was already 85 per cent of the United States' strength. Stopping new construction was only part of the American plan; older capital ships also had to be scrapped, to bring the relative strengths of the three principal battle fleets to approximate the 5:5:3 ratio upon which the American plan was based. Thus the capital ship ratios in the Washington naval treaty actually resulted from the willingness of both Britain and America to settle for equality with each other, and from their ability to bring Japan to accept the 60 per cent ratio that they believed would leave their Far Eastern interests secure.[55]

In analysing the reasons for the success of the American initiative, Theodore Roosevelt, Jr, concluded that timing had been the key. In his view, the American plan had come at the only time when such a ratio among the naval Powers was possible. 'If we had attempted it before', he wrote to the American ambassador in London, 'our fleet would not have been large enough. If we had waited another year, Congress would have abandoned our building program, on which our claim to this proposition is based'.[56] Secretary of State Hughes and President Harding surely made a shrewd political judgment in deciding to reject the General Board's plan, and to present a 'stop now' proposal. From then on, however, it took both naval expertise and political astuteness, in the co-operation between Roosevelt's committee and Hughes's delegation, to plan the world's first successful limitation of naval armaments. By this and the other Washington treaties, Britain, the United States and Japan managed to stabilise the Pacific and Far East for almost a decade, and to stop almost all capital ship construction until the inter-war naval settlement collapsed and rearmament began again after 1935.

Notes

1. A perceptive analysis of Alfred Thayer Mahan's seapower doctrine can be found in Paul Kennedy, *The Rise and Fall of British Naval Mastery* (New York, 1976).
2. See George T. Davis, *A Navy Second to None: The Development of Modern American Naval Policy* (New York, 1940).
3. Cabinet Office Records 23/15, W.C. 616A, 15 Aug. 1919, Secret ('A' Minutes), Public Record Office, London (hereafter cited as CAB, with appropriate filing designations). These developments are discussed in excruciating detail in J. K. McDonald, 'Lloyd George and the Search for a Postwar Naval Policy, 1919', in A. J. P. Taylor (ed.), *Lloyd George: Twelve Essays* (New York, 1971).
4. 126, Official Report, House of Commons Debates, Fifth Series, 2301 (17 Mar. 1920); hereafter cited as H.C. Deb. 5 s.
5. 139 H.C. Deb. 5 s. 1766ff. (17 Mar. 1921).
6. See Ian Nish, *Alliance in Decline: A Study in Anglo–Japanese Relations 1908–1923* (London, 1972).
7. CAB 32/2 Part 2: E. 14th Mtg, 4 July 1921, Most Secret. Actually, Japan had only five capital ships under construction, with two more about to be laid down.

8. CAB 24/126: Cabinet Paper 3137, 15 July 1921, Secret.
9. CAB 23/26: C.67(21)3, 15 Aug. 1921, Secret. Foreign Office Records, Class 371, 6705: Hankey to Curzon, 19 Aug. 1921 (F3166/2905/23), Public Record Office, London (hereafter cited as F.O. 371, with appropriate filing designations). CAB 21/218: Hankey to Prime Minister, 19 Aug. 1921.
10. F.O. 371/6705: Crowe to Hankey (draft), 30 Aug. 1921 (F3166/2905/23).
11. See, for example, V. Wellesley's long 'General Survey', 20 Oct. 1921, *Documents on British Foreign Policy, 1919–1939*, 1st Series, Volume XIV, R. Butler and J. P. T. Bury (eds) (London, 1966), No. 404; and the Foreign Office paper on a tripartite agreement, 22 Oct. 1921, ibid, No. 405.
12. CAB 4/7: C.I.D. [Committee of Imperial Defence] 277-B, 'The Washington Conference', 5 Oct. 1921, Secret. Although the report was actually submitted to the Standing Defence Sub-Committee, these meetings were later redesignated as C.I.D. meetings.
13. The Naval Staff was aware of Japan's interest in a *status quo* agreement for the western Pacific; see F.O. 371/5622: Admiralty to Foreign Office, 1 Nov. 1921, Secret, enclosing Naval Attache Report, Tokyo, 22 Sept. 1921 (A8132/18/45).
14. CAB 4/7: C.I.D. 277-B, 5 Oct. 1921, Secret.
15. Ibid. In Secretary of State Hughes's original proposal the US Navy was to keep 18 capital ships aggregating 500 650 tons, and the Royal Navy 22 capital ships totalling 604,450 tons. (US Senate, *Conference on the Limitation of Armament*, Sen. Doc. 126, 67th Cong., 2nd sess. (Washington, 1922), pp. 56–63.)
16. CAB 4/7: C.I.D. 277-B, 5 Oct. 1921, Secret.
17. Ibid. Of course, the two percentages are not strictly comparable, since the British figure refers to numbers of capital ships, and the American figure to total tonnage.
18. Ibid.
19. CAB 2/3: C.I.D. 145th Mtg, 14 Oct. 1921, Secret (Ex-Standing Defence Sub-Committee [S.S.], 10th Mtg Minutes).
20. CAB 4/7: C.I.D. 280-B, 24 Oct. 1921, Secret.
21. Ibid. CAB 2/3: C.I.D. 145th Mtg, 14 Oct. 1921, Secret (Ex-SS/10th Mtg Minutes); and C.I.D. 146th Mtg, 21 Oct. 1921, Secret (Ex-S.S./11th Mtg Minutes). Churchill was then Colonial Secretary, and hence a member of the C.I.D.
22. CAB 23/27: C.83(21)2, 1 Nov. 1921, Secret.
23. *The Times* (London), 18 Oct. 1921.
24. Denby to General Board, 30 June 1921, File No. 420-2 (Ser. No. 1083), Records of the General Board, Operational Archives, Naval Historical Center, Washington, D.C. (hereafter cited as RGB, with appropriate filing designations).
25. General Board to Secretary of the Navy, 15 July 1921, File No. 420-2 (Ser. No. 1083), RGB.
26. In addition to these proposed three capital ships, the board's programme also called for beginning construction in the fiscal years 1923–1925, of three aircraft carriers, one aircraft tender, 18 cruisers, 18 destroyer leaders, 18 gunboats and 12 submarines.
27. Roosevelt to General Board, 27 July 1921, File No. 438 (Ser. No. 1088) WNCP.I, RGB.
28. Ibid.
29. Hughes to Secretary of the Navy, 1 Sept. 1921, File No. 438 (Ser. No. 1988), WNCP.I, RGB; Rodgers to Secretary of the Navy, 17 and 27 Sept. 1921, ibid.
30. Rodgers to Secretary of the Navy, 12 Sept. 1921, enclosing Report of the General Board of the Navy, The Limitation of Armaments, Part I, File No. 438 (Ser. No. 1088), WNCP.I, RGB.

31. The report's Part IV was submitted in several dozen segments from 18 Oct. 1921 to 11 Jan. 1922.
32. Report of the General Board, The Limitation of Armaments, Part I, 12 Sept. 1921, File No. 438 (Ser. No. 1088), RGB.
33. Ibid.
34. Ibid. Part II, 17 Sept. 1921, File No. 438 (Ser. No. 1088-A), RGB.
35. Ibid. Part III (1st Portion), 3 Oct. 1921, File No. 438 (Ser. No. 1088-B), RGB. Great Britain had already scrapped all her pre-dreadnoughts; according to the General Board tables, the Royal Navy had 1,015,825 tons in existing dreadnought capital ships, while the US Navy had 500,650 tons.
36. Ibid.
37. Ibid. The General Board estimated the four projected British 'super-*Hoods*' at 43,000 tons each; in this case, the six US battlecrusiers at 43,500 tons each would be the world's largest warships when completed.
38. Roosevelt to Secretary of the Navy, 16 and 19 Sept. 1921 and 3 Oct. 1921, Box 39, Theodore Roosevelt, Jr, Papers, Manuscript Division, Library of Congress, Washington, D.C. (hereafter cited as Roosevelt Papers, with appropriate filing designations). Denby to Secretary of State, 10 Oct. 1921, State Dept. Decimal File No. 500.A41a/110, Record Group 59, National Archives, Washington, D.C. (hereafter cited as RG 59, with appropriate filing designations).
39. Minutes of the American Delegation to the Washington Conference, 1st Meeting, 12 Oct. 1921, State Dept. Decimal File No. 500.A41/12, RG 59. Hughes to Secretary of the Navy, 13 Oct. 1921, State Dept. Decimal File No. 500.A41a/110, RG 59.
40. Hughes to Secretary of the Navy, 6 Oct. 1921, State Dept. Decimal File No. 500.A41a/130e, RG 59. Rodgers to Secretary of the Navy, Modification of General Board Plan, 14 Oct. 1921, File No. 438 (Ser. No. 1088-D), WNCP.I, RGB. Rodgers to Secretary of the Navy, Analysis of Plan for Limitation of Armament, 14 Oct. 1921, File No. 438 (1088-E), RGB.
41. Diary of Theodore Roosevelt, Jr, Roosevelt Papers.
42. Navy Dept. Plans I, II, and III, n.d., Washington Naval Conference Materials, Advisory Book No. 1, William Veazie Pratt Papers, Ms. Collection 24, Naval War College Archives, Newport, Rhode Island.
43. Minutes of the American Delegation, 2nd Meeting, 21 Oct. 1921, State Dept. Decimal File No. 500.A41/12, RG 59.
44. Diary of Theodore Roosevelt, Jr, 20 Oct. 1921 and 5 Oct. 1921, Roosevelt Papers; Roosevelt to George Harvey (American ambassador in London), 20 Oct. 1921, ibid.
45. Minutes of the American Delegation, 3rd Meeting, 24 Oct. 1921 at 10 a.m. and 4th Meeting, 24 Oct. 1921 at 4 p.m., State Dept. Decimal File No. 500.A41/12, RG 59. Diary of Theodore Roosevelt, Jr, 25 Oct. 1921, Roosevelt Papers. Hughes to Secretary of the Navy, 25 Oct. 1921, copy attached to Rodgers to Secretary of the Navy, 26 Oct. 1921, File No. 438 (Ser. No. 1088-O), WNCP.I, RGB.
46. Diary of Theodore Roosevelt, Jr, 26 Oct., 1921, Roosevelt Papers. Naval Advisory Committee, 'A Limitation and Reduction of Armaments on the Principle of "Stop Now",' 26 Oct. 1921, Advisory Book No. 1, WNCP.I, RGB. Draft letter, Denby to Secretary of State, Explanatory of 'Stop Now' Proposals, 26 Oct. 1921, ibid.
47. Rodgers to Secretary of the Navy, 'Proposal to scrap all US capital ships under construction with corresponding reduction by Great Britain and Japan', 26 Oct. 1921, File No. 438 (Ser. No. 1088-O), RGB.

48. Rodgers, Memo. for Chief of Naval Operations, 28 Oct. 1921, ibid.
49. Minutes of the American Delegation, 5th Meeting, 31 Oct. 1921, State Dept. Decimal File No. 500.A41/12, RG 59; 7th Meeting, 2 Nov. 1921, ibid. Diary of Theodore Roosevelt, Jr, 2 Nov. 1921, Roosevelt Papers.
50. Minutes of the American Delegation, 7th Meeting, 2 Nov. 1921, State Dept. Decimal File No. 500.A41/12, RG 59.
51. Diary of Theodore Roosevelt, Jr, 4 and 19 Nov. 1921, Roosevelt Papers.
52. Hankey to Prime Minister, 14 Nov. 1921, Private, F/62/1/2, Lloyd George Papers, House of Lords Library, London.
53. The text of the Washington Treaty for the Limitation of Armament can be found in Harold and Margaret Sprout, *Toward a New Order of Sea Power* (Princeton, 1946), pp. 302–11.
54. Minutes of the American Delegation, 18th Meeting, 15 Nov. 1921, State Dept. Decimal File No. 500.A41/12, RG 59.
55. See note 35 above. The United States and Japan each had some pre-dreadnought capital ships still in commission.
56. Roosevelt to Harvey, 29 Dec. 1921, Roosevelt Papers.

11 'Are We Ready?' The Development of American and British Naval Strategy, 1922–39[1]

Malcolm H. Murfett

Every naval project which takes account neither of the foreign relations of a great nation, nor of the material limit fixed by its resources, rests upon a weak and unstable base. Foreign policy and strategy are bound together by an indestructible link.[2]

AMERICAN STRATEGIC PLANNING FOR A WAR AT SEA

Despite the momentous nature of the event, or perhaps because of it, the Washington Conference aroused strong emotions among naval men on both sides of the Atlantic. Many felt that it had managed to create more problems than it had solved. Apart from the dark mutterings about it being a bad bargain that ought not to have been accepted, opponents of the treaties claimed to find sufficient evidence, either in the decisions reached or those postponed, to regard the whole affair with serious misgivings.

One man who rapidly distanced himself from the proceedings at Washington was Admiral Robert Coontz, the Chief of Naval Operations. Although a member of the US delegation, Coontz played a key role neither in the decision-making process behind the scenes nor in the conference sessions. Frustrated by his inability to exert much influence upon Charles Evans Hughes, the American Secretary of State and leader of his delegation, the CNO reacted adversely to what he saw as the surrendering of legitimate naval interests by the United States for the sake of geopolitical considerations.[3]

That Coontz professed little sympathy or confidence in this type of political expediency was very evident. His sense of disenchantment was heightened still further by the suspicion he entertained that the British had once again been able to out-manoeuvre the Americans during the negotiations and had secured for themselves a more advantageous settlement than their position deserved. Unlike Sims or Pratt, Coontz could never be accused of being a committed Anglophile. If anything he harboured a brooding suspicion of them, a feeling nurtured over many years and one that had been aggravated by the outcome of the conference. He particularly resented the determination of the British not to yield on the question of cruiser, destroyer and submarine ratios and looked with disfavour upon the terms of the capital ship tonnage quotas which still enabled the Royal Navy to retain a larger fleet than that of the Americans for some years to come.[4]

This sour reaction, mirrored as it was by others in the US Navy Department, did little to improve Anglo-American relations or force the abandonment of war planning against the British.[5] On the contrary, existing naval war plans, revised in the aftermath of the First World War, were to be kept up-to-date and modified in line with any future developments. From Holloway Frost's blueprint entitled 'Strategy of the Atlantic', which he devised in September 1919, until the successful conclusion of the London Naval Conference in 1930, American naval war plans against *Red* (the British Empire) were something more than just theoretical yardsticks against which the US Navy might be compared.[6] It would be a mistake to dismiss these plans as being merely quaint exercises in imaginative flair or just the stuff of fevered war-gaming played out in the rooms of the Naval War College. Instead, for several years at least, they represented realistic scenarios to officers such as Coontz, Hughes, Hilary Jones, Knox, McNamee, Rodman and Schofield – all of whom tended to expect the worst from the British in those areas where Anglo-American interests conflicted. For these influential individuals war between the two power blocs could not be ruled out as inconceivable.[7]

While they did not seek any form of military confrontation with the British, the Americans were aware of the possibility that such a conflict might arise out of the desire of both Powers for economic and commercial expansion in the Far East, a search that could result in fierce competition for spheres of influence between them. Even the abrogation of the Anglo-Japanese Alliance did not reassure them unduly and a feeling persisted within the US Navy Department that if matters came to a head between the United Kingdom and the United States over, say, trading rights in the Pacific basin or in China, the Japanese would not refrain from entering a war on the side of their former ally. A *Red–Orange* (British Empire–Japan) combination would have been bad enough at the best of times but, in the light of the non-fortification provisions of the Washington Conference, such a simultaneous two-front war would obviously pose a formidable threat to the Americans if it ever materialised.[8]

Although the Navy Department did not seek to shirk the responsibility for coming to terms with this worst-case scenario, the war planners placed this contingency as second in importance and therefore somewhat less likely than a war fought solely against the Japanese. This view of the war planners was subsequently endorsed by Admiral Coontz who, in his capacity as CNO, used this advice as the basis for reorganising the US Navy in December 1922.[9]

Believing that the existing structure was unsound and inefficient, Coontz persuaded Secretary of the Navy Denby to agree to a number of significant changes both in the configuration and deployment of the naval forces at their disposal. Dispensing with the need for separate Atlantic and Pacific fleets in favour of a single US Fleet, the CNO divided his new creation into four major elements, of which by far the largest was the main battle fleet. It was intended that this modern arm of the Navy should operate in the Pacific where it would be given logistic and training support by a Fleet Base Force. Eschewing Mahanian orthodoxy, Coontz wished to retain a scouting fleet and a control force consisting of cruisers, light defence ships and a few of the older battleships in the Atlantic.[10] Despite the division of forces, the US Fleet came together each year to conduct its annual manoeuvres on lines and in locations suggested by the war planners.

None the less, it must have been a sobering thought for all concerned that regardless of these reforms the US Fleet was still no match for the Royal Navy and would not be for many years to come. If a worst-case scenario had to be envisaged, the propsects were uncomfortably bleak for the Americans. This sobering message was underlined by Captain J. M. Reeves, the Chief of the Department of Tactics at the Naval War College, who reported in 1925 that the US Fleet could not engage the Royal Navy in war at that time with any likelihood of victory.[11] Reeves knew only too well that, in every simulated battle played out at Newport between 1923 and 1925, the capital ships of *Red* had always been able to cripple those of *Blue* (the United States). This was hardly surprising given the marked overall superiority in such vital areas as fleet size, speed, gunpower and armour enjoyed by the Royal Navy.[12] Far from being an exaggeration, Reeves's assessment was one with which the General Board of the US Navy reluctantly concurred. Although this inferiority impelled the Americans to do everything in their power to close the gap on *Red* by increasing gun elevation, armour-plating and fleet speed, the results of their endeavours in these areas would take some time to have an effect. For the rest of the decade, therefore, the Royal Navy would remain pre-eminent, although the gap between the two fleets of capital ships began to shrink with each passing year.[13]

In the meantime, of course, American war planning against the British remained largely an exercise in wishful thinking. Even the General Board's Basic Readiness Plan of 1924 seemed to presume a level of strength which the Navy Department was incapable of exercising at that time. This had called for a US Fleet of sufficient strength to enable it to engage and defeat either the British in the Atlantic or the Japanese in the Pacific if called upon to do so.[14] At no stage throughout the 1920s, however, did the Americans possess a fleet of sufficient size or superiority to achieve these ends. Apart from anything else, neither the British nor the Japanese were prepared to accept the idea of a naval holiday for all classes of ship and were both intent on adding to their stock of cruisers. If the United States wished to compete with either of these Powers, therefore, it would obviously have to be willing to lay down at least a comparable number of keels to those of its main naval rivals.

While the US Navy Department was keen enough to do just that, Congress easily resisted the temptation. Influenced both by its aversion to war and the drive for disarmament, Congress systematically supported efforts made by the Harding and Coolidge administrations to reduce Service estimates to a level commensurate with its isolationist foreign policy. This meant in practice that Secretary Denby's naval estimates came in for fairly savage pruning at the hands of those manning the newly created Bureau of the Budget. His annual departmental allocations were drastically cut, insistent appeals for modernisation expenditure went largely unheeded and urgent demands for the construction of 16 heavy cruisers were brushed aside.[15] Once this pattern of economising had been set it continued for much of the Coolidge presidency, regardless of who was at the helm in the Navy Department.

As a result, Curtis D. Wilbur, the surprising choice to succeed Denby in March 1924, was hard put to make out a case which was convincing enough to persuade a reluctant president and budget director to abandon their policy of military austerity in favour of approving a big spending programme of naval construction and modernisation. Labouring under this major handicap, Wilbur none the less succeeded in this endeavour by repeatedly pointing out to anyone who took the trouble to listen that, unless something was done to correct the existing imbalance of forces, the outlook for the US Navy was far from that envisaged by Charles Evans Hughes at the Washington Conference. Assisted by Admiral Edward Eberle, his hard-working Chief of Naval Operations, Wilbur provided Congress with an almost constant stream of evidence which underlined the persistent trend of American naval inferiority towards the British, as well as a shrinking numerical advantage over the Japanese in auxiliary classes of ship. In the end, although it took years to accomplish, the cumulative effect of this sustained effort by the navy secretary was such that congressmen and senators alike began insisting upon a new phase of limited rearmament.[16]

It was a call which even the Coolidge administration found particularly hard to resist in the wake of the notorious Geneva Naval Conference of 1927. By failing so abjectly to agree on extending the Washington system to other classes of naval vessel and in finding no common ground on cruiser quotas, tonnage and gun calibre, the three leading naval Powers may be accused of displaying a cynical disregard for the needs of others and of seeking solely to pursue their own selfish interests to the exclusion of reaching a settlement based on compromise and good sense. A grisly diplomatic failure from start to finish, the Geneva Conference was to reveal the existence of an underlying hostility in Anglo-American naval relations that had been simmering in private for several years but which had now found public expression.[17]

As one who had regularly subscribed to the thesis of 'Perfidious Albion' throughout the twenties, Frank Schofield, the Director of the Naval War Plans Division, could hardly claim to be an impartial witness of what had taken place at Geneva. Even so the acrimony and resentment present in the conference sessions had been such that few of those present would have argued with his conclusion that in managing to plumb the depths in Anglo-American naval relations, the Geneva Conference had ironically brought the day of that once distant and all but inconceivable *Red–Blue* war a good deal closer. Pointing specifically to the vexed and highly contentious issue of cruiser strength, about which the British had adamantly and consistently refused to grant concessions to the Americans, and in claiming to see evidence of an insidious Anglo-Japanese understanding on naval matters generally, Schofield felt perfectly justified in recommending a drastic course of action to his superiors. This was to take the form of a reassessment of US naval priorities in both Pacific and Atlantic oceans and a refinement of their existing war plans directed against *Red*.[18]

Far from being alone in pushing such a strategic review, Schofield was merely echoing what the army war planners had been saying rather extravagantly for several years.[19] As a result of what had happened at Geneva and without much thought about the Kellogg–Briand Pact, the Joint Army and Navy Board was now prepared to turn the attention of its Joint Planning Committee to devising a basic war plan that could be successfully implemented against *Red*, if need be, with the minimum of delay. What emerged finally from these discussions was an operational plan that combined many of the strategic features sought by the army planners with those objectives desired by their naval counterparts.[20]

In essence, the Joint Army and Navy Basic War Plan *Red*, which received its final departmental approval only in May 1930, envisaged a long drawn-out conflict on land and sea before *Red* could be brought to its knees out of sheer economic exhaustion. In order to achieve that favourable result, however, *Blue* would have to knock *Crimson* (Canada) out of the war so as to deny *Red* the opportunity of receiving active logistical support from this strategically important quarter.[21]

Whatever its strategic merits may have been on paper, the Joint Army and Navy Basic War Plan *Red* was shot through with a number of serious practical flaws, perhaps the most important of which were the major assumptions, surely of doubtful validity, that underpinned the entire scheme of naval operations. It would not have taken much probing to have revealed certain basic weaknesses that lay at the heart of this plan, yet no attempt was made on behalf of the joint military authorities to carry out a fundamental revision of it in the years which followed.[22] An explanation for what would otherwise constitute a policy of neglect is readily available in the vast and growing improvement discernible in Anglo-American relations from 1929 onwards. Much of the credit for rescuing the old Atlantic friendship from the deep trough into which it had sunk in the months after the Geneva Conference must be given to J. Ramsay MacDonald, the wily British Prime Minister of 1929–35. Standing resolutely at the head of a government pledged to a policy of disarmament and the maintenance of peace, he strove to repair the damage wrought by others in the past to the old wartime partnership. Investing much time and effort in search of these goals, he was largely responsible for ensuring a successful conclusion to the protracted negotiations carried out between the leading naval Powers in London in 1930.[23]

While the decisions reached at this conference were far from popular with the naval authorities on either side of the Atlantic, the talks themselves had shown that Anglo-American co-operation was not just a thing of the past but stood as a realistic option for the future. To some extent, therefore, the Basic War Plan *Red* appears to have been overtaken by events and looks from the date of its departmental approval in May 1930 to have already become something of an anachronism. It was certainly not an instrument of national policy which President Herbert Hoover or William Veazie Pratt, his Chief of Naval Operations, wished to use. Both were altogether more optimistically inclined and regarded the thought that war might break out with the British Empire as being nothing more than the most remote and improbable of contingencies.[24]

As the years passed this became the conventional view, not least because the Americans had come to believe that they had nothing to fear from the Royal Navy. This growing self-assertiveness in naval thinking was a new and welcome development, representing a maturity which had been a long time in coming to the fore. The degree of confidence which the Navy Department began to exude in the thirties had an important effect in helping to crystallise its thinking along more realistic lines than it had followed in the past. Given this change in emphasis and analysis, there was really never any pressing need for the Joint Committee to revise the Basic War Plan *Red*. It remained on the active file until 1939, but had been seen by the US Navy for many years prior to this as nothing more than an interesting, if rather bizarre, piece of theory.[25]

Unfortunately the same comforting conclusion could not be made of the latent threat posed by the Japanese. Generally regarded as being a more probable enemy than the British had been at any stage of the inter-war period, even at the height of Anglo-American animosity in 1928, the Japanese came to assume an increasingly sinister role as sole enemy of the United States for much of the 1930s. War planning against them became a matter of practical necessity rather than an object of abstract theory that bore little relevance to the existing state of international relations or American foreign policy. Ironically the clear existence of this threat managed to inhibit the very planning process which had been established to thwart it. Despite having the considerable advantage of concentrating their collective attention against a single identifiable enemy, the US war planning agencies still managed over the years to produce operational schemes for use against Japan that lacked such essential qualities as vision, candour, clarity and realism.[26]

It had not always been so. War planning in the second decade of the twentieth century, for instance, had been marked by intellectual ability, foresight and integrity of a very high order. It was only in later years that standards began to fall as modifications and refinements were introduced to the existing war plans. Although revisions were necessary from time to time, it is exceedingly difficult to see any military virtue in some of them. Those which rested on shaky strategic or tactical grounds appear to have been unduly influenced by political departmental expediency; circumstances, in other words, which could not be expected to do much more than compromise and devalue the whole planning exericse. Despite this overall deterioration in quality, War Plan *Orange* retained the allegiance of the US military until the international situation in the wake of the Munich crisis persuaded the Joint Army and Navy Board to set new guide-lines for the drawing up of an entirely different set of war plans.[27]

Undoubtedly part of the fixation the military had with War Plan *Orange* came from the clarity and persuasiveness of the original plan. Initially devised in 1911 by Rear-Admiral Rodgers and studied by successive waves of naval graduates at Newport in the years thereafter, the first *Orange* plan had both a simplicity and logic about it that could hardly be faulted. It was not hedged in with nuances or cloaked, as later revisions were, by a veil of ambiguity. It presupposed the fall of the Philippines at an early stage of the war and the necessity this imposed upon the Americans to recapture the islands at a later date. It did not wax eloquent about the need to retain Manila Bay or imply that massive reinforcements would be sent immediately or subsequently to relieve the overburdened garrison on Luzon. It assumed with the prescience which marked the entire plan that the Japanese would use the advantage of relatively close geographical proximity to good effect, bringing a naval task force south to over-whelm the American and indigenous defenders of this strategically important island chain at an early stage of the war.[28]

This being so, Rodgers's plan envisaged a sequence of strategic steps to deal with the problem of waging war in the vast expanse of the Pacific against an exuberant, if over-extended, opponent. Beginning by assembling the fleet at Hawaii, the 1911 scheme dictated the adoption of a cautious approach by the task force through the central Pacific using an island-hopping procedure that would assist the process of securing American control over the Marshall and Caroline Islands before launching any major assault to recover the Philippines from Japanese occupation. Servicing the fleet throughout its extended campaign, for Rodgers was not blinded to the fact that it was likely to be a long and costly war, would be a mobile, advanced base with dry-docking facilities that might enable it to undertake capital ship repairs if need be. Orchestrated in this way, the plan was designed to bring the Japanese finally to their knees through the implementation of an economic blockade achieved by the concentration of naval superiority and military dominance in the western Pacific.[29]

Far from being outdated, the Rodgers plan appeared to possess the singular advantage of timelessness; it remained as relevant in 1922 as it had been when first mooted over a decade before. If anything, the agreements reached at Wshington, which ensured Japanese naval pre-eminence in the western Pacific for the foreseeable future, gave it added significance. As long as the US government and military continued to perceive the Japanese as constituting a long-term threat to the United States and of being its most probable enemy, a suspicion that even the most rabid Anglophobes would scarcely reject, War Plan *Orange*, or some close variant of it, was likely to be the officially approved means of combatting and eventually defeating them.

What emerged finally in 1924 as the Joint Army and Navy Basic War Plan *Orange*, however, was far from ideal for this purpose. Lacking the intellectual rigour and plain commonsense of earlier studies, this new war plan looked exactly what it was – an inferior hybrid. Bowing to external political pressure, the Joint Board and its planning committee had re-examined and reversed some of the critical assumptions underpinning the original Rodgers thesis. Their revisions had only served to highlight the deficiencies of the new plan compared with its more illustrious predecessor, debasing the old conceptual framework by substituting rash optimism for constructive realism.[30] It was as though a law of diminishing returns had set in.

Under the terms of the 1924 plans, for example, the United States would adopt an offensive strategy in the far Pacific at the outbreak of the Japanese war. This would involve the Navy in transporting some 500,000 troops to the Philippines without delay in order to prevent the fall of both the small American army garrison and undeveloped naval base on Luzon. This plan was wildly impractical and logically unsound. Apart from committing at least a third of the Army's fighting strength at that time, the plan assumed that the naval base in Manila Bay was able to offer the fleet reasonable facilities. Nothing could have been further from the truth. Neither the facilities available at Cavite or those at Olongapo could have provided anything other than a range of skeletal services for ships of the line and both places would have been simply overwhelmed by the needs of any American task force that had to remain in Manila or Subic Bay for any length of time. This mistake was compounded by the fatuous belief that the war would be a short glorious affair rather than a long drawn-out one of attrition.[31]

Plainly the political unacceptability of relinquishing American bases in the Philippines not only distorted but also made a mockery of the entire planning process. From then onwards, in various revisions which were made to the *Orange* plan, the problem of what was to be done as far as the Philippines were concerned was never clearly or adequately spelt out. While it made no strategic sense, the whole sensitive issue was deliberately left by the military and politicians in a fog of uncertainty until this was eventually dispelled by Admiral Stark's famous Plan *Dog* Memorandum of November 1940.[32]

As a result of the prolonged sense of vagueness and ambiguity surrounding the fate of the Philippines, the Basic War Plan *Orange* was left bereft of a convincing strategy. Agonising over whether the United States ought to adopt an offensive or defensive strategy in the Pacific became a perennial problem which was never really satisfactorily resolved by either the two services or their war planners in the period 1924–38. It was evident, for instance, that the navy was always inclined to adopt a more robust stand against the Japanese at the outbreak of war than the army felt was prudent under the circumstances. Far from relishing the prospect of waging an adventurous and possibly reckless campaign in the western Pacific, the army much preferred at the outset of any war to establish a solid, defensive position based on the strategic triangle, Alaska–Hawaii–Panama. This would have the advantage of ensuring the defence of the United States from hostile attack, while giving American forces time to reach a state of readiness for action, enabling them to respond to any threat which might materialise from any quarter whatsoever.[33]

It was unfortunate that, in the disturbed international climate of the 1930s when American war planning needed t be unequivocal, the two armed services could not agree on the best policy to adopt. In the absence of such an agreement, elements of both service schemes were grafted together to offer what was in the end a rather Quixotic mixture of an offensive strategy with defensive priorities for use against the Japanese in the event of war. If the US government was unduly perturbed by what at first sight might seem a strategy of mutually contradictory elements, there is little evidence to suggest that it did much to articulate its concern. Whether justifiable or not, the military planning agencies were allowed to drift along at their own pace, revising their ideas as they went.

This 'hands off' policy is all the more surprising in the wake of the Mukden incident when Japan's abandonment of democracy for militarism and its cavalier attitude towards international opinion had become so evident. Nevertheless, even after Japan's withdrawal from the League of Nations in 1933, there was not an immediate sense of impending doom. American foreign policy, shaped as it was by the forces of congressional isolationism, was confidently expected to stave off the threat of war in the Pacific for years to come.

In the meantime, however, the march of totalitarianism on the world stage and the failure of the General Disarmament Conference were used by President Roosevelt as a convenient pretext for relaxing the tight budgetary control over the navy that had existed for more than a decade, so as to bring the fleet at last up to treaty strength and beyond. As a result of the National

Recovery Act of June 1933 and the passing of the Vinson-Trammel Bill of March 1934, large and increasingly expensive programmes of new naval construction and replacement were initiated. By the end of the 1930s naval appropriations amounting to roughly one billion US dollars annually were being passed in order to finance this important phase of the American rearmament programme. It was just as well that they were because without this significant expansion the navy would not have been able to accomplish the tasks which the joint planners had set it to do in the event of war with the Japanese.[34]

Adherence to the maxim of deterrence through strength, so implicit in the Vinson-Trammel Act, grew in the succeeding years as confidence in the protection afforded by the geographical location of the United States slowly began to ebb away in the face of a relentless advance by the forces of Fascism in Europe and Asia. By the autumn of 1938 it had been proved that independence was no guarantee of safety and that democracy was under serious threat of extinction from the activities of Germany, Italy and Japan: totalitarian states described graphically by Roosevelt as the three bandit nations against whom the free world must defend itself.[35] In these circumstances, with the European powers in disarray and with the Open Door in China gravely imperilled by the Japanese invasion, the United States drew what little comfort it could from the fact that it was actively rearming and that time might still be on its side.

Meanwhile, however, the strategic notion that the Americans had only a single enemy, Japan, to worry about had become almost impossible to sustain. This was particulary true in the charged atmosphere of the post-Munich era when the sense of disenchantment with appeasement was strong and concern for the future was growing. Given the unstable situation in the world and the Roosevelt administration's deep conviction that peace could only be bought from the Axis powers at an unacceptably high price, it is small wonder that the Joint Board at last stirred itself from its lethargy and conceded belatedly that the *Orange* plans had outlived their usefulness. It had taken a long time for this feeling to sink in but now that it had the Joint Board recognised that something completely different was required if the United States was going to be successful in countering the menace of Fascism in the future.[36]

Although it almost defies belief, the fact remains that, before November 1938 when the Joint Planning committee began wrestling with this formidable strategic equation, no systematic attempt had been made by the US military to solve the problems posed for the democracies by a Germany, Italy and Japan bent on achieving world domination. Nor had it sought to evaluate what its response should be if this hostile coalition of powers was prepared to engage the Americans in a war fought on at least two fronts simultaneously. Whatever its motive was, overconfidence or lack of foresight, dilatory behaviour of the kind demonstrated by the US military was inexcusable, particularly when the existence of such a real threat ought to have been obvious for several years.

Once engaged upon its task of compiling a report on the Axis military threat, the Joint Committee found that it was able to rely on some of the operational framework previously developed by the Services for use against two enemies in widely separated theatres of war. In the *Red–Orange* series, to which the Army had been largely responsible during the twenties and early thirties, the needs of American defence had demanded something more than just an even-handed approach from the Services in tackling their enemies in a two-front war. According to the *Red–Orange* plan of 1930, for instance, *Blue* was expected to defeat *Red* before embarking upon an offensive strategy against *Orange*. This emphasis on dealing with the Atlantic or European theatre first, while being prepared to maintain a defensive posture in the Pacific at the same time, a policy first accepted rather unenthusiastically by the Navy in 1932, was endorsed by the Joint Planning Committee in its report to the Joint Board on 21 April 1939. In sounding the death-knell for the *Orange* series, Captain Crenshaw and Colonel Clark, the authors of the 1939 study, virtually ensured that a new, rational and constructive phase in American war planning would being.[37]

By the time the first and most basic *Rainbow* plan had made its appearance, Europe was on the verge of war; by the time it had received presidential approval, Poland had been crushed. After barely surviving this inauspicious start, *Rainbow No. 1* soon lost its unilateral defensive appeal even to the American war planners and became, therefore, the first planning casualty of the war. It was replaced by the second plan in the series and one which had the singular advantage of assuming that the United States would be acting in concert with the British and French in any future war and that such a combination would enable the Americans to adopt an offensive strategy in the western Pacific and involve little in the way of a commitment by them in the Atlantic or European theatre. Although it lasted for the duration of the Phoney War, *Rainbow No. 2* could not survive the *blitzkrieg* offensive on the western front which opened in the spring of 1940. Then, as the Axis forces were rampaging across vast tracts of France with devastating effect, the idea that the democracies could be relied upon to retain any sort of control over events in Europe seemed out of the question. *Rainbow No. 2* was rapidly forsaken in favour of *Rainbow No. 4* a more denfensive scheme similar in some respects to the now defunct *Rainbow No. 1*, but with wider implications since it was based on the sobering belief that Britain and its empire would soon go the way of France. When it became clear after the Battle of Britain that the empire was prepared to strike back, the Americans were obliged to think again and in doing so *Rainbow No. 4* was eventually passed over to the fifth and final plan of the series and the one which would most resemble the role the United States would ultimately play in the Second World War.[38]

Support for an Atlantic first policy, which *Rainbow No. 5* advocated, was provided by Admiral Stark, the Chief of Naval Operations, in his famous Plan *Dog* Memorandum of 4 November 1940. As far as Stark was concerned, American defence and security interests were bound up with the continued existence of the British Empire and that accordingly the United States ought to be prepared to do everything in its power to assist the Churchill government to survive against the Axis Powers. In fact, Plan *Dog* envisaged the lending of such material support to the British that the Germans and Italians would eventually be defeated, thus releasing American forces for their long-awaited offensive against the Japanese in the Pacific.[39] It was powerful stuff from an influential source. In the past the Navy had been the more conservative of the two Services and the one most firmly wedded to its beloved Pacific strategy. Stark changed all that. His memo was bold, imaginative and decisive; it did not pull any punches or try to create any comforting illusions; it did not rely on exaggeration but on plain common-sense. It was a message that in peace-time the planners would have rejected as being too controversial. In the exigencies of war, however, it won rapid approval from General Marshall, the Chief of Staff and from the members of the Army War Plans Division.[40] Over the next few months, as the war developed in Europe, Plan *Dog* came to be accepted as the way ahead by all the military committees whose brief was to review it. Warmly endorsed by the allies, after the news of it was deliberately leaked to them, accepted without much reserve by the secretaries of War and the Navy, this new strategic plan was thought to reflect President Roosevelt's ideas most accurately. Out of this unanimity was forged *Rainbow No. 5* – the flesh on the Plan *Dog* skeleton.[41] It had taken months of warfare and several plans to achieve but in the end the strategy devised by the Joint Planning Committee and Admiral Stark was accepted by the government and the military as the best and most effective one available, even if it was not always as well understood by the querulous American public.

THE BRITISH EXPERIENCE

Whatever their limitations, and some of these were considerable as we have seen, American naval war plans were developed in a far more centralised, detailed and systematic fashion than the rather *ad hoc* arrangement which the British relied upon during the twenties and thirties to cater for their future needs.

Far from being a preserve of the Admiralty Board, whose collective wisdom often left much to be desired, operational planning had always been considered as something much better left to senior officers afloat; men, in other words, whose intelligence and up-to-the-minute knowledge of local conditions usually far surpassed that of the naval staff in Whitehall. It was assumed that fleet commanders would be best able to direct resources where they would be most needed in an emergency and periodic conferences between these individuals ensured that the basic schemes of bringing relief to certain areas of the empire were discussed and understood by those who would necessarily be intimately involved in mounting such operations. Unfortunately the grave weakness of this system was cruelly exposed if and when men of limited intellectual ability were appointed to these crucial positions. It was a sad fact of life that worthy time-servers, such as Howard Kelly or Roger Keyes, for example, were no substitute for men of vision, especially as far as strategic planning was concerned. Those who adopted too narrow, confident or dismissive an approach to these tasks managed unwittingly to undermine the old system and hasten the day when operational planning responsibilities would be entrusted to a Chiefs of Staff committee based in London.

Despite the existence of a Plans Division within the Admiralty, much of the work of the section had very little to do with war planning as such, incongrous though this may seem. In fact, far from devoting themselves to the conception and development of operational strategy, all too frequently the personnel manning this section found themselves frustrated by the bureaucratic demands of the department and the ease with which they were assigned to duties that bore only a tangential relevance to the business of preparing naval policy for use in a future war.[42] Even if one accepts the notion that professional war planning of the kind indulged in by the United States military was against the historic tradition of the Admiralty, it in no way excuses the Board for failing to utilise its resources in the most effective way possible.

As one might expect, however, there was some method in what appears to be its madness. In the past, war planning of the American type had been discouraged by the British mainly because it was believed to be exceedingly difficult, if not impossible, to predict accurately months or years in advance the precise form which the defence of their global empire should take. This was especially pertinent since most of the vital factors that would have to be taken into consideration when framing these plans were of a variable as opposed to a fixed nature and subject disconcertingly to change over the course of time. Long-term planning was seen by the Admiralty, therefore, as being essentially a leap into the dark, since the validity of the assumptions upon which it would be based could not be tested in advance. It could neither safely predict the extent and type of opposition it would be confronting, nor the existence or otherwise of friends and/or allies it might have in some future war; it could not guarantee the exact location in the empire where the enemy's initial blow would fall or which sea routes would be available for the Navy to use in an emergency. In such a fluid situation the Admiralty much preferred to remain flexible rather than to try and prepare detailed war plans which might have the effect of encouraging rigidity in strategic thinking and a commitment to specific action in advance, two features that both the military and the government wished to avoid at all cost.

In the absence of such plans at either the departmental or Chiefs of Staff level, civil servants, politicians and military alike could all afford to take shelter behind general and often ambiguously worded statements of intent that looked more substantial than they proved to be in practice. The value of having nothing specific to disclose to one's friends could be seen at the various Imperial Conferences during the inter-war period. Controversy was kept at bay, the dominions remained quiescent, lulled into a false sense of security by the language of diplomacy and the British kept their options open on what to do and when to do it. Nothing could have suited them better.

A useful illustration of the stark contrast existing between the formulation and development of American and British naval strategy lies in the marked reluctance of the Admiralty to engage itself in long-term war planning. Whereas in the United States the existence of militarily inspired and orchestrated war plans tended to influence the shape and direction of the administration's naval strategy, virtually spelling out for the government what could and could not be contemplated under certain set conditions, the story is completely different in the case of the United Kingdom.

From the end of the First World War onwards, the British government came to assume a dominant role in the construction of naval policy. Whether in the adoption of the ten year rule, or in its programmes of economic restraint or active disarmament, all of which affected naval policy profoundly, the government led the way and the fighting Services, unable to thwart the Cabinet, had to grin and bear it. One need only look at the way in which naval strategy was framed or how keenly the annual battle over the departmental estimates was fought to see this contention being borne out in practice.[43]

Aware of the special status of the Royal Navy in any system of imperial defence it might seek to devise, the government had few qualms about closely monitoring developments involving its senior Service, or the uses to which its strength and vitality could be put. Defence matters were considered to be too serious a business for decision-making on major issues to be left solely in the hands of the military. Equally the idea that strategic principles guiding the present and future deployment of the fleet could be somehow made in isolation by the politicians was rejected for roughly the same reasons. Although the First Sea Lord and the rest of the naval staff were not without infleunce and the Chiefs of Staff (COS) and their various committees could exert considerable pressure on occasion, the final decision would always rest with and be taken by the Cabinet, after receiving advice on the matter from its most influential policy-making and review body the Committee of Imperial Defence (CID). Interaction betweeen government ministers and the COS who sat on this committee was guaranteed, but since the numerical advantage lay with the politicians it was they who ultimately decided what was to be passed on up the line to the full Cabinet for its consideration and approval. If the CID could be persuaded to place its imprimatur on any issue large or small, the odds were that the Cabinet would be likely to support its recommendation. This, of course, reflected the fact that the most senior figures in the government also sat on the CID. In theory, therefore, and often in practice too, policy formation as something of a collaborative effort, if short of being a true marriage of equals.

Unfortunately the legacy of this rather uneven relationship, though apparent from the outset, was only really discovered at some cost subsequently in the 1930s when the Royal Navy, shorn of its former glory, was faced with the expanding threat of the Fascist dictatorships in widely separated parts of the globe. It was then almost too late to rue the day when optimism for the future, mixed with a sincere desire to make a fresh start in international relations, had triumphed at the expense of a more cautious bilateralism founded upon a strong navy and rooted in the Anglo-Japanese Alliance. In truth, however, there had been little else that the British could have done at the time. When the Powers conferred at Washington during the winter of 1921–2, the United States had become the greatest industrial and economic nation in the world. While standing aloof from the League, the USA, the world's largest creditor nation, was clearly in a position to exert a prodigious amount of influence over those who still owed it a small fortune in war debts. Whether by compulsion or subtle bribery, the suspicion was the same, namely, that the Americans could usually get their way on those issues which they felt most strongly about.

In the case of the United Kingdom, for example, the Washington Conference did more than merely give formal effect to the collapse of the naval ascendancy it had enjoyed for more than a century over its main rivals; it also brought to an end the twenty-year-old alliance with Japan that had proved so invaluable during the war, the loss of which was to prove incalculable for the British in the coming years and gravely weaken their system of imperial defence. That two such crucial pillars of British strength should have been removed at a stroke, basically as the behest of the Americans, was bound to stir up a certain tide of resentment against the United States in some quarters. Significantly, however, it did not persuade either the military or the government to cast aside their firmly stated belief that war between the United Kingdom and the United States was out of the question. Consequently no war plans were developed by the British for use against the Americans, regardless of how unsatisfactory their relationships became at various stages of the 1920s.

If war against the Americans could be safely ruled out, the same might not be said of the Japanese, a Power who stood unrivalled in the Far East and supreme in the western Pacific since the Washington Conference. Despite the very serious potential threat Japan now posed to British trading interests and imperial possessions in the region, the government of Lloyd George did not do anything to amend the ten year rule, that comfortable notion which circumscribed military expenditure for the rest of the decade. Such was its seductive attraction that even Winston Churchill, surely the unlikeliest chancellor of any Conservative administration in the twentieth century, fell victim to its beguiling appeal. His advocacy of its retention beyond 1929, the year in which it was originally set to lapse, proved to be crucial in persuading Baldwin's government to move it forward on a rolling year-by-year basis until such time as the Cabinet felt it ought to be abandoned.[44]

Apart, therefore, from the controversies surrounding the builing of a first-class naval base at Singapore, British governments regardless of party label continued throughout the twenties to remain obsessed with the need for financial restraint and convinced by the merits of collective security, even though these had yet to be tested in a crisis involving one of the world's leading Powers. While the COS and the Admiralty fought tenaciously in favour of maintaining as large a treaty navy as possible, the best they could do was to mount a rearguard action delaying the inevitable for as long as possible, since the momentum, particulary in the era of Locarno, remained with those who pursued disarmament. In spite of British intransigence at Geneva in 1927/8, their success proved to be only a short-lived affair.[45]

Insistent demands by the Americans for equality in cruisers, though still resisted in some quarters, could not fail to evoke strong sympathy in politicians such as Ramsay MacDonald who were committed to disarmament and an improvement in international relations. Once he had succeeded Stanley Baldwin as Prime Minister in 1929, MacDonald worked hard at fashioning an international agreement as a complement to and extension of the original Washington Naval Limitation Treaty. In view of his unbridled enthusiasm and unflagging energy, the Prime Minister was able to achieve a significant breakthrough on two fronts at the London Naval Conference in 1930, obtaining a further measure of disarmament, as witnessed by the reduction in British cruiser strength from 70 to 50 and the beginnings of a marked improvement in Anglo-American relations.[46]

His successful linkage of naval and foreign policies had merely reconfirmed the age-old truism that an interdependency of sorts existed between the two. Although hardly a radical concept in itself, government ministers appeared to show remarkable ignorance of the effects that a reckless use of the one might have upon the other. They seemed to forget that, while they might be able to adapt their foreign policy at virtually a moment's notice to take account of sudden changes occurring on the international scene, naval policy could not be so readily accommodated to such rapid or wild fluctuations of political will. Aircraft-carriers and capital ships took years to build and any shortfall in cruiser or destroyer strength was not something which could be made up instantaneously, regardless of whether older vessels could be recommissioned or not. While the spirit of Locarno continued to thrive in western Europe and the Japanese remained quiescent in the Far East, all was well. Once the Wall Street Crash occurred, bringing militarism to the fore, the deleterious effects of planning military policies on a ten year rule were bound to be recognised, but by then considerable damage had been done to all three Services that would take years to offset.

Nowadays it is customary for historians to describe the abandonment of the Anglo-Japanese Alliance and the conversion of this former relationship into one of hostility and contempt as being perhaps the single most important blow to British foreign policy and naval strategy in the entire inter-war period.[47] It was not immediately seen as such because the potential for mischief on the part of the Japanese was deliberately, if genuinely, played down by British cabinet ministers. For years after the Washington Conference had ended, they remained satisfied that no serious damage had been done to their relations with the Japanese by the forced abrogation of the alliance in 1922. Whenever the question of imperial defence had been raised and discussed in the twenties senior cabinet figures were invariably on hand to express confidence in the pacific intentions of the Japanese. Experienced statesmen such as Austen Chamberlain, Winston Churchill and Ramsay MacDonald all regarded the idea of war between the two Powers as, if not unthinkable, nearly so. When pressed on the matter the most they would concede was that an Anglo-Japanese war was only a faint spectre in the far distance and not something which the Admiralty need feel perturbed about at this stage.[48] This heady optimism was, of course, rudely dispelled by the Mukden incident in September 1931 and in its tumultuous aftermath.

Even before the sheer enormity of what was taking place in Manchuria had started to sink in, the COS had begun redoubling their efforts to persuade their political masters to abandon the ten year rule on the ground that it was hopelessly out of date. At the same time they proceeded to catalogue the serious weaknesses in Britain's hallowed system of imperial defence which had been exposed by the Japanese *démarche*. Spelling out the appalling consequences that flowed from more than a decade of benevolent neglect, the COS etched a grim pictue for the CID in their annual review for 1932.[49] Apart from the plight of Hong Kong, whose defences were in a pathetically vulnerable state, the naval base at Singapore, subject as it had been to a history of political wrangling and discontinuity, was both inadequate and unfinished and would remain so for several years to come. Talk of a 38-day period before relief was fatuous when the base was incapable of providing much more than a temporary anchorage for any British fleet that might have to be sent out to do battle with the Imperial Japanese Navy in the Asia–Pacific region. Until it had been invested properly, so that its facilities could be brought up to standard and its defences improved to withstand attack by an enemy Power, Singapore would remain a hostage to fortune and the Far Eastern aspect of imperial defence a joke in rather poor taste.[50]

Once collective security had been seen to fail ingloriously over the

Manchurian episode, the serene confidence of the British government about the future began to evaporate. It was a feeling accentuated by the collapse of the General Disarmament Conference and the decisions of both Japan and Germany to withdraw from the League. By 1933 the Cabinet was at last facing up to the unenviable prospect that it might be compelled at some future date to fight a war either at long distance or on two major fronts simultaneously. Gone were the days when it could concentrate its undivided attention on European affairs, leaving its Far Eastern interests to the friendly protection of the Japanese. While war with Japan could not now be discounted and perhaps remained the most likely possibility, the Treasury protested bleakly to the CID that the United Kingdom simply did not have the economic, financial or military means to prosecute a major war in the Far East.[51] Whether the non-military constraints on British strategic policy were as chronic and debilitating as the Treasury insisted that they were is a moot point. Its claim of military weakness is, however, virtually incontestable. Despite the fact that the government had insisted repeatedly during the postwar period that the Asia–Pacific region rated second in importance to the security of the United Kingdom, the despatch of a major battle fleet to the Far East would leave it with a naval force in home and Mediterranean waters inferior to that of France. Although no danger was expected to come from this quarter, the situation was not one that could be safely allowed to continue indefinitely.[52]

One way of addressing this acute strategic problem on a long-term basis was to provide funds in order to make good Britain's deficiencies so that the Services might be better able to cope with these extra responsibilities. It was basically for this reason that the Defence Requirements Committee (DRC) had been established by the Cabinet in November 1933.[53] When its unanimous and highly controversial report was issued in February 1934, the latent threat of the Japanese, though recognised in the programme of naval building recommended by Chatfield, the First Sea Lord and a member of the DRC, was surprisingly glossed over and relegated in importance behind that of the Germans.[54]

While the DRC could write grandly about hoped-for improvements in Anglo-Japanese relations, the Admiralty was not disposed to alter its Far Eastern strategy or downgrade the existence of the Japanese threat. In a memo to the CID drafted in March 1934, the Admiralty spelt out its vigorous oppositon to the retention of a one-Power standard of naval strength on the basis that it was simply not sufficient to satisfy even the minimum strategical requirements of the fleet. These demanded a navy of such size that it could be divided, if necessary, between Far Eastern and European waters without incurring defeat in either region. Although devised as a positional paper for the anticipated London Naval Conference of 1935, the Admiralty memo reiterated Chatfield's earlier contention to the DRC that the Royal Navy's existing strength was insufficient for it to deal with a war on two fronts involving the Japanese and a European power simultaneously. It was with this in mind that he had recommended a return to a modified two-power standard and had submitted a five year plan of new construction to assist in bringing this about.[55]

Once the Cabinet had passed the DRC report to a special ministerial committee for consideration, Neville Chamberlain, the Chancellor of the Exchequer, launched a wide-ranging attack upon it and the Admiralty's plans for new ships. In his opinion Britain could not afford such an outlay and it was unrealistic to expect otherwise. Chamberlain had very little sympathy for any Far Eastern strategy and considered the Singapore base to be an extravagance which far exceeded British needs, particularly if relations with the Japanese could be improved. His persuasive influence on the committee was strong enough for him to obtain a reduction of 13 million on the naval deficiency programme and to give no encouragement to Chatfield over the Admiralty's five year building plan.[56] Chamberlain's victory on this occasion, though total, was not long-lasting. Within a year the international situation had deteriorated to such an extent that rearmament had come back into vogue.

Japan's announcement at the end of December 1934 that it was giving two years' formal notice of its intention to withdraw from the obligations of the Washington Naval Limitation Treaty spurred the Admiralty on to seek naval agreements with other leading Powers. Undoubtedly the most controversial of these compacts was the one signed with the Germans in June 1935. Although it appeared to make good numerical sense at the time, the treaty, which restricted the German Navy to a figure of 35 per cent of the British capital ship strength but allowed it under certain circumstances to achieve parity in submarine tonnage, was only valuable if the Germans were prepared to accept it as a binding commitment. Immediately they refused to see it in these terms, a matter largely excluded from British calculations at the time, the bonus of having prevented an expensive and potentially dangerous arms race from beginning would disappear. Whether the advantages of this bilateral agreement were worth the damage done to Britain's international reputation by its willingness to do secret deals behind the backs of its friends remains a matter of considerable speculation.[57]

As tension rose in Europe over Italy's scarcely veiled plans for Abyssinia, so the vital nature of the Mediterranean theatre began to assert itself in British naval strategic thinking. Although it had always been given a lower priority than the Far East, the Mediterranean and the Middle East could not be ignored in the future. Italian belligerency in the Horn of Africa, followed less than a year later by Fascist violence in Spain, suggested that the Mediterranean might become a 'no-go area' for the British if their enemies managed to establish themselves in such a way as to control both the western and eastern sectors of this strategically important waterway. This added a new and worrying dimension to British naval policy; it was bad enough having to devise a strategy to deal with a strident Japan, while keeping a wary eye on Hitler's Germany, but if Italy and/or Spain now had to be added to the list of probable enemies the scale of the problem would become immense and totally beyond the ability of the United Kingdom to solve alone.[58]

In the light of the recent Italian war scare and the problems encountered by the Admiralty in what amounted to only a partial mobilisation of the fleet in the autumn, the DRC decided to strike a radical pose in its final report issued in November 1935. Stating unequivocally that the strategic assumptions which it had relied upon in the past were no longer valid, the DRC recommended that the future needs of the country demanded an entirely new standard of naval strength. This would have to be not only capable of providing a strong fleet designed for defensive operations in the Far East and for safeguarding its interests in the region, but also large enough to maintain a force in home waters sufficient to deal, if need be, with an actual threat from Germany at the same time. In the belief that the existing strength of the Royal Navy was simply not up to providing a fleet-in-being worthy of the name in the Far East, the DRC endorsed the Admiralty's proposals for a substantial increase in new construction, the sheer size and cost of which was almost bound to cause the Chancellor something akin to apoplexy.[59] Once again the tempo of the DRC's ideas were too fast for the Cabinet's taste. Although parts of the report were given a grudging acceptance in February 1936, the main issue of vastly increased naval strength was skirted without undue difficulty both then and subsequently. In fact, so successful was the government at temporising that the two-Power naval standard was not accepted even in principle before the outbreak of war in 1939.[60]

Being far from convinced that a military solution could be obtained to its intractable strategic dilemma, the government sought refuge in advocating the use of high-level diplomacy to ease some of its burdens. It was a policy which would become synonymous with the name of Neville Chamberlain. Appeasement, though nowadays a pejorative term, did seem to offer a relatively painless way out of Britain's acute international difficulties in the 1930s. Converting enemies into friends by removing the causes of friction between them does have a simple appeal, not least because it is almost certain to cost less than a massive programme of rearmament. From a strategic point of view it was hard to fault providing the spirit of conversion lasted; immediately the spell wore off or the convert became less zealous and more fractious, the advantages of this policy would be lost.

Although Chamberlain had been in favour of seeking a resumption of friendly relations, if not an alliance, with the Japanese, the government found it virtually impossible to lessen the hostility between them. Unable to do much about their potential enemies in the east, the British paid ever more attention to the European theatre in which the Italians and Germans were restive and becoming more closely identified with each other, a suspicion confirmed by the announcement of the Rome–Berlin Axis on 1 November

1936. Animated by a desire to do something about this worrying development and by the news received shortly afterwards of the establishment of an Anti-Comintern Pact linking Germany and Japan, the Cabinet grasped the initiative and supported diplomatic efforts to procure an agreement with the Italians over the Mediterranean.[61] If the Gentlemen's Agreement of 2 January 1937 did not live up to expectations, forcing Anthony Eden, the British Foreign Secretary, to despair of ever appeasing Italy, the CID took on the whole a more sanguine view based, one suspects, on the feeling that anything was better than nothing. While this may smack a little of cynical desperation, it is perhaps understandable in the context of the time.

Further justification for the government's appeasement policy came in the shape of the COS Review of Imperial Defence issued in February 1937. A singularly depressing document, it re-emphasised the underlying weakness of the British if they were called upon to defend themselves against more than one enemy at a time regardless of whether or not they were supported by allies. In this situation the COS welcomed any diplomatic accord which would reduce the scale of their military liabilities overseas.[62] They had no difficulty in recognising the beneficial effects of such a policy or in stressing its virtues as their reports, strategic appreciations and memoranda reveal in the period up to the outbreak of war in September 1939.

In acknowledging the importance attached to the security of Singapore for the survival of the Commonwealth, the COS had reconfirmed that a fleet would be sent to the Far East in the event of a war with Japan.[63] Although it may have reassured the Australasian dominions, it did not deceive the Admiralty into believing that this was a settled policy. In a memo drafted in April 1937 for the Defence Plans (Policy) Committee, the Admiralty put this plan into perspective:

> When the capital ships now building in Europe are completed, it would not be possible, on our existing standard of naval strength, to safeguard the Empire in the Far East if already engaged in war in Europe; even with Germany limited to 35 per cent of our own strength, we could never take the risk of despatching to the Far East a sufficient fleet to act as a deterrent to Japanese aggression.[64]

If the naval staff were correct and the Singapore Strategy could not be taken for granted, the government was still not prepared to admit as much for fear that the dominions would react adversely to the news by refusing to make any future finanical or military contribution towards imperial defence.[65] Instead the delicate nature of the problem was left in the lap of the COS. It was they who first mentioned the possibility of a delay in sending the fleet out east and raised the period before relief from 38 days to 70.[66] A disarming mixture of candour and disingenuousness employed by a variety of government spokesmen at the Imperial Conference in May and June 1937 left the dominions guessing about the specific nature of the British naval guarantee.[67] This was exactly what the Cabinet wanted because it bought extra time for a more satisfactory, long-term policy to be found. If such an elusive thing existed, grasping it successfully proved impossible for the British over the next two years.

All lingering hopes about securing a friendly accommodation with the Japanese were removed in the weeks following the Marco Polo Bridge incident of 7 July 1937. This renewed belligerency, but on a much larger scale than before, prompted Anthony Eden to seek diplomatic, economic and military assistance from the United States. Over the next six months the British Foreign Secretary went to inordinate lengths to try and lure the Americans into taking an active role in the Far Eastern crisis and a stronger line with the Japanese.[68] Apart from the naval staff conversations held in London during January 1938, however, there was little tangible reward for his enthusiastic efforts to secure a joint naval initiative with the United States in the western Pacific.

Once Eden's dramatic hijacking of British naval policy had finally come to grief in February 1938, without securing any substantial improvement in his country's strategic position in the Far East, the search for a diplomatic settlement shifted elsewhere. Further encouragement for the Prime Minister's more restrained policy of European appeasement came in the shape of the latest military appreciation drawn up by the COS and issued, ironically, on the very day that Eden resigned as Foreign Secretary. Harping on the now familiar theme of military inadequacy, the COS left the Cabinet in no doubt as to what they felt about the prospects of fighting a simultaneous three-front war against Germany, Italy and Japan, even if the French and Russians were on their side from the outset.[69] Short of building something in excess of the new standard fleet, a project which the government had little difficulty in resisting on financial grounds, or of persuading the Americans to look after British interests in the Far East on their behalf, a possibility considered so remote that it was hardly mentioned in the report, there appeared to be little else for the United Kingdom to do other than to appease its potential rivals both in Europe and the Far East. This was the line which the COS held consistently throughout the Austrian and Czechoslovakian crises, believing that any reduction in Britain's potential enemies was correspondingly a positive accretion to its strength.[70]

British naval strategy, which had limped along unconvincingly since the ending of the war, was not immediately altered to take account of the Munich settlement; the priorities remained the same, that is, home defence, followed by the Far East with the Mediterranean coming third. None the less the COS readily conceded that the degree of naval strength that could be provided for the protection of British interests in any foreign theatre was strictly dependent upon the stability or otherwise of the European situation. A war with Germany, for instance, would be such as to affect materially the size of fleet which the government could afford to send to the Far East in an emergency. Mention was made of whether the fleet would be adequate for its defensive tasks, but the COS stopped short of saying that the Singapore Strategy was fast becoming an unworkable instrument of policy and might have to be abandoned. Far from being dispelled, the myth of the Grand Fleet steaming out east to do battle with Japan was still maintained even by those on the Admiralty Board who felt it made little strategic sense any longer.[71]

Sir Robert Backhouse was in the forefront of the movement to breathe a little realism into naval strategy. He considered that a blind, obligatory commitment to the dominions was dangerous and outdated, given the relative weakness of the Royal Navy and the great demands that could be made upon it in war. His views on giving precedence to the Mediterranean theatre over that of the Far East gained in popularity over the winter months as the European situation became increasingly unsettled. Supported by Lord Stanhope, the First Lord and Sir Andrew Cunningham, the Deputy Chief of the Naval Staff, what might be termed the Backhouse–Drax school of strategy offered an interesting alternative policy to that of the traditionalists.[72] At long last, therefore, the Admiralty was initiating rather than merely responding on strategic matters. Tragically the influence of the First Sea Lord and his imprint on policy-making within the COS was cut short by ill health; even so by the time he resigned in June 1939 a substantive change had occurred in strategic thinking. Although the Far East was not to be abandoned, the actual size of the task force which would be sent there in the event of war with Japan could no longer be determined in advance. This decision would only be made in the light of the situation prevailing in the Mediterranean, the nature of the Japanese war strategy and the reactions of both Russia and the United States to the idea of a war breaking out in the Pacific. In the conclusion of Cunningham's memo to the Strategic Appreciation Committee in April 1939 the point was made that there were too many variable factors in this equation for it to be solved in advance.[73] Even Chatfield, for so long an advocate of sending the Grand Fleet to Singapore, was persuaded by the collapse of European appeasement that times had changed and the British ought to begin thinking seriously about risking their position in the Far East temporarily in the hope of first being able to settle matters in the Mediterranean.[74]

Although for a few weeks it looked as though the Italian card was likely to be played in preference to that of the Far East, a suspicion seemingly confirmed by the COS recommendation of raising the period before relief at Singapore from 70 to 90 days on 1 June 1939, the developing crisis in Tientsin, which gathered pace later in the same month, succeeded in switching the limelight back to China and the Pacific theatre. From apparently condoning the use of a 'flying squadron' of two capital ships for the Far East on 18 June, the COS were to state their opposition to this idea only a few days later. This bewildering inconsistency typified the strategic mess in which the British found themselves at this time.[75]

Aware of their own weakness in the face of a formidable triumvirate of Fascist Powers, the British cast around for support from the democracies. Overtures went out to the French and the Americans in a bid to ease their strategic burdens in the Mediterranean and the Far East respectively. At the same time the British were engaged in appeasing the Japanese by opening discussions in Tokyo over the Tientsin affair.[76] Neither ploy worked particularly well or did much to improve the United Kingdom's somewhat beleaguered strategic position. In the end this was unexpectedly transformed for the better, not by anything which the British did for themselves, but by the sudden disintegration of the Anti-Comintern Pact in late August.[77] Thereafter Japan's decision to remain neutral and that of Italy to assume an attitude of non-belligerency at the outset of hostilities did more for British naval strategy than anything else in the 17 years which had elapsed since the ending of the Washington Conference. A deferment of the Singapore Strategy coupled to the absence of any immediate crisis in the Mediterranean were the most welcome gifts from the unlikeliest of donors.

WORKING HARD AT IMPROVING THE THREE Rs – READINESS, REALISM AND RELEVANCE: NAVAL STRATEGY AND THE COMING OF WAR

When the General Board conducted a searching examination into the state of the US Navy's readiness for war in August 1939, it found a situation which was hardly reassuring. While there was a bare sufficiency in capital ships, aircraft-carriers and destroyers to meet immediate needs, cruiser and submarine strength was below that deemed necessary to wage war in two oceans simultaneously. In addition, American bases to the west of Hawaii, such as Guam or Cavite, were seriously deficient, being under-developed, vulnerable to attack and impossible to rely upon, either as forward areas for mounting naval operations in the western Pacific, or as parts of an extended defensive chain to slow up an enemy's advance through the central part of the ocean.[78]

Although the situation was bad enough for the Americans, it was far worse for the British. In early August they faced the prospect of a war on three fronts with wholly inadequate resources at their disposal. While the influence of Mahan had gradually diminished during the thirties, the Royal Navy still remained to some extent an embodiment of his philosophy. The Admiralty had not worked the idea of a Jutland-style major naval engagement out of its system. The battleship was still regarded by many as the final arbiter of victory at sea, while the age and crucial importance of naval aviation and long-range shore-based aircraft had yet to come or be fully appreciated.[79]

Habits died hard within a service that had such a long and vivid history; the *Dreadnought* mentality was ingrained too deeply for it to be summarily rejected on the merest whim or fancy, even for startling new developments in weapons or machine technology. As a result, it took the Admiralty longer than the US Navy Department to recognise that a revolution in naval design, system and construction had taken place since the ending of the First World War, with enormous consequences for the evolution of maritime strategy and tactics.[80] Although only guessed at in 1939, it took the Battle of the Coral Sea and that of Midway to make it clear that in future epic duels at sea would no longer be fought between lines of battleships drawn up for the purpose of achieving that one conclusive and smashing victory that would determine the very outcome of the war.

Fortunately for both the Americans and the British when war came to Europe in September 1939, the military situation was nothing like as complicated as either feared that it might be less than a fortnight before. Gone was the horrendous prospect of an immediate two- or three-front war being fought, following the startling withdrawal of both Japan and Italy before the fray commenced, which simplified things in the most dramatic fashion possible. Consequently the United Kingdom entered the war in far better shape than it ever had a right to expect. Its aversion to detailed war planning had ultimately paid off and the relative frugality and slowness of the rearmament programme had failed to have a crippling effect on the prosecution of its war effort. For its part the United States was to be given more than a two-year reprieve to sort out its own war strategy, time which for the most part was well spent. Even so the military still failed to recognise the growing need to make sufficient prepartions for amphibious and combined operations which they would need to rely upon increasingly once they had been pitched rudely into the war in December 1941.

It is doubtful whether any nation that is neither initiating nor seeking war is ever entirely prepared for it until it happens. To this extent strategic planning of a responsive kind carries none of the certainty or conviction implicit in a system that is conditioned by aggressive intent. Although the Americans and the British were cast in this complex defensive role for the entire inter-war period, each, as we have seen, adopted a vastly different and fallible approach to a dynamic problem whose sheer volatility ensured the maximum difficulty for those seeking its solution.

Despite these considerable drawbacks, the methods employed by the two Powers to prepare themselves for future war yielded some successes. One has only to think of the convoy arrangements for merchant vessels which were settled in advance and implemented speedily once the war began to see how even the British, usually so disdainful of pre-planning, benefited from the exercise. On the American side, the stimulus given to carrier development and the suspicion, confirmed later, that future naval warfare would be dictated as much by considerations of air power as of purely surface power were notable achievements in themselves.

Just how long strategic plans can expect to be relevant is, of course, a matter of intense debate and speculation. Ironically the Rodgers Plan of 1911 was more relevant to the American experience of the Pacific campaign in the Second World War than any of the later versions of the *Orange* plan would be. By the time the Japanese struck at Pearl Harbor in December 1941, the Americans had not only long since abandoned their reliance upon any of the eight versions of the *Orange* series, but had also discarded four of the five *Rainbow* plans which had taken its place in their quest to find the most appropriate plan for use in a dynamic and changing environment. Their final choice lay in a mixture of improvisation and a return to the sound strategic theory of an earlier age. While not in itself an unqualified endorsement of the quasi-fatalist approach adopted by the British, the American experience suggested that the days of flexible response were far from over. It was a refrain that the British knew well and had repeated for years.

Notes

1. 'Are We Ready?' was the title given to a survey conducted by the General Board of the US Navy on 8 August 1939, classified as General Board 425, Serial 1868, cited by J. Major, 'The Navy Plans for War 1937–1941' in K. J. Hagan (ed.), *In Peace and War: Interpretations of American Naval History 1775–1978* (Westport, Conn., 1984) p. 247.
2. A. T. Mahan, *Naval Strategy* (Westport, Conn., 1975) p. 20.
3. L. H. Douglas, 'Robert Edward Coontz' in R. W. Love Jr (ed.), *The Chiefs of Naval Operations* (Annapolis, Md, 1980) pp. 23–6.
4. Ibid.
5. M. Vlahos, *The Blue Sword: The Naval War College and the American Mission 1919–1941* (Newport, RI, 1980) pp. 99–112; W. R. Braisted, 'On the American Red and Red–Orange Plans, 1919–1939', in G. Jordan (ed.), *Naval Warface in the Twentieth Century* (London, 1977) pp. 167–85.
6. Ibid. For an entirely different interpretation, see L. Morton, *Strategy and Command: The First Two Years* (Washington, DC, 1962) pp. 31–3.
7. Vlahos, *The Blue Sword*, pp. 99–112; Braisted, *Red and Red–Orange Plans*, pp. 167–85.
8. Ibid. For additional information on the background to and importance of the Washington Conference by other historians, see J. Kenneth McDonald's chapter in this book and the following works; T. H. Buckley, *The United States and the Washington Conference* (Knoxville, Tenn., 1970); R. Dingman, *Power in the Pacific* (Chicago, 1976); G. E. Wheeler, *Prelude to Pearl Harbor* (Columbia, Miss., 1963).
9. Douglas, *Coontz*, p. 33.
10. Ibid; P. E. Coletta, *The American Naval Heritage in Brief* (Washington, DC, 1980) pp. 302–3.
11. Vlahos, *The Blue Sword*, pp. 107–8.
12. Ibid.

13. Ibid., p. 108.
14. Navy Basic Readiness Plan (W.P.L.8) 1924, Basic Joint, Combined and Navy War Plans, Naval Historical Center Archives, Washington Navy Yard, Washington, DC.
15. Coletta, *American Naval Heritage*, pp. 301–2.
16. Ibid., pp. 303–6; R. W. Turk, 'Edward Walter Eberle', in Love, *Chiefs of Naval Operations*, pp. 39–46.
17. S. W. Roskill, *Naval Policy Between the Wars*, vol. I (London, 1968) pp. 498–516; Wheeler, *Prelude to Pearl Harbor*, pp. 131–57.
18. Braisted, *Red and Red–Orange Plans*, pp. 171–4.
19. Ibid., pp. 169–74.
20. Ibid., pp. 174–8.
21. Ibid.
22. Ibid., p. 178–81.
23. D. Marquand, *Ramsay MacDonald* (London, 1977) pp. 501–17. S. W. Roskill, *Naval Policy Between the Wars*, vol. II (London, 1976) pp. 30–66.
24. C. L. Symonds, 'Williams Veazie Pratt', in Love, *Chiefs of Naval Operations*, pp. 69–88; Wheeler, *Prelude to Pearl Harbor*, pp. 159–86; R. H. Ferrell, *American Diplomacy in the Great Depression* (London, 1957) pp. 68–105.
25. Braisted, *Red and Red–Orange Plans*, pp. 180–2.
26. L. Morton, 'War Plan ORANGE: Evolution of a Strategy', *World Politics* 11 (1959), 221–50.
27. M. Matloff and E. Snell, *Strategic Planning for Coalition Warfare 1941–1942* (Washington, DC, 1953) pp. 1–8.
28. Vlahos, *The Blue Sword*, pp. 118–21.
29. Ibid..
30. Morton, 'War Plan ORANGE' pp. 221–50.
31. Ibid., pp. 231–2.
32. L. Morton, 'Germany First: The Basic Concept of Allied Strategy in World War II', in K. R. Greenfield, *Command Decisions* (Washington, DC, 1960) pp. 11–47.
33. L. Morton, *Strategy and Command*, pp. 24–44.
34. P. T. Rosen, 'The Treaty Navy, 1919–1937', in K. J. Hagan, *In Peace and War* pp. 232–3.
35. R. Dallek, *Franklin D. Roosevelt and American Foreign Policy 1932–1945* (New York, 1979) p. 148.
36. Morton, 'Germany First', pp. 20–7.
37. J. Major, 'The Navy Plans for War, 1937–1941', in K. J. Hagan, *In Peace and War* pp. 243–6.
38. Morton, 'Germany First', p. 38.
39. Ibid.; P. Abbazia, *Mr. Roosevelt's Navy* (Annapolis, Md, 1975) pp. 119–23.
40. Morton, 'Germany First', p. 38.
41. Ibid., pp. 37–47.
42. A good objective history of the Plans Division has still to be written. What little information has been published hitherto about its operations is extremely sketchy. See, for instance, P. Beesly, *Very Special Admiral* (London, 1980), p. 63. Undoubtedly the fact that several Directors of Plans died without leaving any personal papers has complicated this issue, for example, Pound, Danckwerts, Tom Phillips.
43. Both volumes I & II of Roskill's *Naval Policy Between the Wars* are instructive in this regard, as is the impressive tome by N. H. Gibbs, *Grand Strategy* vol. I, *Rearmament Policy* (London, 1976).
44. M. Gilbert, *Winston Churchill*, vol. V, *1922–1939* (London, 1976) pp. 289–92.

45. Gibbs, 'The Naval Conferences of the Inter War Years: A Study of Anglo-American Relations', *Naval War College Review* 30 (1977) 50–63.
46. Roskill, *Naval Policy*, vol. II, pp. 30–66.
47. D. N. Dilks, 'Appeasement Revisited', *The University of Leeds Review* 15 (1972) 28–56.
48. Gibbs, *Rearmament Policy*, pp. 55–6; Marquand, *Ramsay MacDonald*, pp. 315–17.
49. Gibbs, *Rearmament Policy*, pp. 78–87.
50. In the meantime Malta remained the nearest first-class naval base to the Far East at 5926 nautical miles' distance from Singapore.
51. The extent to which the Treasury influenced government expenditure on defence and foreign policy is best described by G. C. Peden in his excellent book *British Rearmament and the Treasury 1932–1938* (Edinburgh, 1979).
52. Gibbs, *Rearmament Policy*, p. 118.
53. Apart from the three Chiefs of Staff, the DRC consisted of the permanent secretaries of both the Treasury (Fisher) and Foreign Office (Vansittart) along with the Secretary of the CID (Hankey).
54. Roskill, *Naval Policy*, II, pp. 164–93.
55. Gibbs, *Rearmament Policy*, pp. 118–20.
56. Roskill, *Naval Policy*, pp. 171–2.
57. Gibbs, *Rearmament Policy*, pp. 155–70.
58. Ibid., pp. 189–222. The Italian dimension in British strategy is well covered by L. R. Pratt, *East of Malta, West of Suez* (Cambridge, 1975); a doctoral thesis by P. R. Stafford, submitted to Oxford in October 1984 and entitled 'Italy in Anglo-French Strategy and Diplomacy', to which there is restricted access until August 1988, is also reputed to cast some interesting new light on this problem.
59. Gibbs, *Rearmament Policy*, pp. 254–61; Roskill, *Naval Policy*, pp. 216–21.
60. Ibid., pp. 323–62, M. H. Murfett, *Fool-proof Relations: The Search for Anglo-American Naval Cooperation During the Chamberlain Years 1937–1940* (Singapore, 1984) pp. 5–9, 11, 16, 19, 29, 166, 169–72.
61. Gibbs, *Rearmament Policy*, pp. 380–6.
62. COS 560, 'Review of Imperial Defence', 22 Feb. 1937, Cab 24/268, PRO, Kew Gardens, London.
63. M. H. Murfett, *Fool-proof Relations*, pp. 3–26.
64. Admiralty Memorandum, 'A New Standard of Naval Strength', 26 April 1937, submitted as a paper for the Defence Plans (Policy) Committee, DP(P)3, para. 10, Cab16/182.
65. Murfett, *Fool-proof Relations*, pp. 3–39.
66. Gibbs, *Rearmament Policy*, pp. 415–20.
67. Murfett, *Fool-proof Relations*, pp. 27–39.
68. Ibid., pp. 41–161.
69. COS 691, 'Mediterranean, Middle East and North East African Appreciation', 21 Feb. 1938, WO 33/1507.
70. COS 683 'Military Preparations in Relation to Imperial Defence Policy', 11 Feb. 1938, also DP(P)20, para. 2, Cab 16/182.
71. Gibbs, *Rearmament Policy*, pp. 420–1; M. H. Murfett, *Fool-proof Relations*, pp. 187–215.
72. Murfett, *Fool-proof Relations*, pp. 187–215.
73. Paper S.A.C. 16, 5 Apr. 1939, DP(P)48, Cab 16/183A.
74. Gibbs, *Rearmament Policy*, pp. 423–31.
75. Murfett, *Fool-proof Relations*, pp. 249–68.
76. Ibid., pp. 216–68.

77. Ibid., pp. 266–8.
78. Major, *The Navy Plans for War*, p. 247.
79. An interesting account of the development of the Fleet Air Arm and a revealing comparison of the stages of its growth in comparison with that of its American equivalent is offered by G. Till in his book, *Air Power and the Royal Navy 1914–1945* (London, 1979).
80. The pioneering work of Rear-Admiral W. A. Moffett, Chief of the Bureau of Aeronautics, is best described by J. J. Clark in his book, *Carrier Admiral* (New York, 1967) and the early phase of carrier development is most persuasively discussed by C. M. Melhorn, *Two-Block Fox: The Rise of the Aircraft Carrier 1911–29* (Annapolis, 1974).

12 Anglo-American Naval Co-operation in the Second World War, 1939–45

Marc Milner

The outbreak of war in 1939 was looked upon by many at the time as a logical continuation, and culmination, of the earlier 'German' war. Not surprisingly then the initial operations and strategy of the Allies harkened back to the First World War. Much as had been the case in 1914, the Royal and French Navies blockaded Germany, swept her trade from the seas, kept a wary eye on the Italians, safeguarded the movement of men and material to the Western Front and checked the Germans' campaign against Allied shipping. Outside Europe, it is true, the strategic situation was different. It was the Japanese who complicated planning in 1939, and it was their hostility which represented such a marked difference from the situation in 1914–18. Japan was now openly hostile and expansionist, although for the time being she was preoccupied with a debilitating and costly war in China and her sea power was held in check by the Americans. Britain was committed to a strategy of containment and continental war alongside the French, trusting in the Italians to remain neutral and hoping that the Japanese could be put off or appeased. Otherwise, in the European scene the naval strategy and pattern of operations in 1939 were a logical continuation of 1918.[1]

Within this apparent sameness and the precarious global balance of forces, however, there was much that was genuinely new. The First World War gave rise to two new elements in sea power, the submarine and aircraft. By 1918 the RN was well steeped in both. The essential lessons were there to be drawn from anti-submarine (A/S) and defence of trade operations. The introduction of escorted mercantile convoys, supported by extensive maritime patrol aircraft, held Germany's U-boats in check during the last eighteen months of the war. What was needed by 1918 was a reliable form of underwater detection that would provide tactical information accurate enough to allow the delivery of depth-charges to the target. The solution, an active sound location system known as Asdic in the British service (and now known by its American acronym Sonar) had to wait until 1921.[2] Asdic promised a more efficient use of A/S forces and, more importantly, a very much higher loss rate among submariners – something which would have implications for both practice and morale among submarine fleets. Aircraft remained a crucial component in the Anti-Submarine Warfare (ASW) equation, since it was aircraft which denied submarines surface mobility and forced submariners into the waiting grip of Asdic and depth-charge-equipped surface vessels.[3] The third leg of this triad – the convoys – was also reasonably well appreciated as an essential in war, although the British did not feel during the inter-war years that it was necessary to practise the art of escorting mercantile convoys. The First Sea Lord, Admiral Chatfield, felt sufficiently confident of his ASW preparations by 1936 to describe them as 80 per cent effective in handling the submarine threat.[4] Trade would be protected through proper organisation while submarines would be dealt with by an active policy of search and destroy.[5] And if all else failed there was the German signing of the Declaration of London in 1936 that restricted submariners to the Prize Laws, a body of regulations governing the conduct of trade war which had cramped German submarines before 1917 and promised to do so again.

Much of the apparent 'failure' of pre-1939 planning for ASW can be attributed to an unfounded (and untested) faith in new technology and a healthy measure of wishful thinking based on the belief that no nation would risk international sanction by resorting to the 'piracy' that brought America into the war against Germany in 1917. Thus despite these obvious lessons of the First World War the Admiralty began the Second with a business-as-usual approach to merchant ship movements, waiting for German intentions to be made clear.[6] In the event they did not have to wait long. The torpedoing of the liner *Athenia* on the first day was taken as evidence that Germany would take up where she had left off in 1918, and the movement of escorted convoys was begun. What was so profoundly different between 1917 and 1939 was that the global system of Naval Intelligence and Naval Control of Shipping (NCS), so laboriously constructed in 1914–18, had never been entirely dismantled or forgotten. In the thirties, under the able direction of Paymaster Rear Admiral Sir Eldon Manisty, the man who had organised convoys in 1917, the British system of trade control and the structuring of British port and rail systems for handling cargoes was thoroughly prepared. Although wartime emergencies, such as the closure of the Port of London in 1940, pointed to gaps in the planning process, the NCS system of Britain, her Commonwealth and Empire constituted the foundation of Allied ship movements for the entire war.[7] It was also the area of operations which brought the earliest direct links with the USN. The use of the sea as a highway, what Mahan called 'a great common', the commerce which moves across that great common and the ability to use – or to deny use of – the highway in war is what sea power is all about. It bears emphasising then that, regardless of what – as Sir Julian Corbett aptly described them – 'historians greedy of dramatic effect' may write,[8] the orderly movement of shipping based on good intelligence and under the general cover of Anglo-American naval superiority remained the principal means of trade defence during the war and therefore the very foundation of Allied victory.

The lion's share of trade defence was thus the task of that enormous gang of 'boffins and bureaucrats' who would make an undramatic yet absolutely vital contribution to the war. Fortunately for the Allies their personnel in lab coats and their pencil-pushers were, on the whole, markedly better than those on the other side. It was just as well, for there were some serious institutional prejudices and structural problems within the Allied armed forces both before and during the war.

For the British the gravest failing was the neglect of many of the lessons of the First World War, particularly those in regard to air power. In addition to their innovative use of aircraft in trade defence the British had led the world in the development of the aircraft-carrier, and by the end of the First World War had begun to use shipborne aviation in an aggressive way.[9] The design and building of *Hermes*, the first purpose-built aircraft-carrier to be completed, followed logically from the RN's wartime experimentations with fixed-wing aircraft at sea. Unfortunately for the RN, British zeal to strike a blow at the Germans who were bombing London manifested itself in the creation of the Royal Air Force in 1918, and the placing of all air-related matters, including aircraft development, under the new Service. At a stroke the RN's lead in maritime air power was checked and the Navy was robbed of its ability to control the development of naval air power during the succeeding years. Inter-war penury and the RAF's intent to justify its existence by concentrating on a strategic bomber force crippled naval aviation in Britain and reduced land-based maritime air power to a pathetic state by 1939.[10] Carrier aviation, tied as it was to support of the battlefleet in a spotting and reconnaissance role and restricted by both an absolute ceiling in numbers and the small hangar decks of British carriers, did not regain its lost ground until after the Second World War. The fleet as a whole remained wedded to a battle concept epitomised by Jutland and trusted in its own guns for air defence. The advent of the all-metal monoplane aircraft in the late thirties radically shifted the balance of hitting power and survivability in favour of land-based air power, but the legacy of the inter-war period could not be shaken. Decrepit aircraft types, such as the biplanes Albacore and Swordfish, and the limited carrying capacity of British carriers left the RN vulnerable to land-based aircraft for most of the war.[11] This in turn restricted fleet movements near land, hampering the Arctic convoys, for example, and reduced the RN's ability to make an equitable contribution to the Pacific war.

In terms of air power the USN was measurably better off, but the war held surprises for Americans as well. American carrier aviation, it is true, evolved along different lines from the British, but this was at least partially owing to chance. The opportunity after the Washington Conference of 1921 to convert battlecruiser hulls to aircraft carriers gave the USN the *Saratoga* and *Lexington*, two very large and fast vessels (the Japanese did the same with *Akagi* and *Kaga*), and they allowed the benefits and uses of massive carrier strikes to be worked out (the two British fast carriers converted after Washington, *Courageous* and *Glorious*, were only about two-thirds as big). However, while the airmen were convinced of the new wave in naval warfare, USN flyers, like those in the British and Japanese navies, remained shackled to the battle line: spotting, doing reconnaissance, and wearing the enemy down with bombs and torpedoes prior to the final culmination of naval battle – the gunnery dual between battlefleets. Although the vastness of the Pacific put a premium on air power and aircraft would be necessary to the central Pacific thrust through the Marshalls and Carolines as envisaged by *Plan Orange*, the battleship admirals were very much in control of things in 1939. Their position had weakened by December 1941, but the carrier vs battleship debate in the USN was only solved by the Japanese, when the battle line was sunk at Pearl Harbor and the USN was forced to rely on its carriers for major fleet actions.[12]

American naval airmen had their difficulties over land-based maritime air, too, and for much the same reason as the British. The US Army Air Corps, like the RAF, was bent on building a role for itself in defence structured on a bomber force that would either deter or deal with threats to US security. The bomber lobby managed to convince Congress that all land-based aviation was a matter for the USAAC, and that naval aviation from bases, as distinct from ships, should be limited to seaplanes. By the time of American entry into the war, then, both the USN and the USAAC were busy flying patrols to seaward, with no provision for co-ordinated effort or a common doctrinal approach to the problems of maritime air power.[13]

The greatest weakness in the USN's readiness for war in 1939 lay in its failure to allow for defence of maritime trade short of a decisive Mahanist-style battle between main fleets. Although its First World War experience was almost exclusively in small ships, guarding merchant vessels and chasing submarines, this aspect of naval war was almost wholly neglected in the inter-war years. While American neglect of trade defence can be traced to many things, it is at least evidence that America was not a maritime empire in the traditional sense, or she would not have been able to indulge such neglect. The British, it is true, were not much better prepared materially but, as Morison points out, the British were 'somewhat prepared to fight U-Boats' – while the USN was not. The RN had 219 warships fitted with Sonar in 1939; only 60 vessels carried the sets in the USN and most were only recently acquired. Much of British interest in limiting the size of battleships and cruisers especially had also been driven by the need to defend long imperial communications against a variety of threats.[14] It would be 1942 before the shortcomings in America's preparations for war were demonstrated. The

British, in the meantime, learned many of the old lessons over again the hard way.

The prewar strengths of the two Navies reflect markedly different approaches to the use and importance of sea power. Britain was the heart of a maritime empire which spanned the world. Her main arteries were the Mediterranean, which could be dominated at its choke points by land-based air power – British or Axis – and the Atlantic which could be endangered by the heavier units of the German navy – if they could escape the blockade – or by Germany's small submarine fleet. The essential point is that defence of trade and communications were the very foundation of British power and however much the material aspects of this were thrust aside during the penurious inter-war years the need to use and defend shipping remained central to Britain's war effort. Fortunately for the RN the shift in threat from surface raiders in 1939 to U-boats by 1941 developed slowly enough for it to react. The British therefore matinained their First World War lead in ASW and further developed their proprietory interest in both the Atlantic and trade movements. The USN, in contrast, was primarily concerned with defence of America against external aggression and with the ability to project sufficient power across vast ocean spaces either to deter or to redress acts of aggression. The American interest in sea power was thus primarily a military one, a luxury which the resources of a continent and distance from major threats permitted. The war against Japan was very much in this vein: a war of power projection, a military use of sea power against a powerful, yet vulnerable, maritime empire in which carrier air power would prove to be an awesome weapon.

These then were the strengths, weaknesses, and interests of the British and Americans on the eve of war. It remains for us to explore how they were played out in the great game.

At a practical level American and British interests met in two places, the Atlantic and South East Asia. The latter was remote from both nations and so presented the greatest difficulty. Prewar discussions on how to handle the Japanese foundered on the inability of Britain to contribute much more than rhetoric to the defence of South East Asia. Constrained in resources and facing the dual threat of Italian and German naval power closer to home, the British had sought to draw the Americans into defence of the so-called Malay barrier against a possible Japanese thrust. Their scheme had little chance of success. The Americans had wrestled with defence of the Philippines since before the First World War and had never come up with a workable solution. The US possession was too far removed from North America to be quickly reinforced, too vast to be adequately defended, and too close to Japan to be effectively screened from attack by superior forces. The best the US Army could hope for was time to circle the wagons before settling in to wait for the cavalry. Even then the best estimates of Army planners for holding out never approached the time estimated by the USN to effect a relief. For the USN the Philippines were hostage to fortune: Malaya might well have been on the moon. Failure to reach an accord on defence of South East Asia eventually forced the Americans into preparations for a multi-front war, and a series of 'Rainbow' war plans – a radical departure from earlier planning.[15] The bulk of American naval power none the less shifted westward, from San Diego to Hawaii, in April 1940, confirmation of the view within the Service that the Pacific was the USN's natural theatre of operations. But the winds of change soon blew the other way.[16]

As early as April of 1940 planners at the US Naval War College had begun to advocate a 'Germany first' policy, while the line against Japan in the Pacific would be held.[17] In the event, both British and American planners seriously underestimated Japan's capabilities. In the meantime, the British strategy of containment worked well enough as long as the war continued as a replay of 1914–18. Attempts by the British to devise and implement a peripheral strategy of attacks on Germany failed, owing to insufficient resources.[18] Fortunately the Germans lacked resources at sea, too, although they had enough to secure local control for the invasion of Norway while the British found that, in the absence of proper air support, traditional sea power alone was not enough to check the German advance. But apart from the Norwegian campaign and a few fugitive sorties by large units, the German surface fleet proved little more than a fleet-in-being. The significant point is, however, that even before the catastrophes of May and June 1940 the USN had begun to move towards a plan of tackling German power prior to dealing with Japan. The fall of France and the entry of the Italians into the war with, as Paul Kennedy describes it, 'a jackal's sense of occasion', brought the naval situation in the Atlantic to a crisis.[19] Now Britain was not only shorn of French naval support, she faced an alliance she could barely handle, a serious threat of invasion and danger to her crucial maritime communications. At stake was British survival and, over the medium term, her existence as a base of operations against an Axis-dominated Europe. The possibility of collapse of British power would have grave implications for the global balance. Not surprisingly, then, British survival was quickly identified with American fortunes in the summer of 1940. By November a clear policy of co-operation with Britain had been articulated as the basis of planning by Admiral Stark, the Chief of Naval Operations, and significant steps had already been taken to bolster the RN and blend Anglo-American activities in the Atlantic.[20] With the British thrown off the continent and virtually all of Western Europe arrayed against her, the situation was now more reminiscent of 1805 than 1914–18, and the Anglo-American coalition forged as a consequence was a fundamentally maritime one. The British reacted by pursuing the policy of resource accumulation and satisfied themselves with pin-pricks at Germany's continental might until the German attack on

Russia in June 1941 gave Britain the continental ally so fundamental to the proper exercise of traditional British maritime strategy.

Among the many problems facing planners in 1940 two were paramount: first, how to ensure British survival for the moment, and second, how to marshal the resources needed utimately to defeat the Axis. There were no easy solutions to either, but as Britain weathered the invasion threat and the Blitz and cowed the Italian Navy in the Mediterranean, it became clearer that she would hold on. American assistance was forthcoming in the form of destroyers for bases, American Neutrality Patrols which broadcast the positions of belligerent ships in plain English, and the dispatch of Admiral Ghormley as a 'Special Naval Observer'. The European crisis of 1940 thus brought the British – the survivor of the collapse of Western Europe – and the United States together in a common cause. Not surprisingly, then, the destroyers were soon followed by more substantial aid in the form of lend-lease in early 1941 as America agreed to provide Britain with the tools to 'do the job'. The arrangement of material aid coincided with the first major staff talks between the two nations. The agreement hammered out in Washington in early 1941, ABC-1, formed the basis of Anglo-American strategy for the balance of the war. It adopted a policy of Germany first, a goal earnestly sought by the British and endorsed by the USN as well, and it committed the Americans to a substantial naval build-up in the Atlantic to meet that objective. American movements into the Atlantic would, in turn, permit the shifting of British forces to Singapore as part of an attempt to deter the Japanese (the USAAC was to move bombers to the Philippines as a deterrent force as well).[21]

The ABC-1 agreement led directly to the formulation of a new US War Plan, *Rainbow 5*, which covered a coalition war against the Axis Powers based on a Germany-first strategy.[22] Not surprisingly, then, senior American naval and political planners were in agreement in the spring of 1941 that the US had to get more involved in the Atlantic. Stark, who had been on Admiral Sims's staff in the First World War, wanted USN forces in place before any formal declaration of war, and in any event by April 1941 he viewed the situation in the Atlantic as 'critical'.[23] The British had survived the winter with difficulty and the Atlantic was now under the double threat of major German surface units and the new and deadly U-boat wolf packs. By the end of the month Stark had ordered major transfers from the Pacific and had instructed Admrial E. J. King, the C-in-C of the Atlantic Fleet, to prepare to defend shipping in the Western Atlantic.[24] By the end of May, as American flyers operating from their new bases in British colonies joined RAF and Canadian aircrew in search of the *Bismarck*, Roosevelt declared an 'unlimited national emergency'. By the end of the summer US Marines were in Iceland (relieving British and Canadian troops),[25] closer liaison in Naval Control of Shipping had been established through Canada, and the Atlantic fleet moved forward to escort trade between North American ports and Iceland. The British, who were thereby relieved of tremendous responsibilities in the Western Atlantic, might have hoped for faster action, but Roosevelt had moved with consummate skill and not a little haste. His country was still at peace, his navy was not.

The details of British–American naval co-operation in the North Atlantic were settled at Argentia, Newfoundland, in August 1941, when Roosevelt and Churchill carved up the world into two strategic spheres.[26] The Western Atlantic, including Iceland, west to Singapore became an American responsibility, an agreement which infringed not a little on a number of existing bilateral defence arrangements between Britain and the Dominions of her Commonwealth. In 1941 this placed Canada, Australia and New Zealand – all of them belligerents – under the wing of a neutral country. For the two Antipodean states this meant little, except comfort, in 1941, while Canada had already concluded an agreement on North American defence with the United States a year earlier.[27] The operational pitfalls of this arrangement remained for 1942 to reveal. For the moment a major objective of British policy had been achieved in bringing the United States closer to direct belligerency. More importantly here, the commencement of USN escort operations to Iceland in mid-September marked the onset of true Anglo-American naval integration, and it was here, in the North Atlantic, that some of the basic differences between the RN and USN approach to war would have to be ironed out.

Since in 1941 the war in the Atlantic was less about power projection than it was about shipping, the emphasis in Anglo-American co-operation was defence of trade. American involvement in naval operations began just at the time that the character of the Atlantic war was shifting from a balanced threat which included major surface units, to a small-ship anti-submarine war. There had, in fact, been no Jutland – nor would there be – and battleships were now reduced to forming the core of larger task forces of various types, or to providing direct anti-raider escort of convoys.[28]

It was the U-boats which brought the greatest challenge and which demonstrated the major flaws in Britain's prewar preparations. The RN, under Churchill's urgings as First Lord and later Prime Minister, spent much of the first two years of the war searching feverishly for U-boats in poorly conceived offensive patrols.[29] These served merely to confirm the value of convoys as both a defensive and offensive strategy, but in the meantime the fast carrier *Courageous* and much valuable shipping were lost. It was not until April 1941 that a sound doctrine for escort operations was settled upon. In that month the RN adopted 'safe and timely arrival of the convoy' as the principle for A/S escorts, an emphasis in trade defence which was not altered for the rest of the war, even if better intelligence, organisation and greater resources allowed a more flexible ASW doctrine to develop after 1943.[30].

The haphazard approach to the submarine threat and the inability to cope initially with submarine attacks on the surface at night – a situation which British prewar doctrine had not foreseen – underlines the importance of other strategic considerations prior to 1942. These included the continuing threat from Germany's surface fleet, the handling of operations following the French collapse and Italian entry on the Axis side, and the facing of the threat of invasion in 1940. Indeed it had been all of these elements telescoped into a few short months in the summer of 1940 that had drawn the RN and the USN together into the coalition which would fight the naval war.

While the character of the war in the Atlantic was being resolved, the basic organisation and movement of escorted and independently routed shipping continued to develop. As mentioned, the British Commonwealth began the war with a well-developed global Naval Control of Shipping and Intelligence network. This network extended to the United States in 1939 in the form of Consular Shipping Agents, actually ex-naval officers, who ran a merchant shipping control system directed from Ottawa and Jamaica (for the Gulf coast). It seems evident that USN authorities were well aware of this network, and in early 1941 following the ABC-1 talks they were brought into its workings. USN 'Port Directors' were appointed and made their contact with the local British agent, while copies of Special Publications and Confidential Books on Naval Control of Shipping (NCS) were issued to the Port Directors from Ottawa. According to Canadian sources, the Consular Shipping Agents were instrumental in teaching the Americans how the system worked and were even moved to within easy distance of American offices to facilitate liaison. When the United States entered the war officially in December of 1941, the system was unmasked, the Agents donned their uniforms, changed their titles to British Routing Liaison Officers, and worked hand in glove with the USN Port Directors to manage the movement of shipping. Ottawa then developed as a clearing house for information from the British NCS system, passing along condensations of intelligence to Washington until the USN's own links were established by July 1942. Direct links between Ottawa and Washington were also developed in 1941, as a Canadian trade specialist was assigned to liaison duty in Washington. The new US Naval Attache to Ottawa, appointed in 1940, had busied himself with mastering what information was available in Canada on trade defence. The whole business of Naval Control of Shipping remains an obscure and little-known aspect of the war at sea, but upon it rested the ultimate success of Allied operations. The gradual integration of the USN into the British system during 1941 seems to have been remarkably free from the petty problems and jealousies which sometimes marred other facets of wartime co-operation.[31]

American involvement in North Atlantic escort operations in 1941 was predicated on the pursuit of a Germany first strategy, and it was anticipated that responsibility for the western Atlantic would therefore remain a USN task. The Canadians, for example, who had defence arrangements with the

British which included trade defence in the western Atlantic and who in the fall of 1941 had agreed with the USN to concentrate on escorting slow convoys between Newfoundland and Iceland, were advised that responsibility for oceanic convoys would ultimately pass to the USN and that Canadian forces would be free to move to the eastern Atlantic to work directly with the RN. In the meantime, neither the declaration of a 'non war zone' in the western Atlantic nor the presence of American warships reduced Canadian escort operations in the area, nor did they keep the Germans from roaming as far west as Cape Race.[32] In October 1941, as U-boats probed the shoreline of Newfoundland, Canadian and USN airmen and sailors fought the convoys through the waiting packs while the B-17 bombers of the USAAC searched the ocean vastness for raiders long bottled-up in French, Norwegian and German ports. The USAAF (as it became) eventually switched its emphasis in maritime air patrols to seeking and sinking U-boats, enemies it searched the vastness of the Atlantic to find. Canadian forces, USN and most particularly Coastal Command of the RAF – the model for all land-based maritime patrol organisation in the Atlantic – had by then found the waters around convoys to be the best hunting grounds. Problems with the USAAF were only resolved when its anti-submarine wings were integrated into naval commands.[33]

American participation in the naval war in 1941 released RN forces and essentially kept the RN and USN physically separated, but from then on complete 'interchange of equipment, teaching devices, doctrine and publications between the U.S.N., R.N. and R.C.N.' became the norm.[34] Many of these contacts were made through Canada, where many of the senior officers, such as the Director of Trade Division and the Rear Admiral of the Halifax-based 3rd Battle Squadron, were Royal Navy officers. Equally important, the professional officer corps of the prewar RCN was fully integrated into the brotherhood of the British Navy, even to the point of inclusion in the RN's *Navy List*. Sorting out what was Canadian and what was British north of the border was by no means easy, even for many Canadians.[35] Moreover the emergence of distinctly national naval Services within the British Commonwealth proved to be one of the important features of the naval war of 1939–45, and this complicated what was otherwise a tidy Anglo-American scene. The Canadians, in particular, put much store in the battle for independence and recognition during the war; at times they found the Germans almost incidental to their main struggles against British and American tutelage.[36] Historians have tended to overlook this facet of the war, but it held deep consequences for Anglo-American co-operation. The RCN, for example, in the fall of 1941 was in the midst of its most hectic period of wartime expansion and it failed miserably in its primary role of convoy protection – by its own admission. Unfortunately this was also the only period of the war when the RCN and the USN operated together in the same theatre on something like equal terms and the Canadians offered a poor example of the 'British' experience in convoy operations.

Indeed it could be said that the Canadians had a pernicious influence on inadequate American reactions to German U-boat attacks in early 1942: one of the major Allied calamities of the war. The problem was that, while the RN passed along the lessons learned from the U-boat war, particularly the vital importance of escorted mercantile convoys, the Americans seem to have utterly ignored them. British historians have long been at a loss to explain this,[37] but they would have been less mystified had they considered the nature of the shared Canadian–American experience in the North Atlantic in the fall of 1941. While the RN told the Americans that convoy – plain and simple – was the solution, the Canadian failures from September to November 1941 suggested that a poorly-defended convoy was an invitation to disaster: a suspicion already strongly held within the USN. Until 1943 this was, in fact, true of lightly escorted convoys in the mid-Atlantic air gap, but it was not a principle applicable to areas where air cover prevented the adoption of mobile pack tactics, as, for example, along the coast. The inability – or unwillingness – of senior American officers to make the distinction between inshore and oceanic A/S escort was largely to blame for the enormous waste of shipping off the US east coast in 1942 and the reliance on long discredited offensive operations.[38]

In doctrine as well the navies were poles apart in 1941 and early 1942 when it came to A/S escort. As already stated, the British had arrived, after nearly two years of bitter wartime experience, at 'safe and timely arrival of the convoy' as the primary escort role by April 1941. After all, if the convoy got through, the U-boat had not done its job. The USN would have to endure its own trial by fire before it reached the same conclusion. In the meantime 'conduct of the convoy clear of the enemy' came dead last on the USN escort's list of priorities in late 1941 and early 1942. The USN was out to sink subs as the best way to defend trade, a Mahanist doctrine that was at least consistent with that of the fleet as a whole, even though the British had tried that for two years and failed.[39]

A workable common doctrine in the North Atlantic for use by all the Allied navies was never really achieved, but much progress was made. By September 1942 there had been a meeting of minds between the USN's CTF-24 in Argentia and the RN's C-in-C Western Approaches, as the American Admiral, saw the wisdom in safe and timely arrival. The RN's new *Atlantic Convoy Instructions*, published in that month, reflected the new commonality of purpose, and included for the first time some USN screening diagrams and signals procedures.[40] None the less, along the main trade routes the USN remained the odd man out, particularly after the withdrawal of virtually all American forces north of New York in early 1942. Other Allied navies followed British procedures, while in some things, like code words for standard escort manoeuvres, the USN stuck to its guns, and even the lack of a common phonetic alphabet for radio communications was occasionally a problem. Much work was done, and there developed a great sharing of expertise, but in the end problems of doctrine remained. These were mitigated in 1943 when distinctive national spheres of operations for the Canadians, Americans and British were adopted following the Washington Convoy Conference,[41] and when an increasingly flexible and sophisticated blending of A/S resources – thanks largely to Ultra and the maturation of command structures – allowed the Allies to mix safe and timely arrival of trade with operations designed to destroy U-boats. Co-operation was also fostered in 1943 by the establishment of a joint Anglo-American Allied Anti-Submarine Survey Board (AA/SSB) to review ASW procedures, throughout the Atlantic and make recommendations on standardisation of tactics, doctrine and the like. The AA/SSB was as close as the Allies got to a 'unified' command in the Atlantic in the Second World War.[42]

The British contend, with some justification, that they were well out in front of the USN in ASW by the end of the war, and that the RN had put the Americans on the right track in 1942. Certainly retired senior Canadian and British ASW officers claim that it was their expertise, distributed liberally to the USN in 1942, that gave impetus to what became by 1944–5, a very successful A/S navy. One RN officer even recalls that, as late as August 1942, the USN still had no standard depth-charge drill and individual captains were at liberty to develop and use their own systems.[43] The same men will also admit that the Americans adapted with frightening speed. If the Commonwealth navies held any edge at the end of the war it would seem to lie in inshore ASW, which in 1944–5 came to dominate anti-submarine operations as the Germans moved into UK waters.[44]

In the absence of good modern scholarship on either RN or USN ASW operations during the war there is little direct evidence to support the British contention, although Canadian archival material suggests the contention is valid. Whether or not this is so by 1941 the British had a proprietary interest in both the Atlantic and ASW, since both were essential to the life-blood of the nation and Empire. The same cannot be said of the Americans who, resting secure in the great land mass of North America, need have no fear of being cut off from anything vital to national survival – except perhaps the global system of free trade upon which the well-being of all industrial nations depended. For the Americans the Atlantic was not so much a lifeline as a front line: an embattled route at the end of which lay an island fortress off a hostile shore. What the British cherished as 'the heart of the whole resistance to the enemy' even Roosevelt once rather callously compared to Greenland, Noumea and other outposts.[45] In any event, the preponderance of British sea power in the Atlantic, the RN's proprietary interest in that ocean, and the reduction of the threat to one which could be handled by small ships and aircraft helped to reduce sharply USN involvement and interest in that theatre after December 1941.

It was, after all, in the Pacific that the USN's heart lay, although it must be said that neither the military nor the politicians advocated any shift in strategic emphasis in the wake of the Japanese attack. At the Arcadia Conference in Washington in late December 1941 and early January 1942, the British came prepared to battle for the retention of the Germany first strategy. They were pleasantly surprised to find that no alteration of the plan was seriously considered – yet.[46] Both the US Army and USAAF were, in any event, bent upon taking the war to the Germans as soon as possible, and the USN, scrambling to make something of the defence of south-east Asia with inadequate forces demurred for the time being. However, by March 1942 the speed and breadth of the Japanese conquests convinced the new CNO, Admiral King, that 'Japan had to take first priority'.[47] The British agreed that the Japanese must be stopped, that the integrity of Australia and New Zealand be preserved and that the communications to the two Dominons be kept open. They willingly placed the conduct of the Pacific war into the hands of the American Joint Chiefs of Staff – the only body with the power to do anything. The British retained some control over the Pacific and over the making of strategy generally, with the formation of the Combined Chiefs of Staff (CCS), an amalgam of the Joint Chiefs of Staff (JCS) and senior British staff representatives who were to oversee Anglo-American strategy from Washington for the balance of the war. As one historian has written, the CCS formed the basis of 'the most successful coalition in the history of warfare'.[48]

The major problems facing that coalition in 1942 were how to stop the Japanese advance and how to bring the war home to Germany now that the United States was officially in. While these were by no means mutually exclusive objectives, there were only limited resources in 1942 and a very great deal depended upon available shipping – shipping to build up assault forces in Britain for the cross-Channel invasion longed for in 1942, shipping to build up the bomber forces that would make that landing unnecessary, and shipping to move men and supplies to the south Pacific to stop Japanese attempts to cut off Australia.

The importance of shipping in virtually all aspects of Anglo-American planning underlines the essential fact that it was a maritime alliance. To this alliance the British brought, in 1942, their empire of bases, communications networks, resources, their traditional preference for a peripheral strategy shaped by their traditional dearth of military hardware and men, and Churchill's well known predilections for a Mediterranean strategy – a case, perhaps, of a too-zealous reading of history. Britain, quite clearly, needed to be maintained as a base of operations and arsenal for many fronts; the Russians had to be supplied and so the Arctic convoys had to be maintained; and the Mediterranean demanded attention, because its closure necessitated diversions via the Cape Town route, which created an enormous drain on shipping. Apart from possibly opening the Mediterranean and bombing Germany there seemed to be few European options in 1942, and this was precisely the case made to King and Marshall when they went to London in July 1942 to discuss strategy. The British were able to convince them, and Churchill to persuade Roosevelt, that the coat had to be cut to fit the cloth. It was not a matter of what should be done, but what could be done, and in 1942 the only possible second front was North Africa.[49]

Few Americans, least of all the US Army, wanted to land in North Africa in 1942, and Americans remained rightfully sceptical of Churchill's Balkan machinations through to the end of the war. King at least was prepared to use British insistence on a North African landing as a way of excusing the United States from its commitment to a Germany first strategy and thereby obtaining more resources for the Pacific. Just such a trade occurred at Casablanca in January 1943, when the British obtained a further statement of agreement on the Germany first strategy in exchange for an increase in forces in the Pacific. On the whole, though, the Casablanca conference was a disappointment for the Americans, because the JCS shopping list, which included a 1943 cross-Channel invasion, a Pacific offensive and a combined strategic air offensive against Germany – a plan which King's recent biographer describes as JCS 'daydreaming' – fell a little short of fruition.[50]

The problem was that there was still a major gap between American desire and Allied capabilities, and the British consistently advanced very eloquent arguments, deftly prepared by superb staffs, explaining just why ambitious American operations could not be carried out. By 1943, however, the writing was on the wall for the British, and it proved the last year in which they were able to dominate strategic planning. The balance shifted dramatically by 1944, by which time the enormous productive capacity of America had given the JCS all the leverage it needed.[51]

Evidence of growing American power can be found in the sphere of merchant shipping as early as 1942 and in the British import crisis which came the following winter. Under the terms of lend-lease the British had ordered a large volume of their merchant shipping from American yards in 1941, thereby allowing the British to concentrate on repairs and warship construction. By the time of Pearl Harbor about 7 million tons of new shipping was projected from American yards during 1942, most of it destined for British use. In the end virtually all of it was absorbed into US service during that crucial year, leaving the United States with a net increase in available shipping by December.[52] At the same time Britain was counting on new American shipping to redress her earlier losses and meet those projected. Her needs were intensified by the fact that the bulk of the heavy shipping losses during 1942 came in the Atlantic from British registered or chartered tonnage. The widening gap between need and tonnage available was further exacerbated in late 1942 by the disruptive effects of the North African invasion, which reduced arrivals in British ports and drained British reserves of more material, in particular oil, than had been planned. In the end the British were forced to strip the Indian Ocean of shipping to keep supplies moving in the Atlantic, a move which magnified the effects of famine in the Indian sub-continent in early 1943.[53]

Thus, through a very complex chain of cause and effect, starvation in India in 1943 owed some of its origins to decisions on ship construction taken two years before as a means of beating the Germans. British historians contend that part of the problem was lavish American use of merchant shipping in the Pacific during 1942 and the essentially 'military' American management of merchant shipping which tended to neglect the civilian needs of Britain's maritime empire. C. B. Behrens, the author of the British civil series of official histories volume on merchant shipping, claims that by VE-Day American mismanagement of shipping had cost the Allies about 9 million tons annually: about three times the actual American tonnage lost during the entire war. The proper management of merchant shipping is one area where, according to Morison, the Americans failed utterly to learn from the British, while Roskill – echoing Behrens – concludes that 'on this issue the two principal maritime Allies never achieved a properly coordinated policy'.[54]

Part of the 1942 problem over shipping was that the Pacific, as Roskill freely admits, was a maritime war, and its call on ships of all types proved greater than any anticipated. The European theatre was essentially a continental war fought at the end of fixed sea routes from well-developed bases. Strategy in the European theatre, although based in part on the erroneous view that it could be determined by aerial bombardment (what Roskill called 'the biggest error by us in the realm of strategy in the war'), centred on the imperative of a direct assault on Germany through landings in north-west France. In the final analysis the war had to be fought and won on land through the defeat of the German army, a situation perfectly well understood by the British (and Ernie King) prior to 1944 even if they also knew that they – and the Americans – lacked the means to speed that process along.[55] It also bears emphasising that the final amphibious assault on Europe put ashore a heavily mechanised, massive continental army, an army like that which the British had long advocated as necessary for dealing with the Germans. It was not the comparatively light forces which could have been put ashore in 1942–3 and which had been favoured by Pacific practitioners on the basis of their experience with poorly supported Japanese forces.[56]

Of all the areas of historical importance in the Second World War, few are more in need of serious scholarship than the whole sphere of merchant shipping. Much as generals are alleged to do with the sweep of a hand over a map, so, too, do historians expound on strategy while glazing over the contours of available tonnages and rates of build-up like so many printed lines laid flat on the surface of a table. The short of it is, no major landing was possible in north-west Europe before the end of 1943 because the build-up, operation BOLERO, was crippled by shipping shortages and disruptions in sailings as escorts and resources were juggled to support what little was undertaken.[57] It is here, in the simple availability of tonnage – a concept any railway planner would find familiar – that the European and Pacific campaigns were linked from 1942 to 1943.

The Atlantic was, and remained, largely a British sphere, with the USN's interest limited to the extent that operations there 'directed American men and material from the region where it had its own great task to perform'.[58] By the time major USN fleet units were assigned to the Atlantic the likelihood of confrontation with comparable German units was all but past, and the British were out in front in the A/S war. American ships none the less made a significant contribution to European and Atlantic theatres throughout the war and readily adapted themselves to British procedures where need be. The Americans' easy professionalism and generosity contrasted with the more formal and austere Royal Navy, but apart from the occasional bar-room disagreement or wardroom grouse the two Navies functioned well together. The whole process was eased along by the Americans' willingness to share their lavish stores with British sailors who could, in their turn, provide the alcohol forbidden aboard USN ships.

While some tended to look upon the Pacific as perhaps a mirror image of the European war, with China holding down the bulk of Japanese forces in the way that Russia preoccupied the Germans,[59] the comparison is not accurate. Serious threat to the Japanese home islands could only come from another maritime (or air) power, and in 1942 that could only mean the United States. It was, then, not surprising that control of the Pacific war passed to the JCS. But making the Pacific an American war did not leave the United States at liberty to follow through on its prewar planning. *Plan Orange*, the war plan for Japan, had called for a central Pacific offensive driving on the Philippines to relieve the American garrison. Key bases in the Marshalls and Carolines would have to be won from the Japanese, while either in that process or later in the Philippines Sea, the great decisive naval engagement of the war would have to be fought between the two main fleets. The Pacific was to be, in the words of MacArthur's biographer, 'an Admiral's war', culminating in a duel between opposing battle lines previously worn down by strikes from auxiliary craft, submarines and carriers, among others.[60]

The problem with the Pacific war was that it did not go according to plan. The scope of enemy action was already well beyond the limits of the *Orange* plan by 1941, as Japan moved in on the weakened empires of conquered European states with the Philippines now but a part of a much greater Japanese expansion. The Japanese also wrecked the plan by sinking the USN's battle line at Pearl Harbor. By the time of the checks at Coral Sea and Midway in mid-1942 the speed and breadth of the conquests had left even the

Japanese drunk with victory fever, and plans were afoot to stretch the defensive perimeter of the new empire further to cover what had been taken. It was the drive to secure – or to cut off – Australia and New Zealand that brought the substantive change to earlier planning for the Pacific war.[61]

Australia and New Zealand came to replace the Philippines as the object of immediate American action. Unlike the Philippines, though, they were not cut off, nor could they be allowed to suffer siege while the war with Germany was pursued. The fundamental assumption of the Germany first strategy, that Japan could be allowed to simmer inside a small sphere of conquest, was therefore undone by the virtual collapse of opposition. By mid-1942 the United States was forced to secure a very long and tenuous line of communications across the south Pacific, a line that was soon directly threatened by the Japanese. Instead of husbanding resources within the Alaska–Hawaii–Panama perimeter, as the USN had earlier preferred,[62] it was necessary to pour men and material into the Solomons. An already complex situation was further aggravated by the promise to Australia that it would be part of a major Allied command. Thus, instead of the unified command of operations which was possible under American direction, two distinct commands emerged, the Central Pacific under Nimitz in Pearl Harbor, and the South West Pacific Area under MacArthur, who was crafty enough to manipulate both American and Australian public opinion to secure an independent command.[63] Here, too, the problems of absorbing the old British empire into the new American sphere of influence proved a mixed blessing. It is difficult to see how, apart from the appointment of a supreme commander, the often conflicting interests of Nimitz and MacArthur could have been fully resolved. Attempts by the JCS to balance interests were not always successful, not least because of King's intractable belief in the Pacific as the USN's war. The most recent historian of the Pacific campaign concludes that the diversion of responsibilities was wasteful and inefficient, and he is right. But it is easier to see that now than it was to claim it then in the face of entrenched interests.[64]

Two main lines of thrust – the 'new' South West Pacific campaign under MacArthur based on Australia and the 'old', original *Plan Orange* central Pacific thrust run by an Admiral based in Hawaii – therefore developed in the Pacific war, when there were few resources for either. Both were utterly dependent upon both sea and air power for successful movements. Under these conditions, and in the absence of the battle line, the USN blossomed into a Service built around large carriers with large airwings embarked. As in the European theatre, battleships soon took on a lone and almost brooding character, forming the 'base' upon which carrier air power rested, providing escorts, bombarding landing beaches, and adding the final say in a number of dramatic surface gunnery actions. But here too there was no Jutland, and the USN was indeed fortunate that the scheme for a 'Two Ocean Navy', passed in June 1940, contained a major increment of carriers.[65]

In 1942 the Japanese advance was finally stopped at Guadalcanal, and MacArthur's SWPA forces made gains in the New Guinea area, but Admiral King was not pleased with the slow pace, nor with the prospects of the Japanese gaining time to consolidate their victory. At Casablanca the Americans exchanged a continued commitment to the Germany first strategy for a modest increase in men and material for the Pacific and the go-ahead for the central Pacific thrust by early 1944. King was also able to obtain British reassurances that they would not abandon the war against Japan after the defeat of Germany.[66] The RN's willingness to participate in the Pacific war had already been demonstrated by the loan of the carrier *Victorious* to the USN at the end of 1942. As one of only four modern fleet carriers available to the British her absence for nearly a year was a considerable sacrifice on the RN's part, and she saw the Pacific fleet through a difficult period in May–July 1943, when Nimitz was down to only one fast carrier, the *Sarotoga*.

The despatch of *Victorious* to the Pacific would seem to have been a major learning experience for the RN, as she underwent a prolonged working-up period, and conformed to USN carrier doctrine. Unfortunately, little is known of what was learned or how it was applied, and the Japanese failed to take advantage of their superiority in numbers to test Task Force 14.[67] More importantly, her departure coincided with the arrival of the first *Essex* and *Princeton* class carriers and the start of the Pacific offensive. The central Pacific drive at least approximated the scenario in *Plan Orange* in being 'direct', 'familiar', and offering the 'maximum scope for the employment of great fleets'.[68] And great fleets they were, stretching from horizon to horizon and by 1944 embodying massive carrier air power.

The Pacific is best remembered, then, as a carrier war, although there were only five true carrier-versus-carrier battles. Indeed, much of what the US fleet engaged in was good, traditional naval gunnery actions against the Japanese. But carrier air power was essential to the suppression and isolation of successive island garrisons, and thereby to the establishment of the string of bases that allowed the war to be brought home to Japan. Senior Japanese planners had known before Pearl Harbor that they could not hope to win a war of attrition against the United States, and their lack of depth, particularly in naval air power, allowed the newly won empire to be steadily picked apart.[69] Air superiority meant surface control, and as the Japanese naval air force was ground down so too was its navy. By the time of the Marianas 'Turkey Shoot' in March 1944 the battle of attrition had been won by the USN, as massive carrier task forces roamed at will. The pace of the war now came to be set by other elements, particularly the speed at which resources could be accumulated for the next round of island assaults – or the invasion of the Japanese home islands.

For a maritime empire the loss of command of the air was, by the Second World War, a fatal blow, particularly when engaged against another maritime Power which was able to win command of the air for itself. The Japanese collapse was so complete that by the time bombers of the USAAF began a major campaign against Japan's industries and cities in early 1945 they were able to operate with comparative impunity.[70] But the collapse of Japanese maritime power was not due entirely to carrier air power. Rather, it owed much to the USN's successful submarine campaign. In this the Americans had learned a valuable lesson from the Atlantic war, and within hours of Pearl Harbor Roosevelt sanctioned an unrestricted submarine campaign against Japan. Torpedo failures marred the first year-and-a-half of the campaign, but in late 1943 when good torpedoes were matched with excellent intelligence and the adoption of a variation of German wolf pack tactics, losses inflicted on Japan's maritime commerce sky-rocketed. In 1944 alone USN submarines sank more shipping than they had in 1942–3 combined, and by the end of the war had accounted for 55 per cent of total Japanese losses.[71] The failure of the Japanese to take effective countermeasures against submarine attack remains one of the great enigmas of the war.

It is a moot point whether the submarines and non-atomic air attacks could by themselves have brought the Japanese to terms in 1945. What is more certain is that the movement of the front was due to the flexibility and enormous power of American carrier aviation. Command of the sea now meant at least local command of the air as well and, without supporting land-based aircraft, carriers were the only means of ensuring that naval power could function. Air power was, of course, vital to European amphibious operations as well, but in the absence of major carrier fleets no amphibious landings took place beyond the range of land-based air support – especially fighters.[72] The RN, which retained primary responsibility for European operations, did respond to the new warfare by planning a major expansion of its fast carrier fleet within the very circumscribed limits of the British economy. The *Illustrious* and *Implacable* classes were good ships, roughly equivalent to the USN's *Enterprise* class, although with fewer aircraft and a shorter radius of action. Although vastly outnumbered by the USN carrier fleet, the RN's carriers' ability to absorb punishment – a benefit of their armoured flight decks and enclosed hangars – allowed carriers of the British Pacific fleet to stay in the line when American carriers had to retire.[73]

The fundamental difference between RN and USN carrier doctrines arose from a number of things, not least of which were different threats faced by each navy before the war. It is also fair to say that the limited size of British airwings effectively crippled the development of the concept of air superiority which drove much of American thinking. Despite innovative use of their carriers, such as at Taranto in 1941, the general cowing of the Italian navy, and the use of carrier air power to support the landings on Madagascar in 1942, the British fell well short of the potential of carrier air power. The Arctic convoys, run in the face of heavy German air opposition, might well have been a different story had the British been able to deploy carrier forces along the line of those available to the USN in 1944. Perhaps had the RN not lost so many of its carriers by 1942 it might well have been able to do something against the Norwegian air bases.[74] But even northern Norway, remote as it was, could not be easily severed from its continental base of supply and the great depth and strength inherent in Germany's Norwegian position could not have been overcome by carrier air power alone. As good as the Japanese were in 1941–3, the Germans were markedly better in the air over the long haul.[75]

All this is by way of suggesting that naval air conditions in the European and Pacific theatres were not directly comparable, a situation which does more to explain than to excuse the development of British carrier aviation. What the British had to learn by 1945, and what the Americans had to teach them, was the management of carrier task forces as the principal naval weapon against any and all targets. Achieving the proper mix of aircraft types, weapons load, and co-ordination between decks for an air strike was as much an art as it was a science. Happily, the British proved eager to learn and the British Pacific Fleet willingly adopted USN practices for its operations alongside the USN in the Okinawa campaign of 1945.[76] Nimitz at least professed himself well pleased at having a British task force under his command and made every effort to ensure that the RN – a junior partner in the Pacific – made a maximum contribution.

For their part the British had not only to master the intricacies of a new form of naval warfare, they also had to develop an independence from bases that they had never experienced before. The importance of fleet trains, and the British inexperience with them, had been the basis of Admiral King's objection to a British fleet in the Pacific. At the Quebec conference in 1944, when the fielding of the British Pacific Fleet (BPF) was agreed upon, King had been insistent that it sink or swim on its own.[77] The RN was already aware of the enormous supply problems in the Pacific, and its liaison officers had reported on the elaborate USN fleet trains that made sustained forward opertions possible.[78] Once committed to the Pacific the British 'moved heaven and earth to become self-sufficient',[79] but in the end the BPF went to war on a shoe-string. While the USN relied on a fleet train of naval ships crewed by USN sailors, the BPF fought with a back-up of chartered Allied and British shipping and a desperate shortage of tankers. In addition to the motley collection of ships, the BPF's fleet train was also only about half the size of what the Admiralty estimated it needed to function properly. In this instance civilian authorities of the Ministry of War Transport limited the size of the BPF's train because of the dire needs for shipping elsewhere, and it was not possible easily to obtain ships from American staffs who controlled allocation. The RN made do, but by the time of the Japanese capitulation the shortage of oil supplies threatened to cripple BPF operations. Fortunately the generosity of the USN went well beyond the strictures of King's insistence at Quebec that the RN fend entirely for itself.[80]

The constrained nature of BPF operations in 1945 underscores the fundamental shift in power betwen the two allies that took place during the war. The British had surmounted most of their technical and operational problems, but not without considerable American material aid. The prewar zeal for centralisation of air matters under the RAF had proved, as Admiral Sir Herbert Richmond pointed out repeatedly during the war,[81] a castastrophe for British arms very nearly for Britain herself. Perhaps the British would have muddled through as they always did, but it would have been much more difficult without the Liberators, Catalinas, Hudsons, Venturas, Avengers, Corsairs and Wildcats that filled an enormous void in British maritime air power. Certainly, without the carrier aircraft the BPF would not have been able to compete in 1945. Britain fared better in the anti-submarine war, where both her equipment and quantity of home-built vessels were up to the task. In some areas even here, though, such as in small escort carriers and the Captain class frigates, the RN drew heavily on American support by 1944–5. And it was perhaps in the Atlantic that 'British' sea power in the old sense had begun to disintegrate by 1945, for by then much of the close escort of trade had been taken over by the RCN. The Canadians had reached such a state of importance to Atlantic operations by 1944 that the Admiralty even toyed with the idea of giving over complete responsibility for convoy escort in that ocean to the Canadians while shifting the weight of the RN to the Far East. In the end the Admiralty had to content itself with exercising operational control over the bulk of the Canadian fleet, while keeping the cream of its ASW forces close to home to meet the German submarine threat in early 1945.[82] In truth, Canadian naval forces, and those of the other Commonwealth Dominions, were less British by 1945 than they had been in 1939. Historians who cobble together everything with an 'HM' prefix under the Admiralty's flag miss the essential point that British naval power, while strong by 1945, was an agglomeration of many elements, most of which could not be held together after the end of the war.

If distinctly British sea power had not been a spent force by 1939 it certainly was by 1945. Perhaps its most enduring strength had been the reasoned judgements of men and councils long familiar with balancing global maritime and strategic interests, and the superb organisation of its Naval Control of Shipping and Intelligence systems – the nervous system of the maritime alliance which decided the war. Few would, in any event, deny that the war which began as a coalition of equals ended with the United States and its fleet supreme in virtually every respect. It is perhaps sufficient to point out that Britain fought both of her twentieth-century world wars with battle fleets – battleships, carriers and cruisers – little changed in quantity from what they had been at the outset. In the First World War the need to dramatically expand the battle fleet simply was not there, since the margin of superiority over the Germans was great enough once the prewar programmes were completed. In the Second World War the need for more capital ships certainly was there, and it was constant (though changing), but the resources were not. Impressive though the completion of the *King George V* class battleships and the *Illustrious, Implacable* and *Glory* classes of carriers may have been by British standards, they did not compare with the tremendous outpourings of American industry. In a way reminiscent of Britain in the eighteenth century, the United States did it all and came out powerful and wealthy.

Notes

1. S. W. Roskill, *The Strategy of Sea Power: Its Development and Application* (London, 1962) p. 150, and P. M. Kennedy, *The Rise and Fall of British Naval Mastery* (London, 1976) p. 300.
2. For the definitive account of the development of Asdic see Willem Hackmann's recent *Seek & Strike: Sonar, Antisubmarine Warfare and Royal Navy 1914–54* (London, 1984).
3. See Admiral Sir Reginald Bacon and F. E. McMurtrie, *Modern Naval Strategy* (London, 1940) pp. 148–9 which asumes that submarines were limited to attacking from submerged positions, and S. W. Roskill, *Naval Policy Between the Wars*, volume II (London, 1977) p. 393.
4. Roskill, *Naval Policy*, II, p. 227.
5. Canadian anti-submarine and trade defence doctrine mirrored that of the RN, and on the eve of war the Canadian Chief of the Naval Staff could write with confidence that 'If international Law is complied with, Submarine attack should not prove serious'. See 'Defence of Trade', CNS Memorandum 12 February, 1937, Public Archives Canada (PAC), MG 27, III, B5, v 37, file D-26.
6. Roskill, *Naval Policy*, II, p. 226.
7. 'Outline History of Trade Division 1939–1945', Naval Service Headquarters, Ottawa, p. 1. Directorate of History, National Defence Headquarters, Ottawa, DHist 8280B, vol. 2. See also M. Milner, *Canadian Naval Force Requirements in the Second World War*, Operational Research and Analysis Establishment, National Defence Headquarters, Ottawa, Extra-mural Paper No. 20, December 1981, for discussion of Canadian NCS activity during the war.
8. J. S. Corbett, *England in the Seven Years War*, volume I, pp. 3–4 as quoted in D. M. Schurman, *The Education of a Navy: The Development of British Naval Strategic Thought, 1867–1914* (London, 1965) p. 165.
9. A. J. Marder, *From the Dreadnought to Scapa Flow*, volume 5 (London, 1970) pp. 141–2.
10. For the most recent work on the state of Coastal Command in the early years of the Second World War, see W. A. B. Douglas, *The Creation of a National Air Force: The Official History of Royal Canadian Air Force*, volume II (Toronto, 1986) pp. 468–72.
11. G. Till, *Air Power and the Royal Navy 1914–1945* (London, 1979) pp. 75–7 and pp. 88–9.
12. There are several standard sources on US carrier development both before and during the war, including Clark Reynolds, *The Fast Carriers: The Forging of an Air Navy* (New York, 1969) and James H. and William H. Belote, *Titans of the Seas: The Development and Operations of American Carriers Task Forces During World War II* (New York, 1975). Norman Friedman's *Carrier Airpower* (New

York, 1981) does an excellent job of blending technological change, doctrinal development and national peculiarities for the inter-war years.
13. S. E. Morison, *History of United States Naval Operations in World War II*, volume I (Boston, 1954) pp. 241–2, and Douglas, *The Creation of a National Air Force*, p. 516 and p. 546.
14. Morison, *United States Naval Operations*, I, pp. 209–10, and pp. 213–14.
15. R. G. Albion, in Rowena Reid (ed.), *Makers of Naval Policy* (Annapolis, 1980) p. 550.
16. For an excellent account of the development of American war planning see Malcom Murfett's chapter in this collection.
17. Albion, *Matters of Naval Policy*, p. 551.
18. J. R. M. Butler (ed.), *Grand Strategy*, volume II, *September 1939–June 1941* (London, 1957).
19. Kennedy, *Rise and Fall*, p. 301.
20. Albion, *Matters of Naval Policy*, p. 551.
21. All major works on strategy in the Second World War, including the British, American and Canadian official histories, have accounts of the ABC-1 talks.
22. R. H. Spector, *The Eagle Against the Sun: The American War with Japan* (New York, 1985), pp. 66–7, and Albion, *Matters of Naval Policy*, p. 552.
23. Thomas B. Buell, *Master of Sea Power: A Biography of Fleet Admiral Ernest J. King* (Boston, 1980) p. 137.
24. Ibid., pp. 137 and 193.
25. See D. F. Bittner's excellent *The Lion and the White Falcon: Britain and Iceland in the World War II Era* (Hamden, CT, 1983) especially chapter 5.
26. J. R. M. Butler, *Grand Strategy*, III, pt II, chapter 5, and Patrick Abbazia *Mr. Roosevelt's Navy* (Annapolis, 1975) pp. 217–22.
27. In August 1940 Canada and the United States signed the Ogdensburg Agreement which, through the establishment of the Permanent Joint Board on Defence, for the first time integrated the two nations in the defence of North America. See C. P. Stacey, *Arms, Men and Governments: The War Policies of Canada 1939–1945* (Ottawa, 1970) Part VI, Military Cooperation with the United States, and Col. S. W. Dziuban, *Military Relations Between the United States and Canada, 1939–1945* (Washington, DC, 1959) pp. 27–9.
28. Only actions against the Italian Navy approached the Jutland mould, and even then the number of battleships was small by comparison. The harrying and destruction of the *Bismarck* and *Scharnhorst* by Task Forces of various ship classes was indicative of the sophisticated and flexible integration of fleet capabilities by the Second World War. See S. W. Roskill, *The War at Sea* (London, 1954–61).
29. Churchill's pernicious influence on naval affairs is well recognised; see S. W. Roskill, *Churchill and the Admirals* (London, 1977), pp. 116–47, and P. Gretton, *Former Naval Person: Winston Churchill and the Royal Navy* (London, 1968) pp. 282–3.
30. *Western Approaches Convoy Instructions*, General, Part 300, Instructions for Escorts. Naval Historical Branch (NHB), London, England, N/NHB/10/70.
31. Milner, *Canadian Naval Force Requirements*, see especially pp. 56–8.
32. The best account of USN activity in the undeclared war between Germany and the United States in late 1941 is Abazzia. The Canadian naval side is explored in depth in M. Milner, *North Atlantic Run: The Royal Canadian Navy and the Battle for the Conveys* (Toronto, 1985) chapter 3, while the air side and a more thorough examination of German operations can be found in Douglas, *The Creation of a National Air Force*, chapter 12.

33. Morison, *United States Naval Operations*, I, pp. 241–2.
34. Ibid., p. 206, fn 6.
35. The USN's wartime filing manual placed Canada, and the other fully independent Dominions, under 'British Empire and Colonies'. US services opposed the establishment of staff missions from the Dominions, preferring to deal with the British Commonwealth through the British. The naval situation was further complicated by the presence of senior British officers in key staff posts in Canada and elsewhere; for example, Ottawa's Director of Trade and the Admiral in Command of the 3rd Battle Squadron at Halifax, which provided the oceanic escort for convoys until early 1941, were both RN.
36. The struggle for independence – from both the British and the Americans – and the battle to establish a firm position for the Navy in the Canadian defence firmament are recurrment themes in Canadian historiography. See the seminal chapter by W. A. B. Douglas, 'Conflict and Innovation in the Royal Canadian Navy, 1939–1945', in G. Jordan (ed.), *Naval Strategy in the Twentieth Century* (New York, 1977) and W. Lund's 'The Royal Canadian Navy's Quest for Autonomy in the North West Atlantic', in J. A. Boutilier (ed.), *The RCN in Retrospect 1910–1968* (Vancouver, 1982).
37. See for example, Roskill, *The Strategy of Sea Power*, p. 179.
38. While the British have long been critics of the USN's handling of the east coast convoy issue, no more trenchant critic of the USN during this period can be found than Morison himself: see Morison, *United States Naval Operations*, I, pp. 200–1. For a more recent discussion of the comparative problems of inshore ASW and trade defence see M. Milner, 'Inshore ASW: The Canadian Experience', in W. A. B. Douglas (ed.), *The RCN in Transition* (Vancouver, forthcoming).
39. The USN's escort doctrine was delineated in *Escort-of-Convoy Instructions*, Lantflt 9A, Part v, Primary Duties of Escorts, as amended to 17 November 1941. Naval Historical Center, Operational Archives Branch, Washington Navy Yard, Washington, DC.
40. *Atlantic Convoy Instructions*, September 1942, see Operations Section, Articles 130 and 131, and Communications Section, Articles 370, 375 and 377, NHB, N/NHB/10/70. See also comments by Director of A/S on convoy ONS 92 in Public Record Office (PRO), Kew, England, ADM 199/1338.
41. All the official histories dealing with the Atlantic war cover the Washington Convoy Conference, although its consequences were of greater import to the British and Canadians. Buell maintains that the conference was called 'thanks to King' (p. 292), while Canadians, such as Douglas, *The Creation of a National Air Force*, pp. 548–50 and Lund, 'Quest for Autonomy' contend that it was convened in spite of King.
42. Neither the British nor the Americans were prepared to let the other nominate a supreme commander for the Atlantic, and so co-ordination of effort was entrusted to the Allied Anti-Submarine Survey Board, which visited all Atlantic establishments in 1943 and attempted to bring together their efforts. See Milner, *North Atlantic Run*, pp. 232, 250–2, and PRO, ADM 1/13746.
43. Interview with Rear Admiral P. W. Burnett, RN, Devoran, Cornwall, June 1987.
44. Milner, 'Inshore ASW'.
45. Roosevelt to Churchill, 18 December 1942, PAC, RG 24, 6796, NS 8375-4. For a discussion of the difference in convoy and escort assessments see Milner, *North Atlantic Run*, p. 103.
46. Buell, *Master of Sea Power*, pp. 162–3, Albion *Matters of Naval Policy*, p. 573.
47. Buell, *Master of Sea Power*, p. 171.
48. Ibid., p. 169.

49. For an excellent summary of strategic dilemmas see Maurice Matloff's 'Allied Strategy in Europe, 1939–1945', in P. Paret (ed.), *Makers of Modern Strategy* (Princeton, 1986) pp. 677–702. See also Buell, *Master of Sea Power*, pp. 210–11, and Albion, *Matters of Naval Policy*, p. 576.
50. Buell, *Master of Sea Power*, p. 269.
51. Matloff, 'Allied Strategy'. I am also grateful to D. S. Graham for sharing his current research for a new book on Command in War in the 20th Century. His revelations about the background to the landings in South France confirm the importance of resource manipulation in the development of strategy after 1943.
52. C. B. A. Behrens, *Merchant Shipping and the Demands of War* (London, 1955) pp. 284 and 290, and Appendix XXVII, p. 292.
53. Ibid., chapter 14 and R. M. Leighton, 'U.S. Merchant Shipping and the British Import Crisis', in K. R. Greenfield (ed.) *Command Decisions* (Washington, DC, 1960) pp. 199–223.
54. Roskill, *The Strategy of Sea Power*, p. 150.
55. King believed that Russia was the key to the European war and would 'do nine-tenths of the job of defeating Germany', a traditional British view of the relationship between sea power and continental allies. Buell, *Master of Sea Power*, p. 265.
56. See W. G. F. Jackson, *Overlord: Normandy 1944* (London, 1978).
57. See Leighton, 'U.S. Merchant Shipping'.
58. Albion, *Matters of Naval Policy*, p. 578.
59. King held this view; see Buell, *Master of Sea Power*, p. 266.
60. D. Clayton James, banquet address at the Sixth Naval History Symposium, US Naval Academy, Annapolis, MD, September 1985. See also James's excellent summary of Pacific strategies in Paret's *Makers of Modern Strategy*, pp. 703–34.
61. Albion, *Matters of Naval Policy*, p. 576, Buell, *Master of Sea Power*, p. 205, and Spector, *The Eagle against the Sun*, p. 143.
62. Murfett, Chapter 11, above.
63. Spector, *The Eagle against the Sun*, p. 144; for the Australian perspective see D. M. Horner's *High Command: Australia and Allied Strategy 1939–1945* (Canberra, 1982).
64. Spector, *The Eagle against the Sun*, p. 144.
65. Morison, *United States Naval Operations*, I, pp. 27–30, Albion, p. 548, and Morison's, *The Two Ocean Navy* (New York, 1963) pp. 15–20. For details of the new warships see Paul H. Silverstone, *U.S. Warships of World War II* (Garden City, NY, 1965).
66. Buell, *Master of Sea Power*, pp. 264–79.
67. Information on *Victorious*'s time with Task Force 14 in published sources is thin. See D. Brown, *Carrier Operations in World War II*, volume I, *The Royal Navy* (London, 1973) pp. 104–5, Roskill, *The War At Sea*, II, pp. 230–1, and Reynolds, *The Fast Carriers*, pp. 35, 71 and 75. Remarkably, Morison's volumes on the Pacific war make no mention of *Victorious*'s time with TF 14, see volumes VI and VII.
68. Spector, *The Eagle against the Sun*, p. 252.
69. For a thorough discussion of the air capabilities of major Powers in the Second World War see R. J. Overy's *The Air War 1939–1945* (New York, 1980).
70. L. Kennett, *A History of Strategic Bombing* (New York, 1982) chapter 10.
71. Spector, *The Eagle against the Sun*, pp. 478–87, contains a good summary of the tremendous accomplishments of the US submariners. See also Clay Blair Jr's *Silent Victory; The U.S. Submarine War Against Japan* (New York, 1975).
72. S. E. Ambrose, 'Seapower in World Wars I and II', in B. M. Simpson (ed.), *War, Strategy and Maritime Power* (New Brunswick, NJ, 1977).
73. Reynolds, *The Fast Carriers*, pp. 303–4, and Till, *Air Power*, p. 76.

74. The potential importance of carriers to the Arctic convoys was a particular issue with the late Admiral B. B. Schofield, RN; see his *British Sea Power* (London, 1967) p. 197.
75. Overy, *The Air War*, pp. 109–30.
76. See Richard Humble's *Fraser of North Cape: The Life of Admiral of the Fleet Lord Fraser (1888–1981)* (London, 1983) chapters 20–3 which covers his period in command of the British Pacific Fleet.
77. Buell, *Master of Sea Power*, pp. 4701.
78. Reynolds, *The Fast Carriers*, p. 306.
79. Buell, *Master of Sea Power*, p. 471.
80. Roskill, *The Strategy of Sea Power*, p. 227, Schofield, *British Sea Power*, p. 213, and Reynolds, *The Fast Carriers*, pp. 312–13.
81. Admiral Sir Herbert Richmond, *Statesmen and Sea Power* (Oxford: Clarendon Press, 1946); see especially his chapter IX, and Barry Hunt's biography of Richmond, *Sailor–Scholar: Admiral Sir Herbert Richmond (1871–1946)*, (Waterloo, 1982).
82. Naval Assistant (Policy and Plans) to Chief of the Canadian Naval Mission Overseas 28 July 1944, PAC, RG 24, 11752, CS 346–1.

Part IV
Planning for a Future War in the Nuclear Age

'We have lived with a balance of military power, which also governs other areas of politics, for much of modern history and we are going to go on living with it for the time being. But the calculus of military power is changing. Of the three traditional functions that it served, to promote the economic power of a nation, to promote its ideological objective and to protect the security of itself and its allies, only the third is now accepted as legitimate.'—Alistair Buchan

The relationship between peace-time contingency planning for a future war, and the manner in which the plans proved relevant in the actual conduct of war can be tested for the first half of the twentieth century. For the second half, one can only look back to the experience of the past as nations deal with the changing calculus of military power.

13 Anglo-American Maritime Strategy in the Era of Massive Retaliation, 1945–60

Eric Grove and Geoffrey Till

INTRODUCTION

For the first two decades of the post-Second World War era, strategic thinking in the navies of Britain and the United States was dominated by a number of factors, some traditional and some novel. Of the traditional ones, the geostrategic situation of the two countries was much as it had been before the Second World War. There was also the perennial problem of having to match resources with commitments, and this was complicated by the difficulty of absorbing what seemed to be a permanent revolution in naval technology.[1]

On the other hand, the planning staffs of the two navies faced an unfamiliar world. No one was at all sure what would be the long-term effect of atomic weapons. Some believed they would transform the miltiary scene, perhaps to the extent of eventually making war unthinkable. Others believed atomic weapons were simply another new technology that the Services would absorb in the usual way. It was already clear by 1945 that the hopeful expectations of Churchill and Roosevelt, as enunciated in the Atlantic Charter, were likely to be delayed. Quarrels over Poland, Eastern Europe and the future of Germany were testing the old wartime coalition to destruction.

It was replaced by a growing Cold War between a maritime Western coalition and a continentally-based Eastern one (which might, or might not, include China). On top of this, any hope of the European colonialists that they might now get back to normal business in the administration of their empires rapidly proved to be illusory. Instead there seemed likely to be a period of great instability as the European Powers disengaged from their colonial past.

All these factors, of course, were interdependent: the requirement to build up and maintain the Western economy was considered to be a vital component of Cold War strategy. This in turn soon demonstrated a need for new weapons of maximum cost-effectiveness, exploiting nuclear technology to deter large-scale wars by being prepared to fight them effectively. General wars would be of such unprecedented destructiveness that everyone hoped they would never happen. Beneath this extreme and increasingly unreal level of combat a much more real world of East–West and colonial crises had to be managed, threatening to escalate to limited or 'warm' wars. All such forms of military operation put a new emphasis on the 'power projection' roles of navies. At the same time, more traditional sea control tasks were challenged as a result of advancing technology and, more importantly, as a result of serious questioning of the likelihood of the kind of long war in which naval forces had been important in the past.

The two navies responded with remarkable flexibility and originality. Naval planners demonstrated a readiness to experiment with established truths. By the end of the period examined in this chapter, both the United States and Britain had built navies that were essentially new and which played a vital role in both strategic nuclear deterrence and power projection in more limited third-world contingencies. Before Flexible Response became the agreed strategy of the NATO alliance, it had become the *de facto* strategy of the Anglo-American maritime coalition outside Europe, and it was even being applied, by the United States Navy at least, to the Superpower confrontation in the Atlantic.

THE NEW STRATEGIC ENVIRONMENT

Directly or indirectly, naval policy reflects the strategic environment of the country it defends. Thus, the real explanation for 'naval' policy is found in foreign, economic and political circumstances. For both the United States and for Britain, the post-1945 world was both uncertain and unfamiliar.

The United States was victorious, and, in contrast with nearly all other countries, prosperous and confident with its nuclear monopoly. Whether it liked it or not, the United States was now the world's greatest Power, and simply could not, in the interests of a return to 'normalcy', demobilise and disengage as it had in 1919. The only acceptable alternative to this uncomfortable role was in the brave new world exemplified by aspirations behind the United Nations Organisation. Squabbles with the Soviet Union and the collapse of the Baruch plan effectively put a stop to that by the end of 1946. By then, there had been a large run-down of the military establishment but the pattern thereafter was for a reluctant reversal of the process. In more general terms, the assumption of strategic power was exemplified by political commitment to Western Europe through the Truman Doctrine, economic commitment through Marshall Aid and finally military commitment through NATO. These radical departures from the American norm quickly provided the United States Navy with a new set of objectives and aspirations.

The other major American preoccupation of the time was to determine where the balance should be struck between its European and its Pacific security concerns. The Chinese Civil War was the main but far from the only concern of the time. Paradoxically the famous 'perimeter speech', by Dean Acheson, which signalled the disengagement of the United States in Asia, also had major implications for the future of the United States Navy.

Britain emerged from the Second World War as a victor, but a bankrupted one. While still appearing one of the Big Three, its relative weakness made it inevitable that Britain would have to seek its salvation through collaboration. But with whom? Churchill's celebrated 'Three circles speech' identified the alternatives very clearly:

> The first circle for us is naturally the British Commonwealth and Empire, with all that comprises. Then there is also the English-speaking world in which we, Canada and the other British Dominions and the United States play so important a part and finally there is United Europe.[2]

From the start the realities of Britain's situation were such that the transition from Empire to Commonwealth was going to be faster than expected. India and Burma became independent almost immediately, and the relative nebulousness of the new formation became apparent in divisions over Korea and Suez. By the end of the 1960s, changing trade patterns had made Europe more important, in economic terms to Britain, than was the Commonwealth. The Commonwealth remained a circle but was clearly not one on which Britain could pin its national security.

Gladwyn Jebb's famous Foreign Office paper of June 1944[3] had explored the potential contribution of a new defence grouping in Western Europe to long-term British security, and emphasised the importance of Britain's supporting it since it would provide defence-in-depth and help assure stability in a potentially turbulent area. The British consensus was that the British contribution to Western European solidarity would be from outside. Britain was in Europe but not of it. Yet, through the Brussels Treaty of 1948, Britain was inexorably drawn into new military commitments on the continent. The 1954 Agreements which transformed the Brussels Pact into the Western European Union formalised this substantial commitment of forces: a development which was bound to have a detrimental effect on traditional British maritme preoccupations.

But this was still in the future. In the meantime, Britain's relationship with the United States was the most important dimension of security policy. But, though the relationship was special, it was rarely easy. A 1951 minute by the Permanent Under-Secretary to the Foreign Office, Sir William Strang, encapsulated the matter well:

> The United States administration often behaves insufferably to its allies

... The United States has come out of the two great wars stronger than it went into them, and can think and talk of a third world war more light-heartedly than we Europeans can. The Americans are new to the responsibilities of world power and have not learned to tolerate the frustrations and bitterness of defeat ... The problem should not be an insoluble one, because in the last resort the Americans want the same kind of thing as we do. We have in fact no alternative but to work with them ... Though the Americans often behave as though our views and interest were of little regard to them, in the last resort they know they must rely on us. This strengthens our position in dealing with them ... Our problem is to deflect the Americans from unwise or dangerous courses without making a breach in the united front.[4]

Among the Anglo-American differences of these years were the abrupt cancellation of lend-lease in the Autumn of 1945, the McMahon Act of 1946, and differences over Palestine, China and Korea. Although the British succeeded in their aim of shackling the United States to the political, economic and military defence of Western Europe, it did not take the warning of the possibility of an 'agonising reappraisal' by John Foster Dulles over the European Defence Community (EDC) debacle to remind the British that it would be unwise to take this commitment for granted.

In the narrower naval world, contact between British and American policy-makers was always close. The Second World War had converted officers of the United States and Royal Navies into professional colleagues, and often personal friends. This closeness had been confirmed by the final operations of the British Pacific Fleet, which had effectively acted as an integral component of American naval power in the Pacific. Although this did not rule out differences of opinion, notably over always sensitive questions of command, it did provide a good basis for a growing harmony in strategic and operational thought, especially after the creation of NATO in 1949 and, more especially, its Atlantic Command three years later.

In these circumstances it is hardly surprising that not only equipment and operating procedures could be exchanged, but also strategic and tactical doctrines. The Royal Navy was by now very much the junior partner, but in the first postwar decade still had things to teach its larger ally, for instance in Anti-Submarine Warfare (ASW) and in carrier deck design and operation. The world's 'former naval power' found a substitute for naval supremacy in an especially intimate and influential special naval relationship with its successor. This was entirely consistent with the thrust of British foreign policy which in rather the same way sought to exert influence on the foreign policy of the United States as a substitute for true Great Power status.

VISIONS OF THE SOVIET THREAT

The Soviet Union was seen by the leaders of both countries as the potential enemy right from the end of the Second World War. As early as February 1946, the Soviet Navy was put forward as a threat for the future. At the same meeting of the British Cabinet's Defence Committee it was formally decided that (a) there would be no war in the next two to three years; (b) the United States would be 'probably on our side and not against us' and that (c) 'no fleet capable of menacing Britain would exist, in the next few years'.[5]

More important was the Soviet threat on land: the Red Army seemed to both the Truman and Attlee governments to pose a real threat to the security of Western Europe. A premeditated attack by the Soviet Union seemed unlikely given postwar conditions, the need to recover from the war and the current lack of a Soviet operational nuclear capability. Nevertheless a new world war could not be entirely discounted. American and British force levels on the ground in Western Europe were so meagre that the initial Soviet land offensive was likely to succeed. In short, if it were attacked, continental Western Europe would probably fall, and would subsequently need to be recovered.

If the few long-range bombers available in bases in Britain, the Middle East and the Pacific proved unable to deter attack, they could at least mitigate its effects. The first priority of Western strategy would therefore be to retain these bomber airfields and the land areas which supported them. The indirect defence of the bomber offensive was, therefore, a task for naval power. For this reason, Prime Minister Clement Attlee reluctantly accepted the need for a strong and continued British Mediterranean presence.

Nor would this be the only role for the Western navies in any future conflict with the Soviet Union. Control of the seas would be crucial to bring to bear against the Soviet Union the mobilised might of the coalition of the United States and the British Commonwealth, the latter still being considered a military as well as a politico-economic unit. At the beginning of 1947, in a Staff Conference with Attlee, the British Chiefs of Staff defined the United Kingdom's principles of defence as (a) protecting the Commonwealth's means to fight a major war until an offensive with allies could be developed and (b) holding bases for the offensive. To achieve these objectives, British forces were first to defend the United Kingdom, second to maintain sea communications, and third to keep a 'firm hold' on the Middle East. Without each of these three 'pillars' the Chiefs of Staff thought that the whole edifice would crumble.[6]

Contemporary American thinking had similar priorities. The 'Pincher' plans of 1945–6 postulated a withdrawal to Britain, the Mediterranean islands, Suez and Bahrain: 'the Eastern Mediterranean was to be the major theater of concentration and naval operations at the start of any general war'.[7] As a 1948 General Board study put it, the United States Navy's tasks in any war were 'control of the seas, occupation or seizure of advanced bases, attack on Russian bases and denial of advanced bases to Russia, combined with the enormous logistic supply effort of the other services and our allies ...'[8]

But it was the Prague coup and the Berlin blockade in 1948 which saw a sharp deterioration in the Cold War in Europe. The creation of the Western Union alliance by the Brussels Treaty of March 1948 drew Britain into an increasing commitment to the defence of the European continent. The month the Treaty was signed, a paper suggesting the addition of 'the defence of Europe as far east as possible' to Britain's defence priorities was discussed by the British Chiefs of Staff committee.[9] There was considerable disagreement over how 'vital' various parts of the world were. The First Sea Lord (Admiral Sir John Cunningham, an ex-C-in-C Mediterranean Fleet) considered Greece and Italy more important than Norway.[10] Slowly, however, the formula suggested by the March Treaty began to be added to Britain's defence priorities. It was given considerable attention in the updated defence review presented to the Commonwealth Prime Ministers in September 1948.[11]

One motive for clarification of strategic aims was the beginning of formal defence discussions with the United States. As well as secret discussions on a North Atlantic Pact, joint Anglo-American planning took place with the result that an emergency war plan was agreed in October 1948. This was called *Doublequick*, later *Speedway*, by the British and *Fleetwood*, later *Trojan*, by the Americans.[12] A major priority remained defence of the Middle East as an air base but also as a means of quickly recapturing Middle East oil (a matter of some concern to the United States).[13] The US Army was never very happy with the Middle East, however, due to the vulnerability of sea lines of communication and, as the intelligence assessment of the threat to the area became more optimistic in 1949, the American priority shifted to a build-up in French North Africa.[14] This was enshrined in a new joint plan, *Offtackle* to the Americans, *Galloper* to the British, drawn up in October 1949. British unhappiness with the new Mediterranean priorities led to a delay until March 1950 before finally *Galloper* was recommended to the Chiefs of Staff by the Joint Planners. One reason they felt able to do so was the feeling that full-scale war was not likely. Nevertheless, if general war *had* broken out over the North Korean invasion of South Korea in June 1950, *Offtackle/Galloper* was the way the British and American military staffs believed it would have been fought.[15] Although the prospect of a full-scale Soviet attack on Western Europe was certainly the most serious threat to Western security in the eyes of British and American planners, it was far from being the most likely. In the much shorter term, there arose minor conflicts and disorders all around the world. Some of these were connected with the slow and often painful collapse of the European colonial empires, and many of these required a significant commitment of naval forces, as shown later.

OPERATIONAL PLANNING

Offtackle/Galloper was one of the most thoroughly considered war scenarios of the period, and for this reason, it is worth considering in some detail the role that the American and British navies were expected to play in it. Allied strategy in such a war would be:

a to launch a strategic air offensive, using atomic bombs, against Russia from the outbreak of the war;
b to hold securely the air bases and sea areas for launching this air offensive (Britain, Egypt and Okinawa);
c to defend certain other areas essential to allied strategy (Western Europe, North West Africa, the Middle East and Japan);
d to defend the allied main support areas (North America, Australia, New Zealand, South Africa and South America);
e to control the sea and air communications essential for the security of the above bases and areas.[16]

The planners were still not sanguine about holding on to much of Europe. Although the attempt would be made to stand on the Rhine, the possibility of holding any kind of bridgehead was considered 'problematical'. The main role of the United States base area in North Africa would be the holding of the Pyrennes and, if that failed, the mounting of a re-entry operation into Western Europe from the south. Whatever the extent of Western holdings along the periphery of the Soviet bloc, however, sea communciations were vital for the great world-wide Anglo-American coalition. The threat to these communications was considered to be, in order of priority, mining, aircraft, submarines, and surface raiders. To counter these threats, convoys were to be established on the routes North America–British Isles, British Isles–Gibraltar–Central and South Atlantic, Gibraltar–Port Said, North America–Gibraltar, North America–Central and South Atlantic and North America–Japan/Okinawa. A British–Scandinavia convoy route would continue, protected by units allocated to the North Atlantic, as long as the locals continued to defend a bastion there, and Bahrain, defended by United States Marines, would need supplies for the Persian Gulf. The French were to be responsible for initial control of communications between North Africa and the South of France and for their own feeder convoys connecting with the main Atlantic system. Dutch forces would be integrated with British. Britain and the United States would jointly run the naval war, although the command boundaries were not finally settled.[17]

As much as possible would be done to gain the initiative. It was 'considered most desirable for the control of sea communications for the enemy to be thrown on to the defensive at the outset and that the enemy shall be made to deploy his forces in a defensive role and as widely as possible'.[18]

Certain forces were, therefore, allocated to offensive tasks, although in the Atlantic area they did not stretch much beyond submarines and a few heavy surface units. The main United States carrier task force was allocated to the Mediterranean, and only a single British fleet carrier was available for North Atlantic duties. Its limited-capability air group, with but a single torpedo bomber squadron, could do little more than act as an auxiliary to the British battleship and American battleship (or *Alaska* class large cruiser) allocated with an Anglo-American cruiser squadron of four ships to deal with Soviet surface raiders. The rest of the forces earmarked for the North Atlantic comprised four light carriers (US, Canadian and Dutch, as well as British) and forty-five destroyers and frigates (doubling in six months to about ninety ships), all primarily concerned in convoy escort duties above 32°N. The main escort task was split 50–50 as in the assumption made in 1949 by the British in their 'Revised Restricted Fleet' plan that the United States would bear half the burden of defending Atlantic communications in any future war.[19]

Submarines would have to be relied upon for any offensive close to the Soviet Union itself and no less than forty-nine boats (twenty-two British, twenty-three American and four Dutch) were deemed to be available from Scottish bases to stand off Soviet ports in the opening days of any future war. United States submarine strength was planned to double and then triple as the war progressed, with British strength remaining about the same.[20] Attempts were being made in 1950 to improve the capability of British submarines in the ASW role.[21] Two years before, the British and American naval commands had been able to agree on submarine deployment areas. These were in the Barents Sea off the Kola Inlet, in the approaches to the White Sea, in the Kattegat and in the western approaches to the Baltic.[22]

In addition to the North Atlantic convoy system, a separate Central Atlantic convoy route would be run from the Western Hemisphere to both Gibraltar and the United Kingdom. This was to be an entirely American responsibility with two light carriers and twenty destroyers/destroyer escorts, rising to forty by D+6 on shipping defence duties. In the Mediterranean itself, air cover would be provided within a month by a British light carrier supported soon after by another light carrier and a fully-fledged fleet carrier full of fighters. In addition, Britain would deploy five cruisers, with two more by D+3. The Americans would contribute an increasing force to supplement these ships on shipping defence duties with, within a month, a light carrier, a cruiser and sixteen destroyers/destroyer escorts on station. Within a year, the United States Navy would again be fighting roughly half the Mediterranean shipping defence battle on the Gibraltar–Port Said route with sixty destroyers/destroyer escorts, three cruisers and a couple of small carriers on station.

However the Mediterranean would also see the deployment of the centrepiece of the American naval presence in Eurasian waters, the carrier striking force. This was planned to grow from one fleet carrier, four cruisers and sixteen destroyers on 'D' Day to four carriers by D+1 month and no less than seven by D+3. The carriers would by then be escorted by six cruisers and twenty-eight destroyers. This concentration of fast carrier striking power in the Mediterranean rather than any other theatre is noteworthy. If circumstances were desperate enough, it was agreed that it might be deployed to the Atlantic to help defend Britain, but this seemed unlikely as it contributed the main concentration of offensive and defensive air power protecting the Americans' favoured North African base area. Amphibious forces were also to be sent to the Mediterranean in considerable strength with, some two years into the war, three battleships, two light carriers, ten cruisers and fifty destroyers/destroyer escorts allocated to this duty alone.

Interestingly the Pacific was allocated merely two (later four) cruisers and twenty-four destroyers 'to secure Japan and Okinawa'. In the South Pacific, Australia and New Zealand would be left in control under the ANZAM command arrangements: all British ships would be withdrawn westwards after troops had been safely convoyed to the Middle East.[23]

The defence of the United Kingdom itself absorbed considerable additional naval resources, not only for coastal convoys but for mine countermeasures. The traditional Russian penchant for this type of warfare led to a challenging requirement for over 280 MCM vessels, which was more than twice the 120 ships available. No wonder, therefore, that current British building plans emphasised a new generation of coastal and inshore minesweepers and minehunters. When the Korean War allowed an acceleration, albeit only a limited one, to naval building the MCM vessels retained top priority in the British programme.[24]

By the time *Galloper* was finally approved by the British as an interim short-term Allied war plan, NATO medium- and long-term planning had been in progress for many months. The North Atlantic Treaty came into force on 24 August 1949 and by the end of the year, discussion was in progress on the strategic guidance to be issued by the tripartite US–UK–French 'Standing Group' to the various Regional Planning Groups, the precursors of the integrated NATO commands. The British planners agreed that NATO should adopt as forward a strategy as possible on land both in Western Europe and in Italy. There was also agreement on the concept of the defence of a Scandinavian 'bastion'. Over the Atlantic itself, the British Joint Planners were unhappy at the original American draft aims, viz:

(a) Protect trans-Atlantic lines of communication;
(b) Provide support for anti-submarine, mining and air defence operations;
(c) Prepare broad plans for the defence of Portugal, the Azores, the Madeiras, Iceland and the Faroes.[25]

Interestingly the British wished a greater emphasis placed on offensive operations. Their preferred wording was:

(a) Plan the control of trans-Atlantic lines of communication.
(b) Plan offensive operations to limit the enemy's ability to wage maritime warfare in the North Atlantic.

British planners also wished to add Greenland to the Atlantic group's deliberations rather than to those of the US–Canadian planners. There was also disagreement between the British and the Americans and French over the allocation of responsibility for the defence of sea communications in the Western Mediterranean.[26]

Broad agreement was reached on most issues. It was assessed that the Soviet Union would in war seek to reach the Atlantic seaboard and the Mediterranean and to take the Middle East. The Soviets would also mount air attacks both on Europe and targets in the Western Hemisphere as well as 'initiate naval and air action to sever essential allied lines of sea communication; to establish submarine and mine blockade of important allied ports; and to control her own coastal waters'. All regions shared common tasks, among which were holding securely base areas essential for offensive operations, especially air offensive operations, protecting regional lines of communication, arranging for convoy control and routing, shipping allocation and co-ordination, and defence of coastal waters.[27]

By mid-December 1949, further discussions in Washington had come up with compromise instructions for the North Atlantic Group:

(1) Control trans-Atlantic lines of communication by the necessary offensive and defensive measures.
(2) Prepare plans for the defence of Portugal, the Azores, the Madeiras, Iceland, the Faroes and such other areas as may be decided within the North Atlantic Ocean area.[28]

Agreement seems to have been reached on this, and planning went ahead in 1950. There was some discussion over the nature and extent of the threat. The British Joint Planners played down some of the more alarmist American expectations of the growth of Soviet naval power, and were especially sceptical about the likelihood of carrier construction in the Soviet Union. The British did, however, expect the numbers of 10,000-ton class Soviet cruisers to grow and they thought that the Soviets might have some twenty-five high-speed and seventy ocean-going submarines available for use in the Atlantic by 1954.

As far as the British were concerned, the appropriate response to the naval threat would be offensive operations against the enemy's fleet, shipping, ports and land resources, particularly destruction of the enemy's forces in

Northern Norwegian waters; destruction of U-boats by our submarines; destruction of U-boats, by hunter–killer groups; and offensive minelaying of the approaches to the enemy submarine bases and training areas. Defensive naval operations would be required to protect merchant shipping generally and convoys between the United Kingdom, Caribbean, West Africa, Gibraltar, Norway and North America.

Offensive air operations against enemy surface units would mainly be against light coastal forces operating against our convoys in the Channel and North Sea areas. Offensive minelaying operations would be carried out in the White Sea, Barents Sea, North Sea, Baltic and Scandinavian areas and anti-submarine operations were planned to cover the sea approaches from Iceland to the Orkneys, the Western Approaches, the North Sea, the English Channel and the Straits of Gibraltar where the main threat was anticipated. For defensive convoy escort operations, air escort would be provided by land-based anti-submarine aircraft and deployed so as to cover the convoy routes.[29]

As early as 1949–50, the main lines of the debate about the proper role of sea power in a major war were already beginning to emerge. Over the whole of the postwar period, there has been in naval circles, and more latterly in political and academic ones too, a major debate about the form and the priority that the three main traditional functions of sea power in a serious war would take. The three roles were, and are, Sea Control, Shipping Defence and Power Projection. From the start there was an interesting diversity of early opinion about their relative priority, their interdependence, and the methods by which they could best be achieved. The differences were apparent not merely between the two navies, but within them too. The three roles will be briefly examined in turn.

SEA CONTROL

The United States Navy was determined to retain its offensive carrier warfare as the centre-piece of its naval capabilities. For a variety of reasons, British perspectives on this were different. In the first place, British and American experience in the Second World War had been quite dissimilar. In the Atlantic and elsewhere, the British had successfully conducted a series of campaigns in which fleet carriers, though important, had not played quite so central a role as they had for the Americans in the Pacific. In Germany and Italy, the British had confronted naval adversaries whose main surface units consistently sought to avoid decisive battle and so, in the nature of things, classic battles for naval command were a much less important feature of naval warfare in the European theatre than they had been in the Pacific. Instead, the maritime lesson the British picked up from the Second World War was how much they depended on maritime communications, and how vulnerable those communications could be even to an adversary who attacked them directly by submarine, mining and aircraft, without establishing sea control first. Finally the British simply did not have the resources to construct a first-class navy based on super-carriers. For all these reasons, British naval perspectives were bound to differ from the American.

In the United States, on the other hand, a large and capable carrier force was maintained, even though budgetary constraints were very tight indeed in the 1940s, at least by American standards. The Navy, of course, was determined to add nuclear weapons to its inventory. Despite the pleas of enthusiasts, however, this was not so much to compete with the USAAF/USAF in the strategic bombing role, but to exploit to the fullest degree the capabilities of offensive air operations in the maintenance of sea command.

When faced with stating British views, via the commander of the Sixth Fleet, on the importance of direct defensive operations in the Mediterranean, the Air Warfare Division of the office of the Deputy Chief of Naval Operations (Air) was quite specific on the matter:

> Carrier aviation must retain the bulk of its strength in *offensive power* if it is to support a truly offensive Navy rather than a defensive one. Our Navy must carry out numerous functions other than defensive antisubmarine warfare and must possess the self-contained ability to move at will and wage offensive war against the enemy in the air, on the surface and below the surface.[30]

This emphasis on offensive operations for sea control did provide capabilities that could be used for other purposes. For example, Sixth Fleet carrier groups were considered the primary means of gaining air supremacy and providing offensive air support against Soviet land thrusts.[31] This was a major factor in subsequent disputes over Allied Command in the Mediterranean. In the American view, Sixth Fleet carriers were such an important element in local Allied air power that they could not be allocated to a separate naval command devoted merely to sea control and the defence of communications. The Americans argued that the carrier-based power projection mission must always take precedence.

All the same, British planners, no less than the American, were keen to emphasise the 'forward' and offensive aspects of maritime strategy. The Admiralty's airmen, frustrated in their initial efforts to develop large nuclear-capable bombers, insisted that the new, high-perforance jet fighters should be produced in strike versions. This led to considerable opposition from the Royal Air Force, which saw its forthcoming medium 'V' bombers as the primary means of attacking enemy sea power 'at source'.

In Britain such inter-Service haggling led to the convening of a Maritime Air Defence Committee, chaired by General Sir Gerald Templer, to look into the question of the role of air power in the defence of sea communications in a war against Russia starting at the NATO planning date of 1954.[32] Significantly, the Templar Committee steered away from the vexed question of offensive carrier air operations against enemy bases, both because this was beyond the immediate capabilities of the Royal Navy and because it would have set the Services at each other's throats.

Even the United States had but limited numbers of strike carriers and they still had their Mediterranean preoccupations. Nevertheless, as early as 1949, long-term American war plans had included a North Atlantic carrier task force containing one American and one British attack carrier group that, together with submarines, would carry out 'offensive operations against the source of threat' to sea communications. These attacks were 'considered the most effective and least expensive means of obtaining desired results ...'[33]

The outbreak of the Korean War allowed these plans to come to fruition rather earlier than had been expected. The planned run-down of the American carrier force was postponed, and eventually abandoned. Also in 1950 and early 1951 American carriers began to acquire the beginnings of a nuclear capability with the first deliveries of AJ-1 Savage aircraft and with the Presidential decision in September 1950 to allow the storage of nuclear bomb components in the largest American carriers. Although the first operational deployment of nuclear capable aircraft was, as expected, to the Mediterranean in February 1951, the role of the US Navy's nuclear strike force was also 'to destroy the capabilities of the Soviet surface and submarine fleets in areas within a 500-mile radius of the ... Norwegian and Bering Seas'.[34]

The centrality of carrier forces for sea control and the growing propensity for these to be used in what would later become known as 'Forward Operations' were amply demonstrated in the comprehensive description of the roles of carrier forces produced by the Joint Chiefs of Staff in 1951:

> These forces represent the major striking power of the Navy and are primarily responsible for neutralising at the source the enemy's offensive capabilities to threaten control of the seas. These forces will destroy enemy naval forces and shipping, attack naval bases, attack airfields threatening control of the seas, support amphibious forces and support the mining offensive. As additional tasks the carrier striking forces will defend bases and vital areas against attack through the seas as required.[35]

Although the Sixth Fleet in the Mediterranean still rated special mention, a new and crucially important carrier striking force was about to be born, the Atlantic Striking Fleet, capable of carrying out the above missions beyond the Straits of Gibraltar. Anglo-American haggling held up the creation of NATO's Atlantic Command until 1952. When it was created this new structure, as well as allocating the crucial Eastern Atlantic area to the British Home Fleet Commander, set up a separate Striking Fleet Command with two subordinate carrier groups, one American and one British. The striking fleet was a more ambitious successor to the limited 'covering' fleet of earlier plans. As a British document put it in 1953:

> The Atlantic 'Striking Fleet' consists of British and American Battleships, Carriers, Cruisers and Destroyers. Its role is analogous to the Grand Fleet of World War I and the British Home Fleet of World War II, namely the offensive force for Atlantic and Northern waters and the essential cover under which defensive forces, protecting our shipping from attack by aircraft, submarine and mine can do their work ... Attacks by aircraft from the Carrier Striking Fleet on the sources of the various threats to our sea communications can materially reduce these threats. In this they are complementary to attacks by shore-based air forces. Heavy attacks can be launched with balanced forces of fighters and bombers. The enemy will be forced into a large defensive effort since the direction and height of attack can be varied, and we have the choice of several types of weapon (e.g. atom bomb, torpedo, large rocket).[36]

The new emphasis on 'attack at source' and the echoes of the 1951 American document are noteworthy. This British statement was part of a major tussle being fought out in Whitehall over whether Britain should continue to possess offensive strike carriers. A later paragraph of the same document spelled out the rationale for a British striking fleet contribution that eventually, after a long and bitter dispute, won the day:

> Although the Americans provide the greater part of the Striking Fleet, we cannot leave to an ally complete responsibility for offensive Naval warfare. We must continue to provide our share, on which the Americans – who also maintain powerful striking forces in the Mediterranean and Pacific – are relying, and without which we cannot expect a voice in the employment of these forces. Furthermore, until the American element of the Striking Fleet can reach this side of the Atlantic, the British element will need to hold the ring alone.[37]

The smaller British carriers would be better able to do this, once the British acquired nuclear capabilities of their own. By 1952, it was clear that by the end of the decade small British 'tactical' nuclear bombs would be available. These could be fitted to the carrier fighters planned for that period but, to provide more enhanced capabilities for the 1960s, a relatively small, high-performance jet strike aircraft began to be developed by the British. To allay RAF fears, however, dealing with the Soviet's *Sverdlov* cruiser threat on the high seas was given priority. This was an agreed role for carrier aircraft. The notion of the 'attack at source' remained too controversial to stake the survival of the new NA39 (later Buccaneer) upon it.

THE PROTECTION OF SEA COMMUNICATIONS

The main threat to sea communications came from submarines and aircraft, but there was some disagreement between the British and Americans over the operational doctrine to be employed. Britain tended to emphasise convoy operations as the main priority. As the First Sea Lord, Lord Fraser, put it in 1948: 'Planning can only proceed on something we know we must do: escort safely our convoys'.[38] The escort role took priority, along with a new generation of escort frigates, and a force of fighter and ASW aircraft for a trade protection role. Larger fleet carriers, with higher performance fighters would protect Mediterranean convoys from the attacks of land-based aircraft along the lines of Malta convoys of the Second World War.

More offensive carrier operations were considered, and indeed attempted in exercises, but available equipment kept the aggressive instincts of British naval planners in check. The lack of suitable aircraft in sufficient numbers, and the foreseeable permanence of the deficiency both advised the escort priority. In October 1949 the Chiefs of Staff decided not to proceed with a large carrier strike aircraft.[39]

The Maritime Air Defence Committee, chaired by General Sir Gerald Templer had paid particular regard to the question of the role of air power in the defence of sea communications in a war against the Soviet Union. The Committee looked at the problem in two contexts, with the Russians on their current line and with the Russians in control of the Biscay coast, Scandinavia and the north shores of the Mediterranean, but not Spain and Portugal.

The Committee believed that mining and air attacks on the approaches to ports would account for half total shipping casualties, but the Soviets would also be able to deploy from the outset six large fast submarines in the North Atlantic as far south as the equator, eleven large, slower boats in the North Eastern Atlantic down to the Azores, eleven medium submarines in the North and Norwegian Seas and a dozen small coastal boats in the southern North Sea. This was assessed as three times the U-boats that the Germans deployed early in the Second World War and, given the increase in submarine capabilities since 1945, the equivalent of the U-boat threat at its height in the Atlantic battle in early 1943. In such circumstances, half NATO's convoys would be attacked.

If the Soviets occupied Western Europe, the numbers of submarines in the North Atlantic area would go up from seventeen to twenty-eight. The main threat in the Mediterranean at the beginning of hostilities would come from the air, but between three and six Soviet submarines might operate there. The Mediterranean would probably be closed by the Soviets if they occupied its northern littoral. Whatever the circumstances ten Soviet cruisers might be on the prowl in the area south of Iceland and Greenland down to about 50°N from the outbreak of war.

The Committee concluded that the 'successful defence of our shipping requires both close defence of convoys and offensive operations in the submarine transit areas'. In order to prevent a Soviet submarine build-up, two boats per month had to be sunk in the transit areas and three around convoys.[40]

The British actually believed in convoy. British admirals tended to be shocked at their American counterparts' choice of priorities and evident failure to grasp the convoy principle. In late 1948 Admiral Sir Rhoderick McGrigor, the C-in-C Home Fleet, visited his American counterpart, the C-in-C Atlantic Fleet, Admiral Lynde McCormick. CinClant told McGrigor that until enough escorts were available, merchantmen should sail independently and not in convoys. McGrigor persuaded the Americans that even a weak escort was preferable to none in submarine-infested water. 'It seems difficult', he wrote to Lord Fraser, the First Sea Lord, 'to believe that the USN have not learned this lesson from their experiences on their East Coast in 1942.' McGrigor was also able to get agreement that escort took priority over independent operations for hunter–killer groups. The latter, when originally formed, would be used primarily as support groups for convoys in dangerous areas. The 'safe and timely arrival' of convoys was the main priority, not 'hunting to death of U-boats' as preferred by some American ASW specialists.[41]

POWER PROJECTION

The beginning of 1951 also saw the foundation of NATO's command structure, with the setting up of Allied Command Europe (ACE) under Supreme Allied Commander Europe (SACEUR). The first SACEUR, General Eisenhower, placed great emphasis on the sea and air strike assets available to him from the flanks to counterbalance his existing weakness on the Central Front. Direct naval support to SACEUR thus became an important role for American carriers and, from 1952, nuclear weapons were allocated to this role.[42] The utility of the allied carriers providing support ashore in the Korean War also demonstrated their potential in 'warm' conflicts in the Far East.

From the early days NATO's Northern Flank, Norway and Denmark, was seen to be an area where the early commitment of sea-based aircraft in support of SACEUR was especially vital. The reluctance of both these nations to have foreign troops deployed on their territory in peace-time placed special emphasis on the need for maritime support. The Norwegians, faced with the dilemma of ensuring NATO support in these circumstances, succeeded in obtaining a British admiral, Sir Patrick Brind, as the first NATO Commander Allied Forces North (AFNORTH). This reflected the general Norwegian desire, as Rolf Tamnes has put it, firmly to 'nail' both the United States and Britain to Northern Europe.[43]

Significantly the scenario for the first NATO Atlantic exercise was the use of the NATO Striking Fleet to give AFNORTH support. Four American fleet carriers were assembled and two British, along with a British battleship, an American battleship and five cruisers. Their task was (a) the interdiction and destruction of enemy forces in Norway, (b) air support for NATO ground forces in Norway and (c) air and land support for NATO ground forces in Denmark. A convoy to Bergen was also to be sailed with light carrier escort and covered by the main striking fleet. The various forces sailed from the Clyde and the Forth, and moved up to the Arctic Circle, operating as far north as 68° (the latitude of Vestfjord). Bad weather caused serious difficulties in these waters, and the British carriers proved better able to operate aircraft than the American. This reduced the level of air activity by some 80 per cent. Cruisers and destroyers gave some naval gunfire support against targets ashore and a Canadian cruiser, emerging like a *Sverdlov* raider from the northern fjords, was also successfully dealt with. After this, the Striking Fleet moved down to Denmark to provide air support there and to cover the landings of an amphibious convoy sailed from the Firth of Forth. Again the weather caused difficulties and a new beach had to be found at the last minute. Nevertheless the landings were successfully carried out and another 'raider' trying to emerge from the Skagerrak was dealt with by surface units and land-based air forces.

The following year the canvas for the main Atlantic exercise was wider, involving sea control and shipping defence operations as well as activities in support of SACEUR. The scenario seems to have been rather more pessimistic, with Soviet warships being intercepted in the Denmark Strait, and air and land bombardments being planned against an enemy-held Iceland. The weather in 1953 proved even worse than in the previous year and the carriers were unable to mount their attacks. They were little more successful when they moved out to support SACEUR from the west of Ireland. The vulnerability of the carriers to land-based air attacks shown in this near-fiasco raised doubts about the ability of contemporary carrier battle groups to take on land-based air forces. Direct carrier support (an old British carrier with an ASW/fighter air group) did, however, provide useful cover for another Bergen convoy.[44]

The multi-faceted nature of this exercise was interesting in that, by involving operations across command boundaries, it presaged what was to become one of NATO's major problem areas subsequently, namely the effective co-ordination of the different commands, both at sea and ashore. At one level there was the issue of the relationship between SACEUR and SACLANT. Below this the equally delicate relationship between SACLANT (an American) and CINCEASTLANT (a Briton). Both exercises had been run primarily by CINCEASTLANT, the British C-in-C Home Fleet from shore headquarters at Pitreavie in 1952 and from the new permanent installation at Northwood in 1953. The Striking Fleet, however, was directly responsible to SACLANT in Norfolk. After these two exercises the extent of Striking Fleet's independence from CINCEASTLANT became a matter of some debate. It had been agreed that the Striking Fleet should be under CINCEASTLANT's operational control when operating in his area. The Americans, however, wished to allow COMSTRIKEFLT to participate dirctly in policy decisions in support of the battle ashore owing to his special knowledge of his fleet's capabilities. SACLANT insisted, therefore, that 'Commander Striking Fleet must plan, under the coordination of CINCEASTLANT, for the use of the Fleet, and that he must communicate direct with shore Commanders when operating, under the operational control and coordination of SACLANT and CINCEASTLANT, in support of the land battle.'[45]

In the Mediterranean the division of offensive carrier and direct sea control forces was clearer. In the compromise, reluctantly accepted by Britain at the end of 1952, the American admiral who was CINCSOUTH and therefore responsible to SACEUR for land defence of the area would control his own American carrier and amphibious 'Naval Striking and Support' HQ at Naples. In parallel, a separate joint naval command was set up directly subordinate to SACEUR, C-in-C Allied Forces Mediterranean, under the British C-in-C Mediterranean Fleet at Malta. Mountbatten, the first CINCAFMED, was jealous of his prerogatives. 'I am the sole Allied Naval Command in the Mediterranean', he declared, insisting, '... that this new Strike Headquarters does not start trying to usurp my functions'.[46] There was, indeed, much room for uncertainty and diplomacy in the degree of co-ordination between CINCSOUTH's power projection navy and his sea control and shipping protection fleet.

This quite detailed examination of early naval thinking on the three roles of sea control, the protection of shipping and operations against the shore, shows that many of the issues that were to beset NATO's planners throughout the postwar period were in a sense present at the creation. In particular it shows that the recent debate on both sides of the Atlantic about the relative strategic validity of 'forward operations' north of the Greenland–Iceland–UK gap when compared to that of the direct defence of shipping by convoy-and-escort and other such measures is no new phenomenon. Together with the British inputs into NATO planning mentioned above, it also demonstrates that there was within the Royal Navy, and perhaps despite its experience in the Second World War, a broad measure of agreement with the general desirability for such assertive uses of sea power when resources allowed.

In the same way these early debates raised a second major issue of the whole postwar period, namely the centrality of Anglo-American sea power to the defeat of an Eastern coalition that was seen as still being fundamentally a land power. Could the whale defeat the elephant, and if so, how? Some naval planners on both sides of the Atlantic, in the traditions of Corbett, may have seen the strike carrier as a modern and effective way of exploiting the inherent flexibility of sea power against a land-bound adversary. Others, also in the traditions of Corbett, pointed out that sea power on its own was not enough, and not least because, as these early exercises seemed to suggest, the carrier's capacity to prevail against land-based air power could not be taken for granted. Perhaps then, the true contribution of sea power to victory in the European theatre lay not so much in independent naval operations around the flanks but more in the unglamorous, even humdrum, matter of assuring the arrival of American and other reinforcements from across the Atlantic.

But there was another possible way by which Anglo-American sea power could exert decisive influence on the outcome of a land war in Europe and this was by getting into the business of nuclear deterrence.

THE NUCLEAR REVOLUTION

The defence of Atlantic reinforcements and resupplies seemed predicated on an assumption that the war in Western Europe would last long enough for their arrival to be relevant. But by the early 1950s there was a growing band of sceptics who doubted whether such a war would be either feasible or desirable, or both. Should such views gain political prominence, it would plainly not make sense for naval planners to hitch their wagon to the idea of the long war.

In 1952, as Britain moved towards a national nuclear capability, the British Chiefs of staff were given the task of a full-scale strategic reassessment. Another factor in this re-think was the British recognition that Britain (and perhaps even the United States) could not afford to keep up with the pace of rearmament over the long haul. Already shortages of resources were forcing the British rearmament programme, inspired by the Korean war, to be wound down. It seemed necessary to take advantage of the nuclear revolution to make strategically coherent what was economically inevitable.

In their week's deliberations at Greenwich at the end of April and beginning of May 1952, the Chiefs decided that a full-scale war would begin with a few weeks' hostilities of an unprecedented intensity, when all British efforts should be directed towards the enemy's military capabilities. The United States would, it was assumed, be directing itself in a more broadly-based strategic offensive at the enemy's industries and morale. After this nuclear exchange, the war would enter into a 'broken backed' period in which the two sides would try to recuperate from the damage they had sustained so that a further, more intense, period of hostilities might be possible later to achieve victory. The task of the Royal Navy in the first phase was to add its weight to the initial offensive against the Soviet Union and its navy and to maintain sea communications. The latter would also be necessary in the 'broken backed' phase which might be more intense at sea than elsewhere.[47]

With Britain unable to meet even the Chiefs of Staff's reduced force goals, the logic of global strategy was developed further as a 'Radical Review' of defence policy took place throughout 1953 and 1954. The initial period of hostilities was defined at six weeks and, as mentioned above, a major inter-Service struggle was played out over the relative roles of sea- and land-based air power in this initial stage. Although the British and American navies had different interests and perspectives about such initial tasks as an attack at source on their Soviet counterpart, the key argument saving the British carrier force proved to be the influence Carrier Striking Group 2 exercised in the employment of the whole Striking Fleet.[48] Just as the V-bombers would, it was hoped, give Britain some say in the direction of the main component of American strategic forces, so the carriers would provide the means to influence the maritime component of the nuclear offensive.

When first exposed to the new British ideas, the Americans had been less than impressed at what seemed to them suspiciously like backsliding from agreed Medium Term Plan force goals as substantially reaffirmed at Lisbon. Nevertheless the change of administration in 1953, coupled with a recognition of the economic costs of 'across the board' rearmament, persuaded Eisenhower to follow the lead set by Churchill. Like their British counterparts just over a year before, the Joint Chiefs in July 1953 were set to thinking about strategic priorities and to encourage agreement they were eventually incarcerated in the President's yacht *Sequoia*.

The result was the 'New Look', or what Secretary of State Dulles a few months later called 'Massive Retaliation'.[49] This strategy emphasised the use of nuclear weapons to attack a broad spectrum of targets in general war. Carriers might well play a significant role in this wider offensive. As the recently retired Chairman of the Joint Chiefs, General Bradley, had put it:

> While the main responsibility for strategic bombing must remain with the air force, in my opinion the primary mission of the big carriers is shifting towards strategic air attack. Because the enemy doesn't know where the flat tops are cruising – as he does the location of airfields – their existence is a powerful additional deterrent to totalitarian aggression.[50]

The effect of this on the role of American carriers was signfiicant. As Sokolsky says of the Sixth Fleet: 'By 1954, American aircraft carriers earmarked for SACEUR had begun to shift their primary focus from battlefield support to nuclear strike against targets deep in Warsaw Pact [sic] territory including the Soviet Union'.[51] This created targeting problems for the conduct of the strategic air offensive and full co-ordination between the two offensives only came in 1960–1 with the first Single Integrated Operational Plan (SIOP).[52]

The H-Bomb, whose practicality and awesome power seems to have been first fully appreciated in Britain in 1954, strengthened the nuclear emphasis still further. As Britain decided that year to produce H-bombs of its own, the Chiefs of Staff produced yet another strategic reassessment in the light of the new weapons. This emphasised that 'an immediate and overwhelming counter-offensive with the most powerful nuclear weapons appears the only hope of defeating the enemy's attempt to destroy us and bring the war to an early halt'. Russia, they argued, 'has now emerged as a first class naval power. We can expect that, concurrently with strategic air operations, major attacks will be made by Soviet naval, land and amphibious forces ... against Western Europe and our sea communications'. Attacks would also take place in the Middle East and Far East. 'The scale and progress of these offensive operations will depend on the extent of the preparedness of the forces situated in and readily available for reinforcement of these areas, and on how quickly the allied strategic air offensive can take effect.' Western command of the sea would be obtained by primarily offensive action against the Soviet Union 'destroying her fleet, her mercantile marine and her bases'.[53]

Control of sea communications, however, had a long-term impact, for purposive war-fighting would continue beyond the initial stage. 'In spite of the devastating effect of the initial bombardments on both sides, the war is likely to go on.'[54] The conditions in which it would do so were spelled out by the British Naval Staff's Plans Division in October 1954. As far as Britain was concerned the situation would be desperate indeed: all large towns substantially destroyed, industry practically at a halt, major airfields out of action, the Army at home employed on civil defence duties, and the Navy reduced to those ships and aircraft and men that were abroad or at sea on the outbreak of war.[55]

Despite all this, however, there would be no surrender, and feeding the survivors would be necessary. Indeed, devastated Britain would, as far as possible 'continue to play an offensive role against the enemy'. The Navy would '... seize the initiative at sea by offensive operations so as to:

(a) keep open our sea supply lines to feed the population of these islands;
(b) defend merchant shipping from air attack, including while unloading in this country, where this could not be undertaken by the remnants of the R.A.F.;
(c) ferrying in fighter aircraft from overseas and war stores of all descriptions'.[56]

To quite a large extent, therefore, these British reviews of the strategic priorities of the 1950s seemed to confirm the need for many of the traditional roles of the American and British navies even in the desperate circumstances attending a thermonuclear war between East and West. But in military terms it was hardly an attractive picture, nor one likely to have much appeal in political circles.

In the longer term the Admiralty also wished the Navy to develop nuclear and thermonuclear capabilities of its own so as to be able to add its weight to the nuclear offensive in war and the deterrent in peace.⁵⁷ Carriers would provide the current and medium-term offensive air power and it was expected that shorter-range sea-based missiles would pose fewer problems than long-range intercontinental systems. They could thus be deployed relatively early on seaborne platforms, both surface and submarine.

There were many indications that the Soviet Union had taken an early lead in putting nuclear missiles at sea. Certainly this emerging menace had a strong influence on American perceptions. At the beginning of 1954, Admiral Hughes Hallett, head of the British naval mission in Washington, wrote home with disturbing news that the Americans now seemed to care more about the potential submarine threat to the homeland with nuclear-armed short-range cruise missiles than the traditional submarine threat to sea communications. This threatened to undermine the agreed division of labour in shipping defence between the two nations. Hughes Hallett thought it would lead the Americans to concentrate on the defence of their eastern seaboard, building up barriers of small submarines between Halifax and Bermuda together with the allocation of valuable hunter–killer groups to non-NATO 'Eastern Sea Frontier Commands'.⁵⁸

The British Naval Staff tried to divert this concern for home defence into a forward defence doctrine that would catch Soviet submarines in their bases by air attack and, as they came out, by mine and submarine. There were great hopes for passive sonar detection, especially by fixed arrays covering important areas that Soviet submarines might use like the 'gaps' between the Orkneys, Shetlands, Faroes and Iceland. Indeed the development of modern passive sonar techniques promised in the mid-1950s to revolutionise ASW in the Atlantic generally. Britain had a shallow water system called 'Corsair' under development and the United States was beginning deployment of longer-ranged low-frequency arrays – in effect the beginnings of the SOSUS system. Despite early problems, it was hoped that such developments would give ASW operations more the character of air defence. By 1954, the British naval mission in Washington was aware of SACLANT's 'New Look Atlantic' plan which involved 'underwater sound stations' and 'atomic depth charges'.⁵⁹

With such devices it seemed to both the American and British navies that the nuclear offensive carrier group was the key both to defending the residual sea communications required after the initial thermonuclear strikes and to the defence of the American homeland from an increasingly capable Soviet striking force. Their general agreement on such matters and indeed their ability to co-operate in the development of highly classified technologies illustrate the profundity of the special naval relationship between the two countries.

Despite the attention given to nuclear-armed carriers, it was clear that submarines had a vital part to play in this defence in depth as well. Nuclear-propelled submarines were especially suited to a forward strategy, with smaller, less capable boats providing inner barriers. The British Flag Officer Submarines (FOS/M) controlled the boats in the critical areas closest to the Soviet Union, a situation which the Americans consistently felt would be untenable in war. The logic that turned British carriers into strings with which to pull the Striking Fleet into the directions which the British wanted, applied just as much to submarines. It is not surprising in these circumstances that the Royal Navy wanted its own nuclear submarine as quickly as possible. Only by this means could it expect to keep its vital role in controlling the forward submarine war.[50]

Long-range plans produced by both the American and British navies in the mid-1950s articulated a continuing faith in the role of sea power even in a full-scale nuclear war, offensively and defensively, strategically and tactically. But naval planners on both sides of the Atlantic could not but be aware that their views were regarded with as much scepticism as were those of their putative adversaries in the Soviet Union. Admiral Gorshkov therefore effectively spoke for all sailors when he complained:

> It turned out unfortunately that we had some very influential 'authorities' who considered that with the appearance of atomic weapons the Navy had completely lost its value as a branch of the armed forces. According to their views, all of the basic missions in a future war allegedly could be fully resolved without the participation of the Navy.[61]

The appropriate military (and no doubt political) response to this situation for all the major navies was not only to continue to defend the validity of their traditional roles even in a nuclear conflict, but also to emphasise their new roles in strategic strike and strategic defence. Moreover these roles were plainly not discrete, but mutually supportive. Effective ASW in the Atlantic, for example, would obviously facilitate the effective performance of any or all of these roles. The American and British navies in the nuclear age offered not this role or that, but a coherent package of roles aimed at coping with a wide range of wartime contingencies. It was against this background that the celebrated comment in the British Defence White Paper of 1957 that 'the role of naval forces in total war is somewhat uncertain'[62] should be seen.

Certainly there was no doubt that the Russians had embarked very early on a determined campaign to put nuclear-armed missiles at sea. The idea of their using nuclear-tipped torpedoes against targets in Western ports was taken seriously and in September 1955 they fired their first nuclear-capable missile at sea. These experiments produced the Zulu-V class of 1956–7, the world's first SLBM firing submarine, followed by the Golf and Hotel classes of 1958.[63] In view of this there could hardly be any disputing the need for the British and American navies to follow the lead set by their adversary. This would involve two things.

Firstly, they would need to deal with the menace posed by these submarines, and even more by the much more sophisticated ones that would certainly follow.[64] Secondly, the obvious counter to the Soviet SSBN force was for the West to produce a bigger and better one of its own. Nuclear missile-firing Polaris submarines would be even more hard to locate than land-based ICBMs: together the two forces would provide for mutual deterrence in which pre-emption was impossible. As well as being more stable, a 'finite' American deterrent of this kind would also release resources for enhanced capabilities 'for countering local and peripheral activities which were the most likely form of local aggression'.[65]

However much President Eisenhower might lament its dangers, the size of the American military–industrial complex meant that, once it had been decided to initiate a radical programme, rapid progress would be made. With their Polaris programme, which only began in 1955, the United States Navy had swept into a commanding lead by the end of the decade.

These ideas were echoed in Britain too. Indeed, in 1954, when Rhoderick McGrigor was First Sea Lord, the naval staff had discussed the advantages of 'submersible launching ships' for ballistic missiles. Vessels like this would reduce the deterrent's vulnerability to enemy attack and draw fire away from British territory. Moreover the fact that the missiles in question need not have the range of their land-based counterparts, meant they could be ready much earlier. For such reasons, the Naval Staff believed prophetically that, 'By 1965 the essential steps towards forming a striking force of submarines capable of firing ballistic rockets far into enemy territory might have begun.'[66]

Mountbatten was also to prove sympathetic to such ideas. He thought a few British missile submarines could make an important contribution to a general Western 'finite' deterrent. However Mountbatten was amongst those who had considerable reservations about a completely 'independent' British deterrent, since this might swallow up far too many scarce defence resources.[67] The potential opportunity costs for the rest of the Navy of a British SLBM programme also advised caution against too energetic a pursuit of total independence.

The answer seemed to lie in close co-operation with the United States Navy. Paradoxically it was in this most sensitive of areas that Anglo-American co-operation was at its height. The British had always been interested in nuclear propulsion for submarines and, despite the early opposition of Admiral Rickover, won for themselves an advantageous position in American development of the concept. The same went for the Polaris programme.[68]

PREPARING FOR LESS THAN ABSOLUTE WARS

Both before and in the midst of the era of massive retaliation, the American and British navies increasingly recognised that their main strategic priority was in fact likely to be in less cataclysmic scenarios. In 1947, Britain's economic crisis had caused serious cuts in naval capability and the active fleet had been slashed to maintain mobilisation potential. Naval planners, however, were very aware of the serious consequences that this naval decline had on perceptions of British power around the world. This perception and the deterioration of the Cold War in early 1948, led the British Chiefs of Staff to place much greater emphasis on the maintenance of peace-time forces to maintain prestige and, if necessary, exert limited naval force to sustain Western power in Asia, Africa and South America.

In 1949 the emphasis on Cold War priorities became more explicit. If presented with the choice, preparedness for 'hot war' was to be sacrificed to Cold War tasks. The main priority of the British 1949 Revised Restricted Fleet Plan was to maintain a fleet capable of carrying out the foreign and colonial policy of the government in peace-time. The requirements of such a fleet were not, however, very carefully thought out. Amphibious forces continued to be neglected, greater reliance being put instead on the traditionally flexible cruiser to show the flag and exert limited force when required.[69]

The rationale for the maintenance of naval capacity outside European waters was varied but received wide support from all sides. At this stage Britain still believed itself to be a global Power, if not a Superpower, with colonies, dependencies and interests to protect in a wider world. At a time when the Royal Navy was extensively involved in anti-immigration patrols off Palestine, was active in the Chinese Civil war, and played a significant part in the naval dimension of the Korean War, there were few to dispute so obvious a role.[70]

Despite the frustrations of the Korean War, the concept of limited war or, as the British called it, 'warm war', began to loom large in Anglo-American naval planning. The 1952 British Global Strategy Paper put considerable emphasis on the primary need to maintain forces for lesser purposes. In a supporting Paper, the Foreign Office stressed the need to maintain prestige at all costs in order that the United States could be encouraged gradually to take up the burden of Britain's part of the maintenance of Western interests.[71] The 'cold' and 'warm' war roles, as proved in Korea, were also emphasised in the carrier debates of 1952–4, and so were the possible political implications of the possible command changes that could be brought about by Britain's abandoning a carrier role. As Britain's naval programmes were repeatedly cut by Churchill's administration, the peacetime role took greater priority still: the minesweeper programme was cut to maintain the fleet carriers; modernisation of the anti-aircraft armament of cruisers was sacrificed still further, and larger cruisers retained instead of smaller ones, in order to sustain shore bombardment capabilities and the general 'presence' of the remaining fleet. The battleship *Vanguard* was maintained in commission, but without ammunition and only at three months' notice for action, in order to keep up appearances.[72]

As the more limited naval role took priority, greater thought and substance began to be given to it. In 1956, the First Sea Lord, Lord Mountbatten, skilfully emphasised the limited war role of the Royal Navy in the Eden Government's new, even more swinging defence review. The Suez fiasco was converted into a magnificent illustration both of the weaknesses of Britain's existing maritime intervention capabilities and of the potential of new techniques, for example the use of carrier-borne helicopters in vertical envelopment operations. The role of the large fleet carrier in limited war was also vindicated. This all stood the Royal Navy in good stead when the new Prime Minister, Harold Macmillan, brought the long story of Conservative defence reviews to a climax with the appointment of Duncan Sandys to the Defence Ministry in 1957. The new Minister's powers were enhanced to allow him to engage in root-and-branch reform.[73]

Mountbatten was able to build on the work of his able predecessor, Rhoderick McGrigor, and his Naval Staff, who had already defined and articulated the need for a 'cold/warm war' priority in 1954.[74] Now the argument was made even more forcefully and skilfully. The Chiefs of Staff were pressed to give the carrier their unanimous endorsement as a weapon of 'cold' and limited war 'East of Suez'. Although it offended the Navy in other respects, the 1957 Defence White Paper at least spelled out a continued need for British sea power. 'On account of its mobility', the paper asserted, 'the Royal Navy, together with the Royal Marines, provides another effective means of bringing power to bear in peacetime emergencies or limited hostilities'.[75] Maritime intervention capabilities were also to be improved, the lessons of Suez having led to plans permanently to convert light fleet carriers into 'commando carrier' assault vessels. Although the purely conventional aspects of these interventions might themselves be limited, the commitment was clearly made to a maritime strategy of limited means to maintain Britain's remaining commitments around the world.

In the United States the peace-time utility of sea power and naval presence was never ignored, although it tended to be regarded as a side-effect of a navy that was essentially designed for 'hot' war. The explosion of the Soviet nuclear bomb, and the re-thinking of American strategy that ensued, led to more careful thought being given to this subject. NSC-68, the strategic policy paper that set out the intellectual basis for the build-up of American military power that Korea later facilitated, stated that limited aggressions by the Communists would only meet a limited response. In a world of two nuclear Superpowers, it argued (quoting Federalist No. 28), 'the means must be measured to the extent of the mischief'.[76]

In its first report of December 1955, the Long Range Objective Group (Op-93) envisaged a 'retreat' from a primarily nuclear strategy. 'The United States, facing a powerful Soviet nuclear force, would probably seek a tacit or overt agreement limiting the use of nuclear weapons. That in turn would limit the US ability to deter conventional attack, and the LRO saw a need for increasingly powerful non-nuclear forces'.[77] Admiral Arleigh Burke had been appointed CNO the previous August and he was a long-standing critic of massive retaliation. He strengthened LRO and its role, and in January 1958 Op-93 promulgated a vital new paper, 'The Navy of the 1970 Era'. This forecast that the primary mission of the fleet would be to deter or fight limited wars.[78]

Clearly, thinking in the two navies took a very similar path on what a later era was to call 'out-of-area' concerns. This reflected not merely the close relations of the two navies but a general coincidence of view in the respective foreign policies of the two countries. Indeed the British believed that their contribution to the defence of Western interests in such places as the Indian Ocean was in some ways a premium whose payment guaranteed close relations with the United States, and so would buttress British security back home. But the Suez affair of 1956 showed that this cosy relationship had its limits; moreover the way that the Sixth Fleet sought to interfere with the British conduct of the operation showed that the two navies could easily become involved in the tensions such quarrels created.

As the 1950s and 1960s developed, there arose many external confirmations of the importance for the British and Americans in maintaining and expanding their capacities for limited war and naval diplomacy generally. In the Soviet Union, the Khruschev regime placed new emphasis on the idea of peaceful economic competition with the West and of the resolute defence of the inevitable growth of world socialism, especially in those areas recently liberated from the yoke of colonialism. The prospect of Western interests around the world being enveloped by the growth of Soviet power and influence seemed at the time to be alarmingly likely. From the early 1960s onwards, indeed, the Soviet Navy itself began to develop as a significant instrument for 'defence of the forces of peace and progress' wherever they should seem threatened. The Soviet Navy made its first serious debut in that guise in 1967, during the Arab-Israeli war.[79]

Not surprisingly, therefore, both navies found themselves, through the 1950s and 1960s, engaged in a series of sometimes quite demanding activities outside the main area of strategic confrontation, for example, off the Lebanon in 1958, the Chinese Offshore Islands Dispute of 1958, the defence of Kuwait in 1961, the Confrontation with Indonesia 1962-6 and, most obviously, the Vietnam War. The requirements of such distant operations included foreign bases, extensive replenishment and amphibious capacities, and, above all, the kind of organic air support that only carriers could provide.

In 1962, against the US Navy's wishes, carriers were officially removed from the SIOP, the strategic nuclear war plan. As Secretary of Defense Robert McNamara put it to Congress:

The principal use of the attack carriers in the years ahead will be in the limited war role. As we acquire larger forces of strategic missiles and Polaris submarines, the need for the attack carrier in the general war role will diminish. However they will still retain a significant nuclear strike capability which could augment our Strategic Retaliatory Forces. But in the Limited War and Cold War roles, the attack carrier force provides a most important and unique capability.[80]

One novel form of limited war that began to be explored at this stage was the idea of a Superpower confrontation confined to the oceans. Prompted by the Berlin Crisis of 1959, Arleigh Burke ordered feasibility studies to be made of limited naval responses to harassments. By 1962, the US Atlantic Fleet Commander had an operational plan to take maritime reprisals against Warsaw Pact shipping, both naval and civilian.[81] Paul Nitze developed the idea further when he was Secretary of the Navy from 1963 to 1967. Nitze 'visualised such a maritime war as presenting not only a lesser chance of deterioration into nuclear war against homeland targets, but a wholly plausible alternative on its own merit'.[82] By 1967, the CINCLANT had 'OPLAN 2300' for 'War at Sea'. This envisaged operations 'specifically designed to apply a measure of force in support of a national policy of determined persuasion' or alternately which might 'be implemented as a controlled response to Soviet military aggression short of a strategic nuclear attack'. Military force was to be applied in 'measured' ways with possible escalation to operations of 'the highest intensity' in which the American Fleet in the Atlantic 'would be in complete confrontation with Soviet forces at sea in warfare short of the strategic use of nuclear weapons'.[83]

As the United States Navy's flexible response strategy was being thus developed for northern waters as well as warmer climes, American and British officers faced the more mundane but immediate questions of resource allocation and equipment procurement. In the era of 'cost-effectiveness' that began with McNamara's arrival in the Pentagon, increasingly specific mission definition was probably inevitable. The traditional flexibility of naval forces had to be broken down into 'roles and missions' for the systems analysts to do their work. In Britain too, such considerations contributed to an emphasis, and possibly an over-emphasis, on the Navy's limited war role in distant waters. In 1962, in the aftermath of the Kuwait operation, the role of the Royal Navy had been described in the Admiralty's 'Statement on the Naval Estimates' wholly in terms of a landing operation.[84] This emphasis on both amphibious warfare and the 'East of Suez' power projection role of the Royal Navy thus dominated the new round in the perennial debate, which the Wilson Government inherited on taking office in 1964, about Britain's carrier programme.

The desire for a new carrier programme was a theme running through the whole of Britain's postwar policy. Carriers were seen as essential for the conduct of serious warfare at sea since they were 'the strength upon which all naval activities depend'.[85] In particular, carriers were seen as the backbone of the kind of balanced fleet which could hope to win sea control against serious naval opposition. Moreover, in peace-time too, the Royal Navy had consistently argued against sceptics in the Air Ministry and the Treasury that carriers were central to the conduct of a real role 'East of Suez'.

The problem was that some of these limited operations were in fact so demanding that they could not necessarily be improvised out of forces essentially designed and provided for other purposes. The confrontation with Indonesia which occupied the attention of one-third of Britain's surface fleet and half its carrier capacity, showed all too clearly that such minor commitments could absorb significant proportions of Britain's naval strength. The Royal Navy began seriously to worry about what it began to call 'overstretch', where the pressure of work was beginning to have its inevitable consequences on personnel retention and so forth.[86]

By the middle of the 1960s, in short, the British were beginning to feel a real strain in reconciling such conflicting demands. The perhaps inevitable consequence of all this was the cancellation in February 1966 of the Royal Navy's CVA-01, its projected 53,000-ton carrier. To the government, land-based aircraft seemed a more cost-effective way of providing air support 'East of Suez'. This was a major shock for the Royal Navy, especially when it was followed at the beginning of 1968 by the abandonment of the 'East-of-Suez' role which had justified it. British naval officers had perforce to turn their attention to matters nearer home.[87]

The United States, fully stretched as it was in the Vietnam War, had seen Britain's 'East-of-Suez' role as part of a coherent Anglo-American response to the challenge of insurgency, and had exerted considerable pressure on the British not to abandon it. The Vietnam War seemed to show that the world was not the neat and tidy polarised one so clearly envisaged in the 1950s; since it also suggested (as did such events as the Pueblo incident of 1968) that the accumulation of great forces at sea did not necessarily lead to desired outcomes on land, the out-of-area role was losing a good deal of its glamour for the American Navy too. In a sense it was fortunate for both Services that at the very moment Britain was deciding to withdraw from 'East of Suez', NATO was substituting flexible response for massive retaliation. In these new circumstances, the more traditional war-fighting aspects of naval power could receive new emphasis, especially as the Soviet Navy was by now clearly becoming so much more formidable than it had ever been before.

CONCLUSIONS

This brief review of British and American naval thinking during the first half of the postwar period shows the extent of the coincidence of view and 'purpose of the two navies', in itself a natural reflection of the closeness of the two countries themselves. Certainly there were disagreements and quarrels (of which the Suez affair was clearly the worst) but the two navies maintained the very special relationship they had achieved in the Second World War. Both sides benefited. The Royal Navy's truly global role was prolonged; the American Navy's capacity to take over was greatly facilitated.

There were also many similarities in the way the two navies adapted to the new realities of the world in which they found themselves. Both navies engaged in a series of major policy reviews in which matters of high policy were thought about strategically. Both navies were guided in their decisions on operation doctrine and building programmes by their understanding of the lessons of the recent past and by their best endeavours to predict an uncertain future. But if this was the thinking and conceptual side of their policy-making, there was another side to it too. This was bureaucratic, incremental and instinctive; it involved naval decision-makers, subject to the overwhelming press of daily business, lurching from one administrative crisis to another. In this last aspect of naval policy-making the habits of cooperation learned in the Second World War proved to be particularly resilient, especially perhaps for the Royal Navy.

Notes

1. For a unique and well-informed survey of the way technical developments affected naval policy in the postwar period, see N. Freidman, *The Postwar Naval Revolution* (London, 1986).
2. Churchill, speech to Conservative Party Conference, *Llandudno*, 9 Oct. 1945.
3. Sir Gladwyn Jebb, in Public Record Office (PRO) FO 371, June 1944.
4. Minute by Strang, 3 Jan. 1961, Public Record Office (PRO) FO 371/92067.
5. Minutes of the meeting of the Defence Committee (Operations), DO (46) 5th Meeting, Public Record Office (PRO) CAB 131/1.
6. Chiefs of Staff Memorandum COS (47)5 in DEFE 5/3 and Minutes of COS Meeting of 13 January 1947, DEFE 4/1.
7. Quoted in L. B. T. Ross 'Chester William Nimitz' in R. W. Love, Jr (ed.), *The Chiefs of Naval Operations* (Annapolis, 1980) p. 188.
8. Quoted in D. A. Rosenberg, 'American Postwar Air Doctrine and Organisation: The Navy Experience', A. F. Hurley and R. C. Ehrhart (eds), *Air Power and Warfare: The Proceedings of the Eighth Military History Symposium, United States Air Force Academy 1978* (Washington, DC, 1979).
9. 'Strategy', COS (48)58, DEFE 5/10.
10. COS (48) 39th Meeting, DEFE 4/11.
11. 'Defence Review – Report of the Chiefs of Staff', 14/9/48, Memo to Defence Committee, DO (48)61, CAB 131/6.
12. Status of Emergency Plans: Annexe to JP (50)9(Final), 13/1/50, DEFE 6/12.
13. Speedway itself JP (48)131 is still closed in the British archives. Comment on American Service attitudes comes from the reports of the meeting between US and British planners, JP (48)130, DEFE 6/12.
14. 'Unsolved Difference of Opinion Between British and United States Concepts', JP (49)134, DEFE 6/11.

15. 'General Report by the Director of Plans' Annexe I to JP (49)133 Final, DEFE 6/11, pp. 2–3.
16. 'Plan Galloper', Annexe to JP (49)134 Final, 1 March 1950, DEFE 6/11.
17. Ibid.
18. Ibid., para. 88.
19. Ibid., appendices detail naval forces. For 'Revised Restricted Fleet' see Board Memorandum B590 in Admiralty Board Minutes and Memoranda ADM 167/133.
20. 'Plan Galloper', Appendix B.
21. For an interesting account of exercises see ADM 1/25252.
22. See note 41 below.
23. 'Plan Galloper', DEFE 6/11; for details of ANZAM, see Annexe to JP(49)160, DEFE 6/11.
24. For British naval rearmament see 'Shape and Size of Fleet, Fraser Plan', Memo B 671 and ADM 167/135 and the Parker Committee papers in DEFE 10/65.
25. 'Strategic Guidance From the Standing Group to the Regional Planning Groups of the North Atlantic Treaty Organisation', JP (49)149 (Final), DEFE 6/11.
26. Ibid., and 'Brief for the United Kingdom Representative on the Standing Group – Strategic Guidance for the North Atlantic Regional Planning Groups', JP (49)151, ibid.
27. Draft of 'Strategic Guidance for North Atlantic Regional Planning', Appendix to JP (49)151, ibid.
28. 'Strategic Guidance to the North Atlantic Treaty Regional Planning Groups, JP (49)161, ibid. This contains at Appendix A a late draft of 561/3, the document in the title.
29. 'British Proposals for the Organisation of Command in the Atlantic Ocean', Annexe 1 to JP (50)43 (Final), DEFE 6/12.
30. Quoted in Rosenberg, 'American Postwar Air Doctrine', p. 262.
31. See para 9, 'Views of Chiefs of Staff of Plan Sandown', JP (48) 109 DEFE 6/7.
32. For discussion of this, se E. J. Grove, *Vanguard to Trident: British Naval Policy Since World War II* (Annapolis, 1987) pp. 65–8.
33. The published version of the 'Dropshot' 1949 long-term war-plan edited by A. Case Brown under the title *Operation World War II* (London, 1978) p. 163.
34. Rosenberg, Hurley and Ehrhart, *Air Power and Warfare*, pp. 264–5.
35. JCS 1800/166 of 7 September 1951 quoted Rosenberg, ibid., p. 265.
36. 'The Role of Aircraft Carriers: Memorandum by the First Lord of the Admiralty', 9 November 1953, ADM 1/24695.
37. Ibid.
38. Holograph minute 'Maritime Policy as it Affects Trident' by First Sea Lord to 5th Sea Lord 14/9/48, ADM 205/69.
39. Memorandum CDS(40)350 in DEFE 5/17 sets out the history of this period: its recommendations to cancel were accepted at COS (49) 164th Meeting, DEFE 4/18.
40. The Report and Proceedings of the Committee are at DEFE 8/23.
41. Letter from McGrigor to Fraser 24/11/48, ADM 205/70.
42. J. J. Sokolsky, *Seapower in the Nuclear Age: NATO as a Maritime Alliance*, Doctoral Dissertation presented to Harvard University, 1984, pp. 65, 68–9.
43. R. Tamnes, 'Norway's Struggle for the Northern Flank, 1950–2', in O. Riste (ed.), *Western Security: The Formative Years* (Oslo: Norwegian University Press, 1985).
44. For 'Mainbrace', see *Brassey's Naval Annual*, 1953, pp. 159–66. For accounts of

'Mariner', see *Naval Review*, Vol 41, pp. 365–73 and *Brassey's Annual 1954*, pp. 285–8.
45. Letter Deputy SACLANT to First Sea Lord, 20 July 1954, ADM 205/102.
46. Quotation P. Ziegler, *Mountbatten, the Official Biography* (London, 1985) p. 519.
47. Grove, *Vanguard to Trident*, pp. 82–5.
48. Ibid., pp. 96–115.
49. Paul R. Schratz, 'Robert Bostwick Carney', in Love (ed.), *The Chiefs of Naval Operations*, p. 246.
50. Quoted in the paper by the British First Lord of the Admiralty, 'The Role of Aircraft Carriers', 9 November 1958, ADM 1/24695.
51. Sokolsky, *Seapower*, p. 126.
52. Ibid., pp. 126–7.
53. 'United Kingdom Defence Policy', D (54) 43, 23 Dec. 1954, CAB 131/14. This was an expurgated version of the new strategic assessment prepared for the Commonwealth Prime Ministers.
54. Ibid.
55. 'The Navy and Hydrogen Bomb War', ADM 205/102.
56. Ibid.
57. 'The Navy of the Future', 2 March 1954, ADM 205/102.
58. Hughes Hallett to First Sea Lord, 7 Jan. 1954 and DCNS Paper 'US Views on Submarine Warfare', ADM 205/102.
59. ABJSM Washington to Admiralty, 24 Sep. 1954, ADM 205/102.
60. For United States fears about the vulnerability of FOS/M, see 'Extract from the Report of Visit of DCNS to USA and Canada – Oct/Nov 1953', ADM 205/102; for British attitudes to nuclear propulsion, Grove, *Vanguard to Trident*, pp. 229–33.
61. G. G. Gorshkov, quoted in R. W. Herrick, 'Soviet Naval Strategy' (Annapolis, 1968) p. 68. For United States Navy nuclear war fighting strategy, see the description of the 1955 First Report of the Long Range Objectives (LRO) Group in Friedman, *The Postwar Naval Revolutions*, pp. 49–55.
62. Minister of Defence, *Defence Outline of Future Policy, April 1957*, CMND 124 (London, 1957), paragraph 24.
63. B. Ranft and G. Till, *The Sea in Soviet Strategy* (London, 1983) pp. 108–9.
64. Ibid., p. 160.
65. D. A. Rosenberg, 'Arleigh Albert Burke', Love (ed.) *The Chiefs of Naval Operation*, p. 293.
66. See note 55 above.
67. Ziegler, *Mountbatten*, p. 561.
68. Ibid., pp. 560–1.
69. For a more detailed and annotated account of this process, see Grove, *Vanguard to Trident*, chapters 1–3; the 'Revised Restricted Fleet' plan is Memorandum B 590 in Adm 167/133.
70. Grove, *Vanguard to Trident*, chapter 4 surveys these world-wide operations.
71. 'British Overseas Obligations', C (52) 202, CAB 129/53.
72. Grove, *Vanguard to Trident*, Chapter 3.
73. Ibid., Chapter 5.
74. See the beginnings of this in ADM 205/102, notably a very prescient paper by the Controller, Sir Ralph Edwards, 'Future Strategy', 6 May 1954.
75. See note 58 above, paras 37–9.
76. NSC 68: A Report of the National Security Council, reprinted in *Naval War College Review*, May–June 1975, p. 60.

77. Friedman, *The Postwar Naval Revolution*, p. 49.
78. Rosenberg, note (63) above.
79. Ranft and Till, *The Sea in Soviet Strategy*, pp. 194–5.
80. U.S. Congress, House Appropriations Committee, *Hearings on the Fiscal Year 1963, Defense Budget* 87th Congress, 2nd Session, 1962, 9 66.
81. Sokolsky, *Seapower*, p. 141.
82. P. R. Schratz, 'Paul Henry Nitze' in P. E. Coletta (ed.), *American Secretaries of the Navy*, Vol II 1913–1972 (Annapolis) p. 945.
83. Sokolsky, *Seapower*, p. 141.
84. Cmnd 1629, para 2.
85. This comes from the classic formulation of the role of carriers as the 'fists of the fleet' in Explanatory Statement on the Navy Estimates 1955–56 (Cmnd 9396).
86. Grove, *Vanguard to Trident*, Chapter 7.
87. Ibid., pp. 269–79 covers the carrier controversy; Chapter 8, the withdrawal from 'East of Suez'.

14 Anglo-American Maritime Strategy in the Era of Flexible Response, 1960–80

Joel J. Sokolsky

INTRODUCTION

The dawn of the Cold War seemed to bring at once a Mahanian dream and a nightmare. On the one hand the United States and its allies held unquestioned 'command of the seas'. American sea power was, Admiral Chester Nimitz noted at the time, 'more absolute than ever possessed by the British ... so absolute that it is sometimes taken for granted'.[1] On the other hand, this superior sea power was not merely taken for granted by some; its very relevance was doubted. The advent of the atomic bomb appeared to make navies obsolete – superfluous in any future war against the most likely enemy, the Soviet Union. 'How could enough time be allowed for seapower to take its effect where war was characterized by strategic bombing by nuclear weapons?' asked one of the leading military thinkers of the day. Nations, their land and air forces as well as their economies would 'disappear in the first blow'.[2] Mahan had said that sea power had greatly influenced the course of history. Now it seemed that the match of events, political, strategic and technological would end that influence.

Sea power as an element of national power did not disappear in the nuclear age. Quite the contrary. The two great navies of the West, the United States Navy and the Royal Navy, remained major elements in the global balance of power soon to face a growing challenge from the ever-improving Soviet Navy.

This would not have surprised Mahan's contemporary and critic, Fred T. Jane. Jane argued that the influence of sea power depended upon larger strategic and political considerations and that what history showed was merely how some states made use of the sea to influence the political and military situation ashore. Sea power being defined as the ability of states to secure, deny and exploit the seas for military and political purposes, in war and peace, the destruction of the enemy fleet was just one means by which these tasks were accomplished, not the sole object of maritime forces.[3]

In the Cold War, the new atomic age, postures and strategies were adjusted to reflect the changed political, strategic and technological circumstances. Foremost amongst these adjustments was the deployment of nuclear weapons to maritime forces. The acquisition by the USN of an atomic delivery capability, first from aircraft-carriers and then from nuclear-powered ballistic missile submarines (SSBN), represented a new way in which the seas were exploited to influence the situation ashore. As John J. Clark observed, the carrier and SSBN underscored 'the modern strategic role of seapower formerly manifested in the silent blockading squadrons and amphibious operations of the Royal Navy'.[4]

While nuclear weaponry endowed maritime forces with a power and importance which eclipsed that of previous ages, the postwar era also generated demands for general purpose conventional forces at sea. The United States undertook an array of 'transoceanic' alliances, with its commitment to Europe through NATO being the most important and demanding. As the European nations rebuilt their armed forces under the American nuclear guarantee, they included construction of modern maritime forces. NATO was, from its very beginning, a 'maritime alliance'. When it created its integrated multilateral command structure in the early 1950s, Allied governments were called upon to earmark conventional maritime forces for the Supreme Allied Commander, Atlantic, (SACLANT), the Commander in Chief, Channel (CINCHAN) and a number of commands subordinate to the Supreme Allied Commander, Europe (SACEUR). Indeed, for the European navies (including the RN) and for the Royal Canadian Navy (RCN), NATO became their modern-day *raison d'être*.

Outside the European arena, the postwar era saw maritime forces employed in limited wars from Korea to Suez to Vietnam. Nor was 'gunboat diplomacy' a thing of the past as tension and crisis, such as in the Persian Gulf, would often bring warships offshore to back up diplomacy.[5]

In short the obituaries of sea power made in the late 1940s were spectacularly premature. The postwar era was a Mahanian dream to the extent that maritime forces emerged as key components in the global balance of conventional and nuclear power. So important did sea power become that, when the Cold War ended in the late 1960s, the problem for the West was not that it had too much, but that its maritime forces might be insufficient and new adjustments were necessary.

This essay deals with those adjustments as they relate to NATO, placing them in the larger strategic and political context of the impact of flexible response and also discusses them with reference to the emergence of *détente*. Flexible response did not fundamentally alter the role of maritime forces in NATO, which had been to support the exercise of power ashore in a war of indeterminate length and character. The new Allied strategy, with its emphasis upon conventional deterrence, only increased the importance of maritime forces in the overall Allied posture. As Dov Zakheim noted in 1976 with regard to the United States Navy, a global maritime posture which 'presumes a prolonged conventional war in the Atlantic/Mediterranean region, generates requirements for large forces'.[6]

During the late 1970s, NATO did take steps to improve its maritime posture commensurate with the new strategy, yet by the end of the decade there were grave doubts about the Alliance's ability to secure use of the seas because of the continuing build-up of Soviet maritime forces. NATO had adopted an overall strategy conducive to a margin of maritime superiority it no longer enjoyed. Why had the West not kept pace with the Soviets at sea in view of its desire to maintain a flexible strategy? One answer might be that the adoption of the new strategy coincided with the ending of the Cold War and the emergence of *détente* with its promise of reduced East–West tensions and less military spending. Although this was surely a factor, the relatively less favourable maritime situation in the late 1970s can be better attributed to the very nature of sea power in the nuclear age and in particular its role in the NATO Allaince. Sea power was important and became even more so with the flexible response strategy. But there were simply limits as to the extent to which adjustments in the Allied maritime posture could add flexibility and hence credibility to the overall strategy.

MARITIME FORCES AND FLEXIBLE RESPONSE

The familiar debate within the strategic studies literature about the Soviet Navy centres around whether the continued build-up of the USSR's maritime forces was defensively or offensively motivated. Michael MccGwire and others have argued that the Soviets' main objective was to add a maritime layer to the traditional Russian concern about protection of the homeland. Thus, as the Soviet Navy acquired a long-range sea-based nuclear capability, its maritime forces were given the task of protecting the SSBN fleet.[7] Others have contended that the Soviets were (and are still) seeking a blue-water maritime capability to pursue global ambitions and that such a navy is commensurate with its status as a superpower co-equal with the United States.[8]

Whatever the underlying rationale, the continued build-up of Soviet maritime forces throughout the Cold War years was steadily eroding the Western margin of maritime superiority. Moreover the maritime forces which the Soviets were putting into service were aimed at denying the West use of the sea, with a particular emphasis upon seaborne missile forces. The number of Soviet ships and naval aircraft, and their fighting capabilities represented 'a significant shift in the balance of maritime power by ending the era in which the United States and its European allies could confidently use the seas without the fears of effective challenge'.[9]

By itself the shifting maritime balance was not overly detrimental to the

Allied deterrent posture, which still stressed nuclear weapons, especially the central strategic systems of the United States. Yet here, too, the balance was in flux. The Soviets were nearly at parity with the Americans and long-held doubts about the credibility of relying almost exclusively upon the American strategic nuclear forces for deterring both nuclear and conventional attack began to surface. As early as the Kennedy administration these doubts influenced policy as the United States sought a more flexible posture for itself and for its NATO allies. The spectrum of deterrence had to be broadened to include conventional forces if all elements of it were to retain their credibility. In December 1967, the North Atlantic Council approved a 'revised strategic concept' submitted to it by the Military Committee as set forth in MC 14/3, and 'following the first comprehensive review of NATO's strategy since 1956':

> This concept, which adapts NATO's strategy to current political, military and technological developments, is based upon a flexible and balanced range of appropriate responses conventional and nuclear to all levels of aggression or threats of aggression. These responses, subject to appropriate political control, are designed, first to deter aggression and thus preserve the peace; but should aggression unhappily occur, to maintain the security and integrity of the North Atlantic Treaty area within the concept of forward defense.[10]

The problems, inconsistencies and internal contradictions of the flexible response strategy are well-known and will not be rehearsed here. There is no reason to believe that the politicians and military leaders who fashioned MC 14/3, or those after them, were unaware of the strategy's shortcomings. And there is much to Leon Sigal's observation that flexible response is 'less a strategy than an agreement not to disagree over strategy'.[11] Nevertheless there could be no turning back to massive retaliation and the implications for NATO's land and air forces were real and required posture changes.

The implications of flexible response for the NATO maritime posture have received less attention, but they were very much a subject of concern at SACLANT, because the doctrine posed fundamental challenges to the Allied position at sea. The adoption by NATO of flexible response increased the Alliance's need to exploit the strategic value of the seas. It did so spatially, temporally and operationally.

Since NATO wanted to deter and defend against a wide spectrum of possible Soviet actions, including limited conventional incursions along the flanks, much more sea space became crucial. Under a massive retaliation posture, the Alliance would not necessarily have to allocate many resources to the defence of the immediate coastal waters. Nor was the naval balance in seas such as the Baltic particularly important. A strategic nuclear attack could be launched from the United States or from British or French soil. Sea power would be important if SSBNs and nuclear-armed carriers participated in the strike, but in these instances NATO would only need limited 'working control' of the sea around the weapons platforms allowed for launching. To be sure, in a pre-hostilities period it would be important to secure sea-based nuclear weapons platforms from pre-emptive attack, but there would be less of a need for defence of the sea lanes of communication (SLOC), or for the coastal waters that gave access to the land areas where a conventional war would be fought. Under flexible responses, these logistic avenues became crucial.[12]

While the strategy of flexible response seemed to apply first to the Central Front, it had important implications for the northern and southern flanks. These were the least densely defended areas and the most in need of immediate Allied reinforcement, including air power projected from the sea. Sea-based support for Norway and the Eastern Mediterranean became necessary when the Allied ability to control the seas in order to support forces ashore in these regions appeared to be diminishing.

This concern with sea control extended the areas of importance back across the Atlantic and throughout the world. While it was generally agreed that the main Soviet threat would come close to the Eurasian land mass, Soviet naval movements beyond the immediate waters could not be ignored. Cuban and African bases afforded the Soviet Union a wider surveillance capability as well as an enhanced capability to strike on the wider oceans. Western concern with oil shipments increased.

Temporally flexible response demanded a pre-hostilities mobilisation of Allied maritime forces in order to commence surveillance and to be in a position to meet the Soviet attack if and when hostilities began. The securing of sea control had to continue for as long as necessary and was dependent upon the nature of the land war and political decisions regarding Allied responses. The greatest demands upon the Alliance's collective maritime forces would come in the event of a conventional conflict which lasted longer than a few weeks, or in a limited nuclear confrontation. Since NATO cannot know for certain what the length of a conflict with the Soviet Union would be, flexible response necessitated greater assurance that the Alliance would be able to exploit the strategic value of the seas from the outset and for an indefinite period. As then CINCSOUTH, Admiral Horacio Rivero, USN, noted in 1972, in reference to flexible response and the Allied posture in the Mediterranean: flexible response meant 'readiness on D-day' and 'staying power'.[13]

The time factor was a basic assumption in the whole strategy of flexible response. Control of the vital sea lanes for the purposes of reinforcement and resupply, and to allow conventional air power to be projected ashore, might give NATO a better chance of having to avoid either early surrender or escalation to the nuclear level. In a war in which major sea battles accompanied conflict on land, it would be a race between NATO's ability to secure use of the seas against Soviet sea-denial forces and the heavy attrition of conventional forces ashore.

In terms of the scope of operations, 'readiness on D-day' and 'staying power' implied, it would appear that flexible response finally validated the predilection of Allied naval leaders since 1949 to maintain a capability which was as broad as possible. They had long held that the uncertainties associated with a future war involving the Soviet Union and Europe (uncertainties as to the use of nuclear weapons, as to the Soviet intentions, and as to the responses of the Alliance), required that the Allied navies maintain the capability to meet as wide a scope of scenarios as resources would allow.[14]

Not only did flexible response explicitly call for meeting an attack at any level, the uncertainty as to what exactly the NATO response would be meant a broadening in the range of possible maritime contributions to deterrence and defence. Thus, in the late 1960s, the attack carrier again assumed a conventional war support role while maintaining a tactical nuclear capability. Submarine-launched missiles were brought into the theatre nuclear equation. By the early 1970s NATO began to revise its plans for the mobilisation of Allied merchant shipping and convoying. A re-emphasis on shipping also raised the problem of harbour defence and countermine measures.

Flexible response demanded that Allied maritime forces be able to secure and exploit the seas in support of the NATO land/air posture in a war of indeterminate length and character. It was precisely because of this that the continued expansion of the Soviet Navy was so significant. For by the late 1960s and early 1970s the Soviets had extended their maritime defence zone, taking in water further and further out from the European land mass. Their maritime capabilities, though not exceeding those of the Allies, were growing. In a conventional war at sea NATO might eventually win, but the question was whether it would be able to overcome Soviet sea denial forces in time to influence the situation ashore. Thus just at the moment when NATO began to look to its maritime forces to keep options open, and thereby strengthen deterrence, the Soviet ability to close off these options, and thereby weaken the credibility of the Allied deterrent posture, seemed to be on the increase.

This situation did not demand fundamental reformulation of Allied maritime strategy which had always been directed towards supporting the NATO posture on land, whether through projection of forces ashore or through conveyance of reinforcement and resupply. In its earliest formulations, the Allied maritime strategy had emphasised forward defence because of the nature of Soviet naval forces. The spatial, temporal and operational demands of flexible response did not remove the need for pressing the Allied naval effort in the forward areas, which was where sea control had to be ultimately achieved and sustained. Rather it required that NATO give greater attention to the maritime aspects of its overall strategic posture. More so than in the past, NATO had to be a maritime Alliance.

ADJUSTMENTS TO THE NATO MARITIME POSTURE

Characteristic of the nature of NATO, the steps taken to improve its maritime posture constituted less of a well-planned programme guided by an overriding and widely accepted 'strategy', and more of a series of organisational and force adjustments. One of the first steps that had to be taken was to convince Allied government leaders of the existence of a maritime threat. This task was undertaken by SACLANT and his staff. A briefing showing the nature of the growing Soviet maritime challenge was prepared and given to various Allied governments. In January 1968, SACLANT presented the North Atlantic Council with his assessment of the threat. This led the then Secretary-General Manlio Brosio to direct SACLANT to undertake a study of the relative maritime strengths of NATO and the Warsaw Pact and the maritime strategic doctrines of the two sides.[15]

The *Brosio Study* was presented to the Secretary-General on 19 March 1969. It was a wide-ranging study which examined not only the respective strengths of the two maritime forces, but the economic and political contexts in which each was developed. Included as well was an evaluation of one particular conflict scenario, a limited conflict along the northern flank. This scenario was run for forces existing at the time of the study and again for estimated forces in 1977. Overall the *Brosio Study* stressed the new importance attached to maritime forces as a result of the flexible response strategy, an importance which demanded adequate peace-time arrangements and the ability to control and use the seas throughout the entire conflict spectrum. The study found the NATO maritime forces to be still superior to those of the Warsaw Pact and likely to win the war at sea. However it warned that in future years it would take the Alliance longer, and cost more in terms of losses, to secure the seas. NATO had to face the prospect of major sea battles concurrent with land and air battles if it was going to be able to exploit the strategic value of the seas for reinforcement and resupply and for the projection of force ashore.

In the 'comprehensive' study, *Allied Defence in the Seventies*, presented to the Defence Planning Committee (DPC) in December 1970, attention was directed to the maritime threat facing the Alliance. The DPC called for 'better maritime surveillance and anti-submarine forces, more maritime patrol aircraft and seaborne missile systems and the replacement of overage ships'.[16]

Accompanying this call for greater attention to the Allied posture at sea were a number of command reorganisations and the creation of more readily available maritime forces. On 5 June 1967, the position of Commander-in-Chief Allied Forces Mediterranean was abolished. All Allied maritime forces (with the exception of the US Sixth Fleet) were placed under a new command subordinate to the Commander-in-Chief South (CINCSOUTH). The mission of Commander Naval Forces South (COMNAVSOUTH) was to defend and control the sea lines of communication in the Mediterranean and to conduct submarine and ASW operations in the Black and Mediterranean Seas. In November 1968, the DPC created another new command, subordinate to COMNAVSOUTH, Maritime Air Mediterranean (MARAIRMED) under whom were brought the land-based maritime air units of the United States, Britain, Italy, Greece and Turkey. By placing maritime air under the control of the commander who controlled the surface and submarine units, it was hoped that the Alliance would be better able to control the sea lines of communication. In peace-time, MARAIRMED provided a basis for co-ordination of day-to-day surveillance and reconnaissance.[17]

In the Atlantic, SACLANT had been conducting the Matchmaker exercises which saw several ships from different nations sail together over an extended period. At the same meeting in which the North Atlantic Council adopted the flexible response strategy the Matchmaker concept became a permanent Standing Naval Force Atlantic (STANAVFORLANT). This force, composed mainly of destroyer-type vessels was intended by virtue of being continuously operational, to 'enhance existing cooperation between naval forces of member countries'.[18] Members of SACLANT's staff, in particular Admiral Richard G. Colbert who had championed the idea, viewed the decision to create the force as 'a great success for us in our efforts to strengthen the Alliance by reorganization and employment of existing naval forces already available in peacetime'.[19]

STANAVFORLANT was activated on 13 January 1968 at Portsmouth, England. The original composition included ships from Britain, Norway and the Netherlands. In subsequent years, between four and eleven destroyer-type ships, and occasionally submarines, would sail with the force as member nations contributed ships as part of their normal training cycles. An oiler accompanied the force. Command of the force rotated yearly. Formally under SACLANT's operational command, STANAVFORLANT would come under CINCEASTLANT's (Commander-in-Chief, Eastern Atlantic) operational control when it was in European waters.

As described in formal briefings,[20] STANAVFORLANT had four main functions: first, it would provide training experience for joint operations enabling Allied navies to improve 'naval operational proficiency and NATO tactical development and evaluation'. Second, by its very existence, STANAVFORLANT would give evidence of Allied solidarity. Third, the force would provide NATO with a multinational ocean surveillance capability to monitor Soviet naval exercises and movements.

The fourth function of STANAVFORLANT would be to provide SAC-

LANT with an immediately available combined force to be deployed 'to the scene of any possible contingency to reaffirm the solidarity of the NATO alliance and provide a visible deterrent ...' STANAVFORLANT would move 'quietly to a threatened area, or just out of sight over the horizon', and thus be ready to respond to higher political and military direction while at the same time exercising the right of freedom of the seas. The force could also provide the initial elements around which a 'more powerful and versatile NATO force could be formed' if tensions continued to escalate. In sum, this multinational squadron was viewed as being useful as a low-level Allied response 'ready to be used in operations intended to deter Soviet aggression under a NATO strategy of controlled response'.[21]

The Maritime Contingency Force (MCF) concept was more in line with the nature of NATO's maritime posture, which relied upon earmarked national ships being made available subsequent to a collective decision. As a supplement to the 'day-to-day availability' of STANAVFORLANT, the MCF consisted simply of 'specially tailored multinational task forces' which could be called up in advance of the bulk of earmarked forces. Pursuant to a decision by the DPC, the MCFs could be called up to support various contingency plans, or as part of a graduated mobilisation as the Alliance moved from 'simple alert' to 'reinforced alert'. According to a 1972 statement by then SACLANT, Admiral Charles Duncan, the MCF was one of 'the primary tools that SACLANT has to carry out the NATO strategy of Flexible Response, short of general war'.[22]

In April of 1969, the DPC authorised the creation of a naval-on-call-force in the Mediterranean (NAVOCFORMED) under COMNAVSOUTH. First activated in April 1970, NAVOCFORMED was something between STANAVFORLANT and MCF in the Atlantic in that it consisted of a multinational squadron of three to five destroyers called together periodically. As with the standing force in the Atlantic, this new force was meant primarily as a means of demonstrating Allied solidarity and to further training and inter-naval familiarisation with NATO operating procedures.[23] Commenting on the situation in 1972, then Sixth Fleet Commander Admiral Isaac Kidd noted: 'NATO works in the Mediterranean. It is working daily in the invaluable exchange of information and perfecting of operating techniques at sea on bilateral and multilateral exercises'.[24]

The emphasis on improving NATO's peace-time posture at sea so as to better support a strategy of flexible response was also apparent in Channel Command. Here the Alliance wanted to be able to keep crucial ports open to allow for reinforcement and resupply and for continued civilian imports. Thus in May 1973, a Standing Naval Force Channel (STANFORCHAN) was commissioned. Operating permanently under the CINCHAN, the force consisted of mine countermeasure vessels from Belgium, Denmark, Germany and Britain. American and Norwegian ships would also join STANFORCHAN from time to time.[25]

Other steps were taken to reflect the impact of flexible response. For example, when Admiral Horacio Rivero USN became CINCSOUTH in February 1968, he changed the primary mission of the Sixth Fleet (which became NATO's Striking Force South upon declaration of a reinforced alert), from one of nuclear strike to support for the air and land battle in defence of Greek, Turkish and Italian territory. This task was subordinated only to the neutralisation of those Soviet maritime forces which posed a direct threat to the carriers. According to Rivero:

> The relative force situation was such that success in the battle for territorial defense depended critically on establishing and maintaining local command of the air over the battlefield, something which the indigenous air forces could not do without a substantial infusion of U.S. airpower in the earliest stages of the battle. The Sixth Fleet carriers, plus deployed U.S. Air Force squadrons at Avino, Italy and Adana, Turkey and the additional USAF squadrons that would immediately deploy from the U.S., were to provide this reinforcement of modern aircraft to supplement the less capable indigenous air forces. Since the immediate use of the deployed USAF squadrons could not be assured because of the QRA* requirement for nuclear attack assigned to them (and from which the Sixth Fleet squadrons were removed), I had to count primarily on the Sixth Fleet to provide the modern aircraft needed to influence the critical early stages of the land/air battle.**[26]

In the 1970s, NATO maritime exercises became larger and more complex and emphasised early mobilisation and controlled, flexible responses particularly along the flanks. *Exercise Strong Express*, conducted in 1972, was the largest-ever combined exercise involving some 300 ships, 700 aircraft and 64,000 personnel from twelve nations. It tested amphibious landings, projection of air power ashore in support of northern flank operations, convoy protection and ASW in the Norwegian Sea, North Sea and English Channel.[27] The exercise simulated maritime movements during a period of

---

*Quick Reaction Alert. A number of aircraft, Pershing missiles and SLBMs in the European theatre are always readied and kept on alert to deliver designated nuclear strikes on short notice.
**As late as 1976, the combined land-based air forces of Italy, Greece and Turkey included just over 400 capable aircraft. Facing NATO in the south were nearly 5000 Warsaw Pact tactical aircraft belonging to the air forces. Soviet naval aviation disposed of another 650 tactical aircraft, 700 long-range naval aircraft of which 200 were Bear, Bison and Backfire bombers.
The two Sixth Fleet carriers brought 48 fighters, 46 attack aircraft, 24 all-weather planes and 8 early warning planes to NATO. These were the most modern F-14, A-7 and A-6 aircraft in the NATO inventory. An additional carrier was earmarked for the Mediterranean during the War, thus increasing by 50 per cent the contribution of carrier-based air power. (US Congress, Senate Armed Services, Committee Print, *U.S. Naval Forces in Europe*, Report by Sen. Hart, 95th, 1st Sess. Washington, DC, GPO, 1977, pp. 3–4.)

strategic warning lasting two weeks during which time the following steps were taken:

Sept. 3   Allied Command Europe (ACE) mobile force units in Italy, Canada, the UK, Germany (the USAF), Netherlands and Luxembourg are put on alert.

Sept. 11   Information is received of a definite attack and the first elements of NATO's Air Mobile Force begin deploying to Norway.

Sept. 15   The eastern Atlantic is covered by long-range patrol aircraft flown from Britain, Iceland, Netherlands, and Germany. A British carrier task force, including amphibious forces moves toward Norway. An American carrier task force moves in from the Western Atlantic. Britain and Belgium begin anti-mine operations in the Channel area.

Sept. 16   Amphibious forces from the Netherlands, Britain and the United States make unopposed landings. Mine-sweeping operations at the Baltic approaches. Continued airlift of ACE mobile force.

Sept. 18   The Soviets attack in Norway.[28]

Emphasis upon the pre-hostilities movement of maritime forces was necessary not only to provide for the early protection of force ashore from carriers and amphibious forces but also to provide for protection of convoys carrying reinforcement and resupplies. NATO exercise tested close convoy protection, long an Allied maritime task but now receiving a new emphasis under the flexible response strategy. During *Strong Express* six convoys were organised, some moving from German and Danish ports across the North Sea while a Western Atlantic convoy of 10 ships sailed to Europe from Halifax and Boston escorted by Canadian and American destroyers. A NATO-wide control of shipping organisation provided convoy operational briefings throughout the exercise.[29] In exercise *Ocean Safari 77*, a reinforcement convoy on its way to Europe amid a deteriorating political situation was first shadowed and then attacked once general hostilities began. Until the initiation of hostilities, NATO escort forces had to avoid any provocation or 'aggressive act'.[30]

As the range of Soviet anti-shipping missiles increased, it became clear that close convoy protection would be insufficient to protect the merchant ships from attack. Towards the end of the seventies, NATO exercises incorporated extended coverage reviving an old concept of 'defended sea lanes':

> The basic principle is that anti-submarine forces, notably surface ships equipped with helicopters and tactical arrayed sensors and maritime patrol aircraft, should keep a close passive sonar watch in sea areas on either side of the route being transited by a convoy. The distance of the areas under surveillance from the convoy would be greater than that of the range of known enemy submarine-launched anti-ship missiles.[31]

The United States and NATO were also concerned about the state of Allied plans for the organisation and control of merchant shipping in the event of war. Despite the emphasis on airlift and predispositioning begun in the 1960s, NATO still viewed it as necessary that provision be made for the massive movement of American reinforcements and resupplies by sea, in convoy if necessary. In 1972, the office of the Assistant Secretary of Defense for Program Analysis and Evaluation released a study which looked at American requirements and capabilities to meet a NATO sealift. The *Sealift Procurement and National Security*[32] (SPANS) study found that the government-owned fleets and privately owned United States merchant fleets would be unable to provide the necessary bottoms for such a sealift. It concluded, however, that the difference would be made up by NATO-flag shipping which would be made available during a crisis.

The problem was not the lack of adequate shipping, but timely acquisition. During the 1970s, the United States and NATO engaged in several measures to ensure that adequate Allied-flag shipping could be quickly brought to American ports for the movement of American military cargo. In September 1973, the Departments of Defense and Commerce entered into a new agreement with NATO 'to increase the availability of NATO flag shipping in the event of a major deployment of forces to Europe'. Emphasising that the sealift problem was 'not so much a matter of total capacity as early availability', then-Secretary of Defense James Schlesinger reported to Congress in 1974 that 300 'suitable' NATO flag ships (some roll-on, roll-off, but mostly break-bulk), 'which normally frequent U.S. East and Gulf coast ports would be "earmarked" in peacetime to facilitate their acquisition in a contingency'. These ships would be directed to American ports 'in response to specific U.S. deployment requirements'.[33] In later years, NATO's Planning Board for Ocean Shipping (PBOS), refined its procedures. In 1977 a new NATO shipping organisation, the Civilian Sealift Group (CSG), was created. This was a group of representatives from the major NATO shipping companies who would assist the United States in marshalling some 600 NATO flag vessels earmarked for reinforcement sealift.

In the late 1970s, the major NATO commanders completed a series of reinforcement studies directed towards identifying measures for improving airlift, sealift, and other aspects of reinforcement. In exercises such as the *Reforger* and *Wintex* series, and *Nifty Nugget*, the United States and NATO tested sealift mobilisation capability as it had not been done in the past.[34]

Another maritime area which received greater attention in the 1970s was Allied co-operation in the development and production of weapons platforms and advance technologies including surface-to-surface and surface-to-air missiles, missile defence systems, communications data links and mine warfare capabilities. The Long Term Defence Programme (LTDP) set forth by the DPC in 1977, identified co-operation in this area as an important element in improving the Allied posture at sea. At the May 1978 DPC meeting, attention was called to the continuing installation of active sonars now carried by most of the Alliance's surface ships, to the planned increase in the stocks of lightweight torpedoes capable of being dropped from aircraft (that is, the US MK-46 Mod 5 Neartip), and the efforts of the NATO Naval Armaments Group (NNAG), to develop a new lightweight torpedo and an advanced acoustic sensor.[35]

The LTDP sub-area on maritime command, control and communications addressed the further implementation of Link 11, 'a standardized NATO automated computer to computer digital data link to convey tactical information between maritime forces'. By 1980, Belgium Britain, Canada, France, Italy, the Netherlands, Norway, the United States and West Germany had already installed or were planning to install Link 11 in surface ships. Some had also put the system into maritime patrol aircraft. Another area of NATO efforts at inter-operability was sonobuoys. In 1978, the French Navy hosted a demonstration which indicated a 98 per cent inter-operability of American, French, West German, Canadian and British sonobuoys with American, French, British and Canadian maritime patrol aircraft.[36]

Co-operation extended to major vessels such as the jointly produced Dutch–German frigate used in the navies of those two countries as well as by Greece. The Alliance was looking into a follow-on to this type which might be used to replace ASW frigates in the 1990s. A number of countries had co-operated in the development of the NATO Patrol Hydrofoil Missile Ship (PHMO), and the United States and Canada began testing a Canadian-designed variable depth sonar which could be towed by high-speed ships like the PHM.[37] One joint approach to missile defence was the NATO Sea Gnat project. This was a co-operative effort by Britain, the United States, West Germany, Norway and Denmark to develop a decoy system. A major project designed to enhance Allied surveillance was the Azores Fixed Acoustic Range (AFAR), which involved implanting transmitting and receiving antennae on the ocean floor. The range was activated between May 1972 and May 1979.[38] With funding from the NATO infrastructure programme the Alliance developed two Naval Force Sensor and Weapons Accuracy Check Sites (FORACS), one off Norway and the other near Crete. The object here was to 'acquire, equip and operate ranges for the purpose of checking the accuracy of all sensors connected with shipborne weapon systems'.[39]

Efforts to standardise or at least to increase the compatability of platforms and weapons used by the Allies were accomplished by an expansion of efforts to standardise procedure and tactical doctrine. Common manuals were being used by the NATO navies. In 1980, the major NATO commands (SACEUR, SACLANT, CINCHAN), completed a joint study which produced a forma-lised agreed 'concept of maritime operations' (CONMAROPS). It would be the core document for NATO maritime forces. According to the SACLANT, Admiral Harry Train II, the concept:

identifies NATO maritime interests and assesses threats to these interests, considers the types of confrontation that can be expected and the associated allied priorities; establishes the principles to be used by NATO forces, and finally, outlines the campaigns that are likely to be waged and the involvement of various types of forces. The three principles are – containment, defense in depth and keeping the initiative.[40]

The United States Navy was particularly anxious to have its allies contribute more to NATO's maritime posture. The number of ships in the American fleet had been declining and, although the newer vessels were more potent than the ones replaced, the Navy viewed its global commitments as stretching its capabilities in the event of war. It might not be possible for the Navy to meet its NATO and other responsibilities. Thus in 1970, Chief of Naval Operations Elmo Zumwalt asked the Naval War College to develop a plan designed to improve the ASW capabilities of the NATO allies. The *Newport Study* was undertaken with the assistance of American naval commanders then associated with NATO naval commands.[41] It was completed in April of 1971.

In a letter to Zumwalt, dated September 1971, Admiral Colbert (by then SACLANT Chief of Staff), reported that he was working with Admiral Rivero (CINCSOUTH), on implementing the recommendations of the Newport Study. He wanted the Defense Department to support their efforts by persuading the Allies to 'carry a heavier burden at sea'. Colbert called for the elimination of the alleged United States policy of 'downgrading NATO navies'. It was also important to establish with the American Joint Chiefs of Staff 'the fact that the shift in the balance of the threat has been to seaward and that MAP [Military Assistance Program] allocations to strengthen allied naval forces need to reflect this'.[42]

Throughout the 1970s, the total number of Allied maritime forces declined. However it would appear that the concerns raised by NATO naval leaders did help to persuade the NATO governments to upgrade their maritime forces. The Europeans and Canadians continued and intensified their traditional specialisations in the areas of ASW, mine warfare and coastal defence.[43] Some navies, such as those of the British and Dutch, reduced their blue-water capability, with the Royal Navy in particular reducing its attack carrier force.

The Royal Navy continued its general withdrawal from distant global obligations. This included the Mediterranean where, by the early seventies, the standing British presence had been reduced to one destroyer, two frigates and two submarines. By 1976, Britain had withdrawn all naval units earmarked for NATO in the Mediterranean although British forces continued to participate in exercises and periodically contributed to NATO's on-call force when present.[44] In a sense, NATO benefited from the contraction of the British maritime posture since it meant that the Royal Navy would be able to provide immediate sea control units in the North Atlantic.

Nearly all Allies began major replacement or upgrading programmes. Belgium commissioned four Wielingen Class frigates in the mid-1970s, significantly improving its contribution towards protection of shipping in the Channel. West Germany began to replace its 1950s era frigates with the German-built Bremen Class frigate and its submarine fleet with the German-built 'Type 210' as well as a new generation of fast patrol boats with modern vessels carrying the American Harpoon missile.[45] Canadian naval forces took delivery of four new helicopter destroyers in the early 1970s. Overall the Alliance's maritime forces moved to increase their firepower through deployment of surface-to-surface missiles such as Penguin and Exocet.[46] A number of European navies, as well as the Canadian, acquired modern long-range patrol aircraft for ASW operations.

The improvement made in the capabilities of the Allied navies during the 1970s meant that, as one American Admiral told a Congressional hearing, non-United States units still supplied 'substantial maritime forces for the common defense'. Nearly 65 per cent of all 'ocean-going' NATO maritime forces and 25 per cent of major combatants would be drawn from Europe and Canada.[47] The United States Navy continued to supply NATO with essential protection and projection forces, including the seaborne nuclear deterrent. But in terms of conventional forces in anti-submarine warfare, mine warfare, and coastal defences, other Allies would play an important role.[48]

Allied naval leaders had always stressed the global nature of the Soviet maritime threat, particularly to Europe's oil lines of communications from the Persian Gulf. NATO's political leadership was reluctant to extend the Alliance's sphere of concern, even below the Tropic of Cancer. This did not mean that several Allies, acting in co-operation with one or two other nations, would not co-operate out of the NATO area. In fact, during the 1970s, the United States, Britain and France did begin joint exercises and other forms of collaboration in the Indian Ocean. Several NATO steps were taken, however, in relation to out-of-area threats. SACLANT was authorised to be prepared to protect shipping below the Tropic of Cancer as necessary, and to proceed with contingency planning in headquarters a Maritime Exercise Information Group was established to collect and distribute information on the movements of Allied navies throughout the world.[49]

Consistent with the emphasis on the flexible response strategy, the thrust of the efforts to improve NATO's maritime posture was directed towards enhancing the Alliance's ability to conduct conventional war. However, the overall strategy did not rule out the first use of nuclear weapons in the event of conventional resistance not succeeding. In its use of nuclear weapons, NATO would target military facilities and formations. This was consistent with shifts in American nuclear doctrine which had progressively moved towards greater flexibility. The 'Schlesinger Doctrine' of 1974 stressed the importance of 'limited nuclear options'.[50]

While here, as in the entire nuclear question, there continued to exist a wide area of disagreement between the United States and its allies on the ultimate wartime meaning, NATO during the 1970s did improve its sea-based nuclear strike posture. By the end of the decade some 400 Poseidon Sea Launched Ballistic Missiles (SLBMs) had been allocated for SACEUR targets. The Royal Navy was co-ordinating its SLBM targeting with NATO. American aircraft-carriers retained a nuclear strike role and exercises run for the northern and southern flank commitments still included provisions for the use of carrier-based tactical nuclear weapons. Also entering service in the early 1980s were American Sea Launched Cruise missiles (SLCM) which could strike at targets in Eastern Europe and the Soviet Union from ranges exceeding a thousand miles. Indeed the Alliance briefly considered the SLCM option as an alternative to the Ground Launch Cruise Missile (GLCM) and Pershing II for the modernisation of the intermediate-range nuclear forces. Although the options were rejected, the continuing deployment of SLCM on American ships afforded NATO a new theatre nuclear capability.[51]

The adoption by NATO of the flexible response strategy did not change the role for maritime forces in the overall Allied deterrent posture. Since 1949, those forces had the traditional tasks common to all maritime forces at all times: to exploit the strategic value of the seas for the purposes of influencing the military and political situation ashore. As with the entire panoply of Allied preparations, those in the maritime sphere operated under the unavoidable cloud of uncertainty as a NATO Warsaw Pact war was one of indeterminate duration and character. Compounding this strategic uncertainty was the fact that, as a coalition of states, whose maritime strength varied from that of a Superpower to states with all but no maritime forces, co-operation and co-ordination were a matter of delicate politics as well as of strategic planning.

None of this changed with flexible response. What did change was the attention which the Alliance as a whole was giving to its posture at sea. The driving force behind this renewed emphasis upon the maritime balance was the adoption of a strategy which called for a larger measure of conventional deterrence on land. The adoption of this position only heightened the threat now posed by growing Soviet maritime capabilities because the Soviet Union was now in a better position to challenge NATO for control of those seas that would be crucial in the support of a protracted conventional struggle in Central Europe and along the flanks.

LIMITS TO ADJUSTMENT

The continued improvements in Soviet maritime capabilities cast doubt upon the actual effectiveness of the adjustments made by NATO in its maritime posture, particularly in terms of lending credibility to the flexible response strategy. United States Navy assessments in the early 1970s concluded that NATO would have a difficult time winning the war at sea. Winning did not entail destruction of the Soviet Union's naval forces; rather, it was gauged upon the ability of the combined American and Allied forces to protect shipping 'necessary to resupply and reinforce the U.S. and allied forces conducting a conventional defence' and to protect and secure the northern and southern flanks 'while the land war is fought in the center'.[52] The Navy's assessments were supported by the President's Foreign Intelligence Advisory Board.[53]

These assessments had the United States and Allies undertaking all missions simultaneously. In the context of an evolving conventional conflict wherein the central front is the focus of hostilities NATO might, with greater chances of success, confine its initial actions to securing sea control for reinforcement purposes and holding projection. This, at least, was the conclusion of a 1976 assessment undertaken by the Congressional Budget Office (CBO).[54]

The CBO study argued that the help of European allies would be needed to secure control of the seas for reinforcement and resupply. This would entail a conflict of several weeks, perhaps two months, and involve heavy losses to both naval units and merchant shipping, but in the end NATO would win. In attempting to secure the sea lines of communication (SLOC) the major threat would be the Soviet submarine force. Other elements of the Soviet Navy, surface ships and naval aviation, would constitute less of a threat because of the distances they would have to cover to mount a concentrated attack on allied shipping.[55]

Projecting forces ashore would require that NATO carrier task forces move close to the Soviet Union. Within a range of 500 kilometres, these forces would come under concentrated attack, for example in the Norwegian Sea and eastern Mediterranean. Under these circumstances:

> Combined Soviet systems are likely to exert enough pressure on naval forces to force them to be preoccupied with their own survival rather than with the projection of power alone.
> There are serious doubts that even self defense would be successful given the intensity of attacks that Soviet shore and medium range defenses can mount. Finally, attack of such Soviet targets as can be reached from the sea would not be likely to affect the outcome of the war in central Europe significantly.[56]

This general assessment of the higher risks associated with projection, as compared to securing the SLOC, was expressed in United States Defense Department Congressional testimony in the later 1970s. In 1977, Secretary of

Defense Brown stated that NATO had enough forces to secure the sea lanes in order to allow for reinforcement, while acknowledging the threat to carrier forces in the eastern Mediterranean.[57] Testifying a year later, the Deputy Secretary of Defense noted that: 'For the present, we believe that the U.S. Navy can carry out the sea control mission in concert with our allies.'[58]

The Navy's view was similar, but more guarded. According to the Chief of Naval Operations, 'the U.S. could probably retain control of the North Atlantic sea lanes to Europe, but would suffer serious losses to both American and Allied shipping in the early stages' of a conflict. He put the ability of Allied forces, particularly the Sixth Fleet, to operate in the eastern Mediterranean as 'uncertain at best'.[59]

The degree of risk inherent in these assessments was considerable. Firstly, regarding the danger of attempting to project force along the flanks, it should be noted that, even if NATO did not strike at targets within the Soviet Union (and this was not then the primary mission of carrier forces), the concentrated fire-power of the Soviets could prevent effective support of the land battle. Under flexible response all NATO territory was to be defended initially with conventional forces. In the eastern Mediterranean and in northern Norway, projection forces were to play an important role in this defence. Moreover these flanks were viewed as the most likely areas of limited Soviet attacks because of the risk of nuclear escalation along the central front. Clearly a limited, and appropriate, NATO response in the event of such an attack was becoming more and more problematic.

The second point relates to the implication for the wider sea battle of a loss of the flanks to conventional land forces. Should the Soviets win the air and land war near the Turkish straits or in northern Norway, they would be able to move their maritime air cover forward and provide a more secure environment for other maritime forces. In the north the combination of a successful strike against allied carriers and advances on the ground could result in NATO losing the battle of the Norwegian Sea. According to SACLANT, 'control of the Norwegian Sea by NATO forces is a vital part of allied defences against Soviet submarines, since the level of threat posed to the Atlantic SLOC will be a function of the Norwegian Sea battle outcome'.[60]

This in turn had led one naval analyst to point out that:

> A war between NATO and the Warsaw Pact cannot be won either at sea or on the flanks. It must be won on the primary battlefield, the central front. But who wins in the center and the ability of the winner to realize the benefits of victory could both be determined by events on and around the northern flank. Either side could lose the battle that it must fight there and thereby lose the war.[61]

The third point is that, while the Soviets might be prevented from mounting concentrated surface, sub-surface and air attacks on convoys and

Allied maritime forces in the mid-Atlantic and the western Mediterranean, the same situation would not necessarily hold true in the coastal waters and harbour areas of northern Europe. In a major war in Europe the most important transatlantic military and economic shipping would converge on the English Channel and pass through to the North Sea ports of Belgium, the Netherlands and Germany. 'Given the opportunity, the Warsaw Pact could be expected to concentrate both submarine and air attacks in those waters.' The Channel sea lanes and North Sea ports would also be 'excellent sites for Soviet minefields'.[62] Isaac Kidd has pointed out that, with their surface ship and air-launched mines, the Soviets 'will be able to cover all the northern European sea lanes'.[63] Thus short-range Soviet capabilities would also put into question the Alliance's ability to land reinforcements, regardless of the level of sea control obtained through combat on the open seas.

As noted, most assessments foresaw the United States and its allies eventually securing use of the seas for reinforcement and resupply. Yet here too the costs were expected to be high, in addition to the fact that sea control would take some time to establish. Estimates of shipping losses varied with assumptions as to how much warning time NATO had and the extent to which the Soviets would move their submarines out. In the late 1970s Kidd was predicting that 'well over a third and probably more of the merchant ships at sea would be destroyed or prevented from delivering their cargoes the day the shooting starts'.[64] A study by the United States Atlantic Council, under the direction of former Secretary of the Navy Paul Nitze, estimated that between 300 and 600 allied merchant ships and escorts would be lost within the first four to twelve weeks of a major war at sea. This study, which was said to be based on statistics supplied by the Navy's Center for Naval Analysis, assumed a pre-deployment of allied maritime forces and Soviet anti-shipping forces in forward positions.[65] Another analysis undertaken by the Carnegie Endowment suggested that, if the Soviets moved significant submarine forces to open seas, it might take a month for the SLOC to be fully secure.[66] Most projections of relative maritime strength gave the long-run edge to NATO so that 'if the conventional NATO defence should be successful for more than a month or so, then the West should be able to regain the use of essential sea lanes at acceptable attrition rates'.[67]

The problem is that NATO may require substantial sea-lift well before a month is out and could not wait for the outcome of a protracted battle for control of SLOC. Even with a period of pre-hostilities mobilisation and commencement of air- and sea-lift, the tonnages able to get through in time could be insufficient. A 1982 report issued by the North Atlantic Assembly's military committee stressed that the 'gross tonnage required for concentrated conflict lasting more than a few days would have to come by sea'. Existing stocks could be drained 'within as little as 2–3 days'.[68] In his book, former American Secretary of Defense Harold Brown argues that NATO does not have the capability to fight conventionally 'for a reasonable period (say a month or more)'. The Alliance could not hold on to the inter-German border. According to Brown, 'the Soviets are probably not certain of being able to drive to the Rhine, the North Sea, and the English Channel in a month's time'. 'Their confidence of doing so', he points out, 'probably exceeds the NATO countries' of being able to stop them. That leaves NATO with an uncomfortable reliance on the threat of nuclear escalation.'[69]

Moreover high rates of attrition at sea coupled with a rapidly deteriorating situation on land will only add to the problem of maintaining Allied cohesion in the event of war. With major combat on land and sea, there would have to be priorities in the allocation of merchant ships for military use and of escort forces. Not all fronts could receive immediate reinforcements, not all shipping would receive close protection and decisions would have to be made about the level of protection, if any, to be dedicated to civilian economic shipping. This could lead to divisions amongst national governments as each sought to support its forces and supply its populations.

Ironically, as NATO became more of a maritime alliance in the 1970s as a consequence of the adoption of the flexible response strategy and the growth in Soviet sea power, its maritime forces, which had been considered one of the strongest elements in the overall posture, came to share many of the uncertainties long associated with its conventional land and air forces. Was there enough? Could they perform their tasks? The apparent inability of the Alliance's posture at sea to keep pace with the new demands might be attributed to another change in the international environment, the emergence of *détente*. Along with the new strategy of flexible response came the end of the Cold War and a lessening of East–West tensions.

As President Nixon and Henry Kissinger found out, the pursuit of *détente* and the maintenance of adequate military forces was a problem. Under the more tense conditions of the Cold War there would have been more concern, particularly in the Congress, about the growing power of the Soviet Navy. During the early 1970s the United States Navy had to defend its budget request against charges that it was exaggerating the Soviet naval threat.[70]

With the United States itself cutting back on overall defence expenditures, it is not surprising to find support amongst Allies for major improvements lacking at times. SACLANT's efforts to alert Allied governments about the Soviet maritime threat reflected a concern that, after twenty years of Cold War and containment, governments had to be convinced anew of the need for defence, at sea and elsewhere. From the United States perspective, Allies would have to shoulder more of the burden as American forces became stretched too thin. While *détente* may have eased tensions, the scope of American global commitments had not contracted. Indeed, with the Carter Doctrine occasioned by threats in the Persian Gulf, the United States appeared to expand those obligations. A 1980 study found that the NATO Allies were unable to fill gaps created by the decline in American forces and the need to meet out-of-area threats. In the area of convoy escorts, where the

United States had always counted heavily upon Allied contributions, the study concluded that there was a serious shortfall and, therefore: 'U.S. defensive forces – already required for protection of U.S. carrier task forces, underway replenishment groups, amphibious groups and perhaps convoys to Asia – could also be required for transatlantic convoy escort'.[71]

It is not hard to find similar deficiencies in the Allied maritime posture during the *détente* years. It is difficult, though, to draw a strong relationship between the emergence of *détente* and the decidedly less favourable maritime situation in the 1970s. As shown above, NATO did take steps to improve its posture at sea. If these adjustments were insufficient, factors other than *détente* contributed. Much effort was going into improvements in the conventional land and air forces, increasing their flexibility. Air-lift and pre-positioning had to complement improvements in sea-lift and indeed were necessary if the forces in place were to hold out in a conventional struggle until the impact of sea-lift could take effect. By the end of the decade, the NATO Allies had committed themselves to three per cent annual real increase in defence expenditures. Some of this was going into maritime forces but other demands were equally pressing.

Not only were maritime force improvements competing against other demands upon NATO's posture resulting from the flexible response strategy, the case for larger general-purpose forces at sea ran up against the very nature of the Alliance's deterrent posture. Nuclear weapons, and in particular strategic nuclear weapons, continued to constitute the most important element in the Allied arsenal. To be sure, maritime forces contributed to NATO's nuclear posture at the tactical theatre as well as the strategic level. But in the presence of massive atomic fire-power on both sides of the East–West balance, the relative importance of conventional sea power in the calculations of the balance would always be circumscribed. Without nuclear weapons, projections as to the likely course of a war in Europe would involve more or less traditional calculations as to the strengths of the land and air forces and the ability of NATO to reinforce by sea in a protracted struggle. The deterrent value of the Alliance's still present margin of maritime superiority would be far greater. But these forces were not thought the exact equivalent of the British fleets in the Napoleonic wars nor of the combined Allied fleets of the First and Second World Wars. No adjustments in the NATO conventional maritime strategy or posture could lessen the importance of strategic nuclear weapons.

The same can be said for the Alliance's conventional land and air posture. Flexible response did heighten the need to improve in this area and progress was made. Yet the conventional imbalance remained along the central front. This imbalance, in turn, provided a further limitation on the overall importance of sea power. The ability of NATO's maritime forces to exploit the strategic value of the seas so as to have a favourable impact upon a conventional land and air war depended upon the early stages of such a conflict. Sustained conventional resistance would require massive sea-lift, but even with a pre-hostilities movement large-scale support might have to await the outcome of the initial battles at sea. In the meantime, the various land and air fronts will have to hold. Unfortunately the prospects here are uncertain without a major successful sea-lift in the first weeks of a war. The war at sea could be won, yet the Alliance would still find itself in a difficult position if this victory were achieved after large-scale losses of forces and territory. In a real sense, the credibility of NATO's maritime posture, as with other aspects of the whole flexible response strategy, had become hostage to the conventional land and air imbalance.

CONCLUSION

The adjustments made in the NATO maritime posture as a result of the adoption of the strategy of flexible response reaffirmed the importance of sea power in the nuclear age and in particular to the North Atlantic Alliance. The manner in which those adjustments were made, on a somewhat *ad hoc* basis involving various national and intra-Alliance compromises, reflected the nature of NATO itself, In flexible response, the Alliance had an overall strategy more conducive to a measure of maritime superiority it no longer enjoyed and, despite real improvements in the posture at sea, the 1970s did not see a regaining of the earlier dominant position there.

To a certain extent the emergence of *détente* and a relaxation in East–West tensions may explain the lack of will to provide greater numbers of maritime forces. But, as in the past, governments had to choose and maritime forces had to compete with other pressing needs occasioned by the new strategy. NATO was a maritime Alliance and had become more so with flexible response, yet with the ultimate objectives ashore it was not surprising that most attention was drawn there. The improvements in land and air posture did not redress the imbalance ashore, and hence limited the impact the adjustments made at sea. Those adjustments did lend more credibility to the flexible response strategy, but they could not overcome by themselves its inherent deficiencies. Indeed, with the continued improvement in Soviet maritime capabilities, NATO's maritime forces came to share many of the uncertainties associated with the land and air posture.

The existence of a rough balance in strategic nuclear forces at once compelled NATO to become more of a maritime alliance while circumscribing the relative importance of its collective conventional sea power. *Détente* or no *détente*, flexible response or no flexible response, strategic nuclear weapons would have continued to constitute the core of the Allied deterrent posture. No adjustments in maritime strategy, organisation or posture could have changed this.

As in the past, sea power continued to derive its importance and confront its limitations, in war and peace, from the nature of the broader strategic and political environment.

Notes

1. Fred T. Jane, *Heresies of Sea Power* (London, 1906) p. 1.
2. As quoted in Geoffrey Till, *et al.*, *Maritime Strategy and The Nuclear Age* (New York, 1982) p. 56.
3. Bernard Brodie, *A Guide to Naval Strategy* (New York, 1965) p. 226.
4. John J. Clark, 'Merchant Marine and the Navy: A Note on the Mahan Hypothesis', *Journal of the Royal United Services Institute* (RUSI) vol. 112, no. 646 (May 1967) p. 164.
5. See, for example: Jonathan Howe, *Multicrises, Sea Power and Global Politics in the Missile Age* (Cambridge, Mass. 1973); B. Blechman, S. Kaplan, *Force Without War: U.S. Armed Forces as a Political Instrument* (Washington, DC, 1978); B. Dismukes, J. McConnell (eds), *Soviet Naval Diplomacy* (New York, 1979); E. Luttwak, *The Political Uses of Seapower* (Baltimore, 1974); James Cable, *Gunboat Diplomacy* (New York, 1981).
6. Dov Z. Zakheim, *U.S. Naval Force Alternatives*, Staff Working Paper, Congressional Budget Office (CBO) (Washington, DC, 26 March 1976) p. 79.
7. Michael MacGwire, 'The Evolution of Soviet Naval Policy, 1960–1974', M. MacGwire, K. Booth, J. McDonnell (eds), *Soviet Naval Policy: Objectives and Constraints* (New York, 1975).
8. On Soviet naval developments, see: Paul H. Nitze, Leonard Sullivan, Jr and the Atlantic Council Working Group on Securing the Seas, *Securing the Seas: The Soviet Naval Challenge and Western Alliance Options* (Boulder, Col., 1979); Paul J. Murphy (ed.), *Naval Power in Soviet Policy*, United States Air Force Studies in Communist Affairs, vol. 2 (Washington, DC, 1978); M. MacGwire (ed.), *Soviet Naval Developments: Capability and Context* (New York, 1973); M. MacGwire, J. McDonnell (eds), *Soviet Naval Influence: Domestic and Foreign Dimensions* (New York, 1977); Edward Wegner, *The Soviet Naval Offensive* (Annapolis, 1975); Elmo R. Zumwalt, Jr, *On Watch* (New York, 1976); Barry M. Blechman, *The Changing Soviet Navy*, Staff Paper (Washington, DC, 1973); Norman Polmar, *Soviet Naval Power* (New York, 1972); Siegfried Breyer, *Guide to the Soviet Navy* (Annapolis, 1970); Robert Kilmarx, *Soviet–United States Naval Balance* (Washington, DC, 1975); United States Congress, Senate, National Ocean Policy Study, Committee on Commerce, Committee Print, *Soviet Oceans Development*, 94th Congress, 2nd Session (Washington, DC, 1976); Bruce W. Watson, *Red Navy at Sea: Soviet Naval Operations on the High Seas* (Boulder, Col., 1982); S. G. Gorshkov, *The Seapower of the State* (Annapolis, 1979).
9. Till, *Maritime Strategy*, p. 68.
10. *NATO Final Communiques, 1949–1974* (Brussels, 1981) p. 197.
11. Leon Sigal, *Nuclear Forces in Europe* (Washington, DC, 1984) p. 14.
12. See Capt. John Morse, USN Ret., 'Questionable NATO Assumptions', *Strategic Review*, vol. 5, no. 1 (Winter, 1977) p. 22.
13. Admiral Horacio Rivero, USN, 'The Defense of NATO's Southern Flank', *RUSI Journal*, vol. 117, no. 2 (June 1972) p. 7.
14. Till, *Maritime Strategy*, pp. 182–3.
15. The full title of the Brosio Study is: Supreme Allied Commander, Atlantic, *Report of Study: Relative Maritime Strategies and Capabilities of NATO and the Soviet Bloc* (Norfolk, Virginia: 1969). Much of this study remains classified. The author was allowed to read it in its entirety on the condition that only general summary reference would be made to its contents.
16. NATO, *Final Communiques*, p. 271.

17. On MARAIRMED, see: John Marriott, 'NATO and the Mediterranean', *Navy*, vol. 72, no. 12 (December 1968).
18. NATO, *Final Communiques*, pp. 197–8.
19. The Richard G. Colbert Papers (CP), Naval Historical Collection, US Naval War College, Newport, Rhode Island, Series I, Box 19, Folder 366, Letter to Rar Admiral J. H. Adams, RN, 20 December 1967. Citations to the Colbert Papers will follow the location of the documents as listed in the *Register of the Richard G. Colbert Papers* compiled by Dr Evelyn Cherpak. For security reasons a number of documents have been removed from those available to the public. Therefore, while the documents cited in this study are in the folders noted, they may not presently be in the boxes indicated.
20. CP, Series I, Box 18, Folder 337, 'Naval War College Looks At Standing Naval Force Atlantic', enclosure to a letter to Rear Admiral L. Geis, 18 February 1969; Series II, Box 21, Folder 39, 'SNFL Briefing for CINCLANT/CINCLANFLT Officers' (undated).
21. CP 'SNFL Briefing'.
22. Admiral Charles K. Duncan, USN, 'The Maritime Equation: SACLANT in the 1970s', *NATO Fifteen Nations*, vol. 17, no. 1 (February–March 1972) p. 35.
23. *NATO Review* (July–August, 1972) p. 1.
24. Admiral Isaac Kidd, USN, 'A View From the Bridge of the Sixth Fleet Flag Ship', *United States Naval Institute Proceedings* (USNIP), vol 92, no. 2 (February 1972) p. 29.
25. *The North Atlantic Treaty Organisation: Facts and Figures* (Brussels: NATO Information Service, 1981) p. 140.
26. Letter from Admiral Rivero to author, 16 May 1983. See also: Philip A. Dur, 'The Sixth Fleet: A Case Study of Institutionalized Naval Presence 1946–1968' (unpublished Doctoral Thesis, Harvard University, 1976); Desmond P. Wilson, *The Sixth Fleet and the Conventional Defense of Europe*, Professional Paper No. 160 (Alexandria, Virginia, September 1976).
27. 'Exercise Strong Express in Retrospect', *International Defense Review*, No. 6 (1972).
28. Ibid. See also: John Marriott, 'Exercise Strong Express', *NATO's Fifteen Nations*, vol. 18, no. 2 (February–March, 1973).
29. 'Exercise Strong Express in Retrospect'.
30. Canada, Department of National Defence, Directorate of History, General Files, J. D. F. Kealy, *Report on Exercise Ocean Safari 77 16–27, October, 1977* (Access Number, 78/44).
31. Desmond Wettern, 'Defended Lanes vs. Convoys', *Navy International*, vol. 86, no. 12 (December 1981) p. 718.
32. United States, Department of Defense (DOD), Office of the Assistant Secretary of Defense, Program Analysis and Evaluation, *Sealift Procurement and National Security* (Washington, DC, August 1972).
33. United States, DOD, *Annual Report for FY 1975 and FY 1975–1980 Defense Program* (Washington, DC: GPO, 1974) p. 165.
34. United States, DOD, Office of Secretary of Defense, *An Evaluation Report of Mobilization and Deployment Capability Based Exercises Nifty Nugget-78 and Rex 78* (30 June 1978).
35. North American Assembly Papers, *NATO Anti-Submarines Warfare: Strategy, Requirements and the Need for Co-operation* (Brussels, 1982) p. 32.
36. Ibid., pp. 32–3.
37. Ibid.
38. *NATO: Facts and Figures*, p. 172.

39. Ibid., p. 169.
40. Admiral Harry Train, USN, 'Challenge at Sea: Naval Strategy for the 1980s', *NATO's Fifteen Nations*, vol. 27, Special Edition (1982) p. 24.
41. CP, Series II, Box 21, Folder 45, Letter from Admiral Elmo Zumwalt to Colbert, 6 September 1970.
42. CP, Series I, Box 18, Folder 348, Letter to Zumwalt, 3 September 1971. As of this writing, further information on the *Newport Study* remains classified.
43. United States Congress, Senate, Committee on Armed Services, Hearings, *Department of Defense Authorization for Appropriations for Fiscal Year 1979*, Part Two, 96th Congress, 2nd Session (Washington, DC: Government Printing Office, 1978), testimony by Admiral Crowe, p. 1737.
44. Assembly of the Western European Union (AWEU), 19th Session, Part Two, *Security and the Mediterranean*, Report, J. Jung Rapporteur, Document 624 (7 November 1973), p. 8; AWEU, 22nd Session, Part One, *Security in the Mediterranean*, Report, Mr. Buck, Rapporteur, Document 708 (19 May 1976) p. 15. See also: Michael Chichester, John Wilkinson, *The Uncertain Ally: British Defence Policy 1960–1980* (London, 1982).
45. Stephen S. Roberts, 'Western Europe and NATO Navies', *USNIP*, vol. 107, no. 3, March 1981) p. 35.
46. John L. Underwood, *Conflict in the Eastern Mediterranean*, Memorandum (Alexandria, Virginia, 20 August 1979) pp. 15–16.
47. US Congress, *Fiscal Year 1979*, testimony by Crowe, p. 1737.
48. Brian Longworth, 'The Case for a Maritime Strategy', *Defence*, vol. XIV, no. 2 (February 1983) p. 88.
49. Sayre A. Swartztrauber, 'The Potential Battle of the Atlantic', *USNIP*, vol. 105, no. 5 (May 1979) p. 116.
50. Charles A. Sorrels, *U.S. Cruise Missile Programs: Development, Deployment and Implications for Arms Control* (New York, 1983) p. 72.
51. Ibid., pp. 80–1.
52. US Congress, Senate, Committee on Appropriations, Hearings, *Department of Defense Appropriations for Fiscal Year 1975*, Part 3, Department of the Navy, 93rd Congress, 2nd Session (Washington, DC: Government Printing Office), testimony by Admiral Zumwalt, p. 88.
53. Zumwalt, *On Watch*, p. 465.
54. US Congress, CBO, *Planning U.S. General Purpose Forces: The Navy*, Budget Issue Paper (Washington, DC: CBO, December 1976).
55. Ibid., p. 24.
56. Ibid., pp. xv, 12.
57. US Congress, Senate, Committee on Armed Services, Subcommittee on Manpower and Personnel, Hearings, *NATO Posture and Initiatives*, 95th Congress, 1st Session (Washington, DC, 1977), testimony by Secretary of Defense Harold Brown, p. 74.
58. US Congress, *Fiscal Year 1979*, testimony by Deputy Secretary of Defense Charles Duncan, p. 1135.
59. Ibid., testimony by Chief of Naval Operations, Admiral James Holloway, p. 1235.
60. North Atlantic Assembly Papers, *NATO Antisubmarine Warfare*, p. 25.
61. Robert W. Weinland, *Northern Waters: Their Strategic Significance*, Professional Paper 328 (Alexandria, Virginia, December 1980) p. 2.
62. US Congress, CBO, *Shaping the General Purpose Navy of the Eighties: Issues for Fiscal Years, 1981–1985* (Washington, DC, January 1980) pp. 48–9.
63. Admiral Isaac Kidd, USN, 'For Want of a Nail: The Logistics of the Alliance',

Kenneth Myers (ed.), *NATO: The Next Thirty Years* (Boulder, Colorado, 1980) p. 200.
64. Ibid.
65. Nitze, *et al.*, *Securing the Seas*, pp. 374, 381.
66. Carnegie Panel on US Security and the Future of Arms Control, *Challenges for U.S. National Security, Assessing the Balance: Defence Spending and Conventional Forces, A Preliminary Report*, Part II (Washington, DC, 1981) p. 126.
67. Nitze, *et al.*, Securing the Seas, p. 381.
68. North Atlantic Assembly Papers, *NATO Anti-submarine Warfare*, p. 15.
69. Harold Brown, *Thinking About National Security: Defense and Foreign Policy in a Dangerous World* (Boulder, Col. 1983) pp. 101–2.
70. United States Congress, *Congressional Record*, 12 June 1972 (Washington, DC, 1972) p. 20493. In 1972 Senator Proxmire and the Chief Of Naval Operations, Elmo Zumwalt, engaged in an exchange of letters regarding the American–Soviet naval balance. The senator claimed that the United States Navy was still far more powerful than the Soviet fleet measured in terms of the quantity and quality of forces. Zumwalt stressed that the missions of the two navies were different with the American Navy having a protective and projective function and the Soviets a sea denial and therefore the United States needed better forces.
71. CBO, *Shaping the General Purpose Forces of the Eighties*, p. xvii.

15 Fleet Renewal and Maritime Strategy in the 1980s

Robert S. Wood

As the United States maritime strategy was developed and articulated in the 1980s, some critics and commentators argued that it was not in fact a military strategy but a programmatic document to justify the 600-ship navy. Moreover, it was asserted, to the degree that the strategy was intended to govern the actual employment of naval forces, it was inconsistent both with nationally approved concepts of operations and war plans and with Alliance commitments.[1] Although these charges were not without substance, they failed to grasp the significance of the maritime strategy in shaping national security perspectives and fleet operations.[2]

The fact that the maritime strategy was used to undergird budgetary claims should surprise no one. Justification of claims on the Federal treasury is, after all, at the heart of national politics. Moreover strategy should shape the size and structure of one's forces. In this sense, all strategic concepts are force-builders. The only interesting question is whether the unfolding concepts of the strategy were also sensitive to the forces in being or reasonably projected and were intended to govern the use of these forces. Furthermore national and coalition strategies and war plans are not and should not be static. The proponents of the maritime strategy thus argued that, not only were the various dimensions of the strategy designed to shape fleet operations, but they were part of the continuing evolution in national and coalition thinking on the nature of the threat and the appropriate military responses.

Within this context, the maritime strategy can most accurately be seen as a set of concepts for employing joint forces in maritime theatres in support of US national policy and strategy and of alliance, including NATO, commitments. A critical supposition of these concepts is that both deterrence and warfare have fundamentally a coalition character. These general concepts are being translated into a variety of campaign options for crucial maritime theatres so that US and allied forces can be exercised in a range of scenarios. The exercise of such options is the essence of readiness – reinforcing deterrence by demonstrating the ability to concentrate and to employ forces flexibly in war-fighting situations.

The articulation of the general strategic concepts and their exercise in campaign options should in turn provide the basis for force choices and development. It is hoped that this evaluation will keep strategy and force characteristics in harmony with each other and with the actual geopolitical and technological environment. The fact that bureaucratic and fiscal considerations shape these relationships in practice does not lessen the importance of injecting broader strategic perspectives into the political process.

It is thus important to sketch the geopolitical and policy underpinnings of US national strategy and to establish the link between these foundations and the general concepts of the maritime strategy. It is equally important to examine the connection between these general points and the role of allied forces within the framework of the commitments of the North Atlantic Treaty.

THE GEOPOLITICAL SETTING AND NATIONAL POLICY

The most striking aspects of the geopolitics of the United States are the unity and relative tranquility of the political order and security from external invasion. These circumstances, joined with the fact that a high percentage of US external interests and friends lie across vast expanses of water, are the foundations of the maritime character of American military strategy. As the United States is united, secure from invasion, and possessed of important trans-oceanic interests, US strategy is naturally more inclined towards power projection than direct continental defense. The fact that the primary threat to those trans-oceanic interests emanates from a vast Eurasian empire, authoritarian and militarised, dictates that the critical strategic problem for the United States should be to strengthen the states on the periphery of that empire and link them together through the consistent projection of US military power into that periphery, as well as through co-ordinated values and economic links.[3]

The central issues of American strategy, at least as regards the Soviet Union, are clear. The terms of that strategy are dictated, however, not only by geopolitics but by internal sociopolitical circumstances. The United States is a commercial, pluralistic democracy with both constitutional limits on public power and social limits on the propensity to sacrifice welfare benefits and individual discretion in peace-time. Hence national leadership seeks political arrangements, strategies, and technologies that will avoid the starkness of a 'guns versus butter' choice and will forestall the militarisation of society. Economic growth has, since the Second World War allowed such a relatively painless approach. Reduced rates of growth and expanded entitlement programmes led in the 1970s to reduced defence capabilities; reduced rates of growth, still large entitlement programmes and a major defence build-up led in the 1980s to a budget deficit. The issues of the 1990s will be whether the still large deficit will force changes both in national policy and national strategy – and whether the challenges of the external world are compatible with such changes. In any case, up to this moment, national defence has not forced major alterations in domestic government programmes nor personal discretionary spending.

NATIONAL POLICY AND STRATEGY

In simple terms, US policy since the Second World War has been animated by four missions: (1) deter a direct attack on the continental United States; (2) protect the American security zone in North and Central America, including the Caribbean; (3) maintain the central Eurasian balance; and (4) manage global political and economic interests.

The deterrence of direct attack on the United States is analytically, at least, relatively simple. If a direct invasion of the United States appears improbable, the destruction of the country by nuclear attack is far less so. In the absence of means of preventing or neutralising such an attack, US strategy continues to be centred on a secure second strike retaliatory capability, and the critical role of the long-range submarine force in executing that strike remains the least controversial aspect of the US force structure. However it should be noted that every president in the nuclear age has also continued to insist as well on a relatively secure but, most importantly, accurate controlled counter-force in order to forestall the cataclysmic choice of a generalised strike against the enemy's populations. With recent developments in guidance and warhead technology, it may be that the submarine force will also be central to this role. Finally, presidents and their advisors tend to believe that a direct deterrence strategy is, in an important psychological sense, dependent on the ability and willingness to respond to lesser threats with appropriate conventional force. It has been felt that, if the United States is unable to sustain a conventional defence of its wide-flung interests, it may be unwilling to engage in nuclear strikes when more direct challenges to the US position as a Great Power are posed. In any event, a direct attack on the United States has not been the most complex challenge facing US defence planning.

The protection of the US security zone in North and Central America and the Caribbean has been less of a direct military problem than a political one. The issue is not strength on US borders but weakness. Political and economic travail south of US borders, with the potential for civil war and external manipulation of internal disarray, could put demographic pressures on US frontiers and create a climate of insecurity so profound as to limit the willingness and perhaps ability to sustain at current levels commitments in Eurasia. The Soviet–Cuban link and the attachment of the Nicaraguan regime to the Soviet Union exacerbate what would already be a difficult situation. The national security problem of the United States has thus been to sustain viable political and economic orders in these areas while providing to those regimes military and police equipment and training to contain internal disruptions and to resist or put on the defensive Cuban and Nicaraguan mischief. Again, in pure theoretical terms, one can appreciate the complexity of this problem as compared with the mission of direct deterrence.

Following from the above, the maintenance of the central Eurasian balance depends in the first instance on the confidence of the American government and people that a direct attack can be forestalled and that its frontier and immediate environs are friendly and secure. This elementary fact is often forgotten by US allies. The precondition of any power projection by a maritime state is its internal unity and proximate external security. Once established and maintained, the strategy of such a state is three-fold: (1) *Coalition construction and management.* This is not simply a matter of military alliances but the political, diplomatic, and economic demands of protecting the integrity and relative indivisibility of the member-states. (2) *Forward force deployments.* With the political collapse of Europe and the destruction of Japanese military power during the Second World War, the basic foreign and national security policy facing the United States was to convert its involvement in the Eurasian balance from an episodic to a constant element. The presence of the United States Army and Air Force in Europe and naval forces in the Norwegian Sea and the Mediterranean are testimony to the success of this conversion. (3) *Maintenance of the sea and air lines of communication, control of critical choke points, and protection of the terminus points where US forces and equipment will be deployed.* These missions ultimately involved not an equality of friendly and hostile forces in these air, sea and adjacent land links but early superiority of US and allied forces.

Apart from these classic elements of power projection, US and NATO strategy has also been premised on the early use of nuclear weapons should initial conventional defence prove unable to dissuade Soviet–Warsaw Pact forces from continuing their advance. Consistent with judgements of NATO commanders that there is a severely finite period of time during which the West could resist on the conventional level, the progression from conventional to battlefield and theatre nuclear to intercontinental nuclear warfare has been seen as quite short. And, indeed, many politicians and defence analysts considered this extension of the American nuclear deterrent capability as the ultimate guarantor of the peace.

It is true that it is precisely the short war thesis and the meaning of the extended nuclear deterrent that was raised in the unfolding development of the maritime strategy. It must be emphasised, however, that maritime strategists were not alone in raising these questions. Influential policy-makers and defence analysts – including critics of the maritime strategy – were also asking troublesome questions about NATO's nuclear strategy and suggesting other perspectives.[4] The maritime perspective on these issues will be made explicit in the pages to follow.

Finally, US policy and strategy have been faced since the Second World War with the task of supporting friends, protecting interests, and opening political and economic opportunities in a world in which Soviet threats are only a part, and sometimes a relatively small part, of the problem. In effect, the United States has been cast in the classic role of a regulatory state. And, as with the United Kingdom in the nineteenth century, naval power has been central to this role – and, as with the nuclear deterrent role at the other end of the spectrum, this task has been rather well accepted by defence analysts.

It is in the area of the maintenance of the central balance and the type of deterrent and war-fighting postures this requires that the role of naval forces has raised the most heated controversy – and which makes the unfolding of the maritime strategy in the 1980s most interesting.

THE ELEMENTS OF THE MARITIME STRATEGY

It has been correctly observed that most elements of the maritime strategy were well founded in naval thinking long before their integrated articulation in the 1980s. It is also worth emphasising that these concepts are compatible both with the American geopolitical posture and evolving overall strategic thought in the United States. Yet it was not simply the budgetary battles which the maritime strategy was called upon to sustain that made these concepts controversial. The development and articulation of the strategy did illuminate in sometimes painful ways the fault lines in US and NATO strategy and did publicly enunciate Navy roles that many found excessive or dangerous.

As a recent study by John Hattendorf shows, the maritime strategy is anything but an orphan.[5] Paternity is claimed everywhere – and with apparently perfect sincerity. What this may demonstrate is the existence of a general climate of strategic opinion in the 1980s with multiple expressions. Although these multiple expressions led to charges that it was impossible to identify clearly the exact meaning of the strategic approach, certain clear themes were fairly well defined by the mid-eighties. If it cannot be said that the ideas associated with the maritime strategy were specifically reflected in NATO doctrine or national war plans, they were visible, on the one hand, in semi-official national defence documents such as *Discriminate Deterrence* (the Iklé Report)[6] and, on the other hand, in campaign plans, theatre concepts of operation, and exercises.

What are the common assumptions and strategic approaches rising out of the US maritime strategy and what issues are associated with these concepts? Critical to maritime thinking in the 1980s was that the nuclear threshold had been raised. The existence of nuclear weapons continued to inhibit thoughts of general war between the superpowers and to undergird the security of those areas where their most vital interests met, that is, Europe. As strategists on both sides thought through actual combat should deterrence fail, they had a difficult time identifying battlefield conditions that would be improved by the *actual* use of nuclear weapons; that is, the credibility of extended deterrence had lessened. At the same time, some commentators, such as John Mearsheimer and Barry Posen – neither of whom is friendly to the claims of the proponents of the maritime strategy – argued that conventional deterrence was not an impossible dream but depended on a force structure and strategic concepts geared towards conventional defence.[7] While their conclusions diverged in terms of the relative size, structure and role of naval forces, the general thrust of their argument was not inconsistent with ideas being developed in naval circles – an early cataclysmic nuclear retaliatory option should not constitute the basis of US and allied defence planning.

In simple terms, the critical assumption undergirding reflections on the maritime aspects of national strategy was that one must be prepared to confront the Soviets with a protracted, global, largely or exclusively conventionally-fought war during which intra-war nuclear deterrence would be effective. The crucial notion was that deterrence would best be served if the Soviets understood that even at the conventional level they could not expect a rapid, decisive war confined to a single theatre but would be faced with an uncertain conflict prosecuted at many points.

Central to these ideas was the ability of the United States to control vital maritime theatres – choke or access points the domination of which would reduce Soviet threats to the sea and the air lines of communication, and would favour at one and the same time our ability to sustain the war on the central front while threatening high-value Soviet targets (such as logistic lines, industrial facilities, follow-on echelon forces, sea-based nuclear retaliatory systems). These maritime theatres included not only sea areas such as the Norwegian Sea, the eastern Mediterranean and the Japanese seas but the air and land areas contiguous to them. Hence the control of these theatres requires a combination of naval and land-based forces if our forces are to survive and prevail. As will be illustrated below, one of the theatres where these concepts have been most thoroughly considered and exercised is the Norwegian Sea.

There are at least six persistent issues associated with this approach: (1) the early employment in wartime of the fleet in forward operations versus missions directly designed for maintaining the sea lines of communication and convoy protection; (2) the concentration on the carrier forces relative to attack submarines; (3) the conscious policy of putting the Soviet ballistic missile fleet at risk; (4) the cost of the naval build-up relative to spending on land, and land-based air forces designated directly for the central European front; and (5) the stability of nuclear deterrence in the conduct of war.

Forward fleet deployments in key 'maritime theatres' rather than exclusive concentration on transatlantic convoys were dictated in the minds of naval analysts by the broad purposes that naval forces would have to serve in conflict and by the most economical way to ensure the Atlantic sea lines of communications themselves.[8] Put simply, the control of areas such as the Norwegian Sea, the so-called GIUK or GIN Gaps (Greenland–Iceland–United Kingdom; Greenland–Iceland–Norway) guarantees a number of important strategic objectives: (1) the difficulty or inability of Soviet forces to transit freely back and forth into, for instance, the Atlantic – and hence limiting their reload capability; (2) in conjunction with control of adjacent land area, again, for instance, in Norway, the protection of convoy routes and key British air bases from aerial attack; and (3) the ability as the war progressed to launch strike campaigns against important Soviet targets via those same access points.

This concentration on key theatres and access points increases the relative importance of carrier aid in gaining and maintaining air control and, as the campaign unfolds, in attacking selected military targets. At the same time, for the carriers to operate in the areas at all, the submarine threat has to be severely reduced. And, if the carrier battle forces were needed early, then the attrition or distancing of that threat was essential. Up to now, the protection of the Soviet ballistic missile submarines by the other components of Soviet naval forces in areas close to the Soviet Union, has suggested the wisdom of a strategy that would press hard against those ballistic missile submarines, thus reinforcing the Soviet defensive naval posture – and at the same time holding at risk their reserve force. Moreover the declaration of an anti-submarine warfare zone by the Norwegians in their territorial waters would also favour the early arrival of the carrier battle force.

However, as improvements in range and the quieting of Soviet submarines in general – attack and ballistic missile – takes place, some argue that Soviet attack submarines may be 'untied' from the ballistic missile submarine, allowing increased numbers of attack submarines of higher quality to operate in places like the Norwegian Sea and beyond. It can be appreciated that in an era of limited resources legitimate debate can ensue on the shape of the naval budget as regards, for example, submarine development and production, and carrier forces. Even proponents of the maritime strategy disagree on this tough issue.[9]

Beyond the argument on the appropriate naval balance is, of course, the broader argument on naval versus other forces. In brief, maritime proponents argue that, without maritime superiority, the ability of the United States to sustain the land conflict in Europe is degraded or lost and that, in any case, marginal improvements on the central front should come from those most immediately affected – the continental NATO partners. Whatever the relative strategic merits of the debate, it is probably worth observing that the willingness of Congress to increase substantially US force improvements in Europe is not increasing but declining.

Two important problems internal to the maritime strategy also become apparent. First, once the battle force is assembled, and assuming success on the US–allied part, would not the Soviets be tempted to launch a nuclear strike on that force on the assumption that nuclear war at sea can be separated from other forms of nuclear combat?[10] This raises the question of how to maintain intra-war deterrence. Many answers have been suggested but analytically they boil down to three: (1) the need for precautionary deployment patterns; (2) the development of (acknowledged) equivalent retaliatory measures; and (3) political limits on the political objects of the war by both sides. A second issue is the ability of the US industrial base to sustain a protracted war or to retain access to and protect other industrial bases (such as Japan) that could also sustain the combat. It should be apparent that both this problem and the issue of intra-war deterrence are dilemmas that not only must engender greater thought in the years ahead but will require important national-level decisions.

At this point, the dimensions of the maritime strategy can best be illustrated by reference to one paradigmatic campaign associated with the strategy – the Norwegian campaign.[11] At the same time, it is important to understand the possible implication of the strategic approach for the NATO Alliance members.

THE NORTHERN FLANK CAMPAIGN

In the early Reagan years, naval leadership concentrated its public discussions of the maritime strategy largely on the European theatre, particularly on the northern flank. This was not only because of the strategic significance of this theatre for US support to Europe, but because it was felt it could be used to build the strongest case in the budget debates. The unfortunate effect of this political strategy was that it tended to equate a prototypical campaign in the north Norwegian Sea with the conceptual entirety of the maritime strategy. None the less it did provide one of the better scenarios for looking at the dimensions of the maritime strategy within a theatre of operations. It might well be useful, therefore, to explore the thought undergirding this campaign.

Our deterrence posture is based on denial of Soviet objectives and, failing that, punishment. Because of the uncertain risk of escalation, this has thus far been an effective deterrent. Moreover, given the current force balance in Central Europe, the former Supreme Allied Commander Europe General Bernard Rogers had characterised his options as 'escalate or capitulate'. In either case, however, war termination with Warsaw Pact forces on NATO territory would call into question the *raison d'être* of the Alliance and might well result in the Soviets achieving their fundmental aim of the dissolution of NATO. Furthermore escalation to nuclear weapons may not prove to

NATO's military advantage. The threat of intercontinental exchange as part of our deterrent posture may be persuasive. But, in the event of war itself, we may prefer a broader set of options, since it is unclear how such a strike would reverse the battlefield situation in Europe. Compared to a strategy of either escalating to nuclear warfare or capitulation, a strategy that allows global, conventional and extended warfare has merit both from a deterrent and a war-fighting perspective. Such an approach maximises the utility of the economic and human potential of the West and does not convert an initial loss of NATO territory into either the dissolution of the Alliance or Armageddon.

It would remain true that the nuclear dimension of even a prolonged conventional war between NATO and the Warsaw Pact would remain paramount. In the first place, the Soviets may well view conventional warfighting as a stage that precedes nuclear war and would have fighting the war for the nuclear advantage a foremost objective, that is, the strategic balance at the conclusion of fighting. Moreover the existence of a large proportion of dual capable systems, as well as nuclear systems that are indistinguishable from conventional systems, implies that even conventional exchanges will necessarily result in the reduction of nuclear forces and could hence shift elements of the nuclear balance. Secondly, because Soviet general purpose forces have as a primary mission the protection of their strategic nuclear forces, as well as their borders, any threat to these targets should reduce the Soviet forces available to contest NATO command of the sea and perhaps prevent the commitment of some forces to the central land campaign. Soviet concerns for the strategic balance and for the ability to control theatre combat assigned forces may not only reinforce the US deterrent posture in peace-time but may well provide a basis for a negotiated termination of war should it occur.

Central to such a strategic perspective are Alliance cohesion and willingness to take the necessary steps to assert and maintain command of the seas. Control of northern Norway is vital to establishing command of the Norwegian Sea and North Atlantic, as is control of the Baltic Straits. Particularly in the far north, application of maritime and air power initially contributes to the command of the seas necessary for the defence of the central front and ultimately provides NATO with an option to escalate Soviet risks short of the use of nuclear weapons. To make credible such a posture, we must conduct exercises in peace-time with our combined forces to indicate the capability to deploy early and aggressively and the will to do so. As has been pointed out many times, this capability and will does not mean a foolhardy rush of surface forces into the Norwegian Sea but rather a sea, land and air campaign partially sequential in character. The viability of various mixes and sequences now requires examination through intense campaign planning, war gaming and exercises.

To prevent Soviet control of the vital sea and air spaces translates into control not only of the Norwegian Sea and the Baltic Straits but also the Bosporus and the Japanese straits. Control of the Baltic and its straits primarily rests with the Danish, the German, the Swedish and the Norwegian forces. This control is probably more threatened by Warsaw pact advances through Schleswig-Holstein and Jutland than by the Soviet Baltic Fleet. The success of Soviet and Warsaw pact forces in Jutland compared to the success of Soviet forces in northern Norway may in the event determine where naval power projection forces are best directed. Given the difficulty and dangers of these choices, a set of campaign options clearly needs to be developed and exercised.

Should NATO forces hold the littorals on the Norwegian Sea, sea control could be established in the northern Norwegian Sea without the presence of a carrier battle force. In this circumstance Soviet surface forces and submarines west of North Cape could be defeated by NATO SSNs and Maritime Patrol Aircraft (armed with Harpoon) assisted by land-based reconnaissance and naval attack aircraft, while those submarines south of the G–I–N gap were worked over by the full range of NATO ASW forces. Soviet surface combatants are not likely to be in the Atlantic at the start of hostilities. An important point to keep in mind is that Soviet attack submarines in the North Atlantic will have a priority for targets. Anti-SSBN and anti-carrier missions are expected to be top priorities, followed by strategic cruise missile and sea lane interdiction missions. Keeping SSBN, CVBG, and convoys geographically separated would prevent Soviet submarines from accomplishing more than one mission at a time, and would permit our forces to concentrate on the area where they were aggregated to accomplish their priority mission.

Presumed in the situation above is that defences in northern Norway would hold, the air bases would remain largely intact, and that there would be sufficient sorties for land-based aircraft to conduct close air support, defensive (and perhaps offensive) counter air and battlefield air interdiction, and also to conduct strikes at sea against Soviet amphibious and other naval forces. Should the available aircraft and facilities *not* be able to support all of these missions, the Atlantic Fleet Striking Force might be the best alternative available to carry on the battle. Though the time of year and weather will largely determine the pace of events this far north, should there be any shortfall in the USAF, USMC or Canadian aircraft assigned to the region, support from the Striking Force might be required immediately for the successful defence of northern Norway.

Just as control of northern Norway assures NATO control of the Norwegian Sea, control of the Norwegian Sea is necessary to sustain the fight in northern Norway. Limited facilities will tax the logistics pipeline in a future battle as they did in the Second World War. Movement by sea is the only viable means of supplying the material needed. Therefore we cannot afford to think of the Norwegian Sea as the Soviets' backyard, too risky a place to operate. It seems perverse to think of a sea, whose only littorals are NATO territory, as under Soviet purview. The risk is in not committing enough forces to what is admittedly a relatively small theatre of conflict compared to the central front, but which has such strategic significance.

Should the war begin under conditions where neither forward defences nor Alliance cohesion are likely to hold, the strategy must call for something else to achieve termination acceptable to NATO. A polar view of the world reveals another aspect of the strategic importance of the north. From waters contiguous to the Soviet Union the newer classes of Soviet SSBNs can aim their missiles under the protection of their own naval forces and ice. Reversing the direction, the flight-path from strategic bomber bases in the United States to Moscow passes right over the Kola Peninsula. In addition to their role as protectors of SSBNs, with the introduction of fourth generation aircraft, the surface forces of the Soviet Northern Fleet play an increasing role in extending the northern air defence zone against strategic bomber attack. Destruction of both the SSBNs and their covering forces affect the Soviet calculation of the nuclear balance. Regarded principally as strategic reserve, the loss of Soviet warheads at sea directly affects both targeting and the Soviet's perception of their ability to prevail should the United States launch a first strike. A reduction in air defences also enters into the calculations through the increased number of bombers and cruise missiles that could penetrate the Soviet Union to their targets.

To some extent operations to gain control of the sea affect the nuclear balance by reducing the total forces available to the Soviets to commit to strategic defence. However, should the situation warrant, specifically assigning NATO SSNs to the destruction of Northern Fleet strategic forces operating in the Barents and under the ice would directly alter the nuclear balance and raise Soviet risks associated with not reaching a termination agreement.

Planning for the employment of any of the above options, or others that may develop, is already well advanced, They are in some aspects dependent on three operational requirements: (1) early deployment of Striking Fleet Atlantic; (2) operations in the Norwegian Seas and Fjords to reduce and counter the threat to our forward deployed forces; and (3) employment of the combined might of Striking Fleet carriers, ASW forces, amphibious forces and marines, and land-based airpower.

As noted earlier, if the key battle for the control of the North develops early, both as a deterrent and in war-fighting terms, it is important that NATO respond to warning in a timely and orderly way by ordering the early deployment of maritime forces. Such early deployment requires attention to the defence of the forces, which explains recent attention to the co-ordination of land- and sea-based air defence. Operating in Norwegian territorial waters prior to hostilities also excludes Soviet forces, thus reducing the prospect of pre-emption. The submarine threat may remain the most difficult. But deployment adjacent to Norway has the added advantage of allowing the Striking Fleet to concentrate its ASW forces in small areas, thus heightening the prospect of success. The exercise *Ocean Safari 85* and subsequent exercises further suggested the importance and feasibility of operating with allies and of exploiting geography to reduce the threat. With the attrition of the immediate threat, the striking power of the combined forces could indeed be formidable.

Critics of the Striking Fleet Atlantic's concept of operations may be missing the point. If containment remains the policy of the NATO allies and the forward strategy is the cohesive cement of the Alliance in both political and military terms, there are few acceptable alternatives but to develop and test these various options. No one can predict what combination of forces and options would be used at the moment of battle. The political and military context will be decisive. The improvement of one's ability to survive and to operate aggressively in this area is, however, an important element of deterrence and provides the campaign discipline to respond flexibly in the event of war.

THE MARITIME STRATEGY AND NATO

We have discussed so far in broad terms the maritime elements of US global strategy in support of its NATO interests and commitments. Let us now focus on how these concepts might relate to Alliance thinking and how the NATO maritime partners might fight in concert should deterrence fail – and, just as important, how the allied maritime elements of NATO strategy and the war-fighting capabilities that underwrite its credibility, bolsters deterrence in peace and crises.[12]

The trend towards greater emphasis on the conventional phase of flexible response is clear. Whereas flexible response generally refers in the Central European context to a series of steps ranging from conventional defence to limited nuclear strikes to intercontinental nuclear response, demands for greater flexibility in both geography and time are being placed on NATO strategy as conventional forces pick up greater burdens for deterrence and forward defence.

Put simply, neither the US nor the Soviets have the forces for maximum sustained war-fighting in all theatres simultaneously. Against rigid defence plans covering all NATO borders the Soviets could concentrate in one theatre and overwhelm the defences, either through sheer numbers or by sustaining combat for longer periods. Strategy and plans that would permit economy of force efforts in theatres under limited or no attack, while concentrating forces in the theatre under direct attack, offer the best prospects for successful forward defence.

Though greater flexibility for the employment of forces to confound and defeat Soviet attacks in the AFCENT region could be realised (such as redeployment of heavier German and US forces to the north, and lighter forces to the south should the threat be oriented that way), AFNORTH and AFSOUTH provide greater possibilities for flexible employment of forces. These theatres are essentially maritime in nature, characterised by relatively thin strips of land where the depth and the lines of communication in the theatre are at sea. Reversing this perspective, these are also the theatres where massed naval power projection forces can, in conjunction with land-based forces, rapidly alter the correlation of forces in the air and on adjacent land areas. Truly flexible use of these forces in response to the situation actually faced, rather than adherence to set plans, is a key determinant of successful forward defence, and thus deterrence. This type of thinking is a critical element in the maritime strategy, but is moreover a way to put more teeth into flexible response.

If conventional flexibility is the key, what implications does this have for allied force requirements? Developments in concepts of strategic needs have evolved with changes in the nuclear balances and force postures, and are not revolutionary. Therefore there is no radical shift in the Alliance roles, though some things need to be emphasised.

On the broadest conceptual level, geography dictates that the things necessary for immediate defence be in place, that the things that take the longest time to bring to the battle be closest to the battle, and that the means to sustain the battle be preserved. In general this would mean that the European allies should concentrate on the development of heavy ground forces which take time to ferry across the Atlantic, and which are potentially escalatory if sent to a theatre during a crisis. Without reducing the current US commitment in theatre, the ability of America's European allies to provide for initial forward defence on the ground and in the air should be a top priority. Inter- and intra-theatre lift to permit flexible use of these forces anywhere in Europe should be a goal. The United States cannot assume full responsibility for these forces because of the size of the forces required and the need for US forces to look after global interests and responsibilities.

In the naval realm, the forces that meet the above prescription are small ships (such as minesweepers, diesel submarines, and inter-coastal ferries) that are not readily transferred across the Atlantic. In addition, the European allies should contribute to control of the seas adjacent to their littorals so that power projection forces can be applied. As the size of their respective navies required for near sea control by most NATO members is already consistent with their definition of their global responsibilities, no change in force structure is contemplated by this observation. Finally, inter-operability between allies defending forward on land, sea and in the air, and power projection forces coming to their support, is a critical concern.

The tasks implicit in the trans-Atlantic maritime commitment are enormous. The region stretches from the Eastern Black Sea to North Cape to the west; it stretches across the North Atlantic all the way through the Florida Straits, to the Gulf ports of the United States. In fact, if we consider the growing defence industrial support capacity in Japan and other Pacific Rim countries, a new strategic map emerges. (One with America in the middle instead of 'at the left edge' of the map.) Instead of envisioning SLOCs running solely from the US East Coast to NATO Europe, for some key war materials, these supply lines could now stretch across the United States, across the vast Pacific to countries such as Japan which could augment NATO's defence industrial capacity in a major NATO/Warsaw Pact war.[13]

In recent years many attempts have been made to better utilise increasingly scarce defence resources; a frequent suggestion has been to employ the concept of defence specialisation. Although there are difficult practical and political problems with this idea, NATO's maritime states have made substantial progress in harmonising their individual contributions to collective defence by avoiding redundancies and by emphasising comparative advantages. As a result, therefore, the role and significance of individual navies in this Alliance – and ultimately the success of deterrence and defence – can only be judged within the context of the NATO Maritime Strategy that synergistically weaves these individual contributions into a whole that is greater and more powerful than its aggregate components. Many people (particularly armchair strategists) when commenting on the US/NATO Maritime Strategy, focus on high-visibility warfare areas: carrier battle group, battleship and SSBN operations; however, senior allied officers know that these are only the tip of the strategic iceberg.

In the Black Sea, for example, it is Turkish forces that provide NATO's forward defence. An aggressive defence in this area would not only protect the Turkish Straits, Anatolia and Thrace but would also force the Soviet Union to consider the vulnerability of its southern flank, and not to concentrate 100 per cent of its combat power on the central region. An aggressive allied defence in this region would also bottle up close to 600 Warsaw Pact naval vessels, including major Soviet combatants; isolate one of the Soviets' major ship-building and repair and logistics facilities; provide a major contribution to reducing Soviet global power; and even support the war in the Pacific by severing at its source one of the two main logistics lines to the Soviet Far East. Without the Soviet Southern Sea route, which starts in the Black Sea, the only link between the heartland of Soviet Europe and the Far East is the fragile Trans-Siberian Railroad and the Baikol Amur (BAM). Finally, Turkish control of the straits coupled with Greek control of the southern gate to the Aegean – the Crete Channels – would effectively provide a 'cordon sanitaire' within which US Carrier Battle Groups could bring air power to bear for the air defence of Thrace, the Straits and Northwest Anatolia.

To the West, the Italian Navy, particularly when augmented with organic air power, provides early warning and forward defence of Southern Italy (especially if the Soviet Union uses Libya as a pre-stocked forward operating base). The Italian Navy also has key roles in keeping important NATO re-supply ports open, maintaining the integrity of the SLOC to the Eastern Mediterranean and guarding the flank of US battle groups and other allied forces operating forward in the Aegean/Eastern Mediterranean area.

Powerful French naval forces, when correlated with NATO's defence, would provide an additional flexible element to NATO's power projection and ASW potential. Further, the participation of France would dramatically improve security and flexibility of reinforcement and re-supply to NATO Europe. Provision of French ports to the southwest of the central front would, through numbers and geographic dispersion, reduce the threat on the vulnerable SLOC Termini and thus free additional NATO naval forces to take the initiative. (Additionally, the French sea-based nuclear deterrent force and the independent decision authority that controls it, may further reduce the already minimal incentive for the Soviets to employ their limited ASW assets – primarily SSNs – in an effective attack on Western sea-based nuclear systems.)

Spain – with its substantial high-capability forces, including modern Maritime Patrol Aircraft and new programmes such as the AV-8 'BRAVO' VSTOL A/C and F18s – guards the maritime approaches to the Mediterranean, thus assuring the flow of reinforcements and re-supply to France, Italy, Greece and Turkey. Together with her Iberian neighbour, Portugal, Spain provides enormously valuable strategic depth to support NATO's defence.

The Portuguese Navy, particularly with newly developing capabilities, such as the P-3 Maritime Patrol Aircraft, has a vital role of guarding the southern SLOCs in the IBERLANT area and protecting the Azores that are a vital link in NATO air lines of communication.

To the North, the Belgian Navy has a similar mission in the Channel area, with emphasis on mine warfare and maintaining access to the BENELUX ports. These and other Channel Command maritime forces, particularly ASW forces, would provide NATO with the option, if necessary, to bring in US carrier battle groups to support the air battle in the Jutland/TWOATAF area – and in later phases to carry the fight to the Warsaw Pact in the Baltic.

Dutch forces, including submarines, new maritime patrol aircraft and modern frigates, would also make a major contribution in this region.

With forces and a strategy to secure the southern SLOCs, the ports of debarcation, the logistic bases in the Azores, Spain, France, the UK and the BENELUX, small but politically and militarily potent Dutch and UK Marines can be moved forward – early – along with North American maritime forces to support the defence of Norway; the defence of Norway, in turn, is the key to the success of the NATO Maritime Strategy (CONMAROPS – NATO's concept of maritime operations) and ultimately the defence of Europe.

Norwegian naval forces would work with other allied units to maintain control of the Norwegian Sea, defend the amphibious approaches to Norway and keep the Fjords and Leads clear and available for the forward movement of logistics and Norwegian allied ground forces. Aggressive ASW prosecution by Norway, along with the UK ASW group and other NATO ASW forces, would allow US carrier battle groups – in concert with Norwegian and other land-based air power – to establish air superiority over the Norwegian Sea and North Norway. Maintaining control of the air space over North Norway and the Norwegian Sea would allow UKAIR to turn its full effort to the East, press continental air forces forward and thus contribute significantly to the successful air battle for the central region. Additionally air superiority over the Norwegian Sea would allow allied MPA to join the ASW campaign.

Across the Atlantic, in WESTLANT, additional US and Canadian forces would protect the approaches to North American ports and, through intensive ASW, severely limit Soviet strategic and operational incentive to place their cruise or ballistic missile submarines in forward positions, reinforcing the Soviets' predisposition to keep these nuclear assets 'close to home', increase warning time and thus further ensure the integrity of the North American-based strategic leg of NATO's Triad.

In the Baltic, Danish and German maritime forces defend the third cornerstone of the Forward Maritime Strategy (Thrace/Turkish Straits, and North Norway being the other two). These three maritime cornerstones share a common trait: all possess an element of vulnerability as well as an element of opportunity. In the Baltic, without a strong forward maritime defence, Jutland could be lost and, as a result, NATO's central front could be outflanked. Alternatively, with success in this campaign, allied forces could press forward in the Baltic, cut off the increasingly important Soviet SLOC to East Germany, threaten the northern flank of the Soviet advance, and force the Soviet Union to calculate the vulnerability of her own homeland.

CONCLUSION

As indicated at the beginning of this chapter, the intellectual framework established by the maritime strategy development has resurrected campaign and combined arms thinking and has posed a series of questions and strategic dilemmas that may well provide the grist for national and Alliance policy mills into the 1990s. No matter how these strategic patterns may unfold, the complex *global* dimensions of NATO strategy are likely to be given new emphasis.

The maritime dimensions of the US and NATO strategy will be global because the highly improbable event for which it is designed could only occur in a gravely deteriorating international environment, and would involve an unprecedented confrontation among states possessing nuclear weapons. It will be global because the interests of the NATO states would be global in such circumstances. It will be global because US and other friendly and allied maritime forces positioned forward in defence of their interests will be in contact with Soviet units: it is implausible, for example, to imagine shooting in the Norwegian Sea and saluting Soviet units in the Northwest Pacific. Most significantly, the strategy is global so that the Soviet Union cannot believe that it would be possible to confine an attack against the land areas of Central Europe. In all this, the maritime strategy has broadened the strategic dialogue both within the United States and in NATO.

Notes

1. See, for instance, R. Komer, *Maritime Strategy or Coalition Defense* (Cambridge, Mass., 1984); J. Beatty, 'In Harm's Way', *The Atlantic Monthly* (May 1987) pp. 37–53; J. M. Collins, *U.S.–Soviet Military Balance, 1980–1985* (Washington, 1985), especially chapters 9, 11, 12, 16; William W. Kaufmann, *A Thoroughly Efficient Navy* (Washington, DC, 1987); John J. Mearsheimer, 'A Strategic Misstep: The Maritime Strategy and Deterrence in Europe', *International Security* (Fall 1986) pp. 3–57.
2. For authoritative statements on the maritime strategy, see The Maritime Strategy Supplement to the US Naval Institute *Proceedings* (January 1986) and Admiral C. A. H. Trost, 'Looking Beyond the Maritime Strategy', US Naval Institute *Proceedings* (January 1987) pp. 13–16. For a recent comprehensive and sympathetic study, see N. Friedman, *The Maritime Strategy of the U.S. Navy: Concepts and Operations* (London, 1987).
3. See C. S. Gray, *Maritime Strategy, Geopolitics, and the Defense of the West* (New York, 1986).
4. See, for instance, J. Mearsheimer, *Conventional Deterrence* (Ithaca and London, 1983).
5. J. Hattendorf, 'The Evolution of the U.S. Navy's Maritime Strategy, 1977–1986', *Naval War College Review* (Summer 1988).
6. *Discriminate Deterrence* – Report of the Commission on Integrated and Long-Term Strategy, delivered to the Secretary of Defense and the Assistant to the President for National Security Affairs, on 11 January 1988 (Washington, DC, 1988).
7. J. Mearsheimer, *Conventional Deterrence* and B. Posen, 'Measuring the European Conventional Balance: Coping with Complexity in Threat Assessment', *International Security* (Winter 1984/5) pp. 47–88. For a critique of this view, see E. A. Cohen, 'Toward Better Net Assessment: Rethinking the Conventional Balance in Europe', *International Security* (Summer 1988).
8. For an examination of the notion of maritime theatres, see Captain Dennis Blair, USN, 'The Significance of Maritime Theaters', *Naval War College Review* (Summer 1988).
9. The Chief of Naval Operations, Admiral Carlisle Trost is keenly sensitive to this issue. See, for instance, Trost, 'Looking Beyond'.
10. For varying views on this subject, see N. Polmar, 'The Soviet Navy: Nuclear War at Sea', US Naval Institute *Proceedings* (July 1986) pp. 111–13; Captain L. Brooks, USN, 'The Nuclear Maritime Strategy', US Naval Institute *Proceedings* (April 1987) pp. 33–9; Ronald O'Rourke, *Nuclear Escalation, Strategic Anti-Submarine Warfare, and the Navy's Forward Maritime Strategy*, Congressional

Research Service (Washington, DC, 27 February 1987); B. A. Posen, 'Inadvertent Nuclear War?: Escalation and NATO's Northern Fleet', *International Security* (Fall 1982) pp. 28–54.

11. For an in-depth examination of campaigns in this theatre, see R. S. Wood and J. P. Hanley, Jr, 'The Maritime Role in the North Atlantic', *Naval War College Review* (November–December 1985) pp. 5–18 and Vice Admiral H. C. Mustin, 'The Role of the Navy and the Marines in the Norwegian Sea', *Naval War College Review* (March–April 1986) pp. 2–6.

12. Commander S. V. MacKay, RN, 'An Allied Reaction', US Naval Institute, *Proceedings* (April 1987) pp. 82–9; Lt. Gen. T. Huitfeldt, RNA, *NATO's Northern Security* (London, 1976) and 'The Threat from the North – Defense of Scandinavia', in *NATO's Sixteen Nations* (October 1986) pp. 26–32; R. S. Jordan, 'The Maritime Strategy and the Atlantic Alliance', *Journal of the Royal United Services Institute for Defense Studies* (September 1987) pp. 45–54.

13. For a more detailed examination of the US industrial base and the role of Japan, see R. S. Wood, 'Conventional Deterrence and the American Industrial Base: Security Challenges for the Nineteen-Nineties', in *Business in the Contemporary World* (H. Sawyer, ed.) (Washington, 1988).

16 Conclusions Maritime Strategy and National Policy: Historical Accident or Purposeful Planning?

John B. Hattendorf and Robert S. Jordan

> Fortunately as regards other states, we [in the United States] are an island power, and can find our best precedents in the history of the people to whom the sea has been a nursing mother.
>
> A. T. Mahan

In our view, the balance of power is a means to an end in international politics, not an end in itself. It is the means by which a state can prevent another from dominating world politics. At the same time, a balance of power creates a situation which allows a state to ensure its own safety and to promote its own interests and objectives. This system imposes limits on the degree and the range of objectives which a state can pursue, and this is true even if a state does not self-consciously pursue a balance of some sort. A balance of power is inherently self-limiting. It prevents hegemony by any single Power, and operates within the context of political pluralism.

In the twentieth century, both Britain and America have used maritime strategy as a sub-set of grand strategy in order to deal with balance of power issues. In regard to Europe, Britain was the traditional balancer who allied herself with the weaker Powers against whichever continental state threatened to predominate. Maritime power was always a key element in traditional British usage, but it was rarely if ever successfully used without reference to the military, economic and diplomatic factors of power. Thus, maritime strategy does not stand alone among the strategies which may be employed to achieve a balance of power, yet it is a subject which is complex enough to deserve its own in-depth analysis.

We can understand the means by which Britain and America have used their maritime power in terms of the balance of power through the four topics of this book: first, the development of the British model of decision-making by which maritime strategy was linked to other national, strategic concerns and to international peace-keeping; second, in terms of the development of naval theory by British and American students of it as they sought to provide an abstract explanation of applications of maritime power; thirdly, in terms of the relationship between peace-time planning for a future war at sea and the actual practice of maritime strategy when that war came. And fourth, in the light of these first three topics, the planning that has gone on since 1945 in regard to the use of navies to maintain the balance of power, both as a deterrent to war and as a participant in a possible future war.

BRITISH AND AMERICAN NOTIONS OF THE BALANCE OF POWER

The influence of Britain on twentieth century coalition warfare has been profound, not only because of the ideas that have been generated about coalition war and international peace-keeping, but also because of the intimate connection these have had with notions of the balance of power – notions developed in the seventeenth, eighteenth and nineteenth centuries by British thinkers in response to Britain's imperial role. The whole issue was summarised by Carsten Holbraad in this way:

> The balance of power theorists, conscious that national security depended on European equilibrium, insisted on the right to intervene to prevent a rival power from gaining dangerous aggrandizement. Their opponents, convinced that the welfare of the people had nothing to do with the balance of power, allowed intervention only when national interests were threatened directly. The balance of power theorists rested their case on the traditions of European politics. Their opponents took their stand on the roles of Christian morality. Here the conflict was between those who liked to control the existing political system and those who wanted to develop a new international order.[1]

These two conflicting, or perhaps more accurately, complementary, viewpoints have been an integral part of the American foreign policy tradition as well. In America, the debate has raged since the turn of the century, when President McKinley revealed that his decision to acquire the Philippines came as a result of prayer, and when interventions in Central America were justified as bringing civilisation and Christianity to otherwise irresponsible and hapless peoples. In one sense, Britain's 'splendid isolation' towards Europe coupled with interventionist actions elsewhere, have been paralleled by American 'isolationism' towards Europe coupled with interventionist actions elsewhere. On both counts, strategies have been invoked which embraced the use of naval force as a concomitant of notions about the balance of power.

These strategies have expressed the concept of balance of power in two ways. First, it has been used to cloak the employment of extra-continental power, in which naval power has been central, to redress an unfavourable balance of power on the European continent. Second, balance of power has been used to compare localised or regional force strengths. Analysts have examined both the Far East and the Caribbean in this way. Since the end of the Second World War, however, American rationalisations for intervening in Europe have changed. They were initially based on creating a regional balance of power *vis-à-vis* the Soviet Union. Later, this rivalry became global in nature, and so the rationalisation for American intervention in Europe has come to encompass both regional and global notions of the balance of power.

Another derivative of British notions about the balance of power in the seventeenth, eighteenth and nineteenth centuries is the idea that coalition warfare can best be conducted through collective security mechanisms. These mechanisms have taken the form of international peace-keeping efforts as provided in the Covenant of the League of Nations and the Charter of the United Nations. They have also taken the form of peace-time treaties of alliance. Although they do not strictly reflect collective security, they have evoked the notion of 'like-minded and peace-loving' peoples standing together collectively against a 'law-breaking and warlike' adversary. Along with this, international organisations have created peace-time planning machinery based initially on the model of the British Cabinet secretariat, and have used it to give credibility to their capacity to carry out international mandates in much the same way that the Cabinet secretariat gave credibility to a national mandate. NATO is a noteworthy example. This development has transformed the way states behave towards one another in their respective pursuits of self-interest. Since the United States emerged as a dominant force in world politics at the end of the First World War and then exerted that force systematically after the Second World War, this pervasive British influence on American thinking and practice is noteworthy. At the same time, the procedures that have arisen from these influences have helped to create a characteristic common approach to the use of naval power.

Because both Britain and America have envisioned the heart of their security as being their respective navies, it is consequently no accident that the two most influential thinkers on the ways in which naval force can be coupled with national power and aspirations should have been Mahan and Corbett. In fact they were both thinkers and publicists who sought to make that connection. The basic foundations which Mahan laid, through his application of Jomini's ideas about land warfare, have been fundamentally altered. Most importantly, they were altered by Sir Julian Corbett's work in applying Clausewitzian theory to maritime affairs. Corbett subsumed and refined Mahan's ideas in the process of laying out a wider theoretical analysis of war at sea. Further refinements to the theory of maritime strategy have been made in reaction to the changing nature of international politics and the increasing impact of technological development on the capabilities of navies. Most importantly, this has meant emphasis on the use of naval power as an instrument of persuasion and deterrence in peace-time, linking it to the entire spectrum of national power. Modern naval theory has thus expanded from the old ideas of major and clearly definable battles at sea between major naval combatants. It now includes the consideration of a much wider range of circumstances in which naval theorists no longer exalt naval power above other forms of armed force or claim an independent role for it. Naval power involves a specialised application of force and is a particular type of military instrument which is used within the context of general theories of strategy.

Following Mahan and Corbett, command of the sea has remained the practical justification for both Britain and America in building up and using their navies. In the mid-1970s, American naval writers began to use the term 'sea control' as a modern application of the older idea. Nevertheless it is the characteristic concept that identifies the Anglo-American tradition of naval thought and, in fact, has repeatedly been used by the predominant naval power. Mahan and Corbett were products and reflections of the first years of the twentieth century. Their ideas were grounded upon an explanation of past practice and combined with their own vision of the future. Nevertheless they could not explain what would follow. Their ideas have continued to serve as guides, but have been modified in interaction with practice. As is often the case with theory, those who use it tend to concentrate on only a particular portion of it, setting aside those other portions which seem too abstract or too far beyond the common expectations of the moment.

THE RELATIONSHIP BETWEEN PREWAR PLANNING AND THE CONDUCT OF WAR AT SEA

In examining the relationship between prewar planning for war and the actual conduct of war in the period between 1898 and 1945, we can see quite clearly that peace-time plans tend to be rigid, with a focus on a particular concept of the way a war should be fought. In the period leading up to the First World War, the dominant concepts were those which reflected the experience of the Spanish–American War and the Russo-Japanese War. But, when the Great War came, there was no decisive battle between fleets which made a major contribution to deciding the issues, such as at Santiago, Manila Bay or Tsushima. The plan to concentrate on the offensive use of large warships was too narrow a concept to prepare for the varied use of naval forces which actually occurred.

Yet the battle of Jutland, however indecisive it was in strategic terms, sustained the vision of great fleet actions that had occurred in previous wars, and continued to capture the imagination of many naval planners. Germany's abrupt change in naval strategy after Jutland, to an offensive war with submarines, demonstrated the effectiveness of a new form of technology in which Germany had the edge initially. If other new technological developments for anti-submarine warfare had not been quickly developed to counter that threat immediately, it might well have been the decisive factor in the war. As it was, however, the use of submarines had not been foreseen by theorists either and they could only link their employment, in abstract terms, to the seventeenth- and eighteenth-century experience of the privateers' war against trade. With a different vision, theorists might have linked the same use of submarines to either a broad concept of blockade or a disputed use of the sea. Such concepts would have made interpretation of the events clearer, but that was not the case.

During the inter-war years of 1919–39, naval planners imagined the future along the lines which they thought the past had suggested. At the same time there were clear indications in the naval events of the First World War that suggested the paths of the future. In some respects the interpretation of those trends was faulty and in other cases it was entirely absent. Naval officers in the inter-war period were still searching for another Jutland, but one which, this time, would bring a decisive victory. The accompanying emphasis on battleships tended to obscure thought about the importance of logistics planning and stockpiling, naval aviation, submarine and anti-submarine warfare, minesweeping, convoy and combined and amphibious operations.

Plans for a war in the Atlantic were based on fighting an enemy similar to the German High Seas Fleet of 1914–18. Plans for a war in the Pacific against Japan were closer to the events which actually occurred, but even they did not fully consider the submarine campaign or the role of aircraft-carriers. When the Second World War came, it brought with it unexpected threats and weapons as well as unexpected tasks for navies to perform.

Thus the contrast between the preparation for war and the actual conduct of it revealed not only the limitations in the war planners' ability to predict the future from existing indicators, but it also revealed the real restraint in peace-time that the intermix of international affairs and domestic politics, together with national finance, can impose on the creation of an armed force capable of meeting the full range of anticipated wartime threats and demands. In peace-time, it is not only very difficult to foresee what a future war might bring, it is also hard to justify large expenditures on a force that might not appear to be immediately necessary. Consequently, as the experience of the first half of the twentieth century shows, the British and American navies did not develop the flexible force capabilities that were needed when war broke out and they were thus unprepared for the adjustment to new strategies which the Second World War required. Without preparation, the two navies were then called upon to provide new equipment, new procedures and new capabilities to meet the new demands with which they were faced. Much of this has been historical accident, but it illustrates also the limitations on purposeful planning which obtain in peace-time.

In the Anglo-American democratic tradition, which contains an inbred suspicion of standing military forces, domestic public opinion may not be willing, at any particular moment, to accept the cost or the concept of wide-ranging, flexible preparations for war. In the distant past, that suspicion most obviously applied to the Army and involved the debate over the control of militia and standing forces. While the navy has been more often, but not always, free of that suspicion, both Parliament and Congress have often required 'a clear and present' threat before they would authorise costly naval forces. With that in mind, it is no wonder that naval leaders have sometimes stressed the potential of offshore threats during peace-time in order to justify expenditure.

At the same time, professional Anglo-American naval leaders have been caught in a dilemma in trying to reach several goals at once. They must meet the immediate demands of peace-time naval operations and the expected peace-time crises. They must additionally try to predict prudently what a future war might look like in order to prevent a future war breaking out, and, further, they must provide an assessment of a future threat which can be used to persuade their legislators to finance the basic and necessary long-term investment in naval equipment. Often these diverse efforts do not reflect the same image of naval requirements. In peace-time, the result is either a compromise among them or an emphasis on one aspect at the expense of the others.

POST-SECOND WORLD WAR MARITIME BALANCE OF POWER CONCEPTS

As suggested earlier, the principles of balance of power theory are naturally opposed to some traditional Anglo-American ideas of political freedom and national liberty. In the national debate naval expenditure for balance of power purposes may conflict with domestic social expenditures. It is not easy to make the connection between domestic social concerns and the international concerns of the balance of power and the state of international politics. But the continued joining together of these English-speaking nations in a relationship that now sees the subordination of one to the formerly subordinate and now predominant newer nation, remains at the centre of contemporary Great Power politics. Justifications for naval force levels, fleet configurations and grand and lesser maritime strategies have reflected this special relationship.

Even at those times in recent history when the British people debated whether they could, or should, continue to aspire to Great Power maritime influence, their decision has been in the affirmative. For example, when the United States continued to opt for big carriers, Britain followed suit until withdrawal East of Suez made its justification politically difficult. Furthermore the reliance on the nuclear-powered and nuclear-armed ballistic missile-carrying submarine, following on from the manned bomber strategic force, was unequivocally an attempt to remain in the Great Power maritime league. Even though budgetary and technological restraints have limited British freedom of national action in this respect, there is still the lingering notion that Britain needs this force to affirm its essential national presence in the councils of the West as well as in the overall calculations of national power and prestige. If the fall of British naval mastery can be attributed to historical accident, purposeful planning has without a doubt replaced it as a means to extend British naval power and influence in the postwar period.

The rise of the Soviet Navy in recent times has introduced a renewed interest in naval strategy and naval concepts. Corbett was quite right to correct Mahan's notions of command of the sea by pointing out that the most common situation in wartime is that neither side has the command. The normal position, he said, is an uncommanded sea in which the command is in dispute. The point is particularly important today when the opposing superpower blocs contain several navies, designed to combine in various ways to meet divergent naval strategic needs. For example, the SSBN navies of the United States, Britain, France and the Soviet Union can be tactial as well as strategic and global in function. They perform such roles as deterring attack on coastal installations and surface fleets, or threatening land warfare through the use of SLCMs. This leads to their involvement in amphibious warfare and the immediate considerations of battle.

The use of the carrier battle groups, still the official backbone of the American navy, to threaten the Soviet navy in both ASW and AAW dimensions, and also to support land based engagements ashore also has a political use in reinforcing the will of the NATO allies to resist Soviet threats or, if necessary, to repel a Soviet incursion. Yet, even though there may well be differing capabilities among the navies of NATO, with some forms of expertise, such as mine warfare and anti-submarine warfare more refined in one allied state's naval force than in another, none the less their broad strategic mission remains similar, even if their capabilities differ. The same is true of the nuclear capability of both the French and British navies which have similar missions, even if their respective relationship to overall NATO planning differs.

In one sense, the Soviet notion of correlation of forces is yet another expression of the balance of power. However, the calculation of the maritime correlation of forces is at present undergoing a reassessment, not only because of changing technologies but, equally important, because of the continuing arms control negotiations between the two Superpowers. In this situation, both the similarities and differences to the experience of the 1920s and 1930s is instructive. In the first part of the century, opposing navies duplicated each other's roles. This may have been one reason why battle between them was indecisive, as it was at Jutland. In contrast to the earlier periods, the respective ship configurations of the two Superpowers today are not symmetrical. The underlying strategic rationale of each navy presents a much more complicated picture, especially when we consider how naval strategy relates to national policy. Nevertheless it is clearly essential that the United States continue to formulate its naval strategy within the context of the NATO coalition. This context helps to rectify the deficiencies in its own configuration of forces. At the same time we need to remember that the manifold requirements for the use of a naval force transcend the Superpower rivalry. No national navy, however large, is capable of performing by itself all of the possible missions assigned to it. In this respect, it is still a wise admonition to choose one's allies wisely and to conserve one's enemies carefully.

Note

1. Carsten Holbraad, *The Concert of Europe: A Study in German and British International Theory 1815–1914* (London, 1970), p. 7.

Index

Abyssinian crisis (1935), 44, 232
  Admiralty, Board of: and the Colonial Defence Committee (CDC), 26–7; and defence of colonies, 28–9; and coast defence, 30; and amphibious operations, 38; and relations with the Committee of Imperial Defence (CID), 38, 167; and Director of Naval Intelligence (DNI), 38; and Winston Churchill, 39, 167; and the First World War, 41, 244; and Director of Plans, 41, 226ff; and British maritime growth, 100; and Julian Corbett, 113, 120, 167; and the Washington Conference, 194ff; and the Singapore strategy, 234; and the British Naval Staff (BNS), 291–2, 294
Adriatic Sea, 181
Afghanistan War (1979–88), 147
Albemarle, Duke of, 107
Alanbrooke, Field-Marshal Lord, as Chairman of the Chiefs of Staff, 46–7
Alexander-Sinclair, Admiral Sir Edwyn, plate 3
Allied Maritime Transport Council, 64
Amery, L. S., 59, 61
Anglo-American maritime relationship, *see* Maritime Strategies
Anglo-Japanese Alliance, 192ff, 215, 228, 230
Anti-Comintern Pact, 234, 237
Anti-Submarine Warfare (ASW), 244, 247, 250ff; and Anglo-American Allied Anti-Submarine Survey Board (AA/SSB), 254; and NATO, 274, 293, 311, 314ff, 318, 354; and passive sonar techniques, 292, 314; and the First World War, 352
ANZAM, 279
Army War Plans Division (US), 225
Arnold, Matthew, 144–5
Asdic, 243–4
Asquith, Herbert Henry (later Earl of Oxford and Asquith), 39, 60, 77n20, 169

Atlantic Council, 322
Attlee, Clement, 48, 275; and post-Second World War principles of defence, 275
Australia, 63, 250, 255, 259, 277, 279
Austro-Hungarian Navy, 181
Azores, 280

Backhouse, Admiral Sir Roger, 236; and the Backhouse–Drax school of strategy, 236
Bahrain, 277
Balance of Power: and the Anglo-American maritime relationship, 1ff, 304, 353; and the multiple balance, 1ff; and simple balance, 1ff; and the distribution of power, 2ff; and the Western hemisphere 8–11; and nuclear weapons, 149–50, 156, 324, 338; and naval balance of power, 189ff, 305, 306–7, 324–5; and the Second World War, 248–9; and balance of military power, 269; and Central Eurasian balance, 333; as means to an end, 348; and Soviet correlation of forces, 354
Baldwin, Stanley, 43, 229
Balfour, Arthur James (Earl), 25; and creation of the Committee of Imperial Defence 1902 (CID), 32, 34, 38; and Admiral Fisher, 171; and Washington Conference, 198; plate 5
Ballard, Captain George, 120; and war plans committee, 121
Baltic Sea, 26
Barbados, 27
Barnes, George N., plate 5
Batt, William, 75
Beatty, Admiral Sir David (Earl), 42, 174, 176–7, 183; and Julian Corbett, 113; and Washington Conference, 195, 197, 208, plates 3, 4
Behrens, C. B. A., 257
Belgium, 40, 312, 318
Bellany, Ian, xv

357

358

Index

Benson, Admiral William S., 178, 181, plate 4.
Beresford, Admiral Lord Charles, 112, 120
Berlin blockade (1948), 15, 276
Berlin crisis (1959), 298
Best, Richard, 16
Boer War, 26, 31–2, 38, 56, 85 (*see also* South Africa)
Booth, Kenneth, 141, 149–52
Borden, Sir Frederick, 34
Borden, Sir Robert, plate 5
Boyle, Marshal of the RAF Sir Dermot, 49
Bradley, General of the Army Omar, 290
Braudel, Fernand, 97
Bridge, Admiral Sir Cyprian, 113
Bridges, Sir Edward, 70
Bright, John: and the Royal Commission on the Defence of British Possessions and Commerce Abroad, 23–4
Brind, Admiral Sir Patrick, 286
Britain, *see* United Kingdom
Brosio, NATO Secretary-General Manlio, 310
Brooke, *see* Alanbrooke
Brown, Admiral Charles R., 146
Brown, Secretary of Defense Harold, 321, 322–3
Burke, Admiral Arleigh, 297, 298
Burma, 11, 273
Burton, Hon. M., plate 5

Cabinet (UK): and interdepartmental coordination, 26, 37; and Committee of Imperial Defence, 26ff, 57ff, 227–8; and the Colonial Committee, 27; and record keeping, 27–8; and Defence Committee (1895), 31–3; and Defence Committee (1946), 47–8, 275; and creation of the Cabinet Office, 35; and Defence and Overseas Policy Committee, 50; and the Chief of the Defence Staff, 51; and War Council, 60; and Dardanelles Committee, 60; and War Committee, 60; and creation of a 'cabinet office', 61–2; and Imperial War Conferences, 63, 227, 234; and the League Secretariat, 68–9, 350; and NATO, 73ff; and 'Ten Year Rule', 191, 227, 229; and post-First World War capital ship construction, 194–5; and Washington Conference, 208; and Defence Requirements Committee (1933), 231–3; and Cabinet secretariat, 350
Cable, Sir James, 5, 141; on coercive diplomacy, 150
Cam Rahn Bay, xiii
Campbell-Bannerman, Sir Henry: and the Hartington Commission on the Administration of the Naval and Military Departments, 24; view of the Prussian General Staff, 24–5
Canada, 48, 63, 126, 193, 218, 287; and the Atlantic in the Second World War, 249, 250ff; and anti-submarine warfare, 250ff, 263; and Anglo-American maritime relations, 252ff; and the Royal Canadian Navy, 305, 318
Cape of Good Hope, 23, 26
Caribbean, 9, 168, 170–1, 173, 281
Calder, J. A., plate 5
Carnarvon Commission, 23, 26–7, 99
Carney, Admiral Robert D., plate 9
Carnegie Endowment, 322
Caroline Islands, 220, 246, 258
Carrier warfare, 260ff (*see also* Royal Navy, US Navy)
Carrington, Lord, as Minister of Defence, 52
Carson, Sir Edward, as First Lord of the Admiralty, 41
Carver, Field-Marshal Lord, 53
Casablanca Conference, (1943), 256; and Germany First strategy, 260
Castlereagh, Lord, 7, 23
Cavite, 231
Center for Naval Analyses, 322
Cervera y Topete, Admiral Pascual, 90–1
Ceylon, 23, 26
Chamberlain, Austen, 230, plate 5
Chamberlain, Neville, 232; and parity deterrence, 43, and inter-Service rivalry, 44–5
Chanak crisis (1922), 42
Chancellor of the Exchequer, and Colonial Defence Committee (CDC), 27; Lord Randolph Churchill, 29–30

Chatfield, Admiral. Sir Ernle (later Lord), 42, 236; and inter-Service rivalry, 43; and Military Co-ordination Committee, 44–5; and Washington Conference, 195, 197; and Defence Requirements Committee report, 231–2; and submarine warfare, 244

Chatham, Lord, 28, 118–20

Chief of Naval Staff (CNS), 43; and Munich, 44

Chief of the Defence Staff, UK (CDS): creation of, 49; and strengthening of, 50–3

Chief of the Imperial General Staff, UK (CIGS), 38; and Sir Neville Lyttelton, 38; and Sir Henry Wilson, 38; and Lord Kitchener, 39; and Sir William Robertson, 40; and inter-Service rivalry, 43, 49

Chiefs of Staff (UK), 42; sub-committee of Committee of Imperial Defence, 42–3; and inter-Service rivalry, 42–3; and Italo-Abyssinian crisis, 44; and Germany, 44ff; and Munich, 44; and the Second World War, 45–7, 227; and creation of Chairman, 48–9; and creation of Chief of the Defence Staff, 49; and interwar naval policy, 229ff; and Review of Imperial Defence (1937), 234; and post-Second World War principles of defence, 275; and *Galloper* war plan, 276; and carrier strike aircraft, 285; and nuclear weapons, 289ff; and H-bombs, 291; and less than absolute wars, 294ff; and Defence White paper (1957), 293, 296

Chiefs of Staff Committee, UK (COS), 70–1, 227ff; and three-front war, 235; and Singapore strategy, 234, 236–7; and Brussels Treaty (1948), 276

Chile, 9

China, 215; and war with Japan, 236–7, 243, 258; and Tientsin affair, 236–7; and Cold War, 271; and the Civil War, 273, 295

Churchill, Lord Randolph: as Chancellor of the Exchequer, 29–30; and the Hartington Commission, 29–30

Churchill, Sir Winston, 11; as Lord of the Admiralty, 39, 44, 174, 175, 250; and Lord Kitchener, 39; and Dardanelles campaign, 39–40, 178–9; on maritime leadership, 40, 44ff, 70; as Minister of Defence, 70; and Admiralty War Staff, 167; and Washington Conference, 198; and Plan Dog Memorandum, 225; and 'Ten Year Rule', 229; and Japanese naval threat, 230; and Argentia Meeting (1941), 250; as Prime Minister, 250, 255; and North Africa, 256; and the Atlantic Charter, 271; and nuclear war, 290; and 1952 naval cuts, 295

Clark, Colonel, 224

Clark, John J., 305

Clarke, Sir George Sydenham, (later Baron Sydenham of Combe): and defence of the colonies, 29; and the British secretariat tradition, 27–9, 58; and Julian Corbett, 114; and Admiral Fisher, 167

Clausewitz, Carl von, 84, 95, 165–7; and Julian Corbett, 115–16, 123–4, 126, 139–40; and influence, 124–5, 139–40, 142, 350

Clémençeau, Georges, 65

Cobden, Richard, 23

Colbert, Admiral Richard G., 311, 317

Cold War 2, 6, 137, 271, 276, 295; and détente, 304–6, 323–5

Colonial Defence Committee, 1878 and 1885, (CDC), 26ff; and Committee of Imperial Defence (CID), 28–33; and functions of, 28; and strategic value of the Cape, 99–100

Colonial Office: and interdepartmental co-ordination, 26ff; and Colonial Defence Committee (CDC), 28ff

Combined Chiefs of Staff (CCS), 255

Committee of Imperial Defence (CID), 23; and origins of, 26ff, 37, 57; and Colonial Defence Committee (1878 and 1885) (CDC), 28–33; and Overseas Defence Committee (1911) 28; and functions of, 28, 33–6, 37–8, 59, 227–8; and Hartington Commission (1898) 29–30; and Joint Naval and Military Committee on Defence (1891), 30–1; and the Defence Committee of the Cabinet (1895) 31–2; and

CID—*contd.*
  composition of, 33–5, 38, 59; and Sir Maurice Hankey, 37; and relations with the Admiralty, 38–9, 167, 227–8; and War Council, 60; and Admiral Fisher, 112, 167; and Invasion Inquiry 1907–8, 120, 130; and Washington Conference 1921, 194–5, 208; and Anglo-Italian Gentleman's Agreement, 234

Commonwealth, British, 250; and Naval Control of Shipping and Intelligence, 251, 254, 263; and transition to, 273; and possible war with the Soviet Union, 275ff

Commonwealth Conferences, 63

Concert of Europe, 7; and Congress System, 2; and the balance of power, 7–8; and the creation of the League of Nations, 8; and the Treaty of Vienna, 23

Conolly, Admiral Richard L., 12, 19n30, plate 8

Constantinople, 26

Cook, Sir Joseph, plate 5

Coolidge, President Calvin, 217

Coontz, Admiral Robert E.: and the Washington Conference, 204–6, 208, 214; and war with Britain, 215; and naval reorganisation, 216; and war with Japan, 215–16

Coral Sea, battle of, 238, 258

Corbett, Sir Julian S., xiiff; portrait plate 2; and security of communications, xiii, 115–18, 174; and dual role of sea power, xii; and limited control of the sea, 5, 127, 184; and 'historical' school of strategists, 110–11, 114–15, 122; and comparison with Mahan, 110–11, 115, 128, 130–1, 350, 354; and 'British Way in Warfare', 111; and Hankey, 112, 121; and *Naval Operations*, 112–13, 182; and Jellicoe, 112–13, 132; and Admiralty Committee of Enquiry, 113; and Royal Naval College War Course, 114, 121; and 'Green Pamphlet', 16, 114ff; and Offensive–Defensive, 115–16, 125ff; and limited–unlimited warfare, 116, 125; and command of the sea, 116–17, 127; and Pitt's system, 118–20; and Ballard's war plans committee, 120, 121, 167; and principles of maritime strategy, 122ff, 163, 169, 182, 288–9, 351; and Clausewitz, 124, 139, 169, 350; and combined operations, 126, 130, 172; on Peninsular War, 126; on fleet-in-being, 130–1; on submarines, 129–30; and CID Invasion Inquiry, 120, 130; and Henry Spenser Wilkinson, 131–2; and Mahan, 110–11, 128, 130–1, 139, 350 and US maritime strategy, 147ff, and Admiral Fisher, 111–12, 114, 131–2, 183

Crenshaw, Captain John S., 224

Crimean War, 9, 25, 125, 126

Crowe, Sir Eyre, 194–5

Crowl, Professor Philip A., 96

Cuban Missile Crisis (1962), 140

Cunningham, Admiral of the Fleet Sir Andrew (later Viscount Cunningham of Hyndhope), 236

Cunningham, Admiral Sir John, 276

Curzon, George (Marquis Curzon of Kedleston), as Foreign Secretary, 193, plate 5

Custance, Admiral Sir Reginald, 112, 113, 174

Czechoslovakia, 15; and Prague *coup* (1945), 276

Dardanelles campaign, 39–40, 178–9

Dardanelles Committee (1915), 60–1

Defence Committee (UK), origins of, 45; and policy making, 50

De Lattre de Tassigny, Marshal, and Western Union, 47

Denby, Secretary of the Navy Edwin, and Washington Conference, 199–201, 203–5, 208; and Navy Department reorganisation, 216; and budget cuts, 217

Denmark, 286–87, 312

Devonshire, Duke of (Spencer Compton Cavendish, Marquis of Hartington), and Defence Committee of the Cabinet (1895), 31–3

Dewar, Commander Kenneth, 128

Dickson, Air Chief Marshal Sir William, 49

Dill, Field-Marshal Sir John, 45

Director of Naval Intelligence UK
  (DNI), 38
Directorate of Naval Mobilisation UK,
  38; and War Division, 38
Disarmament, 189ff
Disraeli, Benjamin, and the Royal
  Commission on the Defence of
  British Possessions and Commerce
  Abroad, 23
Dogger Bank, battle of, 174
Drake, Sir Francis, 174
Drax, Admiral Sir Reginald A. R.
  Plunkett–Ernle–Erle, 236
Drummond, Sir Eric, 66; and League
  Secretariat, 69; and office of
  League Secretary General, 69–70;
  and United Nations, 72–3
Dulles, Secretary of State John Foster,
  274; and Massive Retaliation, 290
Duncan, Admiral Charles, 312

Eaton, Vice-Admiral Sir John,
  frontispiece
Eberle, Admiral Edward, 217
Eccles, Rear Admiral Henry E., 146–7
  and relationship between economic
  and industrial factors, 146–7;
  quoted, 81
Eden, Sir Anthony (later Earl of Avon),
  and creation of Chairman of
  Chiefs of Staff, 48–9; and Anglo-
  Italian Gentleman's Agreement,
  234; and efforts at Anglo-American
  joint naval initiative in the Far
  East, 235; and limited war role of
  the Navy, 296
Egypt, 44, 86, 277 (*see also* Suez)
Ehrman, John, 98–9
Eisenhower, Dwight D., as Supreme
  Allied Commander Europe, 286; as
  President, frontispiece photograph;
  and the 'New Look', 290; and
  nuclear weapons at sea, 294
Esher Committee (1904), 31, 35, 58, 178
European Defence Community (EDC),
  274
Evan-Thomas, Rear-Admiral Sir Hugh,
  plate 4

Falkland Islands: and Falklands/
  Malvinas War (1982), xii, 7; and
  the Battle of the Falklands (1914),
  174

Faroe Islands, 279–80
Field, Admiral of the Fleet Sir
  Frederick L., 43
First Sea Lord, *see* Admiralty
First World War, xi, xiii, 1; and
  balance of power, 2ff, 13; and the
  League of Nations, 8; and Anglo-
  German naval rivalry, 9–10; and
  Committee of Imperial Defence
  (CID), 32, 39–41; and Imperial
  War Cabinet, 36; and British
  secretariat tradition, 57ff; and
  Supreme War Council, 65; and the
  Paris Peace Conference, 63–5; and
  Corbett's writings, 111; and war at
  sea, 173ff, 351–2; and British naval
  war planning, 227
Fergusson, Admiral Sir James A., plate
  3
Firth, Professor Sir Charles, 113
Fisher, Admiral of the Fleet Sir John
  (later Baron Fisher of Kilverstone),
  and the Committee of Imperial
  Defence (CID), 38, 112, 167; as
  First Sea Lord, 39, 41, 168; and
  naval reform, 111, 167; and Julian
  Corbett, 111–12, 114, 131–2; and
  Ballard war plans committee, 120–
  1, 167; and Henry Spenser
  Wilkinson, 131–2; and the
  battleship fleet, 170; and
  submarines, 171; and combined
  operations, 172; and view of
  history, 182–3
Flanders, 40
Foch, Marshal Ferdinand, 124
France: and nuclear forces, 2, 354; and
  European hegemony, 6; and post-
  Napoleonic Europe, 7–8; and
  Anglo-American rivalry, 9–10; and
  arms control, 14; and Waterloo,
  23, 25; and Napoleon III, 25; and
  British war planning, 40ff, 60–61;
  and post of Chairman of Chiefs of
  Staff, 48–9; and Wheat Executive
  (1917), 64; and the Paris Peace
  Conference (1919), 65; and naval
  warfare, 97, 104, 107, 354; and
  Jeune Ecole, 102, 104–5; and *Revue
  Maritime*, 103; and *Guerre de
  course*, 104, 107, 120; and
  competition with the Royal Navy,
  107, 180; and Clausewitz, 124; and

France—*contd.*
  Washington Conference, 200, 202–4, 206, 209; and the Second World War, 243ff, 248; and French North Africa, 276; and NATO war planning, 279–81
Fraser, Admiral of the Fleet Sir Bruce (later Lord Fraser of North Cape), 285, 286, plate 6
Frederick the Great, King of Prussia, 85
Frost, Commander Holloway, and the 'strategy of the Atlantic', 215

Geddes, Sir Auckland, 182, 198
General Disarmament Conference, 231
Geneva Naval Conference (1927), 217, 229
Geopolitics, 140, 170, 171, 172, 183
George V, King, plate 5
George VI, King, plate 6
Germany: and European hegemony, 6; and Anglo-American rivalry, 9–10; and the Second World War, 11, 283ff; and arms control, 14–15; and the Committee of Imperial Defence (CID), 39; and UK Chiefs of Staff Committee, 42–3; and the *Oberkommando der Wehrmacht* (OKW), 46, 47; and Mahan, 105–6, 189–90; and Julian Corbett, 124; and Scharnhorst, 124; and Gneisenau, 124; and von Moltke (elder), 124; and von Schlieffen, 124; and High Seas Fleet, 130, 132, 170–1, 176, 189, 190, 340; and U-boats, 131, 174–6, 190, 243, 246; and Second World War naval strategy, 136, 250; and Luftwaffe, 165; and Washington Conference, 196; and withdrawal from the League of Nations, 231; and war with Britain, 231, 243, 247ff; and secret Anglo-German naval treaty (1935), 232, 244; and Germany First strategy, 249ff; and NATO, 312, 318
Ghormley, Vice Admiral Robert L., as 'Special Naval Observer', 249
Gibbs, Professor Norman H., xiv, xvi, 23, 240n43
Gibraltar, 278, 283
Gladstone, William, and the Royal Commission on the Defence of British Possessions and Commerce Abroad, 23–4, 27; and Gladstonian finance, 99
Goodenough, Rear-Admiral Sir William, plate 3
Gordenker, Leon, 68
Gorshkov, Admiral of the Soviet Union Sergei, 293
Greece, 276; and NATO, 311, 313
Greenland, 280, 285
Grenada, xii, 140
Grenville, Professor J. A. S., 172–3, 181
Grey of Fallodon, Viscount, 191
Guadalcanal, battle of, 260
Guam, 171, 192, 207, 237
Guerre de course, 104, 107, 131, 171, 175, 177, 183

Haig, Field-Marshal Sir Douglas, 40
Haggie, Paul, 120–1
Hague Peace Conference, 85
Halpern, Professor Paul G., 179–80
Halsey, Fleet Admiral William F., plate 6
Hammarskjöld, Dag, 73
Hamilton, General Ian, 178
Hankey, Sir Maurice (later Baron Hankey of the Chart), 37; and creation of a Ministry of Defence, 42; and British secretariat tradition, 58ff; and Machinery of Goverment Committee, 63; and the Paris Peace Conference (1919), 65; and office of Secretary General, 67–8; and reconstituted Committee of Imperial Defence (CID), 70; and Julian Corbett, 112; and Ballard war plans committee, 121; and combined operations, 172; and Washington Conference, 194–5, 207–8; plate 5
Hansen, Roger D., 14
Harding, Warren G., 193, 204–5, 209–10, 217
Harris, Air Marshal Sir Arthur, 165–6
Hartington Commission on the Administration of the Naval and Military Departments (1890), 24, 29–32 (*see also* Devonshire, Duke of)
Hattendorf, John B., 108n21, 334
Hawaii, 207, 237, 248; and War Plan

Orange, 220ff (*see also* Pearl Harbor)
Hawke, Admiral of the Fleet Sir Edward (later Lord), 174
Hayes, Rear Admiral John D., 108n21, 139
Healey, Denis, and the Defence Review, 51; and the Defence Council, 52
Heligoland, 23
Henderson, Commander Reginald, 128
Hendricks, Donald D., xv
Heseltine, Michael, as Defence Minister, 52
Hewitt, Admiral F. Kent, plate 7
Holbraad, Carsten, 349
Hollis, Major General R. M., 47
Honduras, 23
Hong Kong, 11, 26, 42, 195, 230
Hoover, Herbert, 219
Horton, Admiral Sir Max, plate 7
Howard, Professor Sir Michael, 16–17, 84
Hughes, Charles Evans, as US Secretary of State, 196; and Washington Conference, 199ff, 214, 217; and 'stop now' plan, 205–9
Hughes, Admiral Charles F., 215
Hughes, William M., plate 5
Hughes Hallett, Admiral Cecil Charles, 292
Hume, David, 4

Iceland, 249–50, 252, 285, 287
Imperial General Staff UK, 172 (*see also* Chiefs of the Imperial General Staff)
Imperial War Cabinet, 36, 62–3, plate 5
Imperial War Conferences (1917–21), 63, 227, 234
India, 42, 63, 86, 257, 273
Indonesia, 297
Inskip, Sir Thomas, 44
Interwar period (1919–39), xiii; and Committee of Imperial Defence (CID), 32, 227–8; and Washington Conference, 210, 228; British and Japanese naval threats, 218, 228, 230; and Imperial Conferences, 227; and Anglo-American defensive war planning, 238, 247
Ireland, 287

Ismay, General Sir Hastings (later Baron), 12; and War Cabinet secretariat, 45, 77n29; and Churchill's wartime leadership, 46; and role in the Second World War, 47, 71, 79n46; and defence reorganisation, 50; and Committee of Imperial Defence (CID), 70, 78n38; as Secretary of State for Commonwealth Affairs, 71; as Secretary-General of NATO, 71, 73–5, 79n54 and n55, 80n65
Italo-Abyssinian crisis (1935), 44, 232
Italy: and Wheat Executive, 64; and Paris Peace Conference (1919), 65; and Second World War naval strategy, 136, 247; and Washington Conference, 196, 200, 202–4, 206, 209; and Abyssinia, 232; and Anglo-Italian Gentlemen's Agreement (1937), 234; and the Second World War, 248; and post–Second World War threat, 276; and NATO, 311, 313 (*see also* Mediterranean)

Jackson, Admiral of the Fleet Sir Henry, as First Sea Lord, 41, 53n13
Jacob, Lieutenant-General Sir Ian, 47, 50
Jamaica, 251
Jane, Fred T., 304
Japan, 11; and war with Britain, 42, 231; and Russo-Japanese War, 90–2, 112, 114, 125, 192; and Second World War naval strategy, 137; and rivalry with the US, 168–73, 189ff, 215ff; and First World War, 173, 180; and Anglo-American naval rivalry, 191ff, 216–17; and Washington Conference, 191ff, 228; and League of Nations mandate, 192, 195, 207; and Anglo-Japanese Alliance, 192ff, 215, 228; and War Plan *Orange*, 220ff, 260; and Manchuria, 230–1; and withdrawal from the League of Nations, 231; and war with Britain, 231ff; and war with China, 236–7, 243; and Pacific War, 258ff; and Soviet threat, 277, 279; and the Sea of Japan, 335, 339

Jebb, Gladwyn, 273
Jellicoe, Admiral of the Fleet Sir John (later Viscount and Earl), as First Sea Lord, 40–1, 45, 112–13, 174, 176–7; and Julian Corbett, 112, 132
Jeune Ecole, 102, 104–5
Johnson, Franklyn, 5
Joint Army and Navy Board, 218, 220; and Joint Planning Committee, 218–19, 224; and War Plan *Red* (1930), 218ff; and War Plan *Orange*, 220ff; and *Rainbow* Plans 224–5
Joint Chiefs of Staff, US (JCS), and Committee of Imperial Defence (CID), 36; and the Pacific War, 255, 258ff; and the Casablanca Conference (1943), 256; and the roles of carrier forces (1951), 283; and the 'New Look', 290; and Single Integrated Operational Plan (SIOP), 290, 297; and NSC–68, 296; and *Newport Study* (1971), 317
Joint Naval and Military Committee on Defence (1891), 30; and coast defence, 30; and Colonial Defence Committee (CDC), 30, 32
Jomini, Baron Antoine-Henri de, 84; and influence on Mahan, 88, 92, 96–98, 102ff, 350; and Corbett, 123, 125, 139
Jones, Admiral Hilary P., 215
Jordan, Jane H., xv
Jordan, Robert H., xv
Jutland, battle of, 113, 132, 170, 174, 182, 197–8, 203, 237, 250, 259, 339, 351–2, 354

Karsten, Professor Peter, 95–6
Kellogg–Briand Pact, 218
Kelly, Admiral W. Howard, 226
Kennedy, John F., 17
Kennedy, Professor Paul M., xvi, 5, 109n36, 165ff, 189; on Mahan, 96, 98, 106; on Italy, 248
Keyes, Admiral of the Fleet Sir Roger (later Baron Keyes of Zeebrugge), 226
Khrushchev, Nikita, 297
Kidd, Admiral Isaac, Jr, 312, 322

King, Fleet Admiral Ernest J., 11, 249, 255, 257; and North Africa, 256; and Casablanca Conference (1943), 256; and Pacific War, 259ff; and British Pacific Fleet, 262
Kissinger, Henry, 140, 323
Kitchener, Field-Marshal Lord, 39–40, 166
Knox, Rear Admiral Dudley W., 215
Korea: and Korean War, xii, 140, 273, 274, 276, 279, 283, 286, 289, 295, 296, 305; and Russo-Japanese War, 91
Kuwait, 297, 298

Lambert, Colonel G., plate 5
Landsdowne, Henry Petty-Fitzmaurice, Marquis of, 35
Law, A. Bonar, plate 5
League of Nations, 8, 17, 228; and British secretariat tradition, 57ff; and Lord Hankey, 64–7; and office of Secretary-General, 66ff; and League Council, 66; and international civil service, 67–9; German and Japanese withdrawal from, 231; and balance of power, 350
Lebanon, 297
Lee of Fareham, Lord, 194, 198
Lend-lease, 17, 274
Lewin, Admiral of the Fleet Sir Terence (later Baron Lewin of Greenwich), 53
Leyte Gulf, battle of, 137
Libya, 140
Liddell Hart, Sir Basil, 172
Lie, Trygve, 72–3, 74, 79n49
Lloyd, Sir W. P., plate 5
Lloyd George, David, as Secretary of State for War, 40; and War Cabinet, 40–1, 60–1; and Imperial War Cabinet, 62–3, 77n25; and Paris Peace Conference (1919), 65; and convoying, 177; and naval budgetary cuts, 182; and Anglo-Japanese Alliance, 193; and Washington Conference, 207–8; and 'Ten Year Rule', 229; plate 5
Locarno, 229
Lodge, Senator Henry Cabot, 203, 207
London, Declaration of (1936), 244

London Naval Conference, 215, 229, 231
Long, Walter, 191; plate 5
Luce, Rear Admiral Stephen B., 84, and influence on Mahan, 101ff; and Naval War College, 96, 101ff
Luttwak, Edward, 141
Lyttelton, General Sir Neville, as Chief of the General Staff, 38

MacArthur, General of the Army Douglas, 258; and Pacific war, 258ff; and South West Pacific command, 259ff
McCormick, Admiral Lynde, 286; plate 9
MacDonald, J. Ramsay, 219, 229; and Japanese naval threat, 230
MacDonald, Admiral Wesley, plate 10
McGrigor, Admiral Sir Rhoderick, 286, 294, 296
McGwire, Michael, 306
Machinery of Government Committee (1918), 63
MacKinder, Professor Sir Halford, 96, 98, 106
McKinley, William, 349
Mackintosh, John P., 62
Maclay, Sir Joseph, plate 5
McMahon Act (1946), 274
Macmillan, Harold (later Earl of Stockton), 17; and organisation of defence policy-making, 49; and creation of Chief of the Defence Staff, 49; and defence reform, 296
McNamara, Secretary of Defense Robert S., 297–8
McNamee, Admiral Luke, 215
Madagascar, 261
Madden, Admiral Sir Charles, plate 3
Mahan, Professor Denis Hart, 84, 97
Mahan, Rear Admiral Alfred Thayer, portrait of, plate 1; and command of the sea, xiii, 58, 104–6, 138, 348, 354; Rear Admiral John D. Hayes on, 139; and his scientific thought, 83ff, 97, 102; and conception of war, 85–6, 96–7; and exercise of naval strategy, 87; and the Spanish-American War, 90; and the fleet-in-being, 91, 189; and Russo-Japanese War, 90–2; as historian, 95ff, 110–11, 138; and influence of British model, 99–100, 167; and West Point, 84, 97, 100–1; and life in USS *Iroquois*, 101; and influence of Jomini, 102–3, 139; and Naval War College, 102–4, 137; and factors conditioning his thought, 104, 141, 145; and Stephen B. Luce, 101ff; and Julian Corbett, 110–11, 128, 130–1, 139, 350, 354; and US maritime strategy of 1980s, 147ff; and influence in US, 136ff, 145, 165, 171, 246, 253, 304–5, 350–1
Malaya, 11, 46, 248
Malta, 27, 285
Manchuria, and Mukden incident (1931), 230ff
Manisty, Paymaster Rear Admiral Sir Eldon, and Naval Control of Shipping and Intelligence, 244
Marianas Islands, 260
Maritime Power, xi; and inherent flexibility, 2, 289; and the US maritime strategy of the 1980s, 148ff; and general theory of war, 153–4, 348; and nuclear war, 289ff, 304ff
Maritime strategies, Anglo-American, 165ff; and peacetime planning, 353; and influence of Mahan, 168, 351; and the offensive, 153–4, 168–9, 174; and the battleship, 169–70; and command of the sea, 169–71, 304, 351; and the First World War, 173, 183, 351–2; and post-First World War naval rivalry, 191–2, 214ff; and the Second World War, 227, 243ff, 251ff; and flexibility, 238–9, 352; and lend-lease, 249; and ABC-1, 249, 251; and Naval Control of Shipping and Intelligence, 249, 251; and Argentia, Newfoundland, agreements (1941), 250; and Atlantic trade defence, 250ff; and Washington Convoy Conference (1943), 250; and *Offtackle/Galloper* war plans, 276–9; and NATO war plans, 279–81, 337ff; and sea control, 281ff; and the protection of sea communications, 285–6; and power projection, 286–9; and the nuclear revolution, 289ff; and

Maritime strategies—*contd.*
nuclear offensive carrier group, 292; and the SLBM programme, 294; and the era of flexible response, 304ff; and the US maritime strategy (1980s), 330ff; and grand strategy, 345; and notions of the balance of power, 1–17, 349ff (*see also* Sea Power)
Marshall Islands, 220, 246, 258
Marshall, General of the Army George C., and Plan Dog Memorandum, 225; and North Africa, 256
Martin, Professor Laurence W., 141–2
Massey, Sir W. F., plate 5
Mason, Roy, as Minister of Defence, 52
Mauritius, 23
May, Captain William J., 112, 114
Mayer, René, 75
Mearsheimer, Dr John, 335
Mediterranean Sea: in the First World War, 179–81; in interwar period, 229ff; in Second World War, 183, 232, 236, 249, 255–6; and post-Second World War period, 229ff; and NATO, 308, 321; and US maritime strategy in the 1980s, 335ff
Meighen, Arthur, plate 5
Midway, battle of, 137, 168, 171, 238, 258
Minister for the Co-ordination of Defence, UK (1936), 44
Minister for Defence Procurement, UK (1972), 51
Ministry of Defence, UK, 35; and origins of, 41; and the Second World War, 45; and post-war organisation, 47–8; and nuclear weapons cost control, 48; and independent nuclear deterrent, 49; and the Defence Council, 52
Mondonah, General Sir G. N., plate 5
Monroe Doctrine, 200–1
Montagu, Edwin B., plate 5
Montgomery, Field-Marshal Bernard L. (Viscount Montgomery of Alamein); as Chief of the Imperial General Staff, 47; as Chairman of Western Union's commanders-in-chief, 47; and Chiefs of Staff Committee, 48; and Chief of the Defence Staff, 49

Morgenstern, Oskar, 142
Morison, Professor Samuel Eliot, 246, 257
Mountbatten, Admiral of the Fleet Lord Louis, and nuclear weapons, 48; and Chiefs of Staff Committee, 48; as Chief of the Defence Staff, 49–51; and CINCAFMED, 288; and nuclear submarines, 294; and limited war role of the Navy, 296
Mulley, Fred, as Minister of Defence, 52
Munich settlement, 235

Nailor, Professor Peter, 56, 76n8
Napoleonic wars, 85, 99, 120, 175; and Julian Corbett, 123–6
Naval War College (US), 84, 215–216; and Alfred Thayer Mahan, 84, 96, 101, 110–11, 137; and influence of technology on war, 145; and need for strategists, 146; and war plan *Orange*, 220; and 'Germany First' policy, 248; and *Newport Study* (1971), 317
Naval War Council (UK), 38
Nelson, Vice-Admiral Sir Horatio (later Viscount), 28, 112, 118, 178; and Corbett, 113, 114–15, 128, 169–70
Newfoundland, and Argentia meeting (1941), 250; and submarine warfare, 252 (*see also* Canada)
New Guinea, 260
Newport, Rhode Island, *see* Naval War College
New Zealand, 63, 250, 255, 259, 277, 279
Nicolson, Sir Harold, 64–5
Nimitz, Fleet Admiral Chester W., 259, 304; and Central Pacific command, 259ff; and British Pacific Fleet, 262
Nitze, Paul, 298, 322
Nivelle, General Sir Henri, 40
Nixon, Richard, and détente, 323
Noel, Admiral of the Fleet Sir Gerard, 112
North Africa, 277ff
North Atlantic Treaty Organisation (NATO): and maritime war, 6–7, 272, 319ff, 354; and CINCHAN, 11, 305, 312, 316; and SACLANT, 11, 287–8, 292, 305, 307ff, 321,

323; and SACEUR, 11–12, 280, 286, 290, 305, 316, 319, 337; and the Mediterranean, 11–12, 282–3, 311, 312; and US maritime strategy (1980s), 13, 330ff, 341–3; and arms control, 14–16; and Committee of Imperial Defence (CID), 36; and Chairman of Chiefs of Staff (UK), 48; and British defence priorities, 51–2; and British secretariat tradition, 57, 74ff; and Atlantic command, 274, 283–4, 287, 288; and Standing Group, 279; and war plan, 279–80, 322, 333–4; and Soviet naval threat, 280–1, 291, 306ff, 320–5; and Allied Command Europe (ACE), 286; and Allied Command North (AFNORTH), 286–7, 341; and AFCENT, 342; and AFSOUTH, 342; and command relationships, 287–8; and CINCEASTLANT, 287–8, 311; and 'New Look Atlantic' plans, 292; and flexible response, 299, 306ff, 338, 341; and MC 14/3, 307; and *Brosio Study* (1969), 310; and *Allied Defence in the Seventies*, 310–11: and COMNAVAIRSOUTH, 311–12, and MARAIRMED, 311; and *Matchmaker*, 311; and Standing Naval Force Atlantic (STANAVFORLANT), 311–12; and Channel Command, 312; and CINCSOUTH, 288, 311, 313; and CINCAFMED, 288; and Lisbon Medium Term Plan, 290; and 'transoceanic' alliances, 305, 331; and massive retaliation 307–8; and conventional naval war, 309, 318, 321, 333–4, 338; and Maritime Contingency Force (MCF), 312; and Defence Planning Committee (DPC), 310ff; and Naval On-Call Force Mediterranean (NAVOCFORMED), 312; and Standing Naval Force Channel (STANAVFORCHAN), 312; and *Exercise Strong Express*, 313–14; and *Ocean Safari 77*, 314; and *Ocean Safari 85*, 341; and merchant shipping, 315; and *Sealift Procurement and National Security Study* (SPANS), 315; and Planning Board for Ocean Shipping (PBOS), 315; and Civilian Sealift Group (CSG), 315; and Maritime Exercise Information Group, 318; and *Winter* Exercise, 315; and *Nifty Nugget* Exercise, 315; and Long Term Defence Programme (LTDP), 315–16; and NATO Naval Armaments Group (NNAG), 316; and command, control and communications (LINK 11), 316; and interoperability, 316, 342; and NATO Patrol Hydrofoil Missile Ship (PHMS), 316; and Sea Gnat project, 316; and Azores Fixed Acoustic Range (AFAR), 316; and Naval Force Sensor and Weapons Accuracy Check sites (FORACS), 316; and 'concept of operations' (CONMAROPS), 316–17; and out-of-area threats, 318–19, 323–4; and nuclear strike posture, 319, 333–4, 338; and North Atlantic Assembly report (1982), 322–3; and détente, 323–5; and Northern Flank campaign, 327–41; and maritime deterrence, 332ff, 354

North Sea, 168–9, 170, 174, 176, 181, 183, 189

Norway, 248, 262, 276, 281, 286–7, 308, 312, 321; and Norwegian Sea, 335ff; and NATO Norwegian campaign plan, 337–41

Nott, John, as Minister of Defence, 52

Nye, General Sir Archibald, 46

Offices of the War Cabinet and of the Minister of Defence (UK), 70

Okinawa, 262, 277, 279

Oliver, Admiral Sir Henry, 39, 53n13, plate 3

Orlando, Vittorio and Paris Peace Conference (1919), 65

Ottawa, 251; and Naval Control of Shipping and Intelligence, 251 (*see also* Canada)

Ottley, Rear-Admiral Sir Charles, 58, 76n4, 114

Overlord, 15

Overseas Defence Committee (1911), 28

Palestine, 273, 295
Palmerston, Lord, 25
Paret, Professor Peter, 96
Paris Peace Conference (1919), and British Empire Delegation, 63; and creation of the League of Nations, 66ff: and Lord Hankey, 64–7; and Shantung Question, 192
Parliamentary Committee on Army and Navy Estimates (1887), 29
Passchendale offensive, 40
Patiala, Maharaja of, plate 5
Pearl Harbor, 246, 256, 258ff
Perrin, W. G., as Admiralty Librarian, 113
Persian Gulf, 305, 318, 323; and Carter Doctrine, 323
Philippines, 168, 171, 172, 192, 349; and War Plan *Orange*, 220ff, 258; and the Second World War, 247–8, 259
Phillimore, Admiral Sir R., plate 3
Pitt, William, *see* Chatham
Plunkett, *see* Drax
Port Arthur, 91, 92, 129
Portugal, 97, 126
Posen, Dr Barry, 335
Pratt, Admiral William V., 219; and Washington Conference, 204, 206–8, 214
Prussian General Staff, 24–5, 36, 100, 124

Quebec Conference (1944), 262

Radford, Admiral Arthur W., 12
Ranft, Professor Brian, 130
Reagan administration, 6, 14, 337
Reeves, Admiral Joseph M., 216
Repington, Lieutenant-Colonel Charles á Court, 120
Rhodesia, 99
Richmond, Admiral Sir Herbert, 112, 128, 130, 169, 182, 183, 263
Rickover, Admiral Hyman, 294
Riddell, Lord, 59, 66–7
Rivero, Admiral Horacio, 308, 313, 317
Roberts, Field-Marshall Frederick (later Earl Roberts of Kandahar), 32, 120
Robertson, Field-Marshal Sir William, 40, 45

Rodgers, Rear Admiral William L., 206, 220, 239; and War Plan *Orange*. 220ff
Rodman, Rear Admiral Hugh, 215; plates 3, 4
Robeck, Admiral Sir John de, plate 4
Rogers, General Bernard, 337, plate 10
Roosevelt, Franklin D., 11, 200, 254; and *Rainbow No. 5*, 225; and 'unlimited national emergency', 249; and Argentia meeting (1941), 250; and North Africa, 256; and submarine warfare against Japan, 261; and the North Atlantic Charter, 271
Roosevelt, Theodore, 5, 84; and the Great White Fleet, 5–6; and American navalism, 105
Roosevelt, Theodore, Jr., as Assistant Secretary of the Navy, 200, 203–4, 207, 210
Root, Elihu, 203, 206, 207
Rosecrance, Richard, 15
Rosinski, Dr Herbert, 110–11, 146; and strategy as comprehensive direction of power, 146–7
Roskill, Captain Stephen W., 257
Rosyth, 170, 176
Rowell, N. W., plate 5
Royal Air Force (RAF), 41–2; and inter-Service rivalry, 42–3, 245; and Chief of Air Staff (CAS), 43, 44, 49; and Italo-Abyssinian crisis, 44; and Coastal Command, 48, 252; and Fighter Command, 130; and its aerial strategy, 165, 182; and Bomber Command, 165, 245; and uses of air power in Second World War, 165–6, 245ff, 262; and 'V' bombers, 282, 290
Royal Commission on Colonial Defence, 27
Royal Commission on the Defence of British Possessions and Commerce Abroad (1879), 23–4, 27
Royal Commission on the Defences of the United Kingdom (1859), 25
Royal Commission on the South African War, 31–2
Royal Naval War College, 111–12; and influence of Corbett, 112; and War Course, 111–14, 132
Royal Navy (RN), and extra-

Index

continental supremacy, 4, 59; and Atlantic sea lanes, 6, 15, 17, 250; and the balance of power, 1–4, 17, 189ff, 305, 306–7, 324–5; and rivalry with the US Navy, 9–11, 106, 189ff; and American naval superiority, 10–12, 219, 263; and US maritime strategy, 13–16; and nuclear weapons, 13–16, 48–9, 284ff; and steam-powered ironclads, 25; and influence of the colonies, 28–9, 107; and Mahan, 97–8, 189–90, 350ff; and British maritime and commercial power, 98–100, 107, 175; and Corbett, 111, 350ff; and the Grand Fleet, 13, 132, 170; and rivalry with Germany, 168–71, 175, 189–90, 245; and combined operations, 172, 178–9; and Jutland 174; and U-Boat menace, 174–6, 184, 190, 246, 250; and Harwich Force, 176; and Channel barrage, 176; and Otranto Barrage, 176, and Northern Barrage, 178; and 'One-Power Standard', 191; and Washington Conference, 215, 228; and inter-war naval rivalry, 217–19, 245; and the dominions, 236; and carrier aviation, 245ff, 261–2, 284, 298–9; and anti-submarine warfare, 247ff, 274, 278; and the Mediterranean, 26, 179–80, 232ff, 247, 249, 275, 278–9, 317–18; and national and imperial defence, 25ff; and convoying, 238, 244, 247, 250, 286; and Malay barrier, 247; and Royal Canadian Navy, 252; and British Pacific Fleet, 262, 274; and lessons of Second World War, 281–2, 300; and Atlantic Striking Fleet, 283–4; and the protection of sea communications, 285–6; and Malta convoys, 285; and power projection, 286–9; and the nuclear revolution, 289ff; and 'broken-backed' war, 289–90; and British Defence White Paper (1957), 293, 296; and Revised Restricted Fleet Plan (1949), 295; and preparing for less than absolute wars, 294; and withdrawal, 317–18; and SSBN, 351

Russo-Japanese War (1904–05), 90–2, 112, 114, 125, 192
Russo-Turkish War (1877–8), 26

St Lucia, 23
St Vincent, John Jervis, Earl of, 28
Salisbury, Marquess of, and Defence Committee of the Cabinet (1895), 31
Sanchez-Navarro, Paul, xv
Sandys, Duncan, as Minister of Defence, 49, 296
Scapa Flow, 170, 173, 176, 178, 183
Schelling, Professor Thomas C., 141
Schlesinger, James, and Schlesinger Doctrine (1974), 319
Schofield, Admiral Frank, 215; and Geneva Naval Conference, 218
Schurman, Professor Donald M., xvii, 95–109, 110, 114, 118
Scott, Admiral Sir Percy, 181
Seager, Professor Robert II, 96
Sea Power, xi; and security of communications routes, xiii, 153, 155; and Mahan's view of, 87; and a modern theory of naval strategy, 148ff, 351; and uses of navies in peacetime, 149–52, 351; and uses of naval power in wartime, 153–6, 304; and command of the sea, 153–4; and nuclear weapons, 156–8, 304ff; and Anglo-American contrasts, 247; and nuclear war, 293 (*see also* Maritime Strategies)
Second World War, xi, 1; and balance of power, 2ff, 333; and Anglo-American maritime balance of power, 10–11, 17; and containment, 13–16; and Allied Combined Chiefs of Staff, 36; and influence of Dardanelles campaign, 40; and British inter-Service rivalry, 44–7, 245–6; and Committee of Imperial Defence (CID), 70; and command of the sea, 136; and Mahan, 136ff, 244; and US Navy, 136ff, 243ff; and British air power, 165–6, 245ff; and maritime strategy, 183, 333; and *Rainbow No. 5*, 224–5, 239, 248–9; and Anglo-American naval co-operation, 243ff; and convoying, 244–5, 250; and plan *Orange*,

Second World War—*contd.*
  220ff, 246, 258ff; and Naval
  Control of Shipping and
  Intelligence, 251, 254, 263
Secretary of State for Commonwealth
  Affairs, 71
Secretary of State for the Colonies, 26–
  8; and Colonial Defence
  Committee (CDC), 28; and the
  Imperial War Conferences, 63
Secretary of State for War, UK, 39–40
Seven Years War, 125
Sherman, Admiral Forrest, 6, 18n13
Ships' names: *Akagi*, 246; *Alaska*, 278;
  B–11, 179; *Bismarck*, 249; *Breslau*,
  174, 179; *Courageous*, 250;
  Dreadnought, 167, 169; *Essex*, 260;
  Glory, 264; *Goeben*, 174, 179;
  Hermes, 245; *Hood*, 196–7, 203,
  205; *Illustrious*, 264; *Implacable*,
  264; *Invincible*, 167; *Iroquois*, 101;
  Kaga, 246; *King George V*, 264;
  Lexington, 246; *Mussudieh*, 179;
  Mutsu, 198, 206; *Princeton*, 260;
  Queen Elizabeth, 169, plate 4;
  Saratoga, 246, 260; *Sequoia*, 290;
  Vanguard, 295; *Victorious*, 260
Sigal, Leon, 307
Sims, Admiral William S., 106, 177–8,
  214, 249
Singapore, 26, 43, 46, 229–30, 249–50;
  and strategic value, 100, 181, 193,
  195, 230, 232, 234; and Singapore
  strategy, 234, 236–7
Sinha, Sir S. P., plate 5
Slade, Rear-Admiral Edmond J., 112,
  114–15, 120; and Ballard war plans
  committee, 121
Slave trade, 99, 107
Slessor, Air-Marshal Sir John, and
  nuclear weapons, 48
Smuts, Field-Marshal Jan, plate 5
Solomon Islands, 259
Sonar, 243, 246
South Africa, 63, 277; and Cape
  Colony, 99; and Simonstown, 99
  (*see also* Boer War)
Soviet Union, *see* Union of Soviet
  Socialist Republics
Spaak, Paul-Henri, 75
Spain, 97; and naval warfare, 97, 126;
  and Britain, 232–3
Spanish-American War (1898), 90, 116,
  124, 172, 199

Spanish Armada, 120
Sprout, Margaret Tuttle, 95–6, 98
Stanford, Peter, 119
Stanhope, Earl, First Lord of the
  Admiralty, 236
Stark, Admiral Harold, and Plan Dog
  Memorandum (1940), 225; and
  Anglo-American naval co-
  operation, 248ff
Staveley, Admiral Sir William, plate 10
Storr, Lieutenant-Colonel Lancelot,
  plate 5
Strang, Sir William, 273–4
Strauss, Rear Admiral Joseph, plate 3
Subic Bay, xiii, 221
Suez, and 1956 crisis, 49, 296, 297, 300,
  305; and the Canal, 99, 273, 278;
  and 'East of Suez', 296, 298, 299,
  353
Supreme War Council, 65–6
Sykes, General, plate 5

Tamnes, Rolf, 286
Templer, Field-Marshal Sir Gerald,
  and maritime air defence
  committee, 282–3, 285–6
Thorneycroft, Peter, as Minister of
  Defence, 50
Thucydides, 167
Thursfield, James R., 113
Tobago, 23
Tracy, Dr Nicholas, conclusions on
  attack on trade summarised, 155
Trafalgar, battle of, 112–13
Train, Admiral Harry II, 316–17
Treasury (UK), and 'Treasury control',
  24, 31, 43; and inter-departmental
  co-ordination, 26; and nuclear
  weapons cost control, 48; and the
  1974–75 Defence Review, 51; and
  war in the Far East, 231
Trenchard, Marshal of the RAF
  Viscount, 165–6
Trinidad, 23
Truman Doctrine, 13, 275
Turkey, and NATO, 311, 313, 321, 339
Tyrell, William, 59, 76n9

Uhlig, Frank Jr, cited, 154
Underwood, Senator Oscar, 203, 207
Union of Soviet Socialist Republics
  (USSR): and foreign military
  bases, xiii; and balance of power,

2ff, 306, 350; and Russian
European hegemony, 6, 331; and
US maritime strategy in the 1980s,
12–13, 330ff; and nuclear weapons,
13–16; and naval power, 15–16,
291, 297, 319–20; and threat to
India, 42; and Russo-Japanese
War, 90–2, 112, 114, 125; and
Cuban missile crisis, 140; and
German invasion (1941), 249, 258;
and visions of the Soviet threat,
275ff, 306ff, 318, 320, 354; and
Offtackle/Galloper war plan, 276–9;
and nuclear missiles at sea, 292–4,
306, 354; and flexible response
(NATO), 306ff; and Baltic Fleet,
339; and Northern Fleet, 340

United Kingdom (UK): and relations
with the US, xiii–xiv, 219, 229; and
balance of power, 1ff, 348ff; and
nuclear forces, 2, 14–16; and
British conceptions of the balance
of power, 7–8, 15; and non-
intervention, 7–8, 350; and
American naval superiority, 10–11,
192ff; and arms control, 14–16,
214ff; and the origins of imperial
defence, 23ff; and 'Treasury
control', 24; and self-governing
colonies, 23–4, 28, 34; and
'Fortress England', 25, 28; and
NATO, 48–9, 51; and Wheat
Executive, 64; and Anglo-Japanese
Alliance, 192ff; and war with
Japan, 230ff; and war with
Germany, 231ff; and war on two
fronts, 231–2; and secret Anglo-
German naval treaty (1935), 232,
244; and Anglo-Italian
Gentleman's Agreement, 234; and
Austrian and Czechoslovakian
crises, 235; and war on three
fronts, 237; and post-Second
World War principles of defence,
275 (*see also* Royal Navy, Royal
Air Force, Treasury)

United Nations (UN): and the balance
of power, 3, 350; and the British
secretariat tradition, 72–3; and the
Cold War, 272

United States of America: and foreign
military bases, xiii; and balance of
power, 1ff, 306, 348ff; and
influence of British strategic
thought, 7–8; and Anglo-American
regional balance of power
concepts, 8–11; and superiority
over Royal Navy, 10–12, 17, 215;
and NATO, 11–13, 332ff; and
containment, 13–16; and post of
Chairman of Chiefs of Staff, 48–9;
and British war-planning 60–1,
215, 238–9, 244ff; and Paris Peace
Conference (1919), 65; and Pacific
rivalry with Japan, 168–73, 189ff,
245ff; and American Neutrality
Patrols, 249; and Naval Control of
Shipping and Intelligence, 251; and
Truman Doctrine, 272; and the
Marshall Plan, 272; and policy
since the Second World War,
332ff; and the Iklé Report, 334;
and conventional war, 306ff, 335

US Air Force (USAF): and nuclear
weapons, 142, 144; and Strategic
Air Command (SAC), 16; and
Army Air Corps/Force, 246, 249,
252, 261

US Navy: and the Great White Fleet,
5–6; and sea lanes, 6, 335; and the
Anglo-German naval race, 9–10,
105, 169; and the Sixth Fleet, 11–
12, 282–3, 197, 311, 312, 313, 321;
and Seventh Fleet, 140; and
nuclear weapons, 13–16, 142–3,
156–8, 283, 289ff, 335; and Mahan,
104–5, 136ff, 178, 304–6; and
model of the Royal Navy, 105–6,
264; and command of the sea, 136–
7, 304, 354; and limited war, 140;
and convoying, 177–8, 238, 144,
147ff; and situations short of war,
140; and Libya 140; and Soviet
naval threat, 141–2, 275ff, 306ff,
318–20, 354; and influence of
technology on naval strategy, 141–
3, 351; and German naval threat,
170–1, 178, 184; and war plans
Orange and *Black*, 171–3, 239, 246;
and Joint Board, 172, 178; and
combined operations, 172; and the
First World War, 173ff, 215; and
US Marines, 179; and the
Mediterranean theatre in the First
World War, 179–81; and
Washington Conference, 189ff,
199ff, 214–15; and War Plan *Red*,
192, 215ff; and General Board,

US Navy—*contd.*
199ff, 216, 237, 275–6; and *Red–Orange* War Plan, 215; and Japanese naval threat, 219ff, and carrier *v.* battleship debate, 245–6; and neglect of trade defence, 246, 250; and rivalry with Japan, 168, 173, 178, 181, 215ff; and 'Two Ocean Navy', 259; and carrier warfare, 260–2; and British Pacific Fleet, 262, 274; and era of massive retaliation, 271ff, 294; and 'Pincher' plans (1945–6), 275; and *Offtackle/Galloper*, 276–9; and Atlantic Striking Fleet, 283–4, 287–8, 339, 340; and protection of sea communications, 285–6; and power projection, 286–9, 320; and Eastern Sea Frontier Commands, 292; and *Polaris* submarine, 294, 354; and Long Range Objectives Group Op-93 (1955), 296–7; and 'the Navy of the 1970 Era' Report (1958), 297;. and OPLAN 2300 (1967), 298; and flexible response, 306ff, 335; and *Sea Lift Procurement and National Security Study* (SPANS), 315; and *Newport Study*, (1971), 317; and *Poseidon* Sea Launched Ballistic Missiles (SLBM), 319; and Sea Launched Cruise Missiles (SLCM), 319; and Ground Launched Cruise Missile (GLCM), 319; and President's Foreign Intelligence Advisory Board, 320; and Congressional Budget Office (CBO), 320; and Carter Doctrine, 323; and Maritime Strategy (1980s), 12–16, 148ff, 330ff; and sea control, 351

Venetians, 97
Venizelos, M., 68
Versailles Treaty (1919), 190, 198 (*see also* Paris Peace Conference)
Vietnam War, xii, 140, 147, 297, 299, 305
Vladivostock, 92

War Cabinet, UK, 40, 60; and the Second World War, 44–5, 70; and Military Co-ordination Committee, 44–5; and Minister of Defence, 45; and the First World War, 60–2, 77n20; and the Cabinet Office, 63
War Committee, UK (1916), 60
War Council, UK (1914), 60–1
War Office, and Cardwell's reforms, 24; and a department of a chief of staff, 24; and inter-departmental co-ordination, 26ff; and defence of the colonies, 28–9; and coast defence, 30; and War Office reform, 31–2; and board system, 37–8; and Lord Kitchener, 39; and the First World war, 41; and the Second World War, 44–5; and Minister of Defence, 45
War of the Spanish Succession, 87
Ward, Sir Joseph, plate 5
Warsaw Pact, 6, 337–9; and NATO naval war, 310ff, 313, 319, 321–2, 333, 343
Washington Conference (1921), 17, 182; and Anglo-American naval rivalry, 191ff; and Anglo-Japanese Alliance, 192ff; and Five Power Naval Treaty (1922), 209, 229; and its aftermath, 214–15, 228, 230, 245–6
Wellington, Duke of, 25, 126
Wemyss, Admiral Sir Rosslyn (later Lord Wester Wemyss), plate 5
West Indian trade, 107
Western European Union, (WEU), 48; and Brussels Treaty (1948), 273, 276
West Point, 84, 97, 100–1
Wier, Sir W., plate 5
Wight, Martin, 1
Wilbur, Secretary of the Navy Curtis D., 217
Wilkinson, Professor Henry Spenser, 24, 131–2
Wilson, Admiral Sir Arthur, 39; and Ballard war plans committee, 121, 167; and Julian Corbett, 121–2; and submarines, 182
Wilson, Harold, 298
Wilson, Field-Marshal Sir Henry, 38; as Chief of the Imperial General Staff, 40
Wilson, Woodrow: and the balance of power, 4; and the Paris Peace Conference (1919), 65, 191; and

convoying, 177; and 1916 naval building programme, 191, 200; and Shantung quarrel, 192
Wilsonianism, 8
Winton, John, 175, 176–7

Wright, Admiral Jerauld, frontispiece
Wylie, Rear-Admiral J. C., 146–7

Zakheim, Dov, 305–6
Zeebrugge Raid, 179